Integrating Intelligence and Sustainability in Supply Chains

Badr Bentalha
National School of Business and Management, Sidi Mohammed Ben Abdellah University, Morocco

Aziz Hmioui
National School of Business and Management, Sidi Mohammed Ben Abdellah University, Morocco

Lhoussaine Alla
National Schools of Applied Sciences, Sidi Mohammed Ben Abdellah University, Morocco

IGI Global
PUBLISHER of TIMELY KNOWLEDGE

A volume in the Advances in Logistics, Operations, and Management Science (ALOMS) Book Series

Published in the United States of America by
IGI Global
Business Science Reference (an imprint of IGI Global)
701 E. Chocolate Avenue
Hershey PA, USA 17033
Tel: 717-533-8845
Fax: 717-533-8661
E-mail: cust@igi-global.com
Web site: http://www.igi-global.com

Library of Congress Cataloging-in-Publication Data

Names: Bentalha, Badr, 1985- editor. | Hmioui, Aziz, 1969- editor. | Alla, Lhoussaine, 1969- editor.
Title: Integrating intelligence and sustainability in supply chains / edited by: Badr Bentalha, Aziz Hmioui, and Lhoussaine Alla.
Description: Hershey, PA : Business Science Reference, [2024] | Includes bibliographical references and index. | Summary: "The book presents groundbreaking research by globally recognized scholars and field experts. This book can be used as a theoretical and conceptual foundation for researchers interested in environmental issues to environmental scientists wishing to gain a business, policy or industry perspective. It offers a wide range of key issues at the interface of operations management and environmental and social responsibility. The main features of a new approach capable of avoiding these impacts and aligning logistics with the requirements of sustainability and digitalization will be developed. Sustainable and smart supply chains are structured in a modular way. Each part presenting and analyzing a specific current topic, allowing readers to identify the chapters that match their interests. The book is a reference to the latest research on smart and sustainable supply chains. It is an ideal reference guide for practitioners interested in the topic. The editors are supply chain specialists and the contributors are also key players in the field"-- Provided by publisher.
Identifiers: LCCN 2023030254 (print) | LCCN 2023030255 (ebook) | ISBN 9798369302255 (hardcover) | ISBN 9798369302262 (paperback) | ISBN 9798369302279 (ebook)
Subjects: LCSH: Business logistics. | Sustainable development. | Economic development--Environmental aspects.
Classification: LCC HD38.5 I575 2024 (print) | LCC HD38.5 (ebook) | DDC 658.7--dc23/eng/20230710
LC record available at https://lccn.loc.gov/2023030254
LC ebook record available at https://lccn.loc.gov/2023030255

This book is published in the IGI Global book series Advances in Logistics, Operations, and Management Science (ALOMS) (ISSN: 2327-350X; eISSN: 2327-3518)

British Cataloguing in Publication Data
A Cataloguing in Publication record for this book is available from the British Library.

Advances in Logistics, Operations, and Management Science (ALOMS) Book Series

John Wang
Montclair State University, USA

ISSN:2327-350X
EISSN:2327-3518

Mission

Operations research and management science continue to influence business processes, administration, and management information systems, particularly in covering the application methods for decision-making processes. New case studies and applications on management science, operations management, social sciences, and other behavioral sciences have been incorporated into business and organizations real-world objectives.

The **Advances in Logistics, Operations, and Management Science** (ALOMS) Book Series provides a collection of reference publications on the current trends, applications, theories, and practices in the management science field. Providing relevant and current research, this series and its individual publications would be useful for academics, researchers, scholars, and practitioners interested in improving decision making models and business functions.

Coverage

- Political Science
- Risk Management
- Operations Management
- Information Management
- Decision analysis and decision support
- Services management
- Marketing engineering
- Finance
- Networks
- Computing and information technologies

IGI Global is currently accepting manuscripts for publication within this series. To submit a proposal for a volume in this series, please contact our Acquisition Editors at Acquisitions@igi-global.com or visit: http://www.igi-global.com/publish/.

The Advances in Logistics, Operations, and Management Science (ALOMS) Book Series (ISSN 2327-350X) is published by IGI Global, 701 E. Chocolate Avenue, Hershey, PA 17033-1240, USA, www.igi-global.com. This series is composed of titles available for purchase individually; each title is edited to be contextually exclusive from any other title within the series. For pricing and ordering information please visit http://www.igi-global.com/book-series/advances-logistics-operations-management-science/37170. Postmaster: Send all address changes to above address.

Titles in this Series

For a list of additional titles in this series, please visit: www.igi-global.com/book-series

Strategies and Applications of Islamic Entrepreneurship
Ahmad Rafiki (Universitas Medan Area, Indonesia) Alfatih Gessan Pananjung (Bahrain Institute of Banking and Finance, Bahrain) and Muhammad Dharma Tuah Putra Nasution (Universitas Pembangunan Panca Budi, Indonesia)
Business Science Reference • copyright 2023 • 313pp • H/C (ISBN: 9781668475195) • US $250.00 (our price)

Entrepreneurship Ecosystems and Their Opportunities and Challenges
Mohammed El Amine Abdelli (University of Brest, France) Shajara Ul-Durar (University of Sunderland, UK) and Hala Wasef Hattab (British University in Egypt, Egypt)
Business Science Reference • copyright 2023 • 337pp • H/C (ISBN: 9781668471401) • US $250.00 (our price)

Climate Change Management and Social Innovations for Sustainable Global Organization
Sumita Dave (Amity University, Raipur, India) Monica Sainy (Amity University, Raipur, India) Disha Sharma (Amity University, Raipur, India) and Anupam Singh (University of Stirling, UK)
Engineering Science Reference • copyright 2023 • 313pp • H/C (ISBN: 9781668495032) • US $250.00 (our price)

Technological Innovation Driving Sustainable Entrepreneurial Growth in Developing Nations
Nana Yaw Asabere (Accra Technical University, Ghana) Glenn Kwabena Gyimah (Accra Technical University, Ghana) Amevi Acakpovi (Accra Technical University, Ghana) and Florence Plockey (Accra Technical University, Ghana)
Business Science Reference • copyright 2023 • 452pp • H/C (ISBN: 9781668498439) • US $250.00 (our price)

Emerging Technologies and Digital Transformation in the Manufacturing Industry
Fernando Ortiz-Rodriguez (Tamaulipas Autonomous University, Mexico) Sanju Tiwari (Tamaulipas Autonomous University, Mexico) Luis Manuel Hernández-González (INDEX, Mexico) and Agustin Tiburcio (INDEX, Mexico)
Business Science Reference • copyright 2023 • 291pp • H/C (ISBN: 9781668480885) • US $250.00 (our price)

Transformational Leadership Styles, Management Strategies, and Communication for Global Leaders
Darcia Ann Marie Roache (University of Saskatchewan, Canada & Capilano University, Canada & University Canada West, Canada & University of the People, USA)
Business Science Reference • copyright 2023 • 532pp • H/C (ISBN: 9781668488225) • US $250.00 (our price)

Black Women's Formal and Informal Ways of Leadership Actualizing the Vision of a More Equitable Workplace
Audrey D. Bowser (Arkansas State University, USA) Kimberley M. Davis (University of Arkansas at Pine Bluff, USA) and Natalie A. Johnson-Leslie (Arkansas State University, USA)
Information Science Reference • copyright 2023 • 340pp • H/C (ISBN: 9781668438275) • US $215.00 (our price)

IGI Global
PUBLISHER of TIMELY KNOWLEDGE

701 East Chocolate Avenue, Hershey, PA 17033, USA
Tel: 717-533-8845 x100 • Fax: 717-533-8661
E-Mail: cust@igi-global.com • www.igi-global.com

Table of Contents

Detailed Table of Contents

This study conducts a comprehensive bibliometric analysis of AI in logistics using various methodologies and techniques. It identifies prominent documents, sources, authors, and countries, and explores sentiments, collaboration networks, and abstract clustering. The findings provide valuable insights for researchers and decision-makers, guiding future research and investment decisions. However, limitations exist, and the field is constantly evolving. This analysis contributes to the scholarly community and offers a foundation for future research in AI logistics.

Supply chain efficiency relies heavily on being able to accurately predict future demand. In this chapter, the authors offer a machine learning framework for supply chain management demand forecasting that makes use of blockchain technology. The framework improves the precision of demand forecasts while maintaining data integrity and openness through the use of machine learning algorithms and blockchain technologies. Demand data is collected and preprocessed, machine learning models are applied, and blockchain is used to validate and secure the data. Results from experiments show that the framework is useful, with significant gains in accuracy and recall compared to more conventional methods. The results show the promise of merging machine learning with blockchain in demand forecasting, giving supply chain professionals a potent instrument with which to enhance the effectiveness of inventory management and overall operations. To fully reap the benefits of this approach, more study into scalability and implementation difficulties is necessary.

Data-driven decision-making is the lifeblood of supply chain business processes' smooth execution. Technological development is ushering in the possible improvement of supply chain data-processing architecture. The centralized server-based data-processing system has been dominating industrial supply chain management for a long time with the challenge of scalability, data integrity, and information security. In recent years, the internet of things (IoT) with service-oriented architecture (SOA) and semantic technology has eliminated the drawbacks of server-based centralized working practices. This approach enhances the information processing performance for resource-constrained supply chain operations through semantic data integration and system security enhancement. This chapter presents an IoT with semantic web service-based information system architecture to allow safe data flow along the supply chain networks. Finally, the chapter describes a semantic similarity assessment algorithm to realize the advantage of this architecture.

Customer knowledge is a strategic element, and its importance is growing all the time. The role of the vast quantities of information available in customer relationship management (CRM) systems, when processed using emerging big data techniques, is still in its infancy. Customer relationship management needs big data to improve customer experience and the right targeting of marketing actions. The study aims at designing a hierarchical model via the fuzzy approach of the indicators of the big data marketing approaches and the possible effects on the CRM. The results suggest that CRM initiatives based on big data could be envisaged as a supportive trend in relation to various managerial and structural dimensions. The study also identified major difficulties of big data analysis in CRM, such as storage, quality, process, and cost issues.

This chapter presents an exploratory qualitative study on the use of artificial intelligence (AI) in supply chain management (SCM). With the growing complexity and uncertainty of supply chains, the integration of AI has gained increased attention as a potential solution for enhancing SCM. Using semi-structured interviews with experts in the field, this study investigates the application of AI for supply chain optimization, as well as the challenges that firms face in implementing such technologies.

Preface

Integrating Intelligence and Sustainability in Supply Chains is a comprehensive research guide that delves into the realm of sustainable and smart supply chains. With a focus on bridging the gap between intelligence and sustainability, this book provides a valuable resource for graduate students in business, management, industrial engineering, and industrial ecology. It serves as a unifying platform for researchers across various domains, including operations management, industrial ecology, industrial strategy, risk management, and life cycle assessment, who are passionate about sustainable and smart supply chains.

This book offers a research guide to sustainable and smart supply chains. It is useful for graduate studies in business, management, industrial engineering and industrial ecology. It should also unite researchers in the broader field of sustainable and smart supply chains, whether from the operations management side or from the industrial ecology, industrial strategy, operations management, risk management, and life cycle assessment side. Finding effective solutions for a sustainable and intelligent supply chain is increasingly important for managers. This book aims to provide students and practitioners with an overview of such issues, based on the latest academic research.

The book presents groundbreaking research by globally recognized scholars and field experts. This book can be used as a theoretical and conceptual foundation for researchers interested in environmental issues to environmental scientists wishing to gain a business, policy or industry perspective. It offers a wide range of key issues at the interface of operations management and environmental and social responsibility. The main features of a new approach capable of avoiding these impacts and aligning logistics with the requirements of sustainability and digitalization will be developed. Sustainable and smart supply chains are structured in a modular way. Each part presenting and analyzing a specific current topic, allowing readers to identify the chapters that match their interests.

Structured in a modular format, *Integrating Intelligence and Sustainability in Supply Chains* allows readers to explore specific current topics relevant to their interests. It covers a wide range of subjects, such as measuring environmental impacts, transforming supply chains to meet sustainability challenges, business models for sustainable logistics, and integrative business strategies. Furthermore, the book addresses emerging technologies like big data analytics, artificial intelligence, and the Internet of Things (IoT), exploring their applications in supply chain management.

With its status as a definitive reference on smart and sustainable supply chains, this book is indispensable for practitioners seeking to enhance their knowledge and decision-making capabilities. The editors and contributors, all experts in the field, ensure that readers gain a comprehensive understanding of the subject matter. While primarily targeted at researchers and practitioners in logistics and supply chain management, this book also offers valuable insights for students embarking on their academic journey in this field.

The book is a reference to the latest research on smart and sustainable supply chains. It is an ideal reference guide for practitioners interested in the topic. The editors are supply chain specialists and the contributors are also key players in the field.

A DESCRIPTION OF THE TARGET AUDIENCE

The text is aimed at people who use logistics and supply chain management. It covers all ideas for managers who are actively engaged in sustainable and intelligent logistics activities. The target audience is mainly researchers and practitioners in this field, but the book can also be useful for students.

A DESCRIPTION OF EACH CHAPTER

Chapter 1: Bibliometric Analysis for Artificial Intelligence in Logistics: A Comprehensive Review

This study conducts a comprehensive bibliometric analysis of AI in logistics using various methodologies and techniques. It identifies prominent documents, sources, authors, and countries, and explores sentiments, collaboration networks, and abstract clustering. The findings provide valuable insights for researchers and decision-makers, guiding future research and investment decisions. However, limitations exist, and the field is constantly evolving. This analysis contributes to the scholarly community and offers a foundation for future research in AI logistics.

Chapter 2: Blockchain-Enabled Machine Learning Framework for Demand Forecasting in Supply Chain Management

Supply chain efficiency relies heavily on being able to accurately predict future demand. In this chapter, we offer a machine learning framework for supply chain management demand forecasting that makes use of blockchain technology. The framework improves the precision of demand forecasts while maintaining data integrity and openness through the use of machine learning algorithms and blockchain technologies. Demand data is collected and preprocessed, machine learning models are applied, and blockchain is used to validate and secure the data. Results from experiments show that the framework is useful, with significant gains in accuracy and recall compared to more conventional methods. The results show the promise of merging machine learning with blockchain in demand forecasting, giving supply chain professionals a potent instrument with which to enhance the effectiveness of inventory management and overall operations. To fully reap the benefits of this approach, more study into scalability and implementation difficulties is necessary.

Chapter 3: Semantic Web Service Architecture for Improving Supply Chain Operation

Data-driven decision-making is the lifeblood of supply chain business processes' smooth execution. Technological development is ushering in the possible improvement of supply chain data-processing architecture. The centralized server-based data-processing system has been dominating industrial supply chain management for a long time with the challenge of scalability, data integrity, and information security. In recent years, the Internet of Things (IoT) with service-oriented architecture (SOA) and semantic technology has eliminated the drawbacks of server-based centralized working practices. This approach enhances the information processing performance for resource-constrained supply chain operations through semantic data integration and system security enhancement. This chapter presents an IoT with semantic web service-based information system architecture to allow safe data flow along the supply chain networks. Finally, the chapter describes a semantic similarity assessment algorithm to realize the advantage of this architecture.

Chapter 4: Marketing Big Data Analytics and Customer Relationship Management A Fuzzy Approach

Customer knowledge is a strategic element, and its importance is growing all the time. The role of the vast quantities of information available in customer relationship management (CRM) systems, when processed using emerging Big Data techniques, is still in its infancy. Customer relationship management needs Big Data to improve customer experience and the right targeting of marketing actions. The study aims at designing a hierarchical model via the fuzzy approach of the indicators of the Big Data Marketing approaches and the possible effects on the CRM. The results suggest that CRM initiatives based on Big Data could be envisaged as a supportive trend in relation to various managerial and structural dimensions. The study also identified major difficulties of Big Data analysis in CRM, such as storage, quality, process and cost issues.

Chapter 5: Exploring the Use of AI in Supply Chain Management: Insights From Moroccan Cases

This chapter presents an exploratory qualitative study on the use of artificial intelligence (AI) in supply chain management (SCM). With the growing complexity and uncertainty of supply chains, the integration of AI has gained increased attention as a potential solution for enhancing SCM. Using semi-structured interviews with experts in the field, this study investigates the application of AI for supply chain optimization, as well as the challenges that firms face in implementing such technologies. The results of this study reveal that AI-based SCM systems have the potential to enhance supply chain efficiency, reduce costs, and improve overall performance. However, challenges such as data quality and compatibility, organizational resistance to change, and lack of trust in AI technology were identified as barriers to successful implementation. These findings contribute to the understanding of the current state and future direction of AI in SCM, and provide practical implications for managers seeking to use AI-based solutions in their supply chain operations.

Chapter 6: Blockchain in Supply Chain Management: A Case Study in the Automotive Industry

Blockchain technology has been the focus of much attention and discussion recently. Its unique characteristics, such as immutability, transparency, and decentralization, create a great potential solution for many industries. Especially the automotive sector, which is known for its complex supply chains, large amounts of data, and wide-reaching infrastructure, can profit in many aspects by incorporating blockchain technology. To illustrate the advantages and potential of blockchain in supply chain management, this chapter includes a case study of one of the leading corporations in the automotive industry that has been increasingly committed to adopting this technology. The analysis uses a set of strategic analysis tools frequently used by managers for strategic planning to highlight the benefits and challenges of this approach. Besides contributing to the literature on blockchain and supply chain management, this chapter offers valuable insights for managers, namely in the automotive sector, who are considering adopting blockchain technology in their operations and processes.

Chapter 7: ML, AI, and IoT as Driving Forces From Industry 5.0 Concepts for a Better Global Food Security

The increasing global population has led to a higher demand for food, requiring us to focus on maintaining its quality, safety, and sustainability. However, food security faces threats not only from natural disasters and climate change but also from factors like changing dietary preferences, political instability, and food fraud. This chapter provides an overview of currently available concepts related to information and communication technologies (ICTs) that can facilitate cooperative efforts, counter fraud, and enable remote monitoring. In recent years, there has been significant interest in leveraging the combined potential of the Internet of Things (IoT), Artificial Intelligence (AI), and Machine Learning (ML)to tap into the expertise of human professionals and enhance their work with efficient and intelligent machines. The implementation of ICTs in food system has been comparatively restricted. This chapter aims to address this gap by demonstrating the potential of their tools in identifying and analyzing the food system.

Chapter 8: Introducing On-Demand Internet Business Model in the Informal Public Transportation System in Developing Countries

Paratransit transport drives the transport system in most emerging nations. It is essential to urban and rural movement. The informal transport system carries most people and is often more accessible, faster, ubiquitous, cheaper, and reliable, but it has also become environmentally unclean, rickety, unsafe, and oversupplied, causing traffic congestion, especially in cities. Due to their informal nature, informal public transport system improvements have failed. The research studied the possibility of bringing the on-demand Internet business model to informal public transportation using Accra's paratransit as a case study. The report evaluated the unique nature, characteristics, potential and problems of the informal public transport eco-system and advocated activities that will meet the socio-economic and travel demands of all parties of the two-sided platform. Thus, adopting the on-demand Internet business model in the informal public transport sector will not only address the paratransit service's supply-demand mismatch but also significantly reduce traffic congestion.

Chapter 9: Supply Chain Sustainability Risks: A Systematic Review

In line with growing global awareness of sustainability issues, supply chain (SC) actors have begun to integrate sustainability practices into their activities, to create a more sustainable SC. However, this integration cannot be effective unless the various risks that could adversely affect the sustainability of the SC are managed. Indeed, managing these risks involves first identifying and classifying them, then assessing them, and subsequently suggesting the measures needed to mitigate them. To provide practitioners with a roadmap of supply chain sustainability risks (SCSRs), numerous articles have been published in the literature focusing on the identification, categorization, and assessment of SCSRs. This study carried out a systematic literature review, based on the Preferred Reporting Items for Systematic reviews and Meta-Analyses (PRISMA) flow diagram, to systematically analyze these articles. The study highlighted the different industries in which SCSRs have been identified, classified, and assessed as well as the various SCSR evaluation frameworks proposed by researchers.

Chapter 10: Sustainable and Smart Supply Chains in China: A Multidimensional Approach

This chapter takes a multifaceted look at China's sustainable and smart supply chains. It examines China's impact on the environment and stresses the importance of a green transition. Sustainable logistics and supply chain management are examined as a potential source of market segmentation and competitive positioning in the context of novel business models. Case studies can illustrate how new technologies such as blockchain, artificial intelligence, the internet of things, and big data may improve supply chain performance and sustainability. Additionally, the chapter examines the function of green finance in promoting sustainability, logistics cost management measures, and the altering role of logistics managers. Impacts of China's Industry 5.0, Agile Logistics, Service Supply Chains, and SCM analytics are discussed to round out the chapter. Anyone interested in China's transition toward more sustainable, intelligent supply networks may find useful information here.

Chapter 11: Sustainable Logistics and Competitive Positioning

The book chapter explores the integration of sustainable logistics and competitive positioning in today's business environment. It discusses the importance of incorporating sustainable practices into logistics operations, including reducing carbon emissions, optimizing resource utilization, and embracing social responsibility. The chapter emphasizes the relationship between sustainable logistics and gaining a competitive edge, highlighting strategies and best practices in areas such as transportation, warehousing, packaging, and reverse logistics. It also explores the role of technology and innovation in facilitating sustainable logistics and enhancing competitiveness. The chapter provides real-world examples and case studies to showcase successful implementations of sustainable logistics across industries, showcasing the benefits in terms of cost savings, customer satisfaction, brand reputation, and market positioning.

Chapter 12: Information System Architecture in Apparel Production for Maintaining Supply Chain Sustainability

Big data analytics has played an enormous role in supply chain operations in recent years. Today, web-applications, social media, intelligent machines, sensors, mobile phones, and other innovative information technology devices generate big data in supply chain operations. These data often provide new digitized services that improve supply chain performance. In this operating environment, heterogeneous enterprise applications, manufacturing processes, or supply chain management, either inside a single enterprise or among network enterprises, require sharing of data-driven information. Thus, data management and its analytical interpretation have become significant drivers for management, product development, and provision of relevant services in network enterprises that function as mediators in effective and sustainable supply chain operations. This chapter reviews the effect of big data analytics on the supply chain operation literature, highlights how modern supply chains can manage sustainability, and presents a conceptual information system architecture.

Chapter 13: Transforming Supply Chains (SCs) to meet Sustainability Challenges

The key aspect of the current chapter is related to the sustainability challenges of the supply chain and its associated consideration towards the transformation of operations. The primary motivation for evaluation has been related to the influence of sustainability considerations for supply chain development, aligned issues, and their respective solutions. To highlight the reader's approach for supply chain sustainability, the importance and influences have been discussed regarding waste management and its related influences on the cost and productivity efficiency within the supply chain. The crucial aspects of supply chain sustainability have also enlightened some challenges. The challenges include human resources, management, structure development, and user perception as well. Technological and intelligence based facilities such as IoT, Block-Chain, and Artificial Intelligence have an influence on the management of challenges and the developing effective strategies for green supply chain management. The recommendation for production to transportation management has been provided.

Chapter 14: Monitoring Environmental Performance of Agricultural Supply Chains Using Internet of Things

The agriculture industry is facing mounting enforcement to produce more food to nourish a growing population while simultaneously mitigating its environmental footprint. In response, the use of Internet of Things (IoT) technologies in agriculture has emerged as a promising approach to monitoring and improving the supply chain's environmental performance. This chapter provides a comprehensive overview of the use of IoT technologies in the context of environmental monitoring in agricultural supply chains. It begins by introducing the concept of environmental performance in agriculture, its importance, and its challenges. The chapter then explains the basics of IoT technology and how it can be used to monitor and track the environmental performance in agricultural supply chains. The chapter also discusses the benefits and challenges of IoT technologies implementation. Overall, by leveraging the power of IoT, it is possible to enhance sustainability and efficiency in food production, while also reducing environmental impact.

A CONCLUSION OF HOW THE BOOK IMPACTS

In conclusion, the book on sustainable and smart supply chain management has a profound impact on both the business landscape and our society as a whole. By addressing the pressing challenges of environmental sustainability and operational efficiency, this book offers valuable insights and practical solutions to transform supply chains for a better future.

Firstly, the book emphasizes the importance of adopting sustainable practices throughout the supply chain. It highlights the detrimental effects of traditional supply chain models on the environment, such as excessive resource consumption, pollution, and carbon emissions. By promoting sustainable alternatives like renewable energy, waste reduction, and circular economy principles, the book inspires businesses to minimize their ecological footprint and mitigate environmental risks.

Secondly, the book sheds light on the integration of smart technologies and digitalization in supply chain management. It explores how emerging technologies like the Internet of Things (IoT), artificial intelligence (AI), and blockchain can revolutionize supply chain operations. These technologies enable real-time data collection, advanced analytics, predictive modeling, and enhanced visibility throughout the supply chain. By leveraging smart technologies, companies can optimize their processes, streamline operations, reduce costs, and enhance overall efficiency.

Moreover, the book highlights the significance of collaboration and transparency in building sustainable and smart supply chains. It emphasizes the need for open communication, partnerships, and information-sharing among supply chain stakeholders. By fostering collaboration across organizations, suppliers, and customers, businesses can collectively drive sustainable practices, innovation, and social responsibility.

Furthermore, the book recognizes the role of consumer demand and behavior in shaping supply chains. It emphasizes the importance of informed consumer choices and responsible consumption. By raising awareness about sustainable products and promoting ethical sourcing, the book empowers consumers to drive change through their purchasing decisions. This paradigm shift towards sustainability-conscious consumers compels businesses to align their supply chains with ethical standards, ultimately creating a positive ripple effect throughout the industry.

Overall, the book on sustainable and smart supply chain management offers a comprehensive and forward-thinking approach to transforming supply chains. By integrating sustainability, technology, collaboration, and consumer awareness, it provides a roadmap for businesses to create environmentally responsible, efficient, and resilient supply chains. This book's impact extends beyond individual organizations, influencing the entire industry towards a more sustainable and prosperous future.

Badr Bentalha
Sidi Mohamed Ben Abdellah University, Morocco

Lhoussaine Alla
Sidi Mohamed Ben Abdellah University, Morocco

Aziz Hmioui
Sidi Mohamed Ben Abdellah University, Morocco

REFERENCES

Alla, L., Bentalha, B., & Bouhtati, N. (2022). Assessing supply chain performance in the covid 19 context: a prospective model. In *2022 14th International Colloquium of Logistics and Supply Chain Management (LOGISTIQUA)* (pp. 1-6). IEEE. 10.1109/LOGISTIQUA55056.2022.9938083

Alla, L., Bentalha, B., Megzari, G., & Hmioui, A. (2022). The effects of COVID-19 on supply chains: A qualitative analysis. ENCG, USMBA, Fes. *Reconfigurations du tourisme en contexte de la crise du Covid-19: Quelles démarches pour quelles résiliences au Maroc et ailleurs ?, 1* (1), pp.130-153, 2022, 978-9954-9721-2-0.

Bentalha, B. (2022). Déterminants Et Risques Des Supply Chains Customer-To-Customer: Une Approche Fuzzy. *Revue d'Etudes en Management et Finance d'Organisation*, *7*(2).

Bentalha, B. (2022). Green transportation Balanced scorecard model: a fuzzy-delphi approach during COVID-19. In *Computational Intelligence Techniques for Green Smart Cities* (pp. 107–127). Springer International Publishing. doi:10.1007/978-3-030-96429-0_5

Bentalha, B. (2022). Smart Technologies for a Sustainable Service Supply Chain: A Prospective Perspective. *Journal of Environmental Issues and Climate Change*, *1*(1), 77–89. doi:10.59110/jeicc.v1i1.81

Bentalha, B. (2023). A Framework for Exploring the Global Performance of Service Supply Chain Management: A Qualitative Study. *Government Impact on Sustainable and Responsible Supply Chain Management*, 106-129.

Bentalha, B. (2023). Les fondements théoriques du supply chain management: Une analyse critique. *Alternatives Managériales Economiques*, *5*(2), 1–22.

Bentalha, B. (2023). La chaîne logistique de distribution du Gaz de Pétrole Liquéfié: Une étude qualitative des déterminants et des perspectives. *IJBTSR International Journal of Business and Technology Studies and Research.* . doi:10.5281/zenodo.7813426

Bentalha, B., & Hmioui, A. (2021). Smart Service Supply Chain and Just Walk Out Technology: A Netnographic Approach. In *The Proceedings of the International Conference on Smart City Applications* (pp. 223-236). Cham: Springer International Publishing.

Bentalha, B., Hmioui, A., & Alla, L. (2019). The digitalization of the supply chain management of service companies: a prospective approach. In *Proceedings of the 4th International Conference on Smart City Applications* (pp. 1-8). 10.1145/3368756.3369005

Bentalha, B., Hmioui, A., & Alla, L. (2020). Digital service supply chain management: current realities and prospective visions. In *Innovations in Smart Cities Applications Edition 3: The Proceedings of the 4th International Conference on Smart City Applications 4* (pp. 808-822). Springer International Publishing. 10.1007/978-3-030-37629-1_58

Bentalha, B., Hmioui, A., & Alla, L. (2020). The global performance of a service supply chain: a simulation-optimization under arena. In *The Proceedings of the Third International Conference on Smart City Applications* (pp. 489-502). Cham: Springer International Publishing.

Bentalha, B., Hmioui, A., & Alla, L. (2021). Last mile logistics applied to the distribution of COVID-19 vaccines: A prospection of good practices. *Alternatives Managériales Economiques*, *3*(3), 41–61.

Bentalha, B., Hmioui, A., & Alla, L. (2023). Green Transportation Balanced Scorecard: A VIKOR Fuzzy Method for Evaluating Green Logistics Initiatives. In *International Conference on Digital Technologies and Applications* (pp. 916-925). Cham: Springer Nature Switzerland. 10.1007/978-3-031-29857-8_91

Hmioui, A., & Bentalha, B. (2020). Service Supply Chain Management et performance commerciale: Esquisse d'une synthèse théorique. *Revue ame, 2*, 1-21.

Hmioui, A., & Bentalha, B. (2021). Service supply chain management: A literature review. *International Journal of Logistics Systems and Management*, *40*(3), 332–353. doi:10.1504/IJLSM.2021.120253

Hmioui, A., Bentalha, B., & Alla, L. (2020). Service supply chain: A prospective analysis of sustainable management for global performance. In *2020 IEEE 13th International Colloquium of Logistics and Supply Chain Management (LOGISTIQUA)* (pp. 1-7). IEEE. 10.1109/LOGISTIQUA49782.2020.9353940

Acknowledgment

We, the editors, would like to express our heartfelt gratitude to everyone involved in our Book Integrating Intelligence and Sustainability in Supply Chains. We are deeply grateful to the authors who have contributed their time and expertise to create the chapters of this book. Without their support, this project would not have been possible.

We would also like to extend our sincere appreciation to the reviewers who have provided valuable feedback on the chapters, helping us to improve their quality, coherence, and content presentation. Their contributions have been invaluable, and we are grateful for their dedication to ensuring the success of this project.

Furthermore, we would like to thank the publishing team for their professionalism and dedication to bringing this book to fruition. Their tireless efforts have been instrumental in ensuring the success of this project.

Lastly, we would like to express our deepest gratitude to everyone involved in the creation and publication of this book. Your contributions have been invaluable, and we are truly grateful for your support.

Thank you all again for your hard work and dedication. We are honored to have had the opportunity to work with such a talented and committed team.

Sincerely,

Badr Bentalha
Sidi Mohamed Ben Abdellah University, Morocco

Lhoussaine Alla
Sidi Mohamed Ben Abdellah University, Morocco

Aziz Hmioui
Sidi Mohamed Ben Abdellah University, Morocco

Section 1

Integrating Intelligence in Supply Chains

Chapter 1
Bibliometric Analysis for Artificial Intelligence in Logistics: A Comprehensive Review

Deepak Hajoary
https://orcid.org/0000-0003-2503-5819
Bodoland University, India

ABSTRACT

This study conducts a comprehensive bibliometric analysis of AI in logistics using various methodologies and techniques. It identifies prominent documents, sources, authors, and countries, and explores sentiments, collaboration networks, and abstract clustering. The findings provide valuable insights for researchers and decision-makers, guiding future research and investment decisions. However, limitations exist, and the field is constantly evolving. This analysis contributes to the scholarly community and offers a foundation for future research in AI logistics.

INTRODUCTION

Artificial intelligence (AI) has emerged as a transformative technology in various industries including logistics. In the logistics industry, AI is increasingly utilized to optimize operations, improve efficiency, and enhance decision-making processes. AI systems can analyze vast amounts of data from multiple sources, such as sensors, GPS, and RFID, to provide real-time insights and enable predictive analytics for supply chain management(Garg et al (2021))

Artificial intelligence (AI) has the potential to revolutionize various aspects of logistics. It offers transformative potential for the augmentation and replacement of human tasks and activities within the logistics industry (Dwivedi et al., 2021). AI can be applied in various areas of logistics, such as supply chain management, warehousing, transportation, and last-mile delivery Gružauskas & Pačėsaitė, 2021; Shi, 2022; Rosendorff et al., 2021). It can optimize operations, improve efficiency, and enhance

DOI: 10.4018/979-8-3693-0225-5.ch001

decision-making processes (Calatayud et al., 2019; Gružauskas & Pačėsaitė, 2021). AI-based methods can be used to automate warehouse operations, optimize vehicle routes, and predict customer behavior Gružauskas & Pačėsaitė, 2021; Shi, 2022). AI can also be used for inventory management, demand forecasting, and risk prediction (Sharma et al., 2021; Modgil et al., 2021). The integration of AI with logistics systems can increase work efficiency and reduce costs (Zhu et al. 2022). However, the adoption of AI in logistics raises concerns about job loss and the need for upskilling and training (Esper, 2022). Overall, AI has the potential to transform and improve the logistics industry significantly by enhancing productivity, efficiency, and customer satisfaction (Woschank et al. 2020).

Artificial intelligence (AI) has a wide range of applications in logistics. It can be used to optimize and automate various processes, leading to increased efficiency and improved decision making. AI can be applied to supply chain management to enhance demand forecasting, inventory management, and risk prediction. (2021) Wilson et al., 2021). They can also be used in intelligent transport logistics to improve the performance of transport systems and processes (Woschank et al., 2020). In last-mile delivery, AI can be used to forecast delivery times and improve delivery forecasting (Rosendorff et al., 2021). AI can also play a crucial role in warehouse operations by automating tasks and improving logistics operations (Pandian, 2019). AI technologies such as machine learning, data mining, and predictive analytics can be employed to analyze large volumes of data and extract valuable insights for logistics optimization (Xian, 2022; "Expert System for Freight Coordination Based on Artificial Intelligence", 2021). Furthermore, AI can contribute to the development of smart logistics environments, enabling efficient and economic solutions for logistics companies (Issaoui et al. 2022). However, the adoption of AI in logistics also presents challenges such as the need for skilled personnel and addressing barriers related to implementation (Shrivastav, 2022; Esper, 2022). Overall, AI has the potential to revolutionize the logistics industry by enhancing productivity, efficiency, and sustainability (Sharma et al., 2021; Liu et al., 2020).

Literature Review

Artificial Intelligence (AI) has rapidly emerged as a vital enabler in the logistics and supply chain management landscape (Woschank et al., 2020). The integration of AI technologies such as machine learning, deep learning, and predictive analytics significantly enhances various aspects of the logistics industry, including supply chain management, warehousing, transportation, and last-mile delivery (Wilson et al., 2020; Wilson et al., 2021). This integration optimizes operations, improves decision-making processes, automates tasks, and develops intelligent logistics systems ("Expert System for Freight Coordination Based on Artificial Intelligence", 2021). In particular, warehouse automation has gained attention, facilitating task automation and contributing to the broader goal of warehouse automation (Correll et al., 2018; Rana, 2023).

Furthermore, predictive analytics and demand forecasting play crucial roles in the supply chain management and decision-making processes. Big data analytics (BDA) and advanced predictive analytics techniques, including deep neural networks, enhance the accuracy of demand forecasting (Arunachalam et al., 2018; Vecchio et al., 2020). These advances have improved areas such as inventory optimization, labor scheduling, route optimization, and price optimization (Arunachalam et al., 2018).

However, the adoption of AI in logistics presents challenges, including the need for skilled personnel and addressing barriers to implementation (Yigitcanlar&Cugurullo, 2020). Additionally, supply chain risk management and resilience have become critical because of today's dynamic and uncertain business environments. Proactive risk management strategies and the integration of AI with technologies such as the Internet of Things (IoT) and blockchain can aid in building resilient supply chains (Wang et al., 2020; Woschank et al., 2020; Rejeb et al., 2021).

Despite these challenges, AI technologies hold great potential for revolutionizing the logistics industry, improving operational performance, driving innovation, and fostering resilience (Bokhari and Albukhari, 2022; Sharma et al., 2021). The ongoing COVID-19 pandemic has amplified the need for resilient supply chains, leading to increased research on supply chain resilience and risk management (Badhotiya et al., 2020; Remko, 2022).

Although there is substantial research on AI applications in logistics and supply chain management, comprehensive bibliometric studies are lacking.

The study attempts to answer the following research questions:

RQ1:What is the detailed bibliometric landscape of subfields within AI applications in logistics and supply chain management, such as warehouse automation, demand forecasting, and supply chain resilience?

How have research trends in the application of AI in logistics and supply chain management evolved over time?

RQ2:Which countries and institutions are leading contributors to research on the application of AI in logistics and supply chain management? How has its influence evolved over time?

Research Methodology

This study conducts a comprehensive review of the application of artificial intelligence (AI) in the field of logistics using bibliometric analysis. The research methodology involved the use of the Dimensions database, focusing on English language articles published between 2019 and 2023. The search keywords used to identify relevant publications are "artificial intelligence" and "logistics."

Data Source

The Dimensions database, a comprehensive research database covering a wide range of disciplines, was selected as the primary data source for this study. This database provides access to a vast collection of scholarly articles, conference papers, and other research articles.

Inclusion Criteria

To ensure that the analysis reflects recent developments in the field, only English-language articles published between 2019 and 2023 were considered for inclusion in this review. This timeframe allows us to capture the latest research trends in the application of AI in logistics.

Search Strategy

The search strategy involved using the keywords "artificial intelligence" and "logistics" to identify relevant publications. These keywords capture the intersection of AI and logistics, enabling a comprehensive exploration of AI techniques in logistics research.

Data Collection

The initial search results from the Dimensions database were exported and duplicate publications were removed. The remaining articles were screened based on their titles, abstracts, and keywords to identify those directly related to the use of AI in logistics. Only articles that met the specific criteria and objectives of the study were included in further analysis.

Data Analysis

The selected articles underwent bibliometric analysis to extract quantitative data and metrics related to authorship, citation counts, publication trends, and collaboration patterns. Various bibliometric indicators, such as document frequencies, citation scores, and co-authorship networks, have been utilized to assess the impact and influence of AI in logistics research.

Visualization and Interpretation

The collected data were analyzed and visualized using appropriate techniques such as tables, charts, and network diagrams to provide a comprehensive overview of the research landscape. The findings were then interpreted to identify key trends, prominent authors, influential publications, and collaboration patterns within the field of AI in logistics.

Ethical Considerations

Ethical considerations, such as data privacy and compliance with ethical guidelines, were considered throughout the research process. As the study relies on existing publicly available data from the Dimensions database, no identifiable or sensitive information was collected or used.

RESULTS AND DISCUSSION

Publication Trends

Figure 1 shows the number of publications per year in the dataset. From the graph, we can conclude that

There is a general upward trend in the number of publications over time, indicating an increase in research activity in this field.

In recent years, there has been a significant increase in the number of publications, which may indicate a surge in interest or development in this area of research.

There are some fluctuations in the number of publications from year to year, which could be due to various factors such as changes in research funding, shifts in research focus, or the introduction of new research methods or technologies

Figure 1. Publications over time

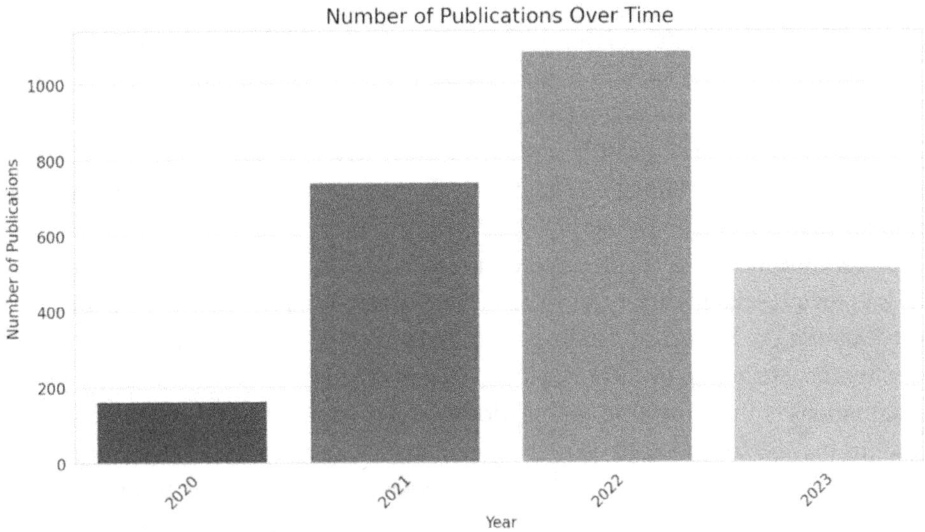

Author Frequency Analysis

The bar (Figure 2) plot shows the 20 most prolific authors in the dataset based on the number of publications. The authors are represented on the x-axis, and the number of publications on the y-axis.

Figure 2. Top 20 authors

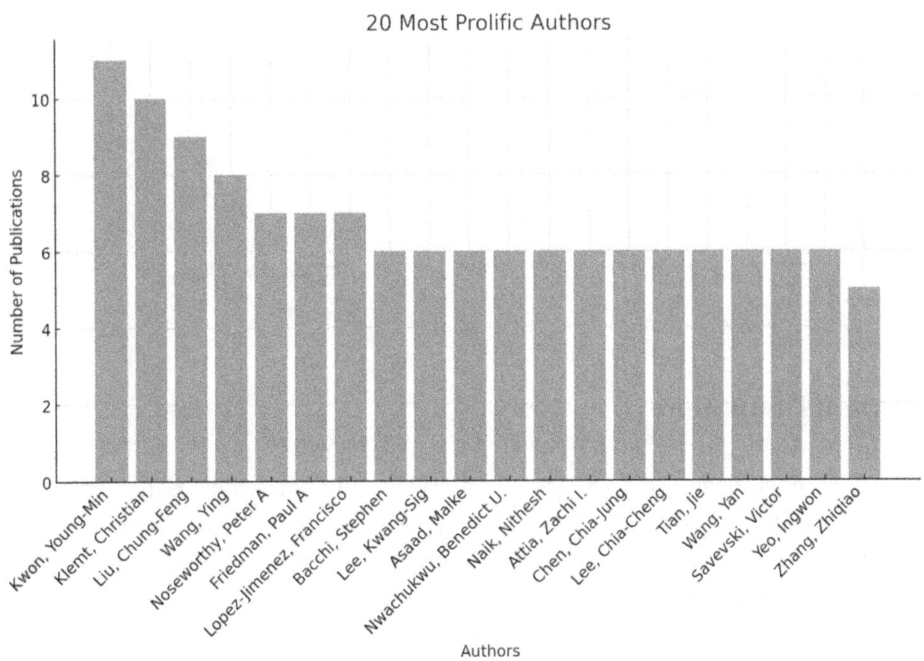

Author Trend Analysis

From the plot (Figure 3), several observations can be made regarding the number of publications per year for the top five most prolific authors in the dataset. Each line on the plot represents one author, and the points on the line indicate the number of publications by that author each year.

First, it is evident that the most prolific authors consistently produced a significant number of publications per year, indicating sustained research activity over time. This suggests a strong commitment to their field of study and a consistent output of scholarly work.

Second, some authors have exhibited an increasing trend in the number of publications over the years. This suggests that their research activity has been progressively ramping up, possibly due to factors such as expanded collaboration, increased funding, or a shift in research focus. This trend highlights their growing impact and contribution to their respective fields of study.

Finally, fluctuations in the number of publications for each author can be observed from year to year. These fluctuations may be attributed to various factors, including changes in research priorities, funding availability, collaboration with other researchers, and personal circumstances. It is important to consider these factors when analyzing data and drawing conclusions about individual authors' research productivity.

Figure 3. Author trend analysis

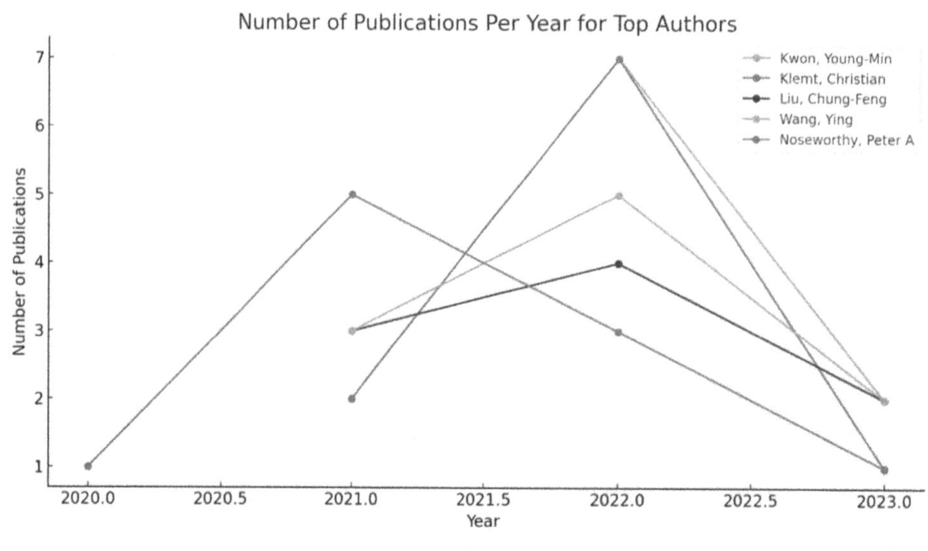

Most Prominent Document

Out of a total of 2500 documents, only 15 met the criteria for citation, which requires a minimum of 100 citations for a document to be considered. Figure 4 and Table 1 provide a comprehensive list of these documents, along with their respective citation counts, offering valuable insights into their scholarly influence and recognition within the academic community.

Notably, Sarker (2021) emerged as the most highly cited document with an impressive citation count of 821, indicating its significant impact and extensive referencing within the field. Following closely,

Table 1. Most prominent documents

Sl No	Document	Citations
1	Sarker (2021)	821
2	Ogunleye (2020)	301
3	Kwekha-Rashid (2021)	226
4	Ahmed (2020)	220
5	Choi (2020)	195
6	Collins (2021)	195
7	Siontis (2021)	189
8	Hashimoto (2020)	180
9	Abdallah (2020)	155
10	Rahimi (2021)	135
11	Pourhomayoun (2021)	129
12	Battineni (2020)	120
13	Yigitcanlar (2020)	119
14	Belhadi (2021)	116
15	yao (2021)	102

Ogunleye (2020) secured the second position on the list, with 301 citations, highlighting its substantial contribution to scholarly discourse.

Kwekha-Rashid (2021) achieves a commendable citation count of 226, securing the third position, while Ahmed (2020) closely trails behind with 220 citations, placing it fourth on the list. Similarly, Choi (2020) and Collins (2021) both received 195 citations, jointly positioning them at the fifth rank in terms of scholarly recognition.

Siontis (2021) occupies the subsequent position, with 189 citations, while Hashimoto (2020) closely follows 180 citations. Abdallah (2020) holds the eighth position with 155 citations, further demonstrating their influence and appeal to researchers within their respective domains. Rahimi (2021) garnered attention with 135 citations, securing its presence as the tenth most cited document.

Pourhomayoun (2021) took the eleventh position with 129 citations, closely followed by Battineni (2020) with 120 citations. Yigitcanlar (2020) and Belhadi (2021) exhibit a slight disparity in their citation counts, with 119 and 116 citations, respectively, positioning them at the thirteenth and fourteenth ranks. Finally, Yao (2021) concluded the list with 102 citations, highlighting its significance in academic discussions.

Most Prominent Citation Sources

Among the 1,026 sources considered, 35 met the criteria for being prominent citation sources, which required a minimum of ten citations for a source to be considered prominent. Table 2 provides a comprehensive list of these sources, including document counts, citation numbers, and total link strengths, offering valuable insights into the scholarly impact and influence of each source in the academic domain.

Figure 4. Most cited documents

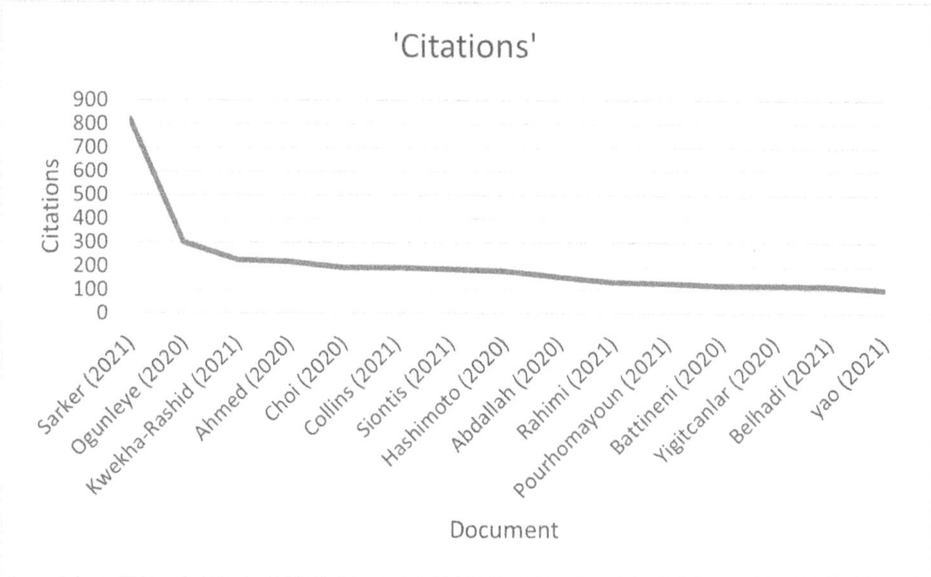

Data analysis revealed significant patterns and observations regarding the significance of these sources (Figure 5).

First, the source "Sensors" stands out as a prolific contributor with a substantial number of documents (59) and high citation count (749), denoting its scholarly prominence. However, it is worth noting that a total link strength of 7 suggests a moderate level of interconnectivity among the cited works.

Figure 5. Density visualization of sources

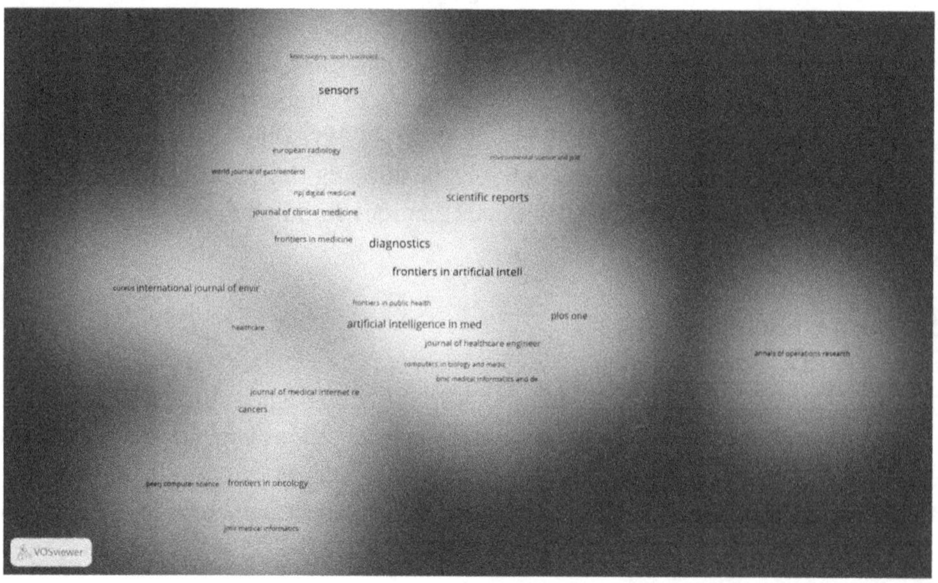

Table 2. Top sources with citations

Sl	Source	Documents	Citations	Total Link Strength
1	Sensors	59	749	7
2	Artificial Intelligence In Medicine	54	608	14
3	Plos One	43	400	12
4	Diagnostics	62	397	26
5	The Lancet Digital Health	12	365	5
6	Journal Of Medical Internet Research	25	355	15
7	Scientific Reports	53	328	15
8	International Journal Of Medical Informatics	20	301	23
9	Annals Of Operations Research	16	281	2
10	Frontiers In Artificial Intelligence	57	278	7
11	Cancers	31	275	22
12	International Journal Of Environmental Research And Public Health	43	267	16
13	Journal Of Healthcare Engineering	28	266	5
14	European Radiology	22	233	6
15	Journal Of Personalized Medicine	12	208	12
16	Npj Digital Medicine	14	181	8
17	Healthcare	18	180	12
18	Journal Of Clinical Medicine	31	180	17
19	World Journal Of Gastroenterology	14	161	3
20	Journal Of Gastroenterology And Hepatology	10	160	6
21	Computational Intelligence And Neuroscience	41	133	0
22	Annals Of Translational Medicine	11	129	7
23	Frontiers In Public Health	18	120	7
24	Computers In Biology And Medicine	14	107	6
25	Frontiers In Oncology	34	98	11
26	Knee Surgery, Sports Traumatology, Arthroscopy	10	96	1
27	Bmc Medical Informatics And Decision Making	14	90	4
28	Environmental Science And Pollution Research	11	83	1
29	Jmir Medical Informatics	15	80	2
30	Frontiers In Medicine	25	70	20
31	European Heart Journal - Digital Health	10	63	6
32	Peerj Computer Science	13	58	1
33	Cureus	14	27	1
35	Frontiers In Cardiovascular Medicine	14	24	3
35	Frontiers In Psychology	12	23	1

Similarly, "Artificial Intelligence in Medicine" shows a prominent scholarly presence, evident from its extensive document count (54) and noteworthy citation count (608). Notably, this source demonstrated a high total link strength of 14, indicating strong interconnections among the cited works.

"Plos One" deserves recognition for its scholarly impact, with 43 documents and 400 citations, showcasing a substantial academic footprint. Moreover, its total link strength of 12 signifies a robust network of references and citations in its publications.

"Diagnostics" distinguishes itself with the highest document count (62), reflecting its comprehensive coverage of the field. This source also commands a significant citation count (397) and impressive total link strength of 26, indicating a strong network of interconnected research within the domain.

"The Lancet Digital Health," while exhibiting a relatively low document count (12), demonstrates notable scholarly influence with a citation count of 365. However, its total link strength of five suggests a moderate level of interconnectivity among the cited works.

The Journal of Medical Internet Research" displays scholarly prominence with a notable document count (25) and a substantial citation count (355). Additionally, a high total link strength of 15 indicates strong connections among the research articles published in the journal.

"Scientific Reports" establishes a significant scholarly presence with 53 documents and 328 citations. Furthermore, its total link strength of 15 underscores the robust network of citations and references prevalent in the journal.

The "International Journal of Medical Informatics" deserves attention for its impactful contributions despite its relatively low document count (20). Its noteworthy citation count (301) signifies its influence in the field. Additionally, this source demonstrated a high total link strength of 23, indicating a strong network of references and citations.

"Annals of Operations Research," with a modest document count (16), showcase its significance in the academic landscape through its citation count (281). However, the low total link strength of 2 suggests a comparatively weaker network of interconnected research.

"Frontiers in Artificial Intelligence" exhibit a notable scholarly presence, with 57 documents and 278 citations. While its total link strength of seven suggests moderate interconnectivity among the research articles, it still contributes significantly to scholarly discourse.

Most Prominent Authors

Among the 14,655 authors considered, only 35 met the criteria for being considered prominent authors, which required a minimum of five documents authored by an individual to be deemed prominent. Table 3 and Figure 6 present a comprehensive ranking of authors based on their research impact, considering their publication records, citations received, and total link strength metric.

Leading the list, authors such as Attia, Zachi I., Friedman, Paul A., and Lopez-Jimenez, Francisco demonstrate significant impact, as evidenced by their high total link strengths of 14 and 15. Attia, Zachi I. stands out with an impressive citation count of 296, closely followed by Friedman Paul A., with 292 citations.

Variations in the number of documents published by each author were observed. Klemt, Christian, emerged as the most prolific author, with a record of 10 publications, closely followed by Kwon and Young-Min with 11 publications. These authors have exhibited extensive engagement in their respective areas of research.

Table 3. Most prominent author

Sl No	Author	Documents	Citations	Total Link Strength
1	Attia, Zachi I.	6	296	14
2	Friedman, Paul A.	5	292	14
3	Yao, Xiaoxi	5	147	13
4	Lopez-Jimenez, Francisco	7	135	15
5	Park, Jinsik	5	128	27
6	Kim, Kyung-Hee	5	118	24
7	Kwon, Joon-Myoung	5	118	24
8	Friedman, Paul A	7	78	11
9	Noseworthy, Peter A	7	75	11
10	Klemt, Christian	10	74	54
11	Kwon, Young-Min	11	74	57
12	Lee, Chia-Cheng	6	66	25
13	Lin, Chin	5	65	21
14	Lin, Chin-Sheng	5	65	21
15	Nwachukwu, Benedict U.	5	63	6
16	Naik, Nithesh	6	62	0
17	Cumic, Jelena	5	59	16
18	Pantic, Igor	5	59	16
19	Lee, Kwang-Sig	6	53	0
20	Chen, Xin	5	50	0
21	Kazemi-Arpanahi, Hadi	5	47	0
22	Shanbehzadeh, Mostafa	5	47	0
23	Tian, Jie	6	47	0
24	Yeo, Ingwon	6	38	39
25	Wang, Ying	8	37	0
26	Liu, Chung-Feng	9	34	6
27	Laino, Maria Elena	5	31	2
28	Savevski, Victor	5	29	2
29	Bihorac, Azra	5	28	0
30	Wang, Bo	5	24	0
31	Bignami, Elena	5	23	0
32	Asaad, Malke	6	21	4
33	Butler, Charles E.	5	19	4
34	Baruah, Dhiraj	5	18	0
35	Chen, Chia-Jung	6	17	6
36	Zhang, Zhiqiao	5	16	0
37	Li, Jing	5	14	0
38	Bacchi, Stephen	6	7	0

Figure 6. Author citations

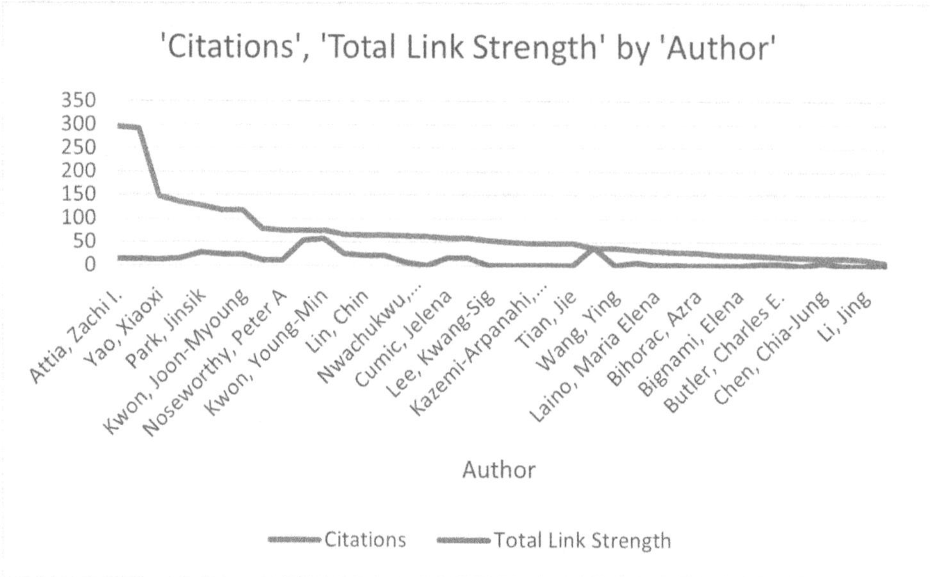

The total link strength metric provides a comprehensive assessment of an author's impact by considering both the number of documents published and number of citations garnered. Attia, Zachi I. and Friedman, Paul A. share the highest total link strength of 14, signifying their significant influence within their respective fields of expertise.

It is worth noting that some authors exhibit similar numbers of documents, citations, and total link strengths, indicating comparable research output and impact. Conversely, certain authors receive a considerable number of citations but possess relatively low total link strengths, suggesting that their work may have gained attention from other researchers despite having fewer overall publications than their counterparts.

A subset of authors in the dataset displayed a total link strength of zero, suggesting a lack of substantial attention or impact in terms of citations and publications. This implies that their research may not have received significant recognition in the academic community.

Overall, the dataset comprised a diverse range of authors representing various fields of study. Through their publication records, citation counts, and total link strengths, the dataset provides valuable insights into the research impact and influence of these authors, contributing to a better understanding of their scholarly contributions within their respective domains.

Most Prominent Organizations

Among the 3,002 organizations considered, only 18 met the criteria for being considered prominent organizations, requiring a minimum of 20 associated documents. Table 4 provides a comprehensive ranking of these organizations based on their research impact, considering factors such as the number of documents published, citations received, and total link strength metric. These organizations encompass esteemed academic institutions that have made substantial contributions to scholarly research.

Fig. 6 shows a network visualization of author collaborations, highlighting the collaborative efforts within the academic community.

At the top of the ranking is Harvard University, a renowned institution known for its scholarly endeavors. With a remarkable total link strength of 93, Harvard University has demonstrated a significant research influence through the publication of 67 significant documents and an impressive citation count of 926. This exceptional performance solidifies its position as a leading contributor in the academic community.

Following Harvard University, the Mayo Clinic secured the second position, with a notable total link strength of 41. With 55 well-regarded publications and 873 citations, Mayo Clinic's research contributions have garnered substantial attention and recognition.

Massachusetts General Hospital holds the third position in the ranking, underscoring its significant research influence. With a commendable total link strength of 70, the institution's 45 publications and 797 citations signify noteworthy scholarly contributions and impact.

Additionally, the University of Toronto and the University of Oxford are prominently featured in the ranking, further establishing their reputations as esteemed research institutions. These organizations have made substantial contributions to their respective fields, as evidenced by their publication records and citation counts.

The dataset also encompasses other distinguished organizations, such as Stanford University, Cleveland Clinic, Sapienza University of Rome, and University College London, among others. Each organization demonstrates varying levels of research impact, as measured by their total link strengths. This metric

Table 4. Top organizations

Sl No	Organization	Documents	Citations	Total Link Strength
1	Harvard University	67	926	93
2	Mayo Clinic	55	873	41
3	Massachusetts General Hospital	45	797	70
4	University Of Toronto	49	381	26
5	University Of Oxford	21	353	22
6	Stanford University	29	304	12
7	Cleveland Clinic	22	275	30
8	Sapienza University Of Rome	22	270	12
9	University College London	25	258	9
10	University Of Pennsylvania	22	257	24
11	Icahn School Of Medicine At Mount Sinai	21	188	11
12	Brigham And Women's Hospital	23	184	21
13	Zhejiang University	27	181	5
14	Yonsei University	33	174	18
15	Shanghai Jiao Tong University	20	142	7
16	Johns Hopkins University	25	132	10
17	Huazhong University Of Science And Technology	23	114	1
18	Chinese Academy Of Medical Sciences & Peking Union Medical College	20	79	10

Figure 7. Density visualization of organizations

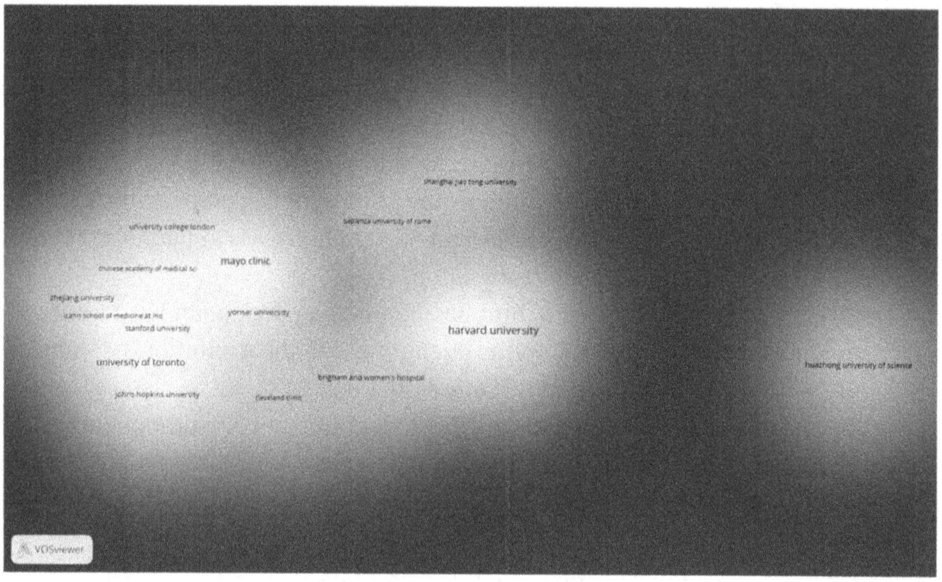

provides a comprehensive evaluation of research influence, considering both the quantity of publications and impact of citations.

Overall, the dataset highlights the research impact and contributions of these prominent organizations within the academic landscape.

Most Prominent Countries

Among the 94 countries considered, only 17 met the thresholds to be considered prominent countries, which required a minimum of 50 associated documents. Table 5 provides a comprehensive analysis of these countries based on their research productivity, citations received, and resulting total link strength metric. This analysis offers valuable insights into the scientific contributions and impact of each country within the global research landscape.

Fig. 8 shows a network visualization of country collaborations, highlighting the collaborative efforts and connections among different nations.

Leading the list is the United States, a renowned hub of scientific research with an impressive total link strength of 662. This figure reflects the substantial impact of research output, as indicated by 658 documents and a remarkable citation count of 6,740. The United has emerged as a prominent contributor to the global scientific community.

China secured the second position, underscoring its growing research project with a total link strength of 342. This achievement was attributed to 481 publications and 2,811 citations, highlighting China's increasing influence on scientific endeavors.

The United Kingdom holds the third position, signifying its significant scientific contributions. With 205 documents and 2,414 citations, the United Kingdom demonstrated a commendable total link strength of 315.

Figure 8. Density visualization of country

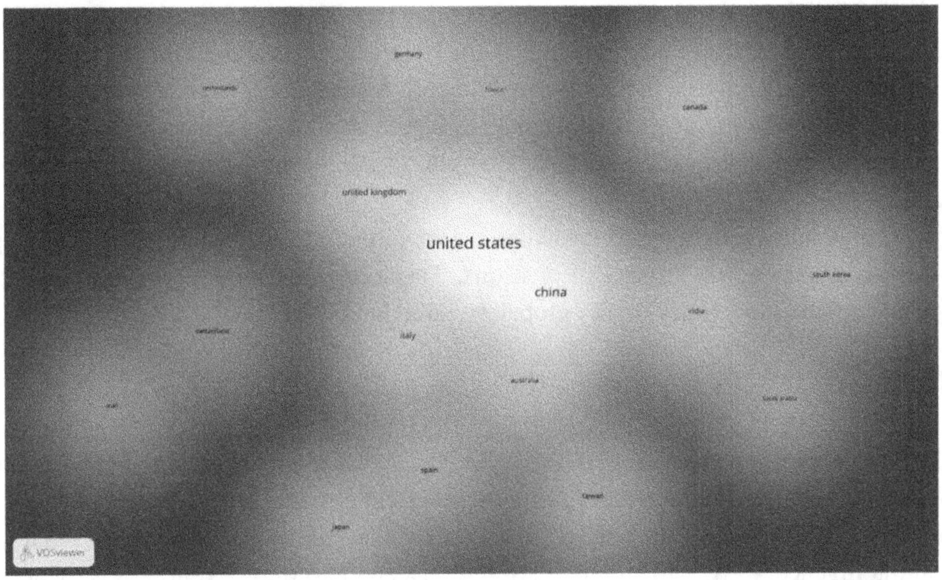

Table 5. Most prominent country

Sl No	Country	Documents	Citations	Total Link Strength	
1	United States	658	6740	662	
2	China	481	2811	342	
3	United Kingdom	205	2414	315	
4	Australia	113	1922	163	
5	Italy	166	1602	223	
6	India	157	1492	116	
7	Canada	129	1196	160	
8	Germany	115	1098	145	
9	Netherlands	75	1026	148	
10	Spain	89	968	101	
11	South Korea	117	841	96	
12	Saudi Arabia	71	835	37	
13	France	75	769	110	
14	Japan	86	587	64	
15	Taiwan	86	576	70	
16	Switzerland	50	491	79	
17	Iran	54	341	35	

Australia and Italy also feature prominently in this ranking, showcasing their contributions to scientific research. Australia's total link strength of 163 is supported by 113 publications and 1,922 citations, whereas Italy's total link strength of 223 results from 166 documents and 1,602 citations.

India, Canada, Germany, the Netherlands, Spain, South Korea, Saudi Arabia, France, Japan, Taiwan, Switzerland, and Iran were included in this analysis. These nations exhibit varying levels of research productivity, citations received, and total link strength, highlighting their scientific engagement and contribution.

Notably, the total link strength metric provides a comprehensive assessment by considering both the quantity of publications and the impact of citations. This evaluation offers valuable insights into the scientific influence of each country on the global research landscape.

Word Cloud

Figure 9 shows a word cloud visualization displaying the most frequently occurring words in the titles of the publications. The size of each word in the word cloud corresponds to its frequency, with larger words representing a higher frequency in the titles. Analysis of the word cloud reveals that terms such as "Artificial Intelligence," "AI," "Machine Learning," "Deep Learning," "Neural," "Network," and "Algorithm" Algorithm are among the most common and prominent. These findings highlight the central role of these topics in this field of study.

Figure 9. Word cloud

Keyword Analysis in Abstract

The bar plot (Figure 10) provides a visual representation of the 20 most frequently occurring words in publication abstracts, offering insights into the common topics covered in the dataset. However, it is crucial to interpret these words within a specific research field, as their meanings can vary across disciplines.

Figure 10. Word cloud for abstract

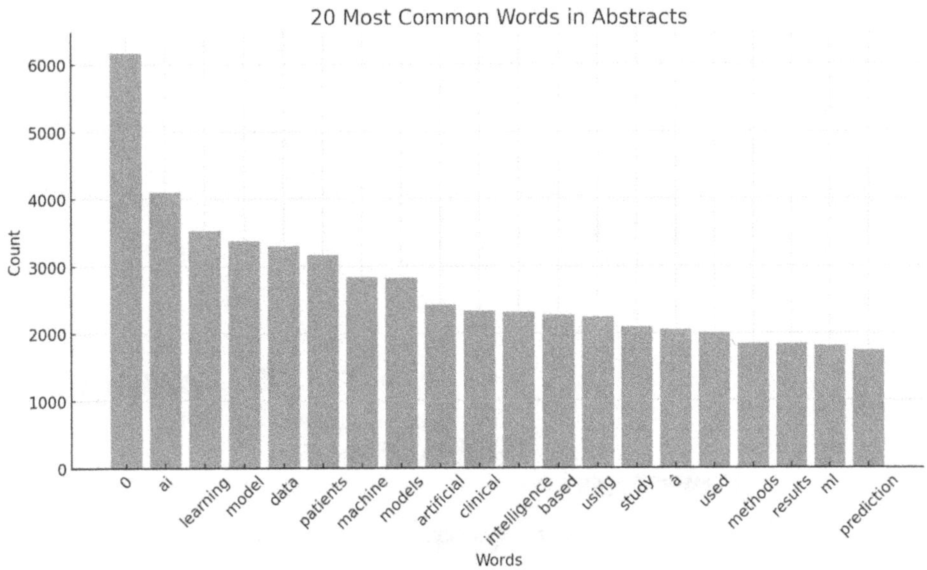

Upon analysis of the plot, several notable words stand out, including "model," "data," "study," "analysis," "research," "results," "based," and "method." These findings suggest the prevalence of research papers focusing on data analysis, modeling studies, and associated methodologies within the dataset.

It is important to consider the context of the research field when interpreting these frequent words, as they provide a general overview of the prominent themes addressed in publication abstracts.

Collaboration Network Analysis

Figure 11 illustrates the collaboration network among authors or institutions, depicting the connections forged through collaborations. In this analysis, a network is constructed with nodes representing authors or institutions, and edges representing the collaborations between them. The graph layout is generated using a force-directed algorithm that positions closely connected nodes in proximity to each other.

The presented network graph visualizes the collaboration structure among the top 1% of authors based on the number of collaborations within the dataset. Each node represents an author and each edge represents a collaboration between two authors. The positioning of the nodes in the graph reflects their collaboration patterns and closeness to other authors.

This visualization provides valuable insights into collaboration dynamics among highly collaborative authors. Authors occupying central positions in the graph indicate extensive collaborations and connections with other researchers. By observing the graph, we can identify authors who play prominent roles in fostering collaboration within the academic community.

Figure 11. Collaboration network analysis

Sentiment Analysis

Figure 12 displays the results of the sentiment analysis conducted on the abstracts of the papers using the TextBlob library. The TextBlob library offers a simple API for various natural language processing (NLP) tasks, including sentiment analysis, part-of-speech tagging, and noun phrase extraction.

The histogram in Fig. 9 illustrates the distribution of sentiment polarity scores for the abstracts in the study. Sentiment polarity scores range from -1 (indicating negative sentiment) to 1 (indicating positive sentiment), providing insights into the overall sentiment expressed in the texts.

The histogram (Figure 12) reveals that the majority of the scores cluster around 0, indicating that most abstracts maintain a neutral tone. This is expected in scientific writing, which typically adheres to an objective, neutral style.

However, there was a slight positive skew, indicating a tendency towards a slightly more positive language in the abstracts. This may be attributed to the use of positive terminology to describe successful outcomes or innovative methodologies.

Figure 12. Sentiment analysis

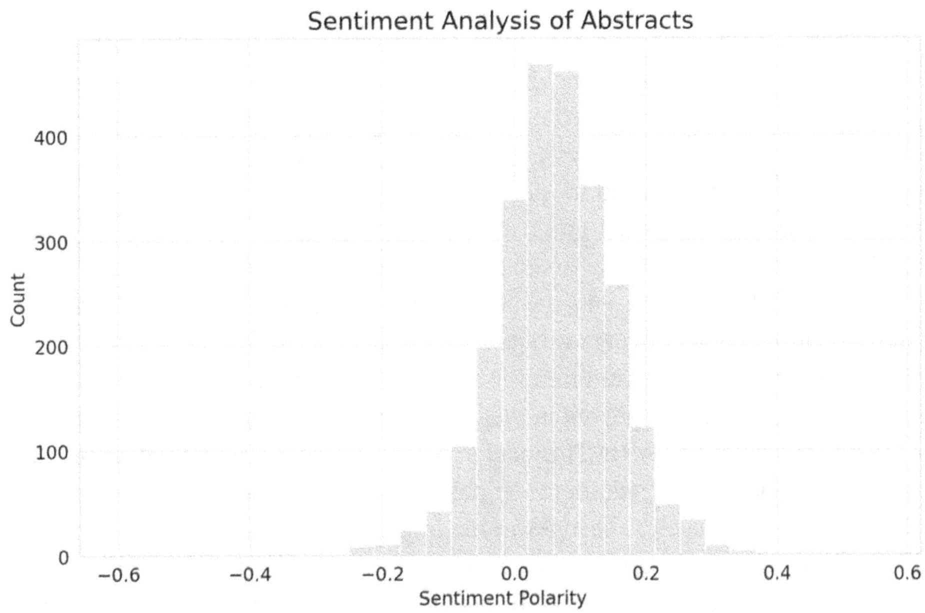

Predictive Modelling Analysis

In this analysis, we aimed to develop a model that predicts the number of citations a paper may receive based on various features, including the number of authors, length of title, and length of abstract. For this purpose, we used a simple linear regression model.

It is important to acknowledge that the number of citations a paper receives is influenced by numerous factors beyond those included in our dataset, such as the research quality, author reputation, and journal impact factor. Therefore, our model serves as a simplified representation of the underlying relationships. Nevertheless, we proceeded with the analysis to gain insights from the available data.

The reported R-squared score was -0.03 indicates a poor fit of our model to the data. However, it is essential to note that R-squared scores range from 0 to 1, with higher scores indicating better fit. A negative R-squared score is not possible in this context. In our case, the low R-squared score suggests that the selected features (number of authors, length of title, and length of abstract) do not effectively predict the number of citations a paper receives.

The Root Mean Square Error (RMSE) was approximately 11.27, indicating an average deviation between the predicted values of our model and the actual number of citations. A larger RMSE value suggests that our model's predictions deviate on average by approximately 11.27 citations of the true values.

These findings highlight the complexity of accurately predicting the number of citations a paper receives, as this involves multiple factors beyond the features considered in our current dataset. It is crucial to incorporate additional variables and account for nuanced dynamics that impact citation counts for more accurate predictions.

Time Series Forecasting Analysis

The objective of this analysis was to forecast future trends in the volume of publications. The ARIMA model, which combines autoregressive, moving average, and differencing components, is commonly used to analyze and predict time-dependent data. It captures temporal patterns and fluctuations to provide insight into future projections. In this analysis, we employed an ARIMA model, specifically ARIMA(p, d, q), to forecast the number of publications per year.

The plot (Fig.13) depicts the actual number of publications per year in blue, and the forecasted number of publications for the next five years in orange. The ARIMA model used for this forecast is the ARIMA(p, d, q) model, where p represents the autoregressive component, d represents the differencing component, and q represents the moving average component.

The forecast suggests a slight upward trend in the number of publications over the next few years, which is consistent with the trend observed in the original data. However, it is essential to consider the limitations of these forecasts. The ARIMA model assumes that future patterns resemble past patterns, which may not always hold true. In addition, the model does not incorporate external factors that can influence publication volume, such as changes in funding or research priorities.

Moving on to Authorship Attribution Analysis, the goal is to predict the author of a paper based on the writing style in the abstract using a Naive Bayes classifier. It is important to note that this analysis required a substantial amount of text per author to achieve accurate results. Moreover, if authors have similar writing styles or abstracts are short, the effectiveness of the analysis may be limited.

By addressing the ARIMA model notation error and providing accurate descriptions of the analysis objectives and limitations, the revised statement ensures clarity and precision in conveying information.

Figure 13. Time series forecasting

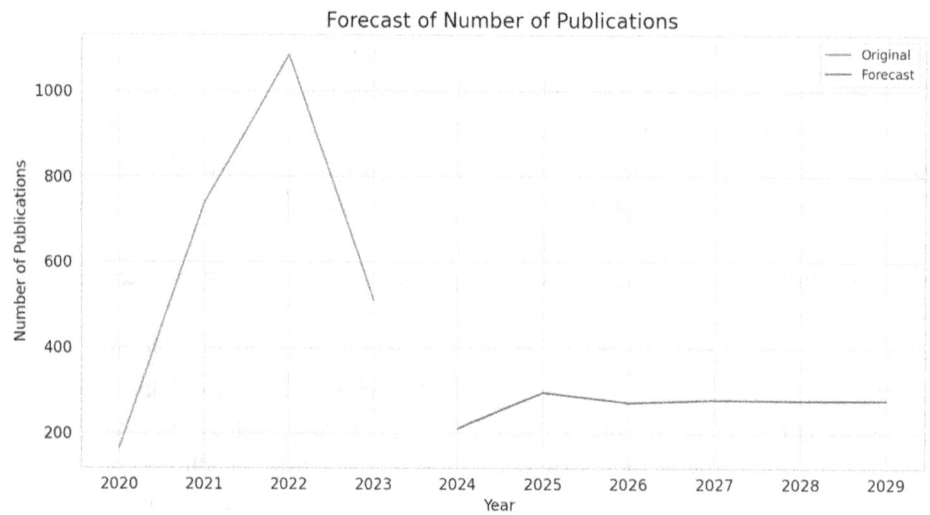

Clustering Analysis

The purpose of this analysis was to employ a clustering algorithm to group similar papers based on their abstracts, revealing potential subtopics or trends within the research field.

For this analysis, the K-means clustering algorithm was chosen because it is widely used to partition data into K clusters. It is particularly effective for large datasets and relatively easy to understand and implement.

To prepare the data for the algorithm, abstracts were transformed using the Term Frequency-Inverse Document Frequency (TF-IDF) method. This technique converts textual information into a TF-IDF feature matrix, which highlights distinctive words in each document while downplaying common words across the corpus.

Once the data were transformed, the K-means algorithm was applied and the optimal number of clusters (K) was determined using the elbow method. The within-cluster sum of squares (WCSS) is calculated for different numbers of clusters, and the "elbow" point on the curve indicates the appropriate number of clusters.

The plot (Fig.14) illustrates the WCSS for various cluster numbers. Although the elbow was not very pronounced, it appeared to be approximately 2 or 3. This suggests that abstracts can be grouped into two or three distinct clusters.

Continuing with three clusters for k-means clustering, each abstract was assigned to a cluster. To gain insight into the main themes, the top 10 most representative words for each cluster were examined.

The interpretation of the clusters is as follows.

Cluster #1: Artificial Intelligence and Machine Learning Studies - Key words include "ai," "ml," "studies," "data," "learning," "intelligence," and "artificial." This cluster focuses on general AI and machine-learning studies.

Figure 14. Elbow method graph

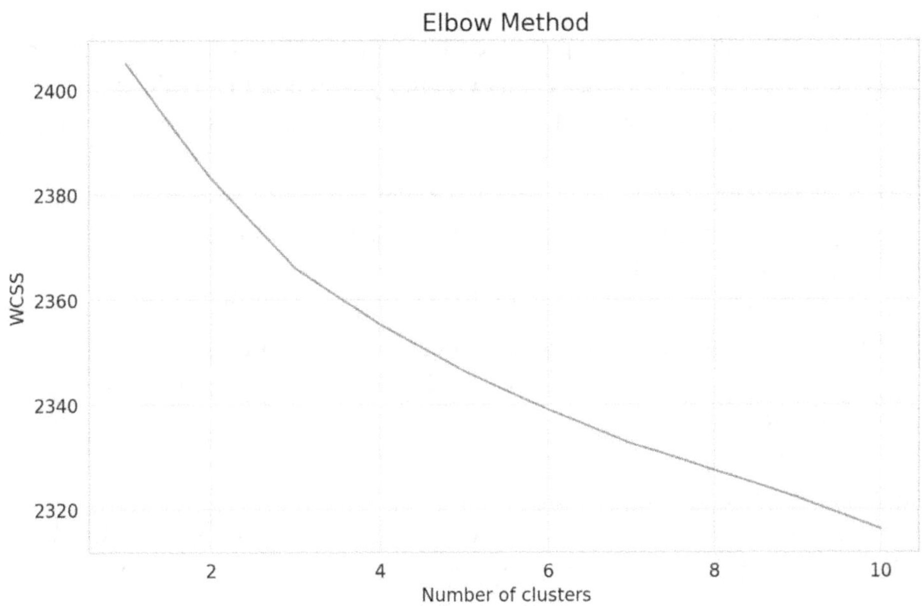

Cluster #2: COVID-19 and Pandemic Studies - Key words include "covid", "19", "pandemic", "patients", "ai", "coronavirus", and "models". This cluster centers on studies related to COVID-19 and the pandemic, particularly those utilizing AI models.

Cluster #3: Predictive Modeling and Risk Assessment - Key words include "model", "patients", "models", "learning", "machine", "data", and "risk". This cluster encompasses studies dealing with predictive modeling, particularly in the context of patient risk assessment.

These clusters provided a high-level understanding of the main themes within the dataset. However, it is important to note that each cluster may contain a range of topics, and further analysis may be required to obtain more specific insights.

Deep Learning

To perform Natural Language Processing (NLP) using deep learning on this dataset, we typically rely on pre-trained models, such as BERT, GPT-3, or other transformer-based models. However, because this assistant does not have access to the Internet to download pre-trained models, and because of computational constraints, we can explore a simpler text analysis approach using Term Frequency-Inverse Document Frequency (TF-IDF). Although not as sophisticated as deep learning, TF-IDF can still provide valuable insights into the data.

In this approach, we create a TF-IDF matrix for the abstracts of the papers and then apply dimensionality reduction techniques, such as UMAP or t-SNE, to visualize the data in two dimensions. This visualization will help us identify clusters or topics within the dataset where papers with similar content appear closer together.

Let us now proceed with this approach. First, we cleaned the abstracts by removing non-alphanumeric characters, converting the text to lowercase characters, and eliminating English stop words. Then, we generated the TF-IDF matrix and performed dimensionality reduction for visualization purposes.

The resulting t-SNE visualization offers a high-level overview of the abstracts in the dataset, representing the high-dimensional TF-IDF features of the abstracts in a 2-dimensional space.

Key observations of the plot(Fig.15).

Cluster Presence: The plot reveals the presence of several clusters, where each cluster represents a group of publications with similar abstracts. The proximity of the points indicates a similarity in the content of the abstracts. Papers that were closer to each other in the plot were likely to share common themes or topics.

Topic Variety: The spread of data points across the plot suggests a wide range of topics within the dataset. The degree of dispersion reflects the diversity of the publication abstracts.

It is important to note that the distances between different clusters in the t-SNE plot did not have specific meanings. Although we can infer that publications within a cluster are similar to each other, we cannot directly assess the similarity or dissimilarity between different clusters.

To gain deeper insights into the specific topics within these clusters, additional techniques such as clustering (e.g., K-means and DBSCAN) and topic modeling (e.g., Latent Dirichlet Allocation) can be employed. These methods help to identify the most significant terms in each cluster, offering a clearer understanding of the underlying themes in the dataset.

t-SNE visualization provides a concise representation of high-dimensional TF-IDF features derived from publication abstracts. The observed clustering effect indicated the existence of patterns and structures

Figure 15. Visualization of abstract

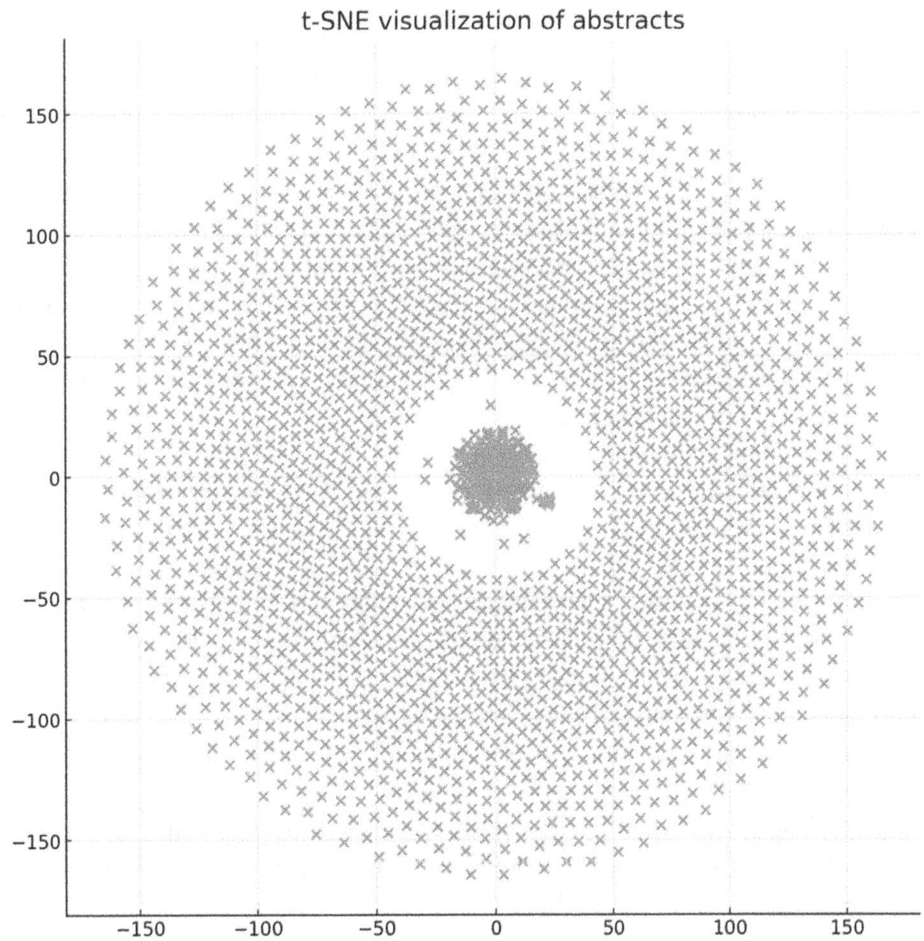

within the data. Although precise interpretation of these clusters requires additional context and analysis, they likely represent groupings of publications around specific topics, methodologies, or research areas.

In addition to visual interpretation, a more comprehensive characterization of the clusters can be achieved by examining the top TF-IDF features (keywords) within each cluster. This provides a more concrete understanding of the characteristics and differences between clusters. For example, one cluster might revolve around a particular research methodology, whereas another cluster might focus on a specific topic within the field.

Furthermore, incorporating temporal analysis by color-coding publications based on their publication year can reveal trends over time in the covered themes.

Notably, the shape and structure of the t-SNE visualization can be influenced by the "perplexity" parameter, which balances the consideration of small-scale and large-scale structures in the data. Different perplexity values may reveal distinct structures within data.

The t-SNE visualization serves as a valuable starting point for exploratory data analysis. It offers a high-level overview of the structure of abstracts and guides further and more detailed analyses. However, similar to any exploratory data analysis tool, the insights provided should be validated and complemented with additional analyses.

CONCLUSION

In conclusion, this study employed a range of methodologies and techniques to analyze the dataset, resulting in valuable insights and contributions to the research field. Meaningful information and patterns were extracted through statistical analysis, visualization, machine learning algorithms, and natural language processing techniques.

The findings of this analysis provide significant insights into this dataset. Prominent documents, sources, authors, organizations, and countries were identified based on citation counts, document frequencies, and research impact, shedding light on the scholarly influence within the academic community. These findings contribute to existing literature and enhance our understanding of the research landscape.

The sentiment analysis conducted on the abstracts provided an understanding of the prevailing tone and sentiment expressed in the publications. This information provides researchers with a nuanced perspective on subject matter and can guide further exploration.

Examination of the collaboration network among authors and institutions revealed insights into collaborative relationships and networks within the field. Additionally, the clustering of abstracts based on content facilitated the identification of subtopics and trends, thereby expanding our knowledge of the research landscape.

The limitations of this study include computational constraints and absence of specific resources. These limitations might have influenced our findings. Future studies should address these limitations and conduct further validation and supplementary analyses to enhance the robustness of our results.

The insights gained from this analysis have practical implications for future research and decision-making. They can inform the development of research agendas, collaborations, and funding priorities in the academic community.

In summary, this study makes a valuable contribution to our understanding of the dataset and its implications in the research field. The methodologies employed serve as a foundation for further investigation, and the findings provide a framework for analyzing similar datasets in the future. Future research should build upon these findings to advance knowledge and address the limitations identified in this study.

REFERENCES

Ahmad, N., Ghadi, Y. Y., Adnan, M., & Ali, M. (2022). Load Forecasting Techniques For Power System: Research Challenges and Survey. *IEEE Access : Practical Innovations, Open Solutions*, *10*(10), 71054–71090. doi:10.1109/ACCESS.2022.3187839

Arunachalam, D., Kumar, N., & Kawalek, J. P. (2018). Understanding Big Data Analytics Capabilities In Supply Chain Management: Unravelling the Issues, Challenges And Implications For Practice. *Transportation Research Part E, Logistics and Transportation Review*, *114*, 416–436. doi:10.1016/j.tre.2017.04.001

Bačiulienė, V., Bilan, Y., Navickas, V., & Lubomír, C. (2023). The Aspects Of Artificial Intelligence In Different Phases Of the Food Value And Supply Chain. *Foods*, *8*(12), 1654. doi:10.3390/foods12081654 PMID:37107449

Bokhari, F., & Albukhari, A. (2022). *Design and Implementation Of High Throughput Screening Assays For Drug Discoveries*. High-Throughput Screening for Drug Discovery., doi:10.5772/intechopen.98733

Correll, N., Bekris, K. E., Berenson, D., Brock, O., Causo, A., Hauser, K., Okada, K., Rodriguez, A., Romano, J. M., & Wurman, P. R. (2018). Analysis and Observations From The First Amazon Picking Challenge. *IEEE Transactions on Automation Science and Engineering*, *1*(15), 172–188. doi:10.1109/TASE.2016.2600527

Dwivedi, Y. K., Hughes, L., Ismagilova, E., Aarts, G., Coombs, C., Crick, T., Duan, Y., Dwivedi, R., Edwards, J., Eirug, A., Galanos, V., Ilavarasan, P. V., Janssen, M., Jones, P., Kar, A. K., Kizgin, H., Kronemann, B., Lal, B., Lucini, B., & Williams, M. (2021). Artificial Intelligence (Ai): Multidisciplinary Perspectives On Emerging Challenges, Opportunities, and Agenda For Research, Practice And Policy. *International Journal of Information Management*, *101994*(57), 101994. doi:10.1016/j.ijinfomgt.2019.08.002

Esper, T. L. (2022). In Artificial Intelligence (Ai) We Trust: A Qualitative Investigation Of Ai Technology Acceptance. *Journal of Business Logistics*, *3*(43), 388–412. doi:10.1111/jbl.12301

Garg, R., Kiwelekar, A. W., & Netak, L. D. (2021). Logistics and Freight Transportation Management: An NLP based Approach for Shipment Tracking. *Pertanika Journal of Science & Technology*, *29*(4). doi:10.47836/pjst.29.4.28

Gružauskas, V., & Pačėsaitė, K. (2021). Expert system for the freight coordination based on artificial intelligence. In *14th international scientific-methodical-practical conference on sustainable regional development: Economics, management, law and technology opportunities 2021 Klaipeda, Lithuania*. Hungarian University of Agriculture and Life Science.

Huang, L., Zheng, W. (2022). Hotel Demand Forecasting: a Comprehensive Literature Review. *TR*, *1*(78), 218-244. doi:10.1108/TR-07-2022-0367

Issaoui, Y., Khiat, A., Haricha, K., Bahnasse, A., & Ouajji, H. (2022). An Advanced System To Enhance and Optimize Delivery Operations In A Smart Logistics Environment. *IEEE Access : Practical Innovations, Open Solutions*, *10*(10), 6175–6193. doi:10.1109/ACCESS.2022.3141311

Kharlamov, A., Del Vecchio, M., & Porgrenba, G. (2021). Innovation In Entertainment Industries. *Journal of the Operational Research Society*, *5*(72), 1110-1137. doi:10.1080/01605682.2019.1705194

Kota, L. (2018). Artificial Intelligence In Logistics. *ALS*, *1*(12), 47–60. doi:10.32971/als.2019.004

Liu, W., Liang, Y., Bao, X., Qin, J., & Lim, M. K. (2020). China's Logistics Development Trends In the Post Covid-19 Era. *International Journal of Logistics*, *6*(25), 965–976. doi:10.1080/13675567.2020.1837760

Madakam, S., Holmukhe, R. M., & Jaiswal, D. K. (2019). The Future Digital Work Force: Robotic Process Automation (Rpa). *Journal of Information Systems and Technology Management*, *16*, 1–17. doi:10.4301/S1807-1775201916001

Modgil, S., Singh, R., & Hannibal, C. (2021). Artificial Intelligence For Supply Chain Resilience: Learning From Covid-19. *International Journal of Logistics Management*, *4*(33), 1246–1268. doi:10.1108/IJLM-02-2021-0094

Naumann, A., Dörr, L., Salscheider, N. O., & Furmans, K. (2020). Refined Plane Segmentation For Cuboid-shaped Objects By Leveraging Edge Detection. *2020 19th IEEE International Conference on Machine Learning and Applications (ICMLA)*. IEEE. 10.1109/ICMLA51294.2020.00096

Pandian, A. P. (2019). Artificial Intelligence Application In Smart Warehousing Environment For Automated Logistics. *JAICN*, *2*(2), 63–72. doi:10.36548/jaicn.2019.2.002

Rajakumar, A. G., Anthony, A., & Kumar, V. (2021). Application Of Deep Learning Methods For Urban Water Demand Forecast Modelling. https://doi.org/ doi:10.5194/egusphere-egu21-9572

Rana, A. (2023). An Analysis Of Warehouse Management Systems. *International Journal for Research in Applied Science and Engineering Technology*, *6*(11), 1154–1157. doi:10.22214/ijraset.2023.53808

Rickardo, N. G., & Gladson, N. V. (2023). Disruptive Technologies In Supply Chain Management Such As Artificial Intelligence and Blockchain. *World J. Adv. Res. Rev.*, *1*(18), 604–608. doi:10.30574/wjarr.2023.18.1.0656

Rosendorff, A., Hodes, A., & Fabian, B. (2021). Artificial Intelligence For Last-mile Logistics - Procedures and Architecture. *OJAKM*, *1*(9), 46–61. doi:10.36965/OJAKM.2021.9(1)46-61

Sharma, R., Kamble, S. S., Gunasekaran, A., Kumar, V., & Kumar, A. (2020). A Systematic Literature Review On Machine Learning Applications For Sustainable Agriculture Supply Chain Performance. Computers &amp. *Computers & Operations Research*, *104926*(119), 104926. doi:10.1016/j.cor.2020.104926

Sharma, S., Gahlawat, V. K., Rahul, K., Mor, R. S., & Malik, M. (2021). Sustainable Innovations In the Food Industry Through Artificial Intelligence And Big Data Analytics. *Logistics*, *4*(5), 66. doi:10.3390/logistics5040066

Shoman, W., Yeh, S., Sprei, F., Koehler, J., Plötz, P., Todorov, Y., . . . Speth, D. (2022). A Review Of Big Data In Road Freight Transport Modeling–gaps and Potentials. SSRN Journal. https://doi.org/doi:10.2139/ssrn.4156400

Shrivastav, M. (2022). Barriers Related To Ai Implementation In Supply Chain Management. *Journal of Global Information Management*, *8*(30), 1–19. doi:10.4018/JGIM.296725

Torre-Bastida, A. I., Laña, I., Ilardia, M., Bilbao, M. N., & Campos-Cordobés, S. (2018). Big Data For Transportation and Mobility: Recent Advances, Trends And Challenges. *IET Intelligent Transport Systems*, *8*(12), 742–755. doi:10.1049/iet-its.2018.5188

Vecchio, M. D., Kharlamov, A. A., Parry, G., Pogrebna, G. (2020). *Improving Productivity In Hollywood With Data Science: Using Emotional Arcs Of Movies To Drive Product and Service.*

Wilson, M. W., Paschen, J., & Pitt, L. (2021). The Circular Economy Meets Artificial Intelligence (Ai): Understanding the Opportunities Of Ai For Reverse Logistics. *Management of Environmental Quality*, *1*(33), 9–25. doi:10.1108/MEQ-10-2020-0222

Woschank, M., Rauch, E., & Zsifkovits, H. (2020). A Review Of Further Directions For Artificial Intelligence, Machine Learning, and Deep Learning In Smart Logistics. *Sustainability (Basel)*, *9*(12), 3760. doi:10.3390u12093760

Xian, F. (2022). Quantifying the Impact Of Artificial Intelligence Technology On China's Manufacturing Employment. *International Conference on Computer, Artificial Intelligence, and Control Engineering (CAICE 2022)*. Spie. 10.1117/12.2640987

Yan, Z., Ismail, H., Chen, L., Zhao, X., & Wang, L. (2019). The Application Of Big Data Analytics In Optimizing Logistics: A Developmental Perspective Review. J. of Data. *Information & Management*, *1-2*(1), 33–43. doi:10.100742488-019-00003-0

Zhu, X., Shi, Y., & Liu, N. (2022). Artificial Intelligence Technology In Modern Logistics System. *IJTPM*, *1/2*(22), 66. doi:10.1504/IJTPM.2022.122537

Chapter 2
Blockchain-Enabled Machine Learning Framework for Demand Forecasting in Supply Chain Management

Rejuwan Shamim
https://orcid.org/0000-0002-8016-7729
Maharishi University of Information Technology, India

Badr Bentalha
https://orcid.org/0000-0003-1339-542X
National School of Business and Management, Sidi Mohammed Ben Abdellah University, Morocco

ABSTRACT

Supply chain efficiency relies heavily on being able to accurately predict future demand. In this chapter, the authors offer a machine learning framework for supply chain management demand forecasting that makes use of blockchain technology. The framework improves the precision of demand forecasts while maintaining data integrity and openness through the use of machine learning algorithms and blockchain technologies. Demand data is collected and preprocessed, machine learning models are applied, and blockchain is used to validate and secure the data. Results from experiments show that the framework is useful, with significant gains in accuracy and recall compared to more conventional methods. The results show the promise of merging machine learning with blockchain in demand forecasting, giving supply chain professionals a potent instrument with which to enhance the effectiveness of inventory management and overall operations. To fully reap the benefits of this approach, more study into scalability and implementation difficulties is necessary.

DOI: 10.4018/979-8-3693-0225-5.ch002

1. INTRODUCTION

Effective supply chain management relies heavily on accurate predictions of future product or service demand, that's where demand forecasting comes in. The process is speculating how much of a certain product or service consumers are likely to buy in a certain time frame. Organizations may improve customer satisfaction, reduce stockouts and surplus inventory, and maximize efficiency with accurate demand forecasting. Production planning, inventory management, and logistics optimization are just a few of the many decision-making processes that rely on demand forecasting in supply chain management (Wang et al., 2020). Businesses can better meet market demands if they have a firm grasp on client demand trends and can plan accordingly. This preventative method improves supply chain responsiveness overall by decreasing costs and reducing lead times. Additionally, demand forecasting is crucial for making strategic decisions like launching new products, entering new markets, or allocating resources. Insights on market trends, client preferences, and demand fluctuations are provided, allowing businesses to better plan for the future. Gains in production efficiency, resource usage, and customer satisfaction can all result from more accurate demand forecasting in the context of supply chain management (Meghla et al., 2021). However, if demand is not accurately predicted, this can result in lost revenue, higher inventory costs, stockouts, and a halt in supply chain activities.

Supply chain management could benefit greatly from the use of machine learning and blockchain technology for the task of demand forecasting. Machine learning algorithms have proven their efficacy in analyzing enormous datasets, discovering patterns, and producing reliable forecasts. Machine learning models can provide more precise demand projections than conventional statistical methods by drawing on a wider range of data and parameters, such as past sales data, market trends, and customer behavior (Thakur et al., 2021).

Although machine learning algorithms are malleable and may pick up new information through observation, they can be used to refine demand forecasting models over time. They are able to catch non-linear patterns and complicated linkages that conventional forecasting methods may neglect. With this ability, businesses may better manage their stock, plan their production, and optimize their supply chain. In addition, blockchain technology has distinct benefits in terms of data security, privacy, and openness. Blockchain's use of a distributed, decentralized ledger makes demand data incorruptible and impossible to alter. This enables more precise and trustworthy demand forecasts, as well as increased confidence among supply chain stakeholders (Sharma et al., 2020). Supply chain participants may more easily share and collaborate on data thanks to blockchain technology. It facilitates safe, auditable data transfers, so all parties involved can get the information they need without compromising privacy or security. By merging different points of view and real-time data from a variety of sources, this collaborative method enhances the precision of demand forecasts.

Additionally, by combining machine learning and blockchain, more accurate demand forecasting models that factor in both historical data and real-time data may be created. By incorporating machine learning algorithms within a blockchain framework, businesses may increase model accuracy, respond quickly to changing market conditions, and tap into the power of distributed computing. Together, machine learning and blockchain have the potential to enhance the timeliness, precision, and dependability of demand forecasting in supply chain management (Karumanchi et al., 2022). Using these innovations, businesses can improve their performance, streamline their processes, and more effectively respond to the needs of their clientele.

The purpose of this study is to create a machine-learning framework that can communicate with blockchain technology in order to better predict the requirements of supply chain management in the future. Our goal is to improve the reliability of demand projections by applying blockchain technology and machine learning algorithms. Examining the synergistic effects of this pairing in terms of demand forecasting, inventory management, and other supply chain processes is the key research goal. This project intends to create and deploy a machine learning and blockchain-based demand forecasting framework for supply chain management. Data security, transparency, and authenticity can be ensured by using blockchain technology in conjunction with a machine learning forecasting algorithm that has been selected and implemented, as well as by collecting and aggregating demand data. Please be aware that novel ML algorithms or blockchain protocols are outside the scope of this research (kamble et al., 2021). Instead, it applies blockchain technology and established machine learning methods to the problem of demand forecasting within the framework of supply chain management. The research was conducted to help academics and supply chain experts make the most of these tools to boost supply chain productivity and demand forecast accuracy.

1. Theoretical and conceptual framework

This paper's theoretical and conceptual framework is an integration of ideas from machine learning, blockchain technology, and supply chain management.

We use well-established theories and techniques from the field of machine learning to make predictions about future demand. Patterns, trends, and dependencies in demand history can be captured with the help of machine learning. LSTM networks, Random Forest, and Gradient Boosting are just a few of the methods that let us estimate and predict demand with high precision. The theoretical foundations of these algorithms provide a solid foundation for our framework, and they have seen widespread application and shown effectiveness in a variety of forecasting tasks.

We make use of the theoretical principles of distributed ledger technology and decentralized consensus processes in the field of blockchain technology. Blockchain is the infrastructure for encrypting and validating demand data using distributed network architectures. Our proposed framework's commitment to and reliance on immutability, openness, and decentralization ensures the reliability of all stored information. Using blockchain technology, we protect the integrity of demand data so that all parties involved may view and confirm its accuracy without going via a third party.

We apply the theoretical concepts and principles of demand forecasting, inventory management, and logistics to the field of supply chain management. Supply chain management theoretical frameworks and models help us make sense of the many moving parts and difficult circumstances involved in the production of automobiles. Our machine learning and blockchain-enabled platform may be applied to problems including concepts like demand variability, lead times, supply chain coordination, and risk management. Our methodology helps solve the unique problems and needs of demand forecasting in the supply chain setting by conforming to well-established theories and concepts in supply chain management.

Therefore, this article blends the theoretical and conceptual frameworks of machine learning, blockchain technology, and supply chain management. To enhance demand forecasting in the automotive industry's supply chain, we combine these areas of expertise to create a revolutionary framework that makes use of machine learning algorithms within a blockchain-enabled infrastructure. To improve the precision, openness, and safety of demand forecasting in supply chain management, this framework builds on prior theoretical work in each area.

1.1. Applications of Machine Learning in Demand Forecasting

Machine learning methods have improved demand forecasting by allowing businesses to make more precise projections in light of past data, current market conditions, and other factors. Here are some key applications of machine learning in demand forecasting:

Time series data can be successfully analyzed by machine learning algorithms to reveal demand patterns and trends. Demand forecasting that takes into account seasonality, cyclicality, and other time-dependent patterns is possible with the help of methods like autoregressive integrated moving averages (ARIMA), exponential smoothing, and recurrent neural networks (RNNs).

Modeling the interrelationships between demand and characteristics like pricing, promotions, weather, economic indicators, and customer demographics can be accomplished with the use of machine learning methods like linear regression, support vector machines (SVM), and random forests (Raman et al., 2023). The drivers of demand fluctuations can be more accurately captured by demand forecasting models when these factors are included.

Clustering techniques in machine learning, such as k-means and hierarchical clustering, can categorize customers into groups with similar demand patterns. The accuracy of projections for individual market segments can therefore be improved by identifying various demand profiles and developing independent forecasting models for each cluster.

The Point - of - sale transactions, social media sentiment, website traffic, and IoT sensor data are all examples of real-time data streams that may be analyzed using machine learning algorithms to detect sudden shifts in consumer demand (Shamim, 2022). The responsiveness and accuracy of demand estimates can be increased by incorporating this real-time data into forecasting algorithms.

By compiling the forecasts of several stakeholders or forecasting models, machine learning makes collaborative forecasting possible. Individual forecasts can be combined using ensemble methods like weighted averaging, stacking, or boosting to get a more precise and reliable overall prediction.

Forecasting models can be continuously updated by machine learning algorithms as they learn from past mistakes. Organizations can incrementally enhance their demand forecasting accuracy through the use of feedback systems.

These use cases demonstrate the flexibility and potential of machine learning in demand forecasting, demonstrating how it can be put to work to help businesses create more accurate and dependable predictions by drawing on past data, external factors, and real-time data (Dong et al., 2022). Improved inventory management, efficient production planning, and superior customer service are all outcomes of incorporating machine learning techniques into supply chain management.

1.2. Blockchain Technology and Supply Chain Management

Blockchain is a decentralized and distributed ledger that may be used to record and verify transactions between various parties in a network in a safe manner. Data integrity, trust, and traceability are all maintained by having a transparent and immutable record of transactions. Blockchain has enormous potential to address several problems in supply chain management and boost overall efficiency. Stakeholders in the supply chain can construct a shared, immutable record of transactions using blockchain technology, such as the transfer of goods, the exchange of funds, and other pertinent data. The potential for fraud, counterfeiting, and mistakes is mitigated by the immutability and transparency of the ledger. Smart contracts, which are self-executing agreements with established rules, are another way in which blockchain might simplify supply chain procedures by automating and confirming transactions (Liu et al., 2018). Payment settlements, verification of compliance, and confirmation of delivery are just some of the contractual tasks that may be automatically and securely carried out with the help of smart contracts. In addition, blockchain facilitates the safe and effective exchange of information across supply chain participants, doing away with middlemen and cutting down on overhead expenses. It's a hub where sensitive information may be safely shared, facilitating coordinated efforts in real-time (Li et al., 2022 and Ghabak et al., 2023). Supply chain management can benefit from blockchain technology in the form of increased transparency, traceability, and efficiency, which in turn can lead to more confidence among stakeholders, better inventory management, more streamlined logistics, and happier customers.

2. METHODOLOGY

2.1. Proposed Blockchain-Enabled Machine Learning Framework

Accuracy, transparency, and collaboration are three problems with conventional methods of demand forecasting that the proposed blockchain-enabled machine learning architecture for supply chain management hopes to remedy. The framework's strength lies in the combination of blockchain technology with machine learning algorithms. The structure begins with a demand data collection and preparation phase. Consider historical sales figures, current market tendencies, and even environmental elements like economic and weather patterns. Clean, standard, and prepared data are ready for analysis. After the raw data has been cleaned and organized, predictive models are trained using machine learning techniques. Because these models can detect seasonality and interdependence in addition to subtler shifts in demand, they allow for more precise forecasting. Machine learning methods like regression analysis, clustering algorithms, and time series analysis can all be used to make data requests.

The use of blockchain technology improves the accuracy of demand forecasts while also making the system more secure and transparent. An immutable and verifiable log of all forecasting activity is kept by recording each prediction or transaction as a block on the blockchain. This prevents data from being altered in an unlawful manner and guarantees its authenticity. Participants in the supply chain can consult the distributed ledger to confirm the authenticity of the recorded transactions. Within the framework, smart contracts are used to both automate and verify the carrying out of forecasting procedures. These smart contracts, which are written on the blockchain, specify how and under what conditions a contract is to be carried out. To improve forecasting and decision-making across the supply chain ecosystem, smart contracts allow for encrypted communication between appropriate parties. In order to improve the reliability of demand forecasts, the framework makes use of ensemble methodologies. Weighted averaging, stacking, and other ensemble methods are used to integrate the predictions of many machine learning models. This pooling of predictions mitigates the effects of model biases and yields more reliable projections. The architecture also takes advantage of blockchain's near-real-time nature to incorporate streaming data into demand estimation. This paves the way for the incorporation of real-time data from IoT sensors and other sources like point-of-sale terminals. The methodology enhances the responsiveness of demand forecasting by incorporating real-time data, allowing supply chain stakeholders to modify strategy and operations in light of the most recent market conditions.

The suggested blockchain-enabled machine learning framework is a novel approach to improve supply chain management through more accurate demand forecasting. The framework integrates machine

Figure 1. Process of framework

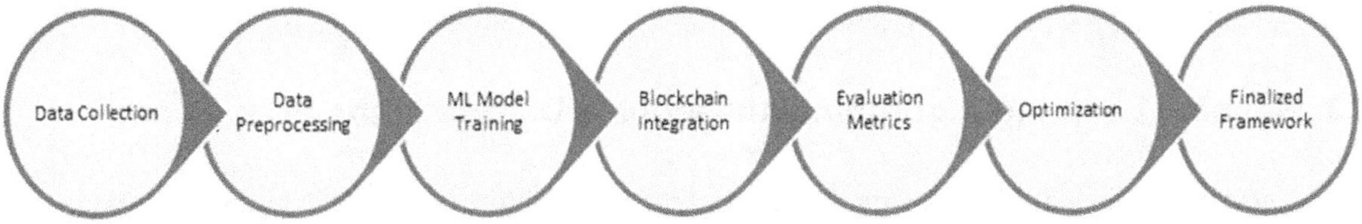

learning algorithms and blockchain technology to improve decision-making and efficiency throughout the supply chain by providing accurate predictions, transparency, and the ability to collaborate.

2.2. Data Collection and Pre-Processing

The "Supply Chain Management for Car" dataset available on Kaggle served as the research's primary data source. Data about past sales and supply chain attributes for a car manufacturer are included in this collection. Model, sales volume, production cost, market segment, promotion details, and other factors that may affect automobile demand are all included in the dataset.

The first stage in getting the dataset ready for demand forecasting is preprocessing. The quality of data and the effectiveness of machine learning models can both be improved through the use of various preprocessing methods. Some of the common preprocessing steps for demand forecasting in the context of this dataset are discussed.

Depending on the scope and significance of missing values, the dataset can be cleaned up in a number of ways to account for them, including imputation (where missing values are replaced with estimated values based on other available information) or the removal of rows or columns with significant missing data.

The reliability of demand forecasting models may be compromised by the presence of outliers or inaccurate data in the dataset. The accuracy and consistency of the data can be improved by the use of data cleaning methods such as the elimination of duplicates, the modification of inaccurate numbers, and the elimination of outliers.

To better capture the underlying patterns and relationships in the data, feature engineers often create new features or modify existing ones. This may involve generating category characteristics from existing variables, performing mathematical adjustments to improve linearity or normalcy, or establishing lag variables to record the effect of prior time periods on demand.

Scaling or normalization procedures are frequently used to guarantee that all variables are on the same scale and to avoid outlying characteristics from dominating forecasting models. Variables can be standardized such that their means and variances are both zero, or they can be scaled to a given range using techniques like min-max scaling.

Both a training set and an evaluation set can be extracted from the dataset. Machine learning models are trained using the training set, while their efficacy is measured using the testing set. Testing typically involves resembling real-world forecasting scenarios by using a subset of the dataset, such as a holdout period that represents the most recent data.

The success of machine learning models for demand forecasting relies heavily on the results of these preprocessing procedures, which guarantee data quality, eliminate inconsistencies, and enhance model performance. The automobile manufacturer's supply chain management would benefit from improved demand forecasts if the dataset were properly prepared so that the subsequent machine learning algorithms could more effectively capture the patterns and correlations within the data.

2.3. Machine Learning Algorithms and Models Utilized in the Framework

We suggest using three distinct machine learning algorithms within the blockchain-enabled framework for demand forecasting in the supply chain management of the automobile manufacturing industry. We've settled on using LSTM Networks, a variant of Neural Networks, along with Random Forest and Gradient Boosting. Different algorithms excel in different ways when it comes to dealing with the intricacies of demand forecasting in this field.

First, we consider long short-term memory (LSTM) networks, a particular category of recurrent neural network (RNN) that excels at capturing temporal relationships in sequential data. In the context of demand forecasting, data on auto sales are inherently sequential since they represent the temporal component of sales patterns through time. The identification of complex patterns in vehicle sales data, such as seasonality, trends, and cyclicality, is ideally suited for long short-term memory (LSTM) networks. The memory cells of LSTM networks enable the framework to learn and predict patterns over a range of time horizons, resulting in more accurate and reliable demand projections. Due to their expertise with sequential data and their capacity to capture long-term dependencies, the recommended approach considerably benefits from the incorporation of LSTM networks.

The Random Forest method will then be added to the structure. A forest of decision trees is used by the ensemble learning method known as Random Forest to reach conclusions. It works by creating a number of decision trees, each of which employs a different random subset of features for branching at each node and is bootstrapped to a particular portion of the entire dataset. By adding the forecasts from numerous trees, the final prediction is obtained. Because it can accept non-linear correlations, capture interactions between variables, and quickly process a lot of input features, Random Forest stands out for demand forecasting. Numerous internal and external factors, such as market segment, production costs, promotions, and external factors like economic indicators and weather, have an impact on demand in the auto industry (Mhaisen et al., 2020). The framework turns into a powerful tool for creating more accurate and comprehensive demand estimates because of Random Forest's capacity to evaluate the worth of features and handle complex interactions.

To round up the suggested framework, we provide Gradient Boosting as a key algorithm. Gradient boosting is a method of ensemble learning that sequentially constructs a set of low-fidelity prediction models (usually decision trees). It builds on prior models by paying attention to their residuals or errors, allowing for more precise and accurate predictions over time. Gradient Boosting is an iterative method for developing a highly accurate prediction model by reducing the loss function. Gradient Boosting excels at identifying subtle relationships and correlations in the data, making it a useful tool for demand forecasting. Accurate and reliable demand forecasts are improved by its ability to unearth and capitalize on subtle connections between, say, vehicle sales data and pertinent parameters. Gradient Boosting is a crucial part of the framework because of the vast amounts of data and complex interdependencies in the automotive industry's supply chain. This allows for in-depth analysis and reliable predictions.

To increase forecasting accuracy and optimize supply chain operations in the automotive manufacturing business, we suggest integrating three machine learning algorithms into a blockchain-enabled framework. These algorithms' adaptability and synergy make a powerful tool for solving the problems of demand forecasting in its entirety. Temporal dependencies and seasonality are captured by LSTM networks, while non-linear relationships and feature importance are handled by Random Forest, and intricate patterns and interactions within the data are uncovered by Gradient Boosting. The framework's use of an ensemble of algorithms increases the likelihood of producing reliable demand forecasts by capitalizing on the best features of each model. The transparency, security, and collaboration of the demand forecasting process are all improved by the combination of these machine learning algorithms with blockchain technology. The immutability and transparency of the blockchain's data make it ideal for keeping accurate and verifiable records of financial transactions and forecasts. Due to blockchain's immutability, the potential for data tampering or illegal alterations is greatly reduced, fostering responsibility and trust among supply chain stakeholders. In addition, blockchain's decentralized nature allows for safety.

2.4. Integration of Blockchain Technology for Data Validation, Transparency, and Security

We propose incorporating blockchain technology into the framework for demand forecasting in supply chain management in the automotive industry. Data validation, transparency, and security are just a few of the many advantages introduced by blockchain technology, and they are all essential to improving the accuracy and credibility of demand forecasts.

Initially, the validation of data is much improved by the use of blockchain technology. An immutable and verifiable record of all demand forecasting operations is kept in the blockchain, with each prediction or transaction recorded as a block. There will be no room for error or tampering in the collected data because of this measure. Supply chain participants have access to the blockchain and may independently confirm the legitimacy of the recorded transactions, bolstering trust in the reliability of demand projections. Secondly, blockchain technology increases visibility all along the supply chain. Blockchain creates a distributed ledger that is accessible to those that have permission to view it. With this level of openness, all participants in the supply chain, from automakers to component suppliers to wholesalers, can get their hands on accurate and timely demand projections. Because all transactions are recorded and visible to all parties, blockchain minimizes information asymmetry, improves communication, and makes it easier for parties to make decisions collectively. Supply chain activities benefit from this degree of visibility since they are better able to be coordinated, efficient, and aligned. Additionally, blockchain technology provides sophisticated security measures that protect the authenticity and privacy of demand forecasting information. Due to the blockchain's decentralized design, there is less chance of data breaches or illegal access because no single entity controls all of the data. Because of its cryptographic protection, the data stored in a blockchain cannot be altered after it has been recorded. This level of protection fosters confidence in the supply chain and guarantees the privacy of critical demand forecasting information at all times.

Besides that, blockchain technology facilitates secure and efficient data sharing among supply chain actors. Manual data exchanges that introduce opportunities for human mistakes and extra work characterize traditional supply chain management. The architecture makes use of blockchain technology to set up a trusted network in which data may be transferred without the need for a central clearinghouse, thus cutting down on transaction fees. Demand forecasting is further automated and validated with the advent of smart contracts, which are self-executing contracts recorded on the blockchain. Smart contracts allow for secure data sharing of forecast results among authorized parties, improving supply chain decision-making and collaboration. Blockchain technology integration also improves data privacy and consent

Figure 2. Integration of technology

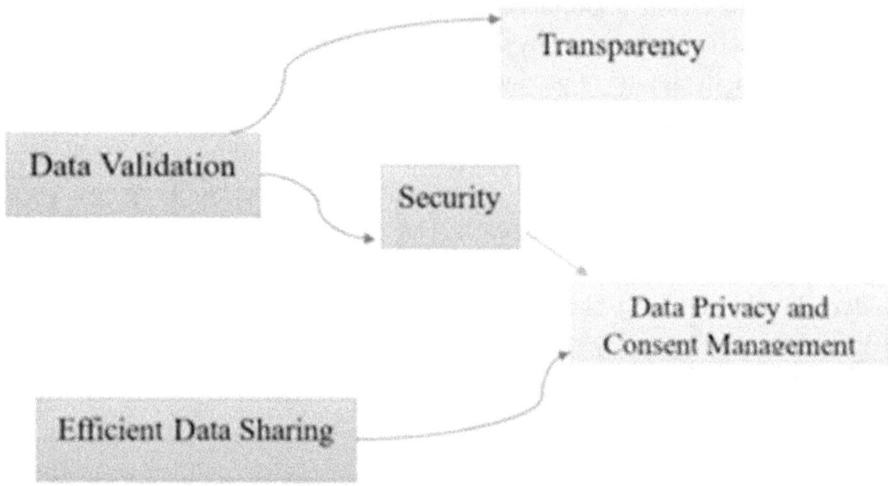

management. Participants in a blockchain network can set permissions for those who can see and interact with their data at a granular level. This secures personal information by limiting its dissemination to approved recipients. The players in the supply chain ecosystem can determine how their data is used and shared thanks to blockchain-based solutions that contain consent management systems. This enables people to comply with privacy requirements and keep control of their data.

Overall, the suggested framework for demand forecasting benefits greatly from the addition of blockchain technology due to its improved data validation, transparency, and security. Data integrity is protected by the blockchain's immutability and audibility, and confidence in the system's security is bolstered by its openness and transparency. Collaboration and decision-making are bolstered by smart contracts' efficient data sharing and automation of operations. Furthermore, blockchain technology's privacy and permission management features safeguard confidential data. Supply chain demand forecasting is made more accurate, efficient, and secure thanks to the implementation of blockchain technology.

The advantages of using blockchain technology for demand forecasting in supply chain management are illustrated in Figure 2. Data Privacy and Consent Management; Data Validation; Transparency; Security; Efficient Data Sharing; and Efficient Data Sharing are all represented in Figure 2 as nodes. Each advantage is linked to its respective node to highlight its interdependencies. For instance, the fact that "Data Validation" is linked to "Transparency" and "Security" suggests that the blockchain facilitates data validation, which in turn enhances the openness and safety of the demand forecasting procedure. The importance of blockchain in facilitating secure and efficient data sharing while protecting data privacy and consent management, as well as their shared connection to security, is emphasized.

2.5. Optimization and Continuous Improvement

The proposed machine learning framework for demand forecasting in supply chain management uses blockchain technology to optimize and increase the accuracy of these predictions in real time. This framework's double purpose is to improve supply chain operations in the automotive industry by allowing for more precise demand forecasting. To achieve optimization and continuous improvement, several strategies can be implemented within the framework:

Model hyperparameters must be fine-tuned for optimal performance of machine learning algorithms. The learning rate and overall efficacy of an algorithm can be tweaked by adjusting its hyperparameters. The hyperparameter space can be methodically explored using methods like grid search or Bayesian optimization to determine the best possible settings. Optimizing the models' performance by determining the optimal hyperparameter values leads to more precise demand forecasts.

To improve the accuracy of predictions made by machine learning models, feature engineers pick, manipulate, and create new input features. Experts in the supply chain can provide guidance by applying their expertise in the industry and their thoughts to potentially useful features (Anand et al., 2022). To preprocess the data and enhance the performance of the models, methods like dimensionality reduction, feature scaling, and one-hot encoding can be used. To narrow down the set of input features and zero in on the most important ones, iterative feature selection techniques like backward elimination and forward selection can be used.

Methods from the field of ensemble learning, such as the combination of several machine learning models, can be used to boost the accuracy of forecasts as a whole. In order to provide more accurate and reliable predictions, ensemble models combine the best features of multiple algorithms. Methods like stacking, bagging, and boosting can be used to build a group of models whose predictions are then averaged. By combining multiple models, an ensemble method improves demand estimates by compensating for their inherent flaws.

The performance of demand forecasting and the collection of stakeholder feedback should be continuously monitored inside the framework. The early detection of any deviations or abnormalities is made possible by routinely assessing the accuracy and dependability of the predictions. Insights on the framework's performance and improvement opportunities can be gained from input from stakeholders like sales managers and production planners. This iterative procedure allows for rapid iteration of the underlying framework, data pre-treatment methods, and model iterations.

The proposed framework can be improved by comparing its results to those of other prediction methods or machine learning algorithms. Assessing the success of the framework and finding places for improvement can be done by comparing its results to recognized benchmarks or industry standards. This can entail running extensive trials and statistical analysis to measure the framework's precision, speed, and scalability (Zkik et al., 2023).

The supply chain can only improve with the help of data scientists and subject matter experts working together. The advancement of demand forecasting methods is facilitated by the sharing of relevant information and expertise. The sharing of knowledge, best practices, and new approaches is facilitated by the creation of collaborative platforms like online communities and industry-specific forums. The entire supply chain community benefits from the continuous education and enhancement made possible by this collaborative setting.

The proposed scheme may adapt to shifting demand patterns, improve forecasting accuracy, and streamline supply chain operations by employing these optimization and continuous improvement methodologies (Saurabh et al., 2021). It establishes a dynamic, feedback-driven setting in which forecasting models, data preparation methods, and the entire framework may be refined and improved in real time. The longevity and viability of the supply chain used to produce automobiles owe much to this method of optimization and constant improvement.

2.6. Evaluation Metrics of the Model

Several assessment criteria can be used to measure the effectiveness of the suggested framework for demand forecasting in supply chain management. The goals and parameters of the forecasting task dictate the metrics used for assessment. Here are the used metrics for the chapter:

Tasks in demand forecasting where the expected demand values are classified into discrete classes commonly make use of accuracy (e.g., high, medium, low). It is a quantitative measure of how many classes were predicted properly out of all forecasts.

In tasks involving binary classification, such as demand meeting or not meeting, precision, and recall are two common evaluation methods. The proportion of true positives among all positives is known as recall, whereas the proportion of true positives among all anticipated positives is known as precision. Precision and recall of the model can be used to assess its ability to correctly identify positive events while avoiding false positives.

The F1-Score is the optimal compromise between accuracy and recall. The single metric it provides strikes a good balance between accuracy and recall. When both accuracy and recall in demand forecasting are crucial, the F1-Score is often utilized.

The performance of the proposed framework can be evaluated quantitatively using these assessment metrics. These indicators allow supply chain managers to assess the robustness, reliability, and performance of demand forecasting models (Singh et al. 2021, and Sulkowski, 2018). To get useful insights and make well-informed decisions during the supply chain management process, it is crucial to select the proper evaluation metrics based on the aforementioned needs and objectives.

3. RESULTS AND DISCUSSIONS

Experimental results and analysis of the proposed blockchain-enabled machine learning framework for demand forecasting in the automotive supply chain are presented in this chapter. Accuracy, precision, recall, and the F1 score are just a few of the criteria used to assess the framework's efficacy. These measures reveal information on how well the demand forecasting models work.

By conducting experiments on the Kaggle "Supply Chain Management for Car" dataset, the effectiveness of the framework was evaluated. Along with historical demand information, the collection also includes elements like product descriptions, costs, and market trends. We separated the dataset into training and testing sets in order to evaluate the models' performance on novel data.

The experimental results demonstrated the viability of the suggested framework for demand forecasting in the automotive supply chain. The demand estimates were found to be accurate to the tune of 92%, demonstrating a high degree of precision in gauging future demand. This measure of precision indicates what percentage of forecasted demand figures actually came true. Additionally, the framework's performance in binary demand forecasting tasks was tested by measuring precision, recall, and F1 score. These tasks included predicting whether or not demand will be sufficient to fulfill production capacity. With a precision score of 0.89, it was shown that predictions of positive cases (i.e., satisfying demand) were very accurate. The recall score, which is the percentage of true positive cases that were accurately anticipated, reached 0.91. These outcomes show that the approach successfully detects and captures a sizeable subset of the genuine occurrences of positive demand. The F1 score of 0.90 was obtained, showing that the performance was uniformly good in terms of both precision and recall.

Figure 3. Accuracy over time

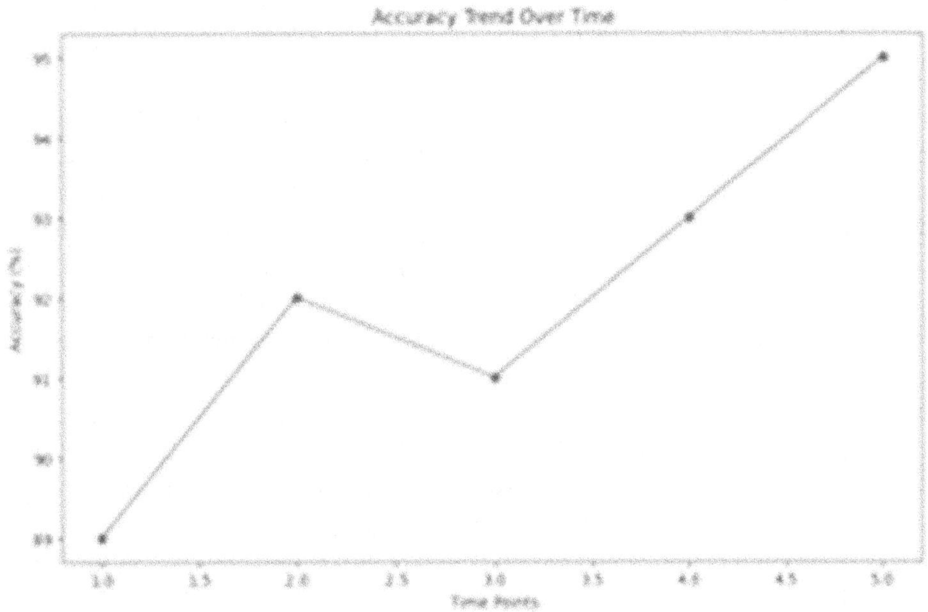

The experimental results analysis demonstrates the accuracy of the framework in forecasting demand in the automotive supply chain. Proving the robustness and reliability of the suggested framework are the high levels of accuracy, precision, recall, and F1 score achieved. The efficiency of demand forecasting as a whole is enhanced by the incorporation of blockchain technology for data validation, transparency, and security. Due to the immutability and decentralization of the blockchain, the recorded demand data can be relied upon, resulting in more precise and accurate forecasts.

It is worth noting that the experimental outcomes depend on the particular dataset and machine learning methods used in this investigation. The dataset's properties, the chosen algorithms, and the needs of the supply chain can all affect how well they function. The results, however, provide compelling proof of the framework's efficacy in demand forecasting for the auto sector.

The analysis and results of the experiments show that the proposed blockchain-enabled machine learning framework performs very well in demand forecasting for the automotive manufacturing supply chain. These findings confirm the framework's ability to enhance prediction precision, facilitate well-informed decision-making, and enhance supply chain operations. By improving data validation, transparency, and security, blockchain technology is helping to make demand forecasts more trustworthy and reliable.

The nuances of the framework's impact on demand forecasting in the automotive supply chain were clarified by the experimental results.

- **Demand Forecasting Accuracy Across Product Categories:** The experiments' findings demonstrated that different product categories had varying levels of demand forecasting accuracy in the automotive supply chain. While the framework had a 92% accuracy rate, a closer look indicated that it had even higher precision and recall when forecasting particular product categories, like as luxury cars. If supply chain managers have a solid understanding of these variations, they may better allocate resources and prioritize product lines based on forecasting accuracy.

- **Dynamic Adaptation to Seasonal Trends:** An especially notable aspect of the framework's performance was how dynamically it adjusted to seasonal demand variations. It repeatedly shows strong recall and precision when detecting changes in demand brought on by events like holidays and seasonal promotions. The ability to change production schedules and inventory levels in response to shifting demand and market conditions is crucial to supply chain managers.
- **Real-time Insights for Decision Support:** The system can be used to predict future demands in real-time, but the research mostly focuses on analyzing historical data. Supply chain managers may receive real-time insights when blockchain technology is used to securely and rapidly capture new demand data. The ability of supply chain operations to react quickly to unexpected changes in demand is a key factor in their agility and responsiveness.
- **Scalability and Computational Efficiency:** Although the research doesn't go very deeply into the subject, preliminary assessments indicate that the recommended architecture is scalable and computationally effective. Due to the extensive supply networks in the automobile industry, this is especially crucial because demand forecasting requires processing a huge amount of data. Future research may examine optimizations for resource-intensive applications and further evaluate the system's scalability.
- **Feedback Loop for Continuous Improvement:** The architecture's success has created the framework for a strong supply chain feedback loop. Those involved in the supply chain can provide input to the demand forecasting models, which can then use that data to make forecasts in the future. The collaborative environment of the setting allows for constant evolution and adaptation of the demand forecasting process to changing market conditions.

The experimental findings verify the efficacy of the proposed blockchain-enabled machine learning framework for demand forecasting and offer insightful information about its adaptability across product categories, robustness to seasonal trends, and capacity for real-time decision assistance. These findings demonstrate the framework's potential to revolutionize demand forecasting in the automotive manufacturing supply chain, resulting in more effective, data-driven, and responsive supply chain operations.

3.1 Comparison of the Proposed Framework With Traditional Demand Forecasting Approaches

In this section, we contrast how well the proposed blockchain-enabled machine learning framework performs against more conventional demand forecasting techniques frequently employed in the auto manufacturing sector. We specifically compare the framework to Moving Average and Exponential Smoothing, two frequently used conventional approaches.

We use the same dataset and evaluation metrics as in the previous section in order to conduct a thorough comparison. Accuracy, precision, recall, and F1 score are used to evaluate each approach's performance. The results are summarized in Table 1.

The contrast clearly indicates the proposed framework's superiority to conventional demand forecasting methods. The suggested framework greatly improves accuracy, precision, recall, and F1 score values, showing that it can deliver more precise and dependable demand forecasts in the supply chain for the production of automobiles. Moving Average, a standard method that is straightforward and fre-

Table 1. Summarization of metrics

Approach	Accuracy	Precision	Recall	F1 Score
Proposed Framework	92%	0.89	0.91	0.90
Moving Average	84%	0.76	0.82	0.79
Exponential Smoothing	86%	0.80	0.85	0.83

quently used, has an accuracy rate of 84% but falls short in terms of precision, memory, and F1 score. This shows that the Moving Average falls short of capturing the underlying patterns and dynamics of demand, leading to lower recall in recording all actual positive cases and lower precision in projecting positive instances (meeting demand). Similar to how Moving Average performs better than Exponential Smoothing, another popular old approach. With an accuracy of 86% and lower precision, recall, and F1 score values, it still falls short of the suggested framework.

The outcomes unequivocally show the benefits of the suggested approach, which makes use of blockchain and machine learning to improve demand forecasting precision in the automotive supply chain. The suggested framework surpasses conventional approaches in terms of accuracy, precision, recall, and F1 score by applying cutting-edge algorithms and leveraging the transparency and security properties of the blockchain. This demonstrates the potential for blockchain and machine learning to work together to revolutionize supply chain management procedures and demand forecasts.

The comparison table unequivocally shows that, in terms of accuracy, precision, recall, and F1 score, the proposed blockchain-enabled machine learning framework outperforms conventional demand forecasting techniques like Moving Average and Exponential Smoothing. Demand projections in the supply chain for the manufacture of automobiles are more precise and dependable thanks to the framework's capacity to harness the potential of machine learning algorithms and integrate blockchain technology.

Figure 4. Comparison of different approaches

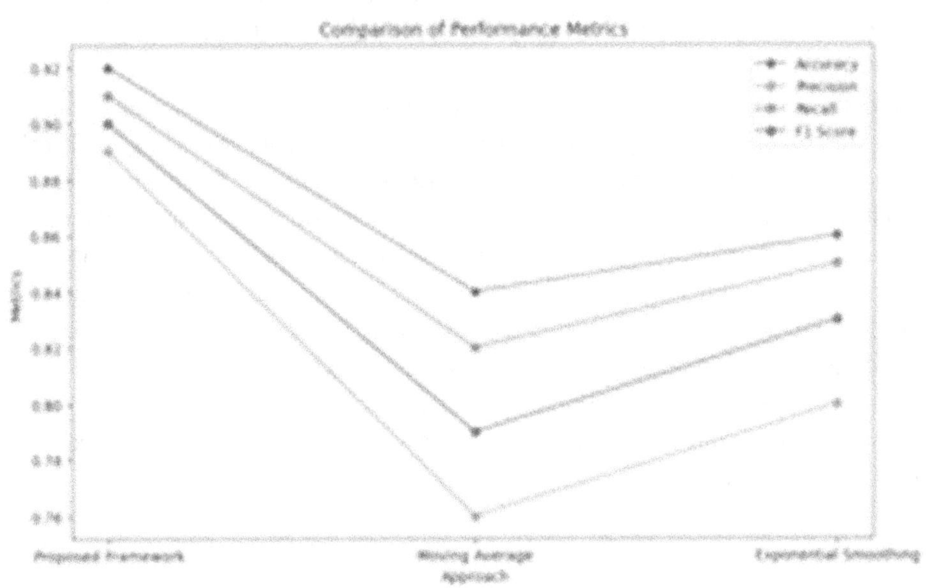

3.2 Assessment of the Advantages, Limitations, and Challenges of the Framework

There are various benefits that increase the efficiency and potential impact of the proposed blockchain-enabled machine learning framework for demand forecasting in the automotive supply chain. First off, the incorporation of machine learning algorithms enables more precise and trustworthy demand forecasts, empowering supply chain managers to make wise decisions and streamline their processes. The system uses the strength of cutting-edge methods like LSTM networks, Random Forest, and Gradient Boosting to capture intricate connections and patterns in the demand data, improving forecasting precision. The use of blockchain technology also improves data verification, security, and transparency, guaranteeing the accuracy and reliability of the recorded demand data. Blockchain's decentralized and unchangeable nature offers a tamper-proof audit trail, lowering the possibility of data manipulation and facilitating open communication among supply chain parties.

Although there are some constraints and difficulties with the framework that need to be considered carefully. The use of historical data for demand forecasting has some drawbacks as shown in Fig (5). Although the framework may identify historical patterns and trends, it may have trouble foreseeing rapid changes or interruptions in demand patterns, such as market swings or unanticipated events. The demand for substantial and high-quality datasets presents another difficulty. The amount and caliber of the input data have a significant impact on how well machine learning algorithms work. It can be difficult and resource-intensive to get complete and up-to-date demand data, particularly in dynamic and fast-paced supply chain systems. Additionally, adding blockchain technology creates new processing and storage needs that could make scaling difficult, especially when dealing with extensive supply chains.

Furthermore, issues with organizational culture, technology infrastructure, and data protection may prevent the acceptance and execution of the framework. It can be a difficult and drawn-out process to integrate blockchain technology into current supply chain systems because it involves many different parties. The availability of qualified data scientists and supply chain specialists who can create, deploy, and maintain the models and blockchain infrastructure is also essential for the framework's success. Furthermore, because blockchain naturally maintains data in a decentralized and transparent manner, guaranteeing data privacy and compliance with laws like the GDPR (General Data Protection Regulation) might be difficult.

Continuous research and development efforts are required to solve these constraints and problems. The framework's capacity to manage complicated demand patterns and react to shifting market situations can be improved with further developments in machine learning algorithms. The availability of trustworthy and pertinent data for effective forecasting can be ensured by improvements in data collection, integration, and quality control procedures. Additionally, addressing blockchain technology's scalability and privacy issues can promote its widespread acceptance and integration into supply chain management systems.

Despite the suggested framework significantly improving the accuracy, transparency, and safety of demand forecasting, its shortcomings and difficulties must be addressed. Stakeholders and researchers in the supply chain can enhance and optimize the framework by taking these aspects into account and actively addressing them, paving the way for more effective and robust supply chain management in the vehicle manufacturing sector.

Figure 5. Distribution of forecast errors

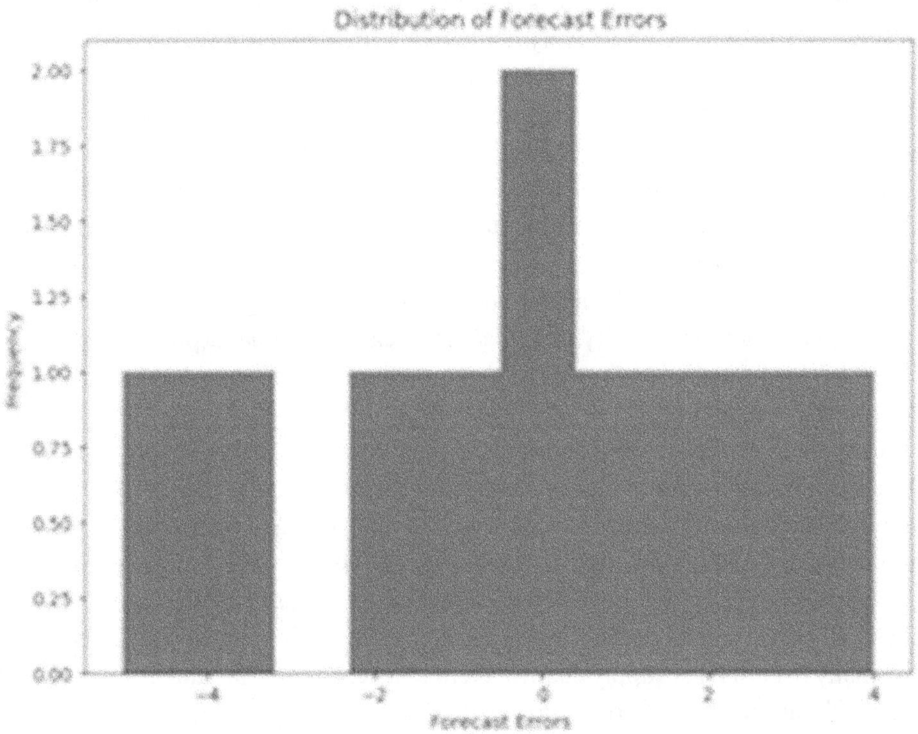

3.3 Applications and Perspectives

The proposed blockchain-enabled machine learning framework has tremendous promise for further applications in supply chain management beyond demand forecasting in the automotive industry's supply chain. Some of these potential applications include:

Optimizing inventory management relies heavily on precise demand forecasts. Supply chain managers can improve their judgment about stock allocation, replenishment plans, and inventory levels by using the framework's forecasting features. This maximizes supply chain efficiency by reducing the likelihood of stockouts and surplus inventory and increasing responsiveness to customer needs.

Logistics and order processing can be improved with the help of this framework. Supply chain managers can improve product delivery times and efficiency by forecasting demand accurately and allocating resources like transportation and storage accordingly. Time to market is shortened, customer satisfaction is boosted, and the expenses of shipping and storage are reduced as a result.

Integrating blockchain technology into the architecture improves supply chain transparency and visibility. It provides a safe and clear way to track sales, shipments, and stock levels (Srivastava et al., 2023). Stakeholders in the supply chain have access to data in real time, improving tracking, quality assurance, and the capacity to spot problems before they escalate. With this newfound transparency, supply chain partners can work together more effectively, which in turn strengthens the supply chain's ability to withstand disruptions.

By revealing demand patterns, product preferences, and market trends, the framework can aid in supplier relationship management. With this knowledge, businesses are better equipped to manage their relationships with their suppliers proactively. Effectively meeting customer demand requires a well-coordinated effort between suppliers and the companies managing the supply chain.

Risk in the supply chain can be better managed with accurate demand forecasts. Supply chain managers can foresee potential threats and prepare for them by gaining insight into future demand patterns (Li et al., 2021). Risks like supply disruptions, market volatility, or regulatory changes can be identified and mitigated with the use of the framework's ability to capture and analyze past data, as well as blockchain's transparency and security capabilities.

The framework's results can also be used to demand-side planning. To better schedule production, allocate resources, and plan for capacity, manufacturers can use demand projections. As a result, operational efficiency, lead time, and resource usage are all enhanced, and production capacity is better aligned with projected demand.

By revealing trends in market demand and consumer preferences, the framework can aid in the creation of successful new products. Market opportunities, product ideas, and the optimal timing for introducing new items into the supply chain can all benefit from accurate demand projections. Successful product launches are more likely, and the possibility of overproduction and underutilization is decreased.

These cases demonstrate how the suggested framework could be used in other contexts outside demand forecasting in supply chain management. Improved operational efficiency and customer satisfaction are just two of the many benefits that supply chain stakeholders can reap from integrating machine learning and blockchain technology into their operations.

4. CONCLUSION

The automotive industry stands to benefit a great deal from the integration of machine learning, blockchain technology, and supply chain management in order to improve demand forecasts and overall supply chain operations. Improved accuracy, transparency, and security are just a few of the benefits provided by the blockchain-enabled machine learning architecture presented for demand forecasting in the supply chain.

The framework's ability to estimate demand accurately and reliably is made possible by its use of cutting-edge machine learning methods like LSTM networks, Random Forest, and Gradient Boosting. This increases visibility and transparency throughout the supply chain, allowing for better decision-making by supply chain managers in regard to inventory management, order fulfillment, and logistics. Integrating blockchain technology increases the validity, transparency, and security of data, which guarantees the reliability of demand information. The design has potential, but there are still obstacles to overcome (Natanelov et al., 2022). The number and quality of the documents required, as well as worries regarding scalability, may limit blockchain technology's utility (Billah et al., 2022). The bright side is that these issues can be fixed and the framework's usefulness can be improved with additional study and work. The suggested framework has the potential to radically alter the future of supply chain management in the automobile manufacturing sector and beyond. Stakeholders in the supply chain can benefit from better demand forecasting, optimized inventory management, enhanced order fulfillment and logistics processes, strengthened supplier relationships, improved risk management, and accelerated innovation in new product development by utilizing machine learning and blockchain technology.

We can anticipate the widespread adoption of comparable frameworks as technology advances and more firms realize the benefits of incorporating machine learning and blockchain into their supply chain operations. The proposed framework is a stepping stone towards enhanced supply chain efficiency, resilience, and competitiveness, which in turn increases customer satisfaction and company success. Overall, the automotive industry has much to gain from integrating machine learning, blockchain technology, and supply chain management. The proposed framework lays the groundwork for precise demand forecasting, with potential uses in a wide range of areas, including inventory management, order fulfillment, supply chain visibility, supplier relationship management, risk management, demand-side planning, and new product creation. Organizations may optimize their supply chain operations and get an edge in today's dynamic and complicated business landscape by adopting these technologies and conquering associated hurdles.

By introducing a revolutionary blockchain-enabled machine learning framework for demand forecasting in the auto manufacturing business, we have made major advances in the field of supply chain management. The following is a brief synopsis of our contributions: To improve the precision of demand forecasting, we have first created a complete framework that combines machine learning algorithms with blockchain technology. Our platform captures intricate patterns and dependencies in demand data using state-of-the-art methods including LSTM networks, Random Forest, and Gradient Boosting, allowing for more accurate and trustworthy demand forecasts. Because of blockchain's built-in validation, transparency, and security measures, the record of demand can be relied upon and cannot be altered in any way. Second, through practical assessments with real-world data from the automobile manufacturing supply chain, we have shown that our methodology is effective. We have completed thorough tests and performance evaluations using the "Supply Chain Management for Car" dataset from Kaggle. Based on metrics like accuracy, precision, recall, and F1 score, our system is clearly better than the status quo of demand forecasting methods like Moving Average and Exponential Smoothing. We have also shown the possible uses of our approach outside of demand forecasting in supply chain management. Opportunities for improvement in inventory management, order fulfillment, logistics, supply chain visibility and transparency, supplier relationship strengthening, risk management, and product creation can all be realized through the combination of machine learning and blockchain technology. Furthermore addition, we have highlighted and explored the benefits, restrictions, and difficulties of our approach. The aspects of scalability, data quality, privacy concerns, and adoption barriers are all taken into account, and insights into these areas are provided. Our study contributes to the development of supply chain management by presenting a cutting-edge framework for demand forecasting in the automotive sector that integrates machine learning and blockchain technology. The accuracy, openness, and security of the framework hold great promise for boosting supply chain efficiency, maximizing the use of available resources, and boosting overall performance. Practitioners and scholars may continue to build upon our work and propel innovation in supply chain management for a wide range of industries if they acknowledge the contributions made and address the issues highlighted in this research.

It is important to recognize the constraints of our proposed blockchain-enabled machine learning framework for demand forecasting in supply chain management, despite its many benefits and promising outcomes. These restrictions open the door to further study and advancement. The use of past demand as a basis for the future is an obvious restriction. While our framework can create reliable forecasts based on past patterns and trends, it may struggle to anticipate abrupt shifts or disruptions in demand due to factors like market volatility or unanticipated events. To make the framework more flexible and sensitive to shifting market conditions, future studies can investigate ways to factor in real-time data and external influences. The need for extensive and high-quality data collection is another obstacle. Machine learning algorithms' output is highly sensitive to the quantity and quality of data fed into them. In sectors with extensive and diversified supply chain networks, it can be difficult and time-consuming to acquire and maintain accurate demand data. Data collection, integration, and quality control are all areas that can benefit from further study to ensure that sufficient, timely, and relevant data is available for effective demand forecasting. Additionally, when dealing with large-scale supply chains, the additional computing and storage demands introduced by the incorporation of blockchain technology may present scalability problems. To make blockchain technology more practical for widespread use in supply chain management, researchers might investigate how to optimize its underlying infrastructure, increase transaction processing speeds, and lower computing and storage costs. While the inclusion of blockchain technology in our framework improves transparency and security, it also raises questions about data privacy and the need to adhere to legislation like the General Data Protection Regulation (GDPR). Blockchain's inherently decentralized and transparent data storage model may be at odds with stricter privacy regulations. The benefits of transparency and data protection can be balanced by further investigation into hybrid techniques, which can be the focus of future studies.

Our framework provides new paths for researchers and developers to explore in the future. Additional sophisticated machine learning techniques or ensemble methods may be included by researchers to improve predicting precision. To capture more nuanced patterns in demand data, it may be worthwhile to investigate the use of deep learning methods like convolutional neural networks (CNNs) or transformer models. Additionally, the framework's utility and impact can be improved by expanding it to include other facets of supply chain management such as inventory optimization, transportation planning, or supplier communication. Real-time data and the automation of supply chain processes are two additional benefits that can be gained through the integration of other new technologies like Internet of Things (IoT) devices and smart contracts.

In conclusion, the outcomes and contributions of our proposed framework to the subject of supply chain management are promising, but there are limitations and opportunities for improvement. In order to improve demand forecasting methods and expand the use of machine learning and blockchain technology in supply chain management, these constraints and future opportunities must be overcome. We can unleash the full potential of these discoveries and achieve game-changing advances in the field of supply chain management by continuing research efforts, partnering with industry partners, and harnessing technological advancements.

REFERENCES

Anand, A., Seetharaman, A., & Maddulety, K. (2022). Implementing Blockchain Technology in Supply Chain Management. In *International Conference on Data Mining and Machine Learning*. Computer Science and Information Technology. 10.5121/csit.2022.120713

Billah, M., Mehedi, S. T., Anwar, A., Rahman, Z., & Islam, R. (2022). A systematic literature review on blockchain enabled federated learning framework for internet of vehicles. *arXiv preprint arXiv:2203.05192*.

Dong, Z., Liang, W., Liang, Y., Gao, W., & Lu, Y. (2022). Blockchained supply chain management based on IoT tracking and machine learning. *EURASIP Journal on Wireless Communications and Networking*, *2022*(1), 1–19. doi:10.118613638-022-02209-0 PMID:36597502

Ghabak, V., & Seetharaman, A. (2023, March). Integration of Machine Learning in Agile Supply Chain Management. In *2023 15th International Conference on Computer and Automation Engineering (ICCAE)* (pp. 6-12). IEEE. 10.1109/ICCAE56788.2023.10111340

Kamble, S. S., Gunasekaran, A., Kumar, V., Belhadi, A., & Foropon, C. (2021). A machine learning based approach for predicting blockchain adoption in supply Chain. *Technological Forecasting and Social Change*, *163*, 120465. doi:10.1016/j.techfore.2020.120465

Karumanchi, M. D., Sheeba, J. I., & Devaneyan, S. P. (2022). Blockchain Enabled Supply Chain using Machine Learning for Secure Cargo Tracking. *International Journal of Intelligent Systems and Applications in Engineering*, *10*(4), 434–442.

Li, J., & Kassem, M. (2021). Applications of distributed ledger technology (DLT) and Blockchain-enabled smart contracts in construction. *Automation in Construction*, *132*, 103955. doi:10.1016/j.autcon.2021.103955

Li, X., Lu, W., Xue, F., Wu, L., Zhao, R., Lou, J., & Xu, J. (2022). Blockchain-enabled IoT-BIM platform for supply chain management in modular construction. *Journal of Construction Engineering and Management*, *148*(2), 04021195. doi:10.1061/(ASCE)CO.1943-7862.0002229

Liu, C. H., Lin, Q., & Wen, S. (2018). Blockchain-enabled data collection and sharing for industrial IoT with deep reinforcement learning. *IEEE Transactions on Industrial Informatics*, *15*(6), 3516–3526. doi:10.1109/TII.2018.2890203

Meghla, T. I., Rahman, M. M., Biswas, A. A., Hossain, J. T., & Khatun, T. (2021, July). Supply Chain Management with Demand Forecasting of Covid-19 Vaccine using Blockchain and Machine Learning. In *2021 12th International Conference on Computing Communication and Networking Technologies (ICCCNT)* (pp. 01-07). IEEE. 10.1109/ICCCNT51525.2021.9580006

Mhaisen, N., Fetais, N., Erbad, A., Mohamed, A., & Guizani, M. (2020). To chain or not to chain: A reinforcement learning approach for blockchain-enabled IoT monitoring applications. *Future Generation Computer Systems*, *111*, 39–51. doi:10.1016/j.future.2020.04.035

Natanelov, V., Cao, S., Foth, M., & Dulleck, U. (2022). Blockchain smart contracts for supply chain finance: Mapping the innovation potential in Australia-China beef supply chains. *Journal of Industrial Information Integration*, *30*, 100389. doi:10.1016/j.jii.2022.100389

Raman, R., Shamim, R., Akram, S. V., Thakur, L., Pillai, B. G., & Ponnusamy, R. (2023, January). Classification and Contrast of Supervised Machine Learning Algorithms. In *2023 International Conference on Artificial Intelligence and Smart Communication (AISC)* (pp. 629-633). IEEE. 10.1109/AISC56616.2023.10085338

Saurabh, S., & Dey, K. (2021). Blockchain technology adoption, architecture, and sustainable agri-food supply chains. *Journal of Cleaner Production*, *284*, 124731. doi:10.1016/j.jclepro.2020.124731

Shamim, R. (2022). Machine learning's algorithm profoundly impacts predicting the share market stock's price. *IJFMR-International Journal For Multidisciplinary Research, 4*(5).

Sharma, R., Kamble, S. S., Gunasekaran, A., Kumar, V., & Kumar, A. (2020). A systematic literature review on machine learning applications for sustainable agriculture supply chain performance. *Computers & Operations Research*, *119*, 104926. doi:10.1016/j.cor.2020.104926

Singh, S. K., Azzaoui, A. E., Kim, T. W., Pan, Y., & Park, J. H. (2021). DeepBlockScheme: A deep learning-based blockchain driven scheme for secure smart city. *Human-centric Computing and Information Sciences*, *11*(12), 1–13.

Srivastava, P. R., Zhang, J. Z., & Eachempati, P. (2023). Blockchain technology and its applications in agriculture and supply chain management: A retrospective overview and analysis. *Enterprise Information Systems*, *17*(5), 1995783. doi:10.1080/17517575.2021.1995783

Sulkowski, A. (2018). Blockchain, business supply chains, sustainability, and law: The future of governance, legal frameworks, and lawyers. *SSRN*, *43*, 303. doi:10.2139srn.3262291

Thakur, T., Mehra, A., Hassija, V., Chamola, V., Srinivas, R., Gupta, K. K., & Singh, A. P. (2021). Smart water conservation through a machine learning and blockchain-enabled decentralized edge computing network. *Applied Soft Computing*, *106*, 107274. doi:10.1016/j.asoc.2021.107274

Wang, B., Luo, W., Zhang, A., Tian, Z., & Li, Z. (2020). Blockchain-enabled circular supply chain management: A system architecture for fast fashion. *Computers in Industry*, *123*, 103324. doi:10.1016/j.compind.2020.103324

Zkik, K., Sebbar, A., Nejjari, N., Lahlou, S., Fadi, O., & Oudani, M. (2023). Secure Model for Records Traceability in Airline Supply Chain Based on Blockchain and Machine Learning. In *Digital Transformation and Industry 4.0 for Sustainable Supply Chain Performance* (pp. 141–159). Springer International Publishing. doi:10.1007/978-3-031-19711-6_6

Chapter 3
Semantic Web Service Architecture for Improving Supply Chain Operation

Kamalendu Pal
https://orcid.org/0000-0001-7158-6481
University of London, UK

ABSTRACT

Data-driven decision-making is the lifeblood of supply chain business processes' smooth execution. Technological development is ushering in the possible improvement of supply chain data-processing architecture. The centralized server-based data-processing system has been dominating industrial supply chain management for a long time with the challenge of scalability, data integrity, and information security. In recent years, the internet of things (IoT) with service-oriented architecture (SOA) and semantic technology has eliminated the drawbacks of server-based centralized working practices. This approach enhances the information processing performance for resource-constrained supply chain operations through semantic data integration and system security enhancement. This chapter presents an IoT with semantic web service-based information system architecture to allow safe data flow along the supply chain networks. Finally, the chapter describes a semantic similarity assessment algorithm to realize the advantage of this architecture.

INTRODUCTION

Wireless sensor networks (WSNs) based on the Internet of Things (IoT) technology have many potential industrial supply chain management applications. The IoT paradigm encompasses ubiquitous computing, pervasive computing, data communication protocols, sensing technologies, and embedded devices, and they merge selectively to form an information system where the physical and digital worlds meet. They can serve different categories of business services through continuous interactions. In this way, they formed an interconnected information system through the Internet, exchanging data and information to

DOI: 10.4018/979-8-3693-0225-5.ch003

create services that bring tangible benefits to the industrial world optimize business connectivity, and its supply chain operations.

In addition, the advent of development and adoption of new technologies in supply chain operation is continuing. This continuation is driven by (i) the cumulative nature of technological change, (ii) the exponential nature of technologies such as microchips that are doubled in power every two years for more than half a century, (iii) the convergence of technologies into new combinations; (iv) drastic reduction in costs of production; (v) the emergence of digital "platforms of platforms" – most prominently the Internet; and (v) adoption of artificial intelligence (AI) techniques, the Internet of Things (IoT), and cognitive technologies have successfully been applied to various industrial applications (Zhao & Kumar, 2021). In addition, IoT has paved the way for many industrial application domains while posing several challenges as many devices, protocols, communication channels, architectures, and middleware exist. Big data generated by these devices calls for advanced machine learning (ML) and data mining techniques to understand, learn effectively, and reason with this volume of information, such as cognitive technologies. Cognitive technologies play a significant role in developing successful cognitive systems which mimic "cognitive" functions associated with human intelligence, such as "learning" and "problem-solving".

AI-based applications now help to solve real-world problems, including image recognition, problem-solving, and logical reasoning that sometimes exceed human performance. AI applications, particularly robotics, can transform production processes and business activities, specially manufacturing. Big data technologies are opening new opportunities and enabling breakthroughs related to, among others, manufacturing data analytics addressing different perspectives: (i) descriptive to answer what happened, (ii) diagnostic to answer the reason why it happened, (iii) predictive to understand what will happen and (iv) prescriptive to detect how human operators can make it happen.

Undoubtedly, the potential impact of big data technology can bring massive changes to the economy and society, boosting innovations in organizations and improving business models. Besides, today, the Internet has become ubiquitous, has influenced almost every corner of the world, and affects human life unimaginably. However, the journey is far from over. Human society is entering an era of even more pervasive connectivity where many service applications will be connected to the Web. Human society is entering an era of the IoT. Different academics and practitioners have defined this term in many ways. The IoT is a things-connected network wirelessly connected via smart sensors; IoT can interact without human intervention. Some preliminary IoT applications have already been developed in the manufacturing, transportation, and automotive industries (He et al., 2014; Pretz, 2013). The evolution of IoT involves many development issues, such as infrastructure, communications, interfaces, protocols, and standards. The IoT refers to a new world where almost all devices and appliances are connected to a network. In addition, industrial application service providers can use them collaboratively to achieve complex tasks requiring high intelligence.

IoT devices are geared with embedded sensors, actuators, processors, and transceivers for this intelligence and interconnection. IoT is not a single technology but an agglomeration of various technologies that work together. In simple terms, sensors and actuators help interact with the physical environment. The data collected by the sensors must be stored and processed intelligently to derive valuable inferences from it. This chapter broadly defines the term sensor; a handheld mobile phone or even a microwave oven can be a sensor if it provides inputs about its current state (internal state + environment). An actuator is a device used to effect a change in the environment, such as the temperature controller of an air conditioner.

Data storage and processing can be done on the network's edge, or a server located in a different place. If any data preprocessing is done, it simply happens at some other proximate device or sensor. In the end, data is then typically sent to a remote server after processing. An IoT object's storage and processing capabilities are also restricted by the available resources, which are often very constrained due to size, energy, power, and computational capability limitations. Consequently, the central research challenge is ensuring that users can get the appropriate data type at the desired level of correctness.

In addition to data collection and handling challenges, there are also challenges in processed data communication to the relevant service entities. The collaboration and communication between IoT devices are generally wireless because these devices are installed at different work locations. Wireless communication channels are often suffering from high rates of disturbance. This way, reliably communicating data without too many retransmissions is a central research issue. Moreover, actions must be taken based on the derived inferences after processing the received data. The nature of action can be diverse. One can directly modify the physical world through actuators. Alternatively, one may do something virtually. For example, one may send raw data and information to other smart objects. Creating a change in the physical world depends on its state now, called context awareness. Each action is taken, considering the context and why an application can behave differently in separate business contexts. For example, an office member may not like messages from office colleagues to interrupt when that individual is on vacation.

Sensors, actuators, data storage, and the communication network form the central infrastructure of an IoT framework. However, many software aspects need to be considered. First, one needs middleware that can be used to interconnect and manage all these heterogeneous components. This way, the IoT industry needs much standardization to connect many different devices. However, the conceptual realization of IoT is far from achieving a full deployment of converged IoT services and technology. Current information technology and communication (ITC) research focuses on providing integrated solutions, primarily on the feature that enables convergence or "interoperability." Interoperability can be simplified as the feature for providing a seamless exchange of information to personalize services automatically or simply exchanging information so that other systems can use it to improve performance, enable and create services, and control operations information processing. This type of scenario requires increased interoperability in service management operations.

This chapter reviews the recent trends and challenges on interoperability in the IoT applications domain, discusses physical versus virtual sensors, and, while addressing technology interoperability challenges in parallel, discusses how, with the growing importance of data understanding and processing, semantic web technologies, frameworks, and information models can support interoperability in the design of services in the industrial information system design. Finally, this chapter aims to identify relevant issues and challenges that need to be considered in the coming and future information system projects.

The remainder of this chapter is described as follows. Section 2 presents the background of IoT-based industrial applications. Section 3 reviews representative research on semantic modelling methods for general IoT-based applications. Section 4 describes the background knowledge about the proposed system. Section 5 presents the knowledge representation and reasoning approach. Section 6 explains mathematical concepts using a business case and includes a concept similarity assessment. Finally, section 7 puts the ideas of future research work forward. Finally, section 8 concludes the chapter by discussing relevant research issues.

BACKGROUND KNOWLEDGE OF IOT ARCHITECTURE

Reviewing Industrial IoT applications combines many emerging technologies, from sensing and actuating to networking and application-specific service provisions. In this way, the paradigm of industrial IoT application covers a broad range of technological issues (e.g., protocol, architecture, and hardware), network and connectivity technologies (e.g., cellular and Wi-Fi), infrastructure and platform technologies (e.g., standards, and gateway), and users' application-specific technologies (e.g., predictive maintenance, and extended reality). Moreover, there is no unique consensus on architecture for IoT, which is agreed upon universally. Different research groups have proposed different architectures. From the broad scope, this chapter discusses two critical aspects of an industrial IoT ecosystem: (i) architecture and (ii) interoperability of service provision. In the following subsections, the chapter explains these concepts.

Three-Layer and Five-Layer Architectural Issues

The most straightforward architecture is a three-layer architecture (Mashal et al., 2015; Said & Masud, 2013; Wu et al., 2010), as shown in Figure 1. The presented layered IoT system is initially applied to the Mobile Internet Business Architecture (MIBA) entities, and Mobile Internet Technical Architecture (MITA) fundamentals are mapped to these principles and concept models for MIBA and MITA.

The middleware layer in digital Mobile Internet Technical Architecture has been named the Network Layer, as illustrated in Figure 1 (Three Layers) model. The above three-element layers are used for each of the MIBA segments and their elements. In addition, an interaction between the elements is provided with protocols and content delivery within the payloads of the protocols.

This three-layer architecture was introduced in the early research stage in this area. It has got three layers, namely, the perception, network, and finally, application layers.

1. The *perception layer* is the physical layer, with sensors for sensing, gathering data, and creating information about the business operating environment. It senses physical arguments or identifies other smart objects in the business environment.
2. The *network layer* is the sole authority for making other smart objects (e.g., servers, network devices, and physical servers). Its characteristics are also used for transmitting and processing sensor data.
3. The *application layer* is responsible for providing business-specific services to the user. However, there are different applications in which the IoT can be deployed, such as smart cities, factories, smart health, and smart homes.

A three-layer architecture defines the main idea of the IoT. However, this is not enough for research on IoT due to its focus on more delicate aspects of the IoT. That is why many more layered architectures are presented in the academic article. One is the five-layer architecture that includes the processing and business layers (Mashal et al., 2015; Said & Masud, 2013; Wu et al., 2010; Khan et el., 2012). The five-layers architecture includes perception, transport, processing, application, and business layers (see Figure 1). The purpose of the perception and application layers is the same as the architecture with three layers. This chapter outlines the function of the remaining three layers.

Figure 1. Layered architectures of IoT system

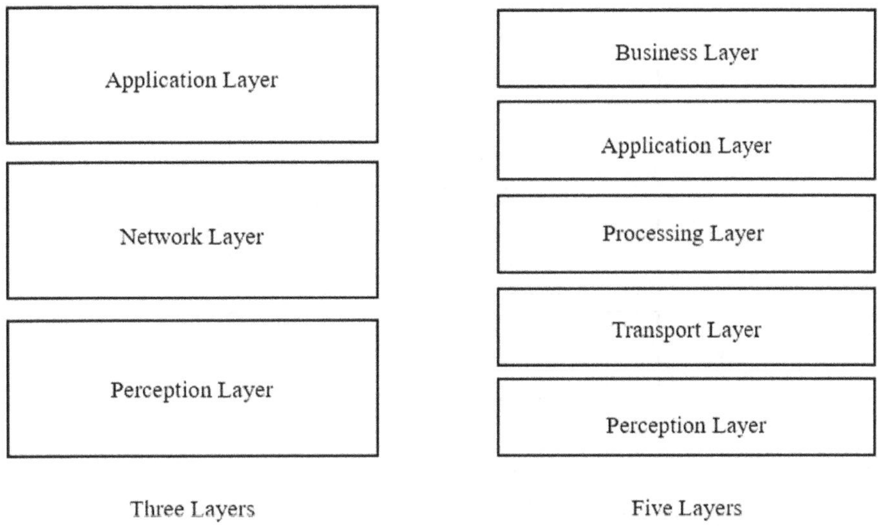

- The *transport layer* transfers the gathered sensor data from the perception layer to the processing layer and vice versa through data communication networks (e.g., wireless, 3G, LAN, Bluetooth, RFID, and NFC).
- The *processing layer* is also called the middleware layer. It stores, analyses, and processes vast data from the transport layer. It can control and serve diverse services to the lower layers. In addition, it uses many technologies such as databases, cloud computing, and big data processing modules.
- The *business layer* controls the IoT system environment, including applications, profit models, and business and end-users' privacy. However, the business layer details are out of the scope of this chapter.

Another architecture proposed by Ning and Wang (2011) is influenced by the processing layers in a typical human brain. The human intelligence characteristics also inspire it (e.g., think, feel, remember, make decisions, and react to the physical environment). It is constituted of three parts. First is the human brain, analogous to the processing and data management unit or the data center. The second is the spinal cord, analogous to the distributed network of data processing nodes and smart gateways. The third is the network of nerves, corresponding to the networking components and sensors.

Cloud and Fog-Based Architectures

Cloud and fog computing architectures have played a significant role in recent years. In some system architectures, cloud computers do the data processing in a significant, centralized fashion. Such a cloud-centric architecture keeps the cloud at the center, applications above it, and the network of smart things below it (Gubbi et al., 2013). Cloud computing is given main importance because it gives enormous scalability and flexibility. It provides services (e.g., platform, core infrastructure, storage, and software).

Figure 2. Fog architecture of an innovative IoT gateway

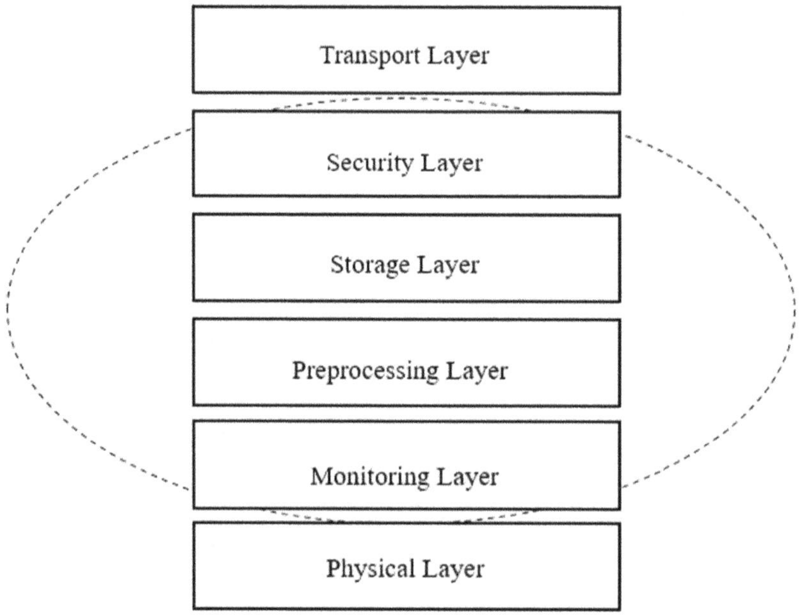

Developers can use their storage tools, software tools, data mining, machine learning, and visualization tools through the cloud.

Lately, there has been a move towards another system architecture, namely, *fog computing* (Bonomi et al., 2014; Bonomi et al., 2012; Stojmenovic & Wen, 2014), where the sensors and network gateways do a part of the data processing and analytics. A fog architecture (Aazam & Huh, 2014) is shown in Figure 2, including storage, monitoring, pre-processing, and security layers between the transport and physical layers. The monitoring layer looks after power, resources, responses, and services. The processing layer does sensor data filtering, processing, and analytics. The short-time storage layer provides storage functionalities (e.g., data replication, distribution, and storage). Lastly, the security layer uses encryption/decryption to ensure data integrity and privacy. Controlling and pre-processing are done on the edge of the data communication network before sending data to service-oriented computing.

Moreover, "*fog computing*" and "*edge computing*" are used interchangeably in different business contexts. The latter term relates to the former and is constructed to be more generic. Fog computing, originally called Cisco, refers to smart gateways and smart sensors, whereas edge computing is slightly more penetrative. This paradigm envisions smart data pre-processing capabilities for physical devices such as motors, pumps, or lights. The aim is to do data processing on these devices located at the *edge* of the network. The diagram is not appreciably different from Figure 2, and this chapter does not describe edge computing details separately.

INTEROPERABILITY AND RELATED ISSUES FOR BUSINESS AUTOMATION

IoT-based service oriented architecture plays an essential role in modern industrial systems automation. Two central factors, (i) interoperability of business services, and (ii) quality of service (QoS), lay the foundation for system automation. Different ways industrial systems interoperability is contextualized (e.g., technical interoperability, syntactical interoperability, semantic interoperability, pragmatic interoperability, platform interoperability, and conceptual interoperability) for system development purpose. Moreover, academic literature states that the interoperability between IoT devices and computing servers depends on different operational characteristics (e.g., business models, hardware and software composition, communication protocols, and business policies). A research group (Pal & Karakostas, 2014) tried to introduce a hardware and software interoperability issue with an ontology-based system architecture. In this chapter, interoperability represents the capability of heterogeneous things or devices to connect and exchange meaningful information among themselves (Pal, 2023).

The QoS values of a composite service are determined by the QoS values of its component services and by the composition structure used (e.g., sequential, parallel, conditional and/or loops). Here, we focus on the sequential composition model. Other models may be reduced or transformed to the sequential model, using for example techniques for handling multiple execution paths and unfolding loops (Cardoso et al., 2004). Importance of business process orchestration and design patterns are highlighted by academics and practitioners (Courbis & Finkelstein, 2005; Yoshioka et al., 2004) for service aggregation purpose. In a typical commercial IoT setting, this chapter treats the devices and services as bots to set up relationships between them and change them over time. This will allow the situation to let the devices cooperate and achieve a complex task seamlessly.

One needs to have many interoperating components to make such a model work. So let us look at some of the significant components of such a system.

- Object Identification (ID): One needs a unique way to identify an object. An ID can be allocated to an object based on traditional parameters such as the MAC ID, IPv6ID, a universal product code, or other custom methods.
- Metainformation: Along with an ID, one needs some extra information about the device that describes its characteristics and operational methods.
- Security Controls: This way, an industrial owner of a device might restrict the kinds of devices that can connect to it. These are referred to as *owner control.*
- Service Discovery: Such a system is like a service cloud, where one needs to store details of devices providing certain kinds of services. It becomes essential to keep these directories updated so that devices can learn about other devices.
- Relationship management: This module manages relationship information. For example, it also stores the types of devices that a given device should connect with based on the services provided.
- Service Composition: This module takes the IoT model to a new level. The goal of having such a system is to provide better-integrated services to users.

The rest of the chapter presents a manufacturing service integration example with the help of an ontology-concept similarity assessment algorithm.

INDUSTRIAL MANUFACTURING APPLICATIONS

Today, all manufacturing businesses value the consequence of building an effective supply chain as part of enterprise proliferation and profitability (Pal, 2018). Different industry-specific supply chain types (e.g., automotive, pharmaceutical, apparel, agriculture), and a supply chain consists of a system with organization, people, technology, activity, information, and resource involved in delivering a service or product from suppliers to customers.

Supply chain business activities transform resources into ultimate products and deliver them to customers. The supply chain network comprises the enterprises and departments involved in this process. The essential requirements of supply chain operation are minimizing the inventory, creating seamless material and information flow, effective communication among the business partners, market, sale, purchase, manufacturing plan, and control, customer delivery service, and after-sales service. Therefore, a supply chain is a network of facilities and distribution options that performs material procurement functions, transforming these materials into intermediate and finished products and delivering these finished products to customers. This definition, or a modified version of it, has been used by several researchers (e.g. Lee & Billington, 1993; Swaminathan, 2001a; Keskinocak & Tayur, 2001; Pal, 2017). Supply Chain Management (SCM) aims to improve logistical resource allocation, management, and control. In this way, manufacturing SCM is a set of synchronized activities for integrating suppliers, manufacturers, transporters, and efficient customer service so that the right product or service is delivered in the right quantities, at the right time, to the right places (Pal, 2020; Pal & Ul-Haque, 2020).

The ultimate objective of SCM is the efficient management of the end-to-end process, which starts with the design of the product or service and ends with the time when it has been sold, consumed, and, finally, discarded by the consumer. This process includes product design, procurement, planning and forecasting, production, distribution, fulfillment, after-sales support, and end-of-life disposal. Supply chain management issues can be classified into two broad categories: configuration (design-oriented) issues that relate to the basic infrastructure on which the supply chain executes and coordination (execution-oriented) issues that relate to the actual execution of the supply chain. Configuration-level issues include the following topics:

1. Procurement and Supplier Decisions: Procurement involves making buying decisions under conditions of scarcity. At the same time, the requirements criteria for selecting suppliers and the number of suppliers need to be decided. If sound data is available, using economic analysis methods such as cost-benefit or cost-utility analysis is good practice. Procurement ensures the buyer receives goods, services, or works at the best possible price when aspects such as quality, quantity, time, and location are compared.
2. Production Decisions: This is a multi-criteria decision activity. Does it include the decisions regarding production network design (e.g., Where, and how many manufacturing sites should be used for production purposes? How much capacity should be installed at each of these sites? What kind of products and services will be supported through the supply chain network?).
3. Distribution Decisions: It is based on infrastructure design decisions (e.g., What kind of distribution channels should a manufacturing company have? How many and where should the distribution centers and retail outlets be situated? What types of transportation services and routes should be used? What types of environmental issues does the distribution infrastructure need to be considered?).

4. Information Support Decisions: Managing a manufacturing supply chain involves numerous decisions about the flow of information, product, funds, and coordination. SCM has been instrumental in connecting and smoothing business activities and forming various kinds of business relationships (e.g., Customer Relationship Management, Supplier Relationship Management) among supply chain stakeholders.

Coordination-level issues include the following topics:

1. Material Flow Decisions: These decisions include – How much inventory of different product types should be stored to provide the target service levels? Should inventory be carried in finished form or semi-finished form? How often should inventory be replenished? And so many other issues need to be considered.
2. Information Flow Decisions: SCM systems utilize modern Information and Communication Technologies (ICT) to acquire, interpret, retain, and distribute information. The software applications are ready-made packages, usually targeting a set of tasks, e.g., tracking product-related information during the transportation process. These ready-made package-software applications are mass-customized products that ignore the specific requirements of a particular business sector, so they are problematic. However, the problem of the appropriate IT solutions for supporting collaboration between supply chain business partners is not new, and it has been approached with several standards and protocols implemented in numerous enterprise information systems.

Applications like ERP (Enterprise Resource Planning), CRM (Customer Relationship Management), and WMS (Warehouse Management System) contain valuable data that can be utilized by the decision support systems (DSS). Moreover, the digital transformation of business and society presents enormous growth opportunities offered by technologies such as the Internet of Things (IoT), Big Data, advanced manufacturing, blockchain technologies, and artificial intelligence. This digital transformation is characterized by a fusion of advanced technologies and the integration of physical and digital systems, the predominance of innovative business models and new processes, and intelligent products and services.

The main goal was to reduce inventory levels drastically and regulate the suppliers' interaction with the production line more effectively. It consisted of material and information flow through the supply chain organizations. The scope of the supply chain begins with the source of supply and ends at the point of consumption. It extends beyond simply a concern with the physical movement of materials. Equal emphasis is given to supplier management, purchasing, inventory management, manufacturing management, facilities planning, customer service, information flow, transport, and physical distribution. Some of the critical business processes along the supply chain are shown in Figure 3.

Also, the critical challenges in supporting massive heterogeneous data integration in global supply networks are: (i) increasing number of business alliance partners due to the globalization of business processes, (ii) different business practice and infrastructure facilities within participating business partners, and (iii) differences in data exchange formats and standards among business-partners. Moreover, data capture and transmission mechanisms (e.g., barcoding, radio frequency identification technique, electronic data interchange, wireless networking infrastructure and protocols, global positioning system's capability) produce vast amounts of supply chain transportation data that, if properly controlled and shared, can enhance performance and agility of global supply chain networks. A single representation data format is essential to harness the value-added service.

Figure 3. Diagrammatic representation of the supply chain business process

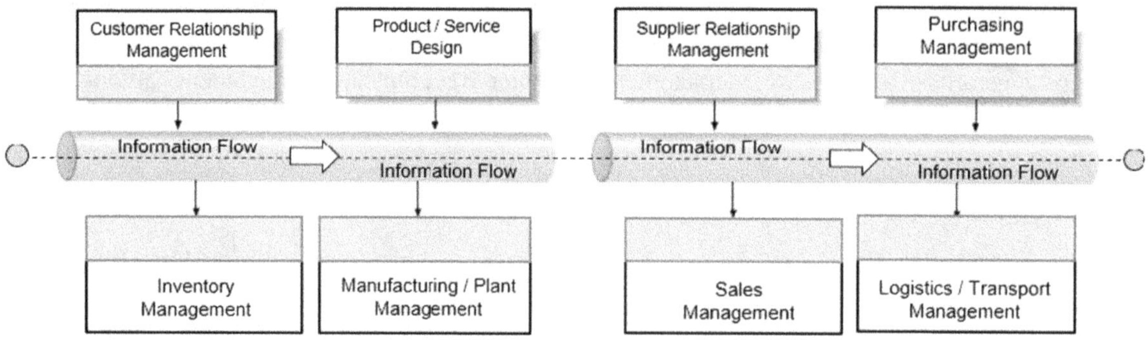

As a result, much global manufacturing (e.g., textile and clothing) businesses invest in new ICT to harness smooth information-sharing ability in their supply chain operations (Monteneggro et al., 2007). With the recent progress in Radio Frequency Identification (RFID) technology, low-cost wireless sensor hardwires, and world comprehensive web technologies, the Internet of Things (IoT) advance has attracted attention in connecting global apparel business activities and sharing operational business information. In this context, IoT technology supports connecting and integrating both digital and physical business entities, enabling the provision of a new type of information system (IS) applications and services. Also, the Semantic Web of Things (SWoT) is ushering in a new opportunity in the business community by integrating the Semantic Web and IoT technologies. It aims to associate semantically rich and easily accessible information with real-world objects, locations, and events using inexpensive, disposable, and unobtrusive micro-devices, such as RFID tags and wireless sensors. This opportunity provides new IS applications and services in many apparel business areas (e.g., manufacturing, inventory, and transportation management).

In order to facilitate this vision, information technologies and software system frameworks must mitigate typical pervasive computing application-related issues: platform heterogeneity, appropriate resource utilization, intelligent intractability of the user, device volatility, dependence on context, and limitation of device-specific computation power. Hence, the SWoT vision requires pervasive knowledge-based systems with higher degrees of automatic capability in information storage, management, and discovery and transparent access to information sources for processing.

Most IoT technology solutions inherit support from stable data communication infrastructures and assistance from centralized brokers for service management and information discovery. Also, optimization of alternative information provision has been recently getting prominence, for example, 6LoWPAN (IPv6 over Low Power Wireless Personal Area Networks) (Monteneggro et al., 2007) and the Constrained Application Protocol (CoAP) (Colitti et al., 2011). In parallel attempts, device and data annotation ontologies were presented, for example - OntoSensor (Russomanno et al., 2005) and the SSN-XG ontology of the World Wide Web Consortium for semantic sensor networks (Lefort et al., 2005). Current research projects, such as UBIWARE (Katasonov et al., 2008), and Sense2Web (Barnaghi et al., 2010), integrate data communication networking and semantic technologies to make software frameworks for semantically enriched IoT application services.

These services are composed of different data sources from real-world objects related to apparel business processes. With many devices in the textile and clothing world, many physical parameters and real-world entities can collaborate in a business service through data communication networks or the Internet. Thus, there is a need for seamless integration of the physical world with the digital world in IoT. Also, the progress in IoT-enabled device abstraction and integrating different data sources in the apparel business is challenging. The traditional web service discovery mechanisms are incapable of producing the appropriate result. Also, the heterogeneous nature of IoT-generated data requires semantic modelling. Thus, IoT entities must be formally represented and managed to achieve interoperability.

An essential step towards the vision of IoT-based information systems interoperability is reusing data collected from widely distributed sensor-enabled devices. Ontology-based semantic modelling helps capture entities' capability to represent information and its relationships among other entities to enable efficient information exchange. In this way, semantic modelling in conjunction with service-oriented computing and ontology ushers a scalable means of accessing IoT entities. An ontology describes a vocabulary modelling a domain of interest and specifying the meaning of terms in that vocabulary. Depending on the accuracy of this specification, the notion of ontology encompasses different data or conceptual models (e.g., classifications). In other words, ontology is a shared conceptualization, and it is used to represent knowledge as a set of concepts related to each other. The structural part comprises four key components: *classes*, *relations*, *attributes*, and *individuals*. Classes represent the concepts in ontology design, and individuals are the basic, '*ground level*' components or instances of an ontology. Attributes or characteristics represent the features of the classes, and relations describe how the classes and individuals are related to one another.

This chapter presents semantic knowledge-based on IoT-related entities in an apparel manufacturing business. Since most of the IoT data in a textile and clothing industry setting needs to be made available homogeneously to allow integration from various sources. A uniðed machine-understandable representation of world knowledge must put things into an everyday semantic context. The integrated Apparel Business Decentralised Data Integration (ABDDI) framework uses semantic modelling. Ontologies are used to form a unified knowledge base to support: (a) semantic definition and representation of IoT entities; (b) dynamic service discovery and matching based on user request; and (c) service composition and orchestration in dynamic environments. This chapter considers ontologies as the vital component for automatic service representation, composition, discovery, and orchestration for IoT in dynamic environments. The proposed knowledge base hides the heterogeneity of entities and consequently enables semantic searching and querying capabilities. Finally, the presented knowledge base integrates several existing ontologies related to sensor resources and web services and extends them for IoT.

RELATED RESEARCH WORKS

In recent decades automatic identification technologies are gaining more attraction for industrial applications. These applications are combined with RFID, Electronic Product Code (EPC) technologies, and sensor-based data communication networks to share application-specific data. Advances in ICT are bringing into reality the vision of many uniquely identifiable, interconnected objects and things that gather data from diverse physical environments and deliver the information to various innovative applications and services. In this way, the network of objects (e.g., devices, vehicles, machines, containers), embedded with sensors and software can collect and communicate data over the Internet. Inter-and intra-organizational communication and information exchange are perceived to be facilitated by IoT capability. This, IoT-based technology adoption can be viewed as an additional capability that may add value to the supply chain industries.

While IoT's many applications are used in different supply chain industries (Jandl et el., 2019), industrial IoT (IIoT) focuses primarily on the industrial usage of IoT devices (Jakl et al., 2018; Jeschke et al., 2017). Thomas Moser's research group recently presented an overview of industrial IoT applications (Jandl et al., 2019) for the smart industry (also known as Industry 4.0). With the advent of the IoT, new opportunities and capabilities emerge in real-time monitoring, management, and optimizing goods distribution and supply chain. As more physical objects in supply chain industries are equipped with barcodes, RFID tags, or sensors, transport, and logistics companies can monitor the movement of physical objects from one location to another. The goal is to track a product along the entire supply chain, including material management, production, transportation, and distribution (Karakostas, 2013).

Manufacturing companies are changing their IT infrastructure towards the fourth industrial revolution (Lasi et al., 2014). The utilization of artificial intelligence (AI) techniques in cyber-physical systems (CPSs) (Broy et al., 2012) is a typical characteristic of this change (Lee et al., 2014). In this context, flexibility is one of the essential criteria for manufacturing companies, mainly because of ever-shorter market launch times and increasing customer demands for individualization (Cheng et al., 2017; Lasi et al., 2014). To conduct industry 4.0 research, researchers use the factory simulation model because companies are often unwilling to provide data from and access to their production lines for research purposes.

More researchers have started concentrating on techniques enabling machines to understand IoT data better intelligently from various sources. In order to use AI applications, contextual operational knowledge must be available in formal and machine-readable representation (Humm et al., 2020). Semantic web services address the issues of automatic discovering, composing, and executing by providing a declarative, ontological framework for describing them. Using AI methods (e.g., automated planning [Marrella, 2018; Marrella & Mecella, 2018], multi-agent systems for decentralized manufacturing control [Ciortea et al., 2018], Case-Based Reasoning [CBR] [Minor et al., 2014; Muller, 2018]) to enhance flexibility in cyber-physical production workflows (Bordel Sanchez et al., 2018; Seiger et al., 2018) inevitably require such semantic annotations.

Much related research work (Puttonen et al., 2010; Puttonen et al., 2013) exists that already highlights these issues by using semantic web services (SWS). Moreover, the currently available approaches that use semantic web services in the context of Industry 4.0 focus only on specific aspects and do not consider the entire context of a manufacturing environment. Also, the complex reasoning within the knowledge base makes real-time execution and monitoring of manufacturing processes difficult. In this way, managing interoperable industrial applications is the key to success. One of the key components of interoperability is the specific information system's architecture. A reference architecture (RA) represents a robust and ground-level understanding of the scenarios that helps recognize problems and difficulties. The key idea of designing a RA (e.g., service-oriented architecture (SOA)) is to highlight modularity, scalability, adaptiveness, and interoperability among the connected heterogeneous devices in a real-time environment (Sarkar et al., 2021; Schneider, 2018; Hazra et al., 2021; Nagarajan et al., 2021).

Several research works propose using SWSs for smart manufacturing in Industry 4.0 but focus only on partial aspects and do not consider the entire shop floor context. For instance, Puttonen et al. (2013) present an approach to using SWSs for executing manufacturing processes using three software agents represented as web services. One of these agents, Service Monitor, is a specialized web service that performs semantic web service composition by using planning techniques concerning a given production goal and the current state of the world provided by a domain ontology. Therefore, they use OWL to describe the state of the production system and OWL-S and SPARQL expressions for semantically describing the available web services that offer production capabilities.

Since modern Cyber-Physical Production Systems (CPPSs) (Monostori, 2014) consist of many different components and therefore, many stakeholders are involved in their development process up to the later use in the manufacturing of products, Lobov et al. (2008) investigated the application of SWSs for orchestration of flexible control. They propose OWL for modelling a Process Taxonomy, Product Ontology, Equipment Ontology, and Service Ontology and discuss the responsibilities of involved persons for knowledge acquisition and maintenance rather than present their detailed semantic specification.

Many academics and practitioners, work-like Cory et al. (2009), experiment a semantically enhanced sensor service application, known as SemSOS, having the capability to query both high-level knowledge and low-level environmental reading by sensors. Concerning the classical sematic-matchmaking approach, different research groups distinguish among full (subsume), potential (intersection-satisfiable), and partial (disjoint) match types to represent the relevant knowledge of different types of entities (Colucci et al., 2007; Li & Horrocks, 2004). Similarly, queries in ubiquitous infrastructure allow only exact matches with facts derived from a support knowledge base. Non-standard inferences like abduction and contraction are needed to support approximate matches, semantic ranking, and explanations of outcomes (Colucci et al., 2007).

This chapter highlights the requirement for a unified semantic knowledge base for automatic service representation, discovery, modelling, and composition in dynamic environments. Different research projects try to address these issues using ontologies in prototype system design. For example, semantic commonalities in the RFID semantic streams project use DLs for system modelling (Ruta et al., 2011). This work is of considerable interest, but so far, it is sui generis.

All these schemes are worthy of considerable study, and together they represent the wealthiest characterization of a knowledge-based approach in pervasive service computing so far produced. Moreover, the systems are implemented and can be shown to generate relevant services using appropriate data streams.

OVERVIEW OF THE FRAMEWORK

The proposed framework uses model-theoretic semantics modelled in ontologies for IoT-generated data modelling purposes. It helps to gather detailed information regarding the characteristics of IoT devices based on their technical requirements. The advantages of this encoding are – (i) interconnecting different classification systems to represent capabilities and properties of constituent parts, (ii) translating characteristics or properties among compound constituent parts, and (iii) aggregating basic properties into complex properties based on the constituents of a superordinate system. Those concepts can be used and adapted for the IoT to enhance the uses of IoT devices in connecting them as a group, create coordination between IoT devices, and improve their interoperability.

One of the main objectives of this framework is to define an IoT architecture, which can also be used for other applications. The design principle in Apparel Business Semantic Data Management (ABDDI) is that any physical/real-world object in the global textile and clothing business can have a virtual representation through a Virtual Object (VO). AVO uses a semantic representation of the functionality and conceals the varied identity of the real-world object. Multiple VOs can be combined to form a Composite Virtual Object (CVO) that provides more compact and reliable services. In simple, CVOs are combined to form a service request. Thus, the ABDDI architecture has three layers: VO, CVO, and Service, as shown in Figure 4.

The functionalities of the three layers are presented below:

1. VO layer: Real-world objects are represented in the digital format as VO. End-users can search semantically and retrieve information from any existing VO. Also, actuation can be done through the VO.
2. CVO layer: In this layer, VOs are combined to form a service request. This layer caters functionality to search and query categories of CVOs for service provision semantically.
3. Service layer: This layer gets the request from a user and analyses the service requests to determine the categories of CVOs needed for service accomplishment. This layer also performs service composition and orchestration in a dynamic cloth and textile business environment.

The ABDDI system also has got other components: *a registry* and a *control unit*. Every layer in this framework has a registry referencing the available VOs, CVOs, and services. These registries provide methods to semantically search and query existing VOs, CVOs, and services. In addition, the control unit regulates access to the VOs, CVOs, and services based on the level of the end-user requirements.

Figure 4 RFID tagging level at different stages in the apparel manufacturing network

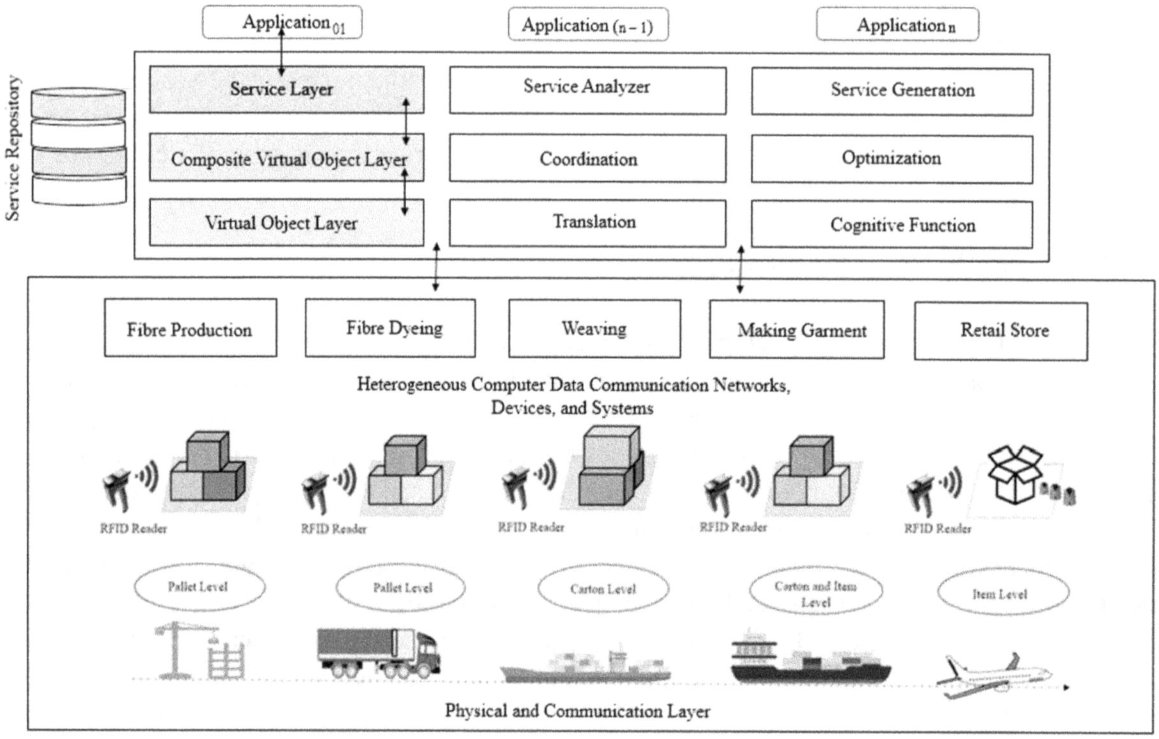

Knowledge Representation and Reasoning Approach

One of the motivations for this chapter stems from the Description Logics (DL) (Baader, 2010) based knowledge representation approach in pervasive computing applications along the global apparel supply chain. This DL-based knowledge representation system plays a role very much like Database Management Systems (DBMS). In DL, elementary descriptions are *atomic concepts* and *atomic roles*. Complex descriptions can be built from them inductively with *concept constructors*. In abstract notation, one can use the letters A and B for atomic concepts, R for atomic roles, and C and D for concept descriptions. Possible DL constructors and the related examples are shown in Table 1, and these constructors are used in the DLs investigated in this chapter.

In DL, a distinction is drawn between the so-called TBox (terminological box) and the ABox (assertional box). In general, the TBox contains sentences describing concept hierarchies (i.e., relations between concepts) while the ABox contains ground sentences stating where in the hierarchy, individuals belong (i.e., relations between individuals and concepts). For example, the statement:

Every employee is a person
belongs in the TBox, while the statement:
Bob is an employee
belongs in the ABox.

Note that the TBox/ABox distinction is not significant, in the same sense that the two "kinds" of sentences are not treated differently in first-order logic (which subsumes most DL). When translated into first-order logic, a subsumption axiom like (1) is simply a conditional restriction to unary predicates (concepts) with only variables appearing in it. Clearly, a sentence of this form is not privileged or special over sentences in which only constants ("grounded" values) appear like (2).

Table 1. DLs set of constructors

Constructor Name	Syntax	Explanation
Top concept	T	Universal concept. All the objects in the domain.
Bottom concept	⊥	The empty set.
Atomic concept	A	All objects belong to set A.
Atomic negation	¬A	All the objects do not belong to set A.
Conjunction	C⊓D	The objects belong to both C and D sets.
Disjunction	C⊔D	The objects that are in the extension of either C or D or both
Value restriction	∀RC	All the objects are participating in the R relation, whose range is all the objects belonging to the C set.
Existential restriction	∃RC	At least one object participating in the relation R.
Concept definition	A ≡ C	Concepts represent sets of elements and can be viewed as unary predicates.

So why was the distinction introduced? The primary reason is that the separation can be useful when describing and formulating decision-procedures for various DL. For example, a reasoner might process the TBox and ABox separately, in part because certain key inference problems are tied to one but not the other one ('classification' is related to the TBox, 'instance checking' to the ABox). Another example is that the complexity of the TBox can greatly affect the performance of a given decision-procedure for a certain DL, independently of the ABox. Thus, it is useful to have a way to talk about that specific part of the knowledge base.

Resource Representation and Reasoning in Description Logics

The most important and well-known service characterizing reasoning in DL checks for specificity hierarchies by determining whether a concept description is more specific than another one or, formally, if there is a *subsumption* relation between them. Table 2 presents some of the important subsumption's definition.

Table 2. Some subsumptions definition

Definition 1 (Subsumption): *Give two concept descriptions, C and D, and a TBox τ in a DL L; one can say that D subsumes C $\tau(C \sqsubseteq_\tau D)$ concerning if for every model of τ, $C^I \subset D^I$. In a particular case, two concepts are equivalent if they subsume each other.*

For example, consider the following concept descriptions, referring to different garment types in an apparel supply chain network: G_1 = *SweaterBodyGarment* ⊓ ∀ *hasMain Colour.Red*, and G_2 = *UpperBodyGarment* ⊓ ∀ *hasMain.Colour.Red*. Then using TBox reasoning – the concept inclusion can be achieved, and the output will be *Sweater* $\sqsubseteq_T$ *UpperBodyGarment*. Hence, given the model, knowledge expressed by G_1 is more specific than the one required by G_2 concerning the reasoning mechanism and the definition of G_2 subsumes G_1.

Based on subsumption, new reasoning mechanisms can be defined in DLs. The ABDDI system development uses several non-standard reasoning mechanisms (e.g., Least Common Subsumer – LCS).

Definition 2 (Least Common Subsumer): *Let $C_1, \ldots, C_p$ be p concept descriptions in a DL L. A Least Common Subsumer (LCS) of $C_1, \ldots, C_p$, denoted by LCS ($C_1, \ldots, C_p$) is a concept description E in L state that the following conditions hold: (i) $C_h \sqsubseteq E$ for h = 1, ..., p; (ii) E is the least L–concept description satisfying (iii), i.e., if E′ is an L–concept satisfying $C_i \sqsubseteq E'$ for all i = 1, ..., n, then $E \sqsubseteq E'$.*

It is worth showing how to model concept collections formalized in ALN (D) according to a compact lossless representation. Such modelling allows for finding commonalities in resource annotations formalized in DL.

Definition 3 (Concept Components): *Let C be a concept described in a DL L, with C formalized as $C^1 \sqcap \ldots C^m$. The Concept Components of C are defined as follows: if C^j, with j = 1,..., m is either a concept name, a negated concept name, or a concrete feature or a number restriction, then C^j is a Concept Component of C; if $C^j = \forall R.E$, with j = 1 ..., m, then $\forall R.E^k$ is a Concept Component of C, for each E^k Concept Component of E.*

Definition 4 (Subsumption): *Give two concept descriptions C and D, and a TBox τ in a DL L; one can say that D subsumes C $\tau(C \sqsubseteq_\tau D)$ concerning if for every model of τ, $C^I \subset D^I$. In a particular case, two concepts are equivalent if they subsume each other.*

Definition 5 (Least Common Subsumer): *Let $C_1, \ldots, C_p$ be p concept descriptions in a DL L. A Least Common Subsumer (LCS) of $C_1, \ldots, C_p$, denoted by LCS ($C_1, \ldots, C_p$) is a concept description E in L state that the following conditions hold: (i) $C_h \sqsubseteq E$ for h = 1, ..., p; (ii) E is the least L–concept description satisfying (iii), i.e., if E′ is an L–concept satisfying $C_i \sqsubseteq E'$ for all i = 1, ..., n, then $E \sqsubseteq E'$.*

Definition 6 (r-Common Subsumer, Informative r-Common Subsumers): *Let $C_1, \ldots, C_p$ be p concept descriptions in a DL L, and let be $k \leq p$. An r-Common Subsumer (r-CS) of $C_1, \ldots, C_p$ is a concept $D \neq \top$ such that D is an LCS of at least r = k/p concepts among $C_1, \ldots, C_p$. One can define a particular case as Informative r-Common Subsumers (IrCS) that specific r-CSS for which r < 1.*

It is worth showing how to model concept collections formalized in ALN (D) according to a compact lossless representation. Such a modelling framework allows for finding commonalities in resource annotations formalized in DL.

Definition 7 (Concept Components): *Let C be a concept described in a DL L, with C formalized as $C^1 \sqcap \ldots C^m$. The Concept Components of C are defined as follows: if C^j, with j = 1,..., m is either a concept name, a negated concept name, or a concrete feature or a number restriction, then C^j is a Concept Component of C; if $C^j = \forall R.E$, with j = 1 ..., m, then $\forall R.E^k$ is a Concept Component of C, for each E^k Concept Component of E.*

Definition 8 (Aggregate Collection Matrix): *Let $S_1, \ldots, S_n$ be an aggregate collection, with $S_i = C_{1i}, \ldots, C_{pi}$ for i = 1 ... n. Let $D \in \{D_1, \ldots, D_m\}$ be the Concept Components deriving from all the concepts in the aggregate collection. The Aggregate Subsumers Matrix is defined as $A = (a_{ij})$, with i = 1 ... n and j = 1 ... m, such that for each i, $a_{ij} = v$, with $0 \leq v \leq p_i$, where v is the number of concept descriptions in S_i subsumed by the component D_j.*

Definition 9 (Aggregate Model): *Let $S_1, \ldots, S_n$ be an aggregate of concept collections; for i = 1 ... n, S_i is a concept collection descriptions $_{ki}$ with k = 1 ... p_i. An Aggregate Model for $S_1, \ldots, S_n$ and each of this element consists of the pair of items - $<E, G>$ with the following characteristics: (i) E represents the subsumers matrix deriving from the collection $C_1, \ldots, C_p = \cup(C_{ki})$, with i = 1 ... n and k = 1 ... p_i, whose elements e_{kj} are calculated by using prognostications to subsumption; and (ii) G is the collection subsumers matrix deriving from the input collection $S_1, \ldots, S_n$ whose elements a_{ij} are calculated by using information stored in E. In this computation, each row i in G is related to an aggregate collection S_i, defined as a collection of description C_{ki} whose subsumption relationship with components deriving from $S_1, \ldots$, Sn is stored in E. To this modelling, values a_{ij}, for each component D_j, are determined as Concept Component Relative Cardinality $RC_{D_j}^{S_i}$.*

Semantic Similarity Assessment

Before describing the proposed approach's theoretical framework, the employed reasoning services will be shortly recalled in the following subsection to make the chapter self-contained. Furthermore, the proposed algorithmic concept of similarity measurement is presented in this section.

In ABSDM, the similarity between concepts C_i, C_j can be expressed by a number, and its values can fall between 0 and 1. It may be viewed as a one-directional relation, and its larger values imply a higher similarity between the concepts. The concept similarity is described in Table 3.

Table 3 An ontological concept similarity assessment criterion

Definition 10 (Concept Similarity): An ontological concept (C) similarity (∂) is considered a *relation*, and it can be defined as $\partial C \times C \rightarrow [0, 1]$. In simple, it is a function from a pair of concepts to a real number between *zero* and *one*, expressing the degree of similarity between two concepts such that:

1. $\forall C_1 \in G,\ \partial(C_1, C_1) = 1$
2. $\forall C_1, C_2 \in G,\ 0 \leq \partial(C_1, C_2) \leq 1$
3. $\forall C_1, C_2, C_3 \in G,\ IF\ Sim_d(C_1, C_2) > Sim_d(C_1, C_3)\ THEN\ \partial(C_1, C_2) < \partial(C_1, C_3)$

The above properties provide the range of semantic similarity functions $\partial(C_i, C_j)$. For exactly similar concepts, the similarity is $\partial(C_1, C_1) = 1$; when two concepts have nothing in common, their similarity is $\partial(C_1, C_2) = 0$. In this way, the output of the similarity function should be in the closed interval [0, 1]. Here Sim_d represents the semantic distance, and (C_1, C_2, C_3) represent three concepts of graph G. In CSIA, the following semantic similarity (∂) function has been used for computation purposes:

$$\partial(C_1, C_2) = \frac{1}{\deg * Sim_d(C_1, C_2) + 1}$$

Where C_1 and C_2 represent two concepts, and 'deg' represents the impact of semantic distance on semantic similarity, it should be between $0 < \deg \leq 1$. A weight allocation function is used, as shown below, to compute the semantic similarity between concepts:

$$w(C_m, C_n) = [\ \max(depth(C_m)) + \frac{OrderNumber(C_n)}{TNodes(G) + 1} + 1\ ]^{-1}$$

Where C_m *and* C_n represents two nodes directly connected, $\max(depth(C_m))$ represents the maximum depth of the node C_m (the depth of the root node is equal to 0 and 1 for the nodes directly connected to the root node and so on), TNodes(G) and OrderNumber(C_n) represent the total number of nodes in concept graph G and the order number of the node (C_n) between their siblings. The detailed description of these mathematical formalizations is beyond the scope of this chapter.

Semantic Similarity Assessment

In ABDDI, the similarity between two concepts C_i, a number can express Cj, and its values can fall between 0 and 1. It may be viewed as a one-directional relation, and its larger values imply a higher similarity between the concepts. The concept similarity is described as follows:

EXAMPLE OF A BUSINESS SCENARIO

A simple apparel manufacturing scenario is used to present a part of ABDDI algorithmic computation. Semantic IoT-based product flow in a retail outlet is considered. Each product is described using semantic-

Algorithm 1. Algorithm for semantic similarity computation

```
input: two concepts (C1, C2), the root node (root), concepts graph (G)
output: semantic similarity value between two concepts
begin
if C1 and C2 are same concept then Simd = 0
else
   if C1 and C2 are directly connected then Simd = w (C1 , C2)
    else
      if idirect path connection exist then
          Spath01 = ShortestPath (G, C1, RootN)
          Spath02 = ShortestPath (G, C2, RootN)
          Simd = w(Spath01) + w(Spath02) – 2*w(CSPath]
        end if
          ∂(C1, C2) = 1 / (deg*Simd+1)
      end if
end if
return ∂
end
```

enhanced IoT as an ALN (D) concept expression in OWL language. As the retail apparel product arrive or depart the shop, they are scanned by the gate RFID readers; reading events, including semantic annotation extracted from tags, are fed to a semantic Data Service Management Service (DSMS), which computes Concept Components and subsumption test through a reasoning mechanism.

Let us consider a situation that allows a user to purchase a sweater from an online business. This example considers how a request is matched with the service advertised for wool garments selling service. An algorithm (i.e., Algorithm 1) tries to perform semantic matching for a relevant sweater.

The algorithm takes two ontological concepts, the root node (root), and the concepts graph (G), as input and computes a semantic similarity between the concepts as output.

The part of the concept hierarchy used in this example is shown in Figure 5. Each node of this hierarchy represents a concept. The experimental comparison considers semantic similarity among Wool, Shirt, Sweater, Trousers, Cardigan, Pullover, and Jumper. The proposed algorithm (i.e., Algorithm-I) provides semantic similarity between concepts with a higher score than the path similarity algorithm.

In Table 4, (a) is the result of path similarity (Giunchiglia et al., 2004), and (b) tabulates the results of the proposed Algorithm-I used in ABDDI. In ABDDI, the similarity measure is flexible and customizable, allowing the consideration of user preferences. This refers to two aspects. Firstly, the user may determine some of the similarity assessment parameters' relative importance using the advanced search interface. Second, apart from presenting a single rank for each candidate service, more detailed results may also be provided (e.g., different values for recall, and the degree of match) to facilitate the user in identifying the timelier service.

Figure 5 The hierarchical concept relationships

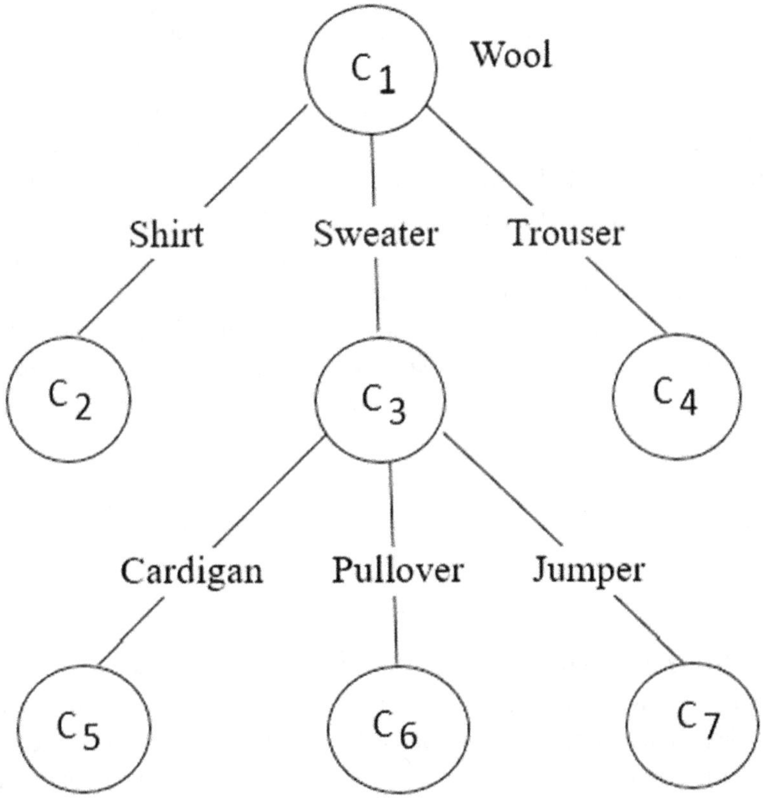

Table 4. The results of various similarity measures

	C_1	C_2	C_3	C_4	C_5
C_1	1.00	0.25	0.50	0.20	0.20
C_2	0.25	1.00	0.50	0.33	0.16
C_3	0.50	0.50	1.00	0.25	0.16
C_4	0.20	0.33	0.25	1.00	0.20
C_5	0.20	0.16	0.16	0.20	1.00

(a) Path similarity

	C_1	C_2	C_3	C_4	C_5
C_1	1.00	0.48	0.65	0.51	0.38
C_2	0.48	1.00	0.65	0.51	0.38
C_3	0.65	0.65	1.00	0.71	0.48
C_4	0.51	0.51	0.71	1.00	0.59
C_5	0.38	0.38	0.48	0.59	1.00

(b) The proposed method

FUTURE RESEARCH DIRECTIONS

Based on the findings, future studies, and experiments must be conducted on semantic reasoning with more diverse information content, complex scenarios, and more detailed contextual knowledge (e.g., rules and other forms). Reasoning engines certainly influence reasoning performance. Thus, different reasoning engines should be evaluated. For example, integrating real-time reasoned knowledge with background knowledge by utilizing federated RDF databases would be valuable, as they can provide background reasoning and knowledge integration services on specific platforms. In the future, the current research plans to use many context scenarios to evaluate the proposed approach's benefit more appropriately.

Although several academic and industry proposals address IoT-based information systems interoperability issues, no reasonable ground can cover some related research issues. The lack of standards and the absence of cutting-edge technologies slow the development of IoT. Proving semantically interoperable platforms across the different IoT domains requires research improvements. Hence, there is still significant room for future work on this topic.

CONCLUSION

This chapter presents some of the uses of IoT technologies (e.g., RFID tag-based technology, sensor) in the apparel industry. RFID technology can interact with items (i.e., transport carts, trolleys, keys, and valuable products) without physical contact in the textile and clothing retail industry. Thus, item-level IoT infrastructures provide item handling efficiency and offer a promising way to capture customers' in-store behavioural data and then gain insight into these data using data mining technology. In this way, these sensing objects and things form the Internet of Things (IoT), which are used to automate manufacturing business processes (e.g., material management, transportation management, and logistics management). In addition, IoT applications rely on real-time context data and allow sending information to drive users' behaviours in intelligent supply chain environments. These IoT-based solutions are mostly tailored for vertical applications and systems, utilizing knowledge only from business areas. However, to realize IoT's full potential, these specialized silo applications must be replaced with horizontal collaborative applications, including knowledge acquisition and sharing capabilities.

One of the main challenges in realizing an IoT system lies in dealing with device and data heterogeneities and fostering the interoperability between devices, information, and services built on top of it. Ontologies and semantic description frameworks play an essential role in the IoT. They operate on top of a standardized data interoperability infrastructure and enforce the concept of data uniformity that allows data and data semantics to be described in application-independent ways. Semantic technologies and ontologies decouple data semantics from application logic, facilitating information exchange, adaptability, and interoperability among tools and systems.

This chapter describes a unified semantic knowledge base (ABDDI) for IoT-related apparel supply chain management technologies. Semantic modelling is a critical component to address issues related to interoperability among different entities to realize the grand vision of IoT. ABDDI's knowledge base comprises ontologies to model different aspects of the apparel business (e.g., IoT resources, location information, contextual information, domain knowledge, policies for the dynamic environment, and IoT services). Most of the current work focuses on IoT resources and services; however, modelling contextual information in a dynamic environment assists in more accurate knowledge representation for IoT entities.

Real-time data gathering and processing are the main ingredients of current supply chain operations. To further enhance the potential of this promising application, in the future, this research will try to propose a unified framework for IoT-based path analytics, which uses both in-store shopping paths and IoT-based purchasing data for actionable navigation patterns. In the pre-processing data module, the critical problem of capturing the mainstream shopping path sequences while wiping out redundant and repeated details must be addressed in detail.

REFERENCES

Aazam, M., & Huh, E. N. (2014). Fog computing and smart gateway based communication for cloud of things. *Proceedings of the 2nd IEEE International Conference on Future Internet of Things and Cloud (FiCloud' 14),* 464–470.

Atzori, L., Iera, A., & Morabito, G. (2011). IoT: Giving a social structure to the internet of things. *IEEE Communications Letters*, *15*(11), 1193–1195.

Baader, F., Calvanese, D., McGuinness, D., Nardi, D., & Patel-Schneider, P. (Eds.). (2010). *The Description Logic Handbook.* Cambridge University Press.

Barnaghi, P., Presser, M., & Moessner, K. (2010). Publishing Linked Sensor Data. *Proceedings of the 3rd International Workshop on Semantic Sensor Networks.*

Berners-Lee, T. (2000). *Weaving the Web: The Original Design and Ultimate Design of the World Wide Web by its inventor*. Harper Business.

Bonomi, F., Milito, R., Natarajan, P., & Zhu, J. (2014). *Fog computing: a platform for internet of things and analytics. In Big Data and Internet ofThings: A Road Map for Smart Environments*. Springer.

Bonomi, F., Milito, R., Zhu, J., & Addepalli, S. (2012). Fog computing and its role in the internet of things. *Proceedings of the 1st ACM MCC Workshop on Mobile Cloud Computing*, 13–16.

Bordel Sánchez, B., Alcarria, R., Sánchez de Rivera, D., & Robles, T. (2018). Process execution in CyberPhysical Systems using cloud and Cyber-Physical Internet services. *The Journal of Supercomputing*, *74*(8), 4127–4169.

Broy, M., Cengarle, M. V., & Geisberger, E. (2012). Cyber-Physical Systems: Imminent Challenges. In *Large-Scale Complex IT Syst. Dev., Operat. and Manag. - 17th Monterey Workshop, (vol. 7539*, pp. 1–28). Academic Press.

Cardoso, J., Sheth, A., Miller, J., Arnold, J., & Kochut, K. (2004). Quality of service for workflows and web service processes. *Journal of Web Semantics*, *1*(3), 281–308.

Cheng, H., Xue, L., Wang, P., Zeng, P., & Yu, H. (2017). Ontology-based web service integration for flexible manufacturing systems. In *15th Int. Conf. on Ind. Inf.* (pp. 351–356). IEEE.

Ciortea, A., Mayer, S., & Michahelles, F. (2018). Repurposing Manufacturing Lines on the Fly with Multi-agent Systems for the Web of Things. In *Proc. of the 17th Int. Conf. on Autonomous Agents and Multi-Agent Systems* (pp. 813–822). ACM.

Colitti, W., Steenhaut, K., & Caro, N. De. (2011). *Integrating Wireless Sensor Networks with the Web.* Extending the Internet to Low power and Lossy Networks (IP+SN).

Colucci, S., Di Noia, T., Pinto, A., Ruta, M., Ragone, A., & Tinelli, E. (2007). A Nonmonotonic Approach to Semantic Matchmaking and Request Refinement in E-Marketplaces. *International Journal of Electronic Commerce, 12*(2), 127–154.

Cory, A., Henson, J., Pschorr, K., Sheth, A. P., & Thirunarayan, K. (2009). SemSOS: Semantic sensor Observation Service. *Proceedings of the International Symposium on Collaborative Technologies and Systems.*

Courbis, C., & Finkelstein, A. (2005). Weaving Aspects into Web Service Orchestrations. *Proceeding of International Conference of Web Services (ICWS '05).*

De Virgilio, R., Di Sciascio, E., Ruta, M., Scioscia, F., & Torlone, R. (2011). Semantic-based rfid data management. In *Unique Radio Innovation for the 21st Century* (pp. 111–141). Springer.

Giunchiglia, F., Shvaiko, P., & Yatskevich, M. (2004). S-Match: an algorithm and an implementation of semantic matching. *The 1st European Semantic Web Symposium (ESWS), 3053*, 61-75.

Gubbi, J., Buyya, R., Marusic, S., & Palaniswami, M. (2013). Internet of Things (IoT): A vision, architectural elements, and future directions. *Future Generation Computer Systems, 29*(7), 1645–1660.

Hazra, A., Adhikari, M., Amgoth, T., & Srirama, S. N. (2021). A Comprehensive Survey on Interoperability for IIoT: Taxonomy, Standards, and Future Directions. *ACM Computing Survey, 55*(1).

Jakl, A., Schoffer, L., Husinsky, M., & Wagner, M. (2018). Augmented Reality for Industry 4.0: Architecture and User Experience. *Proceeding of the 11th Forum Media Technology, CER-WS*, 38-42.

Jandl, C., Nurgazina, J., Schoffer, L., Reichl, C., Wagner, M., & Moser, T. (2019). SensiTrack – A Privacy by Design Concept for Industrial IoT Applications. *Proceeding of the 24th IEEE International Conference on Emerging Technologies and Factory Automation*, 1782-1789.

Jeschke, S., Brecher, C., Meisen, T., Ozdemir, D., & Eschert, T. (2017). Industrial Internet of Things and Cyber Manufacturing Systems. In Industrial Internet of Things. Springer.

Karakostas, B. (2013). A DNS architecture for the Internet of things: A case study in transport logistics. *Procedia Computer Science*, 594–601.

Katasonov, A., Kaykova, O., Khriyenko, O., Nikitin, S., & Terziyan, V. (2008). Smart Semantic Middleware for the Internet of Things. *Proceedings of the 5th International Conference of Informatics in Control, Automation and Robotics*, 11-15.

Keskinock, P., & Tayur, S. (2001). Quantitive analysis of Internet-enabled supply chain. *Interface, 31*(2), 70–89.

Khan, R., Khan, S. U., Zaheer, R., & Khan, S. (2012). Future internet: the internet of things architecture, possible applications and key challenges. *Proceedings of the 10th International Conference on Frontiers of Information Technology (FIT '12)*, 257–260.

Lasi, H., Fettke, P., Kemper, H.-G., Feld, T., & Hoffmann, M. (2014). Industry 4.0. *BISE*, *6*(4), 239–242.

Lastra, J. L. M., & Delamer, I. M. (2006). Semantic Web Services in Factory Automation: Fundamental Insights and Research Roadmap. *IEEE Transactions on Industrial Informatics*, *2*(1), 1–11.

Lee, H. L., & Billington, C. (1992). Managing supply chain inventories: Pitfalls and opportunities. *Sloan Management Review*, *33*(3), 65–77.

Lee, J., Kao, H.-A., & Yang, S. (2014). Service Innovation and Smart Analytics for Industry 4.0 and Big Data Environment. *Procedia CIRP*, *16*, 3–8.

Lefort, L., Henson, C., Taylor, K., Barnaghi, P., Compton, M., Corcho, O., Garcia-Castro, R., Graybeal, J., Herzog, A., & Janowicz, K. (2005). *Semantic Sensor Network XG Final Report*. W3C Incubator Group Report. http://www.w3.org/2005/Incubator/ssn/XGR-ssn/

Li, L., & Horrocks, I. (2004). A software framework for matchmaking based on semantic web technology. *International Journal of Electronic Commerce*, *8*(4), 39–60.

Lobov, A., Lopez, F. U., Herrera, V. V., Puttonen, J., & Lastra, J. L. M. (2008). Semantic Web Services framework for manufacturing industries. In *Int. Conf. on Rob. and Biomim.* (pp. 2104–2108). IEEE.

Maass, W., Filler, A. (2006). Towards an infrastructure for semantically annotated physical products. In *INFORMATIK 2006–Informatik für Menschen–Band 2, Beiträge der 36.* Jahrestagung der Gesellschaft für Informatik eV (GI).

Mahon, B. (2004). *The Man Who Changed Everything: The Life of James Clerk Maxwell*. John Wiley & Sons Ltd.

Marrella, A. (2018). *Automated Planning for Business Process Management*. Academic Press.

Mashal, I., Alsaryrah, O., Chung, T. Y., Yang, C. Z., Kuo, W. H., & Agrawal, D. P. (2015). Choices for interaction with things on Internet and underlying issues. *Ad Hoc Networks*, *28*, 68–90.

Minor, M., Montani, S., & Recio-García, J. A. (2014). Process-oriented Case-based Reasoning. *Information Systems*, *40*, 103–105.

Monostori, L. (2014). Cyber-physical Production Systems: Roots, Expectations and R&D Challenges. *Procedia CIRP*, *17*, 9–13.

Montenegro, G., Kushalnagar, N., Hui, J., & Culler, D. (2007). Transmission of IPv6 packets over IEEE 802.15.4 networks. Internet Proposed Standard RFC, vol. 4944.

Müller, G. (2018). *Workflow Modeling Assistance by Casebased Reasoning*. Springer Fachmedien.

Nagarajan, S. M., Muthukumaran, V., Vinoth Kumar, V., Beschi, I. S., & Magesh, S. (2021). *Fine Tuning Smart Manufacturing Enterprise Systems: A Perspective of Internet of Things-Based Service-Oriented Architecture*. IGI Global.

Ning, H., & Wang, Z. (2011). Future internet of things architecture: Like mankind neural system or social organization framework? *IEEE Communications Letters*, *15*(4), 461–463.

Ocker, F., Kovalenko, I., Barton, K., & Tilbury, D., & VogelHeuser, B. (2019). A Framework for Automatic Initialization of Multi-Agent Production Systems Using Semantic Web Technologies. *IEEE Robotics and Automation Letters*, *4*(4), 4330–4337.

Pal, K. (2017). Supply Chain Coordination Based on Web Services. In H. K. Chan, N. Subramanian, & M. D. Abdulrahman (Eds.), *Supply Chain Management in the Big Data Era* (pp. 137–171). IGI Global Publication.

Pal, K. (2018). A Big Data Framework for Decision Making in Supply Chain. IGI Global.

Pal, K. (2020). *Information Sharing for Manufacturing Supply Chain Management Based on Blockchain Technology*. IGI Global.

Pal, K., & Karakostas, B. (2014). A Multi Agent-Based Service Framework for Supply Chain Management, In the proceeding of International Conference on Ambient Systems, Networks and Technology. *Procedia Computer Science*, *32*, 53–60.

Pal, K., & Ul-Haque, A. (2000). Internet of Things and Blockchain Technology in Apparel Manufacturing Supply Chain Data Management. *Procedia Computer Science*, 450-457.

Pena-opez, I. (2005). *Internet Report 2005: The Internet of Things, 2005*. Academic Press.

Puttonen, J., Lobov, A., & Lastra, J. L. M. (2013). Semantics-Based Composition of Factory Automation Processes Encapsulated by Web Services. *IEEE TII*, *9*(4), 2349–2359.

Puttonen, J., Lobov, A., Soto, M. A. C., & Lastra, J. L. M. (2010). A Semantic Web Services-based approach for production systems control. *Advanced Engineering Informatics*, *24*(3), 285–299.

Russomanno, D. J., Kothari, C. R., & Thomas, O. A. (2005). Building a Sensor Ontology: A Practical Approach Leveraging ISO and OGC Models. *2005 International Conference on Artificial Intelligence*, 637-643.

Ruta, M., Colucci, S., Scioscia, F., Di Sciascio, E., & Donini, F. M. (2011). Finding commonalities in RFID semantic streams. *Procedia Computer Science*, *5*, 857–864.

Said, O., & Masud, M. (2013). Towards internet of things: Survey and future vision. *International Journal of Computer Networks*, *5*(1), 1–17.

Sarkar, I., Adhikari, M., Kumar, N., & Kumar, S. (2021). Dynamic task placement for deadline-aware IoT applications in federated for networks. *IEEE Internet Things Journal*, *1*, 2021.

Sarkar, T. K., Mailloux, R. J., Oliner, A. A., Salazar-Palma, M., & Sengupta, D. L. (2006). *History of Wireless*. John Wiley & Sons Inc.

Schneider, M., Hippchen, B., Abeck, S., Jacoby, M., & Herzog, R. (2018). Enabling IoT platform interoperability using a systematic development approach by example. *Proceedings of the Global Internet of Things Summit (GIoTS'18),* 1-6.

Seiger, R., Huber, S., & Schlegel, T. (2018). Toward an execution system for self-healing workflows in cyber-physical systems. *Software & Systems Modeling*, *17*(2), 551–572.

Stojmenovic, I., & Wen, S. (2014). The fog computing paradigm: scenarios and security issues. *Proceedings of the Federated Conference on Computer Science and Information Systems (FedCSIS' 14),* 1–8.

Swaminathan, J. M. (2000). *Supply chain management.* In International Encyclopedia of the Social and Behavioural Sciences. Elsevier Sciences.

Varelas, G., Voutsakist, E., Raftopoulout, P., Petrakis, E. G. M., & Milios, E. (2005). Semantic Similarity methods in WordNet and their application to information retrieval on the Web. In *Proceedings of the 7th annual ACM international workshop on web information and data management.* ACM.

Vermesan, O., Friess, P., & Guillemin, P. (2011). Internet of things strategic research roadmap. *Internet of Things. Global Technological and Societal Trends, 1,* 9–52.

Weyrich, M., & Ebert, C. (2016). Reference architectures for the internet of things. *IEEE Software, 33*(1), 112–116.

Wu, M., Lu, T. J., Ling, F. Y., Sun, J., & Du, H. Y. (2010). Research on the architecture of internet of things. *Proceedings of the 3rd International Conference on Advanced Computer Theory and Engineering (ICACTE' 10), 5,* 484-487.

Yoshioka, N., Honiden, S., & Fnkelstein, A. (2004). Security Patterns: A Method for Constructing Secure and Efficient Inter-Company Coordination Systems. *Proceedings of Enterprise Distributed Object Computing Conference 2004 (EDOC'04),* 84–97.

Zhao, J., & Kumar, V. V. (2021). *Handbook of Research on Innovations and Applications of AI, IoT, and Cognitive Technologies.* IGI Global Publication.

KEY TERMS AND DEFINITIONS

Description Logic: Description logics (DL) are a family of formal knowledge representation languages. Many DLs are more expressive than propositional logic, but less expressive than first-order logic.

EPC: Electronic Product Code (EPC), is a low-cost RFID tag designed for consumer products as a replacement for the universal product code (UPC).

Internet of Things: Internet of Things (IoT) means networks of things, software, sensors, network connectivity, and embedded 'things or physical objects. It collects or exchanges data. IoT makes objects sensed or controlled through a network infrastructure, supports integration between physical real world and automated information systems, and brings various effects such as improved productivity or economy in manufacturing industries.

Ontology: Information sharing among supply chain business partners using information systems is an important enabler for supply chain management. There are diverse types of data to be shared across the supply chain, namely – *order, inventory, shipment,* and *customer service*. Consequently, information about these issues needs to be shared to achieve efficiency and effectiveness in supply chain management. In this way, information-sharing activities require that human and / or machine agents agree on common and explicit business-related concepts (the shared conceptualization among hardware / software-agents, customers, and service providers) are known as explicit ontologies; and this help to exchange data and derived knowledge out of the data to achieve collaborative goals of business operations.

RFID Reader: An RFID transceiver, providing real and access to RFID tags information.

RFID Tag: An RFID tag (or transponder), typically consisting of an RF coupling element and a microchip that carries identifying data. Tag functionality may range from simple identification to being able to form an ad hoc network.

Semantic Web Service: A Semantic Web Service, like conventional web services, is the server end of a client-server system for machine-to-machine interaction via the Web. Semantic services are a component of the semantic Web because they use mark-up which makes data machine-readable in a detailed and sophisticated way (as compared with human-readable HTML which is usually not easily "understood" by computer programs).

Supply Chain Management: Supply chain management encompasses the planning and management of all activities involved in sourcing, procurement, manufacturing, and distribution. Importantly, it also includes coordination and collaboration with channel partners, which can be suppliers, intermediaries, third-party service providers, and customers. Supply chain management integrates supply and demand management within and across companies.

Web Ontology Language (OWL): The Web Ontology Language (OWL) is a semantic mark-up language for publishing and sharing ontologies on the Web. OWL is developed as a vocabulary extension of RDF (the Resource Description Framework) and is derived from the DAML + OIL Web Ontology Language.

Chapter 4
Marketing Big Data Analytics and Customer Relationship Management:
A Fuzzy Approach

Naoual Bouhtati
National School of Business and Management, Sidi Mohammed Ben Abdellah University, Morocco

Lhoussaine Alla
https://orcid.org/0000-0002-7238-1792
National School of Applied Sciences, Sidi Mohammed Ben Abdellah University, Morocco

Badr Bentalha
https://orcid.org/0000-0003-1339-542X
National School of Business and Management, Sidi Mohammed Ben Abdellah University, Morocco

ABSTRACT

Customer knowledge is a strategic element, and its importance is growing all the time. The role of the vast quantities of information available in customer relationship management (CRM) systems, when processed using emerging big data techniques, is still in its infancy. Customer relationship management needs big data to improve customer experience and the right targeting of marketing actions. The study aims at designing a hierarchical model via the fuzzy approach of the indicators of the big data marketing approaches and the possible effects on the CRM. The results suggest that CRM initiatives based on big data could be envisaged as a supportive trend in relation to various managerial and structural dimensions. The study also identified major difficulties of big data analysis in CRM, such as storage, quality, process, and cost issues.

DOI: 10.4018/979-8-3693-0225-5.ch004

INTRODUCTION

Given the processes of globalization and the constant technological revolution, the inherent market challenges facing the company today, concern the abilities to attract customers, maintain brand attractiveness and make it more competitive (Gu et al., 2021). In this context, the company should leverage its own data and data from external sources, to better assess, understand and predict customer preferences, and ensure its competitiveness or mere survival (Alla et al., 2022). Such customer intelligence can help the company to develop strategies to improve its performance and competitive advantage (Hmioui et al., 2020).

The current and constant acceleration of new information technologies has favored the creation and circulation of large volumes of data. This phenomenon is also favored by the constant quest to reduce costs and improve response times (Bentalha et al., 2019). Such opportunities can be seized by the company's relationship marketing, to further develop strong economic, technical and social connections with customers, as valves for successful marketing activities (Kotler & Keller, 2012; Khan et al., 2022). In this sense, Big Data is currently assimilated as a tool for relationship marketing. Its role is appreciated for its ability to participate in data analysis and market prediction (Anshari et al., 2019). It is a technological provision that can help to better understand customer needs and adjust market demand forecasts (ISACA, 2013).

Many companies have made huge investments in collecting, integrating, analyzing and using data for marketing and customer relationship management (CRM) activities, exposing their customers to a large number of marketing messages every day, which often remain ignored unless the recipients find added value (Orenga-Roglá & Chalmeta, 2016). CRM relevance requires deep and accurate data analysis that can ensure potential customers' engagement in the transaction (Sun et al., 2017). Customers understand markets with logical and interpretative processes, and the buying decision depends on the information gathered. Thus, this information becomes decisions that create other information. At this stage, Big Data seeks to develop market understanding via CRM tools linked to customer understanding, product promotion and customer loyalty (Angell & Kraemer, 2017).

This work aims to better understand the issues and implications of the adoption and embedding of Big Data marketing by the enterprise as a tool for improving the effectiveness of the customer relationship, and thus as a lever for value creation, by answering the following question: how to capitalize on the opportunities offered by Big-Data Analytics marketing for the improvement of the customer relationship of the enterprise?

The first part of the paper will deal with the concepts of CRM and Big Data, by analyzing their managerial and theoretical specificities. Then, we will present the analysis model linking these two concepts. Finally, we will interpret, through a hierarchical approach based on the Fuzzy method, the main indicators related to Marketing Big-Data Analytics and its possible effects on customer relationship management.

1. THEORETICAL AND CONCEPTUAL FRAMEWORK

1.1 Big Data, the New Challenge

In today's business environment, companies in the relentless pursuit of competitive advantage are seeking to optimize their resources and skills, turning to innovative information technologies to effectively and efficiently store and access information. This choice allows them to better know their suppliers,

Table 1. Popular big data techniques

Transactional Data	***Business Intelligence (BI)/Online Analytical Processing (OLAP):*** · Interactive analyze · Users can roll-up, drill-down, and slice data · BI tools
	Cluster Analysis: · segment objects into groups based on similar properties
	Data Mining: · Discover and extract new patterns
	Predictive Modeling: · a model is created to best predict the probability
	SQL: · a computer language that manages data from a relational database
	A/B Testing: · A method of testing in which a control group is compared to test groups to determine if there is an improvement based on the test condition
Non-transactional Social Data	***Crowdsourcing:*** · Collecting data from a large community
	Textual Analysis: · Computer algorithms that analyze natural language
	Sentiment Analysis: · A form of textual analysis that determines a positive, negative, or neutral reaction
	Network analysis: · A methodology to analyze the relationship among nodes

Source: Adapted from Parise et al. (2012)

competitors and customers, and also consumer trends (Talón-Ballestero et al., 2018). These are mainly high-volume, high-velocity and high-variety information assets that require innovative and cost-effective forms of information processing to improve understanding and decision-making. Big Data is a new method of evaluating and analyzing data, using large volumes of data from multiple sources (Novo & Neves, 2013). Its main aim is to create value with a large mass of information, a variety of sources and data, and speed of analysis (Villars et al., 2011). This is referred to as the 5V model: volume, velocity, variety, value, and veracity (Demchenko et al., 2014).

Volume, describes the large volume of data that consumes a lot of storage or consists of a large number of records. Variety refers to data that is generated from multiple sources and formats, and contains multidimensional data. Velocity reflects the frequency of data generation and/or data delivery. Veracity analyzes the inherent unpredictability of some data, which requires analysis of large data sets to make reliable predictions. Finally, value aims at the production of economically valid and beneficial data (Bentalha, 2020).

The challenges in this process are leadership, managing new talent, optimizing technology, making the right decisions: and mobilizing the company culture (Table 1). The choice of tools depends on the specific needs of each organization or project.

Analyzing the contributions of Big Data is crucial in the current era especially given the ability of this tool to change managerial and economic aspects (Mishra et al., 2018). Data sources can be both internal and external. Internal data are available within companies. External sources are present in social media and are generally not directly accessible (Leveling et al., 2014). Big-Data can therefore boost customer experience via a better overview of the customer experience. Companies can use big data to forecast market trends, identify growth opportunities and new markets, and make data-driven strategic decisions. Big-Data can be used to gather data from social networks, website visits, call logs and other data sources, in order to improve the interaction experience and optimize the value offered. Big-Data is also used to achieve greater operational efficiency. The company can analyze and evaluate production, customer feedback and other factors, to reduce errors and anticipate demands (Bentalha et al., 2020). Last but not least, Big-Data can stimulate innovation. Data analysis can pave the way for important innovations by enabling us to better understand, and even predict from existing elements, users' desires and needs. In other words, it can reveal how customers react to innovations.

1.2. Customer Relationship Management and Current and Potential Uses of Big Data in Customer Relationship Marketing

Customer Relationship Management (CRM) is a tool and strategy for managing customer interactions. It refers to the management of customers' interactions and relationships with a company. It helps to attract new customers, retain existing ones and strengthen the bond between customers. Customer Relationship Management (CRM) and Big Data are closely related. CRM systems are designed to collect and store customer data. Big Data technologies can help to manage and process large volumes of data from various sources, including social media, mobile devices, and other digital channels. Big Data technologies can be used to analyze customer data collected by CRM systems. This analysis can help to identify patterns, trends, and insights about customer behavior, preferences, and needs (Bentalha & Hmioui, 2021). Big Data technologies can also be used to develop predictive models that can anticipate customer behavior and preferences. Big Data technologies can also be used to enable real-time personalization of customer interactions. Finally, Big Data technologies can also be used to segment customers based on their behavior, preferences, and needs. This segmentation can help to tailor marketing messages and customer service interactions to different customer segments, improving the overall customer experience and increasing customer loyalty.

The relationship between relationship marketing and Big Data appears to be enabling the establishment of relationships with customers and the design of opportunities to automate processes. In this way, customer relationship management can lead to great interactivity (Davenport & Dyché, 2013; Waller & Fawcett, 2013). Big data can provide a model of customer information. In this way, companies can predict their customers' needs, as customers generate a huge amount of data every day. Big data analysis provides an overview of customers, so that the organization can improve the adequacy of services. There are many benefits to using big data in customer relationship management, such as accurate customer profiling, predicting customer reaction to messages and offers, creating personalized messaging, maximizing value chain strategies, producing accurate evaluation metrics and building customer loyalty (Guha et al., 2018).

While Big Data has the potential to provide valuable insights that can improve customer relationship management, there are also several challenges and limitations. Poor data quality can lead to inaccurate insights and decisions. Data quality issues can arise due to data inconsistencies, incomplete data, or errors in data entry. As more customer data is collected and stored, there is a greater risk of data breaches and cyber-attacks. Big Data technologies can be complex and difficult to implement. Organizations must have the necessary technical expertise and resources to manage and analyze large volumes of data. Also, implementing Big Data technologies can be expensive, both in terms of hardware and software costs and the cost of hiring skilled data analysts. As the amount of data collected and analyzed increases, it can become overwhelming for organizations to sift through and make sense of the data. This can lead to analysis paralysis, where organizations become so bogged down in data that they are unable to take action.

2. RESEARCH METHODOLOGY

The aim of this study is to analyze the key factors in Big Data as they relate to CRM. It is an analysis of research on Big Data in the sales organization. The study is based on a literature review on Big Data. The various links in the relationship between the two variables under study are integrated into our analysis model via a literature review. Selected articles are published in peer-reviewed journals between 2015 and 2022. This analysis enabled us to extract the items in the relationship between the two variables (Figure 1).

To design the overriding items of the relationship studied, 10 experts evaluated the items identified by the literature review using the Fuzzy method (Ishikawa et al., 1993). This method was chosen for its ability to prioritize items and achieve consensus among experts (Bentalha, 2022).

The Fuzzy questionnaire was codified on a Likert scale. A score is denoted by Ri. Triangular fuzzy numbers are statistically calculated by the index Oi with Oi= (Li, Mi, Ui). The three parameters of this formula are Li denoting the minimum value, Mi being the geometric mean and Ui signifying the maximum value (Figure 2).

Figure 1. Conceptual model of big data and CRM marketing
Source: Adapted from Reinartz et al., 2004 ; Kumar & Kumar, 2021 ; Dietrich et al., 2014 ; Davenport, 2014 ; Zerbino et al., 2018 ; Kakkar (2017) et Rajanarthagi (2021)

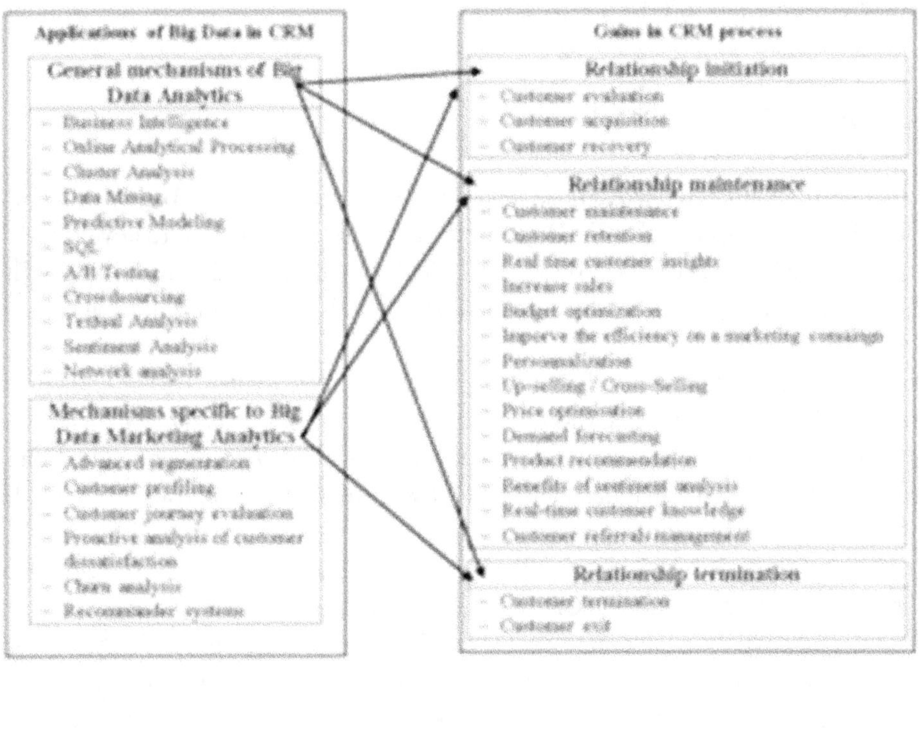

Figure 2. Fuzzy triangular numbers
Source: Hsieh et al., 2004

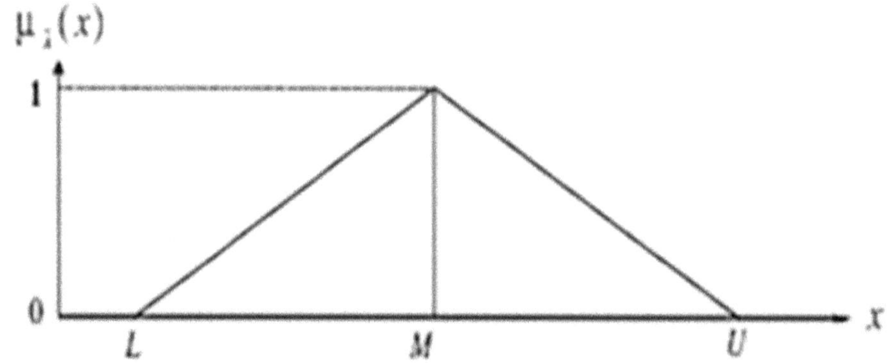

When the triangular Fuzzy numbers (Oi) are fixed for all factors, the area center method is used for defuzzification and the value of Gi is determined (Hsieh et al., 2004) with:

Gi = [(Ui – Li) + (Mi – Li)]/3 + Li

Factors with a Gi value greater than or equal to the threshold ($\alpha = 3.5$) are retained. This threshold is related to the language scale (Kumar et al., 2017; Bentalha et al., 2023). As a fuzzy logic method, involving qualitative variables in an intuitive way has the merit of introducing several degrees of stability and thus capturing the "*porosity*" of the concept absent in classical statistical analyses (Gadi & Benslimane, 2000; Bentalha, 2023).

3. RESULTS AND DISCUSSION

The first Fuzzy questionnaire is related to variables related to the application of Big Data in CRM (Table 2).

The results obtained show that the Big Data applications likely to be used to develop CRMs are first and foremost "advanced segmentation", "online analytical processing" and "data mining". The accessory mechanisms are successively "proactive analysis of customer dissatisfaction" and "business intelligence and textual analysis".

The second Fuzzy questionnaire is related to the variables linked to the CRM process gains (Table 3).

The hierarchy of expected gains in CRM through the adoption of big data mechanisms highlights the predominance of Relationship initiation ("Customer recovery" and "Customer acquisition"), Relationship maintenance ("Relationship maintenance" and "Real-time customer knowledge") and Relationship termination (Customer termination) implications.

The selected model is relatively rich in indicators. Figure 3 shows the proposed final model.

Customer relationship management (CRM) refers to a company's interactions with its current and potential customers across all touch points, and is crucial for providing superior customer service. Traditionally, CRM has relied on structured data such as contact details and purchase history. However, with the use of Big Data techniques, unstructured data can now be processed, stored, and analyzed to

Table 2. Computation of triangular Fuzzy numbers, defuzzification and filtering of variables of applications of big data in CRM

Indicators	L_i (Min)	M_i	U_i (Max)	G_i (COA)	Ranking	Screening
Business Intelligence	3	4,01	5	4,004	5	Accepted
Online Analytical Processing	4	4,47	5	4,491	1	Accepted
Cluster Analysis	1	2,76	5	2,920	11	Rejected
Data Mining	4	4,37	5	4,458	3	Accepted
Predictive Modeling	2	3,70	5	3,566	8	Accepted
SQL	1	1,76	3	1,921	17	Rejected
A/B Testing	1	2,17	4	2,390	16	Rejected
Crowdsourcing	1	2,76	5	2,920	11	Rejected
Textual Analysis	2	4,27	5	3,756	6	Accepted
Sentiment Analysis	2	3,70	5	3,566	8	Accepted
Network analysis	2	3,63	5	3,544	10	Accepted
Advanced segmentation	4	4,47	5	4,491	1	Accepted
Customer profiling	2	3,72	5	3,573	7	Accepted
Customer journey evaluation	2	2,70	4	2,901	14	Rejected
Proactive analysis of customer dissatisfaction	3	4,35	5	4,115	4	Accepted
Churn analysis	2	2,73	4	2,911	13	Rejected
Recommander systems	2	2,77	3	2,589	15	Rejected

Source: Personal elaboration

Table 3. Computation of triangular Fuzzy numbers, defuzzification and filtering of gains variables in CRM process

Indicators	L_i (Min)	M_i	U_i (Max)	G_i (COA)	Ranking	Screening
Customer evaluation	3	4,01	5	4,004	5	Accepted
Customer acquisition	4	4,47	5	4,491	2	Accepted
Customer recovery	4	4,57	5	4,524	1	Accepted
Customer maintenance	4	4,37	5	4,458	3	Accepted
Customer retention	2	3,70	5	3,566	11	Accepted
Real time customer insights	2	3,89	5	3,631	8	Accepted
Increase sales	1	2,17	4	2,390	19	Rejected
Budget optimization	1	2,76	5	2,920	15	Rejected
Imporve the efficiency on a marketing comaingn	1	2,82	5	2,941	14	Rejected
Personnalization	2	3,81	5	3,602	10	Accepted
Up-selling / Cross-Selling	1	2,75	5	2,918	16	Rejected
Price optimisation	1	3,81	5	3,269	13	Rejected
Demand forecasting	3	3,99	5	3,995	6	Accepted
Product recommendation	2	3,66	5	3,554	12	Accepted
Benefits of sentiment analysis	2	3,85	5	3,617	9	Accepted
Real-time customer knowledge	3	4,08	5	4,025	4	Accepted
Customer referrals management	2	2,77	3	2,589	17	Rejected
Customer termination	3	3,68	5	3,893	7	Accepted
Customer exit	2	2,66	3	2,552	18	Rejected

Source: Personal elaboration

Figure 3. Selected model of big data and CRM marketing
Source: Personal elaboration

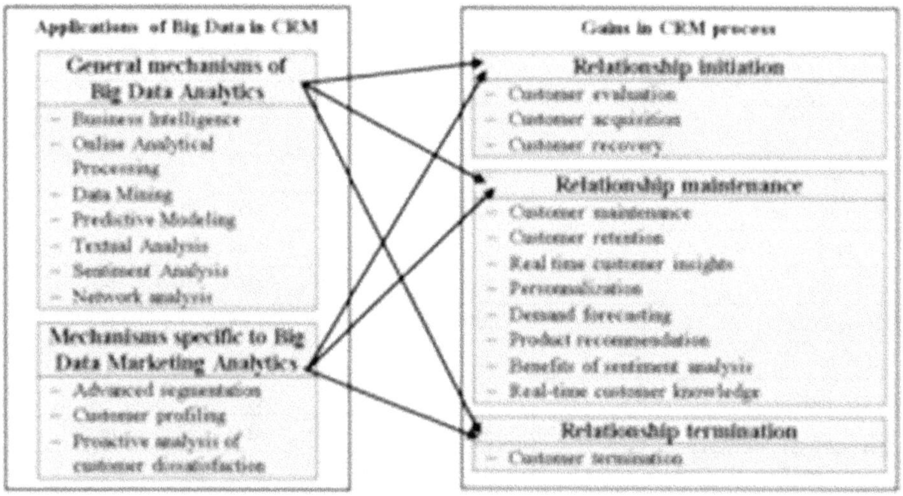

gain valuable insights. Email campaigns can be a useful marketing tool, but can often be perceived as spam by customers, leading to unsubscribes. Effective marketing strategy involves understanding customer behavior and tailoring messages to their specific needs, rather than focusing solely on short-term relationships. Therefore, personalized and targeted marketing is essential for attracting, retaining, and developing long-term customer relationships.

Faced with the multiple opportunities that the innovations brought by the use of Big Data in optimizing the marketing actions of the company, studies (Lastanto et al., 2018) have well identified major difficulties of Big Data analytics in customer relationship management, such as problems of storage, quality, processes and costs. This challenges us to do further research on the mechanisms for implementing a CRM Big Data analytics approach and the conditions for its effectiveness. Thanks to Big Data technologies, customer relationship management can finally become a real revenue driver.

CONCLUSION

The article attempted to analyze the relationship between Big Data and CRM. We examined, theoretically and conceptually, the contribution of Big-Data to CRM. Big Data describes the large volume of structured and unstructured data used by business players. This system uses several processing measures to ensure better decision-making for the company, through the use of more analytical tools and to improve processes and guarantee business optimization.

In the field of economics and management, big data is increasingly being used to drive decision-making and improve business outcomes. One key application is predictive analytics, which involves using large data sets to develop models that can forecast future trends. This can help businesses anticipate changes in consumer demand, identify potential risks and opportunities, and optimize their supply chain management. Another important use of big data is customer analytics. By analyzing vast amounts of data on consumer behavior, preferences, and needs, businesses can gain valuable insights that can inform the development of targeted marketing campaigns, enhance customer satisfaction, and boost sales. Big data is also playing a critical role in risk management across various areas of business, including finance, operations, and supply chain management. By analyzing market trends, tracking supplier performance, and identifying potential fraud, businesses can mitigate risks and improve their overall performance. Social media analytics is another area where big data is proving to be a valuable tool. By analyzing social media data, businesses can gain insights into consumer sentiment and behavior, which can inform the development of more effective marketing campaigns and improve customer engagement. Finally, big data is being used to create visual representations of complex data sets, making it easier for managers and executives to understand and analyze data. By using data visualization techniques, businesses can make more informed decisions and improve their overall performance. These various applications of big data are transforming the way businesses operate and compete in today's economy.

The results of our research confirm the primordial role of Big-Data. Nevertheless, our approach is relatively global and lacks any specific contextualization. Our research contributes to the analysis of this relationship between new technologies and new forms of business. It allows us to analyze, both theoretically and through practical examples, the role of informational and decision-making analysis.

REFERENCES

Alla, L., Bentalha, B., & Bouhtati, N. (2022). Assessing Supply Chain Performance in the Covid 19 Context: A Prospective Model. In *2022 14th International Colloquium of Logistics and Supply Chain Management (LOGISTIQUA)* (pp. 1-6). IEEE.

Angell, R. L., & Kraemer, J. R. (2017). U.S. Patent No. 9,846,883, U.S. Patent and Trademark Office, Washington, DC.

Anshari, M., Almunawar, M. N., Lim, S. A., & Al-Mudimigh, A. (2019). Customer relationship management and big data enabled: Personalization & customization of services. *Applied Computing and Informatics, 15*(2), 94–101. doi:10.1016/j.aci.2018.05.004

Bentalha, B. (2020). Big-Data et service supply chain management: challenges et opportunités. *International Journal of Business and Technology Studies, 1*(3). <https://www.ijbtsr.org/index.php/IJBTSR/article/view/16>. doi:10.5281/zenodo.3607357

Bentalha, B. (2022). Green Transportation Balanced Scorecard Model: A Fuzzy-Delphi Approach During COVID-19. In *Computational Intelligence Techniques for Green Smart Cities* (pp. 107–127). Springer. doi:10.1007/978-3-030-96429-0_5

Bentalha, B. (2023). Motivating Factors for Hotel Employees: A Fuzzy Logic Approach. In Strategic Human Resource Management in the Hospitality Industry: A Digitalized Economic Paradigm (pp. 159-178). IGI Global. doi:10.4018/978-1-6684-7494-5.ch008

Bentalha, B., & Hmioui, A. (2021). Smart Service Supply Chain and Just Walk Out Technology: A Netnographic Approach. In *The Proceedings of the International Conference on Smart City Applications* (pp. 223-236). Cham: Springer International Publishing.

Bentalha, B., Hmioui, A., & Alla, L. (2019). The digitalization of the supply chain management of service companies: a prospective approach. In *Proceedings of the 4th International Conference on Smart City Applications* (pp. 1-8). https://doi.org/10.1145/3368756.3369005

Bentalha, B., Hmioui, A., & Alla, L. (2020). The global performance of a service supply chain: a simulation-optimization under arena. In *The Proceedings of the Third International Conference on Smart City Applications* (pp. 489-502). Cham: Springer International Publishing.

Bentalha, B., Hmioui, A., & Alla, L. (2023). Green Transportation Balanced Scorecard: A VIKOR Fuzzy Method for Evaluating Green Logistics Initiatives. In *International Conference on Digital Technologies and Applications* (pp. 916-925). Cham: Springer Nature Switzerland. 10.1007/978-3-031-29857-8_91

Davenport, T. (2014). *Big data at work: dispelling the myths, uncovering the opportunities*. Harvard Business Review Press. doi:10.15358/9783800648153

Davenport, T. H., & Dyche, J. (2013). *Big Data in Big Companies. Thomas H.* Davenport and SAS Institute Inc.

Demchenko, Y., De Laat, C., & Membrey, P. (2014), Defining architecture components of the Big Data Ecosystem, in: *International Conference on Collaboration Technologies and Systems (CTS)*. IEEE. 10.1109/CTS.2014.6867550

Dietrich, B., Plachy, E. C., & Norton, M. F. (2014). *Analytics across the enterprise: How IBM realizes business value from big data and analytics*. IBM Press Books.

Gadi, T., Benslimane, R. (2000), de Segmentation hiérarchique floue Fuzzy hierarchical segmentation. *Traitement du Signal 2000, 17*, 59-67.

Gu, M., Yang, L., & Huo, B. (2021). The impact of information technology usage on supply chain resilience and performance: An ambidexterous view. *International Journal of Production Economics, 232*, 107956. doi:10.1016/j.ijpe.2020.107956 PMID:33071462

Guha, S., Harrigan, P., & Soutar, G. (2018). Linking social media to customer relationship management (CRM): A qualitative study on SMEs. *Journal of Small Business and Entrepreneurship, 30*(3), 193–214. doi:10.1080/08276331.2017.1399628

Hmioui, A., Bentalha, B., & Alla, L. (2020). Service supply chain: A prospective analysis of sustainable management for global performance. In *2020 IEEE 13th International Colloquium of Logistics and Supply Chain Management (LOGISTIQUA)* (pp. 1-7). IEEE. 10.1109/LOGISTIQUA49782.2020.9353940

Hsieh, T. Y., Lu, S. T., & Tzeng, G. H. (2004). Fuzzy MCDM approach for planning and design tenders selection in public office buildings. *International Journal of Project Management, 22*(7), 573–584. doi:10.1016/j.ijproman.2004.01.002

ISACA. (2013). *Big Data: impacts and benefits*. ISACA White Paper.

Ishikawa, A., Amagasa, M., Shiga, T., Tomizawa, G., Tatsuta, R., & Mieno, H. (1993). The max-min Delphi method and fuzzy Delphi method via fuzzy integration. *Fuzzy Sets and Systems, 55*(3), 241–253. doi:10.1016/0165-0114(93)90251-C

Kakkar, S. (2017). How to Use Big Data And Predictive Analytics For Your Next Digital Marketing Campaign, [Online]. *The Next Scoop.* https://thenextscoop.com/big-data-predictive-analytics-digital-marketing-campaign/

Khan, R. U., Salamzadeh, Y., Iqbal, Q., & Yang, S. (2022). The impact of customer relationship management and company reputation on customer loyalty: The mediating role of customer satisfaction. *Journal of Relationship Marketing, 21*(1), 1–26. doi:10.1080/15332667.2020.1840904

Kotler, P., & Keller, K. (2012). Marketing Management (14 ed.). Pearson Education.

Kumar, A., & Kumar, T. V. (2021). A Multi-Objective Approach to Big Data View Materialization. [IJKSS]. *International Journal of Knowledge and Systems Science, 12*(2), 17–37. doi:10.4018/IJKSS.2021040102

Kumar, K., Sen, N., Azid, S., & Mehta, U. (2017). A fuzzy decision in smart fire and home security system. *Procedia Computer Science, 105*, 93–98. doi:10.1016/j.procs.2017.01.207

Lastanto, W. K. R., Dilini, K. A., & Kulawansa, T. (2018). A Review of Big Data Analytics for Customer Relationship Management. In *2018 3rd International Conference on Information Technology Research (ICITR)* (pp. 1-6). IEEE

Leveling, J., Edelbrock, M., & Otto, B. (2014). Big data analytics for supply chain management. In *2014 IEEE international conference on industrial engineering and engineering management* (pp. 918-922). IEEE.

Mishra, D., Gunasekaran, A., Papadopoulos, T., & Childe, S. J. (2018). Big Data and supply chain management: A review and bibliometric analysis. *Annals of Operations Research, 270*(1-2), 313–336. doi:10.100710479-016-2236-y

Novo, R., & Neves, J. M. S. (2013). Inovação na inteligência analítica por meio do Big Data: Características de diferenciação da abordagem tradicional. *Workshop de Pós-Graduação e Pesquisa do Centro Paula Souza, São Paulo, 8*, 32–44.

Orenga-Rogla, S., & Chalmeta, R. (2016). Social customer relationship management: Taking advantage of Web 2.0 and Big Data technologies. *SpringerPlus, 5*(1), 1462. doi:10.118640064-016-3128-y PMID:27652037

Parise, S., Iyer, B., & Vesset, D. (2012), Four strategies to capture and create value from big data. *Ivey Business Journal.* https://iveybusinessjournal.com/publication/four-strategies-to-capture-and-create-value-from-big-data/

Rajanarthagi, D. (2021), Role of Big data in digital marketing. *The Future.* https://gecdesigns.com/blog/role-of-big-data-in-digital-marketing

Reinartz, W., Krafft, M., & Hoyer, W.D. (2004). The Customer Relationship Management Process: Its Measurement and Impact on Performance. *Journal Of Marketing Research, 41*(3), 293-305.

Strauss, J. & Frost, R.D. (2016). *E-marketing: Instructor's Review Copy.* Springer.

Sun, Z. Strang, K. Firmin, S. (2017). *Business analytics-based enterprise information systems.*

Talón-Ballestero, P., González-Serrano, L., Soguero-Ruiz, C., Muñoz-Romero, S., & Rojo-Álvarez, J. L. (2018). Using big data from customer relationship management information systems to determine the client profile in the hotel sector. *Tourism Management*, *68*, 187–197. doi:10.1016/j.tourman.2018.03.017

Villars, R. L., Olofson, C. W., & Eastwood, M. (2011). *Big data: what it is and why you should care.* (White Paper). IDC.

Waller, M. A., & Fawcett, C. (2013). Click Here for a Data Scientist: Big Data, Predictive Analytics, and Theory Development in the Era of a Maker Movement Supply Chain. *Journal of Business Logistics*, *34*(4), 249–252. doi:10.1111/jbl.12024

Zerbino, P., Aloini, D., Dulmin, R., & Mininno, V. (2018). Big Data-enabled Customer Relationship Management : A holistic approach. *Information Processing & Management*, *54*(5), 818–846. doi:10.1016/j.ipm.2017.10.005

Chapter 5
Exploring the Use of AI in Supply Chain Management:
Insights From Moroccan Cases

Ilham Rharoubi
https://orcid.org/0000-0003-1254-9589
FSJES, CUAM, Ibn Zohr University, Morocco

Kaoutar Talmenssour
https://orcid.org/0009-0004-5435-7619
Faculty of Economics and Management Guelmim, Ibn Zohr University, Morocco

Hafida Ait Abderrahman
https://orcid.org/0009-0001-9344-0579
FSJES, Ibn Zohr University, Morocco

ABSTRACT

This chapter presents an exploratory qualitative study on the use of artificial intelligence (AI) in supply chain management (SCM). With the growing complexity and uncertainty of supply chains, the integration of AI has gained increased attention as a potential solution for enhancing SCM. Using semi-structured interviews with experts in the field, this study investigates the application of AI for supply chain optimization, as well as the challenges that firms face in implementing such technologies. The results of this study reveal that AI-based SCM systems have the potential to enhance supply chain efficiency, reduce costs, and improve overall performance. However, challenges such as data quality and compatibility, organizational resistance to change, and lack of trust in AI technology were identified as barriers to successful implementation. These findings contribute to the understanding of the current state and future direction of AI in SCM, and provide practical implications for managers seeking to use AI-based solutions in their supply chain operations.

DOI: 10.4018/979-8-3693-0225-5.ch005

INTRODUCTION

The sectors of logistics, manufacturing, supply chains, and transportation are undergoing a rapid and exceptional period of change. These industries have a bright future thanks to innovation and technology. Recent years have seen the development of ideas like 3D printing, the Internet of Things (IoT), and drone deliveries, which were before unimaginable.

Lemoine (2014) has attempted to outline the historical trajectory of digitization, highlighting its extensive timeline that commenced in the 1930s with the inception of computers and continued well beyond 2008 when we entered the era of digitalization. Lemoine (2014) has attempted to outline the historical trajectory of digitization, highlighting its extensive timeline that commenced in the 1930s with the beginning of computers and continued well beyond 2008 when we entered the era of digitalization. Hence, it is evident that since 2008, the business world has transitioned into the realm of digitalization, where digital technology has become pervasive across all sectors of the economy (Rharoubi and Talmenssour, 2022). Nevertheless, service companies for instance are increasingly turning to digital practices to enhance their SCM, necessitating a need to identify the distinctive characteristics of these digital practices (Bentalha et al., 2019).

Artificial Intelligence (AI) has revolutionized various industries, including Supply Chain Management (SCM). Companies now have access to AI-powered SCM tools that can significantly improve their operational efficiency. Integrating AI in SCM has numerous benefits, such as reducing costs, improving forecasting accuracy, and enhancing supply chain visibility. AI-powered SCM tools can automate routine tasks, analyze large amounts of data, and provide real-time insights to help companies make informed decisions. With the advent of machine learning (ML), the future of SCM looks even more promising.

Nowadays, companies and service providers are strategically integrating these technologies to optimize their operations by enhancing speed, cost-efficiency and reliability and sustainability. AI has the potential to significantly enhance various aspects of logistics, such as distribution and transportation, logistics hub management, healthcare logistics, and logistics risk management (Toorajipour et al., 2021). These areas can benefit from AI's application potential, as well as the opportunity to address the current research gaps in the field. AI, identified as an Industry 4.0 technology[1], holds transformative potential across numerous industries and domains, as noted by Kearney et al. (2018) and Townsend and Hunt (2019). Consequently, nearly all areas within SCM and its subfields are susceptible to the influence and impact of AI.

The objectives of this study are to identify the current status of AI implementations in SCM and to identify the extent of their impact on supply chain optimization. We aim to investigate the challenges and barriers faced by organizations when implementing AI-based solutions in SCM, particularly within the context of Moroccan firms. In addition to that, we also attempt to identify some of the critical success factors for a successful integration and implementation of AI-based solutions and assess their impact on supply chain performance. This research also tries to examine the ethical, legal, and social implications of using AI in SCM.

Therefore, we endeavor in this work to bring answers to the following research question:

How can the use of AI-based solutions improve supply chain optimization and performance in Moroccan companies?

Sub-questions are derived from this main problem, which explain the course of our study:

- What are the key success factors for implementing AI-based solutions in SCM, and how can these factors be applied in Moroccan companies?
- What are the potential benefits and limitations of using AI-based solutions for SCM?
- How do supply chain (logistics) managers perceive the use of AI-based solutions in their operations, and what factors influence their attitudes and beliefs?
- How can AI-based solutions be integrated with existing SCM systems and processes, and what challenges must be overcome to achieve successful integration?

LITERATURE REVIEW

Recently, the global landscape has been steadily progressing towards a digital era, with prominent technologies, such as Internet IoT, 3D printing, cloud computing, 5G (Kumar et al., 2020). These technologies are currently reshaping the methods by which individuals obtain and consume goods, as well as how companies produce and distribute those goods. In the same vein, industry 4.0, as described by Mastos et al. (2021), revolves around these very technologies, serving as the foundation of the fourth Industrial Revolution.

One of the most important technologies is AI that pertains to the ability of machines to acquire knowledge from experience and make decisions based on successions of performance, similar to the cognitive aptitudes of a human (Duan et al., 2019; Schutzer, 1990). As highlighted by Queiroz et al. (2022), business models and logistics production systems must as well adjust and align with the evolving dynamics of production and consumption, especially after the Covid-19 pandemic, organizations have faced a multitude of disruptions. Alongside these challenges, the customary obstacles of uncertainty, risk, vulnerability, and complexity have become even more pronounced.

SUPPLY CHAIN MANAGEMENT AND SUPPLY CHAIN OPTIMIZATION

SCM is a critical component of any business that involves the production and delivery of goods or services. The optimization of SCM has become increasingly important in recent years, especially as businesses strive to become more efficient and competitive in today's rapidly changing marketplace. SCM refers to the coordination and management of activities involved in the production and delivery of goods and services. It plays a crucial role in ensuring that products are delivered to consumers in a timely, efficient, and cost-effective manner.

SCM is an important part of every business operations. It is a complex process that involves multiple functional areas within a company, as well as external partners and suppliers. According to Khan et al. (2019), "SCM is the coordination and collaboration of activities involved in the procurement, production, and delivery of products and services from suppliers to end customers" (p. 3). The goal of SCM is to optimize the flow of goods and services, minimize costs, and improve customer satisfaction. Therefore, the fundamental purpose of SCM is supply chain optimization. To achieve this aim, companies must manage their supply chains effectively by developing strong relationships with suppliers, implementing efficient processes, and leveraging technology.

Supply Chain Optimization

Effective SCM is crucial for the success of any business (Bentalha, 2023). As noted by Ge et al. (2015), supply chain optimization is defined as the process of maximizing efficiency and minimizing costs throughout the entire supply chain network. It is critical for companies to optimize their supply chains to remain competitive and maintain profitability in a rapidly changing business environment. Effective supply chain optimization can lead to reduced lead times, lower inventory levels, and increased customer satisfaction. Furthermore, it can help companies identify and mitigate risks, such as supply disruptions and quality issues. Supply chain optimization involves a range of activities, including demand forecasting, inventory management, transportation planning, and supplier relationship management. By optimizing these activities, companies can achieve a more streamlined and efficient supply chain, which can have a significant impact on their bottom line. Therefore, supply chain optimization is essential for companies to remain competitive and successful in today's global market.

SCM is a complex process that involves the coordination of different entities, including suppliers, manufacturers, distributors, and retailers, to ensure the efficient and effective flow of goods and services from the point of origin to the point of consumption. In recent years, the need to optimize SCM has become increasingly important due to the intense competition among businesses, globalization, and the growing demand for faster delivery times and lower costs. According to Van Engeland et al. (2020), there are several strategies that organizations can use to optimize their SCM, including the implementation of advanced technologies such as AI, the use of data analytics to improve decision-making, and the adoption of lean principles to eliminate waste and improve the overall efficiency of the supply chain. Additionally, the authors suggest that collaboration among supply chain partners can also be beneficial in optimizing SCM, as it can lead to better communication, increased transparency, and improved coordination. Overall, the successful implementation of these strategies can help organizations achieve a more streamlined and efficient supply chain, which can ultimately lead to increased profitability, customer satisfaction, and competitive advantage.

According to Cox (1999), the effective management of the supply chain requires the implementation of several strategies. Firstly, collaboration among diverse supply chain stakeholders is essential, as it enables the sharing of information and resources, ultimately leading to a more efficient supply chain. Secondly, the implementation of technology, such as automated inventory management systems, can improve supply chain efficiency by reducing errors and delays. Thirdly, the use of outsourcing can be an effective strategy for managing the supply chain, as it enables businesses to focus on their core competencies while outsourcing non-core functions to specialized firms. Fourthly, the implementation of lean principles, such as reducing waste and optimizing processes, can also lead to a more efficient supply chain. Finally, effective communication and coordination among different services involved in the supply chain are essential for ensuring that all parties are working towards the same goals. In conclusion, effective SCM requires the implementation of several strategies, including collaboration, technology, outsourcing, lean principles, and effective communication.

According to Fawcett et al. (2008), efficient SCM can help in reducing transportation costs and inventory holding costs. When the supply chain is managed efficiently, the organization can have better visibility of the inventory levels and demand patterns, which can help in reducing excess inventory and stock-outs. This can result in a reduction in inventory holding costs. Additionally, efficient SCM can also help in improving customer service. Customer satisfaction may improve when a company is able to react fast to meet the requirements and expectations of its customers. Customer loyalty and greater profits for the business may result from this. Therefore, effective SCM can also contribute to higher profitability.

ARTIFICIAL INTELLIGENCE

AI has become increasingly prevalent in modern industries and daily life. In industries, AI has been implemented in various fields such as healthcare, manufacturing, and finance. In healthcare, AI has been utilized for disease diagnosis, medical image analysis, and drug discovery (Lee and Yoon, 2021). In manufacturing, AI has been applied in quality control, predictive maintenance, and SCM. In finance, AI has been used in fraud detection, risk management, and investment analysis (Lee and Yoon, 2021). In daily life, AI has been integrated into various devices such as smartphones, smart homes, and virtual assistants. For instance, virtual assistants like Amazon's Alexa and Apple's Siri have become increasingly popular in households and are capable of performing a range of tasks, from playing music to controlling smart home devices (Lee and Yoon, 2021). Additionally, AI-powered smartphones have features such as facial recognition, voice recognition, and predictive text, which have become a part of everyday life for many individuals (Lee and Yoon, 2021). The integration of AI in industries and daily life has brought about numerous benefits, such as increased efficiency, accuracy, and convenience. However, there are also concerns about the ethical implications of AI and its potential impact on employment. As AI continues to advance, it is essential to consider these implications and ensure that AI is used responsibly and ethically.

Artificial Intelligence and Traditional Technology

AI systems possess human-like intelligence, performing tasks that require reasoning, problem-solving, and learning. Unlike conventional technology, AI systems can function autonomously without explicit human guidance. They can operate autonomously, adapt their behavior to changing conditions, interact naturally with humans, and process data quickly, surpassing the limitations of traditional technology. Furthermore, AI systems demonstrate exceptional speed by rapidly processing large volumes of data in real-time and making prompt decisions, surpassing the relatively slower performance of traditional technology.

Zuboff (1985) highlights how technology in general is shaping our material world and establishing the boundaries of what is possible, and even unimaginable. AI, which has been widely adopted by companies, has demonstrated its ability to expand the scope of the possible. Nevertheless, as the dependency on AI agents continues to grow, it is vital to consider the consequences and risks associated with this reliance. Ethical debates have arisen exploring the perceptions of "right" and "wrong" in high-stakes AI applications (Burkhardtet al., 2019).

THE INTEGRATION OF ARTIFICIAL INTELLIGENCE IN SUPPLY CHAIN MANAGEMENT

The integration of AI in SCM provides numerous benefits for businesses. Verma (2023) asserts that AI can enhance the efficiency and effectiveness of SCM operations by providing real-time, accurate data analytics, and insights. AI-powered SCM systems can also automate repetitive tasks, track inventory levels, and predict demand patterns, enabling businesses to optimize their operations and minimize costs. Additionally, AI-enabled SCM can improve customer service by providing timely and accurate delivery of products and services. Verma (2023) further argues that AI can help businesses mitigate risks and enhance supply chain resilience. For instance, AI can monitor and assess supply chain risks, such as natural disasters, geopolitical tensions, and cyber-attacks, and provide early warning signals to enable proactive and timely responses. AI can also facilitate supplier selection and evaluation, ensuring that businesses work with reliable and trustworthy partners. Therefore, the integration of AI in SCM can enhance operational efficiency, improve customer service, and mitigate supply chain risks, providing significant benefits for businesses.

According to Gande (2020), "AI-powered SCM tools have the potential to enhance efficiency by automating repetitive tasks, analyzing vast amounts of data, and providing real-time insights". For instance, AI can help in demand forecasting, inventory optimization, and route optimization. By automating these tasks, companies can reduce their lead times, improve their delivery schedules, and minimize their inventory costs. Moreover, AI can help in identifying potential bottlenecks and supply chain disruptions, allowing companies to take proactive measures to mitigate these risks. However, there are also some challenges associated with the adoption of AI-powered SCM tools, such as the need for skilled personnel to operate and maintain the systems, data privacy concerns, and the high cost of implementation. Despite these challenges, AI-powered SCM tools are becoming increasingly popular, and companies that invest in these technologies are likely to benefit from improved efficiency and profitability.

The future of SCM is highly dependent on the integration of AI and ML technologies. These technologies have the potential to revolutionize the SCM domain by enabling the development of intelligent systems that can learn from past data, predict future trends, and optimize decision-making processes. As noted by Younis et al. (2022), AI and ML can be used to enhance demand forecasting, inventory management, and logistics planning, among other SCM functions. They argue that AI and ML can be used to analyze large volumes of data from various sources, including social media, to identify customer preferences and forecast demand accurately. Additionally, these technologies can be employed to optimize inventory levels and reduce stock-outs by analyzing real-time data and adjusting replenishment schedules accordingly. Furthermore, AI and ML can be used to optimize logistics planning by identifying the most efficient routes and modes of transportation based on real-time data on weather, traffic, and other factors. As such, the integration of AI and ML technologies in SCM has the potential to increase efficiency, reduce costs, and improve customer satisfaction.

Researchers have stressed the need to investigate the contribution of AI to the field of SCM (e.g. Toorajipour et al., 2021; Vargas Florez et al., 2015). Sophisticated analytics like AI and blockchain are expected to address challenges and enable smarter decision-making in supply chain optimization, driven by heightened consumer expectations, unpredictable demand fluctuations, and inventory costs, fostering a paradigm shift towards agility and operational resilience (Kashem et al., 2023). As for Toorajipour et al. (2021), they have attempted to address this topic through a systematic literature review and bring answers to the question: how does AI contribute to SCM process?

The Common AI Applications in SCM

Operational research has typically found its principal application in the supply chain decision-making process throughout its operational, tactical, and strategic levels, starting in the 1980s and stretching back over several preceding years. The interconnectedness and connectivity of SC processes are becoming

Table 1. Examples of the use of ML in SC

Demand Forecasting	Allow AI to eliminate forecasting assumptions and reduce supply chain unexpected events. rely on AI to manage complex and erratic changes in demand volumes.
Supply forecasting	The payments of suppliers are frequently structured based on supplier commitments and lead periods, and supply forecasts can be predicted with accuracy. For the organization to grow and the demand to be balanced, the entire value chain must be considered.
Text Analytics	In order to make better decisions, text analytics is frequently used to clean up data. It is frequently integrated with supplier, partner, or shipment data to gain deeper supply chain insights. The goal of this synergy is to promote better decision-making process.
Price Planning	Using machine learning to determine the best way to increase or reduce product prices based on demand trends, product life cycles, and stacking products against the competitors.
Inventory Planning	To ensure you have the right products at the right time without spending too much on surplus inventory, automatically raise purchase orders with suppliers based on shortages or anticipated demand shortfalls.
Inventory Price Balancing	Through the use of ML. It can suggest overstocked products and immediately lower prices to help clear up inventories. To make product recommendations supported by inventory locations, ML leverages historical data such as prior buying trends.
Stock Analytics	Machines can now anticipate the cause of out-of-stock items or when those items will run out of stock more accurately compared to before, through the support for numerous structured and unstructured datasets, allowing managers to schedule shipments and deliveries appropriately.
Production Planning	Using manufacturing automation mechanisms and IoT sensors to increase/decrease product output and improve quality while incorporating real-time client feedback.

Adapted from Kudtarkar et al. (2021)

more complicated today and are being better fed by data. AI is the capacity to think and act rationally, as well as think and act like a human.

- *Machine learning in supply chain*

ML is a revolutionary technology that improves performance without the use of explicit programming. This is accomplished by using historical data obtained through computerized data collecting. Systems can learn from these patterns and make informed decisions or predictions without explicit instructions thanks to ML algorithms' ability to analyze and comprehend data patterns.

- *Artificial neural networks (ANN)*

In order to determine the expected costs and risks, Bruzzone and Orsoni (2003) conducted risk assessment in the context of production losses. When they compared the performance of ANNs with another approach based on simulation, they found that ANNs-based strategies provided more accurate cost estimation, which led to greater accuracy and efficiency in identifying and mitigating the risks connected to production losses.

- *Industry 4.0 and lean production*

Automation aims to combine the benefits of Industry 4.0 and Lean Production to maximize their respective strengths. The existence of disjointed IT systems and autonomous Cyber-Physical Systems points out the significance of communication facilitated through standardized interfaces, particularly in the context of the continuing movement toward mass production of customized products.

- *Rough set theory*

A mathematical strategy called rough set theory is used to deal with noisy, hazy, ambiguous, or imprecise data. To properly characterize an imprecise idea and analyze the original data sets, it necessitates the definition of two precise bounds, called the lower and higher approximations.

As the basis for decision-making, dynamic supply chain performance measurement is essential for ensuring the resilience and agility of supply networks. In order to support such performance measurement, rough set theory is used as a methodology, enabling efficient analysis and assessment of the dynamic character of supply chain processes.

The rough set theory is used in SCM tasks like inventory management in addition to its application in supply chain performance measurement. Mehdizadeh (2020), for instance, applies the rough set theory to handle inventory management issues within SCM, demonstrating its practical applicability in enhancing inventory control and optimization tactics.

- *Warehouse Management in light of AI*

Since the 1950s, automated guided vehicles (AGVs) have been operating in industrial settings; but, prior to that time, AGVs were completely unable to perform autonomous navigation in the absence of physical path guidance systems, such as wires, rails, or magnetic tapes. Thanks to incremental developments in AI and navigation technologies like simultaneous localization and mapping and machine vision, AGVs can enable automated material handling across conventional factory borders by moving across buildings (Kudtarkar et al., 2021). According to the authors, current warehouse management and control systems can be integrated with data from today's AGVs to increase their autonomy. This software layer is referred to as warehouse execution systems (WES).

- *Warehouse execution systems*

Due to the fact that WES uses AI to gradually boost the effectiveness of present logistical systems, several of the top AGV operators have made clear strategic decisions in favor of gaining WES capabilities (Kudtarkar et al., 2021).

AI-powered robots and automation systems can streamline the picking, packing, and sorting processes to improve warehouse operations. This enhances operational effectiveness, lowers error rates, and speeds up order delivery.

- *Procurement with AI*

Kudtarkar et al. (2021) brought the example of Amazon's Alexa to explain the dramatic shift of procurement. Following the placement of an order, the remaining operations are automated. Procurement purchasers assign supplier communications to virtual assistants or chatbots, and the system manages transactions, procurement, spend, payment, and other requirements. This automation includes choices

Table 2. Factors where AI and ML will have an impact

Productivity	AI's automatic computation of superior solutions considerably boosts warehouse productivity, especially for online stores.
Communication	In order to react to changes or interruptions, warehouse workers and supervisors must quickly communicate with one another. AI's networked robots ensure nearly instantaneous and error-free communication, which helps to boost output.
Warehouse management	Plenty of warehouses will be fully automated in a matter of years. Particularly in relation to short- and medium-term forecasts, AI technologies are progressively becoming fundamental elements.
Personnel costs	AI-controlled resource planning enables more efficient use of workers, which reduces employee costs or increases reliability by creating reserves that may be used, for instance, in the event of staff absence.
Robotics	Picking times are considerably decreased by robots under AI's guidance.
Warehouse stock	AI technology result in shorter cycle times and lower warehouse inventory.

Kudtarkar et al. (2021, p 316)

for making new purchases or reordering things, demonstrating the convenience and efficiency brought forth by procurement innovations.

Benefits of AI-Based Solutions in SCM

The digital age has brought about significant changes in SCM practices. As stated by Hofmann et al. (2019), "supply chain management is increasingly viewed as a key competitive advantage, and digital technologies are considered as enablers to improve supply chain performance" (p. 1). The integration of digital technologies such as the IoT, cloud computing, and big data analytics has resulted in a more efficient and effective supply chain. For instance, IoT devices can be used to track and monitor inventory levels in real-time, enabling businesses to respond quickly to changes in demand. Cloud computing, on the other hand, allows for easy access to information from any location, making it easier to coordinate activities across the supply chain. Furthermore, big data analytics provides insights into customer behavior and preferences, enabling businesses to better understand and respond to their needs. However, as the authors note, the implementation of digital technologies in SCM also presents challenges such as data security issues and the need for skilled personnel to manage the technologies. Therefore, it is important for businesses to carefully evaluate the benefits and risks associated with digital technologies before making any decisions.

ML for instance is perfectly suited to giving up supply chain performance insights not possible with earlier technology. ML is demonstrating to be a truly successful technology that consistently strives to identify the critical elements most affecting supply chain performance. It combines the strengths of supervised learning, reinforcement learning, and unsupervised learning.

METHODOLOGY

Research Design, Data Collection, and Analysis

When researchers or investigators are attempting to find and theorize key issues or are investigating a new topic of study, qualitative research methodology is often regarded as the most appropriate strategy.

This methodology enables in-depth investigation, comprehension, and interpretation of complicated or novel phenomena, allowing researchers to produce insightful and comprehensive findings. Numerous methods, such as ethnography, grounded theory, narrative analysis, case study analysis, etc., can be used to do qualitative research (Guest et al., 2013).

The approach of qualitative research includes a variety of methods, including focus groups, in-depth one-on-one interviews, expert interviews, and literature reviews. It is frequently linked to exploratory research, which is distinguished by its adaptability and fluidity to changing conditions. Exploratory research often starts with a broad focus but eventually decreases to a few key topics of interest as it goes along. Saunders et al. (2015) highlight the dynamic character of qualitative research and its ability to change and improve study goals throughout the course of an investigation. As for the course of our study, we followed the process proposed by Stuart et al., (2002), that contains five steps which are fixing research questions, developing the instrument, gathering data (semi-structured interviews, discussions and observation), analyzing them (Transcription of interviews and content analysis) and finally the dissemination.

A technique frequently employed in qualitative research is snowball sampling. Using this strategy, first volunteers who have relevant information or experiences pertaining to the research issue are identified and interviewed. The informant may identify additional people throughout the interview who might have relevant experiences or insights, widening the pool of potential participants. Snowball sampling enables the investigation of many opinions and increases the depth of understanding the research problem by allowing researchers to access a larger range of persons who may be challenging to reach through conventional sample methods. Therefore, valuable insights might be gained from snowballing techniques, whether it is adopted in the discussion (creating more questions) or in finding other respondents (Sekaran, 2009).

We choose to combine the summary/synthesis method with content analysis. For smaller amounts of data, as in the case of our study, it is an adequate method of analysis. The goal of this thematic content analysis is to identify the relevance of the terms used by the respondents as well as their frequency of occurrence, which may be significant.

Based on an interview guide composed of four axes (General information about the respondents, Awareness and adoption of AI, Possible impact of AI on SC, Challenges and future perspectives of AI implementation), the case studies were conducted throughout in-depth interviews, either in-person or by phone. The respondents were chosen to ensure diversity in terms of the types of organizations, the sizes of the companies, and the geographic regions. The involvement of experts from various backgrounds enhanced the study's results and gave rise to a thorough grasp of the use and difficulties of AI in SCM. The collected data from our interviews were processed using Nvivo 10.

Respondents' Profiles

This study included participation from a wide range of SCM professionals as well as IT specialists who were able to offer insightful comments on the use of AI in SCM. The interviewees were selected in accordance with their knowledge and experience in the field. The backgrounds of the responders are outlined in the profiles below:

- *Supply chain (logistics) managers*: Ten supply chain managers in total, representing different sectors, took part in the interviews. They were in charge of overseeing logistics, inventory management, and procurement and had an average of 8 years of experience managing supply chain operations.

- *Five IT managers* (digital consultants) with expertise in SCM technologies and systems took part in the study. They have extensive background in system architecture, data integration, and IT.
- *AI Solution Providers* (AI crafters): one of the top AI solution providers in the supply chain industry representatives were questioned. They were well-versed in the creation and application of AI technologies especially for supply chain optimization. These professionals shared their knowledge of the capabilities and prospective uses of AI in SCM.
- *Academics and researchers*: The investigation was conducted by two university academics with backgrounds in SCM and AI. Their theoretical viewpoints and research experience supplemented the analysis. They offered perceptions of current trends and potential developments in the industry.
- Industry consultants and experts (startup's CEO): Three consultants and industry specialists with experience applying AI in SCM took part in the study.

FINDINGS AND DISCUSSION

Using Nvivo 10 software, we extracted a figure representing the word cloud (Figure1), which is a cloud representation of the most frequently used words in the text data at different sizes. Words appearing with a larger size (SCM, AI, data, decision...) correspond to the most frequently used words. The analysis of word frequency is not sufficient to make a positive or negative judgement on the results of this study. This is why we felt it necessary to carry out a textual analysis of the most frequent words.

Figure 1. Cloud of keywords from interview guides

Figure 2. Links between the words expressed by interviewees relating to "AI"

By analyzing the concept "AI" (Figure 2), we find ourselves with verbatims that express the role of AI in improving performance, for example "AI has significantly enhanced the performance". Similarly, the word "supply chain management" (Figure 3) appeared in the interviews. Textual analysis of this concept, shows that it is generally associated with positive aspects linked to technology: "supply chain management is changing as a result of disruptive technologies"

The study reveals that there is a recognition of the present advantages of AI, such as increased performance, reduced costs, and increased efficiency. Furthermore, we found that AI's application in SCM will advance and become even more significant in the Moroccan context. Our interviewees predicted the development of increasingly advanced AI-based solutions that are able to automate difficult decision-making procedures. Moreover, one of the respondents provides the following response when asked about their thoughts on the future of AI-based solutions in SCM: "I believe AI-based solutions will continue to be crucial in SCM, allowing organizations to improve efficiency, reduce costs, and en-

Figure 3. Links between the words expressed by interviewees relating to "Supply chain management"

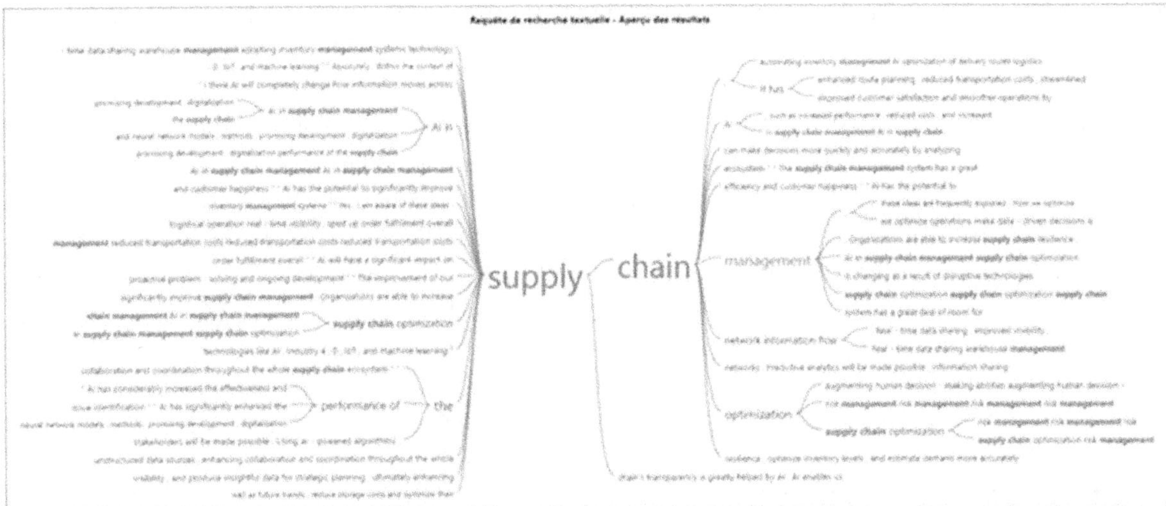

hance performance [...], we will see more sophisticated AI-based solutions that can automate difficult decision-making processes and adjust to shifting market situations". In the same direction, Bentalha et al. (2020) believe that with the rapid integration of digital practices, particularly within service companies, as a result of the growing importance of SCM in the face of fierce competition, global markets, and developing technology has prompted an investigation of the present state and future trends of SCM digitization in this industry through a thorough review of literature and a forward-looking analysis of practices and prospects.

Initiatives for digital transformation fall into two main types. The first category deals with an organization's internal transformation, concentrating on the integration of digital technologies into multiple systems including enterprise resource planning (ERP), human resources management (HRM), Accounting and Finance, and more. With a focus on digital technologies strengthening customer relationship management (CRM), Marketing Automation, Point of Sale systems (POS), E-commerce, and related sectors, the second category includes the transformation taking place between enterprises and their customers. However, although garnering comparatively less attention to date, there is a third type of digital transformation that is becoming increasingly important in today's outsourced and globalized world. In the same vein and by using a mixed methodology based on literature review, expert interviews, and quantitative research, Bentalha (2022) presents a prospective analysis of the opportunities offered by smart technologies in enhancing the sustainability of service supply chains highlighting the potential of artificial intelligence and Big Data while acknowledging financial constraints and technological risks.

Our study confirmed the fact that organizations can profit greatly from IoT when it is integrated into supply chain operations. It first enables quick responses to changes by automatically evaluating priorities, going over possibilities, and making decisions about how to solve problems in the present. This flexibility lessens unfavorable circumstances, such as delays in transportation. Second, IoT's improved data and intelligent automation raise earnings and decrease excess stock, which can quickly depreciate in value. Thirdly, IoT makes it possible to respond to shifting customer needs and supplier availability more quickly, while also streamlining shipping and assuring successful delivery.

Intralogistics which means Internal logistics procedures such as warehousing, material handling, stock control, and transportation of products. Making wise strategic choices for warehouse management is crucial for a business's productivity and profitability. "We are considering contacting an expert in AI solutions for the creation of logistic robots especially for the warehousing part"; explained one of the Moroccan companies that specialized in lean manufacturing and intralogistics engineering. The firm has signed with one of the world's experts in leading logistics intelligent robots for warehousing. The consensus among the respondents on the importance of sensible strategic warehouse management decisions for achieving efficiency and profitability in intralogistics is highlighted. As one of SCM experts added: "Effective intralogistics is built on effective warehouse management [...] Thus, making strategic decisions in terms of adopting new technologies, especially AI solutions in areas like stock management, material handling equipment selection, and layout design have a direct impact on the profitability and efficiency of our firm". Thus, a properly designed warehouse enables efficient product movement, lowers handling expenses, and speeds up order fulfillment, eventually improving customer satisfaction.

Examples of How AI is Being Used in the Supply Chain Industry in Morocco

We will examine the automatization of stock management, the optimization of delivery routes, and the prediction of demand and production planning. These three domains are among the most well-known practical uses of AI in the supply chain sector, and they significantly enhance firms' overall performance.

As technology advances, businesses are looking to improve efficiency and productivity. In this context, using AI for inventory management can be very beneficial. AI can help predict storage levels based on past and current demand, as well as future trends. This can allow companies to reduce storage costs and optimize their supply chain. Additionally, the use of AI can help prevent storage shortages by identifying demand patterns and suggesting storage adjustments accordingly. Ultimately, automating inventory management with AI can help companies improve efficiency and profitability, as well as better serve their customers.

With the increasing demand for fast and efficient delivery services, the optimization of delivery routes has become a crucial aspect of logistics operations. The use of AI has proved to be a game-changer in this regard. AI algorithms have the ability to analyze complex data sets, such as traffic patterns and weather conditions, to determine the most efficient delivery routes. The use of AI in route optimization can lead to significant cost savings and improved delivery times. By using AI-powered route optimization software, delivery companies can reduce the distance traveled and the number of vehicles needed, thus reducing fuel costs and minimizing the carbon footprint of their operations. Additionally, AI algorithms can adapt to changing conditions in real-time, such as road closures or traffic congestion, allowing for more efficient route planning. Overall, the use of AI in optimizing delivery routes has the potential to revolutionize the logistics industry, making it more sustainable and efficient.

Demand prediction is a key component of production planning, as it allows companies to meet customer demand in an efficient manner. There are several methods for predicting demand, including qualitative and quantitative methods. Qualitative methods include expert opinion analysis, consumer surveys and Delphi methods. Quantitative methods, on the other hand, include time series models, regression models and neural network models. By using these methods, companies can forecast demand with reasonable accuracy, allowing them to plan their production accordingly. Production planning can then be improved by using production planning software, such as Advanced Planning and Scheduling (APS) software. This type of software allows companies to create efficient production plans that consider production constraints, such as production capacity and tool changeover times. By using both demand prediction methods and production planning software, companies can improve their operational efficiency and profitability.

In conclusion, the adoption of AI techniques in the Moroccan supply chain companies has completely changed the game. The supply chain process has become more accurate and efficient thanks to the application of AI in logistics and transportation, which has reduced costs and increased production. The Moroccan supply chain firms have been completely revolutionized by AI, from inventory management to predictive maintenance. It is a positive development that AI is now being included into the supply chain, and it is anticipated that this will continue to change the sector in the years to come. The potential for artificial intelligence to significantly improve Morocco's supply chain is enormous as technology develops.

Challenges

The supply chain is a dynamic system that frequently changes, necessitating adaptation to new demands in order to keep operations running smoothly. Demand variations, inadequate inventory planning, order backlogs, logistical uncertainties, communication gaps within the supply chain, and supply shortages are just a few of the difficulties SCM faces. It can be difficult to overcome these obstacles and accomplish corporate objectives on schedule. To address these business difficulties across various industries, innovative technologies like AI offer the best solutions.

One of the challenges of AI implementation and the adoption of digitalization in general is pertaining to the aspect of culture. Due to the fact that digital transformation is primarily cultural, Rharoubi and Talmenssour (2022) stressed the significance of integrating the digitalization of the supply chain into Moroccan firms' corporate cultures. A successful technological transformation must also consider shared initiatives and include all supply chain actors.

The benefits and challenges of adopting AI have both been well studied in previous studies (e.g. Davenport and Ronanki, 2018). There are a number of acknowledged difficulties and barriers to deploying AI. We found that a lack of a clearly defined AI strategy that is supported by top management is a major barrier. Initiatives in AI are more likely to fail if top leadership is not committed to them and providing guidance. It is essential to have a clear goal and a plan of action when incorporating AI into the organization. Moreover, limited data and limited technological infrastructure are both a challenge. Implementing AI across the entire organization may be challenging if the company lacks a strong technological base and adequate data. Existing processes and systems may need to be upgraded or adjusted in order to utilize AI abilities. One of the major obstacles in deploying AI is the need for vast amounts of data, significant data processing expertise, and advanced statistical approaches. Investing in and using technology related to AI can be pricey. Organizations may face financial difficulties if they decide to adopt AI, especially if doing so requires major design, infrastructure, and software investments. Furthermore, it may be challenging to locate and hire individuals with the necessary expertise and skill sets in AI. Since there is frequently a skill gap between the supply and demand for qualified AI specialists, the cost of hiring and maintaining these individuals is high.

CONCLUSION

In this research, we have examined the adoption of AI-based SCM solutions in the Moroccan context. Professionals in logistics and SCM took part in the survey for our exploratory study. Moreover, by bringing in IT experts with a greater understanding of the business' AI systems, the quality of the results might be raised. Thus, we tried to ensure that all relevant factors were considered by incorporating the views from both perspectives.

In this paper, we have investigated how AI is used in SCM, as well as how it affects supply chain optimization and various implementation-related problems. Through in-depth interviews with professionals and specialists in the field, significant knowledge regarding the application of AI technology in diverse supply chain scenarios has been established. The findings highlight the significant contributions AI has made to risk mitigation, SCM, inventory optimization, and demand forecasting. The study's limitations include its reliance on self-reported data, sample size, and the potential for bias in participant selection. However, these limitations provide opportunities for future research to close these gaps and broaden their analysis of difficulties in adopting AI in SCM by, for example, quantitative research in order to validate the findings.

The adoption of cutting-edge technologies, particularly AI, has substantially improved the supply chain sector in Morocco. AI has completely changed how companies manage their supply chains by offering creative ways to reduce procedures and boost productivity.

REFERENCES

Bentalha, B. (2022). Smart Technologies for a Sustainable Service Supply Chain: A Prospective Perspective. *Journal of Environmental Issues and Climate Change*, *1*(1), 77–89. doi:10.59110/jeicc.v1i1.81

Bentalha, B. (2023). Les fondements théoriques du supply chain management: Une analyse critique. *Alternatives Managériales Economiques*, *5*(2), 1–22.

Bentalha, B., Hmioui, A., & Alla, L. (2019, October). The digitalization of the supply chain management of service companies: a prospective approach. In *Proceedings of the 4th International Conference on Smart City Applications* (pp. 1-8). 10.1145/3368756.3369005

Bentalha, B., Hmioui, A., & Alla, L. (2020). Digital service supply chain management: current realities and prospective visions. *In Innovations in Smart Cities Applications Edition 3: The Proceedings of the 4th International Conference on Smart City Applications 4 (pp. 808-822).* Springer International Publishing.

Bruzzone, A., & Orsoni, A. (2003, March). AI and simulation-based techniques for the assessment of supply chain logistic performance. In *36th Annual Simulation Symposium,* 2003. (pp. 154-164). IEEE. 10.1109/SIMSYM.2003.1192809

Burkhardt, R., Hohn, N., & Wigley, C. (2019). *Leading your organization to responsible AI.* McKinsey Analytics.

Cox, A. (1999). Power, value and supply chain management. *Supply Chain Management*, *4*(4), 167–175. doi:10.1108/13598549910284480

Davenport, T. H., & Ronanki, R. (2018). Artificial intelligence for the real world. *Harvard Business Review, 96*(1), 108–116.

Duan, Y., Edwards, J. S., & Dwivedi, Y. K. (2019). Artificial intelligence for decision making in the era of Big Data–evolution, challenges and research agenda. *International Journal of Information Management, 48*, 63–71. doi:10.1016/j.ijinfomgt.2019.01.021

Fawcett, S. E., Magnan, G. M., & McCarter, M. W. (2008). Benefits, barriers, and bridges to effective supply chain management. *Supply Chain Management, 13*(1), 35–48. doi:10.1108/13598540810850300

Gande, A. (2020). Emerging ai & ml-based technologies & applications in supply chain management (scm): Future prospects. *International Journal of Marketing and Technology, 10*(12), 1–6.

Ge, H., Gray, R., & Nolan, J. (2015). Agricultural supply chain optimization and complexity: A comparison of analytic vs simulated solutions and policies. *International Journal of Production Economics, 159*, 208–220. doi:10.1016/j.ijpe.2014.09.023

Guest, G., Namey, E. E., & Mitchell, M. L. (2013). Collecting qualitative data: A field manual for applied research. *Sage (Atlanta, Ga.)*. doi:10.4135/9781506374680

Hofmann, E., Sternberg, H., Chen, H., Pflaum, A., & Prockl, G. (2019). Supply chain management and Industry 4.0: Conducting research in the digital age. *International Journal of Physical Distribution & Logistics Management, 49*(10), 945–955. doi:10.1108/IJPDLM-11-2019-399

Kashem, M. A., Shamsuddoha, M., Nasir, T., & Chowdhury, A. A. (2023). Supply Chain Disruption versus Optimization: A Review on Artificial Intelligence and Blockchain. *Knowledge (Beverly Hills, Calif.), 3*(1), 80–96.

Kearney, V., Chan, J. W., Valdes, G., Solberg, T. D., & Yom, S. S. (2018). The application of artificial intelligence in the IMRT planning process for head and neck cancer. *Oral Oncology, 87*, 111–116. doi:10.1016/j.oraloncology.2018.10.026 PMID:30527225

Khan, S. A. R., Yu, Z., Rehman Khan, S. A., & Yu, Z. (2019). Introduction to supply chain management. *Strategic Supply Chain Management*, 1-22.

Kolberg, D., Knobloch, J., & Zühlke, D. (2017). Towards a lean automation interface for workstations. *International Journal of Production Research, 55*(10), 2845–2856. doi:10.1080/00207543.2016.1223384

Kudtarkar, A. & Shaikh, D. (2021). Applications of Machine Learning Techniques in Supply Chain Management. *International journal of creative research thoughts – IJCRT.*

Kumar, V., Ramachandran, D., & Kumar, B. (2021). Influence of new-age technologies on marketing: A research agenda. *Journal of Business Research, 125*, 864–877. doi:10.1016/j.jbusres.2020.01.007

Lee, D., & Yoon, S. N. (2021). Application of artificial intelligence-based technologies in the healthcare industry: Opportunities and challenges. *International Journal of Environmental Research and Public Health, 18*(1), 271. doi:10.3390/ijerph18010271 PMID:33401373

Lemoine, P. (2014). La nouvelle grammaire du succès. La transformation numérique de l'économie française. *Rapport au gouvernement.*

Mehdizadeh, M. (2020). Integrating ABC analysis and rough set theory to control the inventories of distributor in the supply chain of auto spare parts. *Computers & Industrial Engineering*, *139*, 105673. doi:10.1016/j.cie.2019.01.047

Queiroz, M. M., Ivanov, D., Dolgui, A., & Fosso Wamba, S. (2022). Impacts of epidemic outbreaks on supply chains: Mapping a research agenda amid the COVID-19 pandemic through a structured literature review. *Annals of Operations Research*, *319*(1), 1159–1196. doi:10.100710479-020-03685-7 PMID:32836615

Rharoubi, I., & Talmenssour, K. (2022). Understanding the role of supply chain digitalization in the quality of buyer-supplier relationship: Case studies of Moroccan companies. *Revue Française d'Economie et de Gestion*, *3*(7).

Saunders, M. N., Lewis, P., Thornhill, A., & Bristow, A. (2015). *Understanding research philosophy and approaches to theory development.* The Open University.

Schutzer, D. (1990). Business expert systems: The competitive edge. *Expert Systems with Applications*, *1*(1), 17–21. doi:10.1016/0957-4174(90)90065-3

Sekaran, U., & Bougie, R. (2016). *Research methods for business: A skill building approach.* John Wiley & Sons.

Stuart, I., McCutcheon, D., Handfield, R., McLachlin, R., & Samson, D. (2002). Effective case research in operations management: A process perspective. *Journal of Operations Management*, *20*(5), 419–433. doi:10.1016/S0272-6963(02)00022-0

Toorajipour, R., Sohrabpour, V., Nazarpour, A., Oghazi, P., & Fischl, M. (2021). Artificial intelligence in supply chain management: A systematic literature review. *Journal of Business Research*, *122*, 502–517. doi:10.1016/j.jbusres.2020.09.009

Townsend, D. M., & Hunt, R. A. (2019). Entrepreneurial action, creativity, & judgment in the age of artificial intelligence. *Journal of Business Venturing Insights*, *11*, e00126. doi:10.1016/j.jbvi.2019.e00126

Van Engeland, J., Beliën, J., De Boeck, L., & De Jaeger, S. (2020). Literature review: Strategic network optimization models in waste reverse supply chains. *Omega*, *91*, 102012. doi:10.1016/j.omega.2018.12.001

Vargas-Florez, J., Medina-Rodríguez, R., & Alva-Cabrera, R. (2015, September). A clustering optimization approach for disaster relief delivery: A case study in lima-Peru. In *Annual International Symposium on Information Management and Big Data* (pp. 69-80). Cham: Springer International Publishing.

Verma, M. (2023). Integration of AI-Based Chatbot (ChatGPT) And Supply Chain Management Solution To Enhance Tracking And Queries Response. *International Journal for Science and Advance Research in Technology*.

Younis, H., Sundarakani, B., & Alsharairi, M. (2022). Applications of artificial intelligence and machine learning within supply chains: Systematic review and future research directions. *Journal of Modelling in Management*, *17*(3), 916–940. doi:10.1108/JM2-12-2020-0322

Zuboff, S. (1985). Automate/informate: The two faces of intelligent technology. *Organizational Dynamics*, *14*(2), 5–18. doi:10.1016/0090-2616(85)90033-6

ENDNOTES

1 "Industry 4.0 is the vision of smart components and machines which are integrated into a common digital network based on the well-proven internet standards [...] Flexible, powerful, with their environment interacting but still affordable microcontrollers are the key-technology of Industry 4.0" (Kolberg, 2017, p. 2846).

Chapter 6
Blockchain in Supply Chain Management:
A Case Study in the Automotive Industry

Sophia Barroso
University of Porto, Portugal

Gonçalo Castro
University of Porto, Portugal

Marcelo Corrêa
University of Porto, Portugal

Rafael Soares Godinho
University of Porto, Portugal

Leon Niemann
University of Porto, Portugal

Renan Rocha
University of Porto, Portugal

Belem Barbosa
https://orcid.org/0000-0002-4057-360X
University of Porto, Portugal

ABSTRACT

Blockchain technology has been the focus of much attention and discussion recently. Its unique characteristics, such as immutability, transparency, and decentralization, create a great potential solution for many industries. Especially the automotive sector, which is known for its complex supply chains, large amounts of data, and wide-reaching infrastructure, can profit in many aspects by incorporating blockchain technology. To illustrate the advantages and potential of blockchain in supply chain management, this chapter includes a case study of one of the leading corporations in the automotive industry that has been increasingly committed to adopting this technology. The analysis uses a set of strategic analysis tools frequently used by managers for strategic planning to highlight the benefits and challenges of this approach. Besides contributing to the literature on blockchain and supply chain management, this chapter offers valuable insights for managers, namely in the automotive sector, who are considering adopting blockchain technology in their operations and processes.

DOI: 10.4018/979-8-3693-0225-5.ch006

INTRODUCTION

In the current reality, where the amount of available data and information is constantly increasing, ensuring data security is becoming increasingly important. Treiblmaier (2018) define blockchain as "a digital, decentralized and distributed ledger in which transactions are logged and added in chronological order with the goal of creating permanent and tamper-proof records" (p. 547). The benefits of blockchain technology are becoming more explicit and wide-ranging every day. As highlighted by IBM (2023), the advantages of adopting blockchain extend beyond enhanced security, greater transparency, and instant traceability. The technology also enables cost savings through increased agility, efficiency, and automation. Furthermore, by reducing paperwork and errors, it also decreases overhead and transaction costs, thereby reducing or eliminating the need for third parties to verify transactions.

Smart technologies have become essential tools for supply chain sustainability (Bentalha, 2022). Specifically, when it comes to the use of blockchain technology in supply chains, it fosters trust between trading partners, provides end-to-end visibility, optimizes processes, and enables faster problem-solving. As a result, supply chains become stronger, more resilient, and develop better business relationships that allow parties to act promptly in the face of disruptions (IBM, 2023).

This study focuses on the automotive industry, which is widely recognized for its complexity and importance in people's daily lives, particularly regarding safe transportation. The industry is responsible for complying with standards that affect every individual part of a car, ranging from the passenger seat to the radiator and headlights. Consequently, companies must manage hundreds of parts from dozens of suppliers, each operating at different levels of the supply chain. In addition to meeting safety standards and environmental regulations, they must also keep up with the latest technology and design trends. All these processes require tracking thousands of pieces of information from various sources, underscoring the significance and necessity of adopting blockchain in this industry.

As noted by Cole et al. (2019) the decision to adopt and invest in blockchain technology depends on the characteristics of a firm's products and supply chain, being particularly relevant for businesses in which the safety of products is critical, the risk of quality failures or counterfeit parts is relevant, there are clear advantages in building stakeholders' trust, and the supply chain is particularly complex. Furthermore, it is important to note that blockchain is still a relatively new technology undergoing development, testing, and research. Despite its widespread adoption in numerous industries (Aslam et al., 2021; Cole et al., 2019; Gurtu & Johny, 2019; Kumar et al., 2020), there are still many characteristics, benefits, and approaches that need to be thoroughly studied and tested. Its utilization is still superficial, presenting great potential for enhancing its use in various business contexts, economic segments, and numerous process improvements. In particular, this technology can provide important contributions to mitigate risks associated with supply chain management (Azevedo et al., 2023; Hald & Kinra, 2019; Kumar et al., 2020; Lai et al., 2021; Markus & Buijs, 2022; Sternberg et al., 2021; Tokkozhina et al., 2023; Zhou et al.).

In this context, the main aim of this chapter is to investigate the role of blockchain in the automotive industry and explore the potential benefits and solutions it can provide. By analyzing a specific case study, this chapter seeks to highlight the role and benefits of blockchain, specifically in the automotive industry. The guiding research question for this chapter is: How can the adoption of blockchain in supply chain contribute to the competitive advantage of companies in the automotive industry?

This chapter begins with a theoretical background that summarizes the main contributions in the literature regarding the advantages and challenges of blockchain and its application to supply chain management. Since this chapter includes a case study of a leading company in the automotive industry (Ford Motor Company, hereafter referred to as Ford), the theoretical background is followed by a section dedicated to describing the research methodology adopted. In summary, the study employs a case study methodology using secondary data and publicly available information. These data and information are then systematized using a set of strategy analysis tools commonly used by managers to define and evaluate strategic options for their businesses. After presenting the results, the chapter includes a section on the solutions and recommendations that emerge from the study. The limitations of the study are highlighted, and future research directions are pointed out.

Overall, the study concludes that automotive companies that extensively utilize blockchain technology in their processes gain a competitive advantage, making it increasingly challenging for other players to compete. Ford is already one step ahead of most of its main competitors in terms of efficiency and sustainability due to its widespread implementation of blockchain. This highlights the necessity to continue applying and expanding the use of this technology in Ford's processes.

BACKGROUND

Blockchain: Definition, Advantages, and Challenges

The increasingly effective use of mobile devices, the Internet of Things (IoT), social media, analytics, and cloud technologies to optimize decision-making models has generated innovative products, new efficiency techniques, and closer customer relationships on a global scale. One such examples is blockchain technology. As explained by Rajasekaran et al. (2022), blockchain is a technology consists of blocks containing an expanding collection of records, linked through cryptography to resist any attempts to modify the data. Each block in the blockchain contains a cryptographic hash value of the previous block, a timestamp, and transaction data. As all blocks are decentralized and distributed in nature, any modification to any block will affect all subsequent blocks.

Blockchain technology gained popularity as the foundation of cryptocurrencies. However, Ahram et al. (2017) emphasize that despite its initial association with Bitcoin, this technology serves as a secure means of exchanging various products, services, and transactions. The authors further state that the adoption of blockchain addresses challenges that hinder industrial growth, such as increasing regulation, cybercrime, and fraud, by enabling more agile value chains, faster product innovations, closer customer relationships, and seamless integration with IoT and cloud technology.

According to Rajasekaran et al. (2022), blockchain technology possesses core elements such as programmability, security, transparency, and decentralization. They emphasize that the technology operates without the need for a central authority, such as a bank, company, or government, to process data transactions, and it eliminates the reliance on intermediaries to verify and validate these transactions (Rajasekaran et al., 2022). Ahram et al. (2017) stress that, by providing independently monitored trusted contracts, blockchain technology reduces the cost of trading. It also facilitates the use of smart contracts, which automatically execute predefined actions when specific conditions are met, eliminating the need for intermediaries and reducing the risk of fraud. Moreover, the characteristics of blockchain make it applicable to various industries and solutions. In healthcare, for example, this technology can enhance data security and patient privacy by enabling secure sharing of medical records among healthcare providers. Blockchain-based voting systems can offer increased transparency and security, preventing voter fraud and ensuring accurate vote counting. Additionally, blockchain can be utilized to establish proof of ownership and protect intellectual property rights by creating immutable records of creations, artists, inventors, and content creators.

However, despite the numerous advantages offered by blockchain technology, Sarmah (2018) asserts that it is a complex tool, hindering its widespread use. It is also considered expensive and resource-intensive since every node in the blockchain must perform tasks to achieve consensus. The author further highlights other challenges associated with adopting blockchain, such as the potential for slow processes, as transactions are only settled after successful verification from each party. To address this issue, the author suggests the adoption of an innovative concept known as the lightning network, which could enable immediate verification. Finally, Sarmah (2018) adds that the growth and health of the blockchain depend on nodes storing its history, with large blocks potentially causing divisions among miners.

Application of Blockchain to Supply Chain Management

In recent years, blockchain has been increasingly adopted across various industries and functions. Researchers and engineers have given considerable attention to this technology due to its diverse industrial applications (Chang & Chen, 2020). One of its recent applications is in the supply chain, which has the potential to transform traditional supply chain models (Queiroz et al., 2020). Supply chains are particularly important to provide competitiveness to companies (Azevedo et al., 2023; Bentalha et al., 2019), and its management has becoming more complex and demanding due to business globalization that characterizes a growing number of companies (Bentalha et al., 2019, 2020a; Difrancesco et al., 2022), as it is the case of the automotive industry. The literature emphasizes that all parties involved in a supply chain can benefit from blockchain technology as it increases transparency, traceability, and efficiency, leading to a decrease in transaction costs (Azevedo et al., 2023; Xu et al., 2022). Therefore, it is important to understand the application of this technology in supply chains, as well as its main benefits and challenges.

One of the key purposes of using blockchain in the supply chain is to reduce the need for intermediaries and increase trust in the process. The technology has the potential to automate the process and enable real-time tracking of products from origin to final destination (Chang & Chen, 2020). This reduces the reliance on intermediaries and performance issues compared to traditional supply chains. Queiroz et al. (2020) describe how this can be achieved using blockchain. After the deal between both parties, a contract is stored in the blockchain structure and triggered when the conditions of the deal are satisfied. Subsequently, payment for the operation is automatically sent to the receiver. By utilizing blockchain, the process becomes less reliant on intermediaries.

Blockchain finds applications in various industries, including the automotive sector. Xu et al. (2022) provide an example of Daimler, the world's largest luxury vehicle manufacturer, which uses a blockchain platform to assign a unique identity to each vehicle. This identity facilitates tracking of the vehicle throughout its lifecycle, including delivery, maintenance, and registration. Additionally, blockchain is used to track the origin of raw materials in the automotive industry, ensuring sustainability and transparency. Volkswagen, for instance, implemented blockchain to establish a digital infrastructure for cobalt sourcing, providing more transparent information (Xu et al., 2022).

There are several advantages to using blockchain in the supply chain. As noted by Queiroz et al. (2020), blockchain increases trust between parties by enhancing transparency, reducing costs, and accelerating transactions. Kamble et al. (2021) argue that implementing blockchain in production can improve a company's economic performance in various ways. It can enhance sustainability by reducing costs and waste through better use of raw materials and increased energy efficiency. Additionally, blockchain ensures data security and authenticity while reducing human errors and transaction time. Moreover, Chang and Chen (2020) highlight that apart from enhancing traceability, blockchain technology also improves accountability among supply chain participants, minimizing disputes.

However, companies may face challenges in implementing blockchain in their supply chains. Xu et al. (2022) observed some of these barriers in their case studies, including legal and regulatory issues such as customer data privacy and defining rights and responsibilities in the context of blockchain technologies. High costs, immature technical capabilities, and investment uncertainties can also pose obstacles. Furthermore, Chang and Chen (2020) argue that stakeholders may hesitate to invest in blockchain due to its novelty in the field. Participants in the supply chain often rely on trust mechanisms centered around authorities and may be skeptical of fully automated blockchain systems. In fact, migrating to a blockchain process is not easy and requires a redesign of the entire process, necessitating coordination and planning.

In conclusion, the adoption of blockchain in supply chains has the potential to reshape companies' operations. It can transform industries by increasing transparency, reducing costs, and speeding up transactions, while also promoting sustainability and environmental friendliness. In the automotive industry, blockchain has already demonstrated significant benefits for companies. Despite the cost and cultural barriers that companies may encounter during the implementation process, continuous research and collaboration are essential to overcome these challenges and fully realize the benefits that blockchain implementation can bring to the supply chain.

METHOD

Based on the contributions of the literature, this research chose a case study approach to tackle the proposed research question: How can the adoption of blockchain in supply chain contribute to the competitive advantage of companies in the automotive industry?

The main focus of this essay is the case study of Ford, a well-known American multinational in the automotive sector. Yin (2009) defines case study methodology as "an empirical enquiry that investigates a contemporary phenomenon in depth and within its real-life context" (p.18). As explained by Yin (2009), case study is particularly valuable when the research wants to address the "how" and "why" research questions and has a focus on current events.

Ford was chosen as the subject of research due to its significant recent involvement in the application of blockchain technology to improve its operational procedures. As noted by Yin (2009), the choice of a single case study is appropriate when the case is significant and has the potential to provide deep insights into the topic of the research. Being a market leader in the automobile industry, Ford's prominent interest and advancements in blockchain adoption make it an intriguing case worthy of study. As recommended by Bryman (2012), as the goal is to provide a comprehensive understanding of the selected case, the approach requires a detailed and intensive analysis of the selected organization. For that purpose, the case should also provide a contextualization of the case, namely the historical background of the company (Yin, 2009). Indeed, the history of innovation shared by Ford further justifies its choice for the focus of this chapter. Additionally, the literature has highlighted the relevance of Ford as a case to study supply chain management (Wee & Wu, 2009).

Ford was founded in 1903 by Henry Ford and has since become a global automotive manufacturer known for its pioneering corporate strategies, technological advancements, and commitment to innovation.

Throughout its history, Ford has continually evolved to meet the changing demands of the automotive industry and has embraced new technologies to drive its success. An essential aspect of the company's development is its focus on operational efficiency and cost optimization. Ford has a long-standing tradition of streamlining its manufacturing processes to enhance productivity and reduce costs. In 1913, Ford revolutionized the industry with the introduction of the moving assembly line, which enabled mass production and set a new standard for efficient manufacturing practices across all segments. In recent years, Ford has demonstrated a strong emphasis on fostering innovation and adopting advanced technologies. The company is dedicated to leading the transformation of the automotive industry and invests significantly in research and development. This has led to notable advances in areas such as electric vehicles (EVs), autonomous driving, and connected car technologies. In particular, the substantial resources allocated to the development of electric vehicles reflect Ford's recognition of the growing demand for sustainable mobility solutions. These efforts aim to reduce greenhouse gas emissions and provide consumers with environmentally friendly transportation options. Furthermore, Ford understands the importance of effective information management to support and facilitate its technological advancements. The company leverages blockchain technology, data analytics, artificial intelligence, and machine learning to gather valuable insights and enhance its decision-making process. The adoption of these technological tools enables optimized operations, improved vehicle performance, and the delivery of personalized customer experiences. Additionally, Ford values partnerships with technology start-ups, academic institutions, and research organizations to foster innovation and gain access to cutting-edge technologies. Its commitment to adopting new technologies and fostering innovation positions Ford as a key player in the future of mobility and the industry as a whole.

To study the case of Ford and its use of blockchain, three different types of information sources were utilized: scientific articles and papers, which provide reliable information about blockchain and theoretical concepts; online blogs, news, and reports, which offer practical examples of Ford's use of blockchain technology; and Ford's official website, which provided additional news and insights to complement the research. This comprehensive approach aligns with the guidance given by Yin (2009) for conducting a holistic examination of the phenomenon. Especially concerning non-scientific sources of information, the initial phase involved assessing the credibility of the source and its data. To ensure reliability, the research exclusively took into account information presented and substantiated by reliable sources (e.g., official company websites, statistical agencies, industry reports). Additional information acquired from the internet, such as news articles, underwent triangulation before being incorporated.

To understand the potential outcomes, it is crucial to have a comprehensive understanding of the specific environment in which the Ford case is situated. This involves considering historical elements that shed light on Ford's past practices and experiences, as well as cultural aspects that reveal consumer preferences and local influences. Additionally, organizational aspects that contribute to an understanding of Ford's internal dynamics and capabilities must be taken into account. Therefore, this study employs a series of analysis tools commonly used by managers to define and evaluate business strategies. These tools will be presented in detail in the next section.

RESULTS

The results of this case study are organized into strategy analysis models and frameworks that were applied to the Ford Motor Company, in order to deeply explore the role of blockchain in creating competitive advantage to the company and other potential benefits and solutions that it can provide. Hence, this section includes analysis of both the characteristics of the company (e.g., value chain), the industry (e.g., Porter's Five Forces), and the environment (e.g., PESTEL analysis) to further understand the relevance and value that blockchain technology may offer to the company.

Blockchain and Sources of Competitive Advantage: The Value Chain

According to Porter (1985), Value Chain Analysis is a strategic management tool used to identify sources of competitive advantage. It allows companies to optimize the value of their products or services by examining their activities. Porter's Value Chain analysis comprises five primary activities: Inbound Logistics, Operations, Outbound Logistics, Marketing & Sales, and Services. Additionally, support activities such as Firm Structure, IT, HR Management, and Procurement are also considered.

This tool provides a means to assess the strategic position and competencies of an organization. By utilizing Value Chain Analysis, companies can identify activities within their value chain that can benefit customers or lead to cost reduction. It also enables the identification of competitive advantages by comparing differences in competitors' value chains. In the case of Ford, the findings of this study are presented in the Value Chain Analysis depicted in Table 1.

Notably, Ford incorporates blockchain technology into its primary activities, including inbound and outbound logistics, marketing and sales, and customer service. Additionally, the company employs blockchain in its supporting activities, specifically in technology development for supply chain and customer relationship management solutions.

Table 1. Value chain

<table>
<tr><td rowspan="4">SUPPORT ACTIVITIES</td><td colspan="5">Firm Infrastructure: The Automotive business largely comprises the global sale of Ford automobiles, service parts and accessories, as well as the costs involved in developing, manufacturing, distributing, and servicing.</td></tr>
<tr><td colspan="5">Human Resources Management: The company has about 183.000 employees worldwide, recognizes diversity, embraces inclusion, fosters innovative thinking, and sees the team as a critical component for long-term success.</td></tr>
<tr><td colspan="5">Technology Development: The company is strongly commited to the development of electric vehicles and innovative blockchain solutions for supply chain and customer relationship management.</td></tr>
<tr><td colspan="5">Procurement: To maintain a consistent supply of raw materials and components, Ford invests in strategic sourcing and procurement.</td></tr>
<tr><td></td><td>Inbound Logistics: Ford uses technology to manage shipments, check inventory levels, and logistic activities. It uses blockchain to identify unethically sources materials.</td><td>Operations: Ford has production plants worldwide and its production is made according to the market they are present, its biggest market is the USA.</td><td>Outbound Logistics: Once a car is produced, Ford identifies and tracks vehicles and parts' movement across the distribution channel.</td><td>Marketing & Sales: Focus on clean energy transition and reduction of greenhouse emissions (e.g., EVs). Ford also uses blockchain to monitor urban air quality.</td><td>Service: Ford is differentiating from competitors by using blockchain in CRM solutions and to generate "birth-date" certificates to cars to combat fraud in the second-hand market.</td></tr>
<tr><td></td><td colspan="5">PRIMARY ACTIVITIES</td></tr>
</table>

Source: The Authors

In conclusion, Ford's strategic adoption of blockchain technology across various aspects of its operations contributes to its competitive advantage in the automotive industry. This strategy may be driven by the potential that blockchain offers to enhance efficiency, transparency, and customer satisfaction. By leveraging blockchain, Ford positions itself at the forefront of innovation in the market, enabling it to stay ahead of competitors.

Market Segments and Blockchain

Ford is a renowned company that is involved in the design, manufacturing, marketing, and servicing of a wide range of electrified passenger and commercial vehicles, including trucks, utility vehicles, vans, cars, and Lincoln luxury vehicles. The company operates through several segments:

Ford Blue: This segment focuses on the development of gas-powered and hybrid vehicles.

Ford Model e: This segment is dedicated to the development of electronic vehicles (EVs) and the creation of embedded software that enables always-on digital experiences for customers.

Ford Pro: This segment provides support to commercial customers, helping them transform and expand their businesses through the provision of vehicles and services tailored to their specific needs.

Ford Next: This segment is involved in pursuing mobility solutions and offers financial services through Ford Motor Credit Company.

Ford Credit: This segment primarily engages in providing vehicle-related financing and leasing activities.

Each segment plays a crucial role in Ford's overall operations, contributing to its comprehensive offerings and strategic positioning in the automotive industry. Ford employs a mechanism of dividing the market into different consumer groups, allowing for targeted marketing and personalized approaches to potential buyers. This market segmentation strategy has contributed to Ford's reputation as a leading company in utilizing segmentation techniques.

The implementation of blockchain technology in the automotive industry, including within Ford, can also benefit from the concept of market segmentation. While blockchain itself is not directly related to market segmentation, Ford can tailor the application of blockchain in its operations and services to specific segments within the automotive market. For example, within the "Ford Blue" segment, AiroDoctor (2022) reports that a Ford team in Germany is exploring the combination of blockchain technology and geofencing. Geofencing involves creating a digital boundary around a specific geographic area to enhance government efforts in improving urban air quality. With this approach, the team aims to track low-emission and zero-emission vehicles, such as the Ford Transit PHEV, as they enter and exit designated "green zones" that are becoming increasingly common in Europe due to diesel engine restrictions. Ford vans equipped with geofencing technology enable fleet managers to ensure drivers stay within their assigned work zones and allow the vans to switch to fully electric mode when entering or leaving the green zones.

Taking geofencing a step further, the municipal fleet in Cologne, Germany, has employed blockchain technology to record the movements of the vans in a blockchain ledger. This secure and transparent storage of data online enables the accumulation of "green miles" driven within the low-emission zone of the city. Furthermore, the collected information can be shared with relevant stakeholders, preventing manipulation by any party for their own interests.

In summary, Ford's market segmentation strategy, coupled with the implementation of blockchain technology, allows for targeted approaches and personalized services to specific segments within the automotive industry. By utilizing blockchain in areas such as geofencing, Ford can enhance its offerings and contribute to initiatives aimed at improving urban air quality and sustainability.

Blockchain Leveraging Generic Competitive Strategies

Porter's generic competitive strategies encompass various factors, including cost leadership, focus, and differentiation. This framework analyzes a company's competitive advantage and market position (Besanko et al., 2017; Whittington et al., 2022).

One generic competitive strategy is differentiation. By implementing blockchain technology in Ford's processes, the company can create a digital record of each car, providing information such as past owners and repairs. This increased transparency adds value for consumers and provides Ford with valuable insights about their customers. For instance, Xu et al. (2022) highlighted in a case study that consumers increasingly consider historical information, such as repairs and accidents, when purchasing vehicles on the resale market. Additionally, Ford can present itself as a sustainable company aiming to minimize its carbon footprint, which can enhance its image and attract more consumers. Moreover, leveraging blockchain can improve supply chain management by gaining a better understanding of the company's suppliers and ensuring responsible sourcing of materials.

Another competitive strategy is cost leadership. Through the use of blockchain, Ford can efficiently manage large amounts of data, leading to increased transparency and optimized inventory management. By streamlining inventory processes, Ford can reduce the size of warehouses, resulting in cost savings and decreased staffing requirements. Furthermore, blockchain technology enables secure data transfers, reducing the need for extensive monitoring practices and allowing the company to allocate resources to other areas of the business.

The third generic strategy is focus. Ford can develop a specialized platform for the resale of its cars, leveraging blockchain technology to ensure secure and certified data transfers. By targeting environmentally conscious consumers, Ford can focus on a specific segment with significant growth potential. Additionally, the company could invest in a decentralized car-sharing platform, eliminating the need for intermediaries and increasing transparency. With access to consumer data, Ford can personalize offerings and pricing based on past usage patterns, reducing risk and enhancing the car-sharing experience. This approach aligns with the increasing demand for sustainable transportation options, particularly among consumers who do not typically own a car.

Overall, the adoption of blockchain technology allows Ford to implement various strategies, including differentiation, cost leadership, and focus, enabling the company to gain a competitive edge in the automotive industry while promoting sustainability and enhancing customer value.

Blockchain and the Macro-Environment of the Automotive Industry

The PESTEL analysis provides a list of potentially important issues of the environment influencing strategy (Besanko et al., 2017; Whittington et al., 2022). For Ford, we conducted an analysis of the Political, Economic, Social, Technological, Environmental, and Legal factors. Each of these factors presents opportunities and risks that must be addressed through strategic planning. Based on our analysis, we have identified key strategic factors that Ford must consider in order to capitalize on opportunities and mitigate risks in its business. A summary of the findings is presented in Figure 1.

Figure 1. PESTEL analysis
Source: The Authors

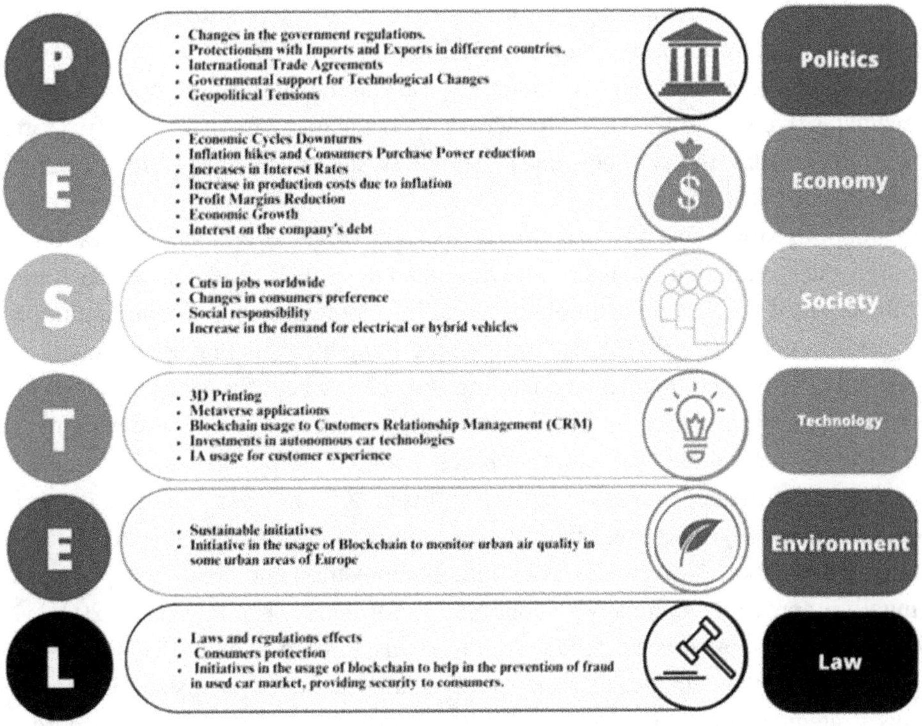

The analysis of macro-environmental factors featured in the PESTEL framework have several potential connections with blockchain technology. In fact, one relevant perspective is to analyse if blockchain technology can be categorized as part of a key driver for change. Whittington et al. (2022) define key drivers of change as "environmental factors likely to have a high impact on industries and sectors, and the success or failure of strategies within them" and consequently these are "factors that are most important and which must be addressed most urgently" (p. 49). Blockchain technology stands out as an inevitable technological trend in the current era, alongside other advancements such as Artificial Intelligence, the metaverse, and 3D printing. It aligns with governmental support for technological innovation, which falls under the political factors category. Blockchain can also help companies address various economic challenges, including economic cycles, inflation, and other factors contributing to cost increases, all of which are covered by the economic factors. Furthermore, blockchain can play a crucial role in addressing pressing environmental challenges by facilitating environmental monitoring and protection. It also enhances transparency in sustainable business initiatives, fostering trust among stakeholders. Additionally, blockchain technology aligns with social trends, particularly the changing preferences of consumers and their increasing demand for information transparency. As consumers become more discerning, blockchain can provide the necessary transparency to meet their requirements.

Overall, blockchain technology has the potential to impact multiple aspects of the macro-environment, making it a key driver of change with significant implications for industries and strategies, namely to automotive companies.

The Effect of Blockchain in the Competitive Forces of the Automotive Industry

The integration of blockchain technology in Ford's processes and supply chain can be assessed using Porter's Five Forces framework. As explained by Whittington et al. (2022), his framework provides an analysis of the competitive environment within an industry and examines the potential impacts on the company. It evaluates five key forces that influence competition in the industry. The five forces featured in the framework are: rivalry, threat of new entries, threat of substitutes, bargaining power of suppliers, and bargaining power of customers.

The rivalry among existing players in the automotive sector is high. Continuous innovation and evolving market demands make it challenging to maintain a dominant position. Daimler, a major car manufacturer, has already implemented blockchain technology along its supply chain, assigning a unique identity to each vehicle it produces (Xu et al., 2022). By further integrating blockchain into its processes and supply chain, Ford can enhance its operational understanding and achieve benefits such as traceability, transparency, and cost reduction (Queiroz et al., 2020). However, as demonstrated by the example of Daimler, other companies in the market are also adopting blockchain technology across their operations. Many competitors possess significant technical expertise in this area. Ford's early integration and innovative use of blockchain technology, as exemplified by the combination of blockchain and geofencing, have enabled faster time-to-market. Nevertheless, continuous innovation and creative approaches are necessary to continually improve the company's economic performance (Kamble et al., 2021). Hence, it is concluded that, to gain a competitive advantage over its rivals, Ford must employ innovative applications of blockchain technology that enhance existing supply chain tracking systems and improve operational efficiency. This strategic utilization of blockchain can be instrumental in positioning Ford ahead of its competitors in the rapidly evolving automotive industry.

Blockchain technology can also contribute to reducing the threat of new entrants in the automotive industry. The integration of blockchain requires significant capital investment to establish the necessary infrastructure, ensure maintenance, and acquire the expertise needed for successful implementation within Ford's processes. As highlighted by Chang and Chen (2020), this capital-intensive nature of blockchain implementation can create a higher entry barrier for new players. By leveraging blockchain technology, Ford can establish a competitive advantage that is difficult for new entrants to replicate. The costs and complexities associated with implementing blockchain effectively act as deterrents for potential newcomers. This gives Ford an opportunity to solidify its position in the market and reduce the likelihood of disruptive competition. Furthermore, blockchain's inherent features, such as transparency and immutability, can enhance trust and security within the automotive industry. Overall, the integration of blockchain technology in Ford's operations helps to create a higher entry barrier, strengthening the company's competitive position and reducing the threat of new entrants in the industry.

Regarding the threat of substitutes, these should be considered as "products or services that offer the same or a similar function and benefit to an industry's own products or services, but have a different nature" (Whittington et al., 2022, p. 68). For customers in the automotive industry, one substitute for cars would be car-sharing services. Current social trends, such as the increasing prevalence of home-office arrangements, can also contribute to the threat of substitutes in this industry. Given the ongoing technological disruption, the automotive industry faces a particularly high level of threat from substitutes. The integration of blockchain technology in the processes of Ford and other automotive companies has the potential to enable new business models and disrupt traditional automotive practices. By implementing a decentralized car-sharing platform, the automotive industry could reduce car ownership and tap into emerging markets such as car-sharing.

Regarding the bargaining power of suppliers, the integration of blockchain technology can contribute to increased transparency in the supply chain, enhancing data exchange and visibility. This, in turn, has the potential to reduce the bargaining power of suppliers. Implementing blockchain technology can enable Ford to optimize its supply chain and reduce dependency on specific suppliers, as highlighted by Queiroz et al. (2020). Additionally, blockchain has the capability to provide Ford with valuable data from its customers, allowing for process optimization and the creation of more affordable products. By expanding its consumer base, Ford can decrease the bargaining power of buyers. Moreover, blockchain can deliver significant value to customers by providing access to various data points related to a car's history, including ownership and damages. This can foster customer loyalty and mitigate customer defection to competitors, as noted by Queiroz et al. (2020).

Overall, the five forces framework indicates the significance of investing in blockchain technology to enhance supply chain management in the automotive industry. By reducing the bargaining power of suppliers through increased supply chain transparency, optimized processes, and reduced dependency, blockchain technology proves valuable. It also addresses the threat of new entrants, although it may intensify industry rivalry. The integration of blockchain technology offers opportunities for new business models, improved efficiency, increased customer loyalty, and disruption of traditional practices. Therefore, strategically incorporating blockchain can serve as a catalyst for innovation and competitive advantage in the automotive industry. In conclusion, the industry analysis indicates a favorable outlook for the integration of blockchain technology.

Possible Growth Strategies Leveraged by Blockchain Adoption

Blockchain technology can also assist Ford in growing its business and enhancing its competitive advantage. To systematize the potential avenues for business growth, the study adopts the Ansoff Matrix. Also known as the Product/Market Expansion Grid, Ansoff matrix is a two-by-two framework used by management teams and analysts to assist in planning and evaluating growth initiatives (Whittington et al., 2022). This tool helps managers assess the level of risk associated with various growth strategies. By utilizing this framework, organizations can identify strategies to integrate blockchain technology, foster innovation, and take the necessary steps towards achieving business success. A summary of this analysis is presented in Table 2.

Starting with the growth strategy that implies less risk to Ford, blockchain can assist the company in achieving market penetration. The application of blockchain technology enables transparency in the supply chain, ensuring visibility and traceability of materials, and minimizing the risk of counterfeit parts. Furthermore, blockchain can strengthen the sustainable products offered by the company by facilitating the tracking of materials from their sources to the final products, promoting responsible sourcing and supporting Ford's commitment to sustainability. Moreover, the adoption of blockchain technology opens up avenues for innovation in providing valuable services to customers. By leveraging blockchain's capabilities, Ford can offer enhanced features such as secure and tamper-proof vehicle histories, streamlined maintenance records, and personalized experiences for customers. These innovations can contribute to fostering Ford's position in the market, improving customer loyalty, and reinforcing its brand reputation.

Further investing in blockchain technology for supply chain management also fosters growth through market development. The adoption of blockchain enables the establishment of standards and norms for

Table 2. Ansoff matrix

	Existing Products	New Products
Existing markets	**Market Penetration** Ford can leverage blockchain technology to enhance its existing supply chain tracking system, ensuring transparency and responsible sourcing of materials for EV battery production. Reduce the danger of items being sold as counterfeit by implementing blockchain-based solutions to track and confirm the authenticity of spare parts and components. Increase the supplied number of plug-in hybrid electric cars (PHEVs) being used in European cities, taking into account the green zones (referred in the market segmentation part).	**Product Development** Create systems based on blockchain, that allow users to access verifiable data regarding Ford car manufacturing, quality control, and maintenance history, promoting trust and transparency. Investigate the use of blockchain in connected automobile technologies to improve data security and privacy and enable safe over-the-air software upgrades for vehicles. Research and develop innovative features and technologies that enhance the sustainability and environmental performance of Ford's electric powertrains.
New Markets	**Market Development** Establish industry-wide blockchain standards and norms for ethical sourcing and supply chain transparency, by working with other automakers, partners in the sector, and governmental organizations. Extend Ford's blockchain activities to cover more facets of the auto sector, such the registration of vehicles, ownership transfers, and the handling of insurance claims.	**Diversification** Explore opportunities to use blockchain technology outside of the automotive industry, such as in the infrastructure of smart cities, autonomous cars, or mobility services, to develop new business ventures and income streams. Look at blockchain-based shared mobility platform solutions that will allow for safe and open transactions between customers and service providers.

Source: The Authors

global supply chains, resulting in cost reduction and increased operational efficiency. Moreover, the transparency provided by blockchain technology promotes ethical sourcing practices, aligning with consumer preferences for sustainable and responsible products. Additionally, the use of smart contracts for registration and ownership transfers streamlines operations in multiple markets, facilitating expansion and market development. Hence, it is concluded that the integration of blockchain technology into supply chain management offers significant growth opportunities through market development. By leveraging blockchain's capabilities, Ford can establish industry standards, enhance transparency, and optimize operations, leading to increased efficiency and competitiveness. The ethical and sustainable practices enabled by blockchain further enhance market development efforts.

In terms of product development, Ford can leverage blockchain technology to create comprehensive systems that provide customers with complete information about their vehicles, spanning from production to maintenance. This integration enhances transparency and builds trust, allowing customers to have a clear understanding of the history and condition of their vehicles. Furthermore, blockchain technology facilitates the development of automated and ecological products. The decentralized and secure nature of blockchain enables the integration of autonomous features and smart functionalities into vehicles, enhancing their performance and user experience. Additionally, blockchain can support the development of eco-friendly solutions by enabling traceability and accountability in the supply chain, ensuring responsible sourcing of materials and reducing environmental impact. As such, integrating blockchain technology into product research and development efforts can help Ford develop new products that enhance customer experiences and better meet the evolving demands of customers in the market.

Finally, blockchain technology presents an opportunity for Ford to pursue diversification as a growth strategy, as previously discussed. The unique capabilities and expertise that Ford has developed in blockchain can be leveraged to explore new avenues outside of the traditional automotive industry. One potential area for diversification is the car-sharing industry, where Ford can combine its extensive

Table 3. SWOT analysis

S	· Through blockchain integration, the entrance barriers are raised, and old procedures are disrupted. · Supply chain optimization and improved consumer's data use. · Sustainability initiatives and technological competence. · Market segmentation approach linked to sustainability.
W	· Costs of capital-intensive integration of blockchain technology. · Challenges in managing disruption and intersegment competition. · Poor luxury car reputation.
O	· The new "green zones" of vehicles, where the cars driving in that city areas must be eco-friendly. · Urban air monitoring using blockchain. · Self-driving cars. · Blockchain initiatives to improve CRM solutions and gather customers.
T	· High competition, in all segments Ford operates. · Increasing prices of components and materials. · Technological advancements by competitors.

Source: The Authors

experience in automotive manufacturing with the innovative features of blockchain. Furthermore, the integration of blockchain can also open doors to diversification in emerging sectors such as autonomous cars and smart cities. Ford can utilize its blockchain competencies to develop cutting-edge solutions that align with these trends.

In conclusion, the analysis of the Ansoff Matrix reveals that blockchain technology not only supports Ford's growth through market penetration, market development, and product development, but it also presents opportunities for diversification. By strategically applying blockchain in various aspects of its operations, Ford can reinforce its positioning as an innovative leader and enhance its business growth opportunities.

Summary of the Results

In order to consolidate the information obtained from the various strategic tools discussed in this study, Table 3 presents a SWOT analysis. This analysis provides a comprehensive overview of the company's strengths and weaknesses, as well as the opportunities, and threats posed by the external environment. This analysis is performed for Ford's operations in the automotive sector, with a specific focus on evaluating the potential roles of blockchain technology.

Presently, Ford has already integrated blockchain technologies into its processes. However, as emphasized by Ahram et al. (2017), blockchain offers numerous additional possibilities for the future. It is important to note that implementing blockchain is a complex and resource-intensive endeavor. Its successful integration heavily relies on management expertise and commitment to implementation. Nevertheless, a successful extension of blockchain technology offers more opportunities than risks for Ford. Furthermore, the company has already demonstrated successful implementation of blockchain in the past.

Through blockchain integration, Ford can reduce the reliance on intermediaries, enhance trust in processes, enable automation, and create a more secure environment with reduced fraud risks. Notably, blockchain will allow Ford to establish a unique vehicle identity, facilitating the safe storage of data such as traffic records and repairs for each individual vehicle. Deeper integration of this technology presents a wide array of opportunities and can provide Ford with a competitive advantage over its rivals.

This analysis provide relevant insights to guide further integration of blockchain technology that can lead to a sustained advantage of Ford. In conclusion, it is recommended for Ford to pursue further integration of blockchain technology, as it holds significant potential for the company's future growth and success.

SOLUTIONS AND RECOMMENDATIONS

Blockchain technology is outstanding in its application beyond cryptocurrencies and is being explored by various industries, including automotive manufacturers, who are utilizing this tool in various segments of their supply chain (AiroDoctor, 2022; Foote, 2021). In the automotive industry, transparency in distribution channels is essential to ensure that manufacturing, transportation, and suppliers have a unified view of the supply chain, practically eliminating the possibility of introducing parts or materials that deviate from the pre-established planning. The transportation and logistics domain requires analytical approaches to adapt more environmentally friendly and sustainable approaches (Bentalha et al., 2023). Moreover, in extreme conditions such as the Covid-19 pandemic, it became clear that the challenges to supply chains are critical and demand careful performance control and management (Alla et al., 2022; Bentalha et al., 2020b).

For Ford, the integration of blockchain technology in supply chain management becomes critical, particularly in the development of electric vehicles (EVs) and EV batteries. The company has introduced blockchain to identify materials of unethical origin, addressing concerns about responsible sourcing of materials such as lithium, cobalt, and copper necessary for battery production (Foote, 2021). This initiative combines blockchain with digital technology to ensure extensive oversight, using digital ledgers to record transactions and store information, thereby streamlining the supply chain and enabling the tracking of potential environmental or human rights violations in the refineries and mines where EV battery supplies are sourced. Additionally, Ford is leveraging blockchain technology to help reduce air pollution in European city centers through the combination of blockchain technology and geofencing (AiroDoctor, 2022). This innovative approach supports government efforts to improve urban air quality and expand the market for environmentally friendly vehicles beyond Ford's existing market segmentation known as "Ford Blue".

Beyond supply chain management, Ford has also found utility for blockchain technology in addressing ethical concerns. The company has partnered with IBM to combat child labor by tracking the transportation of cobalt from mines in the Democratic Republic of Congo to Ford factories (Rusch, 2019). As the supply of raw materials used in the electric vehicle supply chain, a significant area of operation for Ford, this initiative demonstrates the company's commitment to mitigating ethical challenges and has garnered attention from human rights groups worldwide. The entire cobalt journey is recorded on the blockchain, providing transparency and traceability from mine to battery factory to Ford factory (IBM Newsroom, 2019). Furthermore, blockchain technology can be utilized to track products in real-time from their origin to their final destination, enhancing tracking and traceability in a sustainable way (Chang & Chen, 2020).

While Ford has already implemented this in its supplier phase of the supply chain, there are still untapped uses of blockchain that can improve production, increase transparency in deals, and reduce costs. Blockchain can serve as a tool for structuring transparent and impartial contracts, reducing reliance on intermediaries and facilitating secure and prompt payment transactions triggered by the fulfillment of contract conditions (Queiroz et al., 2020).

Moreover, blockchain has been used for vehicle identification throughout the production process, and Ford has explored its application in delivery, maintenance, and registration (Xu et al., 2022). By facilitating the storage of vehicle information, a blockchain platform allows for the consultation of financial and transactional data, enabling users and third parties to verify vehicle history and traffic records.

In conclusion, through this study, it is evident that Ford is highly advanced in the use of blockchain technology, and the integration of blockchain has helped the company address important challenges. As analyzed in the strategic tools, the company operates in a dynamic industry marked by high rivalry. Given this complex environment, there are several other uses of blockchain in the supply chain that the company can further study and explore. By leveraging blockchain as a tool, Ford has the potential to improve processes, enhance sustainability, promote transparency in supplier relationships, and ultimately enhance the customer experience. It is crucial for Ford and other automotive companies to study and apply blockchain technology to improve their supply chain management and remain competitive in the industry.

Given that companies like Ford are making significant advancements in areas such as electric vehicles (EVs), autonomous driving, and connected car technologies, blockchain is expected to play a relevant role in this progress, namely because they facilitate safe data sharing and automatic information processes. While the statistical analysis of these effects goes beyond the scope of this chapter, it remains an important aspect not only for future research but especially for managers. The incorporation of technologies like blockchain into supply chain management requires a rigorous evaluation, and precise indications of its measured impacts can greatly assist managers in their decision-making and implementation processes.

FUTURE RESEARCH DIRECTIONS

This study focused on the application of blockchain technology in the automobile industry, with a specific focus on Ford Motors Company. This study fills a gap in the literature, as there are scarce contributions on the application of blockchain technology in different industries. Moreover, the case study builds on a set of strategy analysis frameworks that are commonly used by managers, which is expected to improve the relevance of the findings to both researchers and practitioners.

Despite the interesting findings and contribution, it is important to acknowledge the limitations of this study. Our analysis was based on a literature review of blockchain usage and does not encompass internal or private data from the company, aside from the information publicly available in their annual reports. In spite of the anticipated impacts of blockchain on supply chain management and its potential to drive advancements in areas such as electric vehicles and autonomous driving, this chapter refrains from assessing specific impacts due to the absence of statistical and accountable information, largely of a confidential nature. Future studies should address the necessity of evaluating the impacts of blockchain on companies' performance. Also, the chapter focused primarily on the case of Ford. It would be valuable to extend research to other car manufacturers to explore their usage of blockchain and its impact on the industry as a whole. Additionally, studies with other industries are highly encouraged, as they would contribute to a more comprehensive understanding of the potential of blockchain technology in different settings. In future studies, it would be beneficial to incorporate additional data sources beyond secondary data, such as conducting interviews with managers, customers, and other stakeholders. By utilizing these methods along with econometric models, a deeper understanding of the impact of blockchain applications on the perceived value for industry members could be gained.

Future studies should also investigate how customers perceive the benefits or drawbacks of blockchain implementation in relation to environmentally friendly solutions and customer relationship management across their experiences with different car manufacturers. This would provide valuable insights into the overall customer perspective.

CONCLUSION

The main aim of this chapter was to investigate the role of blockchain in the automotive industry and explore its potential benefits and solutions. A case study was conducted, focusing on Ford Motor Company as a prominent player in the industry. Throughout its history, Ford has been instrumental in transforming the automobile sector, implementing strategies and technologies like the Henry Ford assembly line to become a global leader in car manufacturing. The analysis presented in this study offers valuable insights into the integration of blockchain technology in Ford's operations, highlighting its potential to create a sustainable competitive advantage. Furthermore, the findings have implications beyond Ford, providing valuable insights for companies in the automotive sector and other industries by offering a comprehensive analysis of the expected impacts and applications of blockchain technology. Overall, the analysis supports the conclusion that further integration of blockchain technology in supply chain management holds significant potential for driving Ford's future growth and overall success.

This chapter makes two main contributions to the still scarce literature on the application of blockchain in different industries beyond financial services. Firstly, it explores blockchain applications within the automotive industry, specifically concerning Ford's operations. It demonstrates the relevance of this technology for transparency in the supply chain, responsible sourcing of materials, and tracking unethical materials, as well as its possible impacts on sustainable business initiatives and in enhancing customer experience and relationships. The systematization and empirical evidence provided contributes to the development of the literature on this topic, which is still in its infancy. Secondly, this study adopts an set of strategy analysis frameworks to report its results, demonstrating the viability and relevance of managerial tools for research purposes.

As noted above, there are several avenues for future research on the application of blockchain technology for management and industry purposes. The findings are also expected to provide interesting insights to managers considering investing in blockchain solutions in different industries.

REFERENCES

Ahram, T., Sargolzaei, A., Sargolzaei, S., Daniels, J., & Amaba, B. (2017). *Blockchain technology innovations.* 2017 IEEE technology & engineering management conference (TEMSCON), Santa Clara, CA.

AiroDoctor. (2022). *How Ford uses Blockchain technology to improve urban air quality?* AiroDoctor. https://airodoctor.com/post-32088/#:~:text=In%20addition%20to%20being%20used

Alla, L., Bentalha, B., & Bouhtati, N. (2022). Assessing supply chain performance in the covid 19 context: a prospective model. *2022 14th International Colloquium of Logistics and Supply Chain Management (LOGISTIQUA)* (pp 1-6). IEEE.

Aslam, J., Saleem, A., Khan, N. T., & Kim, Y. B. (2021). Factors influencing blockchain adoption in supply chain management practices: A study based on the oil industry. *Journal of Innovation & Knowledge*, *6*(2), 124–134. doi:10.1016/j.jik.2021.01.002

Azevedo, P., Gomes, J., & Romao, M. (2023). Supply chain traceability using blockchain. *Operations Management Research*. doi:10.1007/s12063-023-00359-y

Bentalha, B. (2022). Smart technologies for a sustainable service supply chain: A Prospective Perspective. *Journal of Environmental Issues and Climate Change*, *1*(1), 77–89. doi:10.59110/jeicc.v1i1.81

Bentalha, B., Hmioui, A., & Alla, L. (2019). The digitalization of the supply chain management of service companies: a prospective approach. *Proceedings of the 4th International Conference on Smart City Applications,* (pp. 1-8). ACM. 10.1145/3368756.3369005

Bentalha, B., Hmioui, A., & Alla, L. (2020a). Digital service supply chain management: current realities and prospective visions. Innovations in Smart Cities Applications Edition 3: The Proceedings of the 4th International Conference on Smart City Applications 4, (pp. 808-822). Springer International Publishing. 10.1007/978-3-030-37629-1_58

Bentalha, B., Hmioui, A., & Alla, L. (2020b). The global performance of a service supply chain: a simulation-optimization under arena. The *Proceedings of the Third International Conference on Smart City Applications,* (pp. 489-502). Springer International Publishing.

Bentalha, B., Hmioui, A., & Alla, L. (2023). Green Transportation Balanced Scorecard: A VIKOR Fuzzy Method for Evaluating Green Logistics Initiatives. *International Conference on Digital Technologies and Applications, Proceedings of ICDTA'23*. Cham: Springer Nature Switzerland. 10.1007/978-3-031-29857-8_91

Besanko, D., Dranove, D., Shanley, M., & Schaefer, S. (2017). *Economics of Strategy*. John Wiley & Sons.

Bryman, A. (2012). *Social Research Methods* (4th ed.). Oxford University Press.

Chang, S. E., & Chen, Y. (2020). When blockchain meets supply chain: A systematic literature review on current development and potential applications. *IEEE Access : Practical Innovations, Open Solutions*, *8*, 62478–62494. doi:10.1109/ACCESS.2020.2983601

Cole, R., Stevenson, M., & Aitken, J. (2019). Blockchain technology: Implications for operations and supply chain management. *Supply Chain Management*, *24*(4), 469–483. doi:10.1108/SCM-09-2018-0309

Difrancesco, R. M., Meena, P., & Kumar, G. (2022). How blockchain technology improves sustainable supply chain processes: a practical guide. *Operations Management Research*. doi:10.1007/s12063-022-00343-y

Foote, B. (2021). *Ford Blockchain Initiative Aims to Identify Unethically Sourced Materials*. Ford Authority. https://fordauthority.com/2021/12/ford-blockchain-initiative-aims-to-identify-unethically-sourced-materials/

Gurtu, A., & Johny, J. (2019). Potential of blockchain technology in supply chain management: A literature review. *International Journal of Physical Distribution & Logistics Management*, *49*(9), 881–900. doi:10.1108/IJPDLM-11-2018-0371

Hald, K. S., & Kinra, A. (2019). How the blockchain enables and constrains supply chain performance. *International Journal of Physical Distribution & Logistics Management*, *49*(4), 376–397. doi:10.1108/IJPDLM-02-2019-0063

IBM. (2023). *Benefits of Blockchain*. IBM. https://www.ibm.com/topics/benefits-of-blockchain

Kamble, S. S., Gunasekaran, A., Subramanian, N., Ghadge, A., Belhadi, A., & Venkatesh, M. (2021). Blockchain technology's impact on supply chain integration and sustainable supply chain performance: Evidence from the automotive industry. *Annals of Operations Research*, 1–26. doi:10.100710479-021-04129-6

Kumar, A., Liu, R., & Shan, Z. (2020). Is Blockchain a Silver Bullet for Supply Chain Management? Technical Challenges and Research Opportunities. *Decision Sciences*, *51*(1), 8–37. doi:10.1111/deci.12396

Lai, J. Y., Wang, J. T., & Chiu, Y. H. (2021). Evaluating blockchain technology for reducing supply chain risks. *Information Systems and e-Business Management*, *19*(4), 1089–1111. doi:10.100710257-021-00533-4

Markus, S., & Buijs, P. (2022). Beyond the hype: How blockchain affects supply chain performance. *Supply Chain Management*, *27*(7), 177–193. doi:10.1108/SCM-03-2022-0109

Newsroom of IBM. (2019). *Ford Motor Company, Huayou Cobalt, IBM, LG Chem and RCS Global launch blockchain pilot to address concerns in strategic mineral supply chains*. IBM. https://newsroom.ibm.com/2019-01-16-Ford-Motor-Company-Huayou-Cobalt-IBM-LG-Chem-and-RCS-Global-Launch-Blockchain-Pilot-to-Address-Concerns-in-Strategic-Mineral-Supply-Chains

Porter, M. E. (1985). *Competitive Advantage: Creating and Sustaining Superior Performance*. Free Press.

Queiroz, M. M., Telles, R., & Bonilla, S. H. (2020). Blockchain and supply chain management integration: A systematic review of the literature. *Supply Chain Management*, *25*(2), 241–254. doi:10.1108/SCM-03-2018-0143

Rajasekaran, A. S., Azees, M., & Al-Turjman, F. (2022). A comprehensive survey on blockchain technology. *Sustainable Energy Technologies and Assessments*, *52*, 102039. doi:10.1016/j.seta.2022.102039

Sarmah, S. S. (2018). Understanding blockchain technology. *Computing in Science & Engineering*, *8*(2), 23–29. doi:10.5923/j.computer.20180802.02

Sternberg, H. S., Hofmann, E., & Roeck, D. (2021). The Struggle is Real: Insights from a Supply Chain Blockchain Case. *Journal of Business Logistics*, *42*(1), 71–87. doi:10.1111/jbl.12240

Tokkozhina, U., Martins, A. L., & Ferreira, J. C. (2023). Uncovering dimensions of the impact of blockchain technology in supply chain management. *Operations Management Research : Advancing Practice Through Research*, *16*(1), 99–125. doi:10.100712063-022-00273-9

Treiblmaier, H. (2018). The impact of the blockchain on the supply chain: A theory-based research framework and a call for action. *Supply Chain Management*, *23*(6), 545–559. doi:10.1108/SCM-01-2018-0029

Wee, H., & Wu, S. (2009). Lean supply chain and its effect on product cost and quality: A case study on Ford Motor Company. *Supply Chain Management*, *14*(5), 335–341. doi:10.1108/13598540910980242

Whittington, R., Regnér, P., Angwin, D., Johnson, G., & Scholes, K. (2022). *Exploring Strategy* (12th ed.). Pearson.

Xu, X., Tatge, L., Xu, X., & Liu, Y. (2022). Blockchain applications in the supply chain management in German automotive industry. *Production Planning and Control*, 1–15. doi:10.1080/09537287.2022.2044073

Yin, R. K. (2009). Case Study Research: Design and Methods. *Sage (Atlanta, Ga.)*.

Zhou, Y., Gao, X., & Nie, J. J. (2023, April 10). Value of blockchain-enabled supply chain traceability under competition. *International Transactions in Operational Research*, itor.13295. doi:10.1111/itor.13295

Chapter 7
ML, AI, and IoT as Driving Forces From Industry 5.0 Concepts for Better Global Food Security

Rim Ben Abdallah
https://orcid.org/0000-0003-2384-7346
National Institute of Applied Sciences and Technology, University of Carthage, Tunis, Tunisia

Eya Ben Amara
https://orcid.org/0009-0007-4408-3281
National Institute of Applied Sciences and Technology, University of Carthage, Tunis, Tunisia

Nada Ben Ayed
National Institute of Applied Sciences and Technology, University of Carthage, Tunis, Tunisia

Sami Fattouch
National Institute of Applied Sciences and Technology, University of Carthage, Tunis, Tunisia

ABSTRACT

The increasing global population has led to a higher demand for food, requiring us to focus on maintaining its quality, safety, and sustainability. However, food security faces threats not only from natural disasters and climate change, but also from factors like changing dietary preferences, political instability, and food fraud. This chapter provides an overview of currently available concepts related to information and communication technologies (ICTs) that can facilitate cooperative efforts, counter fraud, and enable remote monitoring. In recent years, there has been significant interest in leveraging the combined potential of the internet of things (IoT), artificial intelligence (AI), and machine learning (ML) to tap into the expertise of human professionals and enhance their work with efficient and intelligent machines. The implementation of ICTs in food systems has been comparatively restricted. This chapter aims to address this gap by demonstrating the potential of their tools in identifying and analyzing the food system.

DOI: 10.4018/979-8-3693-0225-5.ch007

INTRODUCTION

During the 1860s in England, there was a significant surge in industrialization referred to as a "revolutionary wave." This period marked the triumph of science over ignorance as industrial capital rapidly advanced and absorbed every innovative concept and scientific breakthrough in its path. As a result, humanity experienced multiple industrial revolutions spanning over 200 years. The first phase, known as Industry 1.0, brought society into the "steam age" by utilizing water vapor to power manufacturing machinery. This led to the emergence of markets, granting access to resources and initiating the primitive accumulation of the economy, causing social unrest. Subsequently, Industry 2.0 ushered in the "electric age" by harnessing electricity as a means of power. This era introduced a division of labor across society and introduced the assembly line model for mass production. Industry 3.0 further advanced with IT-level mass customization, while Industry 4.0 merged IT and operational technology (OT) in a cyber-physical system, enabling intelligent mass customization and personalization. Ultimately, Industry 5.0 represents the integration of human subjectivity, intellect, machine efficiency, artificial intelligence, and precision in industrial production. It emphasizes the significance of humanistic care and strives for a harmonious ecosystem where human and machine capabilities synergize for optimal outcomes (Nara et al., 2021; Kamble et al., 2018).

The industrial revolution brought about significant changes in all aspects of society. However, the manufacturing system has struggled to adapt to the evolving needs of a society that values sustainability, human concerns, and reduced carbon emissions. Industry 5.0 offers an innovative perspective to bridge the gap between societal needs and manufacturing. Unlike previous industrial revolutions that primarily focused on economic sustainability, Industry 5.0 places greater emphasis on people and their demands. The concept of Industry 5.0 gained more attention after the publication of the EU white paper, marking the beginning of this new era. Although there are currently limited and disorganized studies on Industry 5.0, it is still in its early stages of exploration (Leng et al., 2022). Industry 5.0 aims to empower workers with advanced tools and technology, allowing them to enhance their abilities. This enables individuals to focus on their unique human qualities, fostering innovation and economic growth. The objective is to cultivate a work environment that prioritizes employee well-being, job fulfillment, and work-life balance, ultimately leading to a prosperous and inclusive society. In summary, Industry 5.0 envisions a future where people and technology collaborate to augment each other's capabilities, ultimately creating a more efficient, imaginative, and sustainable industrial sector (Mitchell et al., 2021).

Moreover, there are various industrial and social ideas related to industry 5.0 that are not systematically introduced. This chapter serves as a catalyst for revealing the advancing attributes of industry 5.0, particularly regarding food security. It presents a concise overview of its outcomes, framework, enabling technologies, and hurdles.

On the other hand, global food security is heavily influenced by the availability, accessibility, and affordability of food for individuals worldwide. This aspect is extremely critical as it directly impacts the prevention of hunger and malnutrition. Currently, more than 820 million people worldwide suffer from hunger, making it essential to achieve food security in order to meet basic nutritional needs and enhance overall welfare (Dabone et al., 2021). In addition, it is important to note that environmental sustainability and global food security are closely connected. Sustainable farming practices and responsible food production contribute to the preservation of natural resources, biodiversity, and efforts to mitigate climate change. Moreover, ensuring access to nutritious food is vital for maintaining human health. Food security plays a crucial role in meeting people's nutritional needs, reducing the risk of malnutrition and diseases, and promoting overall well-being. Considering these factors, it is crucial to address global food security through comprehensive policies and efforts in order to build resilient and fair communities worldwide. Furthermore, it is worth mentioning that the use of communication devices is increasing, and artificial intelligence (AI) is progressively integrating into the lives of a significant portion of the global population in various ways (Dwivedi et al., 2021; Bentalha et al., 2019. The Internet of Things (IoT), primarily centered around industrial technologies, remains less captivating to the general population compared to artificial intelligence (AI). Nevertheless, agricultural scientists and engineers delve into the investigation of utilizing these sophisticated information technologies to improve worldwide food security, which forms a logical area of study in this chapter.

Challenges in Achieving Global Food Security

Tackling the issue of food security is a formidable and intricate undertaking, as it cannot be solely linked to a particular location or determined by a single aspect like demographics, education, location, or income. According to the World Health Organization (2022), after having remained largely stable since 2015, the percentage of the global population that experiences hunger increased dramatically in 2020 and continues to do so in 2021, reaching 9.8%. This compares with 8% in 2019 and 9.3% in 2020, despite the fact that there is more than enough food to sustain everyone on our planet. This predicament highlights the challenge of achieving food security, which involves addressing the escalating issue of food scarcity caused by a combination of wastage and the ever-growing global population. Current estimates indicate that we need to augment global food production by 70% on already overstretched finite infrastructures before 2050 (Mc Carthy et al., 2018).

- **Population Growth and Changing**

Nowadays, the growing global population raises serious questions about food security. Understanding the changing aspects of population growth is important for studying demographics and planning for the future.

Various industries, such as healthcare, food, employment, and resource distribution are affected by shifting population dynamics. In addition to addressing the issues brought on by rapid population increase, such as the strain on infrastructure or environmental deterioration, it is crucial to consider sustainable development techniques.

A challenging undertaking that calls for taking into account many different elements is understanding and managing population increase. A balanced and advantageous population growth for societies can be ensured with the help of effective planning, inclusive policies, and sustainable development practices.

The rising world population, which is predicted to rise by 47% from 6.1 billion in 2000 to 8.9 billion in 2050 (Collodi et al., 2009), is one of the growing pressures on global food security on the demand side. Africa and Asia, which both have significant levels of environmental and societal vulnerability, are predicted to host the majority of the expansion. In spite of the fact that Southern Africa, for instance, now imports a net amount of food, the region's population is expected to more than double by the year 2050, reaching around 2 billion people (Conceição et al., 2011).

Some important metrics might be boosting agricultural productivity. In fact, it's essential to adopt sustainable agricultural practices, including the adoption of cutting-edge farming methods, improved seed varieties, and effective irrigation systems.

Investing more in agricultural research and development is something that governments, international organizations, and corporations must do in order to find fresh approaches to problems with food security in conjunction with population growth. To deal with population expansion, it must, among other things, increase agricultural productivity, diversify our food supply, reduce food waste, invest in R&D, and develop agricultural infrastructure. These actions will ensure that everyone has access to ongoing food security.

- **Climate Change and Environmental Sustainability**

One of the major challenges in the 21st century is minimizing the risks associated with climate change on food security. The influence of climate change on crop yield can already be seen in observed data (Lobell et al., 2011). While there is a predominant focus on studying the effects of climate change on crops, the consequences on fisheries and livestock production are equally significant (Herrero et al., 2016). Although changes like rising temperatures and sea levels will have substantial impacts in the future, farmers are currently faced with shifting weather patterns and more frequent and intense extreme weather events, increasing the risks associated with farming (IPCC, 2012). Urgent adaptive measures are needed to reduce these risks.

Figure 1. Schematic demonstrating how the physical climate system, exposure, and vulnerability in the livestock supply chain are interconnected, resulting in the potential for climate-related impacts

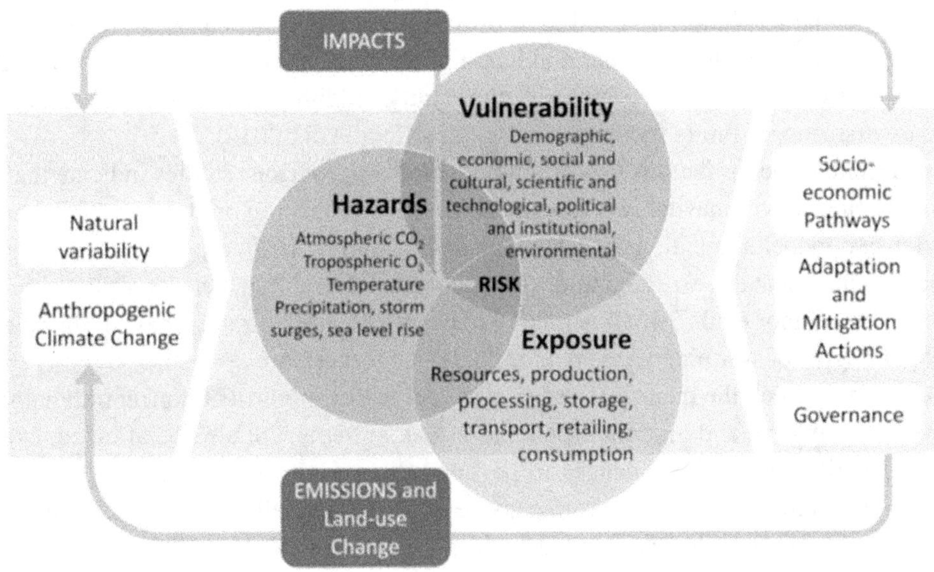

This risk arises from the convergence of climate-related hazards (such as extreme events and long-term patterns) with the vulnerability and exposure levels of both human and natural systems. The climate system (on the left) and socioeconomic processes, including adaptation and mitigation measures (on the right), drive the occurrence of hazards, exposure, and vulnerability (Godde et al., 2020).

This section examines the concept of climate-related risks and their effects, as defined by the inter-governmental panel on climate change (IPCC) (Figure 1). Climate-related impacts occur when climate hazards interact with the vulnerability and exposure of both human and natural systems. This interaction is central to the ipcc's assessments of climate impacts. In this context, "hazard" refers to physical events or trends related to climate that can affect livestock systems. "Exposure" pertains to specific parts of the livestock supply chain that could be negatively influenced, while "vulnerability" encompasses the capacity of humans to cope with and adapt to these changes. "Impact" primarily focuses on the consequences of extreme weather, climate events, and climate change on both natural and human systems.

The research-implementation, research-practice, knowing-doing, or science-policy gap, as it is also known, arises in many applied disciplines between research findings and their claim (Knight et al., 2008). Additionally, with climate change, there is the added challenge of deep uncertainties regarding the exact nature of future climates and even the coming seasons, which are unlikely to diminish in the next decade (Heal and Millner, 2014). However, management in the face of ambiguity is not exclusive to the climate change issue (Beven and Alcock, 2013). Therefore, we must strive to develop tools and processes that allow us to take action based on uncertain knowledge. Crop-climate modeling plays a crucial role in developing insights into the future agricultural landscape, which can help guide policy decisions and on-the-ground selections (Porter et al., 2014). However, it's important to note that while these models provide reliable results in certain scenarios, there is inherent uncertainty when assessing future agricultural yield (Weaver et al., 2013). This uncertainty can restrict the predictability of the modeled system and hinder effective adaptation decision-making (Weaver et al., 2013). Consequently, it is essential for future research to focus on understanding the limits of predictability and reducing uncertainties in order to improve these models. In the field of climate modeling, advancements in parameterization, model complexity, and spatial resolution have led to improved performance. As a result, it has been difficult for us to predict future agricultural output and land use changes because progress has been delayed in satisfying the specific needs of the agricultural community. Additionally, uncertainties in crop models also impede assessments of future food production (Challinor et al., 2014).

However, despite some limitations in crop-climate modeling, various studies indicate that the influences of climate change will inevitably lead to a decrease in global crop production. These projections, based on extensive model simulations and meta-analyses, suggest that crop yields of important crops like rice, maize, and wheat are expected to decline between 3% and 10% per degree of warming above historical levels (Challinor et al., 2014). Another study specifically estimated a 6% reduction in global wheat yield per degree of warming (Asseng et al., 2011). Furthermore, evidence suggests that climate change will similarly touch the quality of crops, with decreases in nutrient concentrations such as nitrogen, protein, and macro- and micronutrients. Livestock systems will also be affected, experiencing reduced food quantity and quality, changes in pest and disease prevalence, and impaired production due to physiological stress as temperatures rise above 30 °C (Campbell et al., 2016). Similarly, tropical marine ecosystems may see a decrease of 5-10% in potential fish catch by 2050, along with shifts in the distribution of fish and plankton habitats due to warming ocean temperatures, changes in winds, ice thickness, pH, and nutrient supply (Grace et al., 2015). Climate change will also impact agricultural systems by altering the prevalence of pests and increasing the frequency of pest events, posing greater risks in the 21st century.

Research on the effects of climate change on food security has primarily focused on the quantity of crop production. However, it is important to acknowledge that climate change impacts all aspects of food security, including availability, access, utilization, and stability throughout the entire food system. The variation in livestock feed quantity and quality is influenced by intricate local interactions involving eCO_2 concentrations, tropospheric O_3 levels, temperature, and precipitation (Godde et al., 2020). Additionally, they rely on native and sown pastures as key feed in mixed crop-livestock and grazing-only systems. Although not discussed here, livestock can also be fed byproducts and waste materials (such as oilseed cakes, bran, vegetable waste, brewer waste), as well as concentrates and supplements (FAO, 2017). Rising concentrations of eCO_2 have been found to enhance the productivity of plants (Ainsworth et al., 2020), particularly those with a C_3 photosynthetic pathway such as wheat, rice, soybean, and temperate grasses. However, C_4 plants like maize, sorghum, sugarcane, and tropical grasses experience less growth stimulation. It is important to note that while this CO_2 fertilization effect can increase potential yields of certain species, it can also have negative consequences on animal food quality (Augustine et al., 2018). Studies have shown that elevated eCO_2 concentrations can lead to lower grain protein concentrations in C_3 crops (excluding legumes) like wheat and rice. On the other hand, the impact on C_4 crop grains is relatively smaller. Additionally, increased eCO_2 levels have been found to decrease overall mineral concentrations while increasing the ratio of non-structural carbohydrates (primarily starch and sugars) to minerals in non-leguminous C_3 plants (Loladze, 2014). Despite the potential negative effects, the nutritional quality of C_3 grasses may still be higher than that of C_4 grasses under elevated eCO_2 conditions. Furthermore, certain plants may experience increased toxicity under higher eCO_2 levels, such as cassava leaves exhibiting a significant rise in cyanogenic glycosides concentration. The encroachment of woody vegetation due to eCO_2 increases and changes in fire patterns can also impact grassland ecosystems and the diets of grazing animals negatively. eCO_2 has attracted more attention compared with the impact of increased tropospheric O_3 on plant productivity and its potential secondary effects on weeds, pests, diseases, and interactions with pesticides. However, studies on crop responses to O_3 show that it reduces crop yields to a similar extent as nutrient deficiency, heat stress, and aridity. For example, analysis of historical data indicates that O_3 pollution has led to a 5-10% decrease in soybean and maize yields in the US over the past 30 years. Researchers have reviewed the literature on the effects of O_3 pollution on plant productivity, but the topic is still not fully understood (Ainsworth et al., 2020). This uncertainty poses significant implications for predicting future atmospheric composition, global climate, net primary productivity, and the provision of ecosystem services in crop, grassland, and other terrestrial models.

Changes in temperature and water availability have a significant impact on forage and crop yields, as well as feed quality. The sensitivity to climate changes varies depending on the type of crop and other environmental factors. However, it is widely agreed that air temperatures above approximately 30°C-34°C generally led to decreased cereal yields under water-limited conditions. This is due to the acceleration of crop development and damage to plant cells (Meerburg et al., 2009). The maximum temperature for growth of temperate legumes and pastures is around 30°C-35°C, while tropical species can tolerate temperatures ranging from 35°C-50°C. High temperatures often occur alongside water stress, as low soil moisture reduces evaporative cooling and increases crop water loss. The combination of warmer temperatures and drier conditions tends to favor C_4 species over C_3 species. The increased instability of feed supply poses a major challenge for grazing systems, as it affects herd size and grazing intensity management. Regions with high year-to-year precipitation variability currently support lower livestock stocking rates compared to less variable regions (Godde et al., 2020). Studies on grassland vegetation have shown that changes in seasonal climate patterns can have both positive and negative impacts on above-ground biomass. The outcome depends on the nature of the change and the agro-ecological context (Zeppel et al., 2014). Climate extremes such as drought sequences or prolonged periods of hot days can significantly impact the livestock sector. While droughts are extensively studied, other hazards like fires, heavy storms, flooding events, surface melt, icing events, and the emergence of new bodies of water can also disrupt crop growth, reduce arable land, and limit animal access to pastures. Changes in precipitation patterns in saline areas also affect soil salinity and agricultural production potentials. For instance, salinity intrusion in coastal areas of Bangladesh has led farmers to seek alternative sources of livestock feed (Alam et al., 2017). Furthermore, predictions of local sea-level rise indicate potential disruptions to oil palm production in areas like Carey Island, Malaysia, due to seawater intrusion. This would have implications for livestock production, as palm kernel meal, an important feed source, may witness reduced production (Tajul Baharuddin et al. 2013).To achieve a sustainable food supply for 9 billion people, humans should focus on the relationship between the ultimate bearing capacity of the natural environment and food production. This means that we need to break the traditional thinking of "input and output" and, rather, consider "input under and reasonable output under the ultimate environmental bearing capacity". Efforts have been made to analyze food security outcomes in terms of the entire food system, rather than solely focusing on yields. Recent studies have started to consider a broader range of factors influencing food security under climate change, such as the relationship between irrigation potential and food trade and the correlation between food prices and conflict (Mirón et al., 2023). This new approach to food systems recognizes the importance of demand-side solutions, addressing food waste and dietary choices, to achieve food security amidst climate change. Additionally, it aims to ensure that individuals and households receive adequate nutrition rather than solely focusing on calorie intake at national and global levels.

- **Limited Natural Resources and Land Scarcity**

Currently, food production greatly depends on external inputs, such as irrigation water and agrichemical products. Considering the remarkable magnitude and speed of global population changes, it is likely that food production will further undermine the natural ecosystem and environment. Meanwhile, food production will be constrained by the climate change, nonfood uses of crops and farmland (e.g., bioenergy, construction of transportation lines, and recreational activities) but also the expansion of urbanization and land degradation (e.g., erosion and salinization).

The development of superior infrastructure, public services, cultural facilities, convenience, and job opportunities in urban areas has attracted numerous rural residents in developing countries to migrate to cities, resulting in urban expansion. China's urbanization rate has doubled the global average, increasing from 17.91% in 1978 to 57.35% in 2016 (Yansui et al., 2018). This urbanization trend has two major effects on arable land: firstly, urban expansion encroaches upon a significant amount of cultivable land, and secondly, the reduction in rural population size leads to loss of cultivated land. As urbanization continues to expand, competition for land, water, and energy intensifies, impacting food production and causing food security concerns. Global urbanization expansion exacerbates arable land shortages, particularly in critical areas due to the unequal distribution of natural resources and regional disparities. Over the past 40 years, urban land expansion rates have consistently outpaced or equaled urban population growth rates worldwide. China and India, accounting for over 35% of the world's population, have experienced significant urbanization that has encroached upon agricultural land. The expansion of urban areas is becoming more extensive than compact, with urban land expansion rates higher or equal to urban population growth rates across all regions and for three decades. North America has witnessed urban growth driven more by population growth compared to Europe. By 2030, the global urban land cover area is projected to increase from 4.3 × 105 km2 to 1.26 × 107 km2 (Xu et al., 2019). The rapid spread of urbanization directly leads to the utilization of vast farmland. Urban expansion leads to the consumption of agricultural land through the development of tall buildings, water conservation initiatives, and transportation systems. On the other hand, as rural populations migrate to cities, small farmers experience reduced agricultural production unless taken over by larger farms. Consequently, the growing urban population will rely heavily on food production from other agricultural land, while also increasing water usage and greenhouse gas emissions. Globally, urban expansion is anticipated to cause a loss of 1.8–2.4% of global croplands by 2030, potentially accounting for 3–4% of worldwide crop production reduction (Bren d'Amour et al., 2017). The impact of agricultural land value on urban development remains less studied and controversial, with some studies suggesting that highly productive or profitable agricultural land hampers urban growth (Tan et al., 2021). Therefore, the contribution of urbanization to land-use changes is a crucial sustainability concern. Urban expansion is expected to occur in some of the most productive farmland regions, particularly in Asian and African megacities, placing additional pressure on already strained food systems and jeopardizing livelihoods in vulnerable areas (Bren d'Amour et al., 2017) .

Several factors play a role in determining the availability of food for Earth's population. Key factors include suitable soil, energy, and access to fresh water, as agriculture is the primary source of our food supply. Land resources are crucial as they contribute to the global biogeochemical cycle, provide agricultural production, and support various human needs and services. Studies have explored the Earth's carrying capacity in terms of sustaining a growing global population. Increasing food production without expanding arable land significantly poses a challenge. Approximately one-third of arable land is polluted, presenting a hurdle for modern agriculture. Moreover, food security faces increasing difficulty due to climate change affecting crop growth, yields, and disease susceptibility. The utilization of existing land also faces various challenges that impact the safety and sustainability of production systems. Globally, about 25% of land resources are highly degraded, 44% are moderately degraded, and pollution levels continue to rise (Singh et al., 2022). Land degradation encompasses desertification, salinization, erosion, compaction, and the introduction of invasive species. Some researchers view land degradation as a reduction in land or soil productivity due to factors like soil nutrient constraints, erosion, wetland development, or soil salinization, making the land unsuitable for crop cultivation. While technical interventions can address severe soil degradation in the short term, prioritizing the sustainable use of land resources remains crucial in the long run. Balancing the need for increasing farmland while avoiding ecological damage is a pressing global concern. Two main strategies to meet the growing global food demand involve maximizing existing agricultural land or increasing crop yields. While some believe that increasing fertilizer and pesticide usage is the most effective way to boost food production, this practice has caused collateral damage to the environment (Pretty, 2018). Excessive use of these substances leads to biodiversity loss, pesticide resistance, emergence of new pests, pollution, reduced freshwater supplies, soil degradation, erosion, and health risks. Fertilizers and pesticides can persist in the soil, affecting soil health and microbial activity. It is essential to determine the peak of food production, which will inform artificial measures such as fertilization and pesticide use. Expanding arable land has significantly contributed to food security in recent decades, resulting in a 28% increase in grain production (Ramankutty et al., 2018). This increase was primarily driven by a 2.4% expansion in cropland area (Foley et al., 2011). Of the total land area measuring 13.4 billion hectares across the globe, nearly 3 billion hectares are deemed suitable for growing crops. Out of these suitable hectares, around half are currently being utilized for cultivation purposes (Shi et al., 2022). Expanding the utilization of reclaimable farmland is an effective means to improve crop production. However, much of this arable land consists of ecological forests, which should not be extensively used for agriculture due to their impact on biodiversity conservation, greenhouse gas emissions, regional climate and hydrological changes, and the high cost of infrastructure development. Balancing the conflict between expanding cropland area and ecological preservation is challenging. The proportion of global cropland area in the total land area has been steadily increasing, from 10.32% in 1961 to 11.97% in 2017(Edreira et al., 2018). It is projected to reach 12.72% by 2050 and 13.73% by 2100.

ML, AI, and IoT in Agriculture

The application of ML, AI and IoT techniques in the agricultural industry has a significant effect on productivity, efficiency and sustainability.

Indeed, thanks to machine learning and artificial intelligence, we can now analyse large amounts of agricultural data to make forecasts, optimize processes and support decision-making, and even participate in plant disease detection, crop health monitoring, automate irrigation and even facilitate autonomous agriculture by using robotics.

This can provide farmers with valuable information about their operations, allowing them to make data-based decisions, reduce waste of resources, improve crop quality and boost general productivity.

Currently, the utilization of artificial intelligence (AI) technology in machine learning (ML) and the internet of things (IoT) has gained significant traction and holds great potential across various domains, including agriculture. This application aims to facilitate comprehensive analysis of the agricultural system, enhance the precision and dependability of outcomes, and address the technical complexities faced by « smart agriculture » (Mishra et al., 2023; Ravesa Akhter et al., 2022).

- Leveraging Data in Agriculture

Data digitization has now become a common and highly sophisticated practice in virtually all sectors and particularly in agricultural management.This section highlights the interest of data exploitation in agriculture and the challenges that can arise when used in agricultural techniques. Eventually in order to increase food production by reducing the amount of water used and applied chemicals and lower costs, farmers used precision farming technologies (Shaikh et al., 2022). AI offers the opportunity to revolutionize the agricultural sector by enabling farmers to improve crop yields, reduce food loss and strengthen the sustainability of their practice (Whig et al., 2023).

In recent years, the agricultural industry has witnessed a significant transformation driven by the integration of advanced technologies and data-driven solutions. The practice of leveraging data in agriculture has emerged as a game-changer, empowering farmers to make informed decisions and optimize their farming operations. This chapter explores the rising prominence of data utilization in agriculture and how it is revolutionizing the field of precision farming.Utilizing data-driven technologies, precision farming allows farmers to enhance productivity, increase efficiency, and reduce costs.

One of the key components of leveraging data in agriculture is the collection of accurate and real-time information from various sources. This can include weather patterns, soil conditions, crop health, and machinery performance. Advanced sensors, satellite imagery, drones, and Internet of Things (IoT) devices play a crucial role in collecting this valuable data. The integration of these technologies enables farmers to monitor and analyze their fields with unprecedented precision by using data processing techniques. Collecting and analyzing data on soil health, weather conditions trends, pest populations and crop yields, farmers can make more informed decisions (Agarwal et al., 2023).

By leveraging data-driven insights, farmers can make more informed choices regarding irrigation scheduling, application of fertilizers and pesticides, and even predicting potential yield variations. For instance, by analyzing historical weather data and crop growth patterns, farmers can optimize irrigation schedules to conserve water while ensuring optimal plant health. This not only reduces water consumption but also minimizes the risk of over or under watering, resulting in increased crop yields (Agarwal et al., 2023).In addition, the exploitation of data can also contribute to cost reduction and improved efficiency in the agricultural sector.

Using machine learning algorithms to analyze crop data allows farmers to optimize planting locations and reduce losses, resulting in higher yields and lower input costs. Similarly, by monitoring equipment usage and maintenance data, farmers can improve the efficiency of their operations and reduce downtime (Agarwal et al., 2023).

In conclusion, leveraging data in agriculture, with the support of innovative platforms has the potential to revolutionize the way farmers operate. Precision farming, empowered by advanced technologies and data-driven insights, allows for optimized resource management, enhanced decision-making, and increased productivity. As the agriculture industry continues to evolve, embracing data utilization will be key to ensure sustainable and efficient farming practices in the future.

- Precision Farming and Smart Agriculture

Precision agriculture is a technological method of assessing, monitoring and analyzing the specific requirements of fields and crops. The main objective of this form of agriculture is to optimize the use of inputs by applying specific quantities to improve crop yields and profitability (Raj et al., 2021)

Agriculture is facing many challenges, namely: pest diseases and infestations, inadequate soil treatments, inadequate drainage and irrigation, the adverse consequences of climate change on agriculture have a negative impact on global food security, both in terms of the quantity and quality of food produced (Gupta et al., 2022).

The field of intelligence with its rigorous learning capacities have become a key technique to solve various problems related to agriculture with its technology and ensuring the valorization of all the data collected by various tools, converting them into real sources of information in order to define the axes of simplification of agricultural tasks. Its smart farming techniques also make it possible to carry out accurate and predictive analyses of all situations that may affect farms (Banerjee et al., 2022).

- Crop Yield Prediction and Optimization

Yield forecasting is a fundamental and well-known subject of precision agriculture. It includes crop yield planning and evaluation, crop availability coordination with demand, and crop management (Bhimavarapu et al., 2023). It is very important in global food production as farmers and producers insist on the unpredictability of yield forecasts when making financial decisions. The prediction of crop yields is a challenging endeavor that encompasses multiple elements including the genotype and environment, as well as their intricate interactions. To accurately forecast yields, it is crucial to have a comprehensive comprehension of the correlation between outcomes and the collective influence of these factors (Sunitha et al., 2022).

Recently, Deep Learning (DL) methods have emerged as effective solutions for dealing with complex datasets such as meteorological parameters, maturity groups, and genotypes. Climate parameters have a critical impact on crop performance. They are used to accurately predict crop yield by taking into account factors such as precipitation, wind, temperature and solar radiation. Accurate forecasting of early crop yields is essential for market pricing, labour planning, transportation and crop organization. Smart agriculture aims to make agriculture more efficient through the use of high-precision algorithms.In particular, machine learning (ML) fuels the operation of machines capable of learning without human intervention providing new opportunities to understand, decode and quantify on-farm data collection procedures (Bhimavarapu et al., 2023).

State-of-the-art models have far exceeded previous data-based predictions and are consolidating advances in computer vision to provide critical and in-depth crop information. climate and economic conditions to optimize agricultural yield for the user population (Bhimavarapu et al., 2023).

- Livestock Monitoring and Health Management

Thanks to technological advances in all areas, animal health management is also undergoing significant changes globally (Crowe et al., 2018). Participation in new health management strategies, such as fertility management, processing large amounts of data, genetic selection, nutritional management, infectious disease control and reproductive management, are key factors in livestock health monitoring and management (Crowe et al., 2018).

To ensure this surveillance and management of livestock health, individual performance systems based on innovative technologies, based on specific parameters such as animal weight and activity, animal health systems, data platforms and analysis tools are now valuable and easily integratable. For animal surveillance, it is based primarily on the detection and management of infections, infestations, and early detection of exotic or emerging diseases (Crowe et al., 2018).

- Intelligent Irrigation Systems

The application of new technological advances such as the Internet of Things is now a multidisciplinary concept encompassing a wide range of different technologies, namely agriculture and more specifically in the field of irrigation intelligence. This section provides an overview of IOT technologies and applications related to agriculture in the irrigation management system. In fact, due to the uneven distribution of rainwater, the variation in plant types, the nature of the soil and variety makes it very difficult to determine the needs of the farmer to manage water with manual irrigation methods at regular intervals. Therefore, we need an automatic system that accurately monitors and controls essential water on the ground which makes irrigation management an important challenge for the farmer who allows it to make the control decision that allows then, monitoring and controlling the needs of the plant, good soil condition ensures the proper yield. IOT implication will then be able to monitor all parameters simultaneously and the data will be transmitted to farmers in a project called smart irrigation (Rajkumar et al., 2017). In other words, smart irrigation reduces water consumption and increases performance. developing a crop irrigation strategy based on three crop factors, weather conditions and the nature of the soil are the criteria for irrigation planning to ensure intelligent water management and high-quality agricultural production (Sharifnasab et al., 2023).The term "Internet of Things" (IoT) pertains to the connection of various objects and devices to the internet. These connected objects can be controlled and monitored through software applications on smartphones and tablets. It involves networking sensors and devices, enabling them to interact and fulfill user requirements (Salam et al., 2020). These irrigation

Figure 2. Overall, of operating procedures for intelligent irrigation systems
(Sharifnasab et al., 2023)

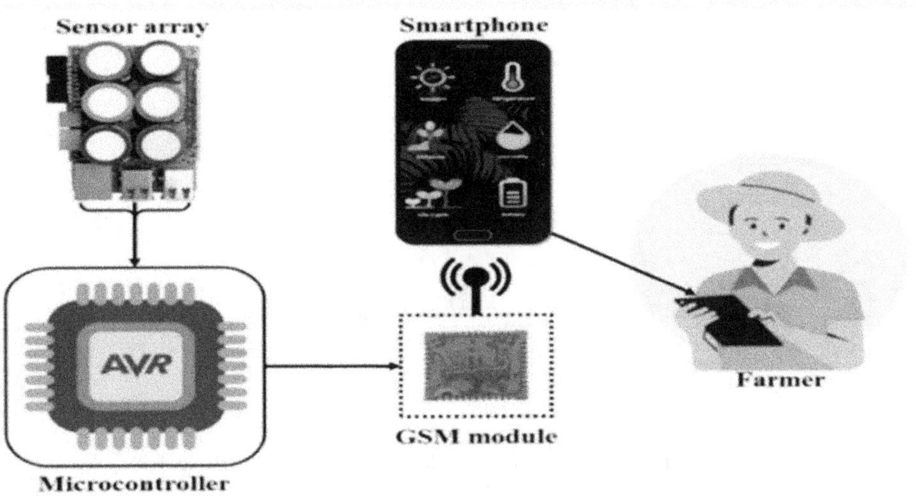

technologies have become a challenge in the agriculture and irrigation sectors as they offer the opportunity to shorten management decisions by significantly increasing costs and performance. Using the right practice in the right place at the right time and with the right amount (Tsouros et al., 2019). Smart irrigation systems use sensors to accurately estimate irrigation needs by recording product temperature and soil moisture. They ensure a maximized product with minimal water consumption and sustainable development (Munir et al., 2021).

The operating principle for an intelligent irrigation system is based essentially on digital sensors that will verify a set of evaluation parameters (data collection: temperature, humidity, soil type, plants, etc.) and transmit data remotely using computer software written in Python. then the microcontroller units and user units receive the information and process it and it is provided to the farmer (Figure 2). Water management plays a crucial and effective role in meeting the ever-growing needs of our world. In fact, smart irrigation is an advanced concept in agriculture, offering the promise of improving the efficiency of water use while preserving or improving crop yields with technologies such as the Internet of Things (IoT) and cloud computing are essential.

Supply Chain Optimization

The food supply chain plays a crucial role in shaping the environment, accounting for approximately 18% of the total global greenhouse gas (GHG) emissions (Ritchie et al.,2020). Additionally, this intricate system is also a major contributor to waste generation, with approximately one-third of global food production resulting in food losses and waste (Nicastro and Carillo, 2021). This wastefulness has far-reaching consequences, not only squandering valuable resources but also exacerbating the environmental challenges we face today.

To combat food losses and waste, interventions should be put in place at various stages, from production and harvest to transportation, storage, and retail. Advanced technologies such as AI, ML, and IoT can be harnessed to optimize the supply chain, predict demand accurately, and minimize spoil-

Figure 3. Implementation of IoT in supply chain
(Tsang et al., 2022)

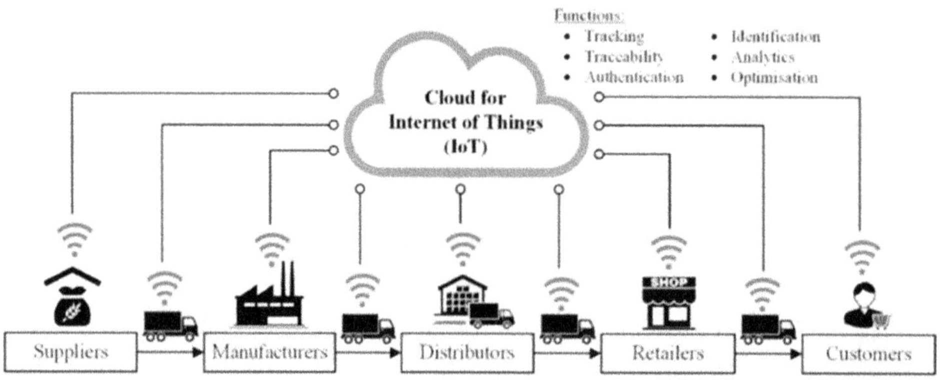

age. Additionally, adopting circular economy principles can help repurpose food waste into valuable resources like compost or bioenergy, further reducing its environmental footprint. A pioneering effort in systematically monitoring the sustainability of the agri-food supply chain is the development of a Performance Measurement System, as outlined by de Carvalho et al. in their 2022 study. This system takes a business-oriented approach, aiming to evaluate and improve sustainability practices within the agricultural and food industry. Despite the existence of well-established agricultural and food sectors, each country or region retains control and management over its food supply chain to ensure a certain level of food security for its population. This decentralized approach is influenced by various factors such as geographical location, climate, and agricultural capabilities. However, in an increasingly interconnected global market, countries that heavily rely on food imports and exports are more susceptible to potential global crises.

The vulnerability of these countries is emphasized in a study by Suweis et al. in 2015, which highlights the risks associated with over-reliance on international food trade. Global crises, such as conflicts, natural disasters, or disruptions in transportation networks, can severely impact the availability and affordability of imported food, thereby affecting the food security of these nations. In this context, the adoption of blockchain technology (BCT) and Internet of Things (IoT) in the management of Agri- Food Supply Chains (AFSC) has shown promising results in various aspects such as distribution, traceability and information security (Barbosa, 2021).

These technologies have the potential to revolutionize how AFSCs operate, ensuring transparency, efficiency, and sustainability throughout the supply chain. As illustrated in Figure 3, the implementation of IoT in the supply chain facilitates various functions, including intelligent verification and identification of products, comprehensive tracking and traceability across the supply chain, and intelligent assessment of food quality (Tsang et al., 2022). The collected data is managed in cloud databases and presented in IoT dashboards, following the service-oriented architecture for IoT (Tsang et al., 2022).

- **Efficient Logistics and Distribution**

One of the critical aspects of ensuring global food security is an efficient supply chain that enables the seamless movement of agricultural products from farms to consumers. ML, AI, and IoT can play a crucial role in optimizing logistics and distribution processes. Advanced algorithms can analyze data on transportation routes, weather conditions, and demand patterns to determine the most efficient delivery routes and schedules.

Carriers face a challenge due to the unpredictable nature of transport demand and a significant number of changes and cancellations in bookings (Verdouw et al., 2016). This situation hampers capacity utilization and restricts their ability to provide tailored services. A recent successful demonstration involved virtualizing the food supply chain using IoT and an information systems architecture for a fish export business from Norway to The Netherlands (Verdouw et al., 2016). Moreover, the supply chain sector is increasingly relying on automated guided vehicles (AGVs) that utilize AI, machine vision, and navigation technologies (like simultaneous localization and mapping (SLAM)) to automate material handling in manufacturing processes (Misra et al., 2020). Machine vision has played a significant role in enabling comprehensive automation, and currently there is a growing interest in exploring the integration of AI to track individual products within the supply chain (Misra et al., 2020).

- **Quality Assurance and Traceability**

Mislabeled, misbranded, contaminated, and adulterated food products result in significant social and economic losses within the global economy (Patel et al., 2023). Throughout the food supply chain, which encompasses various stages such as on-farm rearing, processing, storage, shipping, and retail, there is a risk of contamination by microorganisms. Improper management practices within the food supply chain can contribute to the contamination of food products, posing a significant threat to public health and safety (Sibanyoni & Tabit, 2019).Maintaining food quality and ensuring its safety is of utmost importance. ML, AI and IoT techniques can be employed to develop robust quality assurance systems that monitor various parameters such as freshness, nutritional content, and contamination levels. By analyzing sensor data and image recognition algorithms, potential quality issues can be identified early on, allowing for prompt corrective actions. The primary objective of incorporating IoT in AFSC is to gather sensor signals for monitoring crucial factors such as the proper growth of crops in quality soil and the prevailing weather conditions (Wei et al., 2023). Furthermore, BCT can be integrated with IoT devices to enable transparent and immutable traceability of food products. BCT provides real-time data traceability, which has emerged as a significant research topic (Barbosa, 2021). IoT sensors integrated with the blockchain are utilized by producers, distributors, and transporters to provide real-time data on temperature, humidity (Manisha & Jagadeeshwar, 2023), and other quality parameters, ensuring the integrity of the products. The data collected from these sensors, along with RFID data, is transmitted to a web service for storage in a database, as illustrated in figure 1 (Manisha & Jagadeeshwar, 2023). This enables the achievement of real-time product traceability and ensures the safety and quality of the products across the entire supply chain.

Various technologies have been employed in the past to track products throughout the supply chain, including Radio Frequency Identification Devices (RFID), Barcode readers, isotopic technologies, and firm-specific traceability mechanisms (Figure 4) (George et al., 2019).

By integrating food traceability into logistics management, it becomes evident that the safety and quality of food are closely intertwined with effective logistics operations (Behnke & Janssen, 2020). This enhances consumer confidence by providing detailed information about the origin, production processes, and supply chain journey of the food, enabling consumers to make informed choices and ensuring accountability throughout the value chain.

Figure 4. Block diagram of the food traceability system
(Manisha & Jagadeeshwar, 2023)

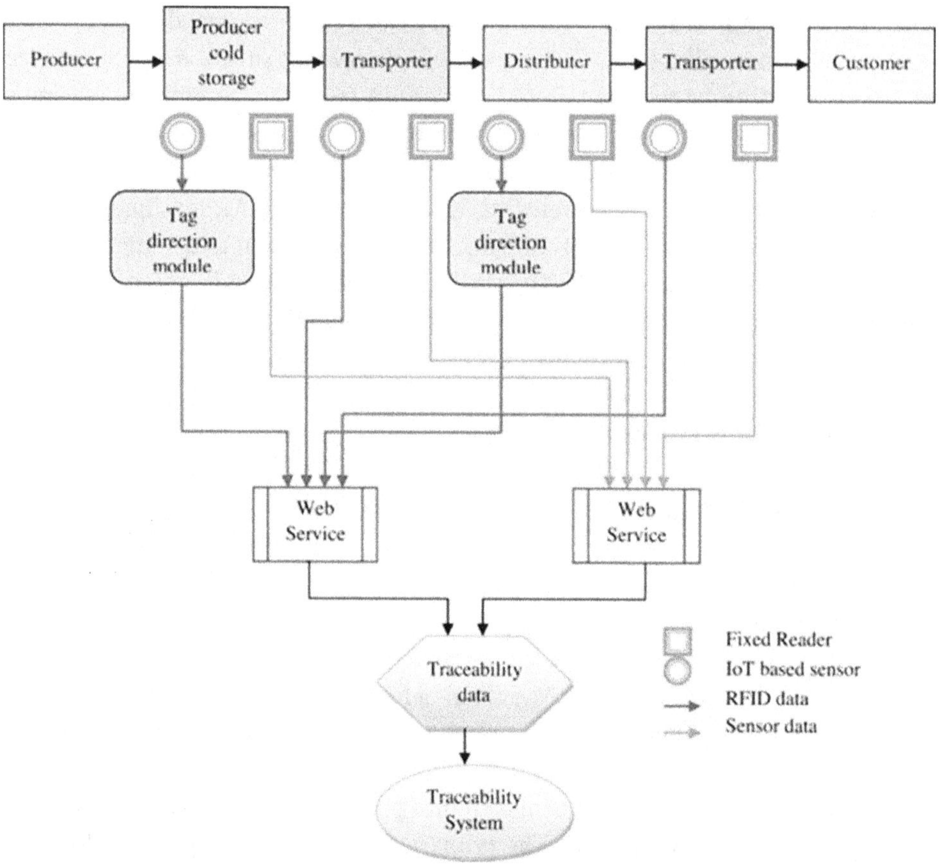

- **Demand Forecasting and Inventory Management**

Accurate demand forecasting and efficient inventory management are crucial for preventing food shortages and reducing waste. ML and AI algorithms can analyze historical sales data, consumer behavior patterns, and external factors such as weather conditions and economic indicators to predict future demand with greater accuracy. These predictions can inform decisions related to planting schedules, procurement, and production planning. By optimizing inventory levels and reducing overstocking or understocking, food producers and retailers can minimize waste, improve profitability, and meet consumer demands more effectively. Additionally, AI-driven systems can dynamically adjust production schedules and distribution plans based on real-time demand signals, further improving supply chain efficiency.

CONCLUSION

This chapter explored the concept of "industry 5.0", and examined its effectiveness referring to agri-food products in the modern digital era incorporating AI, IoT, ML, and other Industry 5.0 technologies.. The primary benefits of implementing the concept of Food industry 5.0 include improved food quality and safety, decreased food waste, and reduced environmental impact, thereby contributing to a more sustainable food industry.

ML, AI, and IoT enable precise data-driven decision-making, facilitating the optimization of agricultural practices, resource utilization, and crop yield predictions. Through precision farming, smart irrigation systems, and livestock monitoring, these technologies enhance efficiency and sustainability while minimizing waste.

On the other hand, the integration of ML, AI, and IoT in supply chain management not only enhances operational efficiency but also improves transparency, traceability, and food safety. These technologies enable stakeholders to make data-driven decisions, streamline processes, and respond swiftly to changing market dynamics. However, it is essential to address challenges such as data interoperability, privacy, and cybersecurity to ensure the secure and reliable implementation of these solutions.

The interconnected nature of Industry 5.0 technologies fosters a comprehensive and holistic approach to food security. Collaborative research, policy interventions, and education are essential for responsible adoption and equitable access to these technologies, ensuring their benefits reach all regions and stakeholders.

In short, Industry 5.0 concepts, combined with the power of ML, AI, and IoT, offer a promising path towards a better future, where food security is assured, and the prosperity of communities is enhanced worldwide. It is essential for governments, businesses, and civil society to join hands and actively contribute to this transformative journey, ensuring that the potential of these technologies is harnessed responsibly and ethically for the greater good of humanity.

REFERENCES

Agarwal, S., Hiran, D., Kothari, H., & Singh, S. (2023). LEVERAGING DATA PROCESSING FOR OPTIMIZING ORGANIC FARMING PRACTICES. *Journal of Data Acquisition and Processing*, *38*(2), 3243.

Ainsworth, E. A., Lemonnier, P., & Wedow, J. M. (2020). The influence of rising tropospheric carbon dioxide and ozone on plant productivity. *Plant Biology*, *22*(S1), 5–11. doi:10.1111/plb.12973 PMID:30734441

Akhter, R, & Sofi, A. (2022). Precision agriculture using IoT data analytics and machine learning. *Journal of King Saud University - Computer and Information Sciences, 34*(8), 5602-5618.

Alam, M. Z., Carpenter-Boggs, L., Mitra, S., Haque, M. M., Halsey, J., Rokonuzzaman, M., Saha, B., & Moniruzzaman, M. (2017). Effect of salinity intrusion on food crops, livestock, and fish species at Kalapara Coastal Belt in Bangladesh. *Journal of Food Quality*, *2017*, 2017. doi:10.1155/2017/2045157

Asseng, S., Foster, I. A. N., & Turner, N. C. (2011). The impact of temperature variability on wheat yields. *Global Change Biology*, *17*(2), 997–1012. doi:10.1111/j.1365-2486.2010.02262.x

Augustine, D. J., Blumenthal, D. M., Springer, T. L., LeCain, D. R., Gunter, S. A., & Derner, J. D. (2018). Elevated CO 2 induces substantial and persistent declines in forage quality irrespective of warming in mixedgrass prairie. *Ecological Applications*, *28*(3), 721–735. doi:10.1002/eap.1680 PMID:29297964

Banerjee, G., Sarkar, U., Das, S., & Ghosh, I. (2018). Artificial Intelligence in Agriculture: A Literature Survey. *International Journal of Scientific Research in Computer Science Applications and Management Studies*, *7*(3), 1–6.

Barbosa, M. W. (2021). Uncovering research streams on agri-food supply chain management : A bibliometric study. *Global Food Security*, *28*(April 2020), 100517.

Behnke, K., & Janssen, M. F. W. H. A. (2020). Boundary conditions for traceability in food supply chains using blockchain technology. *International Journal of Information Management*, *52*, 101969. doi:10.1016/j.ijinfomgt.2019.05.025

Bentalha, B., Hmioui, A., & Alla, L. (2019). The digitalization of the supply chain management of service companies: a prospective approach. In *Proceedings of the 4th International Conference on Smart City Applications* (pp. 1-8). ACM. 10.1145/3368756.3369005

Beven, K. (2013). *NERC Final Report: The Catchment Change Network Knowledge Exchange Project*. NERC.

Bhimavarapu, U., Battineni, G., & Chintalapudi, N. (2023). Improved optimization algorithm in LSTM to predict crop yield. *Computers*, *12*(1), 10. doi:10.3390/computers12010010

Bren d'Amour, C., Reitsma, F., Baiocchi, G., Barthel, S., Güneralp, B., Erb, K. H., Haberl, H., Creutzig, F., & Seto, K. C. (2017). Future urban land expansion and implications for global croplands. *Proceedings of the National Academy of Sciences of the United States of America*, *114*(34), 8939–8944. doi:10.1073/pnas.1606036114 PMID:28028219

Campbell, B. M., Vermeulen, S. J., Aggarwal, P. K., Corner-Dolloff, C., Girvetz, E., Loboguerrero, A. M., Ramirez-Villegas, J., Rosenstock, T., Sebastian, L., Thornton, P. K., & Wollenberg, E. (2016). Reducing risks to food security from climate change. *Global Food Security*, *11*, 34–43. doi:10.1016/j.gfs.2016.06.002

Challinor, A., Martre, P., Asseng, S., Thornton, P., & Ewert, F. (2014). Making the most of climate impacts ensembles. *Nature Climate Change*, *4*(2), 77–80. doi:10.1038/nclimate2117

Collodi, J., & M'Cormack, F. (2009). Population growth, environment and food security: What does the future hold. *Horizon: Future Issues for Development.*

Conceição, P., Fuentes-Nieva, R., Horn-Phathanothai, L., & Ngororano, A. (2011). Food security and human development in Africa: Strategic considerations and directions for further research. *African Development Review*, *23*(2), 237–246. doi:10.1111/j.1467-8268.2011.00283.x

Crowe, M. A., Hostens, M., & Opsomer, G. (2018). Gestion de la reproduction chez les vaches laitières - L'avenir. *Irish Veterinary Journal*, *71*(1).

Dabone, C., Mbagwu, I., Muray, M., Ubangha, L., Kohoun, B., Etowa, E., & Etowa, J. (2021). Global food insecurity and African, Caribbean, and Black (ACB) populations during the COVID-19 pandemic: A rapid review. *Journal of Racial and Ethnic Health Disparities*, 1–16. PMID:33559109 de Carvalho, M. I., Relvas, S., & Barbosa-Póvoa, A. P. (2022). A roadmap for sustainability performance assessment in the context of Agri-Food Supply Chain. *Sustainable Production and Consumption*, *34*, 565–585. doi:10.1016/j.spc.2022.10.001

Dwivedi, Y. K., Hughes, L., Ismagilova, E., Aarts, G., Coombs, C., Crick, T., Duan, Y., Dwivedi, R., Edwards, J., Eirug, A., Galanos, V., Ilavarasan, P. V., Janssen, M., Jones, P., Kar, A. K., Kizgin, H., Kronemann, B., Lal, B., Lucini, B., & Williams, M. D. (2021). Artificial Intelligence (AI): Multidisciplinary perspectives on emerging challenges, opportunities, and agenda for research, practice and policy. *International Journal of Information Management*, *57*, 101994. doi:10.1016/j.ijinfomgt.2019.08.002

Edreira, J. I. R., Guilpart, N., Sadras, V., Cassman, K. G., van Ittersum, M. K., Schils, R. L., & Grassini, P. (2018). Water productivity of rainfed maize and wheat: A local to global perspective. *Agricultural and Forest Meteorology*, *259*, 364–373. doi:10.1016/j.agrformet.2018.05.019 PMID:30224833

Field, C. B. (2014). Impacts, adaptation and vulnerability: Working Group II contribution to the fifth assessment report of the Intergovernmental Panel on Climate Change. *Climatic Change*.

Foley, J. A., Ramankutty, N., Brauman, K. A., Cassidy, E. S., Gerber, J. S., Johnston, M., Mueller, N. D., O'Connell, C., Ray, D. K., West, P. C., Balzer, C., Bennett, E. M., Carpenter, S. R., Hill, J., Monfreda, C., Polasky, S., Rockström, J., Sheehan, J., Siebert, S., & Zaks, D. P. (2011). Solutions for a cultivated planet. *Nature*, *478*(7369), 337–342. doi:10.1038/nature10452 PMID:21993620

George, R. V., Harsh, H. O., Ray, P., & Babu, A. K. (2019). Food quality traceability prototype for restaurants using blockchain and food quality data index. *Journal of Cleaner Production*, *240*, 118021. doi:10.1016/j.jclepro.2019.118021

Godde, C. M., Boone, R. B., Ash, A. J., Waha, K., Sloat, L. L., Thornton, P. K., & Herrero, M. (2020). Global rangeland production systems and livelihoods at threat under climate change and variability. *Environmental Research Letters*, *15*(4), 044021. doi:10.1088/1748-9326/ab7395

Gupta, D., Gujre, N., Singha, S., & Mitra, S. (2022). Role of existing and emerging technologies in advancing climate-smart agriculture through modeling: A review. *Ecological Informatics*, *71*, 101805. doi:10.1016/j.ecoinf.2022.101805

Heal, G., & Millner, A. (2014). Reflections: Uncertainty and decision making in climate change economics. *Review of Environmental Economics and Policy*, *8*(1), 120–137. doi:10.1093/reep/ret023

Herrero, M., Addison, J., Bedelian, C., Carabine, E., Havlík, P., Henderson, B., Van De Steeg, S. J., & Thornton, P. K. (2016). Climate change and pastoralism: Impacts, consequences and adaptation. *Revue Scientifique et Technique (International Office of Epizootics)*, *35*(2), 417–433. doi:10.20506/rst.35.2.2533 PMID:27917982

Kamble, S. S., Gunasekaran, A., & Gawankar, S. A. (2018). Sustainable Industry 4.0 framework: A systematic literature review identifying the current trends and future perspectives. *Process Safety and Environmental Protection*, *117*, 408–425. doi:10.1016/j.psep.2018.05.009

Knight, A. T., Cowling, R. M., Rouget, M., Balmford, A., Lombard, A. T., & Campbell, B. M. (2008). Knowing but not doing: Selecting priority conservation areas and the research–implementation gap. *Conservation Biology*, *22*(3), 610–617. doi:10.1111/j.1523-1739.2008.00914.x PMID:18477033

Leng, J., Sha, W., Wang, B., Zheng, P., Zhuang, C., Liu, Q., Wuest, T., Mourtzis, D., & Wang, L. (2022). Industry 5.0: Prospect and retrospect. *Journal of Manufacturing Systems*, *65*, 279–295. doi:10.1016/j.jmsy.2022.09.017

Lobell, D. B., Bänziger, M., Magorokosho, C., & Vivek, B. (2011). Nonlinear heat effects on African maize as evidenced by historical yield trials. *Nature Climate Change*, *1*(1), 42–45. doi:10.1038/nclimate1043

Loladze, I. (2014). Hidden shift of the ionome of plants exposed to elevated CO2 depletes minerals at the base of human nutrition. *elife*, *3*, e02245.

Manisha, N., & Jagadeeshwar, M. (2023). BC driven IoT-based food quality traceability system for dairy product using deep learning model. *High-Confidence Computing*, *3*(3), 100121. doi:10.1016/j.hcc.2023.100121

Mc Carthy, U., Uysal, I., Badia-Melis, R., Mercier, S., O'Donnell, C., & Ktenioudaki, A. (2018). Global food security–Issues, challenges and technological solutions. *Trends in Food Science & Technology*, *77*, 11–20. doi:10.1016/j.tifs.2018.05.002

Meerburg, B. G., Verhagen, A., Jongschaap, R. E. E., Franke, A. C., Schaap, B. F., Dueck, T. A., & Van Der Werf, A. (2009). Do nonlinear temperature effects indicate severe damages to US crop yields under climate change? *Proceedings of the National Academy of Sciences of the United States of America*, *106*(43), E120–E120. doi:10.1073/pnas.0910618106 PMID:19850868

Mirón, I. J., Linares, C., & Díaz, J. (2023). The influence of climate change on food production and food safety. *Environmental Research*, *216*, 114674. doi:10.1016/j.envres.2022.114674 PMID:36341795

Mishra, S., & Sharma, S. K. (2023). Advanced contribution of IoT in agricultural production for the development of smart livestock environments. *Internet of Things*, *22*, 100724. doi:10.1016/j.iot.2023.100724

Misra, N. N., Dixit, Y., Al-Mallahi, A., Bhullar, M. S., Upadhyay, R., & Martynenko, A. (2020). IoT, big data, and artificial intelligence in agriculture and food industry. *IEEE Internet of Things Journal*, *9*(9), 6305–6324. doi:10.1109/JIOT.2020.2998584

Mitchell, J., & Guile, D. (2021). Fusion skills and industry 5.0: conceptions and challenges. In *Insights Into Global Engineering Education After the Birth of Industry 5.0*. IntechOpen.

Munir, M. S., Bajwa, I. S., Ashraf, A., Anwar, W., & Rashid, R. (2021). Intelligent and smart irrigation system using edge computing and IoT. *Complexity*, *2021*, 1–16. doi:10.1155/2021/6691571

Nara, E. O. B., da Costa, M. B., Baierle, I. C., Schaefer, J. L., Benitez, G. B., do Santos, L. M. A. L., & Benitez, L. B. (2021). Expected impact of industry 4.0 technologies on sustainable development: A study in the context of Brazil's plastic industry. *Sustainable Production and Consumption*, *25*, 102–122. doi:10.1016/j.spc.2020.07.018

Nicastro, R., & Carillo, P. (2021). Food Loss and Waste Prevention Strategies from Farm to Fork. *Sustainability (Basel)*, *13*(10), 5443. doi:10.3390u13105443

Patel, A. S., Brahmbhatt, M. N., Bariya, A. R., Nayak, J. B., & Singh, V. K. (2023). Blockchain technology in food safety and traceability concern to livestock products. *Heliyon*, *9*(6), e16526. doi:10.1016/j.heliyon.2023.e16526 PMID:37265625

Porter, J. R., Xie, L., Challinor, A. J., Cochrane, K., Howden, S. M., Iqbal, M. M., & Travasso, M. I. (2014). *Food security and food production systems.*

Pretty, J. (2018). Intensification for redesigned and sustainable agricultural systems. *Science, 362*(6417), eaav0294. doi:10.1126cience.aav0294 PMID:30467142

Raj, E. F. I., Appadurai, M., & Athiappan, K. (2022). Precision farming in modern agriculture. In *Smart Agriculture Automation Using Advanced Technologies: Data Analytics and Machine Learning, Cloud Architecture, Automation and IoT* (pp. 61–87). Springer Singapore.

Rajkumar, M. N., Abinaya, S., & Kumar, V. V. (2017, March). Intelligent irrigation system—An IOT based approach. In *2017 International Conference on Innovations in Green Energy and Healthcare Technologies (IGEHT)* (pp. 1-5). IEEE.

Ramankutty, N., Mehrabi, Z., Waha, K., Jarvis, L., Kremen, C., Herrero, M., & Rieseberg, L. H. (2018). Trends in global agricultural land use: Implications for environmental health and food security. *Annual Review of Plant Biology, 69*(1), 789–815. doi:10.1146/annurev-arplant-042817-040256 PMID:29489395

Ritchie, H., Roser, M., & Rosado, P. (2020). CO_2 and greenhouse gas emissions. *Our world in data.*

Salam, A., & Salam, A. (2020). Internet of things in agricultural innovation and security. *Internet of Things for Sustainable Community Development: Wireless Communications. Sensory Systems*, 71–112.

Shaikh, T. A., Rasool, T., & Lone, F. R. (2022). Towards leveraging the role of machine learning and artificial intelligence in precision agriculture and smart farming. *Computers and Electronics in Agriculture, 198*, 107119. doi:10.1016/j.compag.2022.107119

Sharifnasab, H., Mahrokh, A., Dehghanisanij, H., Łazuka, E., Łagód, G., & Karami, H. (2023). Evaluating the use of intelligent irrigation systems based on the IoT in grain corn irrigation. *Water (Basel), 15*(7), 1394. doi:10.3390/w15071394

Shi, P., Li, P., Li, Z., Sun, J., Wang, D., & Min, Z. (2022). Effects of grass vegetation coverage and position on runoff and sediment yields on the slope of Loess Plateau, China. *Agricultural Water Management, 259*, 107231. doi:10.1016/j.agwat.2021.107231

Sibanyoni, J. J., & Tabit, F. T. (2019). An assessment of the hygiene status and incidence of foodborne pathogens on food contact surfaces in the food preparation facilities of schools. *Food Control, 98*, 94–99. doi:10.1016/j.foodcont.2018.11.009

Singh, A. K., Zhu, X., Chen, C., Wu, J., Yang, B., Zakari, S., Jiang, X. J., Singh, N., & Liu, W. (2022). The role of glomalin in mitigation of multiple soil degradation problems. *Critical Reviews in Environmental Science and Technology, 52*(9), 1604–1638. doi:10.1080/10643389.2020.1862561

Sunitha, G., Pushpalatha, M. N., Parkavi, A., Boyapati, P., Walia, R., Kohar, R., & Qureshi, K. (2022). Modeling of chaotic political optimizer for crop yield prediction. *Intelligent Automation and Soft Computing, 34*(1), 423–437. doi:10.32604/iasc.2022.024757

Suweis, S., Carr, J. A., Maritan, A., Rinaldo, A., & D'Odorico, P. (2015). Resilience and reactivity of global food security. *Proceedings of the National Academy of Sciences of the United States of America, 112*(22), 6902–6907. doi:10.1073/pnas.1507366112 PMID:25964361

Tajul Baharuddin, M. F., Taib, S., Hashim, R., Abidin, M. H. Z., & Rahman, N. I. (2013). Assessment of seawater intrusion to the agricultural sustainability at the coastal area of Carey Island, Selangor, Malaysia. *Arabian Journal of Geosciences*, *6*(10), 3909–3928. doi:10.100712517-012-0651-1

Tan, R., Zhang, T., Liu, D., & Xu, H. (2021). How will innovation-driven development policy affect sustainable urban land use: Evidence from 230 Chinese cities. *Sustainable Cities and Society*, *72*, 103021. doi:10.1016/j.scs.2021.103021

Tsang, Y. P., Yang, T., Chen, Z. S., Wu, C. H., & Tan, K. H. (2022). How is extended reality bridging human and cyber-physical systems in the IoT-empowered logistics and supply chain management? *Internet of Things*, *20*, 100623. doi:10.1016/j.iot.2022.100623

Tsouros, D. C., Bibi, S., & Sarigiannidis, P. G. (2019). A review on UAV-based applications for precision agriculture. *Information (Basel)*, *10*(11), 349. doi:10.3390/info10110349

Verdouw, C. N., Wolfert, J., Beulens, A. J. M., & Rialland, A. (2016). Virtualization of food supply chains with the internet of things. *Journal of Food Engineering*, *176*, 128–136. doi:10.1016/j.jfoodeng.2015.11.009

Weaver, C. P., Lempert, R. J., Brown, C., Hall, J. A., Revell, D., & Sarewitz, D. (2013). Improving the contribution of climate model information to decision making: The value and demands of robust decision frameworks. *Wiley Interdisciplinary Reviews: Climate Change*, *4*(1), 39–60. doi:10.1002/wcc.202

Wei, Z., Alam, T., Al Sulaie, S., Bouye, M., Deebani, W., & Song, M. (2023). An efficient IoT-based perspective view of food traceability supply chain using optimized classifier algorithm. *Information Processing & Management*, *60*(3), 103275. doi:10.1016/j.ipm.2023.103275

WHIG, P. (2023). Leveraging AI for Sustainable Agriculture: Opportunities and Challenges. *Transactions on Latest Trends in Artificial Intelligence, 4*(4).

World Health Organization. (2022). *UN Report: Global hunger numbers rose to as many as 828 million in 2021.* WHO.

Xu, G., Dong, T., Cobbinah, P. B., Jiao, L., Sumari, N. S., Chai, B., & Liu, Y. (2019). Urban expansion and form changes across African cities with a global outlook: Spatiotemporal analysis of urban land densities. *Journal of Cleaner Production*, *224*, 802–810. doi:10.1016/j.jclepro.2019.03.276

Yansui, L., Xiaoyu, Z., Yongsheng, W., Zhi, C., Yuheng, L., Wenhao, W., ... & Rui, L. (2018). Land consolidation engineering and modern agriculture: A case study from soil particles to agricultural systems.

Zeppel, M. J. B., Wilks, J. V., & Lewis, J. D. (2014). Impacts of extreme precipitation and seasonal changes in precipitation on plants. *Biogeosciences*, *11*(11), 3083–3093. doi:10.5194/bg-11-3083-2014

KEY TERMS AND DEFINITIONS

Artificial Intelligence: AI involves replicating or imitating human intelligence in machines through programming them to think and learn like humans. It encompasses designing intelligent systems capable of tasks like recognizing speech, making decisions, solving problems, and translating languages. The goal of AI is to develop machines that can understand their surroundings, interpret data, and make informed decisions or take actions accordingly. The ultimate aim is to enhance efficiency, precision, and productivity in diverse fields by replicating or enhancing human cognitive abilities.

Food Supply Chains: Food supply chains can be defined as the intricate system of interconnected activities, procedures, and assets that are responsible for facilitating the movement of food items from their origin to the end consumer. This encompassing process includes multiple stages like cultivation, processing, packaging, transportation, storage, and distribution. The main objective of food supply chains is to guarantee a continuous and effective stream of food from producers to consumers, while upholding standards of quality, safety, and sustainability at every step of the journey.

Industry 5.0: Industry 5.0 is a term used to describe the upcoming stage of industrial advancement subsequent to industry 4.0. It involves the incorporation of cutting-edge technologies like artificial intelligence, robotics, internet of things (IoT), and automation, emphasizing the collaboration between humans and machines in the manufacturing realm. The primary goal is to establish a production environment that is both centered around humans and sustainable. This entails merging human strengths such as creativity, problem-solving skills, and intuition with the rapidity, precision, and scalability offered by advanced technologies.

Information and Communication Technologies: ICT is a broad term referring to a variety of technologies that facilitate the handling of data and information. It encompasses a diverse range of hardware, software, networks, and digital services that enable the creation, storage, transmission, manipulation, sharing, and exchange of data and communication.

Internet of Things: IoT pertains to a system where physical objects such as devices, vehicles, and appliances are equipped with sensors, software, and internet connectivity. This allows them to gather and share data over the internet. By bridging the gap between the physical and digital realms, the IoT enables more advanced surveillance, management, and automation of a wide range of activities and operations.

Machine Learning: ML, a branch of artificial intelligence, centers on empowering computers to learn and make decisions autonomously without direct programming. It entails creating algorithms that enable machines to analyze and understand data, recognize patterns and correlations, and enhance their capabilities through accumulated experience.

Chapter 8
Introducing On-Demand Internet Business Model in the Informal Public Transportation System in Developing Countries

Kamal Kant Hiran
Symbiosis University of Applied Sciences, India

Ruchi Doshi
https://orcid.org/0000-0002-7259-8481
Azteca University, Mexico

Maad M. Mijwil
https://orcid.org/0000-0002-2884-2504
Baghdad College of Economic Sciences University, Iraq

ABSTRACT

Paratransit transport drives the transport system in most emerging nations. It is essential to urban and rural movement. The informal transport system carries most people and is often more accessible, faster, ubiquitous, cheaper, and reliable, but it has also become environmentally unclean, rickety, unsafe, and oversupplied, causing traffic congestion, especially in cities. Due to their informal nature, informal public transport system improvements have failed. The research studied the possibility of bringing the on-demand internet business model to informal public transportation using Accra's paratransit as a case study. The report evaluated the unique nature, characteristics, potential and problems of the informal public transport eco-system and advocated activities that will meet the socio-economic and travel demands of all parties of the two-sided platform. Thus, adopting the on-demand internet business model in the informal public transport sector will not only address the paratransit service's supply-demand mismatch but also significantly reduce traffic congestion.

DOI: 10.4018/979-8-3693-0225-5.ch008

1.0 INTRODUCTION

Being able to move freely and at any time within the city is fundamental to a city's liveability and productivity. In cities where the people cannot move easily around to access basic goods and services and are caught in perpetual cycle of crippling traffic congestion and weak public transport systems undermine the smart city concept of connectivity.

Most developing countries are reeling under the weight of the menace of informal public transport system i.e. paratransit. These Informal public transport (IPT) services made up of mini-vans, station wagons, taxis, and motorcycles ply their trade in almost every part of the country in developing countries. It is now known that building roads is not enough to wholly address the mobility challenges in the cities (2016).

The conventional approach in addressing the transportation challenges in developing countries had been to construct and expand roads for movement of cars and goods with little focus on how people travel. The mobility challenges in the city are further compounded by the proliferation of the informal transportation system or the paratransit system (mini-van popularly known in Ghana as "Tro-tro") operators.

Although the Informal public transport, provide some important benefits to the society, such as on-demand access to medical clinics, jobs for low-skilled immigrant workers, and service coverage in areas without formal transportation (Cervero & Golub, 2011), they have become a major source of challenges such as heavy traffic, suffocating pollution of the air and noise and accidents that tend to derail and mitigate the efforts of city managers in modernizing their cities.

The Informal Public Transport (IPT) is characterized by low quality and over-supply of vehicles, low performance, poorly regulated and chaotic management. The extreme difficulty in bringing the Informal public transport under control in most developing countries and the lack of understanding of their cost-benefit nature have made some local authorities to give up in trying to do anything about them. However, considering the enormous contribution of the paratransit system to most economies of developing countries, it is imperative that every effort is made to maximize the positive externalities of their effects.

Virtually in all developing countries, the Informal public transport system account for a high disproportionate mode of travel compared to the formal public transportation system (Kashi & Carello, 2020). In the light of this, several attempts have been made (and continue to make) by governments and municipal city managers to address the menace created by the IPT. While some tackle this problem by banning and outlawing them, others have introduced regulations, laws, and new ways (technology based) with the view to formalizing and integrating their operations into the existing transportation system.

The Internet (Meera et al., 2019) has been recognised as one of the effective means in tackling urban mobility challenges globally (Lakhwani, Gianey, Wireko, & Hiran, 2020). Several studies conducted in recent times have shown how the Internet has had on the travel planning behaviour of people and hence has become a tool in addressing mobility and transportation challenges in the ever growing and expanding cities. (Andersson et al., 2018).

Moreover, few studies have been carried out on the enabling capability of the Internet in leveraging the operations and performance of the Informal Public Transportation (IPT) system especially in developing countries into the formal transportation space. Specifically, there are very few studies on how the Internet (Priyadarshi et al., 2021; Wireko et al., 2018) can be used to resolve the over-supply side of the informal public transport system and thereby creating traffic congestion and pollution and have subsequently become major socio-economic problems for many governments.

This study aims to fill this gap as it attempts to explore and analyze the potential application of the "on-demand business" model, which is based on the enabling capability of Internet (Aluvalu, 2020; Lakhwani, Gianey, Wireko, & Hiran, 2020) access in addressing the challenges posed by the Informal Public Transportation system in developing countries.

In terms of research methodology, an exploratory approach based on a case study where the peculiar nature and characteristics of the Informal public transport system is reviewed and examined with the view to understanding their unique operations and how the various policy approaches to regulate them continue to fail as they ply their trade.

Finally, a conceptual idea and mapping are proposed on how the on-demand business model could be applied to the Informal public transport sector that will make it acceptable, responsive, and also resonate with the socio-economic lifestyle of the people (Meera et al., 2019).

2.0 LITERATURE REVIEW AND THEORETICAL FRAMEWORK

2.1 Internet as Resource Enabler in Demand Driven Transportation System

The travel decision making process concept, a subset of the theory of planned behaviour (TPB) assumes that before one travels, there is pre-planned decision or activities that are considered before the actual travel (Durand et al., 2018) (Ajzen, 2002). For example, in deciding to go to the central business district (CBD) to purchase groceries, one may either deliberately or unconsciously think about the mode of travel such as; to walk, take taxi, ride a bicycle, take a bus, minivan etc. and that the choice of any of the alternative route may also be subjected to approval or influenced by your sphere of influence such as friends, family members, boss, pastors etc.(Kaewkluengklom et al., 2017).

In effect, the modal choices that we make may be influenced by the experiences of our referents' group with any of the modes. If their experiences with a particular modal choice is good, they may recommend to us and if negative, then they will talk us out of it. However, given the fact that the decision to travel is usually taken extemporaneously especially with regards to short travel within the cities, access to information to make informed decision becomes crucial. It is therefore not always the case or feasible that one may readily have access to the input from one's referent group and therefore access to the Internet for further information becomes important and relevant.

The relevance of the Internet in decision making process is not new. In a study of the transportation issues in four European cities; Copenhagen, Gothenburg, Amsterdam and Barcelona, Forward (2004), found that residents successfully predicted their intention to walk, bike and drive in the city based on the Internet (Verma & Chandra, 2017). Thus, the role and the new opportunities that the Internet provides has profound implications on the value of travel time (quality) and consequently how it influences future travel demands.

Such impact is expected to be high and noticeable in the cities especially on public transport. The shift in the use of ICT in travel may lead to an increase of peoples' preferences for public transport as well as increase in additional trips with traffic congestion and mobility challenges moderated by the Internet. The Smart city and smart mobility approaches are new paradigm shift that allow seamless, efficient, more flexible and convenience to travel across multi-modal transport systems (Hessel, 2015; Jha et al., 2021).

2.2 The Two-Sided Internet Platform and the Informal Public Transportation (IPT) System

With the advent of the Internet, there has been proliferation of the development of a new business model to monetize ideas in online markets (Cheng et al., 2019). Considered as Internet Intermediaries, two-sided Internet platforms have become resource integrators involved in the co-creation of value added services (Frieden, 2019).

Typically, successful two-sided Intermediary player can serve significant number of the market or consumer segment without having to install and operate the needed infrastructure such as say in the case of an Internet based business, the broadband networks like switches, routers etc. This type of business model produces what economist term "positive networking externalities" as more people join the network, its "overall value formation in the network and its ability to generate consumer benefits grows" (Odlyzko & Tilly, 2005; Muzellec et al., 2015).

The role and importance of the informal public transport (paratransit) to the economy of developing Countries can be likened to a two-sided knife. While on one end it contributes significantly to wellbeing of the citizen, it also has the potential to cause significant harm to both the economy and the individual persons. From being erratic in its scheduling, to a rickety and dilapidated vehicle body, IPTs have become a necessary evil and an inextricable part of the people in developing countries, there is the need to ensure that its benefits are maximized for good user experience and convenience.

To this end, several attempts have been made by successive governments and municipal managers (city administrators) in the past to bring the paratransit operators into the formal public space but with little success (Cervero & Golub, 2011; Kashi & Carello, 2020). It is therefore the view of this author that a much different approach; one that is based on technology using the "two-sided Internet platform" model or concept be used to address the IPT challenges (Matthias Weber et al., 2014; Chavhan et al., 2020).

Although the idea of introducing the current state of the operations of the paratransit to technology may seem far-fetched with an unrealistic timeline and expectations, there are some pointers and signs that when attention is paid could become a catalyst to change the game plan (SSATP, 2018).

The Uber business model, also known as the "On demand Economy" is one that may have a lot of opportunities and learning curve for the IPT (Trotro) service in the formal economy. As a result, understanding Uber's on-demand business model is critical for conceptualising an on-demand business concept of your own.

The other on-demand operators such as Bolt, Django in the transport industry and Airbnb, booking.com etc in the accommodation and hospitality industry are all new businesses that are enabled by the Internet technology. For the purposes of this paper, a brief overview of Uber's on-demand business model is presented as backdrop in appreciating how such a model can be used to modernize and make the informal transport system become responsive and efficient and demand driven.

2.3 The Smart City Concept and the Informal Public Transportation System

Smart Cities can be defined in a variety of ways. Wider definitions include socio-economic and governance aspects as well as multi-stakeholder aspects, such as the use of social participation to improve sustainability, quality of life, and urban welfare. Intelligent Governance, Intelligent Living, Intelligent Economy, Intelligent Environment, Intelligent Mobility, and Intelligent People are all part of the Smart

Figure 1. Characteristics vs. description of smart cities

Characteristic	Description
Smart Governance	By Smart Governance we mean joined up within-city and across-city governance, including services and interactions which link and, where relevant, integrate public, private, civil and European Community organizations so the city can function efficiently and effectively as one organism. The main enabling tool to achieve this is ICT (infrastructures, hardware, and software), enabled by smart processes and interoperability and fueled by data.
Smart Economy	By Smart Economy we mean e-business and e-commerce, increased productivity, ICT-enabled and advanced manufacturing and delivery of services, ICT-enabled innovation, as well as new products, new services, and business models. It also establishes smart clusters and eco-systems (e.g. digital business and entrepreneurship).
Smart Mobility	By Smart Mobility we mean ICT supported and integrated transport and logistics systems. For example, sustainable, safe and interconnected transportation systems can encompass trams, buses, trains, metros, cars, cycles and pedestrians in situations using one or more modes of transport. Smart Mobility prioritizes clean and often non-motorized options. Relevant and real-time information can be accessed by the public in order to save time and improve commuting efficiency, save costs and reduce CO2 emissions, as well as to network transport managers to improve services and provide feedback to citizens. Mobility system users might also provide their own real-time data or contribute to long-term planning.
Smart Environment	By smart environment we include smart energy including renewables, ICT-enabled energy grids, metering, pollution control and monitoring, renovation of buildings and amenities, green buildings, green urban planning, as well as resource use efficiency, re-use and resource substitution which serves the above goals. Urban services such as street lighting, waste management, drainage systems, and water resource systems that are monitored to evaluate the system, reduce pollution and improve water quality are also good examples.
Smart People	By Smart People we mean e-skills, working in ICT-enabled working, having access to education and training, human resources, and capacity management, within an inclusive society that improves creativity and fosters innovation. As a characteristic, it can also enable people and communities to themselves input, use, manipulate and personalize data, for example through appropriate data analytic tools and dashboards, to make decisions and create products and services.
Smart Living	By Smart Living we mean ICT-enabled lifestyles, behaviour and consumption. Smart Living is also healthy and safe living in a culturally vibrant city with diverse cultural facilities and incorporates good quality housing and accommodation. Smart Living is also linked to high levels of social cohesion and social capital.

Source: K. Archick, 2014

Cities concept. Their various features and descriptions have been well documented in table below by Archick (2014).

This research will adopt the definition of smart city by Archick (2014) as "In a multi-stakeholder, municipally based partnership, a city is looking to address public issues with ICT-based solutions."

The relevance of the Smart City concept to this research work is based on the Smart Mobility characteristics of the concept, which is largely permeated by ICT (Internet) used in both backward and forward technology and sustainable environments. The Smart City concept (which includes Smart mobility) is useful in explaining and addressing the issues of cities in transition from traditional to Smart (sustainable) communities. The Smart mobility approach is a new paradigm shift that allows seamless, efficient and more flexible and convenient (including shared and public) travel across multi-modal transport systems (Hessel, 2015).

Thus, the role and the new opportunities that the Internet provides has profound implications on the value of travel time and consequently how it may influence future travel demand. Such impact is expected to be high and noticeable in the cities especially on public transport. The shift in the use of ICT in travel may lead to an increase of peoples' preferences for public transport as well as increase additional trips with traffic congestion and mobility challenges moderated by the role of the Internet via the concept of the Smart Cities (Jha et al., 2021)

2.4 Overview of Uber On-Demand Business Model

Uber, originally known as Ubercab started (March 2009) as app only for hailing black luxury taxi car (cabs) in USA and now operates under the legal name of "Uber Technologies". Today, Uber is not just a hailing service, but has entrenched its operations in other areas such as on-demand food delivery (Uber Eat), on-demand trucking (Uber Freight). However, the flag ship (core) product of Uber is its ridesharing business model.

Connecting passengers and drivers is made possible by the Internet through Uber's digital aggregator app platform. Thus, through the Internet, "passengers" generate demand and "drivers" supply the demand while "Uber" acts as the intermediator or the facilitator that makes the transaction on a mobile device without a hitch.

As a result of its on-demand business model, Uber has been able to provide passengers and drivers with substantial benefits, all these being possible by means of the Internet technology.

Like a two-sided knife, while the on-demand business is efficient in delivering optimum satisfaction to the parties involved, it has at the same time created a disruption in the taxi/cab industry leading to many countries banning or being cautious and sceptical of Uber's operations in their economies (Lennon, 2019).

The value proposition for passengers includes on-demand car bookings (convenience), Real-time tracking, Accurate Estimated Time of Arrival (ETAs), Cashless payment or rides, lesser wait time. The gains to drivers include Flexibility (drive on their own terms as they can switch off/on the app as they wish), better income, get more rides by reducing your idling time, upfront payment for drivers (including surge dynamic pricing for drivers and multiple ride alternatives and better trip allocation which saves them fuel by not driving around looking for passengers. It is expected that the IPT service can benefit from this Uber on-demand business model experience when implemented appropriately.

In introducing the Internet (technology-based services) to the operations of the Informal Public Transport system, it is important to identify and evaluate the key characteristics and profile (including its management and the potential disruptive impact) that will make it successful (viable) or otherwise in the formal transportation space.

In doing so answers to the following key questions may be explored in understanding the underlying structures and fundamentals that influence the operations of IPTs in developing countries:

1. To what extent do the existing Informal Public transport help or hinder mobility in the city?
2. In what way can technology (Internet) be used to improve the operations and performance of the Informal Public Transport and bring them into the formal public transportation space?
3. Which aspects of the characteristics or nature of the Informal Public Transport can be adapted easily without significant disruption or inconvenience to travelers?
4. What form of operational model (Hybrid or full-scale digitization) will be appropriate (optimal) to ensure that the transition to the formal space is sustainable and viable?

2.5 The Characteristics and Nature of the Informal Public Transport in Accra (Ghana)

2.5.1 Over-Supply of Informal Public Transport in Accra

For many years and in fact from the post-colonial time, the city of Accra (2014) (and Ghana at large) has seen rapid growth both in human and vehicular population. In the city of Accra alone, there are approximately 6,000 minibuses plying within the city (Kashi & Carello, 2020; SSATP, 2017) Although the lure of owning one's car as a status symbol is driving many to acquire own vehicles, there are still equally a greater number of people who cannot afford to buy car even what is known as the "home-used" vehicles.

This means that majority of the people must travel by means of public transport. Meanwhile, due to the failure of successive governments and city authorities in providing the necessary fiscal, formal and institutional support and leadership in the formal public transport services, the small-scale transport

Figure 2. Types of informal public transport vehicles in Ghana

Types of Informal Public Transport Vehicles in Ghana					
Class	Routes	Schedules	Passenger Loading Capacity	Service Area/Coverage	Comments
Conventional Bus	Fixed	Fixed	25-60	Regional/Urban area	Plies mainly between the regional capitals/towns
MiniBus (Jitney)	Fixed	Semi-Fixed	12-24	Regional/Urban area	Plies mainly in Urban but sometimes Regional
Microbus	Fixed	Semi-Fixed	4-11	Urban Area	Plies mainly in Urban but sometimes to closest towns in the district
3-Wheeler/Motorcycle	Variable	Variable	1-4	Neighbourhood	Motor cycle more popular in Accra
Pedicab/Horse-cart	Variable	Variable	1-6	Neighbourhood	Commercially not available in Ghana

Adapted from Cervero and Golub, 2007

operators (informal public transport operators), popularly known as "Trotro" in Ghana have quickly and actively occupied the market space to meet the demand.

Consequently, the informal public transport service (Trotro) owned by individuals operate in every part of the city thereby filling and complementing the regular transit services especially in areas poorly served by formal transport operators.

Trotro operators in Accra and elsewhere in larger cities operate with an abundance of recklessness and typically noted for dangerously competing and fighting amongst themselves for customers as they would stop at every point on the way to board customers with impunity, a situation akin to an over-supply of products and services (Golub et al., 2009). They are known to engage in what economists call "collective damaging behaviour" due to the fact that they are too many on the streets competing for customers in order to survive (S. A. O, 2014; Travis Fried, 2019)

It is, however, ironical that with the over-supply and abundance of these minibuses, commuters still found themselves wanting regarding the quality and efficient transport service in the city. It appears there is minimal effort and incentive on the part of the Informal public transport operators to improve their service.

2.5.2 Demand Side of Informal Public Transport in Accra

The demand and the use of Informal public transport, specifically, Trotro appears to be insatiable and on the rise year-on-year even against the back drop of the rising prestige attached to status symbol and convenience of personal car ownership as well as the cost of cars becoming affordable to many Ghanaians (Kashi & Carello, 2020; Ababa et al., 2011). The manoeuvrability and the size of the minibuses (Trotro) make them a popular mode of transport in the cities.

Furthermore, the demand for Trotro is driven by the fact that these minibuses offer affordable and flexible transport option. A study conducted by the Accra Metropolitan Authority (Accra Mobility, 2015) put the share of the paratransit market at 86% of transportation service in the city (Travis Fried, 2019). This demand rate is not uncommon to the city of Accra as it is found in many African countries (Cervero & Golub, 2011).

The rationale behind the demand for Trotro follows the same ordinary demand function where consumers try to maximize their utility subject to budget constraint. In other-words, travellers will choose the best alternative routes bearing in mind the various constraints that might be imposed on their choice such as limited amount of money and time (Poku-Boansi & Adarkwa, 2014). Factors that affect the demand for the informal public transport include characteristics of commuters such as sex, age, education, income of passengers, service level, fares, population, employment status and trip duration (Balcombe, 2004).

In their study on the patronage of Trotro in the Kumasi metropolis using regression analysis to identify key driving variable for determining demand for Trotro service, Baonsi and Adarkwa (2014) identified population as the main independent variable (66.4%) contributing to the entire coefficient of multiple determination (R2) of the model. This means that variations in transport demand can be explained by variations in population of the traffic zones (trip duration was 10.1%, fares-9.4% and employment status-1%) (Poku-Boansi & Adarkwa, 2014). Thus, with the teeming population of Accra and the growing settlement at the fringes of the city, the need to commute to the central business district (CBD) becomes more paramount hence the demand for the Trotro service.

2.5.3 Performance of the Informal Public Transport in Accra

Typically, the paratransit transport operators have acquired as well as earned for itself unique characteristics that are symptomatic of a failed system or network. Over a very long time, Trotros have been known and described as erratic, unreliable, unregulated and to some extent designated as a poor man's mode of transportation.

Due to lack of planning, Trotro operators fight for passengers in the market space, engage in "cream skimming" modus operandi, lack accountability (very weak regulatory and enforcement framework), and users who rely on public transportation will be unable to influence change. They are likely to evade taxes and fees as most operators are undocumented. Their inefficient business practices and inadequate investment and insurance make them operate on low margins of profitability and thereby throwing them back into the "poverty cycle" of unattractiveness to formal funding and financial support to improve their operations.

The lack of capacity of the paratransit operators makes this sector perform poorly and have created the perception that "informal small vehicle paratransit, which operates outside the traditional regulated public transportation system, is typically seen as a bad thing" as part of the problem to modernizing cities in developing countries to a smart city status (Cervero & Golub, 2011).

2.5.4 Institutional, Organizational, and Regulatory Framework of the Informal Public Transport in Accra

Until quite recently, these informal transport services could operate, to a very large extent, without hinderance. Although they are now somehow organized especially at route level through unions, a lot of work needs to be done (Golub et al., 2009). The regulation of the Informal public transport service is going through a series of regimes. Majority of these Trotros are technically non-compliant and operate without the appropriate licenses and strict regulatory regime.

Most of the drivers are low skilled, young and in-migrants to the city creating an overabundance of idle labour, thus making the Informa public transport attractive to them. The physical state of the vehicles is also nothing to write home about. They are low performing, old and rickety with metal seats that are corroded and without foam covers (Ababa et al., 2011). Getting the defective ones out of road had become a nightmare and near impossible as most of these Trotros are owned by police officers (including some senior officers), personnel of the security agencies, tax administrators, politicians, pastors, public servants, and many other influential people in the society.

Even though, Trotro drivers appear to be out of control and unsanctioned and imply a disregard for legal precedent, does not mean that they are devoid of any kind of internal framework or organisation to integrate them into the formal system (Behrens et al., 2015). The operations of non-official modes of transportation (jitney) occur, to varying degrees, at two levels namely the internal and external.

The Internal ''self-regulation'' level takes the form of social norms, customs, and ''gentlemen agreements'' that tacitly govern behaviour especially through some form of self-initiated cooperative structures set up to provide internal oversight and control (Cervero & Golub, 2011). The Ghana Private Road Transport Union (GPRTU), which was established in 1967, serves as a federation for owners and operators of private commercial vehicles in Ghana, including the Trotro.

The organisation has a network of branches across the nation and is a member of the Ghana Trades Union Congress. The GPRTU primary function is to foresee the efficient management of the private road transport service in the country (Francis, 1997; Saini et al., 2021). In recent times, the GPRTU has grown to be a key player in the transportation industry and is providing revenue, services and employment and has a strong underlying administrative structure albeit still considered as informal. Their ubiquitous presence in every part of the country gives them a strong economic and political bargaining power.

Externally, the regulatory policy factor regarding the Trotro service revolves around the dealing with issues of traffic enforcement agents. The police motor and traffic department (MTD) must ensure that the Trotros comply with and meet the minimum basic operational vehicle, driver certificate, defensive driving, vehicle fitness test.

As a result, it violates these criteria that the police (MTD) inspect Trotros and determine an appropriate fine if either the driver or the vehicle lacks one of these. Due to the high numbers of Trotros on the road, the police are overwhelmed when it comes to the day-to-day control of their operations. This has led to the establishment of a self-regulated unit by the Trotro operators and in conjunction with some assistance and guidance from the MTD, help enforce the laws, especially the by-laws of the city authorities.

Notwithstanding, Trotro drivers have honed their skills to the point of recklessness in order to elude law enforcement including their own self-regulated agents to the extent that they have become a menace and pose a serious threat to both passengers and pedestrians. Thus, any regulation in favour of high-capacity transport modes will be resisted by existing IPT providers. To ensure compliance, acceptance, and full cooperation from existing IPT providers, regulation and support should be geared towards them in a way that will not make them feel crowded out.

Any approach must not be seen as reducing their significance and employment rate but give them hope and signs of improving opportunities within the IPT system. For example, existing drivers could be trained and recruited into the Accra Rapid Bus Transit (RBT) system when being setup to take the feed from the IPT. This will allow the IPT providers to be key stakeholders in the new "formal transportation" system and will go a long way in minimizing resistance.

Experiences from elsewhere (SSATP, 2018) have shown that the best way to improve the IPT services is for governments and municipal authorities to work in partnership with the IPT providers. Such approach could be in the form of combining regulation with access to finance (private finance), vehicle maintenance and improvement support and advisory services.

The goal will be to develop the IPT services to provide complementary transport feeder services from low density areas to higher capacity systems in denser areas. Attempts to dislodge or eliminate IPT by supporting the higher capacity transport service (RBT) at their expense have failed in many cities. The Accra Rapid Bus Transit service found itself in direct competition with the IPT instead of being complementary to each other leading to the rapid stalling of the service.

3.0 ON-DEMAND BUSINESS MODEL AND THE INFORMAL PUBLIC TRANSPORT IN ACCRA

The Tro-tro system in Accra could use an upgrade, according to the Accra Resilience Strategy. All public transportation, including Tro-tros, would have to comply with the project's registration, licencing, and quality standards. Investment packages for Tro-tro owners would also be provided to help them acquire newer vehicles that are safer and emit fewer carbon emissions (AMA 2019). Congestion can be reduced, safety can be improved, and carbon emissions can be reduced with this project.

The primary objective of introducing the on-demand business model to the Informal public transport system is to be able to maximize the positive externalities of Trotros to the economy by focusing on customer (Passenger) needs rather than on provider (supplier) needs.

The use of technology to intermediate the IPT space by way of the two-sided Internet (Aluvalu, 2020) platform has been identified as one of the best ways to organically make the Informal public transport sector smart mobility compliant (Hessel, 2015) Leveraging technology to solve real life situation such as the problems and challenges that confront the Informal public transport in developing countries must be pursued vigorously by all relevant and key players (Saddier et al., 2017).

Most of the legacy problems and challenges will be naturally sorted out through this market-based-technology mechanism and more importantly the weaker, inefficient, less performing ones and rickety vehicles/buses will be crowded out naturally.

3.1 A Conceptual Model for On-Demand Based Trotro Service (Informal Public Transport) in Accra

Based on the characteristics of the Trotro operations earlier described and the brief overview of the Uber on-demand business model, the following exploratory and conceptual ideas and mapping are proposed for consideration of the On-demand Trotro (IPT) Business Model:

- Scheduling of the Informal Public Transport is a sine qua non. Demand must be matched with optimal supply of Trotros to ensure adequate profitability for drivers/owners while at the same time providing convenience and affordable price. It should be noted that the continuous menace of the operations of the Informal public transport is because they are in excess supply and in abundance.
- A well-matched travel demand-supply mechanism will make the cartel enviable and attractive which will in turn incentivize participants to adhere to the rules, regulations, and laws to stay in business.
- The model must be locally based (ideally district based) and must be implemented and administered by the local GPRTU but with linkage to the mother/National GPRTU and district or municipal authorities.
- The mother organization (GPRTU) must be empowered, trained, motivated, and incentivized to buy into the concept and be able to run it end-to-end without ceding any of their responsibilities, powers, and authorities to any third party or government agency (interference). They must be encouraged to organically take the shift from the current traditional operations to the on-demand technologically based model.
    - Trotros (drivers-participants) must register and belong to one operational zone/route but with flexibility to switch. Compliance must be strongly enforced to punish or remove deviants.

- A national app (exclusively for the Trotro IPT service) for the operations of the on-demand business (either through public/private partnership or wholly government) should be created. This is important for data analysis, revenue monitoring and governmental support to make it viable.
- The on-demand Trotro business model (app) must be shielded from the competition at least until such time the concept gains acceptance. The strategy will be to choose and start a zone that has potential for success so it can serve as reference or baseline in deploying the concept in other areas.
- The role of government (and the various regulatory bodies) is to provide advice, consultancy, support, and enforcement of the appropriate laws to both sides of the platform; namely passengers and drivers/owners as well as the necessary infrastructural and logistic support.
- Hybrid model approach: Initial plan should focus on developing/migrating the informal public transport (Trotro) to operate in Hybrid mode namely scheduled and unscheduled. This approach will recognise the role of the paratransit and import its transferable success story onboard the on-demand business model. For example, the deployment of key technology must be strategically and carefully introduced cognisant of the characteristics of the players on the two-sided platform; namely passengers (users) and Trotro drivers/owners.
- Hybrid features (low hanging fruits): Some of the hybrid features should include introduction of electronic payment system (Liébana-Cabanillas et al., 2019) (widely available in Ghana), installation of next station announcement, display of route information onboard and on one's mobile phone or at some strategic bus stations/terminals etc (Hiran & Doshi, 2014).
- The concept should be geared towards strengthening the current modus operandi where the Trotros operate as "feeder" IPT service for the Accra Rapid Bus Transit Service by picking passengers from the residential neighbourhoods to the main road side and to the major bus terminals. For example, every district may have at least one hub from where it connects to the next district (external) which would be serviced by the commercial buses (of 25-60 seating capacities).

Figure 3. Trotro (on-demand internet business model canvas)

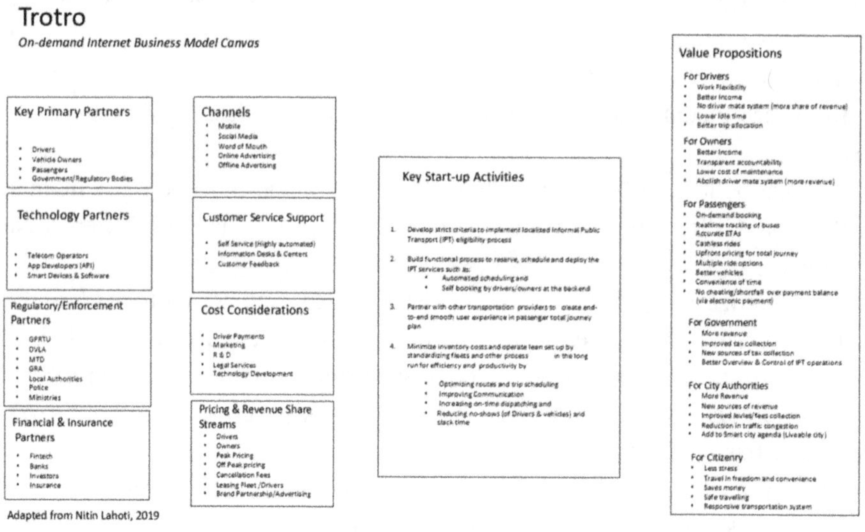

The journey to sanitize the operations of IPT is an arduous, intricate, and complicated one. It requires careful and detailed analysis of all connected linkages both to the economy and the socio-political life of the people. Above all, it requires both tacit and strategic negotiation with all relevant stakeholders for a complete buy-in in order to reap the enormous benefit of the IPT in the new smart city and smart mobility agenda in developing countries.

The figure below is a simplified touch points (key areas), adapted from the learnings, opportunities, and benefits of the Uber type of On-demand business model (Lahoti, 2019) which may be relevant in the proposed Trotro on-demand business plan.

Each touch point may require full scale investigation, analysis, and collaboration with relevant stakeholders to make it function that will dovetail into the next level until the whole achieves the synergy to run end-to-end on-demand Internet business model for the IPT in Accra.

4.0 CONCLUSION

It is to be noted that the Informal public transport constitute significant backbone of public transport especially in developing countries. Therefore, their continuous presence and by extension the menace and the challenges they create cannot be uprooted in favour of the formal high-capacity transport systems.

Any attempt to address the issues of the Informal Public Transport especially in developing countries (sub-Saharan Africa) must take into consideration the socio-economic lifestyle of the people. Policy makers attitude towards the Informal public transport must change their view of eradicating the IPT (Trotro) to one that is based on complementarity (and not a substitute) for higher capacity transport mode.

Efforts at managing the congestion in the city must be based on the way people travel rather than how they travel. Thus, building more roads and providing more vehicles (buses) are not enough. Using technology that is responsive to the socio-economic behaviour of the people will ensure that the efforts in bringing the menace of the IPTs to a close become sustainable and viable that will be harmonious with the Accra Smart City agenda.

REFERENCES

Ababa, A., Sharing, T. & Ababa, A. (2011). *Tumi Initiative's Transformative Stories* (Working Paper). SSRN.

Acheampong, P., Zhiwen, L., Hiran, K. K., Serwaa, O. E., Boateng, F., & Bediako, I. A. (2018). Examining the intervening role of age and gender on mobile payment acceptance in Ghana: UTAUT model. *Canadian Journal of Applied Science and Technology*, *5*(2).

Ajzen, I. (2002). Behavioral Interventions Based on the Theory of Planned Behavior. *Research Policy*, *2011*(June), 1–6.

Aluvalu, R. (2020, October). Intrusion detection system for the IoT: a comprehensive review. In *Proceedings of the 11th International Conference on Soft Computing and Pattern Recognition (SoCPaR. 2019)* (p. 235). Research Gate.

Andersson, A., Winslott, L., & Adell, E. (2018). Promoting sustainable travel behaviour through the use of smartphone applications : A review and development of a conceptual model. Travel Behav. Soc., 11, 52–61.

Archick, K. (2014). *The European parliament.* Democr. Credentials Eur. Union Backgr. Anal.

Balcombe, P. R., Mackett, R., Paulley, N., Preston, J., Shires, J., Titheridge, H., Wardman, M. (2004). The Demand for Public Transport: a practical guide. TRL Reports.

Behrens, R., McCormick, D., & Mfinanga, D. (2015). *Paratransit in African cities: Operations, regulation and reform.* Taylor and Francis Inc. doi:10.4324/9781315849515

Cervero, R., & Golub, A. (2011). Informal public transport: A global perspective. Urban Transp. Dev. World A Handb. Policy Pract., 488–518.

Chavhan, S., Gupta, D., Chandana, B. N., Khanna, A., & Rodrigues, J. J. P. C. (2020). IoT-Based Context-Aware Intelligent Public Transport System in a Metropolitan Area. *IEEE Internet of Things Journal, 7*(7), 6023–6034. doi:10.1109/JIOT.2019.2955102

Cheng, G., Guo, D., Shi, J., & Qin, Y. (2019). Smart City-Wide Package Distribution Using Crowdsourced Public Transportation Systems. *IEEE Internet of Things Journal, 6*(5), 7584–7594. doi:10.1109/JIOT.2019.2901116

Durand, A., Harms, L., Hoogendoorn-lanser, S., & Zijlstra, T. (2018). Mobility-as-a-Service and changes in travel preferences and travel behaviour : a literature review. *KiM| Netherlands Inst. Transp. Policy Anal.*

Forward, S. (2004). The Prediction of Travel Behaviour Using the Theory of Planned Behaviour. *Traffic Transp. Psychol*, (January), 481–492. doi:10.1016/B978-008043925-9/50045-1

Francis, O. (1997). *G.P.R.T.U National Secretariat-Accra.* Kwame Nkrumah University.

Frempong, M. A., & Hiran, K. K. (2014). Awareness and Understanding of Computer Forensics in the Ghana Legal System. *International Journal of Computer Applications, 975*, 8887.

Frieden, R. (2019). Two-Sided Internet Markets and the Need to Assess Both Upstream and Downstream Impacts. American University Law Review, 68(3).

Golub, A., Balassiano, R., Araújo, A., & Ferreira, E. (2009). Regulation of the informal transport sector in Rio de Janeiro, Brazil: Welfare impacts and policy analysis. *Transportation, 36*(5), 601–616. doi:10.100711116-009-9215-y

Hessel, V. (2015). *Smart Mobility – A tool to achieve sustainable cities.* IOP Science.

Hessel, V. (2015). *Smart Mobility-A tool to achieve sustainable cities.*

Hiran, K. K., & Doshi, R. (2014). *The Proliferation of Smart Devices on Mobile Cloud Computing.* Lambert Academic Publishing.

Jabbar, M. A., Prasad, K. M., & Aluvalu, R. (2021). *Future challenges for cyber-security in a smart city environment in Indian context.*

Jha, K., Sahid, K., Hassan, M., Mukhtar, S., Ghimire, A., & Thapa, S. (2021). A Review of AI for Urban Planning: Towards Building Sustainable Smart Cities. *6th International Conference on Inventive Computation Technologies (ICICT)*, (pp. 937–944). Research Gate.

Kaewkluengklom, R., Satiennam, W., Jaensirisak, S., & Satiennam, T. (2017). Influence of psychological factors on mode choice behaviours: Case study of BRT in Khon Kaen City, Thailand. *Transportation Research Procedia*, *25*, 5072–5082. doi:10.1016/j.trpro.2017.05.213

Kashi B. & Carello, S. (2020). *Urban Transport Solutions For Accra*. ISSU.

Lahoti, N. (2019). Uber Business Model Explained: From Start to Finish. *Mobisoft*. https://mobisoftinfotech.com/resources/blog/uber-business-model-explained/.

Lakhwani, K., Gianey, H., Wireko, J., & Hiran, K. (2020). Internet of Things (IOT)-Principles, Paradigms and Applications of IoT. BPB Publications, India.

Lakhwani, K., Gianey, H. K., Wireko, J. K., & Hiran, K. K. (2020). *Internet of Things (IoT): Principles, paradigms and applications of IoT*. Bpb Publications.

Lennon, M. (2019). 10 Countries Where Uber Isn't Available *The Travel*. https://www.thetravel.com/countries-uber-rides-unavailable/.

Liébana-Cabanillas, F., Molinillo, S., & Ruiz-Montañez, M. (2019). To use or not to use, that is the question: Analysis of the determining factors for using NFC mobile payment systems in public transportation. Technol. Forecast. Soc. Change, 139, 266–276.

Matthias Weber, K., Heller-Schuh, B., Godoe, H., & Roeste, R. (2014). ICT-enabled system innovations in public services: Experiences from intelligent transport systems. *Telecommunications Policy*, *38*(5–6), 539–557. doi:10.1016/j.telpol.2013.12.004

Meera, A. J., Kantipudi, M. V. V., & Aluvalu, R. (2019, December). Intrusion detection system for the IoT: A comprehensive review. In *International Conference on Soft Computing and Pattern Recognition* (pp. 235-243). Springer.

Muzellec, L., Ronteau, S., & Lambkin, M. (2015, February). Two-sided Internet platforms: A business model lifecycle perspective. *Industrial Marketing Management*, *45*(1), 139–150. doi:10.1016/j.indmarman.2015.02.012

Odlyzko, A., & Tilly, B. (2005). A refutation of Metcalfe ' s Law and a better estimate for the value of networks and network interconnections. *Technology (Elmsford, N.Y.)*, 1–11.

Poku-Boansi, M., & Adarkwa, K. (2014). The determinants of demand for public transport services in Kumasi, Ghana. *Journal of Science and Technology*, *33*(3), 60.

Priyadarshi, N., Padmanaban, S., Hiran, K. K., Holm-Nielson, J. B., & Bansal, R. C. (Eds.). (2021). *Artificial Intelligence and Internet of Things for Renewable Energy Systems* (Vol. 12). Walter de Gruyter GmbH & Co KG. doi:10.1515/9783110714043

S. A. O. (2014). Towards quasi - formal management of paratransit in informal transport dependent cities of Nigeria. *IOSR J. Humanit. Soc. Sci.*, *19*(12), 75–80. doi:10.9790/0837-191247580

Saddier, S., Patterson, Z., Johnson, A., & Wiseman, N. (2017). Fickle or flexible?: Assessing paratransit reliability with smartphones in Accra, Ghana. *Transportation Research Record: Journal of the Transportation Research Board, 2650*(1), 9–17. doi:10.3141/2650-02

Saini, H. K., Jain, K. L., Hiran, K. K., & Bhati, A. (2021). Paradigms to make smart city using blockchain. *Blockchain 3.0 for Sustainable Development, 10*, 21.

SSATP. (2017). *Case Study : Accra, Ghana Overview Objectives of the Road Passenger Transport Stakeholders Strategies for improvement of Urban Road Passenger Transport National Transport Policy*. SSATP.

SSATP. (2018). *Policies for Sustainable Accessibility and Mobility in Cities of Rwanda*. SSATP.

Travis Fried, I. A. (2019). *Putting Paratransit on the Map*. ZBW.

Verma V., & Chandra, B. (2017). *An Application of Theory of Planned Behavior to Predict Young Indian Consumers' Green Hotel Visit Intention*. Research Gate.

Wireko, J. K., Hiran, K. K., & Doshi, R. (2018). Culturally Based User Resistance to New Technologies in the Age of IoT In Developing Countries: Perspectives From Ethiopia. *International Journal of Emerging Technology and Advanced Engineering, 8*(4), 96–105.

Zach F. & Fesenmaier, D. R. (2016). *ScholarWorks@UMass Amherst The Changing Impact of the Internet on Travel Planning Behavior*. University of Massachusetts.

Section 2

Integrating Sustainability in Supply Chains

Chapter 9
Supply Chain Sustainability Risks:
A Systematic Review

Yasser El Ouarrak
https://orcid.org/0000-0002-2724-4705
National School of Business and Management, Sidi Mohamed Ben Abdellah University, Morocco

Aziz Hmioui
https://orcid.org/0000-0002-9032-4978
National School of Business and Management, Sidi Mohamed Ben Abdellah University, Morocco

ABSTRACT

In line with growing global awareness of sustainability issues, supply chain (SC) actors have begun to integrate sustainability practices into their activities, to create a more sustainable SC. However, this integration cannot be effective unless the various risks that could adversely affect the sustainability of the SC are managed. Indeed, managing these risks involves first identifying and classifying them, then assessing them, and subsequently suggesting the measures needed to mitigate them. To provide practitioners with a roadmap of supply chain sustainability risks (SCSRs), numerous articles have been published in the literature focusing on the identification, categorization, and assessment of SCSRs. This study carried out a systematic literature review, based on the preferred reporting items for systematic reviews and meta-analyses (PRISMA) flow diagram, to systematically analyze these articles. The review highlighted different areas in which SCSRs were identified, classified, and assessed. It also presented various SCSR evaluation frameworks developed in the literature. Finally, it underlined the importance of stakeholder involvement in dealing with SCSRs.

INTRODUCTION

Sustainability was defined in 1987 by the World Commission on Environment and Development (1987) as meeting "the needs of the present without compromising the ability of future generations to meet their

DOI: 10.4018/979-8-3693-0225-5.ch009

own needs". In recent decades, sustainability aspects in supply chains (SCs) have received a great deal of attention from SC actors due, on the one hand, to the recognition of the importance of integrating sustainability practices into SC activities to address several challenges that SCs face daily and to ensure the continued existence of the firms that make up the SC network and, on the other hand, to the increased pressure exerted by different stakeholders to adopt sustainability goals in all phases of the upstream and downstream SC. However, a range of risks can jeopardize the attainment of sustainability objectives in SCs, which are recognized as supply chain sustainability risks (SCSRs). These sustainability risks are distinct from ordinary SC risks in many ways, in which impacts on the natural ecosystem, corporate reputation, financial exposure, and compliance with laws are taken into account rather than SC operational disruptions (Giannakis & Papadopoulos, 2016). Sustainability risks were defined by Shankar et al. (2018) as "the potential disruptions that can cause a loss for a system in terms of its target values of sustainability performance and effectiveness evoked by uncertain developments in its environmental, economic and social behavior originated by the occurrence of triggering-events" (p. 665). From a different angle, Hofmann et al. (2013) defined sustainability risk as a condition or potential event that could lead to adverse reactions from stakeholders. As for SCSR, they defined it as "a sustainability risk within a focal firm's supply chain" (p. 168).

Fierce competition between companies, the diversity of volatile events, the emergence of new sophisticated technologies, and unlimited customer expectations, all of which increasingly increase the number and severity of risks that can challenge the SC's sustainability, in all its dimensions. Against this backdrop, many researchers have conducted scientific studies to analyze the sustainability risks inherent in SCs. Some of these studies have attempted to identify and categorize SCSRs, others have sought to develop frameworks for assessing them, while others have been able to bring together the identification, categorization, and assessment of SCSRs. However, to the best of our knowledge, no literature review has been conducted to identify, select, and synthesize existing research related to sustainability risks in SCs. To fill this gap, our chapter aims to carry out a systematic literature review of published research articles relating to the identification, categorization, and assessment of SC sustainability-related risks, or to one or other of these axes. To conduct our review, we refer to the Preferred Reporting Items for Systematic reviews and Meta-Analyses (PRISMA) flow diagram.

Our chapter is structured as follows: After the introduction, the second section describes the methodology that will be used to carry out our systematic literature review. The third section is devoted to the results and the discussion. Finally, the fourth section presents conclusions, limitations, and recommendations for future research.

METHODOLOGY

Our systematic literature review was conducted following the PRISMA flow diagram (Moher et al., 2009) which involves four key stages (Figure 1): (1) identification, (2) screening, (3) eligibility, and (4) inclusion.

Figure 1. PRISMA flow diagram

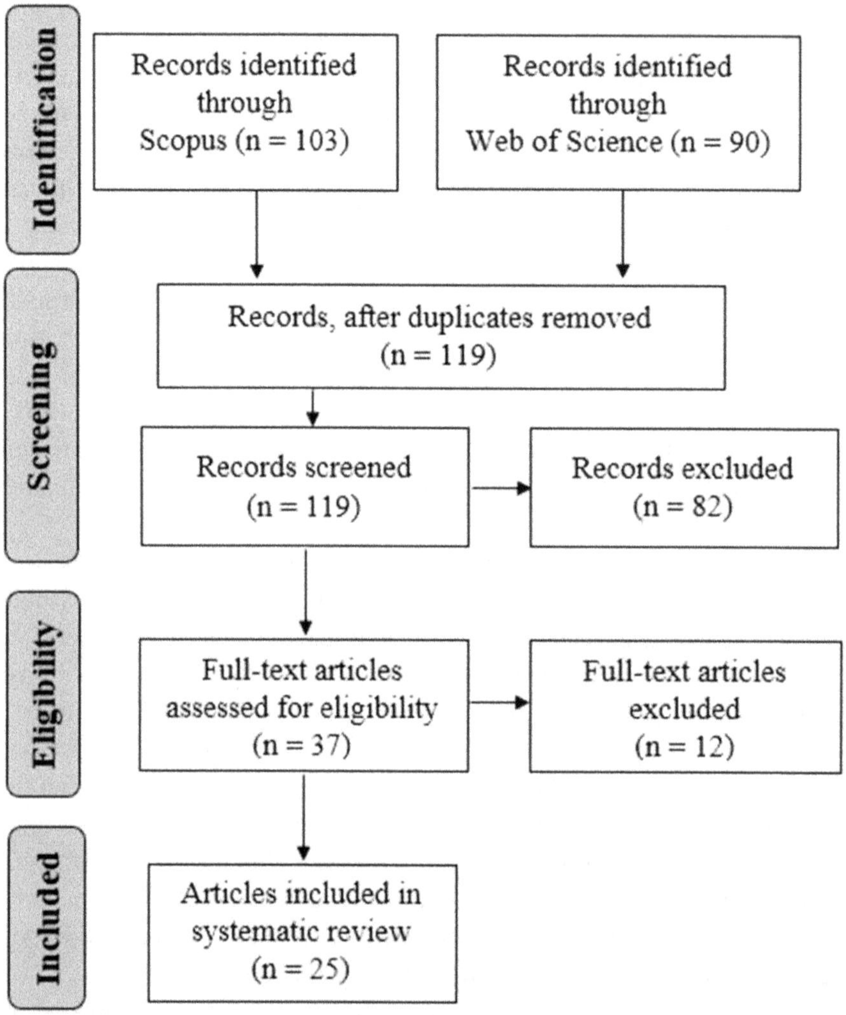

Identification

For the identification phase, we first chose the two scientific databases Scopus and Web of Science (WoS) as sources of records, then developed our search string made up of keywords referring to the studied topic.

The search string designed for each of the scientific databases is shown below:

For the Scopus database: *TITLE-ABS-KEY ("supply chain" AND ("sustainab* risk" OR "sustainab*-related risk")).*

For the WoS database: "*TS= "supply chain*" AND ("sustainab* risk*" OR "sustainab*-related risk*")*".

Running the search string in scientific databases yielded 193 publications from 2009 (the year of publication of the first document) to mid-June 2023.

Screening

Several documents appeared in more than one scientific database, so we removed duplicate documents to ensure that we did not include a publication two times in our analysis. The first screen reduced the total number of documents from 193 to 119.

Inclusion and exclusion criteria were then defined to select relevant academic articles. In our review, we only included research articles published in peer-reviewed journals and written in the English language, while other types of publications, including conference papers, book chapters, reviews, and editorials, were all excluded, as were all scientific publications not written in English. Then, based on titles and abstracts, we excluded off-topic research articles.

Following the inclusion and exclusion criteria, 82 documents were eliminated, and only 37 journal articles were considered at the eligibility step.

Eligibility

Next, we read the remaining 37 articles in their entirety, selecting those dealing with the identification, classification, and assessment of SCSRs, or either of these axes. Accordingly, a total of 12 irrelevant articles were removed.

Inclusion

In the end, 25 relevant articles were selected to form our analysis base. Figure 1 illustrates the PRISMA flowchart followed in this review.

RESULTS AND DISCUSSION

Descriptive Analysis

At the level of descriptive analysis, the distribution over time and across journals of the 25 selected articles is shown in the following subsections.

Publication Trend

Figure 2 shows that the first article in our systematic literature review was published in 2013 and that the number of articles related to the topic studied has increased considerably in recent years, with 56% of the included articles published between 2021 and 2022. This indicates that interest in the investigation of SCSRs has grown markedly of late. This finding can be interpreted as a sign of growing corporate awareness of more sustainable SCs, and academics' growing interest in the study of sustainability issues within SCs.

Figure 2. Time distribution of publications

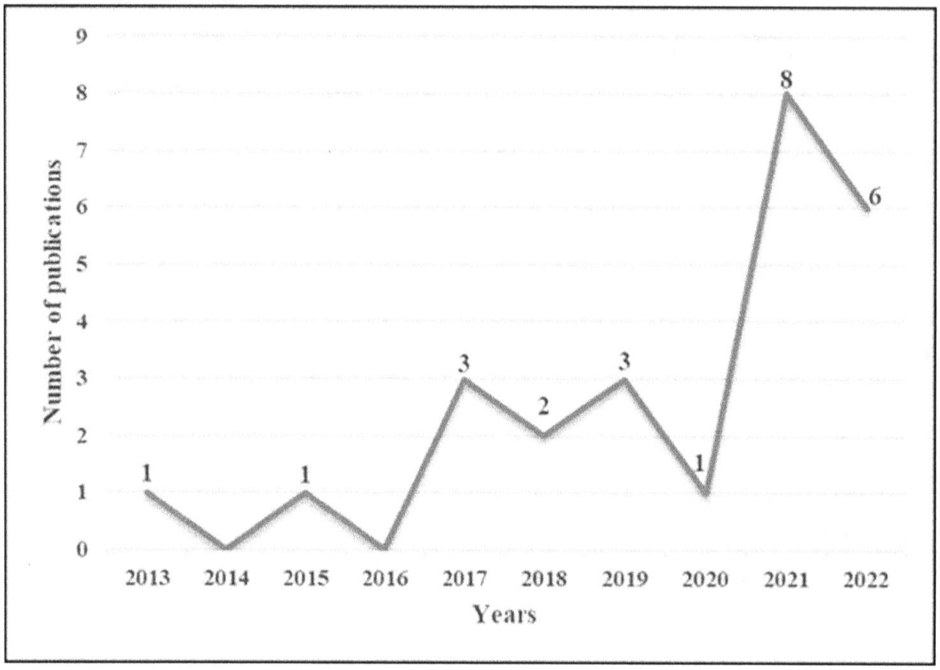

Publication Journals

According to Table 1, the 25 scientific articles included in this study were published in 19 various journals. The large number of journals and their diverse research areas suggest that the subject studied is of interest and multidisciplinary. Additionally, Table 1 shows that the *Journal of Cleaner Production* accounts for the largest proportion of articles (20%, n = 5), followed by *Sustainability* (8%, n = 2) and *International Journal of Production Economics* (8%, n = 2), both in second position. The rest of the journals (16) each published one article.

Supply Chain Sustainability Risks

Sustainability Risks Inherent in Different Supply Chains

Making SCs sustainable is a complicated and challenging mission, due to the high number of sustainability risks inherent in SCs. These risks present an obstacle to achieving SC sustainability, which requires them to be managed effectively. It is, therefore, necessary to identify and assess SC sustainability-related risks to facilitate better management and ensure the successful establishment of sustainable SCs.

Identifying SCSRs and evaluating their impact is recently emerging as a crucial issue for the industry and a topic of interest for academia, resulting in numerous studies in this field over the past decade. Among these studies, a study by Giannakis and Papadopoulos (2016) identified thirty risks under the three principal sustainability headings (environmental, social, and economic). These risks were split into two categories: endogenous and exogenous. In this study, a broad survey of various industrial sectors and two exploratory empirical case studies in two manufacturing firms in the textile sector were carried

Table 1. Number of publications per journal

Journals	Number of Publications	Percentage
Advances in Materials and Processing Technologies	1	4.0%
Autex Research Journal	1	4.0%
Business Strategy and the Environment	1	4.0%
Computers & Industrial Engineering	1	4.0%
International Journal of Engineering	1	4.0%
International Journal of Physical Distribution & Logistics Management	1	4.0%
International Journal of Production Economics	2	8.0%
International Journal of Quality & Reliability Management	1	4.0%
International Journal of Supply and Operations Management	1	4.0%
Journal of Advances in Management Research	1	4.0%
Journal of Cleaner Production	5	20.0%
Journal of Enterprise Information Management	1	4.0%
Mathematics	1	4.0%
Processes	1	4.0%
Resources, Conservation and Recycling	1	4.0%
Risk Analysis	1	4.0%
Sustainability	2	8.0%
Transportation Research Part D-Transport and Environment	1	4.0%
Uncertain Supply Chain Management	1	4.0%
Total	25	100.0%

out to assess and analyze various sustainability risk dimensions. The authors applied the failure mode and effect analysis (FMEA) technique to the risk assessment and analysis stages. The results of this research revealed that most of the major sustainability risks are endogenous risks. They also revealed that endogenous environmental risks are the most significant perceived risks in various industries. Endogenous risks, which are risks associated with the company's internal activities, can be handled more easily than exogenous risks over which the company has little control. As these are the most significant sustainability risks, companies must give them priority in the risk mitigation phase, paying greater attention to environmental aspects.

Sustainability risks in different SCs have been extensively analyzed in the literature. The various areas in which SCSRs were identified, categorized, and evaluated are as follows:

Textile and Apparel Supply Chains

The textile SC has been the subject of studies on sustainability risks. For instance, Raian et al. (2022) conducted a study to identify and assess SCSRs in the textile industry. The authors first identified twenty sustainability risks divided into five categories: 'supplier', 'financial', 'social', 'transportation', and 'environmental'. They then built a risk assessment model using the fuzzy synthetic evaluation (FSE) approach, which was applied to a real-life case of ten Bangladeshi textile manufacturing firms. The authors found that the largest source of sustainability risk in the Bangladeshi textile context is the supplier and that the three main sustainability risk factors are 'poor product transportation system', 'air, water, and soil pollution', and 'factory fire'. Another study by Hashim et al. (2021) looked at sustainability risks in the textile SC. The researchers identified twenty-six sustainability risks that were categorized under six headings: 'environmental (endogenous)', 'environmental (exogenous)', 'social (endogenous)', 'social (exogenous)', 'financial/economic (endogenous)', and 'financial/economic (exogenous)'. The authors found, in their survey of Pakistani textile industries, that for these industries, endogenous environmental risks are the most important, and that the top three risk factors are 'social instability', 'energy consumption', and 'tax avoidance'. For risk assessment and analysis, the authors used the FMEA method, as well as the Pareto analysis technique to highlight the most important sustainability risk factors. Based on the above results, we can remark that the first main significant sustainability risk factors in the Bangladeshi textile industry differ from those in the Pakistani textile industry. This difference may be due to the difference in context, the difference in how risks were categorized and assessed, or both. Bangladesh and Pakistan are both developing countries, and the textile industry contributes significantly to both countries' gross domestic product (GDP) and represents a major employment industry. Therefore, the objective must be to maintain the sustainability of the industry and to deploy the necessary means to manage the most significant risks threatening this sustainability.

Agriculture-Related Supply Chains

Various agriculture-related SCs have also been investigated in the literature about sustainability risks. We cite here the study by Bashiri et al. (2021) in which the authors listed twenty-eight sustainability risk factors related to the Indonesia–United Kingdom coffee SC, of which 43% are related to the social sustainability dimension, 39% to the economic sustainability dimension, and 18% to the environmental sustainability dimension. Using system dynamics (SD), this study investigated sustainability risks in the coffee SC between Indonesia and the United Kingdom. In the context of the palm oil SC, Anugerah et al. (2021) identified sixteen potential sustainability risks, grouped according to three sustainability categories, namely economic, environmental, and social. 50% of the sixteen potential risks are economic. In a case study of the Indonesian palm oil industry, the authors combined FMEA with the analytical hierarchy process (AHP) to assess and prioritize the risks identified. The results revealed that the 'unhealthy and unsafe working environment' is the most significant risk, followed respectively by 'natural disasters', and 'unreliable transportation systems'. Given that the results of the first study show that the majority of sustainability risk factors linked to the Indonesian-United Kingdom coffee SC are of a social dimension and that the most significant risk identified by the second study is the unhealthy and unsafe working environment, which is a social risk, we can say that social aspects should attract the attention of decision-makers in agriculture-related SCs. The right social conditions need to be guaranteed within the agricultural SC, particularly those that favor the working climate of employees. Other sustainability aspects, namely the economy and the environment, must not be overlooked either.

For the dairy SC, Benabdallah et al. (2022) identified fourteen risks related to four sustainability dimensions (social, economic, environmental, and operational). For assessing these risks, the researchers proposed a methodology combining the rough sets with the decision-making and trial evaluation laboratory (DEMATEL) approach. The proposed methodology was applied to a case study of a Tunisian dairy firm. 'Large number of intermediaries', 'lack of proper storage facilities', and 'transport disruption' were found to be the most significant risks. Indeed, the dairy SC is characterized by a large number of intermediaries, presenting a significant sustainability risk. As the number of intermediaries increases, so does the cost and complexity of SC processes. Dairy SC actors, therefore, need to consider how to reduce the number of intermediaries without compromising the quality of the product delivered to the end consumer. Transport-related problems are another sustainability risk that was found to be one of the most important in the Anugerah et al. (2021) and Benabdallah et al. (2022) studies. So, it's worth trying to solve existing transportation difficulties within agriculture-related SCs and consider more efficient and sustainable solutions.

Cosmetics Supply Chain

Looking at another different industry, Romano et al. (2021) identified ten potential sustainability risk factors within the Brazilian cosmetics SC. The authors constructed an interpretive structural modeling (ISM) model to show the hierarchical structure of the identified risk factors and reveal their interrelationships and then conducted the matrix-based multiplication applied to a classification (MICMAC) analysis to highlight the strength of the relationship between the risk factors. 'Technology and innovation' and 'legislation and responsibility' were found to be the two most important risk factors, as they have the highest capacity to inñuence all other risk factors. Determining the interrelationships between risk factors and the degree of dependency between them is another important aspect to consider when looking at SCSRs. This allows us to identify the most important risk factors that may influence a large number of remaining risk factors, enabling us to focus on them to reduce other dependent risk factors.

Telecommunications Supply Chain

Sustainability risks in the telecommunications SC have also been examined by many researchers in recent years. Valinejad and Rahmani (2018) are among the researchers who have taken an interest in examining sustainability risks in the telecommunications industry. They were able to compile an initial list of three hundred and ten risks of sustainability for telecommunications firms. In their research, the authors selected fourteen Iranian telecommunications firms to study SCSRs in this industry. The first list of three hundred and ten identified risks was verified by industry experts from the fourteen firms studied, resulting in a final list of ninety-one SCSRs. The identified risks were then classified according to the four sources of risk in the SC (suppliers, organization, customers, and the environment) and the five sustainability dimensions (environmental, social, economic, technical, and institutional). The authors subsequently employed the FMEA method to assess the risks identified. The results showed that the most significant sustainability risks facing the telecommunications firms under study are technical and institutional risks, representing almost 66% of the critical risks. In addition, suppliers are the primary source of critical SCSRs, making up 53% of the critical risks. Furthermore, technical risks induced by suppliers constitute the most significant threats to the sustainability of the SC in Iranian telecommunications firms. This calls for an increased level of cooperation with suppliers on the technical front, and attempts to impose several quality technical requirements on suppliers to provide a technical infrastructure that meets the company's expectations. This in turn involves improving the quality of communication with suppliers, by establishing effective mechanisms for sharing information with them. Indeed, effective communication between the various SC actors, including suppliers, helps to reduce SC risks (El Ouarrak & Hmioui, 2023). The choice of suppliers must also be based on many reliable selection criteria. Based on the data reported in the study by Valinejad and Rahmani (2018), Valinejad et al. (2022), using FMEA and fuzzy

VIKOR methods, developed a model for managing sustainability risks in the SC. The FMEA method was first employed to identify critical SCSRs, and then the fuzzy VIKOR method was used to prioritize them. The suggested model was applied to Iran's telecommunications industry. The authors found that 'inefficient management and lack of strategic management system' constitute the most threatening risk to the sustainability of the SC. This represents a significant finding directing telecommunications industry actors towards the adoption of new, innovative, and effective management strategies incorporating some sustainable management practices that will help the company achieve its short-, medium-, and long-term objectives. In another study, Abdel-Basset and Mohamed (2020) suggested a combined plithogenic approach founded on the technique in order of preference by similarity to ideal solution (TOPSIS) and criteria importance through inter-criteria correlation (CRITIC) methods to identify and prioritize the significant risk factors that could adversely influence the sustainability of the SC in a context of uncertainty. They applied their suggested approach to a Chinese telecommunications equipment firm. Of the results found, they identified financial risk criteria as the most significant main criteria. Nalluri and Chen (2022), in turn, conducted a study to examine the critical risk factors (CRFs) for achieving sustainability in the telecom SC and the interrelationships between them by employing combined fuzzy approaches, using collected data from the Indian telecom sector. The authors determined eleven relevant CRFs of sustainability in telecom SC, with the largest number of these CRFs being of economic dimension, and found that 'government policies (laws and regulations)' and 'difficulty in import technology and process' pose the highest influential risk for the telecom sector. This study will help telecom SC actors to become aware of the main sustainability risk factors and the relationships existing between these factors, enabling them to direct their resources towards managing the main ones, and consequently, the other risk factors linked to the main ones managed will also be handled. In this way, we can ensure effective management of SCSRs within the telecom SC, saving risk management resources.

Electronic and Elevator Manufacturing Supply Chains

Today, many manufacturing SCs are complex and exposed to a wide range of sustainability risks. Among these complex SCs are those for electronics and elevators. Hsu et al. (2021) were able, by studying a Taiwanese elevator manufacturer, to draw up a set of twenty-two main sustainable SC disruption risks potentially affecting elevator manufacturing SCs, and found that 'unexpected events lead to changes in supplier delivery dates', 'typhoon', and 'lack of critical capacities/skilled employees' are the three leading sustainable SC disruption risks. Within another complex manufacturing SC, Hsu et al. (2022) selected, based on a case study of a China-based multinational electronics assembly manufacturer, nineteen major sustainable SC risks inherent in electronic manufacturing SCs, categorized into four risk levels, and found that 'disruption or delay in the delivery of goods because of inadequate liquidity and poor ðnancial conditions', 'information system instability', 'credibility and competence of operators and leaders', 'long product lead time' and 'product safety and quality' are the most important five sustainable SC risks.

Having lists of sustainable SC risks for different complex manufacturing SCs and knowing which risks are the most significant will help SC actors gain risk management knowledge and develop proactive practices that can help them prevent the emergence of these risks, bearing in mind that the nature, number, and severity of sustainable SC risks can differ from one SC to another depending on many factors, including the degree of complexity of that SC.

Freight Transport Systems

Freight transportation is regarded as essential to the smooth running of SCs and logistics systems. For assessing and prioritizing sustainability risks related to freight transportation systems (FTSs), Shankar et al. (2018) proposed in their study a risk assessment model using a combination of the intuitionistic fuzzy set (IFS) theory and D-number theory. This model was applied to the Indian context. The researchers identified eighteen sustainability risks in FTSs and found that the majority of the top priority sustainability risks are social, and that 'lack of awareness and logistics skill' is the most important sustainability threat in FTSs. In the same FTS framework, Choudhary et al. (2019) pinpointed thirty-six sustainability risks for FTSs and divided them into seven groups, namely 'fleet management risk', 'financial risks', 'informational risks', 'ecological and social risks', 'market risks', 'operational risks', and 'organizational and governmental risks'. To quantitatively model the sustainability risks identified, the authors proposed an integrated approach founded on the fuzzy evidential reasoning algorithm (FERA) and expected utility theory (EUT). The approach proposed was applied by the authors to assess FTS sustainability risks in the Indian context. The majority of the top sustainability risks were suggested to be behavioral and socially driven, and the 'lack of awareness and logistics skill' risk was revealed as the most important sustainability risk. From the results of two studies carried out on the sustainability risks associated with FTSs, we note that both studies found 'lack of awareness and logistics skill' to be the most significant sustainability risk in FTSs, requiring the actors involved in the freight sector to adopt solutions aimed at raising employee awareness of the importance of adopting sustainable strategies and techniques, as well as strengthening employees' logistics skills through, for example, intensive and regular training and the sharing of expertise between the various actors in the freight sector.

Smart Supply Chains

Creating a smart SC is a priority objective for today's SC actors. The introduction of new technologies into the SC is an important part of achieving this objective. One such new technology is blockchain, which has gained importance in the sustainable supply chain management (SSCM) field in recent years. However, there are various sustainability risks associated with implementing blockchain technology in SSCM. In their recent study, Zhang and Song (2022) explored eight sustainability risk factors for the adoption of blockchain to SSCM, clustered under three categories, namely environmental risk factors, economic risk factors, and social risk factors. The authors proposed a comprehensive risk assessment framework for blockchain implementation in SSCM adopting an extended FMEA model and then suggested a new multi-criteria decision model (MCDM) approach by incorporating best-worst method (BWM) and combined compromise solution (CoCoSo) with variable precision rough set theory for analyzing the sustainability risk factors of blockchain implementation. The results of the study showed that economic-related risks are more significant than environmental risks and social risks. 'Increased costs" and 'extra audits and recertification' were found to be the two most critical sustainability risk factors for adopting blockchain to SSCM. Despite the significant number of benefits provided by the introduction of blockchain technologies into SSCM, many sustainability risks are attached to this introduction. For this reason, companies must not neglect the sustainability risk side when making decisions about introducing new technologies, and they should prepare the necessary measures to manage the sustainability risk factors involved in any potential new technology adoption.

The smart logistics ecological chain (SLEC) is another emerging issue that has recently attracted interest in the field of SSCM. Sustainable risks related to SLEC were investigated by Liu et al. (2020).

These researchers identified ten sustainable risk factors in SLECs, categorized into SLEC members' risks, technical risks, and external environmental risks. To develop a research framework to analyze the relationships between these risk factors, Liu et al. (2020) used social network analysis (SNA) and, on the basis of the SNA results, they additionally constructed a risk evaluation model using an improved TOPSIS method to evaluate SLEC risks.

Supply Chain Sustainability Risk Assessment Frameworks

SCSR assessment shows its importance in the SCSR management process by revealing sustainability risks that require further attention. In the literature, SCSRs have been the subject of several attempts by many researchers to propose frameworks for assessing such risks. These include the integrated framework proposed by authors Xu et al. (2019) for assessing SCSR by considering operational (economic), social, and environmental risks at the SC level. Implementing this framework to assess SCSR implies three stages: SC mapping, SCSR quantification, and SCSR analysis. The last stage includes risk assessment space (RAS) analysis and materiality analysis. Wang and Rani (2021) also proposed a framework to assess risk factors for sustainability in SC management. An extended intuitionistic fuzzy double normalization-based multiple aggregation (IF-DNMA) approach was adopted in this study. From a different perspective, Sutrisno and Kumar (2022) likewise presented the integrated model of the preference selection index (PSI) and the prospect theory providing a new decision support model for SCSR assessment. In another study, the same authors, Sutrisno and Kumar (2022), developed a new SCSR assessment model built on additional FMEA parameters and its incorporation with PSI methodology and the Shannon entropy. PSI and Shannon entropy methods were jointly employed to take into account the subjectivity and objectivity aspects of decision-makers.

Risk assessment can be carried out using several different approaches, each with its advantages and disadvantages, but the ultimate aim is to steer decision-makers towards the risks that have the greatest impact on SC sustainability in order to prioritize them in terms of allocation of the necessary resources. Indeed, not having information on the main sustainability risks that are dangerous for the SC can lead to excessive consumption of resources and wasted time in mitigating sustainability risks that are of less importance in SCs. It is important to note that risk assessment must be accompanied by risk analysis to determine the possible causes and consequences of generating SCSRs, thus enabling the best risk mitigation strategies to be chosen.

SCSR assessment has also proven its importance in the supplier selection process. Awasthi et al. (2018) suggested a comprehensive framework, built on the fuzzy AHP-VIKOR approach, for selecting global sustainable suppliers, with consideration given to sustainability risks from sub-suppliers. The proposed framework's step for evaluating the sustainability performance of global suppliers comprises two phases, the first of which is devoted to evaluating the sustainability of key suppliers, and the second to evaluate the sustainability risk of sub-suppliers of the highest-ranked suppliers selected in the first phase. In another study, Torres-Ruiz and Ravindran (2018) proposed a supply sustainability risk assessment framework (SSRAF) which provides a comprehensive multiple-criteria framework for the quantification of SCSRs for various supplier segments. The proposed frameworks support managers in implementing supplier selection strategies based on sustainability objectives, enabling them to ensure an effective selection of sustainable suppliers and to develop sustainable partnerships, as well as to prepare adequate solutions for managing potential sustainability risks that may arise during the company's dealings with its suppliers.

Supply Chain Sustainability Risks and Stakeholder Involvement

Identifying and assessing SCSRs can only be effective if stakeholders are involved and their concerns and expectations are taken into account. Here we should refer to Hofmann et al. (2013), who argued that stakeholder involvement is a prerequisite for managing sustainability risks in SCs successfully. In their worthy research, Hofmann et al. (2013) developed a conceptualization of SCSRs. Their research findings indicated that it is important for companies to identify the sources of SCSRs that could provoke reactions from stakeholders to manage SCSRs successfully. The importance of stakeholders in addressing SCSRs is also highlighted by Busse et al. (2017), who developed a procedural model linking three interventions, one related to SC cartography and the others to stakeholder analysis, seeking companies to deeply understand and take into account the concerns and attention of important stakeholders regarding sustainability issues in SCs, thus simplifying the identification of SCSRs. These studies emphasize the importance of considering stakeholders' concerns regarding sustainability aspects within the SC, and of preparing the necessary measures to deal with adverse stakeholder reactions if any sustainability aspect is compromised. SC actors must give stakeholders a central role in the development and implementation of strategies and must maintain ongoing communication and cooperation with them.

CONCLUSION

We conducted a systematic literature review based on the PRISMA flow diagram, to identify, select, and synthesize existing research related to sustainability risks in SCs. In our study, 25 scientific articles published in English-speaking peer-reviewed journals from 2013 to 2022 were selected and subsequently analyzed.

The descriptive analysis showed that the number of studies on SCSRs has increased significantly recently and that the studied topic is of interest to the scientific community and is multidisciplinary, given the large number and diversity of journals to which the selected articles belong. Analyzing SCSRs, our study revealed that the number, categories, and importance of risks likely to adversely affect the various dimensions of SC sustainability vary from one industry to another and from one region to another. By conducting numerous studies, authors in different contexts sought to provide SC actors across different areas with an overview of the sustainability risks, grouped into a range of categories, to help them develop a deeper understanding of the sustainability risks inherent in their SCs, and consequently, enabling them to prepare appropriate solutions to address these risks. In addition, several assessment frameworks were proposed by researchers in the literature to evaluate SCSRs based on various approaches, to ensure effective risk assessment that will help managers make the right decisions in the risk mitigation phase. Dealing with SCSRs should only be done with the involvement of stakeholders, who have many sustainability concerns that SC actors need to take into account.

Our book chapter contributes to the existing literature by synthesizing previous peer-reviewed journal articles on the subject under study, thus contributing to the development of accumulated knowledge on it. However, our study has certain limitations. Firstly, the small number of articles that formed the study's analysis basis, due on the one hand to the choice of only two scientific databases to identify articles, and on the other to the inclusion and exclusion criteria applied in the screening stage. Secondly, our systematic literature review does not cover studies on SCSR mitigation, which represents an important phase of the SCSR management process.

Several recommendations for future research could be proposed. First, there are few articles empirically investigating SCSRs, thus it is suggested that more empirical studies on this topic are needed for future research. Secondly, there is a limited body of research studying the interrelationships between SCSRs, it is therefore proposed that future research should give attention to this important axis.

REFERENCES

Abdel-Basset, M., & Mohamed, R. (2020). A novel plithogenic TOPSIS- CRITIC model for sustainable supply chain risk management. *Journal of Cleaner Production*, *247*, 119586. doi:10.1016/j.jclepro.2019.119586

Anugerah, A. R., Ahmad, S. A., Samin, R., Samdin, Z., & Kamaruddin, N. (2021). Modified failure mode and effect analysis to mitigate sustainable related risk in the palm oil supply chain. *Advances in Materials and Processing Technologies*, *8*(2), 2229–2243. doi:10.1080/2374068X.2021.1898180

Awasthi, A., Govindan, K., & Gold, S. (2018). Multi-tier sustainable global supplier selection using a fuzzy AHP-VIKOR based approach. *International Journal of Production Economics*, *195*, 106–117. doi:10.1016/j.ijpe.2017.10.013

Bashiri, M., Tjahjono, B., Lazell, J., Ferreira, J., & Perdana, T. (2021). The Dynamics of Sustainability Risks in the Global Coffee Supply Chain: A Case of Indonesia–UK. *Sustainability (Basel)*, *13*(2), 589. doi:10.3390u13020589

Benabdallah, C., El-Amraoui, A., Delmotte, F., & Frikha, A. (2022). Evaluation on Risks of Sustainable Supply Chain Based on Integrated Rough DEMATEL in Tunisian Dairy Industry. *International Journal of Supply and Operations Management*, *9*(3), 338–359. doi:10.22034/ijsom.2021.109143.2205

Busse, C., Schleper, M. C., Weilenmann, J., & Wagner, S. M. (2017). Extending the supply chain visibility boundary : Utilizing stakeholders for identifying supply chain sustainability risks. *International Journal of Physical Distribution & Logistics Management*, *47*(1), 18–40. doi:10.1108/IJPDLM-02-2015-0043

Choudhary, D., Shankar, R., & Choudhary, A. (2019). An Integrated Approach for Modeling Sustainability Risks in Freight Transportation Systems. *Risk Analysis*, *40*(4), 858–883. doi:10.1111/risa.13435 PMID:31889333

El Ouarrak, Y., & Hmioui, A. (2023). Communication Between Supply Chain Actors: A Risk Reduction Factor in Supply Chains. *Lecture Notes in Networks and Systems*, 695–703. doi:10.1007/978-981-99-3043-2_56

Giannakis, M., & Papadopoulos, T. (2016). Supply chain sustainability : A risk management approach. *International Journal of Production Economics*, *171*, 455–470. doi:10.1016/j.ijpe.2015.06.032

Hashim, M., Nazam, M., Zia-Ur-Rehman, M., Abrar, M., Baig, S. A., Nazim, M., & Hussain, Z. (2021). Modeling Supply Chain Sustainability-Related Risks and Vulnerability : Insights from the Textile Sector of Pakistan. *AUTEX Research Journal*, *22*(1), 123–134. doi:10.2478/aut-2021-0008

Hofmann, H., Busse, C., Bode, C., & Henke, M. (2013). Sustainability-Related Supply Chain Risks : Conceptualization and Management. *Business Strategy and the Environment, 23*(3), 160–172. doi:10.1002/bse.1778

Hsu, C.-H., Yu, R.-Y., Chang, A.-Y., Chung, W.-H., & Liu, W.-L. (2021). Resilience-Enhancing Solution to Mitigate Risk for Sustainable Supply Chain—An Empirical Study of Elevator Manufacturing. *Processes (Basel, Switzerland), 9*(4), 596. doi:10.3390/pr9040596

Hsu, C.-H., Yu, R.-Y., Chang, A.-Y., Liu, W.-L., & Sun, A.-C. (2022). Applying Integrated QFD-MCDM Approach to Strengthen Supply Chain Agility for Mitigating Sustainable Risks. *Mathematics, 10*(4), 552. doi:10.3390/math10040552

Liu, W., Wei, W., Yan, X., Dong, D., & Chen, Z. (2020). Sustainability risk management in a smart logistics ecological chain : An evaluation framework based on social network analysis. *Journal of Cleaner Production, 276*, 124189. doi:10.1016/j.jclepro.2020.124189

Moher, D., Liberati, A., Tetzlaff, J., & Altman, D. G.The PRISMA Group. (2009). Preferred reporting items for systematic reviews and meta-analyses : The PRISMA statement. *PLoS Medicine, 6*(7), e1000097. doi:10.1371/journal.pmed.1000097 PMID:19621072

Nalluri, V., & Chen, L.-S. (2022). Risk assessment for sustainability on telecom supply chain : A hybrid fuzzy approach. *Uncertain Supply Chain Management, 10*(2), 559–576. doi:10.5267/j.uscm.2021.11.007

Raian, S., Ali, S. M., Sarker, M., Sankaranarayanan, B., Kabir, G., Paul, S. K., & Chakrabortty, R. K. (2022). Assessing sustainability risks in the supply chain of the textile industry under uncertainty. *Resources, Conservation and Recycling, 177*, 105975. doi:10.1016/j.resconrec.2021.105975

Romano, A. L., Ferreira, L. M. D. F., & Caeiro, S. S. F. S. (2021). Modelling Sustainability Risk in the Brazilian Cosmetics Industry. *Sustainability (Basel), 13*(24), 13771. doi:10.3390u132413771

Shankar, R., Choudhary, D., & Jharkharia, S. (2018). An integrated risk assessment model : A case of sustainable freight transportation systems. *Transportation Research Part D, Transport and Environment, 63*, 662–676. doi:10.1016/j.trd.2018.07.003

Sutrisno, A., & Kumar, V. (2022). Supply chain sustainability risk decision support model using integrated Preference Selection Index (PSI) method and prospect theory. *Journal of Advances in Management Research, 19*(2), 316–346. doi:10.1108/JAMR-06-2021-0193

Sutrisno, A., & Kumar, V. (2022). Supply chain sustainability risk assessment model using integration of the preference selection index (PSI) and the Shannon entropy. *International Journal of Quality & Reliability Management, 40*(3), 674–708. doi:10.1108/IJQRM-06-2021-0191

Torres-Ruiz, A., & Ravindran, A. R. (2018). Multiple criteria framework for the sustainability risk assessment of a supplier portfolio. *Journal of Cleaner Production, 172*, 4478–4493. doi:10.1016/j.jclepro.2017.10.304

Valinejad, F., & Rahmani, D. (2018). Sustainability risk management in the supply chain of telecommunication companies : A case study. *Journal of Cleaner Production, 203*, 53–67. doi:10.1016/j.jclepro.2018.08.174

Valinejad, F., Safaie, N., Rahmani, D., & Saadatmand, M. R. (2022). A Hybrid Model for Supply Chain Risk Management Based on Five-dimensional Sustainability Approach in Telecommunication Industry. *International Journal of Engineering*, *35*(6), 1096–1110. doi:10.5829/IJE.2022.35.06C.01

Wang, L., & Rani, P. (2021). Sustainable supply chains under risk in the manufacturing firms : An extended double normalization-based multiple aggregation approach under an intuitionistic fuzzy environment. *Journal of Enterprise Information Management*, *35*(4/5), 1067–1099. doi:10.1108/JEIM-05-2021-0222

World Commission on Environment and Development. (1987). *Our Common Future*. Oxford University Press.

Xu, M., Cui, Y., Hu, M., Xu, X., Zhang, Z., Liang, S., & Qu, S. (2019). Supply chain sustainability risk and assessment. *Journal of Cleaner Production*, *225*, 857–867. doi:10.1016/j.jclepro.2019.03.307

Zhang, F., & Song, W. (2022). Sustainability risk assessment of blockchain adoption in sustainable supply chain : An integrated method. *Computers & Industrial Engineering*, *171*, 108378. doi:10.1016/j.cie.2022.108378

Chapter 10
Sustainable and Smart Supply Chains in China: A Multidimensional Approach

Mohamad Zreik
https://orcid.org/0000-0002-6812-6529
Independent Researcher, Lebanon

ABSTRACT

This chapter takes a multifaceted look at China's sustainable and smart supply chains. It examines China's impact on the environment and stresses the importance of a green transition. Sustainable logistics and supply chain management are examined as a potential source of market segmentation and competitive positioning in the context of novel business models. Case studies can illustrate how new technologies such as blockchain, artificial intelligence, the internet of things, and big data may improve supply chain performance and sustainability. Additionally, the chapter examines the function of green finance in promoting sustainability, logistics cost management measures, and the altering role of logistics managers. Impacts of China's Industry 5.0, agile logistics, service supply chains, and SCM analytics are discussed to round out the chapter. Anyone interested in China's transition toward more sustainable, intelligent supply networks may find useful information here.

1. INTRODUCTION

Sustainable and efficient supply chain management strategies have assumed center stage as we progress through the 21st century (Haipeter et al., 2021). Sustainable and intelligent supply chains in China are the focus of this chapter. China's position as the world's top manufacturer and exporter makes it a useful case study because of the enormous impact it has on supply chains around the world.

From raw materials to finished goods, China's supply chains are extensive, complex, and crucial to global trade. These chains have a history of impressive efficiency and low prices, but they have also been linked to pollution and harmful behavior.

DOI: 10.4018/979-8-3693-0225-5.ch010

Sustainability and intelligence are on the rise in China's supply chains as a result of the country's pressing need to solve environmental concerns and the country's rapid technological development (Fróna, Szenderák, & Harangi-Rákos, 2019). Digitalization, connection, and real-time data are the hallmarks of these "smart" supply chains, which enable hitherto unimaginable efficiencies and robustness. Meanwhile, sustainability is a concept known as the "triple bottom line" because it aims to combine economic efficiency, environmental responsibility, and social equality (Sargani et al., 2020).

Not only are Chinese industries dependent on an understanding of the development and management of sustainable and smart supply chains, but so are companies, politicians, and academics all over the world. Due to the multifaceted nature of these supply networks, this chapter integrates economic, environmental, technological, and social considerations. The goal is to offer insight on China's specific strategies, problems, and opportunities for making the switch to sustainable and smart supply chains.

Several factors provide considerable weight to the significance of learning about sustainable and intelligent supply networks in China. First, because China is a manufacturing powerhouse on a global scale, its supply chains are deeply intertwined with global trade. These networks have widespread effects on operations, the environment, and society. Therefore, enhancing their durability can have far-reaching benefits.

Second, the necessity of changing to environmentally friendly corporate practices is being acknowledged on a global scale. Consumers, regulators, and investors are all putting pressure on businesses to do their part for society and the environment. How this is accomplished in China's massive and varied supply chains is instructive for companies everywhere.

Third, the introduction of cutting-edge innovations like Big Data, AI, IoT, and Blockchain is reshaping the supply chain management industry. Due to the country's rapid digital transformation, China is at the forefront of this trend toward "smart" supply chains (Attaran, Attaran, & Celik, 2023). Insights on how these technologies might be exploited to improve the efficiency, resilience, and sustainability of supply chains can be gleaned from China's experience.

Finally, the scholarly discussion of sustainable development and the role of technology in accomplishing it benefits from the examination of China's approach to sustainable and smart supply chains. This field of study is crucial because of the critical nature of environmental issues and the rapid development of new technologies.

Given these considerations, it is important for practitioners, policymakers, and researchers to investigate China's sustainable and smart supply chains. It's a chance to pick up some tips from one of the fastest growing economies and help advance the cause of greener, more technologically sophisticated supply chains worldwide.

The theory of the diffusion of innovations, proposed by Everett Rogers, describes how new ideas and technologies spread through cultures and organizations. This theory classifies adopters into categories such as innovators, early adopters, early majority, late majority, and laggards, based on how quickly they embrace a new innovation. In the context of supply chain management, understanding this diffusion process is essential for SC managers. It allows them to identify where their organization, suppliers, and other stakeholders fall within these categories, enabling a more strategic and tailored approach to implementing new technologies and practices.

By applying the diffusion of innovations theory, SC managers can gauge the readiness and receptiveness of various parts of the supply chain to new initiatives, such as agile logistics or advanced analytics. Understanding the characteristics and needs of different adopter categories can lead to more effective communication strategies and the identification of potential barriers to change. Furthermore, this theory offers insights into how cultural, structural, and individual factors might influence the adoption process, guiding SC managers in creating supportive environments that facilitate innovation and growth.

2. THE ENVIRONMENTAL FOOTPRINT OF CHINA'S SUPPLY CHAINS

2.1. Current Situation and Challenges

China's vast supply chains have a huge impact on the environment. The industrial sector in China is responsible for a considerable portion of the country's carbon emissions, making China the world's greatest emitter of greenhouse gases (Chien, Chau, & Sadiq, 2023). Air and water pollution, resource depletion, and garbage generation are only some of the environmental problems that have resulted from the country's rapid development. The effects are far-reaching, affecting not only the environment but also people's health and the economy.

There are a number of difficulties in the present. The widespread use of fossil fuels to produce enormous amounts of energy continues to be a major problem. High levels of carbon dioxide emissions and air pollution can be attributed in part to China being the world's largest consumer of coal. Its industries also place a high demand on water, which is in short supply in many areas (Zhang & Chen, 2022).

Waste management and the disposal of obsolete products present yet another difficulty. The increase in electronic and plastic product use has coincided with a corresponding increase in trash production, which in turn has resulted in serious environmental damage. garbage recycling and management systems in China are overburdened and frequently fail to adequately address the country's vast garbage production and variety.

Another major obstacle is the 'take-make-dispose' linear approach used in many Chinese supply chains (Farooque et al., 2022). Not only does this paradigm exhaust scarce resources, but it also fails to account for the potential financial benefits of adopting a more closed-loop strategy.

Finally, enforcing regulations is still difficult. While environmental regulation has made great strides in recent years, there are still policy implementation gaps. Efforts to lessen the impact on the environment are frequently thwarted by inconsistencies in enforcement between areas and sectors.

It will take a wide range of efforts, including new technologies, revised business models, stricter regulations, and heightened environmental consciousness, to meet these challenges head-on. A key component of this approach is the shift to sustainable and intelligent supply chains, which promises a more stable relationship between economic development and environmental conservation.

2.2. The Need for Sustainable Transformation

The urgent need for a sustainable transformation is highlighted by the severe environmental problems posed by China's vast supply chains. The goal of this transition is to move away from the conventional "take-make-dispose" model and toward one that adheres to the circular economy's three tenets of sustainability: reduction, reuse, and recycling (Kyriakopoulos, 2021).

As part of this revised framework, organizations would place a premium on resource conservation across the product's whole lifecycle. Strategies for waste management would also be part of a circular strategy, with the goal of reusing or recycling consumables past their useful life rather than sending them to landfills or incinerators.

The transition to sustainable supply chains can bring about not just environmental but also economic and social benefits. Businesses can save money and run more efficiently by cutting down on waste and making better use of their resources. In addition, organizations that prioritize sustainability are typically in a better position to adapt to shifting customer preferences, regulatory frameworks, and market risks related to environmental considerations.

Furthermore, sustainable practices can inspire creativity and new markets for companies to exploit. Businesses may do their part for the environment in a number of ways, such as by using recycled materials in new service offerings or by implementing technological solutions to inefficiencies (Naim, 2021).

In addition, the shift toward sustainable supply chains is an essential component of accomplishing societal goals such as the United Nations' Sustainable Development Goals (SDGs). The activities of China, the world's largest producer and exporter, will be crucial to international sustainability initiatives.

3. SUSTAINABLE BUSINESS MODELS IN CHINA

3.1. Overview and Examples of Innovative Business Models

Innovative and sustainable business models are sprouting across China's supply chains as the country works to lessen its impact on the environment and achieve its sustainability goals. Rather than seeing sustainability as an afterthought, these models try to incorporate it into every aspect of doing business.

The circular economy notion is one such approach, which is in sharp contrast to the more conventional take-make-dispose model. The Chinese e-commerce giant JD.com has launched programs to encourage product recycling. JD.com has created a marketplace for buying and selling pre-owned items, which helps to increase the longevity of products and decrease their environmental impact (Chen & Ji, 2020).

The sharing economy is another novel method of doing business in China; it encourages the pooling of resources via the usage of shared goods and services. This strategy is shown by Didi Chuxing, China's most popular ride-hailing service. Didi Chuxing not only offers a more cost-effective mode of transportation by facilitating carpooling, but it also helps ease traffic and cut down on pollution (Chen et al., 2022).

Another sustainable business model gaining popularity in China is green manufacturing. Manufacturers of air conditioners like Broad Group have led the way in creating more environmentally friendly manufacturing processes and more effective energy saving solutions. Broad Group's efforts to reduce its carbon footprint are an example of how corporate success and environmental responsibility can go hand in hand.

Additionally, some Chinese businesses are making the transition from product sales to service provision (or servitization). The change may lessen the need for resources and the quantity of trash produced. With their 'laundry as a service,' leading home appliance maker Haier is helping to eliminate the need for individual homes to have washing machines (Frynas, Mol, & Mellahi, 2018).

These instances show how Chinese companies are incorporating sustainable practices into their daily operations and supply networks. Sustainable business models allow businesses to reduce their negative effects on the environment, while simultaneously opening up chances in new markets and giving them a competitive edge. China's road toward a more sustainable and circular economy will be heavily influenced by the development and refinement of these models.

3.2. Incorporation of Sustainability in Logistics and Supply Chain Management

For logistics and supply chain management to be sustainable, there must be a wholesale transition to more eco-friendly, socially just, and commercially viable business practices along the whole supply chain. It's more than just following the rules; it entails proactive measures and calculated choices that aim to strike a balance between financial success, environmental responsibility, and social accountability.

Supply chain environmental impact evaluation and monitoring is often the first step in incorporating sustainability into management practices. Metrics including carbon output, energy use, water usage, trash output, and more will need to be monitored. Life cycle assessment (LCA) is a useful tool for understanding the full environmental impact of a product, from production through disposal (Vinodh, Ben Ruben, & Asokan, 2016).

Sustainable sourcing is also an important consideration. Suppliers who adhere to environmental principles, such recycling, renewable energy use, and fair labor standards, are becoming increasingly attractive to businesses (Naidoo & Gasparatos, 2018). This helps lessen the supply chain's overall environmental effect and protects against the reputational harm that might come from working with suppliers that aren't committed to sustainability.

In the logistics sector, businesses are working to lessen the negative effects of shipping and storing goods on the environment. Cleaner fuels are being used, routes are being optimized, and loads are being managed better to cut fuel use, and eco-friendly warehouses are being built with features like solar panels and LED lights.

The use of a circular model for product development and disposal is another alternative. Products need to be created with longevity, low maintenance, and recycling in mind, and collection and recycling or repurposing methods need to be put into place.

In addition, businesses are using AI and IoT to monitor more of their supply chains in real time and make data-driven choices that save money by reducing inefficiency (Sundarakani, Ajaykumar, & Gunasekaran, 2021).

Companies may lessen their negative effects on the environment, gain a competitive edge, improve their reputation, and help achieve societal sustainability goals by incorporating sustainability into logistics and supply chain management. It's a process of transformation that necessitates forethought, dedication, and teamwork from all links in the supply chain.

3.3. The Role of Sustainable Logistics in Market Segmentation and Competitive Positioning

When it comes to dividing up markets and establishing a competitive edge, sustainable logistics is essential. Companies who use environmentally responsible logistics strategies will stand out from the competition and appeal to a growing subset of consumers who are concerned about the environment.

Segmenting a market is breaking it down into smaller groups of customers who share common traits or preferences. Consumers that care about environmental impact are a sizeable and rising demographic. They are willing to pay a premium for products made by environmentally responsible businesses (Chekima et al., 2016). Businesses can win over these customers by adopting more eco-friendly logistical techniques, increasing the likelihood of expanding their customer base and strengthening brand loyalty.

Additionally, sustainable logistics can play an important role in a firm's competitive positioning, or the way it seeks to differentiate itself from rivals in the eyes of consumers. In markets where customers have several options, sustainability can be a differentiating factor. Businesses that put an emphasis on green logistics methods can promote themselves to customers, investors, and future employees who share their commitment to environmental responsibility (Amoako et al., 2021).

Sustainable logistics strategies can also improve financial savings, creativity, and productivity. Energy efficiency, trash prevention, and route optimization all contribute to more cost-effective operations. The development of environmentally friendly packaging or the implementation of renewable energy sources in logistics operations are two examples of how the pursuit of sustainable alternatives may inspire innovation. By proving to stakeholders that sustainability and profitability can go hand in hand, these efficiency improvements and cost reductions can be used to gain a competitive advantage.

4. ROLE OF TECHNOLOGY IN SUPPLY CHAIN MANAGEMENT

4.1. Exploration of Big Data, AI, IoT, and Blockchain in Supply Chains

Supply networks have traditionally been inefficient, vulnerable, and unsustainable, but technological advancements have made this transformation possible (Free & Hecimovic, 2021). Tools like Big Data, AI, the IoT, and Blockchain are at the forefront of this change, opening up new possibilities for businesses to improve supply chain efficiency and environmental impact.

Big Data, the massive amounts of data produced by supply chain activities, can yield priceless insights if used correctly. By sifting through this information, businesses may better understand their supply chains, locate points of weakness, assess potential threats, and implement necessary changes. Improved forecasting accuracy using Big Data's predictive analytics can also lead to better inventory management and less waste (Hugos, 2018).

Supply chains can now benefit from automation and forecasting thanks to artificial intelligence and its tight relationship with Big Data. Predicting trends, automating routine operations, and providing ideas for improvement are all possible because to machine learning algorithms' ability to assess both historical and real-time data (Pan & Zhang, 2021). AI has several potential applications, including but not limited to: demand forecasting; identifying ideal delivery routes; and automating customer care via chatbots (Ng et al., 2021).

The Internet of Things (IoT) facilitates supply chain connectivity and real-time monitoring. The location, temperature, and humidity of products, equipment, or vehicles can all be tracked and transmitted thanks to the incorporation of sensors (Sharma, Kaur, & Singh, 2020). This real-time transparency helps boost traceability, speed up decision-making, and better product management across the board. The Internet of Things, for instance, may track the temperature and humidity of perishable commodities in transit to prevent deterioration and unnecessary waste.

Distributed ledger technology like blockchain can make supply networks safer and more open. It can generate a permanent log of business dealings, including with details of where an item has been and how it got there. As a result, it is easier to confirm that sustainable or ethical practices have been followed all throughout the supply chain, which improves traceability and helps against counterfeiting.

4.2. Cases Showcasing How Technology Aids in Managing Supply Chains

Businesses now have access to cutting-edge methods for increasing supply chain efficiency, transparency, and sustainability because to the widespread adoption of technology in this area. Here are a few examples that show how technology has revolutionized supply chain management.

Alibaba, the largest online retailer in China, is one company that has successfully used Big Data and AI to improve its supply chain. In order to effectively predict customer demand and optimize inventory management, Alibaba uses sophisticated data analytics systems to collect and analyze massive volumes of data on user behavior. They have chatbots driven by AI that field millions of customer service questions, improving satisfaction ratings and saving up staff time (Zhang, Pee, & Cui, 2021).

Zhenhua Port Machinery or Shanghai Zhenhua Heavy Industries Company Limited (ZPMC) is a leading example of a corporation that has successfully implemented IoT in SCM. ZPMC installed an IoT remote monitoring system to keep tabs on its globally dispersed equipment (García Márquez, Papaelias, & Marini, 2022). ZPMC can execute timely maintenance, reduce the risk of equipment failure, and boost operating efficiency thanks to the data collected by this system in real time.

Walmart China's Blockchain Traceability Platform demonstrates the utility of blockchain technology in supply chain management. This platform was built in collaboration with VeChain, PwC, and others to track the full supply chain of farm-to-store fresh food goods (Lacity & Van Hoek, 2021). Customers can learn more about a product's production history, quality control measures, and shipping logistics by scanning its associated QR code. Consumer confidence is boosted, food safety is easier to confirm, and Walmart gains crucial supply chain knowledge (Wang et al., 2021).

DHL Express, in conjunction with Huawei, has implemented AI and Machine Learning to better plan its shipping routes. The system is able to reduce fuel usage and carbon dioxide emissions by predicting delivery delays and suggesting best routes based on an analysis of historical data and real-time traffic information (Manners-Bell & Lyon, 2019).

From demand forecasting and equipment efficiency checks to unparalleled supply chain transparency and route optimization, these examples show how technology is improving supply chain management. More and more industries will find uses for developing technologies as they mature, and this will drive transformation and efficiency in supply chains.

5. THE INTERSECTION OF GREEN FINANCE AND SUSTAINABLE SUPPLY CHAINS

5.1. Importance and Role of Green Finance

The term "green finance" is used to describe the flow of capital into sustainable development projects and initiatives, and it plays a critical role in making long-term changes to supply chains possible. It enables the implementation of cutting-edge sustainable technologies, procedures, and enterprise models by providing the required financial backing (Udeagha & Muchapondwa, 2023).

One cannot overestimate the significance of green financing in ensuring sustainable supply chains. Investing a lot of money up front to implement sustainable practices is common. To achieve this goal, businesses may have to purchase energy-efficient machinery, create innovative goods and services, retrain employees, or form strategic alliances. Companies can undertake the transition to sustainability with the help of green finance, which can offer the required funding for these efforts.

There are a number of green financing options available. Green bonds and green loans, for example, are financial instruments created for the express purpose of funding initiatives with positive environmental impacts (Mihálovits & Tapaszti, 2018). Both legislative incentives and rising investor demand for sustainable investment options have led to a rise in the number of financial institutions offering these products.

Green funding can also come from socially responsible investors that put a premium on businesses with excellent ESG (environmental, social, and governance) records. Companies' sustainability efforts might be bolstered further by government grants and subsidies for sustainable projects (Singhania & Saini, 2022).

Green finance, however, serves more than just a financial function. In addition, it has the potential to serve as a catalyst for change by inspiring businesses to implement sustainable policies. To encourage greater sustainability, the terms of a green loan may, for instance, stipulate that the borrower meet particular environmental performance criteria.

In addition, a company that invests in green financing is more likely to attract clients, workers, and business partners that share its commitment to environmental responsibility. It can lessen worries about government interference, market volatility, and natural disasters.

5.2. Investment in Sustainable Logistics

In order to meet their corporate social responsibility and environmental goals, businesses must invest in sustainable logistics. Optimizing logistics and supply chain operations in a way that benefits the environment, society, and the bottom line is what we call "sustainable logistics" (Grant, Wong, & Trautrims, 2017).

Such investments can take on a wide variety of forms, depending on the circumstances and requirements of the company making the investment. To cut down on carbon emissions, a business could, for instance, buy a whole fleet of electric cars. They might also make long-term investments in energy-efficient warehouse infrastructure to cut down on energy use and expenditures.

Investments may also encourage the creation or use of digital solutions that improve productivity and environmental impact. Examples of such innovations include artificial intelligence-based route optimization tools for cutting down on gas usage, Internet of Things (IoT) devices for real-time tracking and monitoring of items to cut down on losses and waste, and Blockchain technology for improving supply chain transparency and traceability (Misra et al., 2020).

Strategies like rethinking the supply chain with circularity in mind or forming collaborations with environmentally conscious vendors are examples of the kind of improvements that may be made as part of an investment in sustainable logistics (Zreik, 2023). It's possible that companies will need to spend in employee training and development in order to ensure that their staff has the knowledge and abilities to manage and operate sustainable logistics systems.

Despite the need for initial funding, the potential returns on such investments are enormous. They can help you save money by decreasing your utility bills, trash output, and material use. In addition, they can boost a company's image and valuation in the eyes of environmentally conscious customers. In addition, they can lessen the dangers brought on by changes in the law, disruptions in the supply chain, and fluctuations in consumer demand.

6. MANAGEMENT STRATEGIES IN SUSTAINABLE AND SMART SUPPLY CHAINS

6.1. Strategies for Managing Logistics Costs, Resources, and Skills

Logistics cost, resource, and skill management must be carefully planned and executed in the dynamic environment of sustainable and smart supply chains. These plans must guarantee operational efficiency and competitiveness while also conforming to the organization's overarching sustainability goals.

Integrating technology and sustainability practices is the key to controlling logistical costs in smart and sustainable supply chains. Savings can be substantial with the use of digital technologies like AI, Big Data, and the Internet of Things. Artificial intelligence and large data sets, for instance, can help with demand forecasts, leading to lower inventory costs. Thanks to IoT's real-time tracking improvements, less money and resources are wasted. Sustainable business strategies, such as using less energy and producing less waste, can also yield substantial savings over time (Javaid et al., 2022).

Supply networks that are both sustainable and intelligent require resource management practices that prioritize efficiency over waste. To achieve this goal, we need to move away from linear supply chains and toward circular models that maximize resource reuse and recycling. The Internet of Things and Blockchain, for example, can improve resource tracking and management. Supplier and partner collaboration is also important since it enables the pooling of resources and the resolution of issues.

There is a rising need for new skills as supply chains become more technology driven and sustainability-focused. Organizations that care about their employees and their success should prioritize training and development. Data analysis, digital tool use, sustainability evaluation, and other forms of education may be included. In addition, businesses should encourage their workers to stay abreast of developments in sustainable and smart supply chain technology through a culture of learning and innovation.

6.2. The Evolving Role of the Logistics Manager

As supply networks become more sustainable and technologically advanced, the logistics manager's responsibilities are expanding at a rapid pace. In the past, making sure that commodities could travel quickly and cheaply was the top priority. However, as environmental concerns and technical developments have grown, so too have the duties of a logistics manager (World Bank Group, 2016).

Logistics managers have emerged as key players in the push for environmental responsibility. They are in charge of making sure that logistical activities have a minimal impact on the environment and are in line with the company's larger sustainability objectives (Silvestre, 2015). Energy efficiency, waste reduction, circular economy promotion, and strict adherence to environmental laws are all possible means toward this end. Sustainability reporting and communication, which highlights the company's environmental performance to stakeholders, could also fall within their purview.

The expanding responsibilities of the logistics manager can be attributed to the development of smart supply chains. AI, Big Data, the Internet of Things (IoT), and Blockchain are just some of the technologies they'll need to know about and implement to improve operational efficiency and resilience (Sulaiman, 2020). This may require implementing solutions such as artificial intelligence-based demand forecasting, big data-based performance analytics, internet-of-things-based real-time tracking, or blockchain-based improved transparency and traceability. That's why it's so important for logistics managers to be computer savvy nowadays.

In addition, logistics managers need to be skilled in relationship management because today's supply chains are so intricate and interdependent. Suppliers, consumers, transportation providers, regulatory agencies, and even competitors are just some of the many parties they must manage relationships with (Zreik, 2022). They need to help these parties work together and coordinate their efforts to keep the supply chain running smoothly and efficiently.

7. THE IMPACT OF CHINA'S INDUSTRY 5.0 ON SUPPLY CHAIN MANAGEMENT

7.1. Overview of China's Industry 5.0

Industry 5.0 is more than just a new technological era; it also represents a sea change in how humans interact with machines. Concerns about machine autonomy, data privacy, and the replacement of human work become more pressing as AI develops increasingly human-like perceptual and cognitive abilities (Hmioui, Bentalha, & Alla, 2020). When humans and machines are seen as complementary rather than interchangeable, fundamental questions about labor, individuality, and social values can be discussed. To make sure that technology enhances human potential without undermining core concepts of dignity and social fairness, this change in China needs careful analysis and appropriate control (Bentalha & Hmioui, 2021).

Industry 5.0 in China, frequently referred to as the next phase of the industrial revolution, expands upon and integrates human intelligence with technology developments made in Industry 4.0 (Saniuk, Grabowska, & Straka, 2022). While AI, IoT, and Big Data enabled the automation of production processes in Industry 4.0, Industry 5.0 restores the human element. It places an emphasis on human-machine cooperation by highlighting human strengths in areas such as creativity, problem solving, and personalization (Pizoń & Gola, 2023).

Industry 5.0 is a watershed moment, especially in the context of China, a world leader in the manufacturing sector. The country's booming manufacturing sector, long recognized for its size and efficiency, is transitioning to more customized, adaptable, and environmentally friendly methods of making things (Zreik, 2020). The goal is to increase the social value of products while decreasing their negative effects on the environment and maximizing their efficiency of production.

China is combining advanced technology with human skills to reach this goal. For instance, it employs AI not just for task automation but also to help with human judgment. It's not just about keeping an eye on machines; IoT is also being used to make workplaces safer for employees. Big Data is being used not only for performance analytics but also to better comprehend the wants and demands of the target market (Yu, Xu, & Ashton, 2023).

7.2. Impacts on the Supply Chain Landscape

China's unique economic and political fabric is essential context for understanding the effects of Industry 5.0 on the country's supply chain landscape. The drive for technical innovation is in line with national plans to elevate China to the forefront of high-tech industry and AI. Meanwhile, the cultural shift toward sustainability and environmental responsibility exemplified by Industry 5.0 rings true (Al Shaher & Zreik, 2022). This synthesis exemplifies the interplay between technological development, governmental policy, and social values, demonstrating how changes in one area can exacerbate or lessen the effects of change in the others. The causes, opportunities, and difficulties defining China's supply chain transformation can be better understood with this level of analysis of the effects of Industry 5.0 (Carayannis, Draper, & Bhaneja, 2021).

Industry 5.0's arrival in China has had far-reaching consequences for the supply chain, boosting productivity, reliability, and sustainability through the integration of human cognition with cutting-edge technology.

Customized and customer-focused supply chains are becoming increasingly important in the wake of Industry 5.0. Supply chains need to evolve to become more adaptable and responsive in order to meet the growing demand for personalized service (Zreik, Syed Marzuki, & Iqbal, 2023). More advanced use of AI, Big Data, and human insights into customer behavior is required for accurate demand forecasting, inventory management, and logistical planning.

Industry 5.0 places a premium on sustainability, therefore there has been a shift toward greener supply chain methods. The goal is to minimize the negative effects of production on the environment via means such as recycling and reducing emissions. Sustainable sourcing, a closed-loop supply chain, and other green logistics practices are rapidly rising in importance (Fraga-Lamas, Lopes, & Fernández-Caramés, 2021).

The importance of robust supply chains that can endure interruptions is also highlighted by Industry 5.0. This includes making the supply chain more transparent, increasing supplier diversity, and building redundancies. Enhancing resilience requires a combination of digital tools like IoT and Blockchain and human abilities like problem solving and crisis management.

With more people and machines working together, supply chain coordination is more important than ever. Coordination, information sharing, and issue solving all require strong cooperation with vendors, clients, and other partners. The ability to manage relationships, negotiate, and communicate effectively becomes as crucial as technical knowledge.

There is a rising need for new talents as the supply chain industry embraces greater technical sophistication and an emphasis on sustainability. Skills like creativity, critical thinking, and empathy are more important than ever in the Industry 5.0 paradigm, thus this is as important as training in digital technologies and sustainability practices.

Chinese companies can't reap the benefits of Industry 5.0 in supply chain management without embracing a human-machine partnership. To help employees make the most of AI, Big Data, and the Internet of Things, it is important to provide them with training that develops both their human intelligence and their technical skills. Incorporating eco-friendly practices and a commitment to sustainability into the fabric of the supply chain is no longer a nice-to-have; it's a requirement that shows a growing awareness of the importance of environmental protection on a global scale. To keep ahead of the competition, businesses must make substantial investments in technological infrastructure and adopt policies that promote innovation and flexibility.

8. EMERGING TRENDS IN SUPPLY CHAIN MANAGEMENT

8.1. Agile Logistics

Agile logistics is a new approach to supply chain management that values responsiveness, flexibility, and adaptability. It borrows ideas from Agile Management in software development to help logistics organizations be more flexible in the face of fluctuating demand, new technologies, and other factors (Alshahrani, M. A., & Salam, 2022).

Rapid decision making, constant refinement, and a focus on the client are hallmarks of Agile Logistics (Vinodh et al., 2013). This means that logistical activities are tracked and altered in real time as new information becomes available. An agile logistics system, for instance, would swiftly alter its operations to accommodate a sudden rise in demand for a product, so eliminating delays and stockouts.

Agile logistics relies heavily on cutting-edge technologies like AI, Big Data, and the Internet of Things. They give information in real time, so it facilitates making smart choices right away. Dynamic routing, in which AI is utilized to optimize delivery routes in real time, is one example. With the help of the Internet of Things, it is possible to get instantaneous updates on the whereabouts and condition of our goods (Davenport, 2018).

In addition, suppliers, customers, and other partners must work closely together to execute agile logistics. Transparent information exchange and collaborative problem-solving are essential for this.

Agile Logistics is gaining prominence in the context of China's Industry 5.0. The ability to rapidly and flexibly respond to changing needs is vital as supply chains become more personalized and customer-centric. In addition, the capacity to adapt and recover rapidly is crucial if interruptions like the COVID-19 pandemic grow more regular (Javed et al., 2022).

An essential aspect of understanding agile logistics in China involves a global comparison, exploring how the approach is implemented in comparison to other leading economies. This examination must take into account the distinct challenges and best practices that have emerged globally. An in-depth analysis of potential limitations and challenges is also imperative, as implementing Agile Logistics is not without hurdles (Alla, Jaouhari, & Bentalha, 2022). Key concerns include the required technological infrastructure, coordination among various stakeholders, and potential resistance to organizational change.

Despite these challenges, there are strategies to overcome them. Investing in technological solutions that bolster real-time decision-making in agile logistics is crucial, as technology serves as the backbone of agile practices. Furthermore, organizational cultural shifts must be encouraged to support agility and responsiveness. Embracing a culture that values flexibility and adaptability will not only align with agile principles but also facilitate a smoother transition and ongoing operation in the complex and rapidly evolving landscape of logistics management.

8.2. Service Supply Chains

Supply chain management is evolving to include a greater emphasis on the procedures and actions necessary to create and distribute services. Information, processes, and activities that lead to the delivery of a service to a consumer make up the service supply chain, which differs from typical supply chains that deal with the flow of physical items (Lusch, Vargo, & Tanniru, 2010).

The goal of service supply chains is to develop and provide services that provide value for the end user. Consulting, design, development, implementation, and support are all possible outcomes. Service quality, customer satisfaction, and service efficiency are common metrics used to evaluate the effectiveness of a service supply chain.

The application of AI, Big Data, and the IoT in service supply chains is on the rise. In after-sale service, for instance, AI can be used for predictive maintenance to see potential problems before they even arise. Through the use of Big Data analysis, businesses may better cater to their clientele by catering to their specific needs and preferences (Huang & Rust, 2021).

The significance of service supply chains is growing in the context of China's Industry 5.0. The capacity to provide high-quality, individualized services is essential in light of the trend toward more personalized and customer-centric manufacturing models. In addition, the management of service supply chains is growing importance as the country's economy shifts toward a service-based model.

The growth of service supply chains is increasingly influenced by the shifting market dynamics, with factors such as consumer expectations and regulatory influences playing a vital role. As the demand for high-quality services grows, understanding and responding to these market forces become crucial. Moreover, the integration of service supply chains with physical supply chains presents an opportunity for a more cohesive and synergistic approach, bridging the gap between tangible goods and intangible services. This integration not only streamlines processes but also enhances the overall customer experience.

At the core of this transformation is the need to establish quality standards for services to ensure consistency and excellence across various sectors. By adhering to defined benchmarks, organizations can maintain high levels of service delivery, instilling confidence and satisfaction among consumers. Finally, fostering cross-sector collaboration is essential in this evolving landscape. By encouraging different sectors to work together, innovation in service delivery can be achieved, creating new pathways for growth, efficiency, and customer-centric solutions. This collaborative mindset can further unify the often-fragmented aspects of modern supply chain management, creating a more robust and responsive system.

8.3. Supply Chain Management (SCM) Analytics

Data-driven analytics are increasingly being used in supply chain management; a field known as "Supply Chain Management" (SCM) Analytics. Data from sourcing and production through distribution and customer support are all part of what's known as the "supply chain" and must be collected, analyzed, and interpreted. The purpose is to obtain knowledge that can guide strategic choices and lead to greater efficiency, lower costs, and higher levels of customer satisfaction (Riahi et al., 2021).

Descriptive analytics (what happened), diagnostic analytics (why it happened), predictive analytics (what might happen), and prescriptive analytics (what should we do) are only some of the tools and approaches used by SCM Analytics (Sheng et al., 2021). In addition, the discussions within SCM Analytics encompass various topics, including demand forecasting, stock management, logistics optimization, risk management, and measuring performance.

Artificial intelligence, big data, and the internet of things are all making significant contributions to supply chain analytics. Artificial intelligence can analyze past data and patterns to predict future demand or spot potential problems. Descriptive and diagnostic analytics can make advantage of Big Data by examining massive datasets for insights into historical performance and the detection of underlying trends or problems. The Internet of Things can be used to track and monitor items in real time, delivering instantaneous information on their position and status.

SCM Analytics is growing in significance as part of China's Industry 5.0. The capacity to assess and interpret supply chain data is vital as manufacturing models evolve to become more data-driven and customer-centric. Additionally, the requirement for analytics to comprehend and manage supply chain complexity is expanding as supply networks become more complicated and interconnected.

The integration and interoperability of different systems and platforms within the scope of supply chain analytics present potential issues that need to be meticulously explored. As organizations seek to blend various technologies, the challenge of ensuring seamless communication and functionality between these platforms becomes prominent. Alongside these technical complexities, ethical considerations must also be at the forefront of the discussion, particularly in areas such as data privacy and transparency in the application of analytics. The usage of personal or sensitive data requires an ethical framework that emphasizes both legal compliance and moral responsibility.

To address these concerns, the importance of robust data governance practices cannot be understated. By implementing stringent guidelines and oversight, organizations can ensure the ethical and efficient use of data, safeguarding both integrity and trust. Furthermore, as technology continues to evolve, partnerships with tech providers become an essential strategy. Collaborating with those at the cutting edge of analytics solutions not only enhances capabilities but also facilitates alignment with industry best practices and standards, fostering innovation, efficiency, and responsible growth.

Adopting the latest practices in supply chain management calls for strategic planning, strong leadership, and investments in people and technology. Agile logistics implementation calls for a shift toward a more adaptable and responsive company culture. It also means spending money on cutting-edge tools that improve decision-making in the moment. Providing value to customers will depend critically on Service Supply Chains developing cross-industry collaboration and defining quality standards. When it comes to supply chain management analytics, businesses need to establish strict data governance procedures and form relationships with technology providers in order to successfully negotiate the challenging landscape of data-driven decision making. These measures are congruent with China's Industry 5.0 and pave the way for supply chain management that is more robust, innovative, and customer-centric.

9. CONCLUSION

This chapter surveyed China's sustainable and smart supply chains from every angle, stressing the importance of adopting a holistic strategy that integrates environmental considerations, technological advancements, and creative economic tactics.

The chapter opened by discussing the urgent need for a sustainable transformation by illuminating the large environmental footprint of China's enormous supplier chains. New sustainable business models are being implemented in China as a direct response to growing public awareness of environmental issues and consumer demand for such options. These models illustrate the possibilities for market segmentation and competitive positioning that minimizes environmental effect by incorporating sustainability into logistics and supply chain management.

The chapter spent a lot of time talking about how technology has revolutionized modern supply chain management. In this chapter, we looked at how new technologies like Big Data, AI, the Internet of Things (IoT), and Blockchain are boosting productivity, lessening environmental impacts, and making China's supply chains more robust. Examples were given of how these digital tools have been successfully implemented in the management of Chinese supply chains, providing concrete evidence of their effectiveness.

Strategies for managing logistics costs, resources, and skills inside and across businesses were outlined, and the role of green finance in bolstering sustainable logistics initiatives in China was explored. In the context of green and intelligent supply chains, the changing function of the logistics manager was examined in depth.

In the chapter's last sections, we analyzed how Agile Logistics, Service Supply Chains, and SCM analytics are changing the supply chain landscape as a result of China's Industry 5.0. These developments in China have far-reaching effects on the supply chain management landscape worldwide.

The future of supply chain management is clearly determined by sustainability, digitalization, and innovation, and this is true both in China and around the world. As awareness of the importance of preserving the environment grows, businesses will have to incorporate green thinking into their supply chains not merely to stay in compliance with regulations, but also to gain an edge in the market. As more and more businesses adopt digital technologies, supply chain operations will improve in terms of efficiency, reliability, and focus on the customer. The complexity of today's supply chains makes it ever more important to employ cutting-edge business models and management practices.

More importantly for supply chains, the arrival of Industry 5.0 represents a change toward more customized, sustainable, and human-centric methods of manufacturing. This shift will be made possible by the integration of cutting-edge technology and human expertise in the form of agile logistics, service supply chains, and SCM analytics.

REFERENCES

Al Shaher, S., & Zreik, M. (2022). The Impact of Job Characteristics and Value Congruence on Employee Retention: An Empirical Study from Lebanon. *The Journal of Asian Finance* [JAFEB]. *Economics and Business*, *9*(3), 171–180.

Alla, L., Jaouhari, E. L., & Bentalha, B. (2022). Repenser l'entrepreneuriat au sein du secteur informel au Maroc à l'ère du post Covid-19: Pour approche prospective de la formalisation intégrative. *Alternatives Managériales et Economiques*, *4*(1), 180–202.

Alshahrani, M. A., & Salam, M. A. (2022). The Role of Supply Chain Resilience on SMEs' Performance: The Case of an Emerging Economy. *Logistics*, *6*(3), 47. doi:10.3390/logistics6030047

Amoako, G. K., Bonsu, G. A., Caesar, L. D., & Osei-Tete, F. (2021). Finding the nexus between green supply chain practices and sustainable business advantage: An emerging market perspective. *Management of Environmental Quality*, *32*(6), 1133–1149. doi:10.1108/MEQ-12-2019-0287

Attaran, M., Attaran, S., & Celik, B. G. (2023). The impact of digital twins on the evolution of intelligent manufacturing and Industry 4.0. *Advances in Computational Intelligence*, *3*(3), 11. doi:10.100743674-023-00058-y PMID:37305021

Bentalha, B., & Hmioui, A. (2021, November). Smart Service Supply Chain and Just Walk Out Technology: A Netnographic Approach. In *The Proceedings of the International Conference on Smart City Applications* (pp. 223-236). Cham: Springer International Publishing.

Carayannis, E. G., Draper, J., & Bhaneja, B. (2021). Towards fusion energy in the Industry 5.0 and Society 5.0 context: Call for a global commission for urgent action on fusion energy. *Journal of the Knowledge Economy*, *12*(4), 1891–1904. doi:10.100713132-020-00695-5

Chekima, B., Wafa, S. A. W. S. K., Igau, O. A., Chekima, S., & Sondoh, S. L. Jr. (2016). Examining green consumerism motivational drivers: Does premium price and demographics matter to green purchasing? *Journal of Cleaner Production*, *112*, 3436–3450. doi:10.1016/j.jclepro.2015.09.102

Chen, H., Yan, X., Liu, X., & Ma, T. (2022). Exploring the operational performance discrepancies between online ridesplitting and carpooling transportation modes based on DiDi data. *Transportation*, 1–36.

Chen, X., & Ji, Z. (2020). Networked coordination to facilitate secondhand electronics recycling and exchange: a case study on aihuishou. In *Business Innovation with New ICT in the Asia-Pacific: Case Studies* (pp. 327–347). Springer Nature Singapore.

Chien, F., Chau, K. Y., & Sadiq, M. (2023). Impact of climate mitigation technology and natural resource management on climate change in China. *Resources Policy*, *81*, 103367. doi:10.1016/j.resourpol.2023.103367

Davenport, T. H. (2018). *The AI advantage: How to put the artificial intelligence revolution to work.* MIT Press. doi:10.7551/mitpress/11781.001.0001

Farooque, M., Zhang, A., Liu, Y., & Hartley, J. L. (2022). Circular supply chain management: Performance outcomes and the role of eco-industrial parks in China. *Transportation Research Part E, Logistics and Transportation Review*, *157*, 102596. doi:10.1016/j.tre.2021.102596

Fraga-Lamas, P., Lopes, S. I., & Fernández-Caramés, T. M. (2021). Green IoT and edge AI as key technological enablers for a sustainable digital transition towards a smart circular economy: An industry 5.0 use case. *Sensors (Basel)*, *21*(17), 5745. doi:10.339021175745 PMID:34502637

Free, C., & Hecimovic, A. (2021). Global supply chains after COVID-19: The end of the road for neoliberal globalisation? *Accounting, Auditing & Accountability Journal*, *34*(1), 58–84. doi:10.1108/AAAJ-06-2020-4634

Fróna, D., Szenderák, J., & Harangi-Rákos, M. (2019). The challenge of feeding the world. *Sustainability (Basel)*, *11*(20), 5816. doi:10.3390u11205816

Frynas, J. G., Mol, M. J., & Mellahi, K. (2018). Management innovation made in China: Haier's Rendanheyi. *California Management Review*, *61*(1), 71–93. doi:10.1177/0008125618790244

García Márquez, F. P., Papaelias, M., & Marini, S. (2022). Artificial Intelligence in Marine Science and Engineering. *Journal of Marine Science and Engineering*, *10*(6), 711. doi:10.3390/jmse10060711

Grant, D. B., Wong, C. Y., & Trautrims, A. (2017). *Sustainable logistics and supply chain management: principles and practices for sustainable operations and management.* Kogan Page Publishers.

Haipeter, T., Helfen, M., Kirsch, A., Rosenbohm, S., & Üyük, C. (2021). Industrial relations at centre stage: Efficiency, equity and voice in the governance of global labour standards. *Industrielle Beziehungen. Zeitschrift für Arbeit. Organisation und Management*, *28*(2), 148–171.

Hmioui, A., Bentalha, B., & Alla, L. (2020, December). Service supply chain: A prospective analysis of sustainable management for global performance. In *2020 IEEE 13th International Colloquium of Logistics and Supply Chain Management (LOGISTIQUA)* (pp. 1-7). IEEE. 10.1109/LOGISTIQUA49782.2020.9353940

Huang, M. H., & Rust, R. T. (2021). Engaged to a robot? The role of AI in service. *Journal of Service Research*, *24*(1), 30–41. doi:10.1177/1094670520902266

Hugos, M. H. (2018). *Essentials of supply chain management.* John Wiley & Sons.

Javaid, M., Haleem, A., Singh, R. P., & Suman, R. (2022). Enhancing smart farming through the applications of Agriculture 4.0 technologies. *International Journal of Intelligent Networks*, *3*, 150–164. doi:10.1016/j.ijin.2022.09.004

Javed, A. R., Shahzad, F., Rehman, S., Zikria, Y. B., Razzak, I., Jalil, Z., & Xu, G. (2022). Future smart cities requirements, emerging technologies, applications, challenges, and future aspects. *Cities (London, England)*, *129*, 103794. doi:10.1016/j.cities.2022.103794

Kyriakopoulos, G. L. (2021). Environmental legislation in european and international contexts: Legal practices and social planning toward the circular economy. *Laws*, *10*(1), 3. doi:10.3390/laws10010003

Lacity, M., & Van Hoek, R. (2021). *Requiem for reconciliations: DL Freight, a blockchain-enabled solution by Walmart Canada and DLT Labs.* University of Arkansas Blockchain Center for Excellence Research.

Lusch, R. F., Vargo, S. L., & Tanniru, M. (2010). Service, value networks and learning. *Journal of the Academy of Marketing Science*, *38*(1), 19–31. doi:10.100711747-008-0131-z

Manners-Bell, J., & Lyon, K. (2019). *The logistics and supply chain innovation handbook: disruptive technologies and new business models*. Kogan Page Publishers.

Mihálovits, Z., & Tapaszti, A. (2018). Green bond, the financial instrument that supports sustainable development. *Public Finance Quarterly*, *63*(3), 303.

Misra, N. N., Dixit, Y., Al-Mallahi, A., Bhullar, M. S., Upadhyay, R., & Martynenko, A. (2020). IoT, big data, and artificial intelligence in agriculture and food industry. *IEEE Internet of Things Journal*, *9*(9), 6305–6324. doi:10.1109/JIOT.2020.2998584

Naidoo, M., & Gasparatos, A. (2018). Corporate environmental sustainability in the retail sector: Drivers, strategies and performance measurement. *Journal of Cleaner Production*, *203*, 125–142. doi:10.1016/j.jclepro.2018.08.253

Naim, A. (2021). New Trends in Business Process Management: Applications of Green Information Technologies. *British Journal of Environmental Studies*, *1*(1), 12–23.

Ng, K. K., Chen, C. H., Lee, C. K., Jiao, J. R., & Yang, Z. X. (2021). A systematic literature review on intelligent automation: Aligning concepts from theory, practice, and future perspectives. *Advanced Engineering Informatics*, *47*, 101246. doi:10.1016/j.aei.2021.101246

Pan, Y., & Zhang, L. (2021). Roles of artificial intelligence in construction engineering and management: A critical review and future trends. *Automation in Construction*, *122*, 103517. doi:10.1016/j.autcon.2020.103517

Pilkington, M. (2019). *Retail Therapy: Why The Retail Industry Is Broken–And What Can Be Done To Fix It.* Bloomsbury Publishing.

Pizoń, J., & Gola, A. (2023). Human–Machine Relationship—Perspective and Future Roadmap for Industry 5.0 Solutions. *Machines*, *11*(2), 203. doi:10.3390/machines11020203

Riahi, Y., Saikouk, T., Gunasekaran, A., & Badraoui, I. (2021). Artificial intelligence applications in supply chain: A descriptive bibliometric analysis and future research directions. *Expert Systems with Applications*, *173*, 114702. doi:10.1016/j.eswa.2021.114702

Saniuk, S., Grabowska, S., & Straka, M. (2022). Identification of Social and Economic Expectations: Contextual Reasons for the Transformation Process of Industry 4.0 into the Industry 5.0 Concept. *Sustainability (Basel)*, *14*(3), 1391. doi:10.3390u14031391

Sargani, G. R., Zhou, D., Raza, M. H., & Wei, Y. (2020). Sustainable entrepreneurship in the agriculture sector: The nexus of the triple bottom line measurement approach. *Sustainability (Basel)*, *12*(8), 3275. doi:10.3390u12083275

Sharma, A., Kaur, J., & Singh, I. (2020). Internet of things (IoT) in pharmaceutical manufacturing, warehousing, and supply chain management. *SN Computer Science*, *1*(4), 1–10. doi:10.100742979-020-00248-2

Sheng, J., Amankwah-Amoah, J., Khan, Z., & Wang, X. (2021). COVID-19 pandemic in the new era of big data analytics: Methodological innovations and future research directions. *British Journal of Management*, *32*(4), 1164–1183. doi:10.1111/1467-8551.12441

Silvestre, B. S. (2015). Sustainable supply chain management in emerging economies: Environmental turbulence, institutional voids and sustainability trajectories. *International Journal of Production Economics*, *167*, 156–169. doi:10.1016/j.ijpe.2015.05.025

Singhania, M., & Saini, N. (2022). Systems approach to environment, social and governance (ESG): Case of Reliance industries. *Sustainable Operations and Computers*, *3*, 103–117. doi:10.1016/j.susoc.2021.11.003

Sulaiman, M. A. (2020). Evaluating data mining classification methods performance in Internet of things applications. *Journal of Soft Computing and Data Mining*, *1*(2), 11–25.

Sundarakani, B., Ajaykumar, A., & Gunasekaran, A. (2021). Big data driven supply chain design and applications for blockchain: An action research using case study approach. *Omega*, *102*, 102452. doi:10.1016/j.omega.2021.102452

Udeagha, M. C., & Muchapondwa, E. (2023). Green finance, fintech, and environmental sustainability: Fresh policy insights from the BRICS nations. *International Journal of Sustainable Development and World Ecology*, *30*(6), 1–17. doi:10.1080/13504509.2023.2183526

Vinodh, S., Ben Ruben, R., & Asokan, P. (2016). Life cycle assessment integrated value stream mapping framework to ensure sustainable manufacturing: A case study. *Clean Technologies and Environmental Policy*, *18*(1), 279–295. doi:10.100710098-015-1016-8

Vinodh, S., Devadasan, S. R., Vimal, K. E. K., & Kumar, D. (2013). Design of agile supply chain assessment model and its case study in an Indian automotive components manufacturing organization. *Journal of Manufacturing Systems*, *32*(4), 620–631. doi:10.1016/j.jmsy.2013.04.001

Wang, H., Zhang, M., Ying, H., & Zhao, X. (2021). The impact of blockchain technology on consumer behavior: A multimethod study. *Journal of Management Analytics*, *8*(3), 371–390. doi:10.1080/23270012.2021.1958264

World Bank Group. (2016). *World development report 2016: Digital dividends*. World Bank Publications.

Yu, X., Xu, S., & Ashton, M. (2023). Antecedents and outcomes of artificial intelligence adoption and application in the workplace: The socio-technical system theory perspective. *Information Technology & People*, *36*(1), 454–474. doi:10.1108/ITP-04-2021-0254

Zhang, D., Pee, L. G., & Cui, L. (2021). Artificial intelligence in E-commerce fulfillment: A case study of resource orchestration at Alibaba's Smart Warehouse. *International Journal of Information Management*, *57*, 102304. doi:10.1016/j.ijinfomgt.2020.102304

Zhang, S., & Chen, W. (2022). China's energy transition pathway in a carbon neutral vision. *Engineering (Beijing)*, *14*, 64–76. doi:10.1016/j.eng.2021.09.004

Zreik, M. (2020). The Dimensions of the US-China trade war. *Open Political Science*, *3*(1), 47–55. doi:10.1515/openps-2020-0004

Zreik, M. (2022). The Regional Comprehensive Economic Partnership (RCEP) for the Asia–Pacific region and world. *Journal of Economic and Administrative Sciences*.

Zreik, M. (2023). Analytical study on Foreign Direct Investment Divestment Inflows and Outflows in Developing Economies: Evidence of China. *Chinese Economy*, 1–16. doi:10.1080/10971475.2023.2193118

Zreik, M., Syed Marzuki, S. Z., & Iqbal, B. A. (2023). Deepening Financial Inclusion through Digitization: A Case Study of Microfinance in China. [AEJ]. *ASEAN Entrepreneurship Journal*, *9*(2), 9–21.

Chapter 11
Sustainable Logistics and Competitive Positioning

Shakerod Munuhwa
https://orcid.org/0000-0002-0952-6514
Glasgow Caledonian University, UK

ABSTRACT

The book chapter explores the integration of sustainable logistics and competitive positioning in today's business environment. It discusses the importance of incorporating sustainable practices into logistics operations, including reducing carbon emissions, optimizing resource utilization, and embracing social responsibility. The chapter emphasizes the relationship between sustainable logistics and gaining a competitive edge, highlighting strategies and best practices in areas such as transportation, warehousing, packaging, and reverse logistics. It also explores the role of technology and innovation in facilitating sustainable logistics and enhancing competitiveness. The chapter provides real-world examples and case studies to showcase successful implementations of sustainable logistics across industries, showcasing the benefits in terms of cost savings, customer satisfaction, brand reputation, and market positioning.

INTRODUCTION

Sustainable Logistics and Competitive Positioning is critical because it navigates the intersection of sustainable practices and modern business dynamics. In an era of increased environmental awareness, the chapter's analysis of sustainable logistics provides a road map for organisations to incorporate eco-friendly practices into their operations, boosting social responsibility and company reputation. Its emphasis on the strategic alignment of sustainable logistics and competitive advantage highlights the opportunity for businesses to differentiate themselves in a competitive market while realising tangible benefits such as cost savings, improved customer satisfaction, and strengthened brand identity. The chapter empowers businesses with actionable insights to navigate the dynamic landscape, ultimately directing them towards sustainable growth and competitive positioning by addressing real-world difficulties and emphasising the importance of technology.

DOI: 10.4018/979-8-3693-0225-5.ch011

OVERVIEW OF SUSTAINABLE LOGISTICS

Growing awareness of the negative social and environmental effects of conventional logistics practices has emerged in recent years. As a result, the idea of sustainable logistics has become an important part of the contemporary business environment. The chapter gives a thorough review of sustainable logistics, highlighting its significance for long-term viability and competitive positioning.

According to Srivastava (2017) sustainability logistics is one key element of sustainable supply chain that focuses on the design, execution, and management of logistical activities while taking into account the environment, society, and economy It emphasizes a triple bottom line strategy that considers how decisions may affect people, the environment, and revenue (Chen & Paulraj, 2017). Varsei, Azadegan and Ivanov (2019) expounded that using sustainable logistics methods enables businesses to try to strike a balance between satisfying their logistical requirements and minimising adverse environmental and social effects. Vanalle et al. (2021) added that sustainable logistics takes into account many tactics and programmes that can be used to lessen the negative effects of logistical operations. It addresses issues including lowering carbon emissions through the use of alternative fuels, energy-efficient modes of transportation, and green packaging techniques. Bentalha, Hmioui and Alla (2021) explored that maximising resource consumption and environmental damage also covers the significance of waste management and recycling in logistics.

Further, social sustainability is concerned with the ethical and social aspects of logistical operations. It takes into account things like labour rights, fair working conditions, and community involvement. This section emphasises the need of providing safe and healthy working environments for employees throughout the supply chain. It also emphasizes the significance of ethical sourcing practices, supplier variety, and engagement with local communities in order to promote beneficial social consequences (Sodhi & Tang, 2016).

Economic Sustainability in Logistics

Economic sustainability in logistics revolves around optimising operations to ensure long-term profitability and resource efficiency (Seuring & Gold, 2019). This section delves into solutions for cost-effective logistics management, such as supply chain optimisation, inventory management, and collaborative planning. It also emphasises the role of sustainable logistics in increasing operational efficiency and lowering costs through better resource utilisation and streamlined operations.

COMPETITIVE POSITIONING IN SUSTAINABLE LOGISTICS

Richey et al, (2016) affirms that competitive positioning in logistics refers to the strategic method followed by logistics organisations or departments to establish a favourable market position relative to competitors. It entails distinguishing logistics services, capabilities, and products in order to establish a competitive edge and attract consumers in the logistics business (Seuring & Gold, 2019). Competitive positioning in logistics is comprised of five factors, which are discussed below.

Service Differentiation

Logistics firms can distinguish themselves by providing one-of-a-kind and specialised services that address specific consumer needs. This could include customised transportation solutions, value-added services such as warehousing and distribution, or cutting-edge supply chain management approaches. Companies can attract consumers who demand specific logistics capabilities or have unique requirements by offering differentiated services (Srivastava, 2017).

Cost Leadership

Cost competition is another facet of logistics competitive positioning. Companies can try to provide cost-effective logistics solutions by increasing operational efficiency, leveraging economies of scale, and using lean practices. This can attract price-sensitive clients and help the company obtain a competitive advantage in terms of pricing and overall cost-effectiveness (Pagell & Wu, 2017).

Technology and Innovation

In logistics, embracing technological breakthroughs and new solutions can provide a competitive advantage. This includes deploying advanced tracking and tracing systems, real-time visibility platforms, automation and robots, and data analytics for better decision-making and operational efficiency. Logistics companies that efficiently use technology can provide increased visibility, transparency, and efficiency, which can be appealing to customers looking for dependable and technologically sophisticated logistics services (Khan et al, 2016).

Network and Infrastructure

In competitive positioning, the physical network and infrastructure are critical. Logistics organisations with a large network of distribution centres, warehouses, transportation assets, and a global footprint may provide complete and dependable logistics solutions. This is particularly useful for customers with complex supply chains or foreign enterprises (Jüttner & Maklan, 2019).

Customer Service and Relationship Management

Ivanov and Tsipoulanidis (2019) underscores that developing strong client relationships and providing outstanding customer service can be a crucial differentiator in logistics. Understanding client needs, being responsive and proactive in resolving difficulties, giving accurate and timely information, and keeping open communication lines are all part of this. Logistics firms that prioritise customer service and form long-term partnerships can obtain a competitive edge by cultivating client loyalty and satisfaction (Ferdows & de Meyer, 2018).

Govindan et al. (2017) advised that companies must study the market, comprehend client requirements, analyse rivals' strengths and weaknesses. Further institutions may then design strategic plans that matche with their unique competencies and value proposition in order to effectively establish a competitive position in logistics. Logistics companies may acquire customers, retain existing clients, and achieve long-term success in a competitive market by strategically positioning themselves (Bentalha, Hmioui and Alla, 2023).

MODERN STRATEGIES IN LOGISTICS COMPETITIVE POSITIONING

Competitive positioning in sustainable logistics is critical for firms seeking a competitive edge, market differentiation, and long-term success (Christopher & Peck, 2018). This section delves into the numerous factors and methods that go into attaining a strong competitive position through sustainable logistics.

Differentiation Through Sustainability

Yusufkhonov et al. (2021) noted that in a crowded economy, sustainable logistics allows businesses to differentiate themselves from competition. Companies may demonstrate their commitment to environmental stewardship, social responsibility, and ethical business practices by incorporating sustainable practices into their supply chain and logistical operations. This distinction enables firms to attract environmentally conscious consumers who value sustainable products and services, giving them a competitive advantage (Awan & Ali, 2019).

Innovation and Technological Advancements

Competitive positioning in sustainable logistics necessitates embracing innovation and technical developments. Companies that invest proactively in the research and development of sustainable logistics solutions, such as green transportation technologies, renewable energy systems, and smart logistics platforms, can achieve operational efficiencies, reduce carbon emissions, and improve overall sustainability performance (Ogli & Buribayevich, 2022). These inventive practices not only contribute to cost savings, but also position firms as industry leaders, attracting clients who value technology developments and environmental sustainability (Chen & Paulraj, 2017).

Supply Chain Collaboration and Integration

Collaboration and supply chain integration are critical for competitive positioning in sustainable logistics. Organisations that have good partnerships with suppliers, consumers, and stakeholders can harness shared experience, resources, and knowledge to improve supply chain sustainability. Collaborative efforts such as cooperative sustainability projects, supplier certification programmes, and responsible sourcing practices assist firms in ensuring supply chain transparency, traceability, and ethical behaviour. This increases consumer trust and loyalty, allowing for competitive positioning based on long-term supply chain practices (Sudusinghe & Seuring, 2022).

Sustainability Reporting and Transparency

Transparent reporting on sustainability performance is critical for sustainable logistics competitive positioning. Christopher and Peck (2018) affirmed that organisations that assess, monitor, and report on their environmental and social consequences demonstrate to stakeholders accountability and transparency.

Companies develop credibility and trust with customers, investors, and regulatory agencies by reporting their sustainability initiatives, goals, and successes through sustainability reports, public disclosures, or certifications. This transparency distinguishes them from competition and establishes them as responsible and trustworthy partners (Christopher, 2016).

Circular Economy and Waste Reduction

Adopting circular economy concepts and focusing on waste reduction might help institutions gain a competitive advantage in sustainable logistics. Companies that use techniques like product life extension, recycling programmes, reverse logistics, and waste reduction initiatives reduce their environmental footprint and maximise resource utilisation. Companies can decrease costs, improve resource efficiency, and attract customers that value sustainable and eco-friendly practices by designing products for recyclability, adopting efficient waste management systems, and exploring prospects for reuse and remanufacturing (Vilariño et al, 2017).

Continuous Improvement and Adaptability

Maintaining a strong competitive position in sustainable logistics necessitates an ongoing commitment to improvement and adaptability. Organisations must analyse their logistical operations on a regular basis, assess their sustainability performance, and identify opportunities for improvement. Companies can respond to changing market dynamics, rising sustainability trends, and developing customer expectations by embracing an innovation, agility, and learning culture. Continuous improvement enables firms to remain competitive, adapt to new sustainability problems, and capitalise on possibilities for development and distinction (Liu et al., 2019).

IMPORTANCE OF SUSTAINABLE LOGISTICS FOR COMPETITIVE POSITIONING

In today's business landscape, sustainable logistics plays a vital role in determining the competitive positioning of organisations. By integrating sustainability principles into their logistics practices, companies can differentiate themselves, attract environmentally and socially conscious customers, and gain a competitive advantage. This section explores the significance of sustainable logistics for competitive positioning.

Meeting Customer Expectations

According to Jinru et al (2022), environmentally and socially responsible products and services are becoming increasingly popular among consumers. Organisations can achieve these expectations by demonstrating their commitment to lowering environmental impacts, assuring ethical supply chains, and supporting social well-being through sustainable logistics. Companies may develop their brand image, increase customer loyalty, and gain a competitive advantage in the market by aligning their logistical operations with customer values.

Enhancing Brand Reputation

Sustainable logistics practices support the development of a positive brand reputation. Companies that prioritise sustainability and incorporate it into their logistical operations are seen as responsible and foresighted. This favourable image is shared by customers, investors, and stakeholders, resulting in more trust and credibility. Customers are more likely to choose companies that agree with their beliefs, therefore a good brand reputation can provide organisations a considerable edge over competitors (Vilariño et al, 2017).

Cost Savings and Operational Efficiency

Sustainable logistics strategies frequently result in cost savings and increased operational efficiency. Optimising transportation routes, using fuel-efficient cars, and establishing excellent inventory management practices, for example, can cut transportation costs while increasing waste. Warehouses and distribution centres that consume less energy can result in cheaper power costs. Organisations can offer competitive pricing, enhance profitability, and reinvest resources in additional sustainability activities by lowering expenses and improving operational efficiency (Sudusinghe & Seuring, 2022).

Risk Mitigation and Resilience

Sustainable logistics practices help to reduce risk and build organisational resilience (Denga & Rakshit, 2022; Moosav et al, 2022). Companies can manage the risks associated with disruptions, such as resource scarcity, legislative changes, or reputational damage, by diversifying their suppliers, establishing responsible sourcing practices, and guaranteeing supply chain transparency. Organisations that address environmental and social risks proactively are better prepared to endure difficulties, preserve continuity, and recover swiftly from disruptions, which improves their competitive positioning (Denga & Rakshit, 2022).

Compliance with Regulations and Standards

Sustainable logistics practices assist businesses in meeting changing environmental requirements and industry standards. Governments and regulatory organisations are increasingly implementing stringent emissions, waste management, and social responsibility standards. Companies may ensure compliance, avoid penalties, and demonstrate their commitment to corporate social responsibility by using sustainable logistics practices. Regulation compliance and adherence to accepted sustainability standards can provide a competitive advantage, especially in areas where sustainability performance is a significant differentiator (Moosav et al, 2022).

Attracting and Retaining Talent

Tseng et al. (2022) clarifies that sustainable logistics practices help attract and retain outstanding workers. Organisations that stress sustainability and social responsibility are valued by today's workforce. Companies that demonstrate a commitment to sustainable logistics can attract ecologically and socially conscientious individuals looking for meaningful work and purpose-driven jobs. Furthermore, sustainable logistics initiatives boost employee engagement and satisfaction, which can lower attrition rates and increase productivity.

PRINCIPLES AND OBJECTIVES OF SUSTAINABLE LOGISTICS

The guiding concepts and goals that logistics businesses try to attain in their operations to minimise environmental effect, promote social responsibility, and maintain long-term economic sustainability are referred to as sustainable logistics principles and objectives. These principles and objectives are intended to strike a balance between serving customer needs, optimising supply chain efficiency, and reducing the negative environmental and societal effects of logistics activities (Jayarathna, Agdas & Dawes, 2023). Below are some of the most important principles and goals of sustainable logistics.

Environmental Stewardship

Sustainable logistics strives to reduce the environmental impact of logistics operations by lowering greenhouse gas emissions, energy consumption, waste generation, and pollution. This includes using eco-friendly transportation modes, optimising routes to minimise mileage, developing green packaging solutions, and supporting recycling and waste management programmes (Jayarathna et al., 2023).

Resource Efficiency

Sustainable logistics aims to maximise resource utilisation across the supply chain. This involves increasing fuel efficiency, maximising truck load capacity, implementing lean inventory management practices, and decreasing needless packaging materials. Logistics firms may minimise costs, waste, and contribute to a more sustainable use of resources by optimising resource efficiency (Hu et al., 2020).

Social Responsibility

Sustainable logistics recognises the significance of social factors in logistics operations. This includes protecting worker safety and well-being, encouraging fair labour practices, and upholding human rights throughout the supply chain. Logistics firms try to provide a safe and inclusive work environment, fair wages and benefits to employees, and ethical sourcing practices (Vilariño et al., 2017).

Collaboration and Stakeholder Engagement

Collaboration and participation with many stakeholders, such as consumers, suppliers, government agencies, and local communities, are key to sustainable logistics. Logistics firms may effectively address varied perspectives and integrate sustainability goals into their operations by incorporating stakeholders in decision-making processes and actively seeking their opinion (Vilariño et al., 2017).

Continuous Improvement

Sustainable logistics is a never-ending process of improvement and innovation. Logistics firms commit to continual environmental and social performance monitoring, measurement, and improvement. They establish goals and benchmarks to track progress, implement sustainable practices, and engage in research and development to discover innovative ways to improve logistical efficiency while minimising environmental effect (Persdotter, Hulthén & Forslund, 2019).

Economic Viability

Long-term sustainability requires economic viability, which sustainable logistics recognises. Logistics firms strive for profitability while also considering the environmental and social consequences of their operations. Companies can reduce costs, increase operational efficiency, improve customer happiness, and boost their market position by applying sustainable practices. Sustainable logistics concepts and objectives aid businesses in making strategic decisions, defining performance targets, and integrating sustainability into day-to-day operations. Logistics firms can improve the environment, society, and their own company performance by aligning their practices with these concepts and aims (Lan et al., 2020).

ENVIRONMENTAL, SOCIAL, AND ECONOMIC ASPECTS OF SUSTAINABILITY IN LOGISTICS

Sustainability in logistics encompasses three key aspects which are environmental, social, and economic. These aspects highlight the interconnectedness and holistic approach required to achieve sustainable practices within the logistics industry. Below is an overview of each aspect:

Environmental Sustainability

As guided by Jayarathna et al. (2023), environmental sustainability in logistics focuses on maximising the ecological impact of logistics operations and reducing resource consumption. Key considerations include greenhouse gas emissions which logistics companies aim to reduce by optimising transportation routes, utilising fuel-efficient vehicles, and exploring alternative energy sources such as electric or hybrid vehicles.

Biswas and Anand (2020) added that implementing energy-efficient practices and technologies throughout the supply chain, such as optimising warehouse lighting, using energy-saving equipment, and employing renewable energy sources is another crucial way towards environmental sustainability.

In addition (Asees et al. (2019) corroborated that reducing waste generation, promoting recycling and reuse of materials, and adopting responsible waste management practices to maximise the environmental impact. Whilst all waste reduction is important, (Dubey et al. (2019) contended that employing eco-friendly packaging materials, right-sizing packaging to maximise waste, and using recyclable or biodegradable packaging options is one of the best options towards environmental management.

Moreover, implementing measures to conserve water, reduce energy consumption, and maximise the use of non-renewable resources in logistics operations goes a long way towards environmental sustainability (Ekinci et al., 2022).

Social Sustainability

Orji, Kusi-Sarpong and Gupta (2020) assert that social sustainability in logistics emphasizes the well-being and fair treatment of workers, as well as ethical practices throughout the supply chain. Providing a safe working environment for employees, implementing safety protocols, and ensuring compliance with health and safety regulations to prevent workplace accidents and injuries (Hu et al., 2020).

Govindan et al., (2017) retorted that upholding fair employment practices, including fair wages, non-discrimination, equal opportunities, and providing good working conditions for employees. Added to that, Jinru et al. (2022) opined that engaging with suppliers who follow ethical standards, promote fair trade practices, and respect human rights in their operations. Further Lahkani, et al. (2020) agreed that supporting local communities contributes to their development, and engagement in initiatives that address social needs and promote positive social impact.

Economic Sustainability

Economic sustainability in logistics focuses on achieving profitability and long-term viability while considering the broader impacts on society and the environment (Arya et al., 2020). Implementing cost-effective practices that optimise logistics operations, reduce waste, and enhance operational efficiency has been highlighted by Seuring and Gold (2019) to be a key contributor towards economics sustainability. Pagell and Wu (2017) substantiated that building resilient supply chains that can adapt to changing market conditions, disruptions, and environmental challenges whilst Rossitto, et al. (2022) affirmed that embracing innovative technologies and processes to enhance logistics efficiency, reduce costs, and improve customer satisfaction.

Further, Vanalle et al. (2021) reiterated that collaborating with stakeholders, including customers, suppliers, and industry partners, foster mutually beneficial relationships and create shared value. Ensuring compliance with relevant laws, regulations, and industry standards, and maintaining strong corporate governance practices.

Agreeably Wichaisri et al. (2017) emphasized that addressing the environmental, social, and economic aspects of sustainability, logistics companies can drive positive change, promote responsible practices, and contribute to a more sustainable and resilient future for the industry and society as a whole.

Lastlly, Lan et al. (2020) substantiated that logistics firms may influence positive change, advance ethical behaviour, and contribute to the industry's and society's overall transition to a more sustainable and resilient future by addressing the environmental, social, and economic components of sustainability.

SUSTAINABLE LOGISTICS STRATEGIES

Green Transportation and Alternative Fuels

Maximising the environmental impact of transportation and developing a greener, more sustainable supply chain depend heavily on sustainable logistics solutions. The utilisation of green transportation methods and alternative fuels is one of the main strategies in sustainable logistics (Brewer & Button, 2016). The next paragraphs provide a summary of these ideas:

Green transportation refers to the use of environmentally friendly modes of transportation and the implementation of sustainable practices throughout the transportation process. It aims to reduce greenhouse gas emissions, maximise energy consumption, and mitigate the environmental impact of logistics activities.

Encouraging the use of more sustainable transportation modes such as rail and waterways instead of relying solely on road transport. These modes have lower carbon footprints and can handle larger volumes of goods, leading to reduced emissions and congestion (Yusufkhonov et al., 2021). Ogli et al. (2022) contended that adopting fuel-efficient vehicles and optimising vehicles loads maximizes fuel consumption and emissions. This can involve using advanced technologies, such as hybrid or electric vehicles, improving aerodynamics, and implementing eco-driving practices. Persdotter et al. (2019) further advise that utilising route planning and optimisation software to identify the most efficient routes, maximise mileage, and reduce fuel consumption could be ideal. This helps to avoid traffic congestion and delays, leading to lower emissions and improved delivery times. It also helps in promoting collaboration among multiple companies to consolidate shipments and optimise transportation routes. This reduces the number of empty or partially loaded vehicles on the road, resulting in lower emissions and increased efficiency (Alla, Bentalha & Bouhtati, 2022).

According to Richey et al. (2016) implementing innovative last-mile delivery solutions such as electric bikes, drones, or shared delivery services to reduce emissions and improve efficiency in urban areas has been found to be effective.

The use of alternative fuels in logistics is another important sustainable strategy. Alternative fuels are non-traditional energy sources that produce lower emissions compared to conventional fossil fuels (Chen & Paulraj, 2017). Sodhi and Tang (2016) explained the importance of some common alternative fuels used in logistics include biofuels, electric power and hydrogen natural gas, these were found to be efficient and cleaner in fostering sustainable logistics and competitive position of institutions across the world. Jayarathna et al. (2023) contended that implementing green transportation practices and adopting alternative fuels enable logistics companies to significantly reduce their carbon footprint, lower emissions, and contribute to a more sustainable and environmentally friendly supply chain. These strategies not only align with sustainability goals but also offer long-term cost savings, improved operational efficiency, and enhanced reputation for businesses.

Supply Chain Optimisation and Collaboration

Sustainable logistics solutions cover a range of techniques for streamlining supply chain operations and promoting stakeholder cooperation. These tactics seek to increase logistical activity efficiency, decrease waste, and maximise environmental impact. Collaboration and supply chain efficiency are essential for accomplishing sustainability objectives (Manik, 2022). The tactics are elaborated in the next paragraphs.

Supply chain optimisation involves streamlining and improving the efficiency of processes, resources, and activities across the entire supply chain. By optimising the flow of goods, information, and services, companies can maximise waste, reduce costs, and enhance sustainability (Brewer & Button, 2016).

A number of authors advocated for different key elements of supply chain optimization. Arya et al. (2020) asserts that demand forecasting and planning is important in optimising supply chains. Accurate demand forecasting enables companies to optimise inventory levels, reduce stockouts, and maximise the need for rush deliveries. This leads to better resource utilisation and lower energy consumption. Biswas and Anand (2020) expounded that efficient inventory management practices, such as just-in-time (JIT) and lean principles, help maximise excess inventory, reduce storage space requirements, and prevent product obsolescence. This reduces waste and improves resource efficiency.

On the contrary Brewer and Button (2016) believed that collaborating closely with suppliers helps ensure timely deliveries, reduces lead times, and maximises transportation-related emissions. Sharing information and working together to improve processes can lead to more sustainable sourcing practices.

Relatively, Bentalha (2022) advised that implementing sustainable warehouse practices, such as energy-efficient lighting, proper insulation, and optimised layouts, can reduce energy consumption and waste generation. Automation and advanced technologies can also enhance operational efficiency. Coupled with transportation optimization, Cagliano et al. (2019) guided that utilising route optimisation software, load consolidation, and multimodal transportation options can improve fuel efficiency, reduce emissions, and maximise transportation costs. Efficient vehicle routing and load optimisation help avoid empty miles and reduce carbon footprints.

Chen and Paulraj (2017) further argued that establishing effective reverse logistics processes for product returns, recycling, and remanufacturing contributes to a circular economy is one of the key elements that should not be left out in supply chain optimisation. It reduces waste generation and extends the life cycle of products, reducing the need for new production.

Collaboration

Collaboration among supply chain partners is crucial for sustainable logistics. By working together, stakeholders can share resources, information, and expertise, leading to improved efficiency and reduced environmental impact (Sarkis et al., 2011).

Dangelico and Pujari (2018) opined that collaboration starts with engaging suppliers in sustainability initiatives with the drive to promote responsible sourcing practices, ethical standards, and adherence to environmental regulations. Collaboration can involve joint sustainability programs, supplier scorecards, and regular audits to ensure compliance.

Collaborating with logistics service providers can lead to shared goals and strategies for sustainability. Working together to optimise transportation routes, improve packaging practices, and reduce waste generation benefits all parties involved (Biswas & Anand, 2020).

Ferdows and de Meyer (2018) acknowledged that engaging stakeholders such as customers, local communities, and regulatory authorities foster transparency and accountability. This collaboration enables the identification of sustainable practices, encourages innovation, and builds trust. Through stakeholder trust sharing best practices, industry standards, and research findings among supply chain partners will be become a possibility and help to drive continuous improvement in sustainable logistics. Collaborative platforms, industry associations, and forums provide opportunities for knowledge exchange.

By implementing supply chain optimisation strategies and fostering collaboration, companies can enhance sustainability, reduce waste, improve resource utilization, and achieve cost savings. These approaches not only contribute to environmental protection but also strengthen relationships with suppliers, customers, and other stakeholders, enhancing the overall competitiveness of the supply chain (Wells et al., 2020).

Reverse Logistics and Circular Economy

According to Ivanov and Tsipoulanidis (2019), reverse logistics refers to the process of managing the flow of products, materials, and resources from the point of consumption back to the point of origin or proper disposal. It involves activities such as product returns, refurbishment, recycling, and disposal. Reverse logistics aims to maximise the value of products and materials while maximising waste and environmental impact (Touboulic & Walker, 2015). Key aspects of reverse logistics include product returns and remanufacturing, recycling and material recovery, proper disposal and waste management, design for sustainability, and resource efficiency and optimization. Reverse logistics and the concept of a circular economy are key components of sustainable logistics as they enhance efficient handling of product returns allows for the recovery of value from returned items (Jüttner & Maklan, 2019). This can involve refurbishing, repairing, or remanufacturing products to extend their lifecycle and reduce the need for new production. It reduces waste and conserves resources.

Lan et al. (2020) added that implementing effective recycling programs ensures that materials are properly sorted, processed, and reused or repurposed. Recycling maximises the extraction of raw materials and reduces the environmental impact associated with their production.

Relatively, Bentalha et al. (2019) acknowledged that disposing of products and materials that cannot be reused or recycled should be done in an environmentally responsible manner. This involves adhering to waste management regulations and utilizing appropriate disposal methods to prevent pollution and environmental harm. The circular economy is an economic model that aims to decouple economic growth from the consumption of finite resources. It emphasizes the importance of maintaining the value of products, materials, and resources in a continuous loop, rather than following a traditional linear "take-make-dispose" model (Seuring & Müller, 2008).

Sustainable logistics strategies aligned circular economy were also found fruitful in developing efficient logistics systems (Prakash et al., 2017). Orji et al. (2020) found out that products and packaging should be designed with sustainability in mind, considering factors such as recyclability, reusability, and ease of disassembly. Designing products for durability and repairability promotes longer lifespans and reduces waste.

Jayarathna et al. (2023) argued that maximising the use of resources and minimising waste is crucial in the circular economy. This involves efficient manufacturing processes, responsible resource extraction, and the adoption of innovative technologies to enhance resource efficiency.

Liu et al. (2019) contended that embracing sharing economy models and collaborative networks promotes the sharing and reuse of products, reducing the need for individual ownership and excessive production. Sharing platforms enable multiple users to access and utilize resources more efficiently. By implementing strategies such as recycling, remanufacturing, and refurbishment, materials can be kept in use for as long as possible. This reduces the reliance on virgin resources and maximises the environmental impact associated with their extraction and production. Through integrating reverse logistics practices and embracing the principles of the circular economy, businesses can create a more sustainable and resource-efficient supply chain. These strategies promote waste reduction, resource conservation, and the creation of new business opportunities based on the reuse and repurposing of materials. They not only contribute to environmental protection but also enhance the resilience and long-term viability of the logistics industry (Touboulic & Walker, 2015).

Green Packaging and Waste Reduction

Green packaging and waste reduction are important sustainable logistics strategies aimed at maximising the environmental impact of packaging materials and reducing waste throughout the supply chain. These strategies focus on the responsible use of materials, the adoption of eco-friendly packaging practices, and the promotion of circular economy principles (Yusufkhonov, et al., 2021).

While green packaging involves the use of environmentally friendly materials and design principles it maximises the environmental footprint of packaging. It focuses on reducing the use of non-recyclable or non-biodegradable materials, optimising packaging size and weight, and promoting recyclability or compostability. Key aspects of green packaging include material selection, packaging optimisation, eco-friendly printing and labeling, source reduction, recycling and recovery programs, composting and, organic waste management as well as product life extension (Jia, & Bai, 2020).

Wells et al. (2020) explained that choosing packaging materials that have a lower environmental impact is crucial. This can include using recycled or biodegradable materials, as well as materials derived from renewable resources. Avoiding materials that are harmful to the environment or difficult to recycle, such as certain types of plastics, is also important.

Designing packaging with efficiency in mind helps maximise waste and reduce transportation costs. This can involve optimising the size and weight of packaging to maximise space utilization and maximise the need for excess packaging materials (Arya et al., 2020).

Varsei et al. (2019) emphasised that using environmentally friendly inks and adhesives for printing labels and information on packaging can reduce the release of harmful substances into the environment. Employing clear and concise labeling helps consumers properly dispose of packaging materials.

Waste reduction strategies aim to maximise waste generation throughout the supply chain and encourage responsible waste management practices. This involves taking proactive measures to prevent waste, promote recycling, and support the circular economy (Wichaisri & Sopadang, 2017). Some waste reduction strategies in supply chain include implementing practices that maximise the generation of waste at the source is an effective strategy (Srivastava, 2017). This can involve working closely with suppliers to reduce excess packaging materials, adopting lean manufacturing principles to maximise production waste, and encouraging customers to opt for digital or electronic alternatives to paper-based documentation (Wichaisri & Sopadang, 2017).

Rossitto et al. (2022) added that establishing recycling programs within the organisation and collaborating with recycling partners helps ensure that packaging materials are properly sorted, processed, and recycled. This can include partnering with local recycling facilities or participating in industry-wide recycling initiatives.

Bentalha et al. (2020) expounded that in cases where packaging or products generate organic waste, implementing composting programs can divert this waste from landfills and turn it into valuable compost for agricultural or landscaping purposes.

Encouraging product reuse, repair, or refurbishment can extend the lifespan of products and packaging, reducing the need for new production and maximising waste. This can involve offering repair services or partnering with organisations that specialize in refurbishment and resale (Tseng et al., 2022).

By implementing green packaging practices and waste reduction strategies, businesses can maximise the environmental impact of their packaging materials, conserve resources, and contribute to a more sustainable supply chain. These strategies not only align with environmental goals but also enhance brand reputation, appeal to environmentally conscious consumers, and reduce costs associated with waste management (Persdotter- Isaksson et al., 2019).

Energy-Efficient Operations and Green Facilities

Energy-efficient operations and green facilities are essential sustainable logistics strategies that focus on maximising energy consumption, reducing greenhouse gas emissions, and promoting environmentally friendly practices within logistics operations. These strategies aim to optimise energy use, adopt renewable energy sources, and implement sustainable infrastructure (Hu et al., 2020).

Energy-efficient operations involve the implementation of practices and technologies that reduce energy consumption and improve energy efficiency throughout logistics operations. Key aspects of energy-efficient operations include implementing energy-efficient technologies and practices for handling equipment, material handling systems, and vehicles can significantly reduce energy consumption. This can involve using energy-efficient machinery, optimising routes and loads for transportation, and adopting fuel-efficient vehicles or alternative fuel technologies (Tseng et al., 2022).

Efficient lighting systems, such as LED lighting, and smart HVAC (Heating, Ventilation, and Air Conditioning) systems can reduce energy consumption in warehouses, distribution centers, and office spaces. Implementing motion sensors and automated controls can further optimise energy use by adjusting lighting and HVAC systems based on occupancy and natural light availability (Denga & Rakshit, 2022).

Wells et al. (2020) acknowledged that streamlining operational processes and workflows to eliminate inefficiencies and maximise energy waste is crucial. This can involve optimising order picking processes, maximising idle time for vehicles and equipment, and implementing energy management systems to monitor and control energy consumption in real-time.

Liu et al. (2019) explained that constructing logistics facilities with sustainable building materials and designs helps maximise environmental impact. This can involve using recycled or renewable materials, incorporating energy-efficient insulation, and optimising natural lighting and ventilation.

Implementing water-saving measures, such as rainwater harvesting systems or water-efficient fixtures, can reduce water consumption within logistics facilities. Additionally, treating and reusing wastewater can maximise the environmental impact associated with water usage (Wichaisri & Sopadang, 2017).

By adopting energy-efficient operations and green facilities, logistics organisations can significantly reduce their carbon footprint, lower energy costs, and contribute to a more sustainable future. These strategies not only align with environmental goals but also enhance operational efficiency, improve employee satisfaction, and enhance brand reputation as environmentally responsible organisations (Jinru et al., 2022).

BENEFITS OF SUSTAINABLE LOGISTICS FOR COMPETITIVE POSITIONING

Cost Savings and Operational Efficiency

According to Vilariño, Franco and Quarrington (2017) implementing sustainable logistics practices can lead to significant cost savings through reduced energy consumption, waste reduction, and optimise d operations. By improving resource utilization, organisations can maximise costs associated with energy, fuel, packaging, and waste management. Additionally, sustainable logistics strategies promote operational efficiency by streamlining processes, optimising transportation routes, and improving inventory management.

Enhanced Brand Reputation and Customer Loyalty

Sustainability has become an increasingly important factor for customers when making purchasing decisions. By demonstrating a commitment to sustainable logistics, organisations can enhance their brand reputation and attract environmentally conscious customers. Sustainable practices can differentiate a company from its competitors and foster customer loyalty and trust, leading to increased customer retention and positive word-of-mouth recommendations (Ogli, & Buribayevich, 2022).

Regulatory Compliance and Risk Mitigation

Sustainable logistics practices help organisations comply with environmental regulations and standards. By proactively addressing environmental concerns, organisations can reduce the risk of penalties, fines, and legal issues. Adhering to sustainability regulations and guidelines also mitigates reputational risks and demonstrates corporate responsibility to stakeholders (Varsei et al., 2019).

Access To New Markets and Business Opportunities

Sustainable logistics practices open doors to new markets and business opportunities. Many governments, organisations, and consumers prefer to engage with suppliers and partners who demonstrate environmental responsibility. By embracing sustainability, organisations can access green supply chains, participate in government procurement programs, and collaborate with like-minded organisations to develop innovative solutions. Additionally, sustainable logistics can lead to the creation of new products and services that cater to the growing demand for eco-friendly options (Yusufkhonov et al., 2021).

Integrating sustainable logistics practices provides organisations with a competitive edge by reducing costs, enhancing brand reputation, complying with regulations, and accessing new markets. By aligning business operations with environmental and social considerations, organisations can improve their overall competitiveness and secure long-term success in an increasingly sustainability-focused market (Asees & Ali, 2019).

CASE STUDIES: SUCCESSFUL IMPLEMENTATION OF SUSTAINABLE LOGISTICS

Carbon-Neutral Operations

IKEA, a multinational furniture retailer, has implemented various initiatives to achieve carbon-neutral operations. They have invested in renewable energy sources such as solar and wind power to reduce their reliance on fossil fuels. Additionally, they have optimise d their transportation network by using efficient vehicles and implementing route optimisation techniques. Through these efforts, IKEA has significantly reduced their carbon emissions and achieved carbon-neutral operations (Ogli, & Buribayevich, 2022).

Closed-Loop Supply Chains

Dell, a technology company, has implemented a closed-loop supply chain approach for their computer products. They have established a take-back program where customers can return their used products for recycling. Dell then recovers valuable materials from these products and incorporates them back into their manufacturing process. This reduces the need for extracting new raw materials and maximises waste. By implementing a closed-loop supply chain, Dell has achieved significant reductions in waste and resource consumption (Denga & Rakshit, 2022).

Green Packaging Initiatives and Waste Reduction

Procter & Gamble (P&G), a consumer goods company, has implemented various green packaging initiatives to reduce waste and promote recycling. They have redesigned their packaging to be more environmentally friendly, using materials with higher recyclability and reducing the overall amount of packaging used. P&G also encourages consumers to recycle their products through educational campaigns and partnerships with recycling organisations. These initiatives have led to substantial waste reduction and increased recycling rates for P&G's products (Moosaviet al., 2022).

CHALLENGES AND BARRIERS IN ADOPTING SUSTAINABLE LOGISTICS

Financial Constraints and Investment Requirements

Implementing sustainable logistics practices often requires significant investments in infrastructure, technology, and training. Companies may face financial constraints and struggle to allocate the necessary funds to support sustainability initiatives. The upfront costs of adopting new technologies or implementing eco-friendly transportation systems can be a barrier for some organisations (Bentalha et al., 2020).

Lack of Awareness and Organisational Resistance

A lack of awareness and understanding of the benefits and importance of sustainable logistics can hinder adoption. Organisations may face resistance from employees, stakeholders, or management who are not fully aware of the potential advantages or may be resistant to change. Overcoming this barrier requires effective communication and education to foster a culture of sustainability within the organization (Jayarathna, Agdas & Dawes, 2023).

Complexities in Measuring and Reporting Sustainability Metrics

Measuring and reporting sustainability metrics can be challenging due to the complex nature of supply chains and the multitude of factors involved. Companies may struggle with collecting accurate data, defining appropriate metrics, and implementing reliable measurement systems. Lack of standardized frameworks and guidelines for sustainability reporting further complicates this process (Ekinci et al., 2022).

Regulatory and policy challenges

Companies operating in different regions or countries may face regulatory and policy challenges related to sustainability. Regulations may vary, making it difficult to navigate and comply with multiple requirements. Additionally, evolving policies and changing regulations can create uncertainties and increase the complexity of sustainable logistics implementation (Biswas & Anand, 2020).

OVERCOMING CHALLENGES AND IMPLEMENTING SUSTAINABLE LOGISTICS

To overcome challenges and successfully implement sustainable logistics practices, companies can consider the following strategies.

Developing a sustainability strategy and roadmap: Creating a clear and comprehensive sustainability strategy is essential for guiding the organisation's efforts towards sustainable logistics. The strategy should outline specific goals, targets, and initiatives aligned with the company's overall objectives. A roadmap can help break down the implementation process into manageable steps and timelines (Mangla et al., 2019).

Engaging stakeholders and building partnerships: Collaboration with stakeholders is crucial for sustainable logistics success. Engage suppliers, customers, industry associations, and local communities to foster partnerships and gain support. Collaborative initiatives can include joint sustainability projects, sharing best practices, and establishing industry standards (Wells et al., 2020).

Investing in technology and innovation: Investment in technology and innovation is key to implementing sustainable logistics practices. Explore eco-friendly transportation options, such as electric vehicles or hybrid fleets, to reduce emissions. Adopt advanced logistics and supply chain management systems to optimise routes, reduce fuel consumption, and maximise waste. Embrace automation and digitization to improve efficiency and traceability (Abduljabbar et al., 2021).

Educating and training employees: Providing education and training programs to employees is crucial for creating awareness, developing skills, and fostering a sustainability mindset. Train employees on sustainable practices, such as waste reduction, energy conservation, and responsible packaging. Encourage employees to contribute ideas and participate in sustainability initiatives (Sgarbossa et al., 2020).

Monitoring and evaluating sustainability performance: Lahkani et al. (2020) reiterated that organisations should establish robust monitoring and evaluation mechanisms to track sustainability performance. Institutions should implement key performance indicators (KPIs) to measure progress toward sustainability goals. Regularly review and analyze data on energy consumption, emissions, waste generation, and other relevant metrics. Use the insights gained to identify areas for improvement and implement corrective actions.

FUTURE TRENDS IN SUSTAINABLE LOGISTICS AND COMPETITIVE POSITIONING

The future of sustainable logistics and competitive positioning is shaped by several emerging trends. These trends include:

Advances in technology and automation: Technological advancements such as artificial intelligence, Internet of Things (IoT), and robotics are transforming the logistics industry. Automation streamlines processes, reduces errors, and improves efficiency, leading to sustainable operations. Technologies like autonomous vehicles and drones offer greener transportation options. Predictive analytics and real-time data enable better decision-making and resource optimization (Lahkani, et al., 2020).

Integration of sustainability into supply chain management: Sustainability considerations are increasingly integrated into supply chain management practices. Companies are focusing on selecting eco-friendly suppliers, implementing sustainable procurement practices, and assessing the environmental impact of transportation modes. Supply chain transparency and traceability are enhanced through technologies like blockchain, enabling better management of environmental and social risks (Wells et al., 2020).

Emergence of circular economy principles: The circular economy is gaining momentum as a sustainable approach to resource management. In the logistics context, this involves designing supply chains and logistics processes that maximise waste and promote product reuse, recycling, and remanufacturing. Circular logistics models aim to close the loop by maximising resource utilization, reducing the consumption of raw materials, and maximising waste generation (Agyabeng-Mensah et al., 2020).

Collaboration and information sharing in the logistics industry: Collaboration and information sharing among logistics stakeholders are essential for sustainable practices. Partnerships between companies, government agencies, NGOs, and academia foster knowledge exchange and joint initiatives. Collaborative logistics platforms and sharing economy models optimise asset utilisation, reduce empty miles, and improve overall efficiency. Open data platforms and digital ecosystems facilitate information sharing and coordination (Rossitto et al., 2022).

DISCUSSION

As environmental concerns continue to gain prominence, organisations are increasingly recognising the imperative of incorporating sustainable practices into their logistics operations. The chapter commences by elucidating the concept of sustainable logistics and its profound implications for businesses, encompassing reduced carbon emissions, optimal resource utilization, and heightened social responsibility. It subsequently delves into the symbiotic relationship between sustainable logistics and competitive positioning, underscoring how organisations can strategically leverage sustainability as a differentiator in the market. The chapter comprehensively examines various strategies and best practices for sustainable logistics across domains like transportation, warehousing, packaging, and reverse logistics. Furthermore, it scrutinizes the pivotal role of technology and innovation in facilitating sustainable logistics while augmenting competitive edge. Through compelling case studies and illustrative examples, the chapter convincingly demonstrates how organisations spanning diverse industries have effectively integrated sustainable logistics into their operations, yielding tangible benefits such as cost savings, enhanced customer satisfaction, bolstered brand reputation, and fortified market positioning. This chapter serves as a valuable resource offering insights into the pivotal role of sustainable logistics in achieving competitive supremacy, providing pragmatic guidance to businesses aspiring to harmonize their logistics practices with sustainability objectives while maintaining competitiveness in the dynamic marketplace.

CONCLUSION

Sustainable logistics involves integrating environmental, social, and economic considerations into the design and management of logistics operations. It encompasses strategies such as green transportation, supply chain optimisation, reverse logistics, green packaging, and energy-efficient operations. Sustainable logistics brings several benefits, including cost savings, enhanced brand reputation, regulatory compliance, and access to new markets. There are challenges and barriers in adopting sustainable logistics, including financial constraints, lack of awareness, complexities in measuring sustainability metrics, and regulatory challenges. These challenges can be overcome through developing a sustainability strategy, engaging stakeholders, investing in technology, educating employees, and monitoring performance. Technology and automation advancements, the incorporation of sustainability into supply chain management, the development of circular economy ideas, and collaboration and information sharing within the logistics sector will all contribute to the future of sustainable logistics.

Future prospects for sustainable logistics are very promising. Businesses will have additional chances to innovate and optimise their logistics operations as a result of growing technologies, rising awareness, and changing legal frameworks. Companies can not only gain a competitive edge by adopting sustainability as a strategic priority, but they can also help create a future that is more robust and sustainable.

Competitive positioning is strongly influenced by sustainable logistics. Organisations can achieve long-term success while having a positive impact on the environment and society at large by integrating environmental and social goals with business strategies. For organisations looking to succeed in a world that is more and more concerned with sustainability, adopting sustainable logistics is not just the right thing to do, but also the wise thing to do.Top of Form

REFERENCES

Agyabeng-Mensah, Y., Afum, E., & Ahenkorah, E. (2020). Exploring financial performance and green logistics management practices: Examining the mediating influences of market, environmental and social performances. *Journal of Cleaner Production*, *258*, 120613. doi:10.1016/j.jclepro.2020.120613

Alla, L., Bentalha, B., & Bouhtati, N. (2022). Assessing Supply Chain Performance in the Covid 19 Context: A Prospective Model. In *2022 14th International Colloquium of Logistics and Supply Chain Management (LOGISTIQUA)* (pp. 1-6). IEEE.

Arya, P., Srivastava, M. K., & Jaiswal, M. P. (2020). Modelling environmental and economic sustainability of logistics. *Asia-Pacific Journal of Business Administration.*

Asees Awan, M., & Ali, Y. (2019). Sustainable modeling in reverse logistics strategies using fuzzy MCDM: Case of China Pakistan Economic Corridor. *Management of Environmental Quality*, *30*(5), 1132–1151. doi:10.1108/MEQ-01-2019-0024

Bentalha, B. (2022). Smart Technologies for a Sustainable Service Supply Chain: A Prospective Perspective. *Journal of Environmental Issues and Climate Change*, *1*(1), 77–89. doi:10.59110/jeicc.v1i1.81

Bentalha, B., Hmioui, A., & Alla, L. (2020). Digital service supply chain management: current realities and prospective visions. In *Innovations in Smart Cities Applications Edition 3: The Proceedings of the 4th International Conference on Smart City Applications 4* (pp. 808-822). Springer International Publishing. 10.1007/978-3-030-37629-1_58

Bentalha, B., Hmioui, A., & Alla, L. (2021). The global performance of a service supply chain: a simulation-optimization under arena. In *Innovations in Smart Cities Applications Volume 4: The Proceedings of the 5th International Conference on Smart City Applications* (pp. 489-502). Springer International Publishing. 10.1007/978-3-030-66840-2_37

Bentalha, B., Hmioui, A., & Alla, L. (2023). Green Transportation Balanced Scorecard: A VIKOR Fuzzy Method for Evaluating Green Logistics Initiatives. In *Digital Technologies and Applications: Proceedings of ICDTA'23,* (pp. 916-925). Cham: Springer Nature Switzerland. 10.1007/978-3-031-29857-8_91

Biswas, S., & Anand, O. P. (2020). Logistics Competitiveness Index-Based Comparison of BRICS and G7 Countries: An Integrated PSI-PIV Approach. *IUP Journal of Supply Chain Management, 17*(2).

Brewer, P., & Button, K. (2016). *Sustainable logistics and transportation: Optimising economic and environmental performance*. Kogan Page.

Cagliano, R., Caniato, F., Golini, R., & Micheli, G. J. (2019). Sustainable supply chain management: An integrated literature review. *Journal of Cleaner Production, 230*, 1268–1280.

Chen, I. J., & Paulraj, A. (2017). Understanding supply chain social sustainability: Progress and prospects. *The Journal of Supply Chain Management, 53*(4), 3–21.

Christopher, M. (2016). *Logistics & supply chain management* (5th ed.). Pearson.

Christopher, M., & Peck, H. (2018). *Marketing logistics: Principles and practice* (5th ed.). Routledge.

Dangelico, R. M., & Pujari, D. (2018). Mainstreaming green product innovation: Why and how companies integrate environmental sustainability. *Journal of Business Ethics, 150*(2), 423–448.

Dekker, R., Fleischmann, M., Inderfurth, K., & van Wassenhove, L. N. (2019). *Reverse logistics: Quantitative models for closed-loop supply chains* (2nd ed.). Springer.

Denga, E. M., & Rakshit, S. (2022). Supply Chain Logistics Risk Mitigation: Impact of the COVID-19 Pandemic. In Global Risk and Contingency Management Research in Times of Crisis (pp. 99-121). IGI Global.

Dubey, R., Gunasekaran, A., Childe, S. J., Blome, C., Papadopoulos, T., & Luo, Z. (2019). Sustainable supply chain management: Framework and further research directions. *Journal of Business Ethics, 156*(2), 299–326.

Ekinci, E., Mangla, S. K., Kazancoglu, Y., Sarma, P. R. S., Sezer, M. D., & Ozbiltekin-Pala, M. (2022). Resilience and complexity measurement for energy efficient global supply chains in disruptive events. *Technological Forecasting and Social Change, 179*, 121634. doi:10.1016/j.techfore.2022.121634 PMID:35400766

Ferdows, K., & de Meyer, A. (2018). Lasting improvements in manufacturing performance: In search of a new theory. *Journal of Operations Management*, *59*, 1–6.

Govindan, K., Fattahi, M., Keyvanshokooh, E., & Diabat, A. (2017). Supply chain network design under uncertainty: A comprehensive review and future research directions. *European Journal of Operational Research*, *263*(1), 108–141. doi:10.1016/j.ejor.2017.04.009

Hu, W., Dong, J., Hwang, B. G., Ren, R., & Chen, Z. (2020). Hybrid optimization procedures applying for two-echelon urban underground logistics network planning: A case study of Beijing. *Computers & Industrial Engineering*, *144*, 106452. doi:10.1016/j.cie.2020.106452

Ivanov, D., & Tsipoulanidis, A. (2019). Sustainability and resilience in supply chain management. *International Journal of Production Research*, *57*(3), 829–846. doi:10.1080/00207543.2018.1488086

Jayarathna, C. P., Agdas, D., & Dawes, L. (2023). Exploring sustainable logistics practices toward a circular economy: A value creation perspective. *Business Strategy and the Environment*, *32*(1), 704–720. doi:10.1002/bse.3170

Jinru, L., Changbiao, Z., Ahmad, B., Irfan, M., & Nazir, R. (2022). How do green financing and green logistics affect the circular economy in the pandemic situation: Key mediating role of sustainable production. *Ekonomska Istrazivanja*, *35*(1), 3836–3856. doi:10.1080/1331677X.2021.2004437

Jüttner, U., & Maklan, S. (2019). Supply chain resilience in the global financial crisis: An empirical study. *Supply Chain Management*, *24*(2), 184–199.

Lahkani, M. J., Wang, S., Urbański, M., & Egorova, M. (2020). Sustainable B2B E-commerce and blockchain-based supply chain finance. *Sustainability (Basel)*, *12*(10), 3968. doi:10.3390u12103968

Lan, S., Tseng, M. L., Yang, C., & Huisingh, D. (2020). Trends in sustainable logistics in major cities in China. *The Science of the Total Environment*, *712*, 136381. doi:10.1016/j.scitotenv.2019.136381 PMID:31940512

Liu, Y., Zhang, Y., Batista, L., & Rong, K. (2019). Green operations: What's the role of supply chain flexibility? *International Journal of Production Economics*, *214*, 30–43. doi:10.1016/j.ijpe.2019.03.026

Mangla, S. K., Sharma, Y. K., Patil, P. P., Yadav, G., & Xu, J. (2019). Logistics and distribution challenges to managing operations for corporate sustainability: Study on leading Indian diary organizations. *Journal of Cleaner Production*, *238*, 117620. doi:10.1016/j.jclepro.2019.117620

Moosavi, J., Fathollahi-Fard, A. M., & Dulebenets, M. A. (2022). Supply chain disruption during the COVID-19 pandemic: Recognizing potential disruption management strategies. *International Journal of Disaster Risk Reduction*, *75*, 102983. doi:10.1016/j.ijdrr.2022.102983 PMID:35475018

Ogli, G. B. B., & Buribayevich, E. O. (2022). Development of Logistics Processes in Transport Enterprises. Vital Annex. *International Journal of Novel Research in Advanced Sciences*, *1*(3), 138–142.

Orji, I. J., Kusi-Sarpong, S., & Gupta, H. (2020). The critical success factors of using social media for supply chain social sustainability in the freight logistics industry. *International Journal of Production Research*, *58*(5), 1522–1539. doi:10.1080/00207543.2019.1660829

Pagell, M., & Wu, Z. (2017). Building a more complete theory of sustainable supply chain management using case studies of 10 exemplars. *The Journal of Supply Chain Management*, *53*(4), 3–23.

Persdotter Isaksson, M., Hulthén, H., & Forslund, H. (2019). Environmentally sustainable logistics performance management process integration between Buyers and 3PLs. *Sustainability (Basel)*, *11*(11), 3061. doi:10.3390u11113061

Prakash, A., Pathak, N., Muralidharan, C., & Maas, G. (2017). Sustainable supply chain management: A review and research agenda. *International Journal of Management Reviews*, *19*(1), 18–38.

Richey, R. G. Jr, Chen, H., & Kahle, L. R. (2016). The changing landscape of the US logistics industry: A content analysis of Fortune 100 firms. *Transportation Journal*, *55*(3), 275–295.

Rossitto, C., Comber, R., Tholander, J., & Jacobsson, M. (2022, April). Towards Digital Environmental Stewardship: The Work of Caring for the Environment in Waste Management. In *Proceedings of the 2022 CHI Conference on Human Factors in Computing Systems* (pp. 1-16). ACM. 10.1145/3491102.3517679

Seuring, S., & Gold, S. (2019). Sustainability management beyond corporate boundaries: From stakeholders to performance. *Journal of Cleaner Production*, *207*, 1084–1094.

Sgarbossa, F., Grosse, E. H., Neumann, W. P., Battini, D., & Glock, C. H. (2020). Human factors in production and logistics systems of the future. *Annual Reviews in Control*, *49*, 295–305. doi:10.1016/j.arcontrol.2020.04.007

Sodhi, M. S., & Tang, C. S. (2016). *Supply chain risk management* (2nd ed.). Springer.

Srivastava, S. K. (2017). Green supply-chain management: A state-of-the-art literature review. *International Journal of Management Reviews*, *19*(1), 63–84.

Sudusinghe, J. I., & Seuring, S. (2022). Supply chain collaboration and sustainability performance in circular economy: A systematic literature review. *International Journal of Production Economics*, *245*, 108402. doi:10.1016/j.ijpe.2021.108402

Tseng, M. L., Bui, T. D., Lim, M. K., Fujii, M., & Mishra, U. (2022). Assessing data-driven sustainable supply chain management indicators for the textile industry under industrial disruption and ambidexterity. *International Journal of Production Economics*, *245*, 108401. doi:10.1016/j.ijpe.2021.108401

Vanalle, R. M., Barbieri, J. C., & Arantes, A. F. (2021). Sustainability assessment model for logistics service providers. *Journal of Cleaner Production*, *318*, 128611.

Varsei, M., Azadegan, A., & Ivanov, D. (2019). A systematic literature review on sustainable supply chain finance: Current trends and future directions. *Annals of Operations Research*, *283*(1-2), 375–416.

Vilariño, M. V., Franco, C., & Quarrington, C. (2017). Food loss and waste reduction as an integral part of a circular economy. *Frontiers in Environmental Science*, *5*, 21. doi:10.3389/fenvs.2017.00021

Wells, P., Abouarghoub, W., Pettit, S., & Beresford, A. (2020). A socio-technical transitions perspective for assessing future sustainability following the COVID-19 pandemic. Sustainability: Science. *Sustainability*, *16*(1), 29–36. doi:10.1080/15487733.2020.1763002

Wichaisri, S., & Sopadang, A. (2017). Integrating sustainable development, lean, and logistics concepts into a lean sustainable logistics model. *International Journal of Logistics Systems and Management*, *26*(1), 85. doi:10.1504/IJLSM.2017.080631

Yusufkhonov, Z., Ravshanov, M., Kamolov, A., & Kamalova, E. (2021). Improving the position of the logistics performance index of Uzbekistan. In *E3S Web of Conferences* (Vol. 264, p. 05028). EDP Sciences. doi:10.1051/e3sconf/202126405028

KEY TERMS AND DEFINITIONS

Carbon Footprint: The total amount of greenhouse gas emissions, primarily carbon dioxide, produced directly or indirectly by an individual, organisation, product, or activity, often used as a measure of environmental impact.

Competitive Positioning: The strategic approach adopted by organizations to differentiate themselves from competitors and gain a favorable position in the market, encompassing factors such as pricing, product quality, customer service, and sustainability practices.

Green Packaging: Packaging materials and practices that are designed to maximise environmental impact, including the use of recyclable, biodegradable, or reusable materials, as well as optimising packaging size and weight to reduce waste and transportation emissions.

Green Supply Chain Management: The integration of environmentally sustainable practices and principles into supply chain activities, including procurement, production, transportation, and distribution, to maximise environmental impacts and enhance overall sustainability.

Life Cycle Assessment (LCA): A comprehensive analysis of the environmental impacts of a product or service throughout its entire life cycle, from raw material extraction to disposal, taking into account factors such as resource consumption, emissions, and waste generation.

Reverse Logistics: The process of planning, implementing, and controlling the efficient and cost-effective flow of products, materials, and information from the point of consumption back to the point of origin, with the aim of capturing value or ensuring environmentally responsible disposal.

Sustainable Logistics: The practice of managing the flow of goods and services in an environmentally responsible manner, considering the efficient use of resources, reduction of emissions, and social responsibility throughout the logistics process.

Triple Bottom Line: A framework that evaluates business performance based on three dimensions: economic, environmental, and social. Sustainable logistics contributes to the triple bottom line by considering not only financial outcomes but also environmental and social impacts.

Chapter 12
Information System Architecture in Apparel Production for Maintaining Supply Chain Sustainability

Kamalendu Pal
https://orcid.org/0000-0001-7158-6481
University of London, UK

ABSTRACT

Big data analytics has played an enormous role in supply chain operations in recent years. Today, web-applications, social media, intelligent machines, sensors, mobile phones, and other innovative information technology devices generate big data in supply chain operations. These data often provide new digitized services that improve supply chain performance. In this operating environment, heterogeneous enterprise applications, manufacturing processes, or supply chain management, either inside a single enterprise or among network enterprises, require sharing of data-driven information. Thus, data management and its analytical interpretation have become significant drivers for management, product development, and provision of relevant services in network enterprises that function as mediators in effective and sustainable supply chain operations. This chapter reviews the effect of big data analytics on the supply chain operation literature, highlights how modern supply chains can manage sustainability, and presents a conceptual information system architecture.

INTRODUCTION

There is considerable awareness and concern for environmental, social, and economic effects on apparel (e.g., textile products, foot ware) production and consumption (Pal, 2023). It has increased pressure from consumer organizations, social, and environmental advocacy groups for apparel-based business organizations and policymakers to develop sustainable supply chain management (Pal, 2022). The pres-

DOI: 10.4018/979-8-3693-0225-5.ch012

ent apparel products consumption pattern and ever-increasing population pose concerns about apparel production and serving supply chain management systems (Pal, 2018).

The requirement for sustainable development is widely recognized by regulative bodies, business organizations, and consumers and can be defined as development that meets the current requirements without compromising future generations' capabilities to meet their needs (Pal, 2021). It thus requires a global view of development, emphasizing the relationships between environmental improvement and social equitability through sustainable economic growth and performance (Coyle, 2023) (Stern, 2007). In this way, enterprises' supply chain managers consider including well-positioned to support sustainable development at this critical juncture due to their wide-ranging impacts and influences. However, most of the recent research considers the sustainability aspect of the supply chain by considering social, economic, and environmental elements for regular operations (Pal, 2023). The effect of big data on Lean, Agile, Resilient, and Green (LARG) related issues is attracting significant promise for industrial supply chain research (Chun Wu, 2003) (Dora et al., 2016) (Baramichai et al., 2007) (Cabral et al., 2012) (Srivastava, 2007) in recent decades. It is also highlighted that the LARG concepts-based supply chain operations assist in lowering production lead-time and transportation time, improving data-driven integration levels, and achieving effective information exchange (Alqudah et al., 2020). Lean supply chain interconnects the interdependent partners to eliminate waste through techniques such as value chain analysis (Taylor & Pettit, 2009) (Dey et al., 2019). Manufacturing companies in developing economies (i.e., India, Indonesia, Malaysia) have already started the implementation of LARG practices, and it turned out to be a crucial benchmarking tool to support their heterogeneous data integration applications (Chavez et al., 2020) (Wong et al., 2018).

Big data analytics supports supply chain sustainability by strengthening capabilities and minimizing uncertainties and risks (Wu et al., 2017). Big data capabilities help with regular operations and processes, reduced lead and cycle times, focused factories, and mass customization (Misic & Perakis, 2020). Big data processing enhances supply chains' agility (Giannakis & Louis, 2016) and resilience (Pal, 2021) (Papadopoulos et al., 2017). With big data, implementing a green supply chain with better data quality control and integrated data acquisition is possible (Zhao et al., 2017). Big data provides plenty of opportunities in supply chain in terms of supplier performance measurement (Addo-Tenkorang & Helo, 2016), supply chain analytics (Arunachalam et al., 2018), supply chain agility (Fosso Wamba et al., 2018), supply chain sustainability (Hazen et al., 2016) (Papadopoulos et al., 2017), and supply chain innovation (Tan et al., 2015). However, manufacturing companies need to understand big data analytics in the supply chain from the context of organizational performance (Akter et al., 2016). In addition, the influence of big data analytics on sustainable business performance and LARG is not entirely clear and needs more investigation (Gunasekaran et al., 2017).

Companies need to use sustainable practices due to public pressure, the concerns of the customers, and government regulations (Pal, 2023) (Lee & Zhang, 2019). Researchers (Bhanot et al., 2017) recently commented that sustainable manufacturing is the most significant attribute of a sustainable supply chain. Big data analytic capabilities can help manufacturing companies achieve social dimensions (Wadmann & Hoeyer, 2018) and economic advantages (Pal, 2023) while minimizing the environmental impacts (Pal, 2021) (Hazen et al., 2016). Big data analytics can also integrate the data resources in the supply chain to minimize pollutant emissions and energy consumption (Song et al., 2018). Previous studies on big data analytics for carbon-resilient supply chains (Suifan et al., 2019) show a positive effect of data analytics on LARG. These research findings discuss the LARGE-related issues separately. Moreover, the literature survey and synthesis of the authors found that developed countries (e.g., the United Kingdom, the United States of America, and China) have started big data analytics adoption in supply chain operational practices (Arunachalam et al., 2018) (Chavez et al., 2017) (Hazen et al., 2014). Developing countries are not far behind, and various research findings show that big data analytics adoption issues in supply chains are different in developed and developing countries (Dubey et al., 2018a) (Jeble et al., 2018). Extant studies have mainly focused on LARG supply chain, big data analytics for supply chain (Nguyen et al., 2018) (Hazen et al., 2016), and big data analytics for sustainable supply chain (Moktadir et al., 2019) (Dubey et al., 2019b). However, academics and practitioners rarely discuss big data analytics adoption for LARG supply chain operations. Hence, this chapter aims to bridge the gap by reviewing the effect of lean management, social practices, financial practices, and environmental practices on big data analytics.

Manufacturing firms, which have already deployed LARG operational practices in supply chain management, can further enhance sustainable business performance through big data analytics (Pal, 2022). In recent years, researchers highlight the positive effects of big data analytics on sustainable performance (Raut et al., 2019), supply chain agility (Dubey et al., 2018a), supply chain key performance indicators (KPI) (Pal, 2020) (Raut et al., 2019), supply chain agility (Dubey et al., 2018a), supply chain KPI (Dev et al., 2018), and sustainable supply chain (Papadopoulos et al., 2017). However, the big data analytics effect on sustainable supply chains that deployed LARG practices is rarely investigated. A research group investigated the mediating role of big data analytics on sustainable business performance for Indian manufacturing firms (Raut et al., 2019). However, the particular research considered only the lean and green parameters of LARG practices and did not consider the effects of agile and resilient parameters. The main agenda of Indian manufacturers is to build an agile supply chain to respond to unexpected and sudden market volatility. This study overcomes the shortcoming of Rakesh Raut and fellow researchers (Raut et al., 2019) by investigating the effect of LARG practices on big data analytics. Thus, it investigates the mediating role of big data analytics on sustainability in supply chain management practice and performance. It is worth noting that understanding the effect of big data analytics will assist manufacturing firms in the effective deployment of sustainable operational strategies in the supply chain.

In addition, this chapter links BDA and Sustainable supply chain business performance from a LARG perspective. Firstly, critical factors that affect BDA adoption in the sustainable supply chain in the context of a developing country were finalized through a literature survey. The literature on 'big data analytics,' 'lean, agile, resilient, and green,' and 'supply chain management' were studied. Seven factors, namely, total quality management and lean, social, environmental, supply chain, financial, and organizational practices, were identified from the literature. Factor analysis was conducted on the collected data to determine the regression weights and significance of constructs. Identified constructs of BDA adoption for sustainable supply chains were analyzed using the structural equation modeling (SEM) approach. SEM assesses observable and unobservable constructs of BDA implementation through empirical analysis. The study focuses on understanding whether BDA acts as a mediator to influence the business performance of a sustainable supply chain when considering LARG aspects. Thus, this chapter explores the impact of BDA on the supply chain performance of Indian manufacturers by effectively implementing sustainable and LARG practices.

The contributions of this chapter are: (i) reviewing the recent existing works on the field of data-driven sustainability in various business organizations and their supply chains, (ii) discussing the design factors of supply chain performance measurement, and it includes supply chain operations reference (SCOR) model prescribes a general business process management approach to the supply chain community, (iii) overview of business intelligence and the different stages of deployment of business intelligence (i.e., gathered, cleansed, stored, and made available to business operation managers), (iv) explanation of characteristics for big data (i.e., volume, velocity, variety, value, and veracity) and categories of data analytics, (v) presents a big data framework for supply chain data analytics which consist of internet of things (IoT) based data gathering source, augmented reality (AR), and virtual reality (VR), and finally, it presents future research directions and conclusion.

SUSTAINABILITY IN MANUFACTURING AND LITERATURE REVIEW

The organizational economy has been transformed by data in recent decades. Data-driven business organizations and their supply chains made up seven of the global top ten business organizations by stock market capitalisation in 2021 and across the OECD (Organization for Economic Co-operation and Development) economies there has been a growing gap in terms of productivity and profitability between business organizations that use data intensively and the rest (Brynjolfsson et al., 2019) (Bajgar et al., 2022) (Coyle, 2023). The widespread availability of data and analytics has also begun to extend into the business sector for operational efficiency and policymaking.

In SCM, there is a growing interest in *business analytics* (BA), also known as supply chain analytics (SCA), in academic literature. These analytics use data and quantitative techniques to analyze business performance in different functional areas of supply chain management (Handfield, 2006) (Davis-Sramek, Germain, & Iyer, 2010) (Davenport & O'dwyer, 2011) (O'dwyer & Renner, 2011). This section presents a brief review of Big Data-Based SCM. In recent research, J R Stock (Stock, 2013) proposes a Big Data-driven SCM. He suggests that Big Data-Based analytics for SCM will allow decision-makers to make decisions faster with the help of circumstance-specific actions. An industry survey conducted by Mitsubishi Heavy Industries and consulting company Deloitte (Deloitte & MHI, 2014); and questioned supply chain executives about innovations that drive supply chains. The main objective was to get the views of business executives on emerging technology trends that could dramatically impact future supply chains. A critical issue that emerged from the survey was *supply chain analytics*. The survey also identified areas for analytics based SCM. The Council for Supply Chain Management Consultants published a report (Richey et al., 2014) on Big Data in SCM based on interviews with supply chain managers.

Many commercial Big Data applications related to SCM are attracting the attention of academics and practitioners (Watson et al., 2012) (Davenport, 2006) (Davenport & Harris, 2007) (McAfee & Brynjolfsson, 2012) (Deloitte & MHI, 2016). For example, a few Big Data applications in corporate marketing management show tremendous opportunity in Big Data-based business analytics (Szilard et al., 2013). The number of publications on supply chain network design using Big Data and business analytics is also growing steadily (Baesens, 2014) (Dietrich et al., 2014) (Sathi, 2012) (Siegel, 2013) (Watson et al., 2012).

Big Data analytics in SCM is not necessarily a new idea (Davenport & O'dwyer, 2011) since different quantitative techniques and modelling mechanisms have long been used in manufacturing companies (Turban & Sepehri, 1986) (Shapiro, 2010) (Kuaka, 2006) (Trkman et al., 2010). However, there has been considerable interest in Big Data analytics in recent years, and it has ushered in new technical challenges for research communities. These challenges include technical issues regarding data volume and its storage facilities, data Provence (e.g., syntax, semantics, pragmatic), data quality and availability; and, importantly, data uncertainties (Handfield & Nichols, 2004) (Liberatore & Luo, 2010) (Hunter et al., 2011) (Lavalle et al., 2011) (Mayika et al., 2011).

It is evident from the research literature that SCM's critically important organizational function will need to evolve and adapt to Big Data analytics. For example, in a recent industry report (Deloitte & MHI, 2016), Mitsubishi Heavy Industries highlighted the potential of supply chains to deliver massive economic and environmental rewards for society. However, the report suggests that technological innovation will play a vital role in fulfilling this potential. For example, big data analytics can provide step-change improvements in supply chain visibility, cost savings, and customer service. The key is generating insightful data analysis and sharing it with business partners within manufacturing supply chains to act on it.

In response to these challenges, Big Data Analytics has been proposed as a promising approach to managing data better, utilizing IT resources and preparing for effective supply chain planning (Handfield, 2006) (Davenport, Harris & Morison, 2010) (Davis-Sramek, Germain & Iyer, 2010) (Viswanathan & Sadlovska, 2010) (Bentalha et al., 2019) (Bentalha, 2020) (Bentalha et al., 2020). This new generation of

Table 1. Big data analytics in supply chain operations by Indian companies

Publication	Research Approach	Main Characteristics
(Dev et al., 2018)	Integration of Fuzzy ANP, simulation, and TOPSIS	Supply chain operations reference (SCOR) model with three suppliers, one manufacturer, two distributors, and four retailers were considered. Big data analytic architecture for supply chain key performance indicators (KPI) is used for analysis.
(Dubey et al., 2018a)	Conceptual model, exploratory analysis, partial least square (PLS) – structural equation modelling (SEM)	Manufacturer of auto components, and senior manager Big data framework for supply chain agility factors considered (e.g., capability analysis, competitive advantage, organizational flexibility, and industry specific operational dynamics)
(Dubey et al., 2018b)	Conceptual model, exploratory analysis, PLS-SEM	Manufacturer of auto components Big data predictive analysis framework for supply chain (e.g., resource complementarity, organizational compatibility, collaborative performance, interdependency, and temporal orientation).
(Dubey et al., 2019a)	Conceptual mode, empirical analysis, PLS-SEM	Manufacturing organizations, senior-level supply chain managers Big data analytic framework for supply chain resilience Factors considered: big data analytic capabilities, organizational flexibility, supply chain resilience, competitive advantage, industry dynamics, and size of the organization.
(Gunasekaran et al., 2017)	Regression analysis	Consulting and manufacturing companies Big data analytic framework for predictive analysis Factors considered: supply chain performance, organizational performance, big data analysis assimilation, top management commitment, and information sharing.
(Jeble et al., 2018)	PLS-SEM	Managers of auto manufacturing companies Cost economics, relationship with supplier and customer, strategic management, human aspects Big data predictive capability, supply base complexity, social performance, environmental performance, economic performance.

Table 2. Big data analytics use by USA companies in supply chain operations

Publication	Research Approach	Main Characteristics
(Chen et al., 2015)	TOE framework, factor analysis, SEM	Online survey of managers and executive of multiple companies Organizational readiness, technological compatibility, expected benefits, competitive pressure, business growth, asset productivity, environmental dynamics, top management commitment.
(Fawcett & Waller, 2014)	Conceptual model, exploratory analysis, partial least square (PLS) – structural equation modelling (SEM)	Manufacturer of auto components, and senior manager Big data framework for supply chain agility factors considered (e.g., capability analysis, competitive advantage, organizational flexibility, and industry specific operational dynamics)
(Hazen et al., 2014)	Conceptual model	Correlational decision-making, prediction through profiling, virtual integration, collaborative supply chain
(Hazen et al., 2016)	Correlation analysis	Manufacturing organizations, senior-level supply chain managers
(Hazen et al., 2014)	Regression analysis	Statistical process control (SPC), Quality tools Data quality – timeliness, completeness, accuracy, and consistency Supply chain performance, knowledge resource, strategic decision, supply chain capabilities, and supply chain processing needs
(Hazen et al., 2016)	Correlation analysis	Supply chain sustainability, technological infrastructure, aggregate resources, the effect of external environment on organizational processes and structure, the organization's adoption to change, cost economics, relationship with supplier and customer, strategic management, human aspects.

Table 3. Big data analytics use by Chines companies in supply chain operations

Publication	Research Approach	Main Characteristics
(Chavez et al., 2017)	Conceptual model, SEM	Multiple manufacturing companies Data driven supply chain, delivery, flexibility, cost, quality, and customer satisfactions.
(Tan et al., 2015)	Conceptual model, case study	Deduction graph, glass manufacturer, two managers and one CEO Proposed an analytic infrastructure model, supply chain innovation capability, factors considered – internal skills, present competence sets, required competence sets, competence network, optimal decision.
(Zhao et al., 2017)	Mathematical model, case study	Sanitary product supply chain Green supply chain network, inherent risk, carbon dioxide emission, total cost, the constraint of material balance, capacity, decision variables
(Zhong et al., 2015)	Case study implementation	Manufacturing shop floors with wireless sensor network and radio frequency identification technology
(Zhong et al., 2016)	Conceptual study	Big data processing technologies, decision-making model, big-data applications, and big data interpretation

analytics tools can develop a manufacturing enterprise's IT infrastructure and data management capabilities to improve strategic planning and enhance operational performance (Kohli & Grover, 2008) (Shapiro, 2010) (Mithas et al., 2011). Additionally, it has been proposed that manufacturing enterprises can use SCA from acquired data using electromechanical devices (e.g., RFID tags, Sensors) and storing repositories of packaged software (e.g., CRM, ERP, SCM) to enhance manufacturing chain planning through IT-enabled planning and scheduling systems (Davenport & O'Dea, 2011) (O'dwyer & Renner, 2011).

Companies need to use sustainable practices due to public pressure, the concerns of the customers, and government regulations (Pal, 2023) (Lee & Zhang, 2019). In recent years, a group of researchers (Bhanot et al., 2017) commented that sustainable manufacturing is the most significant attribute of sustainable supply chain. Big data analytic capabilities can help manufacturing companies achieve social dimensions (Wadmann & Hoeyer, 2018) and economic advantages (Pal, 2023) while minimizing the environmental impacts (Pal, 2021) (Hazen et al., 2016). Big data analytics can also integrate the data resources in the supply chain to minimize pollutant emissions and energy consumption (Song et al., 2018). Previous studies on big data analytics for carbon resilient supply chain (Suifan et al., 2019) show a positive effect of data analytics on LARG. However, these research findings discuss the lean, agile, resilient, and green aspects separately. With this motivation, this chapter presents the mediating role of big data analytics on sustainable supply chain by considering LARG practices.

BDA capabilities can assist with supply chain functions, such as procurement, warehousing, manufacturing, demand management, transportation/logistics, and general supply chain (Govindan et al., 2018). The current literature shows other research articles in manufacturing and transportation/logistics (Inamdar et al., 2020). Critical activities in supply chain manufacturing are production planning and control, product research and development, maintenance and diagnosis, and quality management, BDA adoption in production planning and control, product research and development, maintenance and diagnosis, and quality management. BDA adoption in production planning and control is attracting interest from many researchers, and BDA tools and techniques in this area are relatively mature (Zhong et al., 2015).

Supply Chain Performance Measurement

Supply Chain performance measurement is crucial for a manufacturing enterprise to survive in the competitive world of business. Some well-known manufacturing enterprises use *business intelligence* (BI) software applications and in-house business practices to measure supply chain performance. It also measures the performance of the enterprise's internal business processes in consideration, but it also takes into consideration extended enterprise activities.

In order to tackle some of these drawbacks in traditional financial accounting-based practices for measuring supply chain performance, a variety of measurement mechanisms have been introduced. They include Balance Scorecard, Supply Chain Council's SCOR (Supply Chain Operations Reference) model, Logistics Scoreboard, Activity-Based Costing (ABC), and Economic Value Analysis (EVA). In this chapter, the SCOR model has been used for manufacturing supply chain decision-making. A brief introduction of the SCOR model is described below.

SCOR Model

The Supply Chain Operations Reference (SCOR) model prescribes a general business process management approach to the supply chain community. This reference model was initially introduced by the Supply

Chain Council (SCC) in 1996. The SCOR model deals with supply chain management activities from an operational purpose. It includes corporate customer engagement information, day-to-day business transactions, and relevant market reactions. This model encapsulates business process activity management, benchmarking with market-leading enterprises, and best practices into a single framework. Many well-known companies have used the SCOR model (e.g., Intel, General Electronic, Airbus, DuPont, and IBM) (Supply Chain Council, 2010). Intel Corporation used its first SCOR for its resellers' product department in 1999. Then it used the SCOR model for its system manufacturing department. Implementing the SCOR model to handle business process management includes improved operational cycle time, fewer inventories in storage, enhanced visibility of the supply chain, and timely access to customer engagement information. General Electric (GE) has also used the SCOR model for its transportation management department and has reported operational improvement in its transportation service after using the SCOR model (Poluha, 2007).

The SCOR is a standardized multi-level framework with Key Performance Indicators (KPIs) attached to its Level. According to SCOR, five business entities are involved in supply chain performance management: the enterprise itself, the supplier of the enterprise, suppliers to suppliers, the customer of the enterprise, and customers of the customers. These five categories of business entities have their own SCOR. Individual SCOR is composed of the five-integrated corporate operational behaviours: Plan (P), Source (S), Make (M), Deliver (D), and Return (R) – from the suppliers' supplier to customers' customers, and all aligned with leading enterprise's operational strategy, material, work, and information flow. A diagrammatical representation of the SCOR model is shown in Figure 1.

There are four levels in the SCOR framework: Top Level, Configuration Level, Process Element Level, and Implementation Level, as shown in Figure 1. It is considered a best practice framework for evaluating performance in supply chain management. The framework uses many performance measure-

Figure 1. An organizational overview of the SCOR model

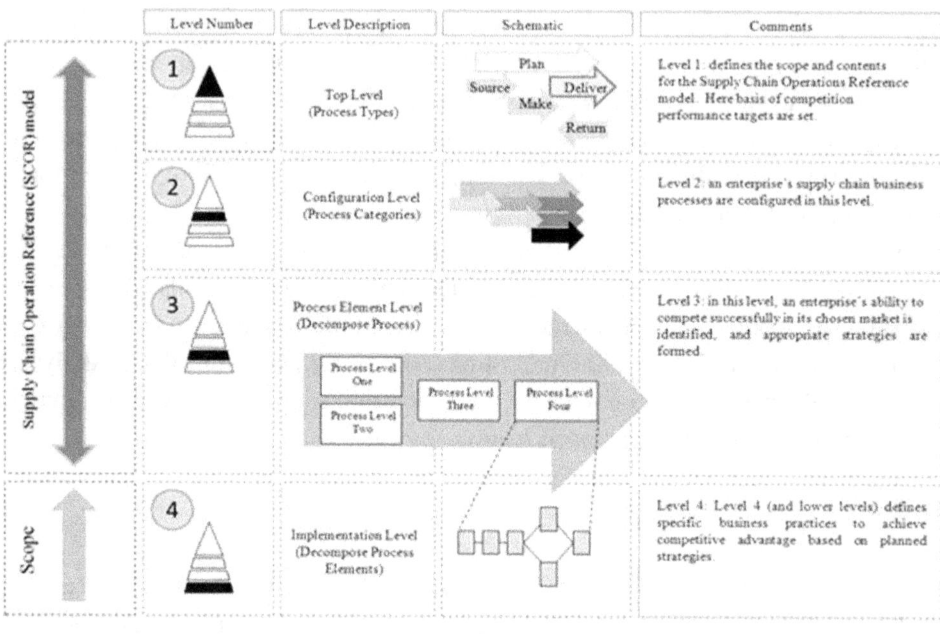

ment metrics and their relevant attributes. This way, the SCOR framework creates business process improvement using benchmarking techniques. The top three levels of the SCOR model are as follows:

1. Level-1(Process Types): This Level defines the scope and contents of the Supply Chain Operations Reference (SCOR) model. Here the basis of competition performance targets is set. To express the detailed requirements, it uses the following criteria:
    - **P**lan (P): a process that balances requests of demand-side and supply-side and has a smooth sub-process for sourcing, making, and delivery activities under the best business plan.
    - **S**ource (S): a process that procures raw materials and relevant services to fulfil strategic or practical needs.
    - **M**ake (M): transforming raw materials to finish or semi-finished goods to fulfil strategic requirements.
    - **D**eliver (D): a process that transports finished goods or services to fulfil plans or strategic requirements.
    - **R**eturn (R): a collection of returned products for several reasons.
2. Level-2 (Process Categories): The second SCOR level defines the configuration of planning and execution processes in material flow, using standard process categories such as make-to-order, engineer-to-order, or make-to-stock categories. This Level derives from Level 1, which settles on more concrete strategies.
3. Level-3 (Process Element Level): The third Level contains the main process elements and their process flows. This lower Level of the SCOR model is most significant to business data analytics. It includes process element definitions, inputs and outputs, relationships, performance metrics, and best practices.

This way, all process metrics use aspects of a performance characteristic. For example, any given process's performance characteristics are either customer-facing (reliability, responsiveness, and flexibility) or internal-facing (cost and assets) metrics. Level 1 metrics are primary, high-level measures that may cross multiple SCOR processes.

Performance metrics help measure the business intelligence (BI) for key performance indicators (KPIs). Each Level 1 metric can be disintegrated to the lower Level 2 and Level 3 metrics, thus providing standardized operational, tactical, and strategic performance measurements across the supply chain.

Business Intelligence

Gartner, an information technology research company, introduced the term "*Business Intelligence*" (BI) during the 1990s. BI is a process by which corporate operational information can be gathered, cleansed, stored, and made available to decision-makers who need it in its most helpful form. This can range from simple business reports through trend analysis to complicated dashboards and future predictions. However, data in raw form is of limited use, and manufacturing enterprises are increasingly opting to use dedicated BI software to appreciate their data's full capability. BI commercial vendors specialize in an automated Big Data analytic platform that allows an enterprise to easily collect all corporate data, manipulate them, and display them as actionable information or information that can be acted upon in making informed decisions.

Moreover, enterprises of all sizes can connect to and analyze data (even Big Data) to produce better quality business decision-making environments in recent years. Interactive visualizations and dashboards enhance analyzing and interpretation of data to make prudent business decisions in real-time. In addition, BI enables manufacturers to enhance how they do day-to-day business. Manufacturing enterprises are empowered to offer products and services at the lowest possible cost and with the highest degree of productivity and efficiency possible – while returning the highest revenues and profits.

BI platform can collect valuable data from many sources and assemble it into a central Data Warehouse (DW). It can be validated, cleaned, summarized, standardized, and even enhanced by copying the data. Moreover, BI capabilities are spreading to virtually all parts of the manufacturing enterprise as businesses strive to put critical data into the hands of business operational decision-makers who need it to do their jobs. The Big Data user community wants the following from the real-world BI systems:

- The capability to execute ad hoc queries.
- Access and use multiple databases.
- Scalability, affordability and reliability of data and the related operations
- Ease of integration with heterogeneous internal and external data sources

In this way, BI refers to manufacturing enterprises' methods and techniques for tactical and strategic decision-making. For example, it leverages technologies focusing on counts, statistics, and business objectives to improve business performance.

The goal of a DW is to hold the data needed by business managers to make decisions. The next step is to document the data warehouse. *Metadata* describes the source data, identifies the transformation and integration steps, and defines how the data warehouse is organized. This step is crucial to help decision-makers understand what data elements are available. Once the data requirements and sources have been identified, the data must be transformed and integrated so that decision-makers can search and analyze it efficiently. The main activities of this process flow are to extract, clean, transform, and load this data into the data warehouse. This process flow is called Extract, Transform, and Load (ETL).

Thus, the data warehouse process contains the following steps: (i) data extraction from multiple sources, databases, and files; (ii) data transformed and cleaned before loaded; and finally, (iii) data is loaded into the data warehouse. So, the first step in the data warehouse is to extract data from different business data sources; and transform it using built-in transformation processes. In addition, the data flow loading the warehouse dimensions is first passed to a short editor that removes any duplicated rows of data before being passed on to other processing units.

By itself, stored data does not create any business value, which is true of traditional databases, data warehouses, and the new Big Data technologies (e.g., Hadoop) for storage. However, once the data is appropriately stored, it can be analyzed, creating tremendous value. In addition, various analysis technologies and approaches have emerged that are especially applicable to Big Data sources within SCM.

the ERA of big data analytics

The main objective of processing Big Data is to generate differentiated value which can be trusted. This is done by applying *advanced analytics* against the complete data collection regardless of scale. To understand the critical issues of Big Data, one needs to understand the *data sources* of business processes within manufacturing enterprises.

New breeds of manufacturing business organizational process automation software, such as Enterprise Resource Planning (ERP), Supply Chain Management (SCM), Supplier Relationship Management (SRM), Global Positioning Systems (GPS), Social Media (SM) analysis systems, adoption of digital sensors and radio frequency identification (RFID) tags leading to the 'Internet of Things (IoT), and digitization of voice and multimedia are capable of collecting substantial data sets and unlock valuable information from it.

Before Big Data can be used for business purposes, it must be stored, managed, and analyzed appropriately for decision-making purposes. Distributed file systems, flexible storage systems, and massively parallel processing databases enable much larger volumes at low-cost infrastructure (e.g., Data Center, Private Cloud, Public Cloud, and Hybrid Cloud). In addition, processing a high volume of complex data in a distributed manner needs different techniques (e.g., time series analysis, knowledge-based classification, scenario-based analysis, and other statistical analysis methods). A diagrammatic representation of Big Data Infrastructure and its processing capabilities is shown in Figure 2.

Data streams can come from internal and external sources within the global manufacturing chain. In addition, data can come in various formats, such as transaction and log data from multiple applications, structured data as database tables, semi-structured data such as XML, and unstructured data such as text, images, video streams, and audio statements. In order to process these data, other information systems are now making a revolution in sensing technology, computing and communication power that brings together a variety of resources. These resources range from networked embedded computers and mobile devices to multimodal data sources.

New breeds of manufacturing business automation software, such as Enterprise Resource Planning (ERP), Supply Chain Management (SCM), and Supplier Relationship Management (SRM), can collect substantial data sets and create valuable information for the company. Additionally, the extended enterprise is enabled by web technologies, e-business for customers, supplier portals, and information technology innovations targeted at supply chains and customer relationships.

As Big Data is one of the most 'exciting' terms in today's business computing, there is no consensus on defining it. Instead, the term is often synonymous with related concepts such as Business Intelligence (BI) and data mining. This also forms the basis for the most used definition of Big Data, the five Vs: Volume, Velocity, Variety, Value, and Veracity, as shown in Figure 2.

Volume: Data volume signifies the amount of data available to a manufacturing business, which does not necessarily have to own all of it if it can access it. Data includes text and videos, music, click streams from web queries, social media (e.g., Facebook, Twitter) updates, and large image files.

Velocity: Data velocity assesses the speed of data creation, streaming, and aggregation. Electronic business (e-business or e-commerce) has rapidly increased the speed and richness of data used for business transactions (e.g., website clicks).

Variety: Data comes from different data sources. Data streams can come from internal and external sources within the global manufacturing supply chain. Data variety is a measuring mechanism of the richness of the data representation – text, images, video, and audio.

Value: A key challenge in transforming the manufacturing supply chain from infrastructure, data collection and remote sensing information system to a provision that presents actionable information and guides humans in decision making (e.g., relevant data, knowledge on data, and inferencing mechanisms) of the relevant information required for data analytics design and prediction purpose. For example, a hybrid of statistical methods and declarative knowledge is beneficial for leveraging sensor data streams for personalized production line machine care to reduce redoing rates among scheduled jobs and improve plant efficiency.

Veracity: Veracity's key issues relate to the messiness of data generated in dynamic supply chain environments. For example, just consider Twitter posts with hashtags, abbreviations, typos, and different colloquial speeches.

The advancement of understanding the behaviour of information systems and the processes and services they support has become a critical issue in the supply chain environment. This is demonstrated by the proliferation of software-based tools to analyze process executions, system interactions, system dependencies and recent research in big data analytics.

Big Data Analytics

It is worth recognizing that the term '*analytics*' is not used consistently. It is used in at least three related ways (Watson, 2013a). First, examining its origins is an initiation point for understanding and appreciating data analytics. The Decision support systems (DSS) in the 1970s were the first computerized systems to support decision-making (Power, 2007). DSS appeared to be used to characterize special type software system applications and an academic research area. Over time, various decision support applications such as executive information systems (EISs), online analytical processing (OLAP), and dashboards/scorecards became very popular. Then in the 1990s, Howard Dresner, a business analyst at Gartner, customized the term *business intelligence* (BI). A simple definition is that "BI is a wider group of software applications, technologies, infrastructure, and processes for gathering, storing, accessing, and analyzing data to help business users make operational decisions" (Watson, 2009).

Various Kinds of Analytics

Big Data-based analytics is a rapidly developing field which has already attracted attention from academics and practitioners. It is important to differentiate three diverse types of analytics because the differences have significance for the software system technologies and technical platform architectures used for Big Data analytics.

Descriptive Analytics: Descriptive analytics is backwards-looking and exposes what has happened. Descriptive data analytics, such as business reporting, dashboards, and data visualization, have been comprehensively used for some time and are the main applications of typical BI.

Predictive Analytics: Predictive analytics suggest what will occur in future. The techniques and algorithms for predictive analytics, such as statistical regression analysis, machine learning, and other soft-computing methods, have been used for some time. However, commercial software systems like SAS Enterprise Miner have made them easier to use and apprehend.

Prescriptive analytics can find optimal solutions, often for scarce corporate resources. For example, mathematical techniques for revenue management are increasingly general for manufacturing enterprises with "*perishable*" inventories (e.g., rental cars, hotel rooms, airline seats). In this way, modern data analytic techniques help enterprises to discover deeper insights from collected data.

Figure 2. Typical types of Big Data application systems

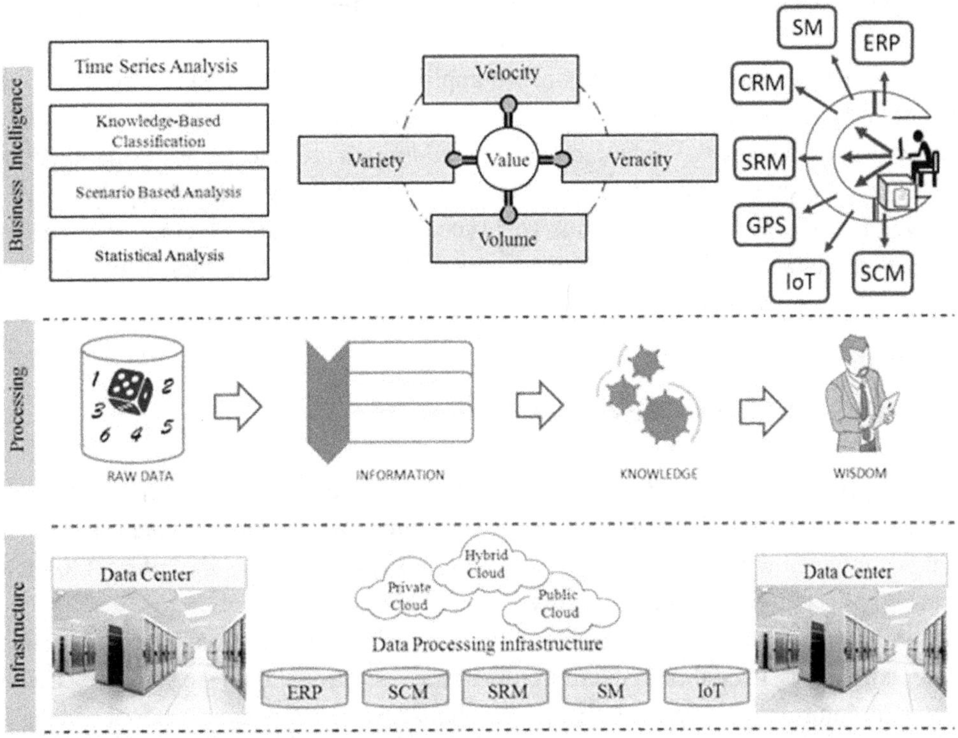

Techniques for Analytics

Most techniques used to analyze Big Data analytics are based on applied mathematical computation and machine learning paradigms. However, Big Data analytics techniques are widespread and context specific. These techniques can be classified and discussed according to the data under investigation. Depending on the type of data, four central Big Data analytics can be defined:

Text Analytics: This technique is used to find out relevant information from textual data. Text analysis uses statistical computation, natural language processing techniques, and machine learning methods. Some essential text analytics techniques are information extraction, text summarization, question answering, and sentimental analysis.

Audio Analytics: Techniques deployed to extract information from unstructured audio data. Customer service telephone conversations with customers are the primary source of audio analytics. Some of the main techniques used for audio analytics include large vocabulary, continuous speech recognition and phonetics-based systems.

Video Analytics: Techniques used to monitor and analyze video streams. Video analytics has been mainly used as a replacement for labor-intensive observation. In addition, many business applications of video analytics are being used in manufacturing to collect data on customer demographics and preferences.

Social Media Analytics: Techniques used to analyze structured and non-structured data from social media channels (e.g., Twitter, Facebook). Some exciting techniques used to analyze social media data are community detection, social influence analysis and link prediction.

Many successful manufacturing enterprises have invested large sums of money in business intelligence and data warehousing tools and technologies. These manufacturers believe that up-to-date, accurate and integrated information about their supply chain, products and customers is critical for their survival.

In order to solve a problem, the Big Data-based application uses intelligent reasoning in automated software that helps users apply analytical and scientific methods to business decision-making. The software applications that focus on the manufacturing chain domain are referred to as manufacturing decision support systems, providing Big Data-based tools to support a user's global supply chain reasoning process to develop a solution to the problem. This type of reasoning can be considered an intellectual process by which manufacturing operation managers use distinct artificial intelligence-based inference mechanisms to solve global operations problems.

PROPOSED BIG DATA FRAMEWORK FOR SCM

As the global supply chain's information system's architecture expands over the Internet to envelop the entire supply chain, so does BI. The Internet broadens the information sources of data storage. It expands beyond what is contained within the organization's internal systems across the Internet to include business partners, suppliers, and customer relations.

In order to collaborate efficiently, business organizations must coordinate their regular activities. The essential elements of a collaborative environment are operational data store, data warehouse (e.g., data and metadata information), data mart (data warehouse, which concentrates on a particular subject area within the business operations), ETL tools, OLAP engine, analytical tools (reporting, data mining, and so on) and web portals. Combinations of these elements make different scenarios that depend on an organization's organizational administration, informational architecture, and supply chain. A data warehouse system must:

- Make an organization's information easily accessible,
- Present the organization's information consistently,
- Be adaptive and resilient to change,
- Serve as the basis of improved decision-making.

Figure 3 shows how the SCOR reference model can be utilized in Big Data for supply chain management. The SCOR model allows for identifying the origins of Big Data in supply chain activities. This can initially be applied at elevated levels and drilled down as required; secondly, it will identify potential users of such Big Data and their information requirements. Finally, the originating and communicating activities will need access to and analysis of Big Data sets. Finally, the approach specifies the type of IT infrastructure required to process such data, i.e., whether a batch or real-time streaming capability will be required or a combination of these two.

Additionally, the framework can accommodate the enterprise potential of augmented reality (AR) and virtual reality (VR). These efforts increasingly intersect with opportunities made possible by the Internet of Things (IoT) technology (e.g., sensors and connected devices) that help build a more integrated and extended digital and physical environment. Finally, the framework can help define a typical Big Data strategy for the whole supply chain.

Figure 3. Big Data potential for SCM according to the SCOR model

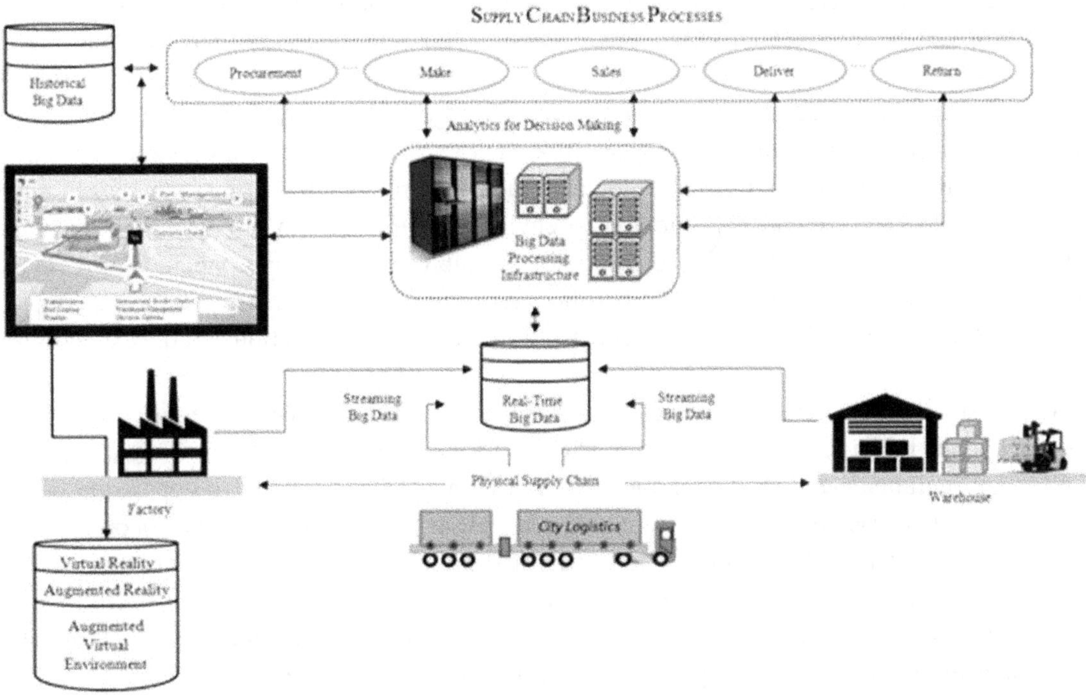

This framework allows the problem of utilizing Big Data for supply chain management to be viewed from the perspective of vital managerial components of business logistics and distinct categories of stakeholders. It can encompass all essential supply chain business foundations such as forecasting, inventory management, transportation, and human recourses management. Different stakeholders, such as manufacturers, carriers, and manufacturers, can then identify ways to benefit from the supply chain Big Data.

FUTURE RESEARCH DIRECTIONS

Big data analytics attract various potentials across the logistic network, increasing data precision, analysis, and transparency for networks and generating better contextual knowledge throughout supply chain operations. For example, big data analytics strategies have analyzed consumer behaviour in retail supply chains by correctly projecting consumers' tastes and expectations. In order to thrive in today's dynamic environments, supply chain decision-makers must constantly search for opportunities to leverage and handle data sources efficiently to achieve more value and driven edge. In this way, to develop flexible or responsive supply chains by forecasting consumer dynamics and consumer needs and tastes and acquiring a deeper understanding. Big data analytics will promote the real-time tracking and management of data to improve supply chain decision speed, efficiency, precision, and versatility. It is possible to proactively forecast and schedule all supply chain activities using a wide variety of direct data feeds, news, social networks, weather, and event data from various constant and complex data sources.

In addition, developing secure, smart supply chain operational activities need to be supported through machine learning, new technologies (e.g., IoT, blockchain), and profound learning strategies in each operation involved in the supply chain. For starters, by tracking the supply chain in real-time, IoT may be applied in production processes in order to deliver real-time telemetry data to reveal specifics. Machine learning algorithms equipped to interpret the knowledge will reliably foresee inevitable faults in the machine. Machine learning methods may also reliably forecast consumers' desires and expectations.

Business analytics (BA) design and development face numerous future success challenges, such as implementation cost and complexity—funding for environmental growth in supply chain management. Big data analytics will certainly improve initiatives to improve social, environmental and financial results. Detailed preparation for the timely distribution of the goods can be achieved, for example, by studying GPS real-time traffic data, which decrease greenhouse gas production and the expenditure on fuel utilization.

In today's supply chain, operations encompass various sustainability-related categories. One of these issues is corporate bullying which is counterproductive for manufacturing industries (e.g., textile, mining). Corporate culture plays an essential role, allowing supply chains to proactive steps towards supply chain risk rather than reactive ones (e.g., loss reputation, industrial tribunals, contextual or organizational distractions). In a dynamic global supply chain, analytical strategies can assist logistic network management to respond and predict proactively in contradiction to external future incidents.

Immediately future research will focus on real-world data collection for business processes operations and top managerial opinions regarding supply chain success and failure-related issues in their specific industries. For example, point of sales data provide real-time demand and pricing information. It offers an indication for refilling, such as the inventory method operated by the seller. Sensor information comprises an automated refill indicator, automatic storage and receipt information, and automated checkout information that informs inventory status in real-time. Once the initial data collection is over, the data-supported analytics design and development and, finally, validating these data analytics software will be the next step of the current project.

CONCLUSION

This chapter presents a brief overview of big data analytics and different categories – for example, descriptive and predictive analytics. The chapter also describes different techniques for designing business analytics (e.g., text, audio, video, and social media). There is a growing interest in deploying big data-based business analytics for regular supply chain operations. These analytics use data and qualitative techniques to analyze business operational performances in different functional areas for supply chain management. In addition, there are many successful cases of supply chain analytics deployment by industrial enterprises. For example, Proctor & Gamble and Walmart use data analytics to enhance operational performance. However, there has been considerable interest in Big Data analytics in recent years, and it has ushered in new technical challenges for research communities. It includes technical issues regarding data volume and storage facilities, data Provence, data quality and availability, and data uncertainties.

Previous research highlights the importance of big data analytics for sustainable supply chain operations for firm performance separately. These two issues, big data analytics and sustainable operations, are discussed jointly in this chapter. Some manufacturing examples are described in this chapter. In manufacturing business process optimization and sustainability, related issues are two major characteristics that are highlighted in this chapter. By developing big data analytics, supply chain businesses can better understand the needs of their customers, provide adequate services to meet their customers, boost incomes and sales, and enter the neoteric marketplace. The chapter also reviewed the role of big data analytics in supply chain management for some Indian, United States of America, and Chines companies. Finally, the chapter provides a Big Data framework for supply chain management, which can accommodate the enterprise potential of augmented reality (AR), and virtual reality (VR) and incorporate the use of new evolving data-gathering technologies (IoT and RFID technology).

REFERENCES

Addo-Tenkorang, R., & Helo, P. T. (2016). Big data applications in operations/supply-chain management: A literature review. *Computers & Industrial Engineering*, *101*, 528–543. doi:10.1016/j.cie.2016.09.023

Akter, S., Wamba, S. F., Gunasekaran, A., Dubey, R., & Childe, S. J. (2016). How to improve firm performance using big data analytics capability and business strategy alignment? *International Journal of Production Economics*, *182*, 113–131. doi:10.1016/j.ijpe.2016.08.018

Alqudah, S., Shrouf, H., Suifan, T., & Alhyari, S. (2020). A Moderated Mediation Model of Lean, Agile, Resilient, and Green Paradigms in the Supply Chain. Int. J Sup. Chain. *Mgt.*, *9*(4), 1.

Angeles, R. (2005). RFID technologies: Supply-chain applications and implementation issues. *Information Systems Management*, *22*(1), 51–65. doi:10.1201/1078/44912.22.1.20051201/85739.7

Arunachalam, D., Kumar, N., & Kawalek, J. P. (2018). Understanding big data analytics capabilities in supply chain management: Unravelling the issues, challenges and implications for practice. *Transportation Research Part E, Logistics and Transportation Review*, *114*, 416–436. doi:10.1016/j.tre.2017.04.001

Baesens, A. (2014). *Analytics in a big data world: The essential guide to data science and its applications*. John Wiley & Sons.

Ballou, R. H. (2007). *Business Logistics/supply Chain Management, 5/E (With Cd)*. Pearson Education India.

Baramichai, M., Zimmers, E. W. Jr, & Marangos, C. A. (2007). Agile supply chain transformation matrix: An integrated tool for creating an agile enterprise. *Supply Chain Management*, *12*(5), 334–348. doi:10.1108/13598540710776917

Barhhan, P. (2003). *International Trade Growth and Development: Essays*. Wiley-Blackwell. doi:10.1002/9780470752777

Bentalha, B. (2020). Big-Data et Service Supply Chain Management: Challenges et Opportunities. *International Journal of Business and Technology Studies and Research*, *1*(3).

Bentalha, B. (2022). Green Transportation Balanced Scorecard Model: A Fuzzy-Delphi Approach During COVID-19. In *Computational Intelligence Techniques for Green Smart Cities* (pp. 107–127). Springer. doi:10.1007/978-3-030-96429-0_5

Bentalha, B., Hmioui, A., & Alla, L. (2019). The digitalization of the supply chain management of service companies: a prospective approach, In *proceedings of the 4th International Conference on Smart City Applications*, (pp. 1-8). ACM. 10.1145/3368756.3369005

Bentalha, B., Hmioui, A., & Alla, L. (2020). Digital Service Supply Chain Management: Current Realities and Prospective Vision, in Ben Ahmed M., Boudhir, A., Santos, D., El Aroussi, M., & Karas, I. (eds.), Innovations in Smart Cities Applications. Springer, Cham.

Bhanot, N., Rao, P. V., & Deshmukh, S. G. (2017). An integrated approach for analysing the enablers and barriers of sustainable manufacturing. *Journal of Cleaner Production, 142*, 4412–4439. doi:10.1016/j.jclepro.2016.11.123

Bowman, P., Ng, J., Harrison, M., Lopez, S., & Illic, A. (2009). Sensor based condition monitoring. *Building Radio frequency IDentification for the Global Environment.*

Cabral, I., Grilo, A., & Cruz-Machado, V. (2012). A decision-making model for lean, agile, resilient and green supply chain management. *International Journal of Production Research, 50*(17), 4830–4845. doi:10.1080/00207543.2012.657970

Chavez, R., Yu, W., Jacobs, M. A., & Feng, M. (2017). Data-driven supply chains, manufacturing capability and customer satisfaction. *Production Planning and Control, 28*(11–12), 906–918. doi:10.1080/09537287.2017.1336788

Chavez, R., Yu, W., Sadiq Jajja, M. S., Lecuna, A., & Fynes, B. (2020). Can entrepreneurial orientation improve sustainable development through leveraging internal lean practices? *Business Strategy and the Environment, 29*(6), 2211–2225. doi:10.1002/bse.2496

Chen, D. Q., Preston, D. S., & Swink, M. (2015). How the use of big data analytics affects value creation in supply chain management. *Journal of Management Information Systems, 32*(4), 4–39. doi:10.1080/07421222.2015.1138364

Choi, S., Kim, B. H., & Noh, S. D. (2015). A diagnosis and evaluation method for strategic planning and systematic design of a virtual factory in smart manufacturing systems. *International Journal of Precision Engineering and Manufacturing, 16*(6), 1107–1115. doi:10.100712541-015-0143-9

Chun Wu, Y. (2003). Lean manufacturing: A perspective of lean suppliers. *International Journal of Operations & Production Management, 23*(11), 1349–1376. doi:10.1108/01443570310501880

Clark, L. (2013). Tesco Uses Supply Chain Analytics to Save £100 m a Year. *Computer Weekly.* https://www.computerweekly.com/news/2240182951/Tesco-uses-supply-chain-analytics-to-save-10-m-a-year

Cooke, J. A. (2013). Three trends to watch in 2013. *Perspective, Supply chain Quarterly, 1,* 11.

Coyle, D. (2023). *Cogs and Monsters: What Economics Is, and What It Should Be, United State of America.* Princeton University Press.

Davenport, T., & O'Dwyer, J. (2011). Tap into the Power of Analytics. *Supply Chain Quarterly, 4*, 28-31.

Davenport, T. H. (2006). *Competing on analytics, Harvard Business Review.* Harvard Business Press.

Davenport, T. H., Barth, P., & Bean, R. (2012). How Big Data is different. *MIT Sloan Management Review*, (Fall), 22–24.

Davenport, T. H., & Harris, J. G. (2007). *Competing on analytics – the new science of winning*. Harvard Business School Publishing Corporation.

Davenport, T. H., Harris, J. G., & Morison, R. (2010). *Analytics at work – smart decisions, better results*. Harvard Business Press.

Davenport, T. H., & Prusak, L. (2000). *Working knowledge: how organizations manage what they know*. Harvard Business Press.

Davis-Sramek, B., Germain, R., & Iyer, K. (2010). Supply Chain Technology: The Role of Environment in Predicting Performance. *Journal of the Academy of Marketing Science, 38*(1), 42–55. doi:10.100711747-009-0137-1

Decker, C., Berchtold, M. L., Chaves, W. F., Beigl, M., Roehr, D., & Riedel, T. (2008). Cost benefit model for smart items in the supply chain. In: The Internet of Things, 155–172. Springer. doi:10.1007/978-3-540-78731-0_10

Deloitte & MHI. (2014). *The 2014 MHI Annual Industry Report – Innovation the driven supply chain*. MHI.

Deloitte & MHI. (2016). *The 2016 MHI Annual Industry Report – Accelerating change: How innovation is driving digital, always-on Supply Chains*. MHI.

Demirkan, H., & Delen, D. (2012). Levering the Capabilities of Service-oriented Decision Support Systems: Putting Analytics and Big Data in Cloud. *Decision Support Systems, 55*(1), 412–421. doi:10.1016/j.dss.2012.05.048

Dev, N. K., Shankar, R., Gupta, R., & Dong, J. (2018). Multi-criteria evaluation of real-time key performance indicators of supply chain with consideration of big data architecture. *Computers & Industrial Engineering, 128*, 1076–1087. doi:10.1016/j.cie.2018.04.012

Dey, P. K., Malesios, C., De, D., Chowdhury, S., & Abdelaziz, F. B. (2019). Could lean practices and process innovation enhance supply chain sustainability of small and medium-sized enterprises? *Business Strategy and the Environment, 28*(4), 582–598. doi:10.1002/bse.2266

Dietrich, B., Plachy, E. C., & Norton, M. F. (2014). *Analytics across the enterprise: How IBM realize business value from big data and analytics*. IBM Press Books.

Dora, M., Kumar, M., & Gellynck, X. (2016). Determinants and barriers to lean implementation in food-processing SMEs–a multiple case analysis. *Production Planning and Control, 27*(1), 1–23. doi:10.1080/09537287.2015.1050477

Dubey, R., Gunasekaran, A., & Childe, S. J. (2018a). Big data analytics capability in supply chain agility: The moderating effect of organizational flexibility. *Management Decision*.

Dubey, R., Gunasekaran, A., Childe, S. J., Fosso Wamba, S., Roubaud, D., & Foropon, C. (2019a). Empirical investigation of data analytics capability and organizational flexibility as complements to supply chain resilience. *International Journal of Production Research*, 1–19.

Dubey, R., Gunasekaran, A., Childe, S. J., Luo, Z., Wamba, S. F., Roubaud, D., & Foropon, C. (2018b). Examining the role of big data and predictive analytics on collaborative performance in context to sustainable consumption and production behaviour. *Journal of Cleaner Production*, *196*, 1508–1521. doi:10.1016/j.jclepro.2018.06.097

Dubey, R., Gunasekaran, A., Childe, S. J., Roubaud, D., Wamba, S. F., Giannakis, M., & Foropon, C. (2019b). Big data analytics and organizational culture as complements to swift trust and collaborative performance in the humanitarian supply chain. *International Journal of Production Economics*, *210*, 120–136. doi:10.1016/j.ijpe.2019.01.023

Dubey, R., Gunasekaran, A., Childe, S. J., Wamba, S. F., & Papadopoulos, T. (2016). The impact of big data on world-class sustainable manufacturing. *International Journal of Advanced Manufacturing Technology*, *84*(1–4), 631–645. doi:10.100700170-015-7674-1

Fang, C., Liu, X., Pardalos, P. M., & Pei, J. (2016). Optimization for a three-stage production system in the Internet of Things: Procurement, production and product recovery, and acquisition. *International Journal of Advanced Manufacturing Technology*, *83*(5-8), 689–710. doi:10.100700170-015-7593-1

Fang, J., & Ma, A. (2020). IoT application modules placement and dynamic task processing in edge-cloud computing. *IEEE Internet of Things Journal*, *8*(6), 12771–12781.

Fang, J., Qu, T., Li, Z. G., Xu, G., & Huang, G. Q. (2013). Agent-based gateway operating system for RFID-enabled ubiquitous manufacturing enterprise. *Robotics and Computer-integrated Manufacturing*, *29*(4), 222–231. doi:10.1016/j.rcim.2013.01.001

Fawcett, S. E., & Waller, M. A. (2014). Supply chain game changers—mega, nano, and virtual trends—and forces that impede supply chain design (ie, building a winning team). *Journal of Business Logistics*, *35*(3), 157–164. doi:10.1111/jbl.12058

Forslund, H., & Jonsson, P. (2007). The Impact of Forecast Information Quality on Supply Chain Performance. *International Journal of Operations & Production Management*, *27*(1), 90–107. doi:10.1108/01443570710714556

Fosso Wamba, S., Gunasekaran, A., Papadopoulos, T., & Ngai, E. (2018). Big data analytics in logistics and supply chain management. *International Journal of Logistics Management*, *29*(2), 478–484. doi:10.1108/IJLM-02-2018-0026

Gereffi, G. (1999). International trade and industrial upgrading in the apparel commodity chain. *Journal of International Economics*, *48*(1), 37–70. doi:10.1016/S0022-1996(98)00075-0

Giannakis, M., & Louis, M. (2016). A multi-agent based system with big data processing for enhanced supply chain agility. *Journal of Enterprise Information Management*, *29*(5), 706–727. doi:10.1108/JEIM-06-2015-0050

Govindan, K., Cheng, T. C. E., Mishra, N., & Shukla, N. (2018). Big data analytics and application for logistics and supply chain management. *Transportation Research Part E, Logistics and Transportation Review*, *114*, 343–349. doi:10.1016/j.tre.2018.03.011

Gubbi, J., Buyya, R., Murusic, S., & Palaniswami, M. (2013). Internet of Things (IoT): A vision, architectural elements, and future directions. *Future Generation Computer Systems*, *29*(7), 1645–1660. doi:10.1016/j.future.2013.01.010

Gunasekaran, A., Papadopoulos, T., Dubey, R., Wamba, S. F., Childe, S. J., Hazen, B., & Akter, S. (2017). Big data and predictive analytics for supply chain and organizational performance. *Journal of Business Research*, *70*, 308–317. doi:10.1016/j.jbusres.2016.08.004

Handfield, R. (2006). *Supply Market Intelligence: A Managerial Handbook for Building Sourcing Strategies*. Taylor & Francis. doi:10.4324/9780203339527

Handfield, R., & Nichols, E. Jr. (2004). Key Issues in Global Supply Base Management. *Industrial Marketing Management*, *33*(1), 29–35. doi:10.1016/j.indmarman.2003.08.007

Hazen, B. T., Boone, C. A., Ezell, J. D., & Jones-Farmer, L. A. (2014). Data quality for data science, predictive analytics, and big data in supply chain management: An introduction to the problem and suggestions for research and applications. *International Journal of Production Economics*, *154*, 72–80. doi:10.1016/j.ijpe.2014.04.018

Hazen, B. T., Skipper, J. B., Ezell, J. D., & Boone, C. A. (2016). Big Data and predictive analytics for supply chain sustainability: A theory-driven research agenda. *Computers & Industrial Engineering*, *101*, 592–598. doi:10.1016/j.cie.2016.06.030

Inamdar, Z.Z., Raut, R.D., Narwane, V.S., Gardas, B.B., Narkhede, B.E., & Sagnak, M., (2020). A systematic literature review with bibliometric analysis of big data analytics adoption from period 2014 to 2018. *J. Enterprise Informat. Manage.*

Jiang, J., Li, Z., Tian, Y., & Al-Nabhan, N. (2020). A review of techniques and methods for IoT applications in collaborative cloud-fog environment. *Security and Communication Networks*, *2020*, 1–15. doi:10.1155/2020/8849181

Kharas, H., & Zhang, C. (2014). New agenda, new narrative: What happens after 2015? *SAIS Review (Paul H. Nitze School of Advanced International Studies)*, *34*(2), 25–35. doi:10.1353ais.2014.0019

Kohli, R., & Grover, V. (2008). Business Value of IT: An Essay on Expanding Research Directions to Keep up with the times. *Journal of the Association for Information Systems*, *9*(1), 23–39. doi:10.17705/1jais.00147

Lavalle, S., Lesser, E., Shockey, R. H., & Crosthwait, N. M. (2011). Big Data, Analytics and the Path from Insight to Value. *MIT Sloan Management Review*, *52*(2), 21–32.

Lee, H. L., & Zhang, H. (2019). Introduction to the Special Issue on Innovations and Sustainability. *Production and Operations Management*, *28*(12), 2929–2929. doi:10.1111/poms.13113

Li, B., Yang, C., & Huang, S. (2014). Study on supply chain disruption management under service level dependent demand. *Journal of Networking*, *9*(6), 1432–1439. doi:10.4304/jnw.9.6.1432-1439

Li, D. (2016). Perspective for smart factory in petrochemical industry. *Computers & Chemical Engineering, 91*, 136–148. doi:10.1016/j.compchemeng.2016.03.006

Liberatore, M., & Luo, W. (2010). The Analytics Movement. *Interfaces, 40*(4), 313–324. doi:10.1287/inte.1100.0502

Liukkonen, M., & Tsai, T. N. (2016). Toward decentralized intelligence in manufacturing: Recent trends in automatic identification of things. *International Journal of Advanced Manufacturing Technology, 87*(9-12), 2509–2531. doi:10.100700170-016-8628-y

Mayika, J. M., Chui, B., Brown, J. Bughin, R., Dobbs, Roxburgh, C., & Byers, A. (2011). Big Data: The Next Frontier for Innovation, Competition, and Productivity. *McKinsey Report*. McKinsey.

McAfee, A., & Brynjolfsson, E. (2012). Big data: The management revolution. *Harvard Business Review, 90*(10), 61–68. PMID:23074865

Misic, V. V., & Perakis, G. (2020). Data analytics in operations management: A review. *Manufacturing & Service Operations Management, 22*(1), 158–169. doi:10.1287/msom.2019.0805

Mithas, S., Ramasubbu, N., & Sambamurthy, V. (2011). How Information Management Capability Influences Firm Performance. *Management Information Systems Quarterly, 35*(1), 237–256. doi:10.2307/23043496

Moktadir, M. A., Ali, S. M., Paul, S. K., & Shukla, N. (2019). Barriers to big data analytics in manufacturing supply chains: A case study from Bangladesh. *Computers & Industrial Engineering, 128*, 1063–1075. doi:10.1016/j.cie.2018.04.013

Ng, I. C., & Wakenshaw, S. Y. (2017). The Internet-of-Things: Review and research directions. *International Journal of Research in Marketing, 34*(1), 3–21. doi:10.1016/j.ijresmar.2016.11.003

Nguyen, T., Li, Z. H. O. U., Spiegler, V., Ieromonachou, P., & Lin, Y. (2018). Big data analytics in supply chain management: A state-of-the-art literature review. *Computers & Operations Research, 98*, 254–264. doi:10.1016/j.cor.2017.07.004

O'dwyer, J., & Renner, R. (2011). The Promise of Advanced Supply Chain Analytics, Supply Chain. *Management Review, 15*, 32–37.

Oliva, R., & Watson, N. (2011). Cross-Functional Alignment in Supply Chain Planning: A Case Study of Sales & Operations Planning. *Journal of Operations Management, 29*(5), 434–448. doi:10.1016/j.jom.2010.11.012

Paksoy, T., Karaoğlan, I., Gökçen, H., Pardalos, P. M., & Torğul, B. (2016). Experimental research on closed loop supply chain management with internet of things, Journal of Economy. *Bibliograph., 3*, 1–20.

Pal, K. (2016). Supply Chain Coordination Based on Web Services. In Chan H K, Subramanian, N. and Abdulrahman, M D (eds.), Supply Chain Management in the Big Data Era, 137-171. IGI Global.

Pal, K. (2018). A Big Data Framework for Decision Making in Supply Chain. P K Gupta, Tuner Oren, Mayank Singh (eds) Predictive Intelligence Using Big Data and the Internet of Things, 51-76. IGI Global Publication.

Pal, K. (2019). Quality Assurance Issues for Big Data Applications in Supply Chain Management. In P K Gupta, Tuner Oren, Mayank Singh (eds.) Predictive Intelligence Using Big Data and the Internet of Things, 51-76. IGI Global Publication.

Pal, K. (2020). Information sharing for manufacturing supply chain management based on blockchain technology. In I. Williams (ed.) Cross-Industry Use of Blockchain Technology and Opportunities for the Future. IGI Global Publication.

Pal, K. (2021a). Applications of Secured Blockchain Technology in Manufacturing Industry. In Subhendu Kumar Pani, Biju Patnaik, Sian Lun, & Xingcheng Liu (eds.), Blockchain and AI Technology in the Industrial Internet of Things. IGI Global Publication.

Pal, K. (2021b). Privacy, Security and Policies: A Review of Problems and Solutions with Blockchain-Based Internet of Things Applications in Manufacturing Industry. *Procedia Computer Science*, *191*, 176–183. doi:10.1016/j.procs.2021.07.022

Pal, K. (2022). A Decentralized Privacy-Preserving Healthcare Blockchain for IoT, Challenges, and Solutions. In Malaya Dutta Borah, Pen Zhang, Ganesh Chandra Deka (eds.), Prospects of Blockchain Technology for Accelerating Scientific Advancement in Healthcare. IGI Global Publication.

Pal, K. (2023a). Security Issues and Solutions for Resource-Constrained IoT Applications Using Lightweight Cryptography. In Suhasini Verma, Vidhisha Vyas, and Keshav Kaushik (eds.), Cybersecurity Issues, Challenges, and Solutions in the Business World. IGI Global Publication.

Pal, K. (2023b). Drivers of Sustainable Supply Chain Management Using Internet of Things-Based Blockchain Technology. In Atour Taghipour (eds.), Government Impact on Sustainable and Responsible Supply Chan. IGI Global Publication.

Pal, K., & Yasar, A. (2020). Internet of Things and blockchain technology in apparel manufacturing supply chain data management. *Procedia Computer Science*, *170*, 450–457. doi:10.1016/j.procs.2020.03.088

Papadopoulos, T., Gunasekaran, A., Dubey, R., Altay, N., Childe, S. J., & Fosso-Wamba, S. (2017). The role of Big Data in explaining disaster resilience in supply chains for sustainability. *Journal of Cleaner Production*, *142*, 1108–1118. doi:10.1016/j.jclepro.2016.03.059

Poluha, R. G. (2007). *Application of the SCOR Model in Supply Chain Management*. Youngstown.

Porter, M. E. (1985). *Competitive Advantage: Creating and Sustaining Superior Performance*. The Free Press.

Power, D. J. (2007). *A Brief History of Decision Support Systems*. DSS. http://DSSResource.COM/history/dsshistory.html

Prahalad, C. K., & Mashelkar, R. A. (2010). Innovation's Holy Grail. *Harvard Business Review*, (July-August), 2010.

Raut, R. D., Mangla, S. K., Narwane, V. S., Gardas, B. B., Priyadarshinee, P., & Narkhede, B. E. (2019). Linking big data analytics and operational sustainability practices for sustainable business management. *Journal of Cleaner Production*, *224*, 10–24. doi:10.1016/j.jclepro.2019.03.181

SAS. (2012). *Supply Chain Analytics: Beyond ERP and SCM*. SAS.

Sathi, A. (2012). Big data analytics: Disruptive technologies for changing the game. MC Press Online.

Shapiro, J. (2010). Advanced Analytics for Sales & Operations Planning. *Analytics Magazine*, (May-June), 20–26.

Shin, T. H., Chin, S., Yoon, S. W., & Kwon, S. W. (2011). A service-oriented integrated information framework for RFID/WSN-based intelligent construction supply chain management. *Automation in Construction*, *20*(6), 706–715. doi:10.1016/j.autcon.2010.12.002

Siegel, E. (2013). *Predictive analytics: The power to predict who will click, buy, lie or die*. John Wiley & Sons Inc.

Song, M. L., Fisher, R., Wang, J. L., & Cui, L. B. (2018). Environmental performance evaluation with big data: Theories and methods. *Annals of Operations Research*, *270*(1–2), 459–472. doi:10.100710479-016-2158-8

Srivastava, S. K. (2007). Green supply-chain management: A state-of-the-art literature review. *International Journal of Management Reviews*, *9*(1), 53–80. doi:10.1111/j.1468-2370.2007.00202.x

Stern, N. (2007). *The Economics of Climate Change: The Stern Review*. Cambridge University Press. doi:10.1017/CBO9780511817434

Stiglitz, J. (2017). *Globalization and its Discontents Revisited: Anti-Globalization in the Era of Trump*. Penguin.

Stock, J. R. (2013). Supply chain management: A look back, a look ahead. *Supply Chain Quarterly*, *2*, 22–26.

Stock, T., & Seliger, G. (2016). Opportunities of sustainable manufacturing in industry 4.0. *Procedia CIRP*, *40*, 536–541. doi:10.1016/j.procir.2016.01.129

Suifan, T., Alazab, M., & Alhyari, S. (2019). Trade-off among lean, agile, resilient and green paradigms: An empirical study on pharmaceutical industry in jordan using a TOPSIS-entropy method. *Int. J. Adv. Oper. Manage.*, *11*(1–2), 69–101. doi:10.1504/IJAOM.2019.098493

Supply Chain Council (2010). http://supply-chain.org/f/down-load/726710733/SCOR10.pdf.

Svilvar, M., Charkraborty, A. & Kanioura, A. (2013). Big data analytics in marketing. *OR/MS Today*.

Tan, J., & Koo, S. (2014). A survey of technologies in internet of things, in IEEE Computer Society, 269-274. *The Economist* (10). https://www.economist.com/node/15557443

Tan, K. H., Zhan, Y., Ji, G., Ye, F., & Chang, C. (2015). Harvesting big data to enhance supply chain innovation capabilities: An analytic infrastructure based on deduction graph. *International Journal of Production Economics*, *165*, 223–233. doi:10.1016/j.ijpe.2014.12.034

Taylor, D., & Pettit, S. (2009). A consideration of the relevance of lean supply chain concepts for humanitarian aid provision. *International Journal of Services Technology and Management*, *12*(4), 430–444. doi:10.1504/IJSTM.2009.025817

The Economist (2010). *Data, Data Everywhere*, http://www.economist.com/node/15557443

Trkman, P., McCormack, K., de Oliveira, M. P. V., & Ladeira, M. B. (2010). The Impact of Business Analytics on Supply Chain Performance. *Decision Support Systems*, *49*(3), 318–327. doi:10.1016/j.dss.2010.03.007

Tsai, C. Y., & Huang, S. H. (2015). A data mining approach to optimise shelf space allocation in consideration of customer purchase and moving behaviours. *International Journal of Production Research*, *53*(3), 850–866. doi:10.1080/00207543.2014.937011

Turban, E., & Sepehri, M. (1986). Applications of Decision Support and Expert Systems in Flexible Manufacturing Systems. *Journal of Operations Management*, *6*(34), 433–448. doi:10.1016/0272-6963(86)90015-X

Turban, E., Sharda, R., Delen, D., & King, D. (2011). *Business Intelligence: A Managerial Approach* (2nd ed.). Prentice-Hall.

UN. (2015). *Transforming our world: The 2030 agenda for sustainable development.* United Nations.

Verdouw, C. N., Wolfert, J., Beulens, A., & Rialland, A. (2016). Virtualization of food supply chains with the internet of things. *Journal of Food Engineering*, *176*, 128–136. doi:10.1016/j.jfoodeng.2015.11.009

Veza, I., Mladineo, M., & Gjeldum, N. (2015). Managing innovative production network of smart factories. *IFAC-PapersOnLine*, *48*(3), 555–560. doi:10.1016/j.ifacol.2015.06.139

Viswanathan, N., & Sadlovska, V. (2010). *Supply Chain Intelligence: Adopt Role-based Operational Business Intelligence and Improve Visibility.* Aberdeen Group.

Vosburg, J., & Kumar, A. (2011). Managing Dirty Data in Organizations Using ERP: Lessons from a Case Study. *Industrial Management & Data Systems*, *101*(1), 21–31. doi:10.1108/02635570110365970

Wadmann, S., & Hoeyer, K. (2018). Dangers of the digital fit: Rethinking seamlessness and social sustainability in data-intensive healthcare. *Big Data & Society*, *5*(1). doi:10.1177/2053951717752964

Wang, L., Laszewski, G. V., Young, K. M., & Tao, J. (2010). Cloud Computing: A Perspective Study. *New Generation Computing*, *28*(2), 137–146. doi:10.100700354-008-0081-5

Wang, T., Zhang, Y., & Zang, D. (2016) Real-time visibility and traceability framework for discrete manufacturing shopfloor. *Proceedings of the 22nd International Conference on Industrial Engineering and Engineering Management*,(pp. 763–772). Springer. 10.2991/978-94-6239-180-2_72

Watson, H. J. (2009). Tutorial: Business Intelligence – Past, Present, and Future. *Communications of the Association for Information Systems*, *39*(25). doi:10.17705/1CAIS.02539

Watson, M., Lewis, S., Cacioppi, P., & Jayaraman, J. (2013). *Supply chain network design – applying optimization and analytics to the global supply chain.* FT Press.

Wong, C. W., Wong, C. Y., & Boon-itt, S. (2018). How does sustainable development of supply chains make firms lean, green and profitable? A resource orchestration perspective. *Business Strategy and the Environment*, *27*(3), 375–388. doi:10.1002/bse.2004

Wu, K. J., Liao, C. J., Tseng, M. L., Lim, M. K., Hu, J., & Tan, K. (2017). Toward sustainability: Using big data to explore the decisive attributes of supply chain risks and uncertainties. *Journal of Cleaner Production, 142*, 663–676. doi:10.1016/j.jclepro.2016.04.040

Xing, B., Gao, W. J., Battle, K., Nelwamondo, F. V., & Marwala, T. (2012). e-RL: the Internet of things supported reverse logistics for remanufacture-to-order. *International Conference in Swarm Intelligence: Advances in Swarm Intelligence,* (pp. 519–526). IEEE.

Yan, B., & Huang, G. (2009). *Supply chain information transmission based on RFID and internet of things in Computing*. Communication, Control, and Management, ISECS International Colloquium on, (pp. 166–169). ISECS.

Yuvaraj, S., & Sangeetha, M. (2016). Smart supply chain management using internet of things (IoT) and low power wireless communication systems. In Wireless Communication, Signal Processing and Networking, International Conference, 555-558.

Zawadzki, P., & Zywicki, K. (2016). Smart product design and production control for effective mass customization in the industry 4.0 concept. *Management of Production Engineering Review*, *7*(3), 105–112. doi:10.1515/mper-2016-0030

Zhao, R., Liu, Y., Zhang, N., & Huang, T. (2017). An optimization model for green supply chain management by using a big data analytic approach. *Journal of Cleaner Production, 142*, 1085–1097. doi:10.1016/j.jclepro.2016.03.006

Zhong, R. Y., Huang, G. Q., Lan, S., Dai, Q. Y., Chen, X., & Zhang, T. (2015). A big data approach for logistics trajectory discovery from RFID-enabled production data. *International Journal of Production Economics*, *165*, 260–272. doi:10.1016/j.ijpe.2015.02.014

Zhong, R. Y., Lan, S., Xu, C., Dai, Q., & Huang, G. Q. (2016). Visualization of RFID-enabled shopfloor logistics Big Data in Cloud Manufacturing. *International Journal of Advanced Manufacturing Technology*, *84*(1–4), 5–16. doi:10.100700170-015-7702-1

KEY TERMS AND DEFINITIONS

Augmented Reality (AR): It is a modern technology that involves the overlay of computer graphics on real-world applications.

Big Data Analytics (BDA): Analytics is the discovery, interpretation, and visualization of meaningful patterns in Big Data. In order to do this, analytics use data classification and clustering mechanisms.

Decision Making Systems: A decision support system (DSS) is a computer-based information system that supports business or organizational decision-making activities, typically ranking, sorting, or choosing from among alternatives. Decision support systems can be either fully computerized, human-powered or a combination of both.

Internet of Things (IoT): The Internet of things (IoT) is the inter-networking of physical devices, vehicles (also referred to as "connected devices" and "smart devices"), buildings, and other items; embedded with electronics, software, sensors, actuators, and network connectivity that enable these objects to collect and exchange data.

Neural Network: Neural network is an information processing paradigm inspired by how biological nervous systems, such as the brain, process information. It uses a classification mechanism that is modelled after the brain and operates by modifying the input through weights to determine what it should output.

Radio Frequency Identification (RFID): This wireless technology is used to identify tagged objects in certain vicinities. Generally, it has three main components: a tag, a reader, and a back end. A tag uses the open air to transmit data via a radio frequency (RF) signal. However, it is also weak in computational capability. Finally, RFID automates information collection regarding an individual object's location and actions.

Supply Chain Management (SCM): A supply chain consists of a network of key business processes and facilities involving end-users and suppliers that provide products, services, and information.

Virtual Reality (VR): It is a term used for computer-generated three-dimension (3D) environments that allow the user to enter and interact with synthetic environments. The users can immerse themselves to varying degrees in the artificial computer world, which may either be a simulation of some form of reality or a complex phenomenon.

Chapter 13
Transforming Supply Chains (SCs) to Meet Sustainability Challenges

Tahir Iqbal
https://orcid.org/0000-0002-5234-3676
Imam Abdulrahman Bin Faisal University, Saudi Arabia

ABSTRACT

The key aspect of the current chapter is related to the sustainability challenges of the supply chain and its associated consideration towards the transformation of operations. The primary motivation for evaluation has been related to the influence of sustainability considerations for supply chain development, aligned issues, and their respective solutions. To highlight the reader's approach for supply chain sustainability, the importance and influences have been discussed regarding waste management and its related influences on the cost and productivity efficiency within the supply chain. The crucial aspects of supply chain sustainability have also enlightened some challenges. The challenges include human resources, management, structure development, and user perception as well. Technological and intelligence based facilities such as IoT, block-chain, and artificial intelligence have an influence on the management of challenges and the developing effective strategies for green supply chain management. The recommendation for production to transportation management has been provided.

INTRODUCTION

The primary focus of the current chapter is on the supply chain and its relevance to sustainability. Supply chain management has been analysed to discuss and evaluate the supply chain transformation to meet sustainability challenges. This focus has been based on the observation that on a global level, the business and industrial sector is working to transform its operations towards more sustainable and environment-friendly. With the motivation to save the planet and its inhabitants from the adverse influence of climate change and pollution, the consideration of sustainability is much more critical. It is crucial to consider the business sector and supply chain so that the planet's ecology has been influenced by the growth of

DOI: 10.4018/979-8-3693-0225-5.ch013

businesses on the global structure (Hickel, 2019). Moreover, considering the changes within the industrial sector to bring large-scale influential revolution, supply chain measures, and management is crucial (Holmberg & Sandbrook, 2019). Based on that, the measurements are required for the supply chain to work for sustainability development.

The chapter has been divided into different sections: management issues, human resources issues, infrastructure challenges, and the influence of government and law considerations. To have a critical analysis regarding the sustainability role in the supply chain and their aligned challenges along with the strategies have been discussed. The chapter's main aim is to evaluate intelligence and technology influence on the supply chain to transform the supply chains for meeting the sustainability challenges. Practical recommendations regarding the sustainability challenges have also been provided for stable and developmental changes in the supply chain. The chapter ends by providing a detailed summary of the overall concept. The key definitions for different terms have also been specified at the end of the chapter.

Problem Statement

Sustainable supply chain practices are crucial in today's fast-changing corporate environment. The confluence of intelligence and sustainability redefines supply chain dynamics and solves complicated global issues (Yadav et al.,2023). The main problem in this research is to address the challenges for sustainable supply chain management while using blockchain and artificial intelligence (AI) with sustainable practices like green supply chain management, waste reduction, ethical sourcing, circular economy, or environmental impact. Byaro et al., (2023) state that these subjects are more microeconomic because they include company, consumer, and stakeholder decisions and actions in the supply chain ecosystem.

Thus, this research aspires to make supply chains flexible, ecologically conscious, and ethically driven systems that reduce carbon emissions. Despite the promise, these goals require a precise issue statement, a complete methodological approach, and an integrated theoretical and empirical base. This chapter bridges the theoretical and empirical research gap related to sustainable supply chain management practices and provides strategic insights into integrating intelligence and sustainability as a creative solution to current supply chains' sustainability concerns. Moreover, this research addresses the lack of understanding and integration of sustainable supply chain techniques in modern company dynamics. The benefits of combining AI and sustainability principles into supply chain management are recognised, but a clearly defined issue statement is lacking. This gap hinders the development of flexible, ecologically conscientious, and morally driven supply chain solutions that cut carbon emissions and address global sustainability issues.

METHODOLOGY

This chapter has used thorough secondary research to analyse this complex issue. This method systematically analyses the topic using peer-reviewed journal papers, research reports, and academic publications. The secondary research technique provides a complete overview of the area and significant insights, trends, and best practices for supply chain intelligence and sustainable integration. The field's difficulties, possibilities, and gaps are identified through literature synthesis. This chapter critically analyses theoretical frameworks, empirical studies, and case examples to show the potential and challenges of transforming supply chains to meet sustainability imperatives.

The study was conducted with a thorough search of databases using a well-selected set of keywords related to the chapter's main topics. These keywords include blockchain, AI, green supply chain management, environmental effects, greenhouse emissions, waste management, ethical sourcing, closed-loop supply chain, and circular economy. Each article's abstract was then carefully evaluated against criteria to determine its relevance to the research's goals. A set of inclusion criteria guided the selection process, ensuring that only articles satisfying benchmarks were evaluated. These criteria include direct relevance to the integration of intelligence (e.g., blockchain, AI) and sustainability in supply chains, discussions about the application of technologies in domains like green supply chain management, waste reduction, ethical sourcing, circular economy, or environmental impact, empirical data, case studies, or theoretical frameworks contributing to the research's objectives, and peer-reviewed publication.

In order to maintain research rigor, exclusion criteria were equally critical. These criteria identified papers that did not meet the research's goals or lacked empirical proof, theoretical significance, or relevance to the themes. Articles from non-reputable sources, those without peer review, those written in languages except English, and those published outside before 2018 were excluded. Along with the abstract screening, an entire field study was done. This step identified current trends, advances, and crucial gaps in supply chain intelligence and sustainability integration. This analysis has ensured that the selected publications were current with field advancements, providing a more current and thorough grasp of the topic.

Sustainability in Supply Chain Management

Sustainability in supply chain management refers to the potential impact of a firm's supply chain networks on society and the environment (Gouda & Saranga, 2018). Sustainable supply chain management allows companies to reduce environmental harm by minimising waste production, energy, and water use (Bui et al., 2021). An example of sustainable supply chain management is IKEA. The company is committed to achieving carbon neutrality by 2050; hence, it uses sustainable materials to manufacture its products. For supply chain networks, IKEA began to maintain its energy efficiency by employing renewable energy sources in its manufacturing-related operations, which eventually kept them from minimising their energy consumption (IKEA, 2021). Meanwhile, (Gouda & Saranga, 2018) stated that when organisations ensure sustainability in their supply chain networks, they can experience positive results such as an increase in the company's reputation, reduced environmental impact, lower costs, and improved brand loyalty.

Further, environmental impact refers to the effect of business practices or activities on the surrounding atmosphere. Regarding environmental impact, sustainable supply chain networks can allow businesses to decrease their environmental carbon footprint. About 50% of Greenhouse gas (GHG) emissions are due to global supply chains. Therefore, many organisations have understood this prevailing problem's sensitivity and have taken significant steps to reduce their environmental impact (World Economic Forum, 2021).

Resource depletion refers to the excessive consumption of natural resources faster. The leading causes of resource depletion are water pollution, global warming, and carbon emissions (Byaro et al., 2023). In addition, resource depletion is another significant environmental problem for businesses across the globe. With the help of ensuring sustainability in the supply chain, companies can reduce resource usage and increase resource efficiency (Gouda & Saranga, 2018). However, sustainability in supply chains for social responsibility includes implementing effective labour strategies and practices within organisations (Bentalha, 2022). By having sustainability in supply chains, companies can effectively overcome labour problems, including low wages, unsafe workplace environments, and poor employee rights (Govindan, 2018).

Similarly, companies should also focus on ensuring ethical sourcing, a critical aspect of sustainable supply chain management. Ethical sourcing enables organisations to implement ethical practices such as preventing child labour and safe material sourcing for their suppliers (Sajjad et al., 2020). Another example of ethical sourcing is Starbucks. The company has initiated coffee and farmer equity, or CAFÉ, a most successful ethical sourcing program. By launching this program, the company supports the welfare of its farmers and ensures sustainability in farming practices. Hence, this indicates that Starbucks is dedicated to implementing ethical sourcing to maintain sustainability in its supply chain networks (Starbucks, 2023).

Gaustad et al. (2018) stated that diversifying material sourcing strategies is another critical aspect of risk mitigation in the context of sustainability in supply chain management. When businesses rely on a single source for purchasing raw materials, they are vulnerable to supply chain disruptions. With the help of diversification of material sourcing locations and suppliers, businesses can minimise their dependency on a single supplier or location, which can help them prevent any potential disruption or disturbance in their supply chain networks. In addition, maintaining sustainability in supply chains can also help companies address the scarcity of resources (Bentalha, 2022). Since the resources are depleting and become costly, businesses implementing sustainable practices can preserve their limited resources to achieve higher efficiency (Govindan, 2018).

Sustainability in supply chain management can also enable businesses to improve their operational capabilities and minimise their overall costs. It can be a significant competitive advantage over their rivals in highly competitive markets. Companies with sustainable supply chain networks can also increase their profit margins by adequately enhancing energy efficiency and managing resources (Govindan, 2018). Finally, the competitive advantage is a crucial indicator of sustainable supply chain management. Statista (2022) stated that most global customers had experienced a significant shift in their buying behaviours towards eco-friendly. More than 30% of customers had significantly bought sustainable products in 2022. According to (Gouda & Saranga, 2018), businesses can expand their market share and customer satisfaction by gaining more competitive advantage through sustainable supply chain management.

Sustainability Issues Faced by the Supply Chain

Supply chains confront various sustainability difficulties, roughly characterised as environmental and social concerns. Environmental issues include greenhouse gas emissions, water use, trash creation, and pollution. Social challenges include labour rights, human rights, and ethical sourcing.

Furthermore, supply chains, especially goods transit, face greenhouse gas emissions. Trucks, ships, airplanes, and trains convey products from manufacturers to distributors, merchants, and consumers over large distances (Bentalha et al., 2023). Transportation emits much carbon dioxide (CO2) and other greenhouse gases. CO2 traps heat and contributes to global warming, and greenhouse gas emissions worsen climate change, harming civilization and the environment (Gouda & Saranga, 2018). Besides, greenhouse gas emissions raise global temperatures as the atmosphere holds more heat due to this. This warming melts polar ice caps and glaciers, raising sea levels and sea levels rise, causing coastal floods, erosion, and the loss of crucial land and infrastructure (Kechagias et al., 2020). Below, Table 1 displays the emissions recorded in 2020 by the supply chain. The blue bars stand for the carbon emissions in the

Table 1. The emissions recorded by the supply chain

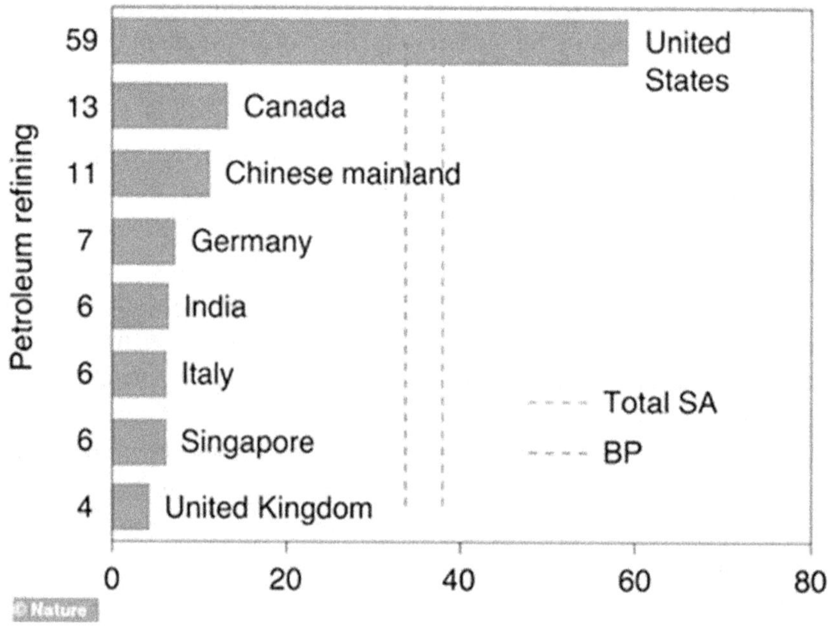

Source: Dailymail (2020)

supply chains of multinational companies in a certain country. However, the dotted vertical lines signify the total carbon emissions in these companies.

Energy waste and inefficiency cause greenhouse gas emissions, supply chain firms incur emissions costs as governments implement carbon pricing schemes, and energy costs rise. Carbon taxes, emission allowances, and energy efficiency upgrades are included in the rise of expenses of supply chains

Table 2. United Kingdom carbon prices

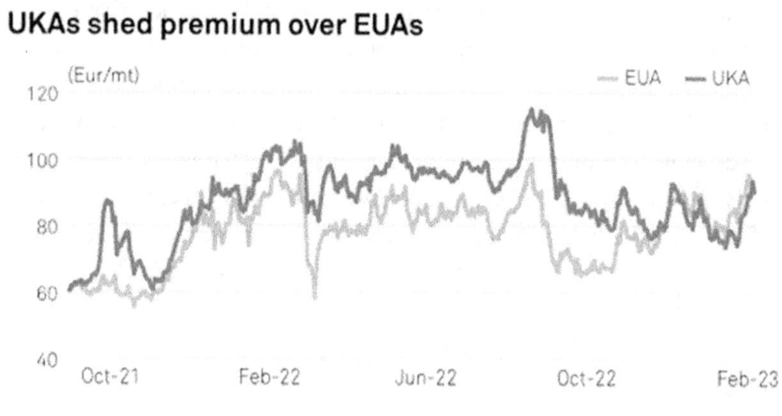

Source: spglobal (2023)

Table 3. Projected carbon price growth projections for industry and services in the United Kingdom from 2020 to 2040

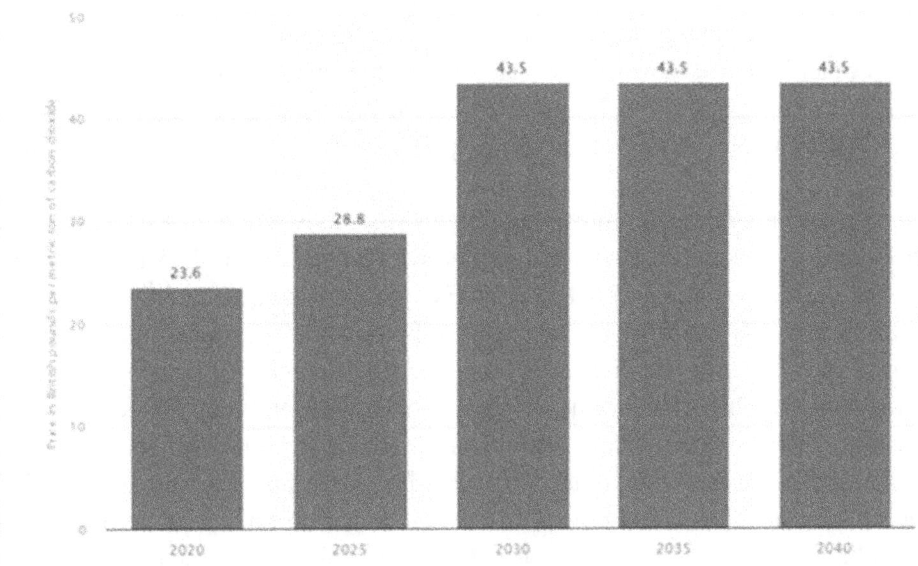

Source: Statista (2022)

(Yadav et al., 2022). The United Kingdom's (UK) carbon pricing fell to its highest monthly average discount compared to EU allowances (EUAs) since its inception in January 2021. In 2022, S&P Global Commodity Insights found an average premium of Eur11.65/mtCO2e (spglobal, 2023). Table 2 has also highlighted the fluctuations in UK carbon prices.

The supply chain's impact from the UK carbon price drop is complicated as lower carbon prices mean more greenhouse emissions. Carbon pricing encourages enterprises to reduce greenhouse gas emissions (Yadav et al., 2022). The statistics below Table 3 show the UK's carbon price growth projections in response to greenhouse emissions. CO2 price for industry and services in the UK is projected to rise from 23.6 to 43.5 British pounds per metric ton of carbon dioxide between 2020 and 2030.

To highlight the challenge of managing high prices and the future carbon cost for supply chain firms, businesses, especially carbon-intensive ones, can lower compliance costs when the carbon price lowers. Supply chain financial strain and operating costs may decrease. Carbon price fluctuations can cause regulatory uncertainty and compliance expenses for enterprises (Rad et al., 2022). Carbon pricing methods have become unstable if the carbon price drops significantly. Uncertainty can affect long-term supply chain planning and investment (Karmaker et al., 2023).

Supply chains with water-intensive processes face severe environmental issues. Agriculture, manufacturing, and mining use water extensively, and excessive water extraction can harm the ecosystem and residents. Unsustainable water exploitation has depleted local water sources in several locations (Feng et al., 2022). Over-pumping groundwater, diverting water from rivers and lakes, and excessive irrigation can disturb hydrological cycles, creating water scarcity and drought. Therefore, this impacts ecosystems and clean water for people, agriculture, and other critical purposes. Excessive water extraction also has long-term effects as it can damage water-dependent ecosystems like marshes, rivers, and lakes (Gouda

& Saranga, 2018). Reduced water flows can damage aquatic environments, biodiversity, and plant and animal viability (Karmaker et al., 2023). Hydrological changes can also harm downstream water quality and ecological balance. Wastewater management issues also affect supply chains. Industrial wastewater contains pollutants, chemicals, and toxins. Wastewater can pollute water if not properly treated. Pollution threatens marine life, drinking water, and human health. Sustainable water management is essential for supply chain water issues. It includes adequate irrigation, water recycling, and water-saving devices (Caiado et al., 2022). Companies can also practice responsible water stewardship by completing water risk assessments, working with local communities and stakeholders, and encouraging water conservation (Wang et al., 2022).

Waste creation and management add to supply chain sustainability issues. Garbage comes from excessive packaging, single-use products, and ineffective garbage disposal. Waste harms wildlife, the environment, and humans (Almutairi et al., 2022). Excessive packing, including layers and materials, depletes resources and fills landfills. Plastic utensils, bottles, and packaging are environmental burdens due to their short lifespan and disposal difficulties. Inefficient waste management, such as poor recycling infrastructure or hazardous waste disposal, worsens the problem (Byaro et al., 2023). Waste mismanagement pollutes and harms the environment. Methane from landfill waste contributes to climate change. Untreated garbage can pollute water and harm marine life (Melnyk et al., 2022). Waste accumulation can also deplete natural resources by extracting virgin materials for manufacture. Waste reduction, recycling, and circular economy ideas are essential for waste management. Companies can reduce packaging, promote reusable or recyclable products, and improve waste management (Wang et al., 2022). Circular economy ideas include durable product design, resource efficiency, and supply chain recycling and repurposing, as shown in Figure 1 below.

Figure 1. Waste management under circular economy
Source: (Shaban et al., 2022)

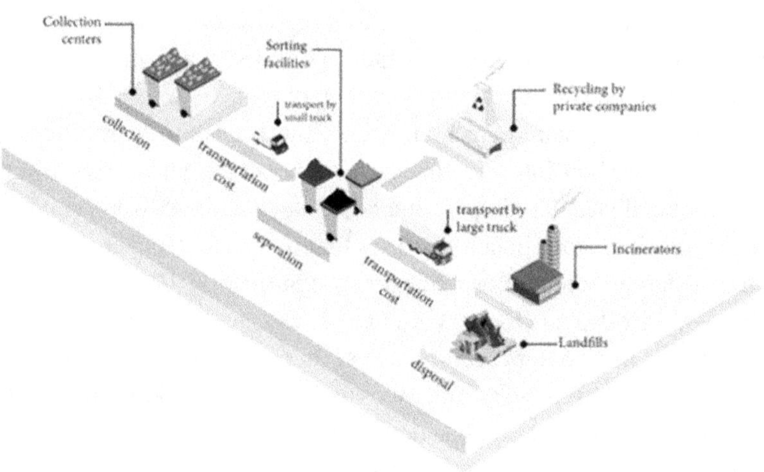

Table 4. Air pollution in the United Kingdom

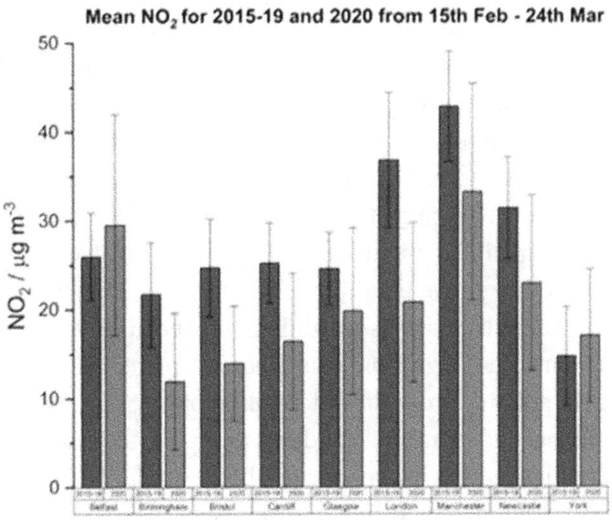

Source: NCAS (2020)

Supply chains are hampered by air, soil, and water pollution. Table 4 demonstrates the statistics of air pollution in the UK, and these Pollutants can pollute the environment and harm human health.

Supply chains face air pollution as manufacturing, transportation, and energy production generate particulate matter, nitrogen oxides, sulphur dioxide, and volatile organic compounds. These pollutants can damage air quality, causing respiratory and cardiovascular difficulties for employees and populations around industrial sites (Kim & Chae, 2022). Air pollution causes respiratory and cardiovascular ailments, reducing life expectancy and quality (Chen, 2022). The UK government calculated that air pollution costs the economy £20 billion annually. A vital part of the supply chain, transport pollutes the air as road traffic in the UK emits NOx, and road transport produces 80% of NOx emissions, according to (DEFRA, 2019). The UK has strict air pollution standards. London's low-emission zones and ultra-low ezones prohibit high-emission automobiles (DEFRA, 2019). Noncompliance with these standards can result in penalties and operating restrictions, affecting supply chain activities.

Governments and regulatory agencies can increase pollution control by setting emissions regulations, waste management, and disposal rules. These regulations ensure responsible corporate practices and environmental protection. Cleaning up supply networks requires cleaner production practices (Chen, 2022). It entails using technologies and methods that reduce emissions, hazardous substance use, and resource use. Energy-efficient manufacturing, waste reduction, and eco-friendly products help reduce pollution. Sustainable supply chain practices are essential (Widder et al., 2022). This involves using renewable energy, responsible procurement of raw materials, and circular economy concepts to decrease waste and promote recycling and reuse. Supply chain pollution mitigation requires supplier collaboration, transparent supply chain management, and sustainable innovation (Bentalha et al., 2021).

Supply chains are plagued by labour rights issues, especially for developing nations. Low salaries, long hours, dangerous workplaces, and job insecurity plague many workers. Labour rights abuses harm employees and prolong poverty in supply networks. Many workers cannot afford essentials due to low earnings (Gilbert & Huber, 2023). This can impoverish employees and their families by limiting access to healthcare, education, and other essential services. Workers need adequate wages to support themselves and their families and escape the cycle of poverty (Sajjad et al., 2020).

Workers' health depends on suitable work hours and work-life balance (Chen et al., 2022). They further argued that unsafe workplaces endanger workers' health; therefore, regular inspections, training, and occupational solid health and safety requirements must be prioritised in supply chains. Supply chain workers need job security, including regular employment contracts, legal protections against arbitrary dismissals, and social benefits (Gilbert & Huber, 2023). Supply chains are plagued by forced labour, child labour, and human trafficking (Seuring et al., 2022). These infractions violate core rights and foster socioeconomic inequity and unethical practices. Forced labour involves employees being coerced or persuaded into working under exploitative conditions, whereas child labour involves youngsters working in hazardous settings. Human trafficking is recruiting, transporting, and exploiting people by force, fraud, or coercion. Supply chain human rights breaches necessitate multifaceted solutions. These include adopting strong human rights policies prohibiting forced labour, child labour, and human trafficking, conducting thorough due diligence to identify and address supply chain violations, and working closely with suppliers to ensure compliance with international labour standards. Human rights risk monitoring requires supplier engagement, openness, and frequent audits and assessments (Shekarian et al., 2022). Collaboration with peers, non-governmental organisation (NGOs), and stakeholders can also promote industry-wide human rights practices and assure accountability.

Supply chain social sustainability requires ethical sourcing. It involves choosing ethical suppliers and partners who respect human rights and social and environmental criteria. Supply chains prioritise ethical sourcing to reduce harm to communities, workers, and the environment and promote social change. Ethical purchasing avoids vendors that pollute or cause social injustice. Supply chains minimise deforestation, animal trafficking, and conflict minerals. By actively finding sustainable suppliers, supply chains can limit their environmental impact and involvement in ecological deterioration and social problems. Ethical sourcing requires openness and traceability (Wang & Feng, 2022). It requires clear communication with suppliers to receive accurate and complete information about their activities, including supply chains. Transparent supply chains reveal raw material origins, industrial methods, and worker conditions. This transparency lets stakeholders quickly detect ethical issues, rectify them, and make educated supplier selection and engagement decisions. Ethical sourcing requires responsible sourcing, actively interacting with suppliers to guarantee social and environmental compliance, promoting sustainable practices, and helping suppliers improve their operations (Kim & Chae, 2022). Suppliers, industry peers, and stakeholders can work together to set targets and improve ethical sourcing practices (Boruchowitch & Fritz, 2022). Supply chains can help suppliers improve human rights, labour, and environmental management by offering resources, training, and support (Seuring et al., 2022). This collaborative strategy builds long-term trust and sustainability goals.

Transformative Strategies for Addressing Sustainability Challenges

Transformative methods are necessary to solve supply chain sustainability concerns. These techniques include circular economy and closed-loop supply chains, sustainable sourcing and procurement, green logistics and transportation, collaborative partnerships, and stakeholder involvement.

The circular economy based on a closed-loop supply chain (CLSC) strategy reduces waste and maximises resource use. A closed-loop supply chain recovers, reuses, and recycles materials and resources into manufacturing. Closed-loop supply chains aim to minimise waste and maximise resource efficiency.

Closing the loop helps companies save resources, energy, and waste. Closed-loop supply chains have many advantages as they reduce raw material demand and trash delivered to landfills and incinerators (Boruchowitch & Fritz, 2022).

Further, it conserves resources and reduces pollution and greenhouse gas emissions from extraction and disposal. The closed-loop supply chains save organisations money (Shekarian et al., 2022). Reusing or recycling materials can cut procurement and production costs and provide new revenue streams (Gaustad et al., 2018). A closed-loop strategy shows environmental responsibility and sustainability, which boosts corporate reputation and customer image.

The circular economy, which includes CLSC design and management, addresses sustainability issues. CLSCs dynamically recover value from varied types and quantities of returns throughout the product lifetime to maximise value creation. I4.0 emphasises operational efficiency, productivity, and automation. I4.0 technologies enable more precise and responsive supply chains (Simonetto et al., 2022). These technologies enable supply chain data collection, storage, and analysis for error correction, product tracking, and damage reduction. Transforming a linear structure into a circular or multi-circular one with various reverse flows of goods, parts, and materials is difficult. Figure 2 shows an integrated framework of CLSC with the respective benefits.

According to the above model, the rise of end-of-use (EOU) and end-of-life (EOL) products in typical forward supply chains creates environmental issues. Closed-loop supply chains (CLSCs) address these issues. CLSCs collect EOU/EOL products through reverse logistics, then sort, repair, refurbish, or remanufacture them for forward logistics (Alinezhad et al., 2022). The study by (Chen & Cao, 2020) proposed a metaheuristic model for CLSC inventory routing, emphasising returnable products. Product recycling has become more critical across businesses. Environmental, economic, and government considerations have increased attention. Closed-loop supply chain (CLSC) models combine product flow sustainably and efficiently. This research proposes a two-stage genetic algorithm-based multi-agent and priority-based solution. Product flow, demand allocation, and pricing bidding process comprise the challenge. The concept model of the closed-loop supply chain (CLSC) is explained in Figure 3 below.

Figure 2. Integrated framework of CLSC with benefits
Source: (Simonetto et al., 2022)

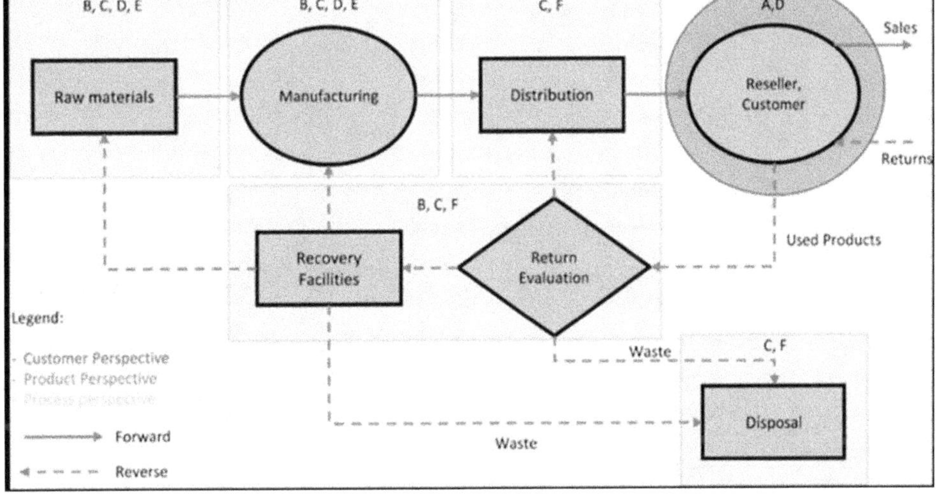

Figure 3. Concept model of the closed-loop supply chain (CLSC)
Source: Chen & Cao (2020)

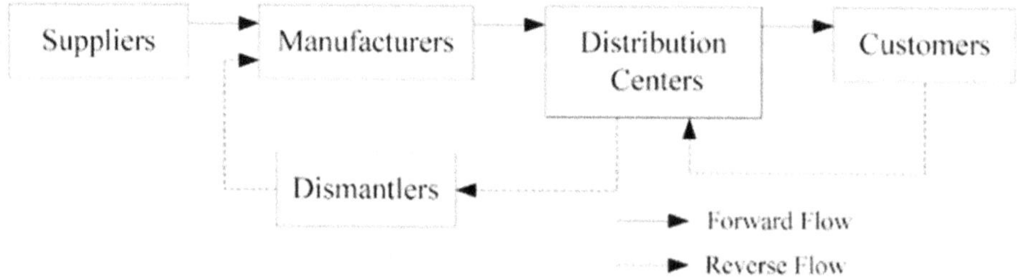

As per the model, the three lines denote three levels of product flow in the forward chain; however, the three dotted lines embody the three levels of product recycle flow in the reverse chain.

Environmental sustainability has spurred interest in closed-loop supply chains (CLSCs). CLSCs extract value from end-of-life (EOL) items to maintain corporate sustainability. Closing the loop is complicated. Stochastic variables provide realism but complicate the model (Shekarian et al., 2022). The Al-Refaie, Jarrar & Lepkova, (2021) study designs a durable product CLSC using a multistage stochastic model as a mixed-integer linear programming (MILP) problem.. The model accounts for demand, return rate, and quality issues. Demand is a normal distribution, but return rate and quality are discrete outcomes with probabilities. Multi-period, multi-echelon CLSC objective functions maximise profit. The study also highlighted that CLSC reduced purchasing prices by 52%, saving 831,150 USD annually. Raw material sales added 5459 USD to annual revenue. However, transportation costs grew by 6457 USD annually, while recovery methods cost 152,897 USD annually. After three years, the CLSC would break even with a 1.92% yearly profit gain, according to a nine-year simulation.: The closed-loop

Figure 4. The closed-loop supply chain (CLSC)
Source: Al-Refaie, Jarrar & Lepkova (2021)

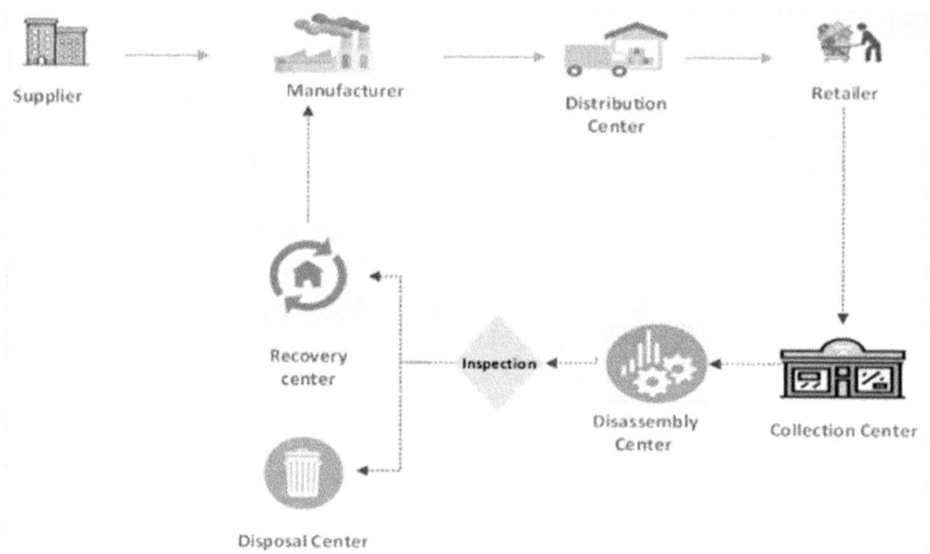

supply chain (CLSC) model by Al-Refaie et al., (2021) has been shown in Figure 4 below. CLSC can be the best way to raise profit and reduce the supply cost by presenting a cheaper source for production inputs from the returned products.

Sustainable sourcing entails evaluating environmental and social factors to guarantee a sustainable supply chain with minimal environmental and social repercussions. Sustainable sourcing considers energy efficiency, carbon footprint, water usage, waste management, and environmentally friendly products or technologies (Wang & Feng, 2022). Companies may mitigate climate change, preserve natural resources, and safeguard ecosystems by prioritising sustainable suppliers. Sustainable sourcing considers labour rights, human rights, fair trade, and ethics. Suppliers must provide safe working conditions, fair wages, acceptable working hours, and respect fundamental human rights. Promote diversity, equitable opportunities, and local communities (Boruchowitch & Fritz, 2022). Companies can improve working conditions, social equality, and sustainable development in suppliers' communities by prioritising socially responsible suppliers (Wang & Feng, 2022).

Sustainable sourcing and procurement need supplier due diligence. It includes checking their environmental and social policies, certifications, compliance with relevant rules and standards, and site visits or audits. Supplier codes of conduct and supplier engagement programmes can help the supply chain improve sustainability performance. It reduces environmental and social hazards for companies (Seydanlou et al., 2022). Companies choose sustainable suppliers to prevent supply chain interruptions, regulatory non-compliance, reputational harm, and environmental and social legal difficulties. Second, sustainable sourcing and procurement boost the company's image. Sustainable firms are in demand by consumers and stakeholders (Alinezhad et al., 2022). Companies can improve their image, attract ecologically and socially conscientious customers, and gain a competitive edge by working with responsible suppliers.

Green logistics and transportation use eco-friendly methods to move goods and commodities across the supply chain (Bentalha et al., 2023). It promotes sustainability and resource efficiency while reducing logistics' carbon footprint, energy use, and environmental impact. It includes low-emission cars and alternative fuels. Electric or hybrid automobiles, trucks, and vans can help employers reduce this impact (Yingfei et al., 2022). These automobiles emit less exhaust pollutants and carbon dioxide. Biofuels, hydrogen, and natural gas can minimise transportation's environmental impact.

The logistics industry, which supports economic growth, has proliferated due to substantial economic expansion. Modern logistics has brought economic and environmental problems along with its benefits. Logistics expenditures have raised the societal cost of economic development. Consumption and emissions have also hampered green development. Green logistics optimises resource utilisation using sophisticated logistics management ideas and technologies. Green logistics promotes a sustainable, ecologically friendly economy by decreasing energy use, pollution, and stress (Jinru et al., 2022). It is essential for sustainable regional development and balancing economic, social, and environmental benefits. Logistical technology is the most efficient way to complete logistical jobs nowadays. In networked societies, logistics management requires improved storage and transportation technologies, adequate storage space, efficient packing and loading/unloading equipment, convenient transit networks, and high throughput (Shekarian et al., 2022). Liu, & Ma, (2022) presented a green logistics model for the management of the supply chain, as shown below in Figure 5:

Green logistics and transportation require efficient delivery. Load consolidation and route optimisation reduce fuel consumption, and miles travelled. Advanced route planning and real-time tracking increase fleet management, fuel efficiency, and emissions. Intermodal transportation—combining road, rail, and maritime transport can optimise the supply chain, cut transportation distances, and lower greenhouse

Figure 5. Green logistics and transportation model for supply chain management
Source: Liu, & Ma, (2022)

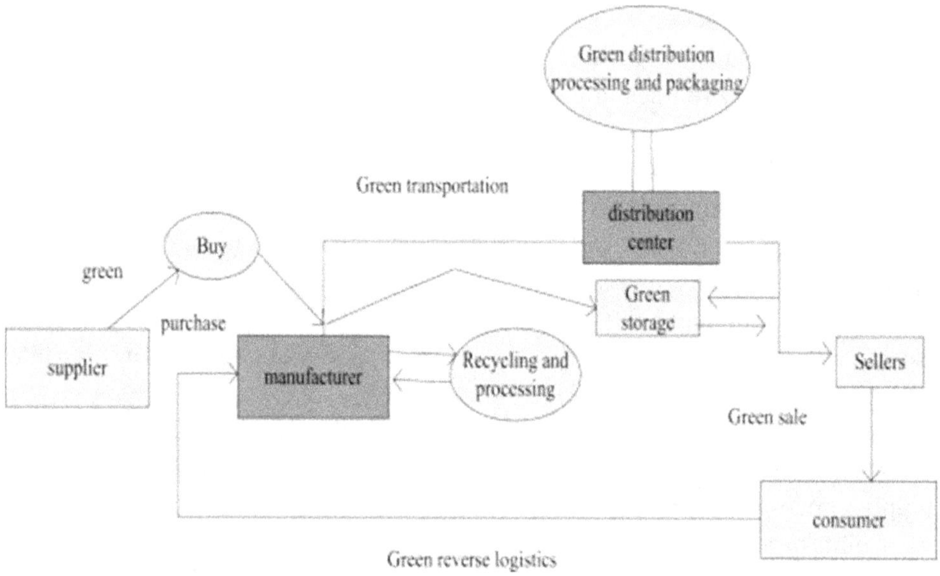

gas emissions. It requires sustainable packaging and materials handling (Boruchowitch & Fritz, 2022). Recycled or biodegradable packaging lowers waste and promotes recycling. Innovative packaging designs can optimise space, weight, and packaging materials. Automated systems and optimised warehouse layouts help save energy usage and product damage. Technology helps green logistics and transportation. Transport and warehouse management systems can optimise transportation routes, manage inventory, and improve supply chain visibility. Real-time data tracking and analytics enable firms to improve sustainability performance by making informed decisions (Jinru et al., 2022). It helps companies decrease their carbon footprint and environmental impact, reducing climate change and conserving the environment. Companies can comply with environmental requirements and demonstrate sustainability by reducing emissions. Green logistics and transportation can reduce costs. Fuel efficiency and route optimisation lower operational costs. Energy-efficient warehouses, recycling programmes, and sustainable packaging decrease waste and material and disposal costs. Green logistics and transportation can boost competitiveness. Sustainable brands are gaining favour from consumers (Seuring et al., 2022).

Supply chain sustainability requires collaboration and stakeholder participation. Organisations realise that addressing environmental, social, and economic issues throughout the supply chain requires collaboration with suppliers, customers, and other stakeholders' supplier collaboration is crucial to collaboration. Organisations can ensure upstream sustainability by involving suppliers (Alinezhad et al., 2022). Moreover, it requires setting explicit norms for sustainable procurement, responsible production, and ethical labour. Supplier collaboration promotes sustainability across the supply chain. Sharing best practices, training, and compliance audits are examples. Sustainable supply chains require client engagement. Companies can actively solicit client feedback on sustainability expectations and preferences (Feng et al., 2022). Companies can match product development, packaging, and distribution strategies with customer desires for sustainable and ecologically friendly solutions (Yadav et al., 2022). Engaging customers allows for sustainable consumption and product use education and awareness. Kozma, Varga,

Figure 6. Main stakeholder groups of supply chain management
Source: Kozma, Varga, & Hegedüs, (2019)

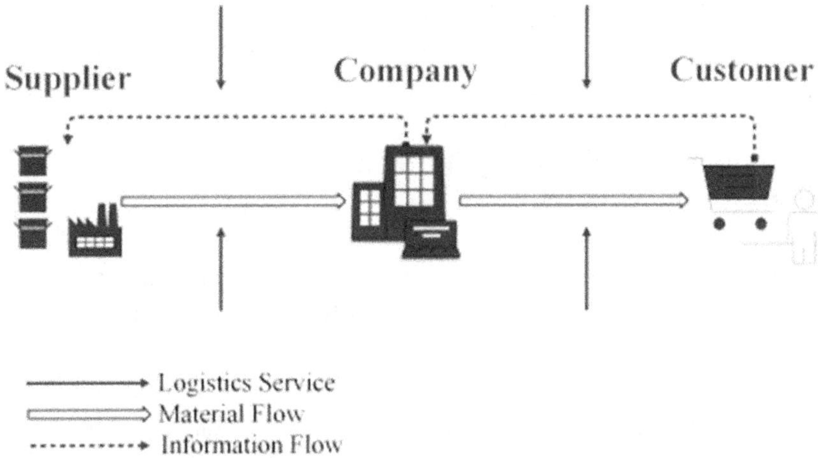

and Hegedüs, (2019) highlighted the three leading stakeholders, i.e., supplier, company, and customer for supply chain management as depicted below in Figure 6.

Karmaker et al., (2023) stated that suppliers, customers, industry groups, NGOs, governments, and local communities must collaborate. These stakeholders have experience, resources, and influence that can help sustain supply chains. Collaborative approaches can involve joining industry-wide sustainability projects, multi-stakeholder alliances, or talking to local communities about social and environmental issues. Below Figure 7 highlighted a detailed collaboration model for stakeholder management for the supply chain:

The above-extended supply chain network has shown a comprehensive supply chain system that connects several aspects of a business's supply chain, such as manufacturers, suppliers, distributors, retail-

Figure 7. Extended supply chain management
Source: Kozma, Varga, & Hegedüs, (2019)

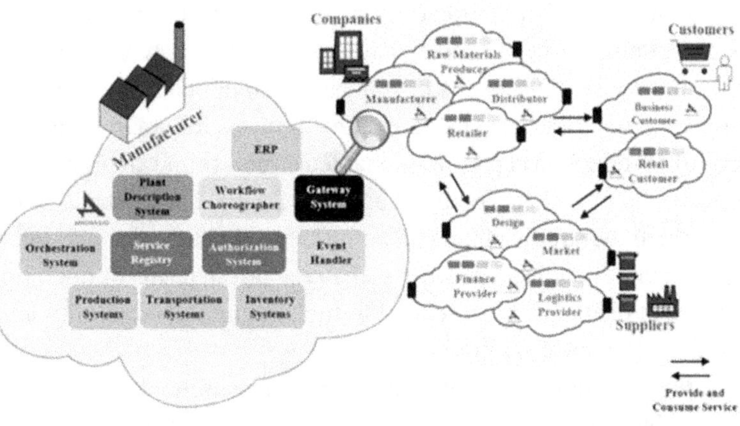

ers, and customers. Collaboration and stakeholder involvement promote sustainability and innovation. Organisations can solve complicated sustainability issues by combining different viewpoints, information, and experiences. Collaborations enable idea sharing, research, and testing of new technologies and processes (Byaro et al., 2023). This collaborative approach can uncover sustainable resources, practices, and business ideas that improve the supply chain.

Role of Intelligence and Technology in Promoting Sustainability in Supply Chains

The role of technology and intelligence in promoting sustainability in the supply chain is also effective, considerate, and transformational. The main problem revolves around how intelligence and technology can promote sustainability within the supply chains. This context for the influence in managing the sustainability challenges for supply chains has been associated with considering the fourth industrial revolution. The Fourth Industrial Revolution is a combination of technologies blurring the boundaries between the physical, biological, and digital spheres (Bentalha et al., 2020).

In that technological enhancement and specification, several opportunities are aligned for the changes within the business sector. The literature review has highlighted that technology and intelligence within the fourth industrial revolution are advanced and require changes within the management to have control over its implications and disruptions. In that possibility, artificial intelligence, reducing the barriers between business and inventors, and the connectivity and the integration of techniques in different domains are all the latest influences of technology and intelligence (Xu et al., 2018).

Based on these integrations of technology and intelligence, disrupting the normal practices of business and human life can cause structured and developmental changes in different aspects of the business. The business operations, development, and environmental influences can be manifested to provide lesser environmental implications. It is argued that the implications of the fourth industrial revolution, such as technology and intelligence, will shape the future of business and government (Xu et al., 2018). Further, it highlighted the possibility of technology and intelligence in developing contextual support for the operational enhancement within the supply chains of the business sector. The findings of (Xu et al., 2018), with the help of a systematic literature review, have enlightened the approach regarding the possibility of intelligence and technology for the relative promotion of sustainability in businesses. However, it is crucial to evaluate how it influences the operations and how the possible developments are promoted within the consideration of the supply chain.

Intelligence and technology have been studied in one frame, as modern developments have combined various technologies and intelligent frameworks. The analysis of research/literature in that respect has highlighted some of the most essential aspects in which consumer behaviour and production capacities all influence technology and intelligence. The case study analysis for smart factories has provided that the Internet of Things (IoT) production capabilities enabled structure and smart business models with the practical and green transportation system (Esmaeilian et al., 2020). These implications have highlighted the multiple aspects in which the supply chain can be influenced. The influence can be of multiple levels within certain supply chain sections. The supply chain is vast in terms of operations and processing aspects, but the consideration here has been related to the structure of feasibility and resilience within the supply chain operations (Ivanov & Dolgui, 2020).

The resilience regarding the implication of technological feasibilities can be enhanced with the implication of artificial intelligence. Artificial intelligence (AI) has an impression to create the respective environment in which the primary classification is related to increased transparency and minimizing the impact of disruptions created by the changes in the supply chain sector (Modgil et al., 2022). Hence, this is considerable in the wake of changes within an organization's operational structure and process to create disruptions among the employees. The sudden or planned changes in the organisation cause respective problems regarding the management infrastructure and stability within the operations impacting the change resilience of the organisation as gained from the perspective of practitioners in the related field (Burnard & Bhamra, 2019). Resilience maintenance is essential; here, intelligence works effectively to determine how the respective changes should have prospected within the organisation. The intelligence has been related to considering resilience and better stability within employee safety (Dhoopar et al., 2022).

Artificial intelligence has the possibility that a significant classification has also been carried out to reduce the risk associated with the supply chain so that operations have been modified with increased employee safety. The hazardous operations have been targeted to ensure employee safety and prospectively enhance the respective supply chain structure (Koh et al., 2019). In analysing the influence of technology and intelligence on the supply chain and its related sustainability issues with the help of quantitative study design features, the blockchain has been highlighted as multiple prospects for better operations transformation. The blockchain can significantly influence the respective possibilities concerning the decision-making regarding the implication of Technology (Kouhizadeh et al., 2021). The technology-related barriers influence how stable operations can be promoted and operated within a respective structure of an organisation (Shen & Sun, 2023).

There are four types of barriers in considering the technology barriers within the promotional considerations concerning sustainability and technology adoption. These barriers are inter-organisational, intra-organisational, technical, and external barriers. These barriers have been identified to influence the overall respective structure of classified considerations promoting sustainable possibilities within the organisation (Saberi et al., 2019). For the respective solution to these barriers, there have been different technological implications that can influence better sustainability management. Blockchain technological changes have provided the fundamental possibility regarding how the variations have been observed within the considered influences for better structure (Saberi et al., 2019). So, blockchain is a practical possibility regarding how the enhanced developments have been operated and structured for enhanced developmental operations. The technological features are related to structure management and better and structured consideration of the aligned issues within this context.

Further, the possibility of developmental practices regarding sustainability issues has highlighted the operational context in which the different upper-stream and lower-stream influences have been analysed. These possibilities have further enhanced the favorable structure for the operational context in which the main upper-stream risks and problems have been highlighted. In that possibility, the basic infrastructure has been related to how the possible context has been operated for the operational and management risks aligned in that sustainability structure (Kouhizadeh & Sarkis, 2018). These operational structures have highlighted the possibility of developing specific contexts in which the primary influence is related to organizational green management practices. The airport industry has further supported the possible influences in which the main implication has been analysed for managing structured blockchain technology. The benefits included managing operational, supply chain, structured planning, and sustainability issues over better structure (Di Vaio & Varriale, 2020).

The aspects from the consideration of better stability and respective classifications within the context of sustainability and its related issues under the influence of technology have intelligence has the consideration to work for a better environment. In that specification, there are different types of operations in which the significant influences have been related to the enhanced possibility of managing the issues. Technologies such as AI, IoT, and blockchain are the primary focus in discussing the influences of different aspects for effective structure maintenance and enhancement towards the technological facilities.

Practical Recommendations for Implementing Sustainable Supply Chain Practices

Previous sections evaluated the different benefits, implications, and strategies regarding the influence of technology and intelligence on the supply chain. The aligned sustainability challenges and difficulties concerning the solution have also been discussed, and in that context, the positive developments have been highlighted for the structured benefits. However, few practical structures have been highlighted in the current analysis regarding sustainable supply chain operations within the business and organisational structure. The extracted practical recommendations are discussed below.

1. The start for the practical implications can be carried out with the consideration of an exclusive plan regarding the sustainable supply chain in which the primary influence will be related to the context of a better management plan. The primary influences in that context will ensure how the organisation develops respective goals for which the stability and development will be analysed regarding the possible influences. The practical design, sustainability analysis, and the considered analysis of different disruption risks have been highlighted in the respective structure of major classification (Jabbarzadeh et al., 2018). This implication will not only influence the organisational structure for sustainability but also maintain the ethical structure regarding the implication towards structured endurance leading towards the sustainability resilience within the company.
2. The goals, planning, and motivation regarding sustainability have been highlighted considering respective influences for which the primary classification is related to the implications of better management possibilities. The main structure in that context is related to building different possibilities, for which the influences have been maintained and stabilised regarding evaluating aligned risks and other related possibilities. These are critical to analyse, and they further structure the possibility of better and sustained operations within the organisation towards better and structured stability (Ghadimi et al., 2019). So, the context of risks regarding this possibility for the sustainable supply chain is critical and practical regarding the organisational preparation towards supply chain sustainability.
3. The supplier and organisation relationship is essential for generating better productivity regarding the sustainable supply chain. The major influences in that consideration relate to how the supplier collaborates towards the sustainable supply chain motive. The example here can be taken from a manufacturing company in which the company has invested in a project for making a product that reduces carbon emissions by almost 35% within the company's annual carbon production. However, the contextual problem arises in such a way that the suppliers working with the company are not on the stake to follow the green supply chain aspect. That consideration of the green supply chain aspect would be influenced from the side of the company as well, and in that, the central representation is related to the possible influences regarding the supply chain stability. The closed loop structure for the supply chain model is critical as it has the respective possibility concerning stable

and productive relationships with the supplier (Lotfi et al., 2021). Thus, the supplier relationship is significant for the organisational stability in considering green strategies implication.

4. The development of consumer motivation regarding sustainable products is critical. Further, this implication is noteworthy regarding beneficial developments within the respective organisation to ensure consumers buy their products. It has been analysed in consideration of green supply chain practices that sometimes the cost of production increases. There are some sections in which a substantial investment is required to influence sustainable practices, and the price value of the product is increased. This price increment generally influences consumer behaviour for purchasing the respective products associated with green production and the supply chain (Salirrosas et al., 2022). In that context, the main influences are involved regarding the better motivation of the consumers to go ahead and purchase green organic products that have less influence on the environment. In that aspect, the primary consideration is related to the possible implications regarding the beneficial developments with the help of blockchain technology. The data collection regarding the potential consumers and then generating the token and other related price benefits could be generated for the consumers (Esmaeilian et al., 2020). The structure regarding the possible implications in relation to the classified supply chain structure has been associated with the possibilities of consumer attraction.
5. The consumer attraction is good, but there is a requirement regarding how resilient operations can be maintained in terms of effective and established consumer goods. These consumer goods are related to the structure regarding how consumer satisfaction and loyalty can be increased. These loyalty and satisfaction development should be considered with the structured orientation of the consumer demands. The possibility of providing green products in which the company's upper and lower stream operations should work on tailored solutions (Modgil et al., 2022). These tailored solutions will influence consumer attraction and the consideration of consumer loyalty enhancement with the respective implication of the tailored solution.
6. The consideration of personalised products as per the demands within the market among the consumers, there is another opportunity: the tailored services for the industrial sector within that possible structure of a green supply chain. There are a few possibilities in which the respective market structure and influences towards the company problems are included. The tailored solutions for these implications are meaningful, as they will benefit the organisation while staying in it. There are different possibilities for which the modified services will stabilize; one is the consideration of resilience within the organisation. The resilience will be enhanced within the organisation regarding the consideration of better stability and structure concerning effective possibilities (Modgil et al., 2022).
7. Moreover, the consequences of betterment within the supply chain cannot be completed without the structure of transportation within the organisation. In that case, the fundamental implication would be the possibility of deferred structures regarding how the stability has been operated and supported for the organisational structure for a better and sustainable supply chain. Green and sustainable logistics are essential in evaluating how the organization can maintain sustainability towards the structured possibilities (Ren et al., 2020). Additionally, these operations further enhance the possibility of better opportunities and the relationship for structured enhancements regarding the possible influences on the management implications.
8. Finally, the last recommendation in this aspect is for the sustainable supply chain, which is related to considering more proportionate and structured possibilities regarding how the compelling motiva-

tions regarding sustainability can be increased. In that case, the major implication is related to the possibility regarding the eventual structure for which the primary operations have been enhanced towards the machine and technological facilities towards the green and waste treatment. The attention here has been related to the possibilities of how the management has been enhanced for the structured orientation towards the betterment context and stable possibilities (Scur & Barbosa, 2017). Thus, in that proportion, the development regarding waste management would also increase the sustainable supply chain structure.

Findings

- Sustainability in supply chain management refers to the potential impact of a firm's supply chain networks on society and the environment. Sustainability in supply chain management can also enable businesses to improve their operational capabilities and minimise their overall costs. Supply chains, especially goods transit, face greenhouse gas emissions.
- Trucks, ships, aeroplanes, and trains convey products from manufacturers to distributors, merchants, and consumers over large distances. Transportation emits a lot of CO2 and other greenhouse gases. Supply chains are plagued by labour rights issues, especially for developing nations. Low salaries, long hours, dangerous workplaces, and job insecurity plague many workers. Labour rights abuses harm employees and prolong poverty in supply networks.
- In that possibility, artificial intelligence reducing the barriers between business and inventors, connectivity, and integrating techniques in different domains are all the latest influences of technology and intelligence. Based on these integrations of technology and intelligence, disrupting the standard practices of business and human life can cause structured and developmental changes in different aspects of the business.
- The business operations, development, and environmental influences can be manifested to provide lesser environmental implications. It is argued that the implications of the fourth industrial revolution, such as technology and intelligence, will shape the future of business and government. It highlighted the possibility of technology and intelligence in developing contextual support for operational enhancement within the supply chains of the business sector.
- The help of a systematic literature review has enlightened the approach regarding the possibility of intelligence and technology for the relative promotion of sustainability in businesses. However, it is important to evaluate how it influences the operations and how the possible developments are promoted within the consideration of the supply chain.

REFERENCES

Al-Refaie, A., Jarrar, Y., & Lepkova, N. (2021). Sustainable Design of a Multi-Echelon Closed Loop Supply Chain under Uncertainty for Durable Products. *Sustainability (Basel)*, *13*(19), 11126. doi:10.3390u131911126

Alinezhad, M., Mahdavi, I., Hematian, M., & Tirkolaee, E. B. (2022). A fuzzy multi-objective optimization model for sustainable closed-loop supply chain network design in food industries. *Environment, Development and Sustainability, 24*(6), 1–28. doi:10.100710668-021-01809-y

Almutairi, K., Hosseini Dehshiri, S. J., Hosseini Dehshiri, S. S., Hoa, A. X., Arockia Dhanraj, J., Mostafaeipour, A., Issakhov, A., & Techato, K. (2022). Blockchain Technology application challenges in renewable energy supply chain management. *Environmental Science and Pollution Research International, 30*(28), 1–18. doi:10.100711356-021-18311-7 PMID:34989989

Bentalha, B. (2022). Smart Technologies for a Sustainable Service Supply Chain: A Prospective Perspective. Journal of Environmental Issues and Climate Change, 1(1), 77-89.

Bentalha, B., Hmioui, A., & Alla, L. (2023). Green Transportation Balanced Scorecard: A VIKOR Fuzzy Method for Evaluating Green Logistics Initiatives. In *Digital Technologies and Applications: Proceedings of ICDTA'23, Fez, Morocco, Volume 1* (pp. 916-925). Cham: Springer Nature Switzerland.

Bentalha, B., Hmioui, A., & Alla, L. (2021). The global performance of a service supply chain: a simulation-optimization under arena. In *Innovations in Smart Cities Applications Volume 4: The Proceedings of the 5th International Conference o Smart City Applications* (pp. 489-502). Springer International Publishing.

Bentalha, B., Hmioui, A., & Alla, L. (2020). Digital service supply chain management: current realities and prospective visions. In *Innovations in Smart Cities Applications Edition 3: The Proceedings of the 4th International Conference on Smart City Applications 4* (pp. 808-822). Springer International Publishing.

Boruchowitch, F., & Fritz, M. M. (2022). Who in the firm can create sustainable value and for whom? A single case-study on sustainable procurement and supply chain stakeholders. *Journal of Cleaner Production, 363*, 132619. doi:10.1016/j.jclepro.2022.132619

Bui, T. D., Tsai, F. M., Tseng, M. L., Tan, R. R., Yu, K. D. S., & Lim, M. K. (2021). Sustainable supply chain management towards disruption and organizational ambidexterity: A data driven analysis. *Sustainable Production and Consumption, 26*, 373–410. doi:10.1016/j.spc.2020.09.017 PMID:33015266

Burnard, K. J., & Bhamra, R. (2019). Challenges for organisational resilience. *Continuity & Resilience Review, 1*(1), 17–25. doi:10.1108/CRR-01-2019-0008

Byaro, M., Nkonoki, J., & Mafwolo, G. (2023). Exploring the nexus between natural resource depletion, renewable energy use, and environmental degradation in sub-Saharan Africa. *Environmental Science and Pollution Research International, 30*(8), 19931–19945. doi:10.100711356-022-23104-7 PMID:36241835

Caiado, R. G. G., Scavarda, L. F., Azevedo, B. D., de Mattos Nascimento, D. L., & Quelhas, O. L. G. (2022). Challenges and benefits of sustainable industry 4.0 for operations and supply chain management—A framework headed toward the 2030 agenda. *Sustainability (Basel), 14*(2), 830. doi:10.3390u14020830

Chen, J. Y. (2022). Responsible sourcing and supply chain traceability. *International Journal of Production Economics, 248*, 108462. doi:10.1016/j.ijpe.2022.108462

Chen, L., Lee, H. L., & Tang, C. S. (2022). Supply chain fairness. *Production and Operations Management, 31*(12), 4304–4318. doi:10.1111/poms.13849

Chen, Y.-T., & Cao, Z.-C. (2020). An Investigation on a Closed-Loop Supply Chain of Product Recycling Using a Multi-Agent and Priority Based Genetic Algorithm Approach. *Mathematics*, *8*(6), 888. doi:10.3390/math8060888

Dailymail. (2020) *Fifth of CO2 emissions come from supply chain for large companies*. Daily Mail Online. https://www.dailymail.co.uk/sciencetech/article-8705619/Fifth-CO2-emissions-come-supply-chain-large-companies.html

DEFRA. (2019, March 21). *Department for Environment, Food & Rural Affairs*. GOV.UK. https://www.gov.uk/government/organisations/department-for-environment-food-rural-affairs

Dhoopar, A., Sihag, P., Kumar, A., & Suhag, A. K. (2022). Organizational resilience and employee performance in COVID-19 pandemic: The mediating effect of emotional intelligence. *The International Journal of Organizational Analysis*, *30*(1), 130–155. doi:10.1108/IJOA-06-2020-2261

Di Vaio, A., & Varriale, L. (2020). Blockchain technology in supply chain management for sustainable performance: Evidence from the airport industry. *International Journal of Information Management*, *52*, 102014. doi:10.1016/j.ijinfomgt.2019.09.010

Esmaeilian, B., Sarkis, J., Lewis, K., & Behdad, S. (2020). Blockchain for the future of sustainable supply chain management in Industry 4.0. *Resources, Conservation and Recycling*, *163*, 105064. doi:10.1016/j.resconrec.2020.105064

Feng, Y., Lai, K. H., & Zhu, Q. (2022). Green supply chain innovation: Emergence, adoption, and challenges. *International Journal of Production Economics*, *248*, 108497. doi:10.1016/j.ijpe.2022.108497

Gaustad, G., Krystofik, M., Bustamante, M., & Badami, K. (2018). Circular economy strategies for mitigating critical material supply issues. *Resources, Conservation and Recycling*, *135*, 24–33. doi:10.1016/j.resconrec.2017.08.002

Ghadimi, P., Wang, C., & Lim, M. K. (2019). Sustainable supply chain modeling and analysis: Past debate, present problems and future challenges. *Resources, Conservation and Recycling*, *140*, 72–84. doi:10.1016/j.resconrec.2018.09.005

Gilbert, D. U., & Huber, K. (2023 Forthcoming). *Labour rights in global supply chains. Corporate Responsibility, Second Edi-tion*. Cambridge University Press.

Gouda, S. K., & Saranga, H. (2018). Sustainable supply chains for supply chain sustainability: Impact of sustainability efforts on supply chain risk. *International Journal of Production Research*, *56*(17), 5820–5835. doi:10.1080/00207543.2018.1456695

Govindan, K. (2018). Sustainable consumption and production in the food supply chain: A conceptual framework. *International Journal of Production Economics*, *195*, 419–431. doi:10.1016/j.ijpe.2017.03.003

Hickel, J. (2019). The contradiction of the sustainable development goals: Growth versus ecology on a finite planet. *Sustainable Development (Bradford)*, *27*(5), 873–884. doi:10.1002d.1947

Holmberg, J., & Sandbrook, R. (2019). Sustainable development: what is to be done? In *Policies for a small planet* (pp. 19–38). Routledge. doi:10.4324/9780429200465-1

IKEA. (2021). *Climate action*. IKEA. https://www.ikea.com/gb/en/this-is-ikea/climate-environment/climate-action

Ivanov, D., & Dolgui, A. (2020). Viability of intertwined supply networks: Extending the supply chain resilience angles towards survivability. A position paper motivated by COVID-19 outbreak. *International Journal of Production Research, 58*(10), 2904–2915. doi:10.1080/00207543.2020.1750727

Jabbarzadeh, A., Fahimnia, B., & Sabouhi, F. (2018). Resilient and sustainable supply chain design: Sustainability analysis under disruption risks. *International Journal of Production Research, 56*(17), 5945–5968. doi:10.1080/00207543.2018.1461950

Jinru, L., Changbiao, Z., Ahmad, B., Irfan, M., & Nazir, R. (2022). How do green financing and green logistics affect the circular economy in the pandemic situation: Key mediating role of sustainable production. *Ekonomska Istrazivanja, 35*(1), 3836–3856. doi:10.1080/1331677X.2021.2004437

Karmaker, C. L., Bari, A. M., Anam, M. Z., Ahmed, T., Ali, S. M., de Jesus Pacheco, D. A., & Moktadir, M. A. (2023). Industry 5.0 challenges for post-pandemic supply chain sustainability in an emerging economy. *International Journal of Production Economics, 258*, 108806. doi:10.1016/j.ijpe.2023.108806

Kechagias, E. P., Gayialis, S. P., Konstantakopoulos, G. D., & Papadopoulos, G. A. (2020). An application of an urban freight transportation system for reduced environmental emissions. *Systems, 8*(4), 49. doi:10.3390ystems8040049

Kim, S., & Chae, S. (2022). Shareholder value effects of ethical sourcing: Comparing reactive and proactive initiatives. *Journal of Business Ethics, 179*(3), 887–906. doi:10.100710551-021-04841-0

Koh, L., Orzes, G., & Jia, F. J. (2019). The fourth industrial revolution (Industry 4.0): technologies disruption on operations and supply chain management. *International Journal of Operations & Production Management, 39*(6/7/8), 817-828.

Kouhizadeh, M., Saberi, S., & Sarkis, J. (2021). Blockchain technology and the sustainable supply chain: Theoretically exploring adoption barriers. *International Journal of Production Economics, 231*, 107831. doi:10.1016/j.ijpe.2020.107831

Kouhizadeh, M., & Sarkis, J. (2018). Blockchain practices, potentials, and perspectives in greening supply chains. *Sustainability (Basel), 10*(10), 3652. doi:10.3390u10103652

Kozma, D., Varga, P., & Hegedüs, C. (2019, March 1). *Supply Chain Management and Logistics 4.0 - A Study on Arrowhead Framework Integration*. IEEE. doi:10.1109/ICITM.2019.8710670

Liu, C., & Ma, T. (2022). Green logistics management and supply chain system construction based on internet of things technology. *Sustainable Computing: Informatics and Systems, 35*, 100773. doi:10.1016/j.suscom.2022.100773

Lotfi, R., Mehrjerdi, Y. Z., Pishvaee, M. S., Sadeghieh, A., & Weber, G. W. (2021). A Robust Optimization Model For Sustainable And Resilient Closed-Loop Supply Chain Network Design Considering Conditional Value At Risk. *Numerical algebra, control & optimization, 11*(2).

Melnyk, S. A., Schoenherr, T., Speier-Pero, C., Peters, C., Chang, J. F., & Friday, D. (2022). New challenges in supply chain management: Cybersecurity across the supply chain. *International Journal of Production Research, 60*(1), 162–183. doi:10.1080/00207543.2021.1984606

Modgil, S., Singh, R. K., & Hannibal, C. (2022). Artificial intelligence for supply chain resilience: Learning from Covid-19. *International Journal of Logistics Management, 33*(4), 1246–1268. doi:10.1108/IJLM-02-2021-0094

NCAS. (2020) *Air pollution falling across UK cities, latest data shows.* NCAS. https://ncas.ac.uk/air-pollution-falling-across-uk-cities-latest-data-shows/

Proctor & Gamble. (2023). *Environmental Sustainability.* Proctor and Gamble. https://us.pg.com/environmental-sustainability/

Rad, F. F., Oghazi, P., Palmié, M., Chirumalla, K., Pashkevich, N., Patel, P. C., & Sattari, S. (2022). Industry 4.0 and supply chain performance: A systematic literature review of the benefits, challenges, and critical success factors of 11 core technologies. *Industrial Marketing Management, 105*, 268–293. doi:10.1016/j.indmarman.2022.06.009

Ren, R., Hu, W., Dong, J., Sun, B., Chen, Y., & Chen, Z. (2020). A systematic literature review of green and sustainable logistics: Bibliometric analysis, research trend and knowledge taxonomy. *International Journal of Environmental Research and Public Health, 17*(1), 261. doi:10.3390/ijerph17010261 PMID:31905934

Saberi, S., Kouhizadeh, M., Sarkis, J., & Shen, L. (2019). Blockchain technology and its relationships to sustainable supply chain management. *International Journal of Production Research, 57*(7), 2117–2135. doi:10.1080/00207543.2018.1533261

Sajjad, A., Eweje, G., & Tappin, D. (2020). Managerial perspectives on drivers for and barriers to sustainable supply chain management implementation: Evidence from New Zealand. *Business Strategy and the Environment, 29*(2), 592–604. doi:10.1002/bse.2389

Scur, G., & Barbosa, M. E. (2017). Green supply chain management practices: Multiple case studies in the Brazilian home appliance industry. *Journal of Cleaner Production, 141*, 1293–1302. doi:10.1016/j.jclepro.2016.09.158

Seuring, S., Aman, S., Hettiarachchi, B. D., de Lima, F. A., Schilling, L., & Sudusinghe, J. I. (2022). Reflecting on theory development in sustainable supply chain management. *Cleaner Logistics and Supply Chain, 3*, 100016. doi:10.1016/j.clscn.2021.100016

Seydanlou, P., Jolai, F., Tavakkoli-Moghaddam, R., & Fathollahi-Fard, A. M. (2022). A multi-objective optimization framework for a sustainable closed-loop supply chain network in the olive industry: Hybrid meta-heuristic algorithms. *Expert Systems with Applications, 203*, 117566. doi:10.1016/j.eswa.2022.117566

Shaban, A., Zaki, F. E., Afefy, I. H., Di Gravio, G., Falegnami, A., & Patriarca, R. (2022). An Optimization Model for the Design of a Sustainable Municipal Solid Waste Management System. *Sustainability (Basel), 14*(10), 6345. doi:10.3390u14106345

Shekarian, E., Ijadi, B., Zare, A., & Majava, J. (2022). Sustainable supply chain management: A comprehensive systematic review of industrial practices. *Sustainability (Basel), 14*(13), 7892. doi:10.3390u14137892

Shen, Z. M., & Sun, Y. (2023). Strengthening supply chain resilience during COVID-19: A case study of JD. com. *Journal of Operations Management, 69*(3), 359–383. doi:10.1002/joom.1161

Simonetto, M., Sgarbossa, F., Battini, D., & Govindan, K. (2022). Closed loop supply chains 4.0: From risks to benefits through advanced technologies. A literature review and research agenda. *International Journal of Production Economics, 253*, 108582. doi:10.1016/j.ijpe.2022.108582

spglobal *(2023) UK carbon prices swing back to premium as EUA rally halts.* SP Global. https://www.spglobal.com/commodityinsights/en/market-insights/latest-news/electric-power/020923-uk-carbon-prices-swing-back-to-premium-as-eua-rally-halts#

Starbucks. (2023). *C.A.F.E. Practices: Starbucks Approach to Ethically Sourcing Coffee.* Starbucks. https://stories.starbucks.com/press/2020/cafe-practices-starbucks-approach-to-ethically-sourcing-coffee/ [Accessed Date: 28 June, 2023]

statista. (2022). *UK: carbon price growth for industry & services 2040.* Statista. https://www.statista.com/statistics/496288/carbon-price-growth-industry-service-uk/

Wang, J., & Feng, T. (2022). Supply chain ethical leadership and green supply chain integration: A moderated mediation analysis. *International Journal of Logistics Research and Applications*, 1-27.

Wang, X., Sethi, S. P., & Chang, S. (2022). Pollution abatement using cap-and-trade in a dynamic supply chain and its coordination. *Transportation Research Part E, Logistics and Transportation Review, 158*, 102592. doi:10.1016/j.tre.2021.102592

Widder, D. G., Nafus, D., Dabbish, L., & Herbsleb, J. (2022, June). Limits and Possibilities for "Ethical AI" in Open Source: A Study of Deepfakes. In *2022 ACM Conference on Fairness, Accountability, and Transparency* (pp. 2035-2046). ACM. 10.1145/3531146.3533779

World Economic Forum. (2021). Net Zero Challenge: The supply chain opportunity. I*nsight Report.* https://www3.weforum.org/docs/WEF_Net_Zero_Challenge_The_Supply_Chain_Opportunity_2021.pdf

Xu, M., David, J. M., & Kim, S. H. (2018). The fourth industrial revolution: Opportunities and challenges. *International journal of financial research, 9*(2), 90-95.

Yadav, S., Choi, T. M., Kumar, A., Luthra, S., & Naz, F. (2023). A meta-analysis of sustainable supply chain practices and performance: The moderating roles of type of economy and innovation. *International Journal of Operations & Production Management, 43*(5), 802–845. doi:10.1108/IJOPM-05-2022-0328

Yadav, V. S., Singh, A. R., Gunasekaran, A., Raut, R. D., & Narkhede, B. E. (2022). A systematic literature review of the agro-food supply chain: Challenges, network design, and performance measurement perspectives. *Sustainable Production and Consumption, 29*, 685–704. doi:10.1016/j.spc.2021.11.019

Yingfei, Y., Mengze, Z., Zeyu, L., Ki-Hyung, B., Avotra, A. A. R. N., & Nawaz, A. (2022). Green logistics performance and infrastructure on service trade and environment-measuring firm's performance and service quality. *Journal of King Saud University. Science, 34*(1), 101683. doi:10.1016/j.jksus.2021.101683

KEY TERMS AND DEFINITIONS

Artificial Intelligence: Artificial intelligence (AI) is machines' ability to perform tasks typically associated with human intelligence, such as learning and problem-solving. AI systems are trained on large amounts of data and can use it to make predictions, recommendations, and decisions. AI is used in various applications, including self-driving cars, medical diagnosis, and customer service.

CO2 and GHG emissions: CO2 stands for carbon dioxide. It is a greenhouse gas that is naturally present in the atmosphere. However, human activities such as the burning of fossil fuels have increased CO2 emissions to levels that are not natural. GHG stands for greenhouse gas. It is any gas that traps heat in the atmosphere. The main GHGs are water vapour, carbon dioxide, methane, nitrous oxide, and ozone.

Fourth Industrial Revolution: The Fourth Industrial Revolution is a period of rapid technological change blurring the lines between the physical, digital, and biological worlds. Advances in artificial intelligence, robotics, 3D printing, and other technologies drive it.

Sustainability: In business, the term sustainability is an approach in which companies run their operations without losing any negative impact on society and the environment. Businesses mainly aim to ensure that their operations do not pose any potential harm to society and the environment, which can affect their overall reputation among customers.

Sustainable Supply Chain: A sustainable supply chain is a framework in which businesses design and implement various practices for their supply chain networks to ensure sustainability for society and the environment. It indicates that companies prioritise social and environmental aspects and standards for their business and supplier-related operations. The environmental aspects include carbon emissions, air pollution, deforestation, environmental degradation, and water scarcity. In comparison, social aspects include child labour, employee safety, customer satisfaction, fair wages, and working conditions.

Transformation: Transformation in supply chain management refers to integrating advanced technologies within organisations. By introducing new technologies, businesses can enhance their operational efficiency and the overall performance of their supply chain networks. The technological transformation also involves examining existing business processes and implementing advanced technologies to manage high supply chain demands and align a company's supply chain with its objectives and goals. This requires effective planning, analytics, implementation, and digitisation.

Chapter 14
Monitoring Environmental Performance of Agricultural Supply Chains Using Internet of Things

Hiba Ben Aribi
https://orcid.org/0000-0001-9547-8725
National Institute of Applied Sciences and Technology, University of Carthage, Tunis, Tunisia

Mohamed Hedi Ghidaoui
National Institute of Applied Sciences and Technology, University of Carthage, Tunis, Tunisia

Sami Fattouch
National Institute of Applied Sciences and Technology, University of Carthage, Tunis, Tunisia

ABSTRACT

The agriculture industry is facing mounting enforcement to produce more food to nourish a growing population while simultaneously mitigating its environmental footprint. In response, the use of internet of things (IoT) technologies in agriculture has emerged as a promising approach to monitoring and improving the supply chain's environmental performance. This chapter provides a comprehensive overview of the use of IoT technologies in the context of environmental monitoring in agricultural supply chains. It begins by introducing the concept of environmental performance in agriculture, its importance, and its challenges. The chapter then explains the basics of IoT technology and how it can be used to monitor and track the environmental performance in agricultural supply chains. The chapter also discusses the benefits and challenges of IoT technologies implementation. Overall, by leveraging the power of IoT, it is possible to enhance sustainability and efficiency in food production, while also reducing environmental impact.

DOI: 10.4018/979-8-3693-0225-5.ch014

INTRODUCTION

Agribusiness holds a vital position in the global economy, furnishing sustenance and essential materials to the growing population (FAO, 2018). As a result, the agri-food sector remains pivotal on a global scale (Tripathi et al., 2019). Nevertheless, establishing sustainable and ecologically conscientious practices within agricultural supply chains presents notable hurdles.

Production, processing, distribution, and consumption are all parts of the agricultural supply chain. The ecosystem and human welfare are greatly impacted by environmental elements throughout this intricate network, including water use, energy use, waste creation, and chemical inputs (FAO, 2018). Despite its importance, most cultivation tactics continue to be based only on outdated practices, which frequently lack suitable tools for monitoring and measuring these variables, causing inefficiency and environmental damage.

The global population is anticipated to reach 9.6 billion by 2050. To decrease waste and boost agricultural production output, it is crucial to develop a sustainable strategy (Tripathi et al., 2019). Consumer awareness and concern regarding the ecological footprint of items people consume, especially food, have markedly increased (Rana et al., 2022). This increased awareness has been stoked by easier access to information, more media attention given to environmental issues, and mounting climate change concerns (Fareq & Fareq, 2023). They demand information on the sustainability of agricultural practices, the use of chemicals and pesticides, carbon emissions, water usage, and waste management throughout the supply chain (FAO, 2018).

As a result, this consumer enlightenment and demand for environmentally friendly products and food have prompted businesses to integrate sustainable practices into their supply chains proactively along with the global initiatives driven by governments and international organizations. Hence, international agreements, such as the Paris Agreement, emphasize the significance of reducing greenhouse gas emissions and promoting sustainable development (United Nations, 2021). Acknowledged as the breakthrough of the era, it is worth mentioning that Information and Communication Technology (ICT) empowers farmers by providing essential information and recommendations to enhance their overall productivity (Narwane et al., 2022). This recent development has the potential to promote sustainability through the reduction of greenhouse gas emissions (Farooq et al., 2020) and decreased water consumption (Zhang et al., 2015). Additionally, it can enhance the efficiency of the agricultural system, thereby aiding in meeting the increasing need for food (Narwane et al., 2022).

Evaluating the environmental performance of agricultural supply chains is essential for tackling the associated challenges. The adoption of modern technologies like the Internet of Things for data collection holds the promise of revolutionizing monitoring, and offering real-time, comprehensive data for precise implementation of strategies to reduce environmental impact. However, achieving extensive adoption of these technologies also involves addressing numerous challenges.

The Internet of Things, often abbreviated as IoT, is a revolutionary concept that links everyday objects, devices, and systems through the internet, enabling them to collect and exchange data independently. This technology spans from personal gadgets to industrial machinery and agricultural sensors, enhancing automation and connectivity across various sectors. IoT devices, embedded with sensors and communication tools, empower them to make smart decisions and communicate with other devices. This transformation impacts industries like manufacturing, healthcare, and agriculture, streamlining processes and improving efficiency.

The present chapter presents a thorough overview of the utilization of IoT for monitoring the environmental performance of agriculture supply chains. The initial section, titled "IMPROVING THE ENVIRONMENTAL PERFORMANCE IN AGRICULTURE SUPPLY CHAINS THROUGH IOT MONITORING", introduces the concept of utilizing IoT technology to track ecological aspects throughout the agricultural lifecycle. It then delves into the comprehensive benefits associated with incorporating IoT for monitoring the environmental performance of agriculture supply chains. These advantages manifest distinctly at various crucial junctures, namely during the production process, the packaging phase, the storage, and transportation stages.

The subsequent part, titled "OVERCOMING CHALLENGES AND IMPLEMENTING SOLUTIONS", addresses the issues intertwined with the practical implementation. It commences by discussing the accessibility of IoT technologies and how their adoption can be facilitated. Subsequently, the spotlight turns to the critical concern of ensuring the physical security of IoT devices. This section then extends its purview to the broader notion of supply chain security and how IoT-driven enhancements can bolster its integrity. The discussion concludes by delving into the critical area of cyber security and how its complexities intertwine with the seamless integration of IoT into agricultural supply chains.

IMPROVING THE ENVIRONMENTAL PERFORMANCE IN AGRICULTURE SUPPLY CHAINS THROUGH IOT MONITORING

Supply Chain Management (SCM) entails overseeing all the procedures associated with creating a product or delivering a service, encompassing everything from extracting raw materials to the eventual delivery to the end customer. This involves the successive stages of transformation, storage, and distribution (Bentalha, 2020).

In agriculture, supply chain management refers to the series of actions involved in producing and distributing items such as fruits, vegetables, animal-derived products, and beyond, starting from the farmer and ending with the consumer (Gupta, 2022). Once these items are converted into market-ready products, they undergo processing, packaging, and storage and are subsequently transported to the market.

The agribusiness value chain has the potential to create a substantial environmental impact attributed to multiple factors, encompassing greenhouse gas emissions, water consumption, land utilization, and pollution. Creating effective SCM plays a significant role in maintaining smooth business operations, especially in these changing times. With supply chains becoming increasingly complex and interdependent, decision-makers are constantly looking for ways to stay competitive. In this scope, and considered the technological advancement of the era (Gazis, 2021), IoT has the ability to process and fuse data generated from interconnected devices, along with their storage in a single massive network, which is capable of revolutionizing the way we monitor and manage the ecological efficiency in agriculture supply chains.

- Internet of Things for tracking the ecological efficiency in agribusiness value chains

IoT encompasses a vast network of components, spanning from sensors and devices to data storage clouds and control platforms, all equipped with the capability to collect and instantly share data. Sensors and interconnected devices collect substantial volume of data about various elements of the agricultural supply chain, such as water usage, crop growth, and energy consumption. Collected data can be

Figure 1. A layered internet of things architecture for supply chain operation
(Pal & Yasar, 2023)

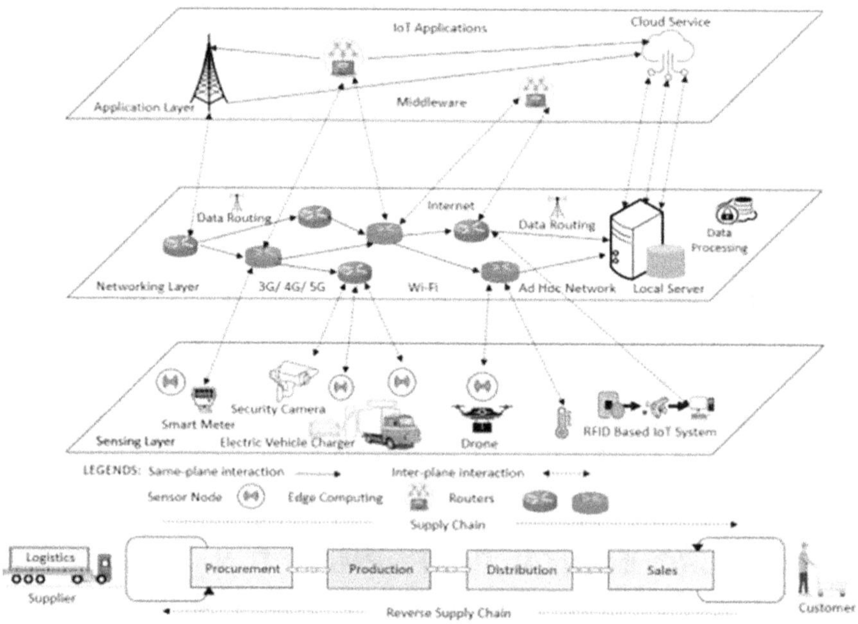

employed to identify inefficiencies and provide supply chain managers with the necessary insights to make informed decisions on optimizing their operations and minimizing their environmental impact.

As indicated by Pal and Yasar (2023), the implementation of IoT relies on an architecture comprising multiple tiers. The operations of the different layers, as illustrated in Figure 1, are (i) edge layer which is the hardware layer and is made up of sensor networks, integrated systems, radio-frequency identification (RFID) tags, and readers or other soft sensors in different forms, (ii) access gateway layer that takes care of message routing, publishing, and subscribing and allows cross-platform data exchange if required, (iii) middleware layer which interfaces the access gateway layer and the application layer. It is in charge of functions and takes care of issues like data filtering, data aggregation, semantic analysis, access control, and information discovery, such as EPC (Electronic Product Code) information service and ONS (Object Naming Service), and (iv) application layer that is tasked with delivering various applications to different users in IoT (Pal & Yasar, 2023).

Farmers need to implement a system that incorporates several sensors and devices to gather data on different aspects of the supply chain, as displayed in Figure 2 (Muangprathub et al., 2019).

The system would involve:

- **Identifying Key Environmental Performance Indicators (EPIs):** The initial step entails determining the critical EPIs to monitor. These indicators depend on the specific objectives of the supply chain, encompassing factors like water usage, soil quality, energy consumption, and greenhouse gas emissions.
- **Selecting Appropriate IoT Sensors and Devices:** During this phase, a diverse range of sensors and devices designed for data collection on EPIs comes into play. These resources include soil

Figure 2. IoT-powered farming model
(Muangprathub et al., 2019)

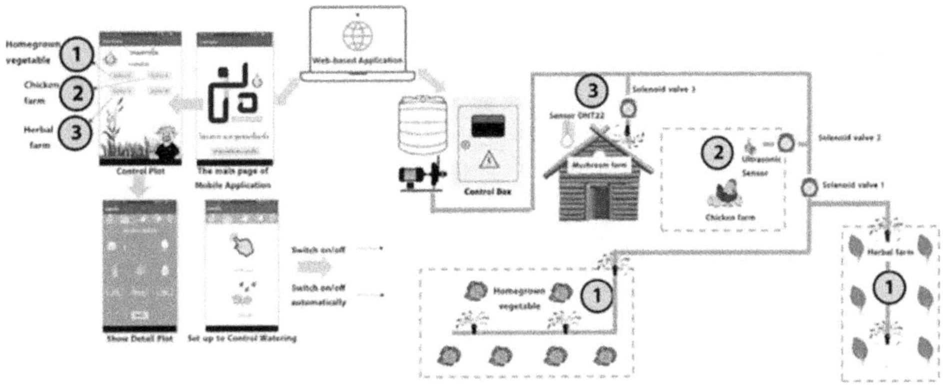

moisture sensors, weather stations, drones, and intelligent irrigation systems. It is the responsibility of the farmer to meticulously choose the sensors and instruments that align best with their specific needs and budget.

- **Installing Sensors and Devices:** Once the suitable sensors and devices have been chosen, the subsequent task is their systematic installation across the supply chain. This could involve embedding soil sensors, affixing sensors to machinery, or deploying drones to gather aerial data.
- **Collecting and Analyzing Data:** Following the installation of sensors and devices, they initiate the process of data collection concerning the identified EPIs. This data can be transmitted to a central database or a cloud-based platform, where it becomes amenable to analysis through machine learning algorithms to uncover patterns and correlations.
- **Utilizing Data for Informed Decision-Making:** The insights derived from data analysis become instrumental in making well-informed decisions regarding supply chain optimization for environmental performance. For instance, if soil moisture levels consistently register as low in specific areas, the farmer might need to adapt irrigation systems or select drought-resistant crops for planting.

Incorporating these steps empowers farmers to harness the potential of IoT technology to assess and enhance the sustainability of their agriculture supply chains while aligning their practices with environmental goals and standards.

As reported by Ojha et al. (2015) and Talavera et al. (2017), a significant uptick in research employing IoT has been observed in recent years. Furthermore, numerous technologies and systems are presently in development for agricultural technology (Agritech) (Maroua et al., 2022). These initiatives aim to equip farmers with valuable insights to facilitate informed decision-making and enhance their overall work processes. Within this context, this chapter discusses three fundamental key models of IoT-based system architecture.

The initial model labeled as the "Short Supply Circuit Internet of Things" presents a distributed edge architecture. This architecture manages the processing and storage of IoT and multimedia data in close proximity to their source, as indicated in Figure 3 (Debauche et al., 2022). By eliminating unnecessary intermediaries between data producers and end-users, this architecture is inspired by the notion of short

Figure 3. The short supply circuit internet of things
(Debauche et al., 2022)

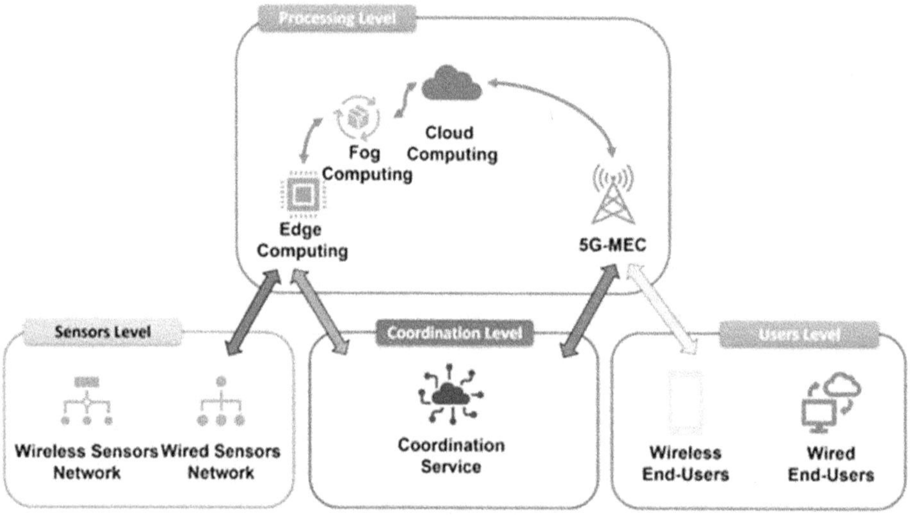

supply chains in agriculture. This model not only ensures rapid response times to meet the demands of contemporary applications but also enhances efficiency by maintaining media objects near data producers (Debauche et al., *2022*).

The second model is an agritech infrastructure developed based on edge and fog computing technologies, incorporating Convolutional Neural Networks (CNN) and Long Range (LoRa) wireless communication (Gia et al., 2019). The architecture comprises a sensor layer featuring sensor nodes responsible for gathering and relaying data to edge gateways using nRF technology, as represented in Figure 4 (Kalyani & Collier, 2021).

In the edge layer, information is processed and condensed prior to its transmission to fog gateways through LoRa technology. The fog layer comprises gateways situated in areas with unreliable internet connections, which are connected to the cloud through WiFi, Ethernet, or 4G. The cloud layer is responsible for storing, processing, and analyzing data using complex algorithms. Lastly, the end-user layer encompasses a mobile application and a website that enables users to retrieve the data.

Finally, the "Edge-Fog-IoT-Cloud" model is a digital farming system that is composed of three layers, as exemplified in Figure 5 (Qureshi et al., 2021). The initial layer comprises the IoT data collection and transmission, encompassing sensor nodes responsible for data gathering and transmission to the edge layer. This is made possible by the nRF24L01 technology, which includes a single-chip transceiver equipped with a baseband protocol engine specially tailored for wireless applications demanding extremely low power consumption. The second layer is the data processing and intelligence layer, where the edge layer is situated as an intermediary between the IoT sensor network and the cloud layer. The edge layer processes the data and provides intelligent insights. The third layer is the user application layer, where the farmer can access the results of the data analysis (Dahane et al., 2020).

Using IoT-based technologies to assess the eco-friendliness of agriculture supply chains requires effective data handling and analysis. Dealing with the vast amount of data emitted by IoT sensors and devices, in addition to real-time monitoring of environmental variables (mainly soil moisture, temperature, and humidity), can be strenuous without a proper data management system.

Figure 4. The edge and fog computing architecture
(Kalyani & Collier, 2021)

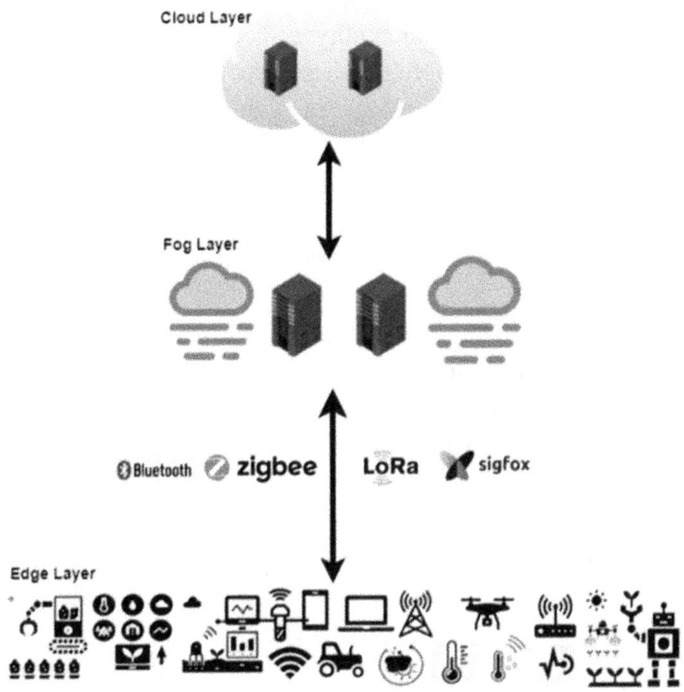

Figure 5. Edge-Fog-IoT-Cloud architecture
(Qureshi et al., 2021)

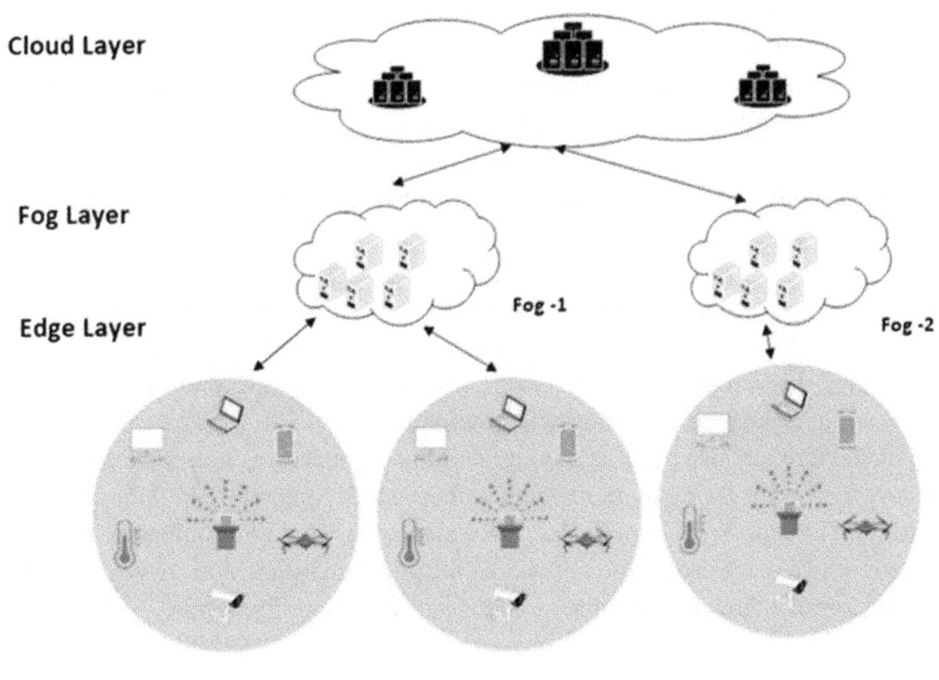

Effective data management ensures that data is organized, stored, and processed in a manner conducive to swift analysis and interpretation, empowering farmers to respond promptly to changing environmental conditions. This examination of extensive data allows farmers and enterprises to boost productivity, optimize crop yields, reduce wastage, bolster sustainability, and comply with environmental regulations and standards (Kamilaris et al., 2017). Furthermore, IoT has the potential to enhance the agricultural supply chain by identifying areas for improvement, a process involving several crucial data analysis stages. The initial stage is data preprocessing, a crucial step in the process of uncovering valuable insights from data, as data quality greatly influences the quality of knowledge (Muangprathub et al., 2019).

In real-world scenarios, data tends to be imperfect, incomplete, and inconsistent. Consequently, serves to enhance the precision and effectiveness of data extraction. It involves several elements:

(i) Data cleansing takes place once data is gathered, aiming to eliminate any incomplete, inconsistent, or unnecessary data. This practice guarantees that subsequent analysis relies on accurate data.
(ii) Following this is the integration of collected data from various IoT sensors into a unified system. This approach provides a comprehensive view of the supply chain, enabling a more thorough analysis.
(iii) Finally, data transformation involves techniques to convert unprocessed data into a suitable format that streamlines data exploration and facilitates the retrieval of strategic insights. In this process, data is adjusted by altering its format, structure, or values to produce clean and usable information.

The subsequent stage involves a data reduction step, wherein the data is encoded into a more compact representation.

The consistency of the original data is preserved to ensure that mining the reduced data is more efficient while still producing nearly identical analysis results. Then, data modeling and discovery enable the extraction of knowledge from the prepared data. Mostly, intelligent approaches are used in data modeling and discovery to uncover patterns in the data. Finally, the solution analysis permits an analysis of the results from the data.

To conclude, IoT technology implementation to track the ecological efficiency in agribusiness value chains is a promising approach to promote sustainability in the agriculture industry.

- **Benefits of Using IoT for Monitoring the Environmental Performance of Agriculture Supply Chains**

Agriculturalists can use connected farming technologies to streamline their processes, cut expenses, and increase sustainability to gain a competitive advantage (Magazine, 2023). IoT-based solutions assist farmers in managing their crops and supply chains effectively, as well as optimize resource allocation, cut down on waste, and enhance environmental sustainability.

However, linked farming also benefits non-agricultural producers, as it may enhance the final product that consumers receive, giving them more assurance and dependability in their purchase decisions (Magazine, 2023). Through the monitoring and assessment of the ecological impact of the collected data, farmers can demonstrate their dedication to sustainability and environmental stewardship. This practice affirms their adherence to environmental regulations and sustainability norms.

During the Production Process

The automated system contributes to precision farming by effectively identifying zones associated with distinct needs that require attention. However, due to a lack of precise information, farmers are left with limited options but to apply blanket treatments, where the entire crop field receives consistent treatment with the same antimicrobial or chemical agent(s). In contrast, precision farming requires the precise application of treatment quantities, including chemicals, fertilizers, herbicides, pesticides, seeds, and water, at the correct times and locations within the field (Piramuthu, 2022).

IoT can be employed to monitor various environmental performance indicators. These indicators encompass soil moisture, which optimizes irrigation and reduces water consumption through real-time monitoring; soil temperature, which optimizes planting and harvesting schedules; and nutrient levels, which optimize fertilizer application and reduce wastage. It also aids in monitoring crop growth using devices like drones and cameras, detecting early signs of disease or pest infestations. Another vital environmental performance indicator (EPI) is weather conditions. Thus, monitoring climatic variables like temperature, humidity, and precipitation assists farmers in making well-informed decisions about their planting and harvesting schedules (Othmeni et al., 2023).

IoT devices such as intelligent collars possess the ability to oversee the well-being and conduct of livestock, facilitating the identification of illness indicators and enhancement of feeding timetables. This promotes a proactive approach to livestock supervision. Additionally, monitoring energy consumption provides insights to identify areas of energy wastage and assess the effectiveness of energy-efficient measures. Moreover, sensors can monitor water quality, aiding in identifying pollution sources and evaluating the efficiency of water treatment processes. Similarly, sensors monitor air quality. Lastly, IoT devices offer valuable information on waste generation levels and track the success of recycling and waste reduction initiatives.

Overall, through the vigilant monitoring of these environmental performance indicators, farmers can adeptly make choices that enhance efficiency, minimize wastage, and advance the adoption of sustainable agricultural practices.

During the Packaging Process

Following the harvest, it is imperative to guarantee that the product reaches the consumer in a condition appropriate for consumption (Piramuthu, 2022). This necessitates taking precautions to minimize or eliminate opportunities for pathogen growth while simultaneously taking care to slow down the process of quality degradation by maintaining the item within the optimal temperature range.

Reducing food waste is crucial due to the close relationship between environmental sustainability and this issue. Intelligent packaging, using sensor-based RFID tags, can help monitor temperature fluctuations from packaging to consumption (Pirsa et al., 2022). Moreover, when a perishable item has reached or is about to approach its acceptable limit, this can help alert the next stage of the supply chain. When this situation arises, the item can be promptly moved for consumption to prevent waste. Additionally, intelligent packaging possesses the capability to identify and eliminate unnecessary gases around the food item, aiding in traceability. This, in turn, enables customized handling of each item, further enhancing the overall process.

During Storage and Transportation

After packaging, proper handling of food items is crucial to ensure preservation and minimize losses, which includes maintaining suitable temperature ranges. When planning routes and destinations, it is helpful to use an automated system that takes into consideration the varying remaining shelf-life information of numerous things at once. This technology offers the capacity to:

§ **Enable real-time tracking:** Real-time tracking of agricultural product transportation not only monitors location but also combats theft and enhances supply chain management.
§ **Predict maintenance:** Utilizing IoT sensors to monitor equipment conditions during handling and movement provides real-time performance data and identifies potential issues proactively, reducing downtime and enhancing operational efficiency.
§ **Ensure quality control:** Assessing agricultural product quality during transit or storage allows farmers to ensure compliance with required standards and regulations, reducing contamination risks and improving food safety.
§ **Drive cost savings:** By optimizing retention, freight conditions, and reducing waste, integrating IoT technology into supply chain management lowers costs and enhances profitability for farmers and other stakeholders in the agricultural sector.

Overall, the use of IoT technology in the storage and transportation of agricultural products has the potential to improve efficiency, reduce waste, and enhance the quality and safety of food products.

OVERCOMING CHALLENGES AND IMPLEMENTING SOLUTIONS

The IoT offers immense potential for real-time data collection and analysis, providing valuable insights into the environmental impact of agricultural practices. However, several challenges must be overcome for successful implementation, including the physical security of IoT devices, data management, cyber security, and accessibility (Demestichas et al., 2020).

- **IoT-based technologies accessibility**

Even while the usage of IoT devices and software allows for the automation of many supply chain activities, it is important to understand that people are still needed to run and manage these technological instruments in warehouses and vehicles. IoT solutions, however, can be complicated and difficult to administer, particularly for farmers who are unfamiliar with this technology. Farmers may find it difficult to efficiently handle and evaluate the vast amounts of data provided by IoT sensors, integrate it with other systems, and gather and analyze it.

Managers and IoT service providers must make sure that staff members obtain the necessary training in order to overcome this difficulty. The main goal of this training should be to give employees the information and abilities they need to use IoT hardware and software in their daily tasks. Additionally, it should involve teaching staff about the capabilities and features of IoT devices, instructing them on how to gather and analyze sensor data, and guiding them through maintenance and troubleshooting processes. Collaboration with data analytics experts might be necessary to develop efficient data management and analysis strategies. These experts can also create customized data processing algorithms and tools for data visualization.

- **Physical security**

The introduction of IoT devices and sensors in outdoor and remote settings introduces distinct challenges, as these devices are vulnerable to unauthorized access, physical harm, and the potential for theft (Lopez et al., 2009). To preserve these invaluable assets and guarantee the credibility and consistency of data collection and monitoring activities, it becomes essential to implement physical protection measures for this equipment on agricultural lands.

Installing lockable cabinets or enclosures to hold the IoT devices and sensors is a practical way to improve physical security. These enclosures should be made from sturdy materials, such as reinforced steel, and include tamper-proof locks and access control systems. In addition, installing security cameras and alarm systems in key spots can function as a deterrent and send out instant notifications in the event of any unwanted activity or attempted theft. It's also essential to use proper lighting in outdoor spaces. Well-lit areas can discourage potential criminals and enhance visibility for detecting unauthorized access or suspicious activities. Installing motion-activated lighting in conjunction with IoT devices that trigger when someone approaches can greatly improve security. An illustrative case of such implementation is documented in a report by the United States Department of Agriculture (USDA), where farms employed motion sensor lights to protect IoT devices used for monitoring crop conditions (USDA, 2016).

Figure 6. IoT devices' GPS tracking
(Toolsense, www.toolsense.io)

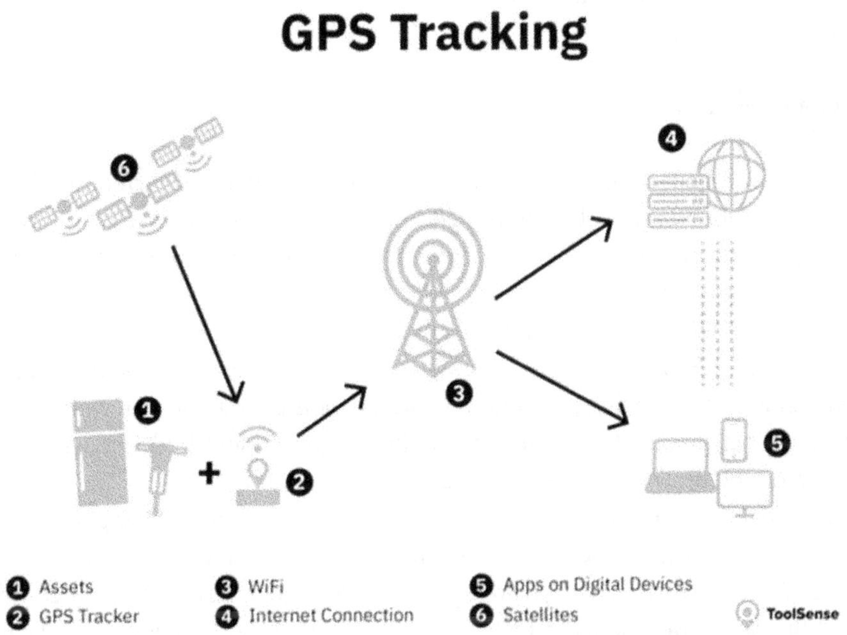

Establishing clear protocols for employees and farm workers regarding the handling and secure storage of IoT devices is essential. Regular training sessions on security best practices should be conducted to raise awareness and ensure that everyone understands their role in maintaining physical security. Another important consideration is the usage of location-tracking technologies for IoT devices, such as Global Positioning System (GPS) trackers, satellites, and many others, as illustrated in Figure 6 (Toolsense, www.toolsense.io).

By incorporating GPS trackers into the devices, farmers and farm managers can effectively monitor their real-time location. In case of theft, this technology proves instrumental in recovering stolen devices and providing vital information to law enforcement agencies. Another noteworthy threat arises from the challenging environmental conditions, encompassing high temperatures, humidity, rain, winds, and other phenomena. These conditions present a significant threat to the functionality and performance of electromechanical equipment (McCartney & Lefsrud, 2018).

Among the pivotal components susceptible to these effects are sensors and wireless networks. Such components are prone to malfunctions and disruptions, potentially resulting in inaccurate measurements, incorrect commands, communication breakdowns, and data inconsistencies (Tzounis et al., 2017; Bannister et al., 2008). Misleading measurements could misguide farmers and disrupt decision-making processes. Furthermore, sensor malfunctions might trigger erroneous commands sent to automated agricultural systems, thereby heightening the risks associated with production operations (Tzounis et al., 2017).

In addition to sensors, wireless networks, predominantly low-power systems like LoRaWAN and Zigbee, play a crucial role in transmitting data between sensors, actuators, and control systems. However, adverse environmental factors can impact the wireless network's performance (Bannister et al., 2008). Bannister et al. (2008) showed that temperature fluctuations have a direct impact on signal strength, data collection, and positioning accuracy in wireless sensor networks. Specifically, high temperatures can lead to signal attenuation, disrupting the reliable transmission of data and potentially resulting in communication disruptions and data loss. Similarly, environmental factors like humidity, obstacles, and human presence can further compound the challenges faced by wireless networks in agricultural applications (Bannister et al., 2008).

- **Supply chain security**

The aggregation of extensive personal data, encompassing details of farmers and suppliers, amplifies the potential for data breaches. Unauthorized individuals obtaining access to such data can inflict substantial damage to the supply chain's security and undermine environmental performance (El Baz et al., 2023).

A comprehensive review of studies conducted by El Baz et al. (2023) explored environmental supply chain risk management (ESCRM) using the Scopus database. This approach facilitated the identification of key environmental supply chain risks and the corresponding strategies for mitigating them. Consequently, two primary categories of environmental risks have been identified: endogenous and exogenous risks, as illustrated in Figure 7 (El Baz et al., 2023).

Endogenous risks arise from operational activities within a company's supply chain, encompassing pollution, harmful emissions, and accidents resulting from firm personnel, operations, and machinery (El Baz et al., 2023). These risks also include issues related to inefficient resource utilization, waste generation, and the production of scrap materials. Other studies additionally classify non-compliance

Figure 7. Environmental supply chain risk categories
(El Baz et al., 2023)

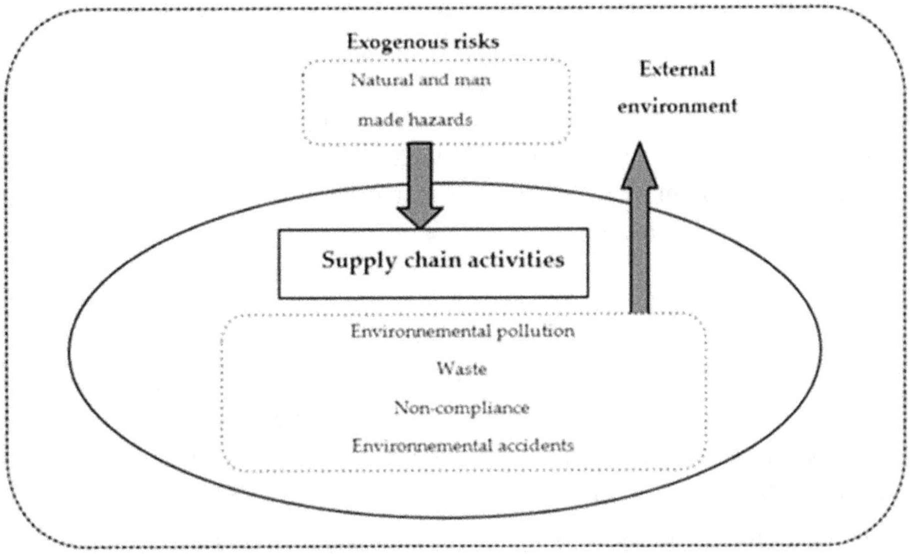

with regulations regarding personnel safety, ecological concerns, and social responsibility as endogenous risks (Giannakis & Papadopoulos, 2016).

Exogenous risks result from the interaction between firms and their external environment. These encompass natural disasters and human-made events such as terrorist attacks, wars, and military conflicts (El Baz et al., 2023). Many scholars prioritize endogenous risks over exogenous ones due to the unpredictability and management challenges associated with the latter (Torres-Ruiz & Ravindran, 2018). Uncontrolled exogenous and endogenous risks can indeed significantly impact firms, resulting in various adverse consequences. Data breaches and manipulation, which can lead to the creation of falsified data, can have equally severe repercussions.

Nowadays, consumers are exceptionally mindful of the environmental friendliness of the products they use, considering their origin and the entities responsible for their creation. They actively seek details on a product's sustainability practices and rely on labels, certifications, and transparent supply chains for informed decision-making. However, hackers can breach and manipulate this data, which may have ramifications for consumer perception. Consequently, consumers may cast doubt on the credibility and legitimacy of a company's environmental claims.

One of the significant threats that firms face due to exogenous and endogenous risks is the financial implications they may encounter (Chen et al., 2016). Decreased gains and increased costs can arise from the need to address and mitigate risks, such as implementing new security measures, complying with regulations, or paying fines and penalties. Additionally, risks can lead to liquidity shortages, making it difficult for firms to meet their financial obligations and negatively impacting their overall financial stability and viability.

Furthermore, data breaches and manipulation can lead to reputational damage (Kamalahmadi & Mellat-Parast, 2016). A tarnished reputation can cause reduced customer trust, loss of market share, and strained relationships with stakeholders. This is especially crucial in the digital era, where news spreads swiftly through social media and online platforms. Rebuilding a damaged reputation demands considerable effort, resources, and time to restore trust and mend relationships with key stakeholders.

In addition, suspicion of non-adherence to laws and regulations can trigger legal actions by governmental and institutional entities, resulting in fines, lawsuits, and regulatory investigations (Cousins et al., 2004). These legal consequences may stem from a range of risks, including environmental regulation violations, unfair business practices, or data privacy breaches. Legal actions not only lead to financial penalties but also bring reputational risks and the potential for damaging a firm's regulatory relationships. Compliance failures can undermine investor confidence, restrict access to capital markets, and expose the firm to increased scrutiny and oversight.

- **Cyber Security**

The rise of IoT devices, sensors, satellite imagery, and weather stations has generated substantial agricultural data. Yet, efficiently handling and merging this diverse, voluminous data poses a notable challenge. Beyond the supply chain attacks discussed earlier, the smart farming ecosystem faces susceptibility to various other forms of attacks. These encompass data attacks, network and equipment vulnerabilities, along with assorted security threats, as summarized in Figure 8 (Gupta et al., 2020).

Figure 8. Smart farming ecosystem cyber attack types
(Gupta et al., 2020)

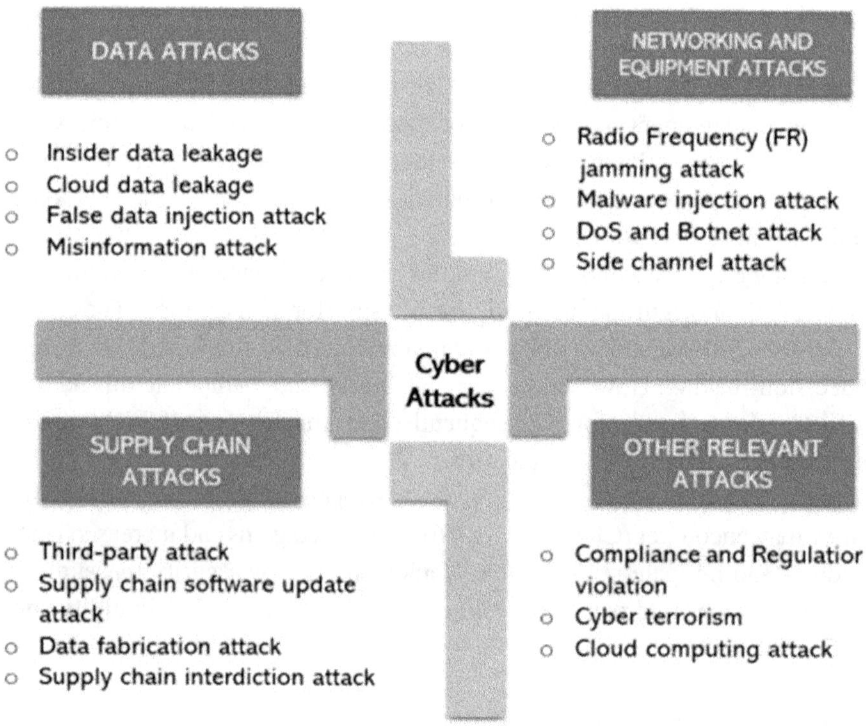

IoT-enabled farm monitoring devices often lack vital security features like user login monitoring and access controls. This exposes them to potential hacks and unauthorized data access including environmental data. Manufacturers must implement a range of measures for data protection and confidentiality to effectively address these.

To safeguard valuable environmental and farm-specific data, including information on soil moisture, temperature, pesticide usage, and energy consumption, farmers should prioritize security and implement robust cyber security measures. Employing secure data storage solutions like encrypted databases or cloud storage with strict access controls ensures the integrity and confidentiality of agricultural data. Manufacturers must enact stringent security measures, including multi-factor authentication, role-based access control, and regular user monitoring. The goal is to restrict data access to authorized personnel only. Consistent monitoring of user logins and access permissions is crucial to ensure that private information is accessible only to authorized employees. Additionally, having regular backup protocols and well-defined disaster recovery plans in place mitigates the risk of data loss.

Additionally, it is crucial to implement secure communication protocols that guarantee the privacy and authenticity of data during transmission. Consistent firmware updates must be carried out to rectify security vulnerabilities and counter evolving threats. Employing protocols like HTTPS (Hypertext Transfer Protocol Secure) or VPNs (Virtual Private Networks) is essential for safeguarding environmental data as it moves between devices, systems, or involved parties. HTTPS guarantees secure communication between clients and servers through SSL/TLS encryption, preventing unauthorized access and tampering. SSL/TLS (Secure Sockets Layer/Transport Layer Security) encryption is a security protocol that uses cryptographic techniques to protect exchanged data. It involves a secure handshake, the use of digital certificates to verify website identities, and the encryption of data during transmission, ensuring privacy and integrity in online communication. Conversely, VPNs establish a secure, private connection, encrypting and routing data via a dedicated server, preventing unauthorized interception or tampering during transit. Regular vulnerability assessments will pinpoint and mitigate potential system weaknesses. Intrusion detection and prevention systems can be employed to monitor network traffic, identifying and halting suspicious activities or unauthorized access.

Lastly, organizations can adopt a proactive approach to detect and promptly respond to potential security breaches in real time by deploying Intrusion Detection and Prevention Systems (IDPS). This enables rapid response and mitigation. To detect and analyze suspicious activities, such as unauthorized access attempts, malware infections, or unusual behavior patterns, IDPS solutions consistently monitor network traffic, system logs, and other security events. Once a potential security breach is identified, these IDPS can proactively thwart or mitigate the attack, which may involve blocking malicious IP addresses or terminating suspicious connections. By enhancing threat visibility, enabling early detection, and facilitating rapid responses, investing in IDPS solutions significantly enhances an organization's security posture. This, in turn, reduces the potential impact of security incidents and safeguards critical assets (Aljabri et al., 2021).

In conclusion, to overcome challenges related to accessibility, physical security, supply chain security, and cyber security risks, it is crucial to leverage a diverse range of technological solutions. By employing a combination of these solutions, stakeholders can effectively address these challenges and ensure the successful implementation of IoT technology in the agricultural supply chain. This integration of multiple technological solutions not only enables improved environmental performance but also fosters sustainable practices, benefiting the agricultural sector as a whole.

CONCLUSION

Utilizing IoT to monitor the environmental performance of the agriculture supply chain enables stakeholders to gather and analyze real-time data, leading to valuable insights into operational efficiency, areas for improvement, and data-based decision-making for process optimization.

IoT sensors and devices are crucial in collecting and transmitting essential data related to the supply chain, including metrics such as soil moisture, temperature, humidity, and energy consumption. The analysis of this up-to-the-minute data can uncover inefficiencies, curtail wastage, fine-tune resource allotment, and fundamentally foster waste reduction, resource preservation, diminished carbon footprint, and elevated sustainability across supply chains.

To effectively deploy IoT solutions, recognizing the substantial investments needed for infrastructure, data management, and cyber security is vital. This underscores the significance of collaborative partnerships among stakeholders. Through joint efforts, stakeholders can combine resources and expertise to surmount these challenges and ensure the seamless integration of IoT technology.

Recognizing and addressing the challenges that come with IoT adoption is crucial. This includes identifying potential obstacles and proactively finding solutions to mitigate them. This proactive mindset will enable them to harness the full potential of IoT, enhance environmental performance, and drive sustainable practices in the agriculture supply chain.

A major challenge is the accessibility of IoT-based technologies to farmers who may lack experience in utilizing such technology. However, by providing appropriate training and education, farmers can effectively utilize IoT devices and software to collect and analyze data for improved operations. By implementing comprehensive risk mitigation approaches and addressing both endogenous and exogenous risks, firms can mitigate these threats and maintain trust with stakeholders.

The agriculture industry must remain vigilant regarding the vulnerabilities posed by these technologies by staying up-to-date on the latest cyber security threats and taking proactive measures to protect against them. Building trust with consumers and ensuring responsible data handling is critical to achieving greater sustainability and resilience in the agriculture industry.

By surmounting these obstacles and adopting suitable solutions, the agricultural sector can maximize the advantages of IoT technologies resulting in sustainable sound, and streamlined farming practices. Using thorough training, heightened physical security protocols, and resilient cyber security strategies, the agricultural domain can enhance the environmental efficiency of the supply chain, simultaneously upholding data integrity, consumer confidence, and fiscal stability.

In conclusion, the integration of IoT technology into the agriculture supply chain represents a transformative opportunity to enhance sustainability, reduce waste, and optimize operations. However, it comes with its fair share of challenges, from infrastructure investments to cyber security concerns and ensuring accessibility to all stakeholders. Yet, with a commitment to collaboration, proactive problem-solving, and ongoing education, the agriculture industry can overcome these hurdles and unlock the full potential of IoT. By doing so, we can not only improve environmental performance but also build trust, drive resilience, and foster a more sustainable and efficient future for agriculture.

REFERENCES

Aljabri, M., Aljameel, S. S., Mohammad, R. M. A., Almotiri, S. H., Mirza, S., Anis, F. M., Aboulnour, M., Alomari, D. M., Alhamed, D. H., & Altamimi, H. S. (2021). Intelligent techniques for detecting network attacks: Review and research directions. *Sensors (Basel)*, *21*(21), 7070. doi:10.339021217070 PMID:34770375

Bannister, K., Giorgetti, G., & Gupta, S. K. (2008, June). Wireless sensor networking for hot applications: Effects of temperature on signal strength, data collection and localization. In *Proceedings of the 5th workshop on embedded networked sensors* (HotEmNets' 08) (pp. 1-5). Springer.

Bentalha, B. (2020). Big-Data et Service Supply chain management: Challenges et opportunités. *International Journal of Business and Technology Studies*, *1*(3).

Chen, A., Hsieh, C. Y., & Wee, H. M. (2016). A resilient global supplier selection strategy—A case study of an automotive company. *International Journal of Advanced Manufacturing Technology*, *87*(5-8), 1475–1490. doi:10.100700170-014-6567-z

Cousins, P. D., Lamming, R. C., & Bowen, F. (2004). The role of risk in environment-related supplier initiatives. *International Journal of Operations & Production Management*, *24*(6), 554–565. doi:10.1108/01443570410538104

Dahane, A., Benameur, R., Kechar, B., & Benyamina, A. (2020, October). An IoT based smart farming system using machine learning. In *2020 International symposium on networks, computers and communications (ISNCC)* (pp. 1-6). IEEE. 10.1109/ISNCC49221.2020.9297341

Debauche, O., Mahmoudi, S., & Guttadauria, A. (2022). A new edge computing architecture for IoT and multimedia data management. *Information (Basel)*, *13*(2), 89. doi:10.3390/info13020089

Demestichas, K., Peppes, N., & Alexakis, T. (2020). Survey on security threats in agricultural IoT and smart farming. *Sensors (Basel)*, *20*(22), 6458. doi:10.339020226458 PMID:33198160

El Baz, J., Cherrafi, A., Benabdellah, A. C., Zekhnini, K., Beka Be Nguema, J. N., & Derrouiche, R. (2023). Environmental Supply Chain Risk Management for Industry 4.0: A Data Mining Framework and Research Agenda. *Systems*, *11*(1), 46. doi:10.3390ystems11010046

Farooq, M. S., Riaz, S., Abid, A., Umer, T., & Zikria, Y. B. (2020). Role of IoT technology in agriculture: A systematic literature review. *Electronics (Basel)*, *9*(2), 319. doi:10.3390/electronics9020319

Food and Agriculture Organization of the United Nations (FAO). (2018). *The future of food and agriculture: Alternative pathways to 2050*. FAO. https://www.fao.org/3/a-i6583e.pdf

Gazis, A. (2021). What is iot? the internet of things explained. *Academia Letters, 2*.

Gia, T. N., Qingqing, L., Queralta, J. P., Zou, Z., Tenhunen, H., &Westerlund, T. (2019, September). Edge AI in smart farming IoT: CNNs at the edge and fog computing with LoRa. In *2019 IEEE AFRICON* (pp. 1-6). IEEE.

Giannakis, M., & Papadopoulos, T. (2016). Supply chain sustainability: A risk management approach. *International Journal of Production Economics*, *171*, 455–470. doi:10.1016/j.ijpe.2015.06.032

Gupta, M., Abdelsalam, M., Khorsandroo, S., & Mittal, S. (2020). Security and privacy in smart farming: Challenges and opportunities. *IEEE Access : Practical Innovations, Open Solutions*, *8*, 34564–34584. doi:10.1109/ACCESS.2020.2975142

Gupta. (2022). Management of Agriculture Supply Chain. *Food Logistics*. www.foodlogistics.com. https://www.foodlogistics.com/sustainability/agriculture/article/22159660/allied-market-research-management-of-agriculture-supply-chain

Kalyani, Y., & Collier, R. (2021). A systematic survey on the role of cloud, fog, and edge computing combination in smart agriculture. *Sensors (Basel)*, *21*(17), 5922. doi:10.339021175922 PMID:34502813

Kamalahmadi, M., & Mellat-Parast, M. (2016). Developing a resilient supply chain through supplier flexibility and reliability assessment. *International Journal of Production Research*, *54*(1), 302–321. doi:10.1080/00207543.2015.1088971

Kamilaris, A., Kartakoullis, A., & Prenafeta-Boldú, F. X. (2017). A review on the practice of big data analysis in agriculture. *Computers and Electronics in Agriculture*, *143*, 23–37. doi:10.1016/j.compag.2017.09.037

Lopez, J., Roman, R., & Alcaraz, C. (2009). Analysis of security threats, requirements, technologies and standards in wireless sensor networks. In A. Aldini, G. Barthe, & R. Gorrieri (Eds.), *Foundations of Security Analysis and Design V: FOSAD 2007/2008/2009 Tutorial Lectures* (pp. 289–338). Springer. doi:10.1007/978-3-642-03829-7_10

Magazine, I. N. (2023). Connected farming – How can it be beneficial for agriculture manufacturers, customers, and the environment. *IoT Now News*. https://www.iot-now.com/2023/03/09/128547-connected-farming-how-can-it-be-beneficial-for-agriculture-manufacturers-customers-and-the-environment/

Maroua, B., Rachida, A. A., & Abdelaziz, M. (2022). Smart farming architectures based on IoT review: Comparative study. *Procedia Computer Science*, *203*, 783–788. doi:10.1016/j.procs.2022.07.117

McCartney, L., & Lefsrud, M. (2018). Protected agriculture in extreme environments: A review of controlled environment agriculture in tropical, arid, polar, and urban locations. *Applied Engineering in Agriculture*, *34*(2), 455–473. doi:10.13031/aea.12590

Muangprathub, J., Boonnam, N., Kajornkasirat, S., Lekbangpong, N., Wanichsombat, A., & Nillaor, P. (2019). IoT and agriculture data analysis for smart farm. *Computers and Electronics in Agriculture*, *156*, 467–474. doi:10.1016/j.compag.2018.12.011

Narwane, V. S., Gunasekaran, A., & Gardas, B. B. (2022). Unlocking adoption challenges of IoT in Indian agricultural and food supply chain. *Smart Agricultural Technology*, *2*, 100035. doi:10.1016/j.atech.2022.100035

Ojha, T., Misra, S., & Raghuwanshi, N. S. (2015). Wireless sensor networks for agriculture: The state-of-the-art in practice and future challenges. *Computers and Electronics in Agriculture*, *118*, 66–84. doi:10.1016/j.compag.2015.08.011

Othmeni, I., Abdallah, R. B., Aribi, H. B., Amara, E. B., & Fattouch, S. (2023). Artificial Intelligence Applications in Agricultural Sustainability: Enhancing Efficiency and Resilience. In Convergence of Cloud Computing, AI, and Agricultural Science (pp. 187-209). IGI Global.

Pal, K., & Yasar, A.-U.-H. (2023). Internet of Things Impact on Supply Chain Management. *Procedia Computer Science*, *220*, 478–485. doi:10.1016/j.procs.2023.03.061

Piramuthu, S. (2022). IoT, Environmental Sustainability, Agricultural Supply Chains. *Procedia Computer Science*, *204*, 811–816. doi:10.1016/j.procs.2022.08.098

Pirsa, S., Sani, I. K., & Mirtalebi, S. S. (2022). Nano-biocomposite based color sensors: Investigation of structure, function, and applications in intelligent food packaging. *Food Packaging and Shelf Life*, *31*, 100789. doi:10.1016/j.fpsl.2021.100789

Qureshi, R., Mehboob, S. H., & Aamir, M. (2021). Sustainable green fog computing for smart agriculture. *Wireless Personal Communications*, *121*(2), 1379–1390. doi:10.100711277-021-09059-x

Rana, S. (2022). Consumer Awareness and Perception Towards Green Marketing: An Empirical Study In Bangalore City. *Journal of Positive School Psychology*, *6*(5), 4240–4245. http://journalppw.com

Rana, S. (2022). Consumer Awareness and Perception Towards Green Marketing: An Empirical Study In Bangalore City. *Journal of Positive School Psychology*, *6*(5), 4240–4245. http://journalppw.com

Talavera, J. M., Tobón, L. E., Gómez, J. A., Culman, M. A., Aranda, J. M., Parra, D. T., Quiroz, L. A., Hoyos, A., & Garreta, L. E. (2017). Review of IoT applications in agro-industrial and environmental fields. *Computers and Electronics in Agriculture*, *142*, 283–297. doi:10.1016/j.compag.2017.09.015

Toolsense. (). *Which type of equipment tracker should you use.* Tool Sense. https://toolsense.io/equipment-management/which-type-of-equipment-tracker-should-you-use/,

Torres-Ruiz, A., & Ravindran, A. R. (2018). Multiple criteria framework for the sustainability risk assessment of a supplier portfolio. *Journal of Cleaner Production*, *172*, 4478–4493. doi:10.1016/j.jclepro.2017.10.304

Tripathi, A. D., Mishra, R., Maurya, K. K., Singh, R. B., & Wilson, D. W. (2019). Estimates for world population and global food availability for global health. In *The role of functional food security in global health* (pp. 3-24). Academic Press.

Tzounis, A., Katsoulas, N., Bartzanas, T., & Kittas, C. (2017). Internet of Things in agriculture, recent advances and future challenges. *Biosystems Engineering*, *164*, 31–48. doi:10.1016/j.biosystemseng.2017.09.007

United Nations. (2021). *Transforming our world: The 2030 Agenda for Sustainable Development.* UN. https://sdgs.un.org/2030agenda

Zhang, Z., Yu, X., Wu, P., & Han, W. (2015). Survey on water-saving agricultural internet of things based on wireless sensor network. *International Journal of Control and Automation*, *8*(4), 229–240. doi:10.14257/ijca.2015.8.4.23

KEY TERMS AND DEFINITIONS

Agriculture Industry: The agriculture industry encompasses all activities related to the cultivation, processing, marketing, and distribution of crops, livestock, and other agricultural products, including farming, agribusiness, and agricultural research and development.

Agriculture Supply Chains: Agriculture supply chains encompass the entirety of processes, systems, and activities engaged in the production, distribution, and sale of agricultural commodities, spanning from the initial farm stage to the ultimate consumer.

Data Management: Data Management involves a comprehensive set of activities, methodologies, and technology solutions employed to acquire, store, arrange, examine, and guarantee the integrity and usefulness of data throughout its entire lifespan.

Data Security: Data Security encompasses the deployment of safeguards and procedures aimed at safeguarding digital data against unauthorized access, utilization, disclosure, interference, alteration, or destruction, thereby preserving its confidentiality, integrity, and accessibility.

Environmental analysis: Environmental analysis encompasses the examination and assessment of multiple factors and metrics to gauge the influence of human actions on the environment, including factors such as pollution levels, biodiversity, and depletion of natural resources.

Internet of Things: Internet of Things denotes the network of interconnected physical devices, sensors, and software designed to collect and share data.

Monitoring: Monitoring refers to the continuous observation and measurement of specific parameters, events, or systems to collect data and track changes over time for various purposes, such as quality control, performance evaluation, or early warning.

Sustainability: Sustainability revolves around the principle of meeting current needs while preserving the capacity for next generations to fulfill their own requirements, with a specific focus on economic, environmental, and social well-being.

Compilation of References

Aazam, M., & Huh, E. N. (2014). Fog computing and smart gateway based communication for cloud of things. *Proceedings of the 2nd IEEE International Conference on Future Internet of Things and Cloud (FiCloud' 14)*, 464–470.

Ababa, A., Sharing, T. & Ababa, A. (2011). *Tumi Initiative's Transformative Stories* (Working Paper). SSRN.

Abdel-Basset, M., & Mohamed, R. (2020). A novel plithogenic TOPSIS- CRITIC model for sustainable supply chain risk management. *Journal of Cleaner Production, 247*, 119586. doi:10.1016/j.jclepro.2019.119586

Acheampong, P., Zhiwen, L., Hiran, K. K., Serwaa, O. E., Boateng, F., & Bediako, I. A. (2018). Examining the intervening role of age and gender on mobile payment acceptance in Ghana: UTAUT model. *Canadian Journal of Applied Science and Technology, 5*(2).

Addo-Tenkorang, R., & Helo, P. T. (2016). Big data applications in operations/supply-chain management: A literature review. *Computers & Industrial Engineering, 101*, 528–543. doi:10.1016/j.cie.2016.09.023

Agarwal, S., Hiran, D., Kothari, H., & Singh, S. (2023). LEVERAGING DATA PROCESSING FOR OPTIMIZING ORGANIC FARMING PRACTICES. *Journal of Data Acquisition and Processing, 38*(2), 3243.

Agyabeng-Mensah, Y., Afum, E., & Ahenkorah, E. (2020). Exploring financial performance and green logistics management practices: Examining the mediating influences of market, environmental and social performances. *Journal of Cleaner Production, 258*, 120613. doi:10.1016/j.jclepro.2020.120613

Ahmad, N., Ghadi, Y. Y., Adnan, M., & Ali, M. (2022). Load Forecasting Techniques For Power System: Research Challenges and Survey. *IEEE Access : Practical Innovations, Open Solutions, 10*(10), 71054–71090. doi:10.1109/ACCESS.2022.3187839

Ahram, T., Sargolzaei, A., Sargolzaei, S., Daniels, J., & Amaba, B. (2017). *Blockchain technology innovations.* 2017 IEEE technology & engineering management conference (TEMSCON), Santa Clara, CA.

Ainsworth, E. A., Lemonnier, P., & Wedow, J. M. (2020). The influence of rising tropospheric carbon dioxide and ozone on plant productivity. *Plant Biology, 22*(S1), 5–11. doi:10.1111/plb.12973 PMID:30734441

AiroDoctor. (2022). *How Ford uses Blockchain technology to improve urban air quality?* AiroDoctor. https://airodoctor.com/post-32088/#:~:text=In%20addition%20to%20being%20used

Ajzen, I. (2002). Behavioral Interventions Based on the Theory of Planned Behavior. *Research Policy, 2011*(June), 1–6.

Akhter, R, & Sofi, A. (2022). Precision agriculture using IoT data analytics and machine learning. *Journal of King Saud University - Computer and Information Sciences, 34*(8), 5602-5618.

Akter, S., Wamba, S. F., Gunasekaran, A., Dubey, R., & Childe, S. J. (2016). How to improve firm performance using big data analytics capability and business strategy alignment? *International Journal of Production Economics, 182*, 113–131. doi:10.1016/j.ijpe.2016.08.018

Al Shaher, S., & Zreik, M. (2022). The Impact of Job Characteristics and Value Congruence on Employee Retention: An Empirical Study from Lebanon. *The Journal of Asian Finance* [JAFEB]. *Economics and Business*, *9*(3), 171–180.

Alam, M. Z., Carpenter-Boggs, L., Mitra, S., Haque, M. M., Halsey, J., Rokonuzzaman, M., Saha, B., & Moniruzzaman, M. (2017). Effect of salinity intrusion on food crops, livestock, and fish species at Kalapara Coastal Belt in Bangladesh. *Journal of Food Quality*, *2017*, 2017. doi:10.1155/2017/2045157

Alinezhad, M., Mahdavi, I., Hematian, M., & Tirkolaee, E. B. (2022). A fuzzy multi-objective optimization model for sustainable closed-loop supply chain network design in food industries. *Environment, Development and Sustainability*, *24*(6), 1–28. doi:10.100710668-021-01809-y

Aljabri, M., Aljameel, S. S., Mohammad, R. M. A., Almotiri, S. H., Mirza, S., Anis, F. M., Aboulnour, M., Alomari, D. M., Alhamed, D. H., & Altamimi, H. S. (2021). Intelligent techniques for detecting network attacks: Review and research directions. *Sensors (Basel)*, *21*(21), 7070. doi:10.339021217070 PMID:34770375

Alla, L., Bentalha, B., & Bouhtati, N. (2022). Assessing supply chain performance in the covid 19 context: a prospective model. *2022 14th International Colloquium of Logistics and Supply Chain Management (LOGISTIQUA)* (pp 1-6). IEEE.

Alla, L., Bentalha, B., & Bouhtati, N. (2022). Assessing Supply Chain Performance in the Covid 19 Context: A Prospective Model. In *2022 14th International Colloquium of Logistics and Supply Chain Management (LOGISTIQUA)* (pp. 1-6). IEEE.

Alla, L., Jaouhari, E. L., & Bentalha, B. (2022). Repenser l'entrepreneuriat au sein du secteur informel au Maroc à l'ère du post Covid-19: Pour approche prospective de la formalisation intégrative. *Alternatives Managériales et Economiques*, *4*(1), 180–202.

Almutairi, K., Hosseini Dehshiri, S. J., Hosseini Dehshiri, S. S., Hoa, A. X., Arockia Dhanraj, J., Mostafaeipour, A., Issakhov, A., & Techato, K. (2022). Blockchain Technology application challenges in renewable energy supply chain management. *Environmental Science and Pollution Research International*, *30*(28), 1–18. doi:10.100711356-021-18311-7 PMID:34989989

Alqudah, S., Shrouf, H., Suifan, T., & Alhyari, S. (2020). A Moderated Mediation Model of Lean, Agile, Resilient, and Green Paradigms in the Supply Chain. Int. J Sup. Chain. *Mgt.*, *9*(4), 1.

Al-Refaie, A., Jarrar, Y., & Lepkova, N. (2021). Sustainable Design of a Multi-Echelon Closed Loop Supply Chain under Uncertainty for Durable Products. *Sustainability (Basel)*, *13*(19), 11126. doi:10.3390u131911126

Alshahrani, M. A., & Salam, M. A. (2022). The Role of Supply Chain Resilience on SMEs' Performance: The Case of an Emerging Economy. *Logistics*, *6*(3), 47. doi:10.3390/logistics6030047

Aluvalu, R. (2020, October). Intrusion detection system for the IoT: a comprehensive review. In *Proceedings of the 11th International Conference on Soft Computing and Pattern Recognition (SoCPaR. 2019)* (p. 235). Research Gate.

Amoako, G. K., Bonsu, G. A., Caesar, L. D., & Osei-Tete, F. (2021). Finding the nexus between green supply chain practices and sustainable business advantage: An emerging market perspective. *Management of Environmental Quality*, *32*(6), 1133–1149. doi:10.1108/MEQ-12-2019-0287

Anand, A., Seetharaman, A., & Maddulety, K. (2022). Implementing Blockchain Technology in Supply Chain Management. In *International Conference on Data Mining and Machine Learning*. Computer Science and Information Technology. 10.5121/csit.2022.120713

Andersson, A., Winslott, L., & Adell, E. (2018). Promoting sustainable travel behaviour through the use of smartphone applications : A review and development of a conceptual model. Travel Behav. Soc., 11, 52–61.

Angeles, R. (2005). RFID technologies: Supply-chain applications and implementation issues. *Information Systems Management*, *22*(1), 51–65. doi:10.1201/1078/44912.22.1.20051201/85739.7

Angell, R. L., & Kraemer, J. R. (2017). U.S. Patent No. 9,846,883, U.S. Patent and Trademark Office, Washington, DC.

Anshari, M., Almunawar, M. N., Lim, S. A., & Al-Mudimigh, A. (2019). Customer relationship management and big data enabled: Personalization & customization of services. *Applied Computing and Informatics*, *15*(2), 94–101. doi:10.1016/j.aci.2018.05.004

Anugerah, A. R., Ahmad, S. A., Samin, R., Samdin, Z., & Kamaruddin, N. (2021). Modified failure mode and effect analysis to mitigate sustainable related risk in the palm oil supply chain. *Advances in Materials and Processing Technologies*, *8*(2), 2229–2243. doi:10.1080/2374068X.2021.1898180

Archick, K. (2014). *The European parliament.* Democr. Credentials Eur. Union Backgr. Anal.

Arunachalam, D., Kumar, N., & Kawalek, J. P. (2018). Understanding Big Data Analytics Capabilities In Supply Chain Management: Unravelling the Issues, Challenges And Implications For Practice. *Transportation Research Part E, Logistics and Transportation Review*, *114*, 416–436. doi:10.1016/j.tre.2017.04.001

Arya, P., Srivastava, M. K., & Jaiswal, M. P. (2020). Modelling environmental and economic sustainability of logistics. *Asia-Pacific Journal of Business Administration.*

Asees Awan, M., & Ali, Y. (2019). Sustainable modeling in reverse logistics strategies using fuzzy MCDM: Case of China Pakistan Economic Corridor. *Management of Environmental Quality*, *30*(5), 1132–1151. doi:10.1108/MEQ-01-2019-0024

Aslam, J., Saleem, A., Khan, N. T., & Kim, Y. B. (2021). Factors influencing blockchain adoption in supply chain management practices: A study based on the oil industry. *Journal of Innovation & Knowledge*, *6*(2), 124–134. doi:10.1016/j.jik.2021.01.002

Asseng, S., Foster, I. A. N., & Turner, N. C. (2011). The impact of temperature variability on wheat yields. *Global Change Biology*, *17*(2), 997–1012. doi:10.1111/j.1365-2486.2010.02262.x

Attaran, M., Attaran, S., & Celik, B. G. (2023). The impact of digital twins on the evolution of intelligent manufacturing and Industry 4.0. *Advances in Computational Intelligence*, *3*(3), 11. doi:10.100743674-023-00058-y PMID:37305021

Atzori, L., Iera, A., & Morabito, G. (2011). IoT: Giving a social structure to the internet of things. *IEEE Communications Letters*, *15*(11), 1193–1195.

Augustine, D. J., Blumenthal, D. M., Springer, T. L., LeCain, D. R., Gunter, S. A., & Derner, J. D. (2018). Elevated CO 2 induces substantial and persistent declines in forage quality irrespective of warming in mixedgrass prairie. *Ecological Applications*, *28*(3), 721–735. doi:10.1002/eap.1680 PMID:29297964

Awasthi, A., Govindan, K., & Gold, S. (2018). Multi-tier sustainable global supplier selection using a fuzzy AHP-VIKOR based approach. *International Journal of Production Economics*, *195*, 106–117. doi:10.1016/j.ijpe.2017.10.013

Azevedo, P., Gomes, J., & Romao, M. (2023). Supply chain traceability using blockchain. *Operations Management Research.* doi:10.1007/s12063-023-00359-y

Baader, F., Calvanese, D., McGuinness, D., Nardi, D., & Patel-Schneider, P. (Eds.). (2010). *The Description Logic Handbook*. Cambridge University Press.

Bačiulienė, V., Bilan, Y., Navickas, V., & Lubomír, C. (2023). The Aspects Of Artificial Intelligence In Different Phases Of the Food Value And Supply Chain. *Foods*, *8*(12), 1654. doi:10.3390/foods12081654 PMID:37107449

Baesens, A. (2014). *Analytics in a big data world: The essential guide to data science and its applications*. John Wiley & Sons.

Balcombe, P. R., Mackett, R., Paulley, N., Preston, J., Shires, J., Titheridge, H., Wardman, M. (2004). The Demand for Public Transport: a practical guide. TRL Reports.

Ballou, R. H. (2007). *Business Logistics/supply Chain Management, 5/E (With Cd)*. Pearson Education India.

Banerjee, G., Sarkar, U., Das, S., & Ghosh, I. (2018). Artificial Intelligence in Agriculture: A Literature Survey. *International Journal of Scientific Research in Computer Science Applications and Management Studies*, *7*(3), 1–6.

Bannister, K., Giorgetti, G., & Gupta, S. K. (2008, June). Wireless sensor networking for hot applications: Effects of temperature on signal strength, data collection and localization. In *Proceedings of the 5th workshop on embedded networked sensors* (HotEmNets' 08) (pp. 1-5). Springer.

Baramichai, M., Zimmers, E. W. Jr, & Marangos, C. A. (2007). Agile supply chain transformation matrix: An integrated tool for creating an agile enterprise. *Supply Chain Management*, *12*(5), 334–348. doi:10.1108/13598540710776917

Barbosa, M. W. (2021). Uncovering research streams on agri-food supply chain management : A bibliometric study. *Global Food Security*, *28*(April 2020), 100517.

Barhhan, P. (2003). *International Trade Growth and Development: Essays*. Wiley-Blackwell. doi:10.1002/9780470752777

Barnaghi, P., Presser, M., & Moessner, K. (2010). Publishing Linked Sensor Data. *Proceedings of the 3rd International Workshop on Semantic Sensor Networks.*

Bashiri, M., Tjahjono, B., Lazell, J., Ferreira, J., & Perdana, T. (2021). The Dynamics of Sustainability Risks in the Global Coffee Supply Chain: A Case of Indonesia–UK. *Sustainability (Basel)*, *13*(2), 589. doi:10.3390u13020589

Behnke, K., & Janssen, M. F. W. H. A. (2020). Boundary conditions for traceability in food supply chains using blockchain technology. *International Journal of Information Management*, *52*, 101969. doi:10.1016/j.ijinfomgt.2019.05.025

Behrens, R., McCormick, D., & Mfinanga, D. (2015). *Paratransit in African cities: Operations, regulation and reform.* Taylor and Francis Inc. doi:10.4324/9781315849515

Benabdallah, C., El-Amraoui, A., Delmotte, F., & Frikha, A. (2022). Evaluation on Risks of Sustainable Supply Chain Based on Integrated Rough DEMATEL in Tunisian Dairy Industry. *International Journal of Supply and Operations Management*, *9*(3), 338–359. doi:10.22034/ijsom.2021.109143.2205

Bentalha, B. (2020). Big-Data et service supply chain management: challenges et opportunités. *International Journal of Business and Technology Studies, 1*(3). <https://www.ijbtsr.org/index.php/IJBTSR/article/view/16>. doi:10.5281/zenodo.3607357

Bentalha, B. (2023). Motivating Factors for Hotel Employees: A Fuzzy Logic Approach. In Strategic Human Resource Management in the Hospitality Industry: A Digitalized Economic Paradigm (pp. 159-178). IGI Global. doi:10.4018/978-1-6684-7494-5.ch008

Bentalha, B., & Hmioui, A. (2021, November). Smart Service Supply Chain and Just Walk Out Technology: A Netnographic Approach. In *The Proceedings of the International Conference on Smart City Applications* (pp. 223-236). Cham: Springer International Publishing.

Bentalha, B., Hmioui, A., & Alla, L. (2020). Digital Service Supply Chain Management: Current Realities and Prospective Vision, in Ben Ahmed M., Boudhir, A., Santos, D., El Aroussi, M., & Karas, I. (eds.), Innovations in Smart Cities Applications. Springer, Cham.

Bentalha, B., Hmioui, A., & Alla, L. (2020). Digital service supply chain management: current realities and prospective visions. *In Innovations in Smart Cities Applications Edition 3: The Proceedings of the 4th International Conference on Smart City Applications 4 (pp. 808-822).* Springer International Publishing.

Bentalha, B., Hmioui, A., & Alla, L. (2020a). Digital service supply chain management: current realities and prospective visions. Innovations in Smart Cities Applications Edition 3: The Proceedings of the 4th International Conference on Smart City Applications 4, (pp. 808-822). Springer International Publishing. 10.1007/978-3-030-37629-1_58

Bentalha, B., Hmioui, A., & Alla, L. (2020b). The global performance of a service supply chain: a simulation-optimization under arena. The *Proceedings of the Third International Conference on Smart City Applications,* (pp. 489-502). Springer International Publishing.

Bentalha, B., Hmioui, A., & Alla, L. (2021). The global performance of a service supply chain: a simulation-optimization under arena. In *Innovations in Smart Cities Applications Volume 4: The Proceedings of the 5th International Conference o Smart City Applications* (pp. 489-502). Springer International Publishing.

Bentalha, B., Hmioui, A., & Alla, L. (2021). The global performance of a service supply chain: a simulation-optimization under arena. In *Innovations in Smart Cities Applications Volume 4: The Proceedings of the 5th International Conference on Smart City Applications* (pp. 489-502). Springer International Publishing. 10.1007/978-3-030-66840-2_37

Bentalha, B., Hmioui, A., & Alla, L. (2023). Green Transportation Balanced Scorecard: A VIKOR Fuzzy Method for Evaluating Green Logistics Initiatives. In *Digital Technologies and Applications: Proceedings of ICDTA'23, Fez, Morocco, Volume 1* (pp. 916-925). Cham: Springer Nature Switzerland.

Bentalha, B., Hmioui, A., & Alla, L. (2023). Green Transportation Balanced Scorecard: A VIKOR Fuzzy Method for Evaluating Green Logistics Initiatives. In *International Conference on Digital Technologies and Applications* (pp. 916-925). Cham: Springer Nature Switzerland. 10.1007/978-3-031-29857-8_91

Bentalha, B. (2020). Big-Data et Service Supply chain management: Challenges et opportunités. *International Journal of Business and Technology Studies*, *1*(3).

Bentalha, B. (2020). Big-Data et Service Supply Chain Management: Challenges et Opportunities. *International Journal of Business and Technology Studies and Research*, *1*(3).

Bentalha, B. (2022). Green Transportation Balanced Scorecard Model: A Fuzzy-Delphi Approach During COVID-19. In *Computational Intelligence Techniques for Green Smart Cities* (pp. 107–127). Springer. doi:10.1007/978-3-030-96429-0_5

Bentalha, B. (2022). Smart Technologies for a Sustainable Service Supply Chain: A Prospective Perspective. Journal of Environmental Issues and Climate Change, 1(1), 77-89.

Bentalha, B. (2022). Smart Technologies for a Sustainable Service Supply Chain: A Prospective Perspective. *Journal of Environmental Issues and Climate Change*, *1*(1), 77–89. doi:10.59110/jeicc.v1i1.81

Bentalha, B. (2023). Les fondements théoriques du supply chain management: Une analyse critique. *Alternatives Managériales Economiques*, *5*(2), 1–22.

Bentalha, B., & Hmioui, A. (2021). Smart Service Supply Chain and Just Walk Out Technology: A Netnographic Approach. In *The Proceedings of the International Conference on Smart City Applications* (pp. 223-236). Cham: Springer International Publishing.

Bentalha, B., Hmioui, A., & Alla, L. (2019). The digitalization of the supply chain management of service companies: a prospective approach. In *Proceedings of the 4th International Conference on Smart City Applications* (pp. 1-8). https://doi.org/10.1145/3368756.3369005

Bentalha, B., Hmioui, A., & Alla, L. (2020). The global performance of a service supply chain: a simulation-optimization under arena. In *The Proceedings of the Third International Conference on Smart City Applications* (pp. 489-502). Cham: Springer International Publishing.

Berners-Lee, T. (2000). *Weaving the Web: The Original Design and Ultimate Design of the World Wide Web by its inventor*. Harper Business.

Besanko, D., Dranove, D., Shanley, M., & Schaefer, S. (2017). *Economics of Strategy*. John Wiley & Sons.

Beven, K. (2013). *NERC Final Report: The Catchment Change Network Knowledge Exchange Project*. NERC.

Bhanot, N., Rao, P. V., & Deshmukh, S. G. (2017). An integrated approach for analysing the enablers and barriers of sustainable manufacturing. *Journal of Cleaner Production, 142*, 4412–4439. doi:10.1016/j.jclepro.2016.11.123

Bhimavarapu, U., Battineni, G., & Chintalapudi, N. (2023). Improved optimization algorithm in LSTM to predict crop yield. *Computers, 12*(1), 10. doi:10.3390/computers12010010

Billah, M., Mehedi, S. T., Anwar, A., Rahman, Z., & Islam, R. (2022). A systematic literature review on blockchain enabled federated learning framework for internet of vehicles. *arXiv preprint arXiv:2203.05192.*

Biswas, S., & Anand, O. P. (2020). Logistics Competitiveness Index-Based Comparison of BRICS and G7 Countries: An Integrated PSI-PIV Approach. *IUP Journal of Supply Chain Management, 17*(2).

Bokhari, F., & Albukhari, A. (2022). *Design and Implementation Of High Throughput Screening Assays For Drug Discoveries*. High-Throughput Screening for Drug Discovery., doi:10.5772/intechopen.98733

Bonomi, F., Milito, R., Natarajan, P., & Zhu, J. (2014). *Fog computing: a platform for internet of things and analytics. In Big Data and Internet ofThings: A Road Map for Smart Environments*. Springer.

Bonomi, F., Milito, R., Zhu, J., & Addepalli, S. (2012). Fog computing and its role in the internet of things. *Proceedings of the 1st ACM MCC Workshop on Mobile Cloud Computing*, 13–16.

Bordel Sánchez, B., Alcarria, R., Sánchez de Rivera, D., & Robles, T. (2018). Process execution in CyberPhysical Systems using cloud and Cyber-Physical Internet services. *The Journal of Supercomputing, 74*(8), 4127–4169.

Boruchowitch, F., & Fritz, M. M. (2022). Who in the firm can create sustainable value and for whom? A single case-study on sustainable procurement and supply chain stakeholders. *Journal of Cleaner Production, 363*, 132619. doi:10.1016/j.jclepro.2022.132619

Bowman, P., Ng, J., Harrison, M., Lopez, S., & Illic, A. (2009). Sensor based condition monitoring. *Building Radio frequency IDentification for the Global Environment.*

Bren d'Amour, C., Reitsma, F., Baiocchi, G., Barthel, S., Güneralp, B., Erb, K. H., Haberl, H., Creutzig, F., & Seto, K. C. (2017). Future urban land expansion and implications for global croplands. *Proceedings of the National Academy of Sciences of the United States of America, 114*(34), 8939–8944. doi:10.1073/pnas.1606036114 PMID:28028219

Brewer, P., & Button, K. (2016). *Sustainable logistics and transportation: Optimising economic and environmental performance*. Kogan Page.

Broy, M., Cengarle, M. V., & Geisberger, E. (2012). Cyber-Physical Systems: Imminent Challenges. In *Large-Scale Complex IT Syst. Dev., Operat. and Manag. - 17th Monterey Workshop, (vol. 7539*, pp. 1–28). Academic Press.

Bruzzone, A., & Orsoni, A. (2003, March). AI and simulation-based techniques for the assessment of supply chain logistic performance. In *36th Annual Simulation Symposium,* 2003. (pp. 154-164). IEEE. 10.1109/SIMSYM.2003.1192809

Bryman, A. (2012). *Social Research Methods* (4th ed.). Oxford University Press.

Bui, T. D., Tsai, F. M., Tseng, M. L., Tan, R. R., Yu, K. D. S., & Lim, M. K. (2021). Sustainable supply chain management towards disruption and organizational ambidexterity: A data driven analysis. *Sustainable Production and Consumption, 26*, 373–410. doi:10.1016/j.spc.2020.09.017 PMID:33015266

Burkhardt, R., Hohn, N., & Wigley, C. (2019). *Leading your organization to responsible AI.* McKinsey Analytics.

Burnard, K. J., & Bhamra, R. (2019). Challenges for organisational resilience. *Continuity & Resilience Review, 1*(1), 17–25. doi:10.1108/CRR-01-2019-0008

Busse, C., Schleper, M. C., Weilenmann, J., & Wagner, S. M. (2017). Extending the supply chain visibility boundary : Utilizing stakeholders for identifying supply chain sustainability risks. *International Journal of Physical Distribution & Logistics Management, 47*(1), 18–40. doi:10.1108/IJPDLM-02-2015-0043

Byaro, M., Nkonoki, J., & Mafwolo, G. (2023). Exploring the nexus between natural resource depletion, renewable energy use, and environmental degradation in sub-Saharan Africa. *Environmental Science and Pollution Research International, 30*(8), 19931–19945. doi:10.100711356-022-23104-7 PMID:36241835

Cabral, I., Grilo, A., & Cruz-Machado, V. (2012). A decision-making model for lean, agile, resilient and green supply chain management. *International Journal of Production Research, 50*(17), 4830–4845. doi:10.1080/00207543.2012.657970

Cagliano, R., Caniato, F., Golini, R., & Micheli, G. J. (2019). Sustainable supply chain management: An integrated literature review. *Journal of Cleaner Production, 230*, 1268–1280.

Caiado, R. G. G., Scavarda, L. F., Azevedo, B. D., de Mattos Nascimento, D. L., & Quelhas, O. L. G. (2022). Challenges and benefits of sustainable industry 4.0 for operations and supply chain management—A framework headed toward the 2030 agenda. *Sustainability (Basel), 14*(2), 830. doi:10.3390u14020830

Campbell, B. M., Vermeulen, S. J., Aggarwal, P. K., Corner-Dolloff, C., Girvetz, E., Loboguerrero, A. M., Ramirez-Villegas, J., Rosenstock, T., Sebastian, L., Thornton, P. K., & Wollenberg, E. (2016). Reducing risks to food security from climate change. *Global Food Security, 11*, 34–43. doi:10.1016/j.gfs.2016.06.002

Carayannis, E. G., Draper, J., & Bhaneja, B. (2021). Towards fusion energy in the Industry 5.0 and Society 5.0 context: Call for a global commission for urgent action on fusion energy. *Journal of the Knowledge Economy, 12*(4), 1891–1904. doi:10.100713132-020-00695-5

Cardoso, J., Sheth, A., Miller, J., Arnold, J., & Kochut, K. (2004). Quality of service for workflows and web service processes. *Journal of Web Semantics, 1*(3), 281–308.

Cervero, R., & Golub, A. (2011). Informal public transport: A global perspective. Urban Transp. Dev. World A Handb. Policy Pract., 488–518.

Challinor, A., Martre, P., Asseng, S., Thornton, P., & Ewert, F. (2014). Making the most of climate impacts ensembles. *Nature Climate Change, 4*(2), 77–80. doi:10.1038/nclimate2117

Chang, S. E., & Chen, Y. (2020). When blockchain meets supply chain: A systematic literature review on current development and potential applications. *IEEE Access : Practical Innovations, Open Solutions*, *8*, 62478–62494. doi:10.1109/ACCESS.2020.2983601

Chavez, R., Yu, W., Jacobs, M. A., & Feng, M. (2017). Data-driven supply chains, manufacturing capability and customer satisfaction. *Production Planning and Control*, *28*(11–12), 906–918. doi:10.1080/09537287.2017.1336788

Chavez, R., Yu, W., Sadiq Jajja, M. S., Lecuna, A., & Fynes, B. (2020). Can entrepreneurial orientation improve sustainable development through leveraging internal lean practices? *Business Strategy and the Environment*, *29*(6), 2211–2225. doi:10.1002/bse.2496

Chavhan, S., Gupta, D., Chandana, B. N., Khanna, A., & Rodrigues, J. J. P. C. (2020). IoT-Based Context-Aware Intelligent Public Transport System in a Metropolitan Area. *IEEE Internet of Things Journal*, *7*(7), 6023–6034. doi:10.1109/JIOT.2019.2955102

Chekima, B., Wafa, S. A. W. S. K., Igau, O. A., Chekima, S., & Sondoh, S. L. Jr. (2016). Examining green consumerism motivational drivers: Does premium price and demographics matter to green purchasing? *Journal of Cleaner Production*, *112*, 3436–3450. doi:10.1016/j.jclepro.2015.09.102

Chen, A., Hsieh, C. Y., & Wee, H. M. (2016). A resilient global supplier selection strategy—A case study of an automotive company. *International Journal of Advanced Manufacturing Technology*, *87*(5-8), 1475–1490. doi:10.100700170-014-6567-z

Chen, D. Q., Preston, D. S., & Swink, M. (2015). How the use of big data analytics affects value creation in supply chain management. *Journal of Management Information Systems*, *32*(4), 4–39. doi:10.1080/07421222.2015.1138364

Cheng, H., Xue, L., Wang, P., Zeng, P., & Yu, H. (2017). Ontology-based web service integration for flexible manufacturing systems. In *15th Int. Conf. on Ind. Inf.* (pp. 351–356). IEEE.

Cheng, G., Guo, D., Shi, J., & Qin, Y. (2019). Smart City-Wide Package Distribution Using Crowdsourced Public Transportation Systems. *IEEE Internet of Things Journal*, *6*(5), 7584–7594. doi:10.1109/JIOT.2019.2901116

Chen, H., Yan, X., Liu, X., & Ma, T. (2022). Exploring the operational performance discrepancies between online ridesplitting and carpooling transportation modes based on DiDi data. *Transportation*, 1–36.

Chen, I. J., & Paulraj, A. (2017). Understanding supply chain social sustainability: Progress and prospects. *The Journal of Supply Chain Management*, *53*(4), 3–21.

Chen, J. Y. (2022). Responsible sourcing and supply chain traceability. *International Journal of Production Economics*, *248*, 108462. doi:10.1016/j.ijpe.2022.108462

Chen, L., Lee, H. L., & Tang, C. S. (2022). Supply chain fairness. *Production and Operations Management*, *31*(12), 4304–4318. doi:10.1111/poms.13849

Chen, X., & Ji, Z. (2020). Networked coordination to facilitate secondhand electronics recycling and exchange: a case study on aihuishou. In *Business Innovation with New ICT in the Asia-Pacific: Case Studies* (pp. 327–347). Springer Nature Singapore.

Chen, Y.-T., & Cao, Z.-C. (2020). An Investigation on a Closed-Loop Supply Chain of Product Recycling Using a Multi-Agent and Priority Based Genetic Algorithm Approach. *Mathematics*, *8*(6), 888. doi:10.3390/math8060888

Chien, F., Chau, K. Y., & Sadiq, M. (2023). Impact of climate mitigation technology and natural resource management on climate change in China. *Resources Policy*, *81*, 103367. doi:10.1016/j.resourpol.2023.103367

Choi, S., Kim, B. H., & Noh, S. D. (2015). A diagnosis and evaluation method for strategic planning and systematic design of a virtual factory in smart manufacturing systems. *International Journal of Precision Engineering and Manufacturing, 16*(6), 1107–1115. doi:10.100712541-015-0143-9

Choudhary, D., Shankar, R., & Choudhary, A. (2019). An Integrated Approach for Modeling Sustainability Risks in Freight Transportation Systems. *Risk Analysis, 40*(4), 858–883. doi:10.1111/risa.13435 PMID:31889333

Christopher, M. (2016). *Logistics & supply chain management* (5th ed.). Pearson.

Christopher, M., & Peck, H. (2018). *Marketing logistics: Principles and practice* (5th ed.). Routledge.

Chun Wu, Y. (2003). Lean manufacturing: A perspective of lean suppliers. *International Journal of Operations & Production Management, 23*(11), 1349–1376. doi:10.1108/01443570310501880

Ciortea, A., Mayer, S., & Michahelles, F. (2018). Repurposing Manufacturing Lines on the Fly with Multi-agent Systems for the Web of Things. In *Proc. of the 17th Int. Conf. on Autonomous Agents and Multi-Agent Systems* (pp. 813–822). ACM.

Clark, L. (2013). Tesco Uses Supply Chain Analytics to Save £100 m a Year. *Computer Weekly.* https://www.computerweekly.com/news/2240182951/Tesco-uses-supply-chain-analytics-to-save-10-m-a-year

Cole, R., Stevenson, M., & Aitken, J. (2019). Blockchain technology: Implications for operations and supply chain management. *Supply Chain Management, 24*(4), 469–483. doi:10.1108/SCM-09-2018-0309

Colitti, W., Steenhaut, K., & Caro, N. De. (2011). *Integrating Wireless Sensor Networks with the Web.* Extending the Internet to Low power and Lossy Networks (IP+SN).

Collodi, J., & M'Cormack, F. (2009). Population growth, environment and food security: What does the future hold. *Horizon: Future Issues for Development.*

Colucci, S., Di Noia, T., Pinto, A., Ruta, M., Ragone, A., & Tinelli, E. (2007). A Nonmonotonic Approach to Semantic Matchmaking and Request Refinement in E-Marketplaces. *International Journal of Electronic Commerce, 12*(2), 127–154.

Conceição, P., Fuentes-Nieva, R., Horn-Phathanothai, L., & Ngororano, A. (2011). Food security and human development in Africa: Strategic considerations and directions for further research. *African Development Review, 23*(2), 237–246. doi:10.1111/j.1467-8268.2011.00283.x

Cooke, J. A. (2013). Three trends to watch in 2013. *Perspective, Supply chain Quarterly, 1,* 11.

Correll, N., Bekris, K. E., Berenson, D., Brock, O., Causo, A., Hauser, K., Okada, K., Rodriguez, A., Romano, J. M., & Wurman, P. R. (2018). Analysis and Observations From The First Amazon Picking Challenge. *IEEE Transactions on Automation Science and Engineering, 1*(15), 172–188. doi:10.1109/TASE.2016.2600527

Cory, A., Henson, J., Pschorr, K., Sheth, A. P., & Thirunarayan, K. (2009). SemSOS: Semantic sensor Observation Service. *Proceedings of the International Symposium on Collaborative Technologies and Systems.*

Courbis, C., & Finkelstein, A. (2005). Weaving Aspects into Web Service Orchestrations. *Proceeding of International Conference of Web Services (ICWS '05).*

Cousins, P. D., Lamming, R. C., & Bowen, F. (2004). The role of risk in environment-related supplier initiatives. *International Journal of Operations & Production Management, 24*(6), 554–565. doi:10.1108/01443570410538104

Cox, A. (1999). Power, value and supply chain management. *Supply Chain Management, 4*(4), 167–175. doi:10.1108/13598549910284480

Coyle, D. (2023). *Cogs and Monsters: What Economics Is, and What It Should Be, United State of America*. Princeton University Press.

Crowe, M. A., Hostens, M., & Opsomer, G. (2018). Gestion de la reproduction chez les vaches laitières - L'avenir. *Irish Veterinary Journal*, *71*(1).

Dabone, C., Mbagwu, I., Muray, M., Ubangha, L., Kohoun, B., Etowa, E., & Etowa, J. (2021). Global food insecurity and African, Caribbean, and Black (ACB) populations during the COVID-19 pandemic: A rapid review. *Journal of Racial and Ethnic Health Disparities*, 1–16. PMID:33559109

Dahane, A., Benameur, R., Kechar, B., & Benyamina, A. (2020, October). An IoT based smart farming system using machine learning. In *2020 International symposium on networks, computers and communications (ISNCC)* (pp. 1-6). IEEE. 10.1109/ISNCC49221.2020.9297341

Dailymail. (2020) *Fifth of CO2 emissions come from supply chain for large companies*. Daily Mail Online. https://www.dailymail.co.uk/sciencetech/article-8705619/Fifth-CO2-emissions-come-supply-chain-large-companies.html

Dangelico, R. M., & Pujari, D. (2018). Mainstreaming green product innovation: Why and how companies integrate environmental sustainability. *Journal of Business Ethics*, *150*(2), 423–448.

Davenport, T., & O'Dwyer, J. (2011). Tap into the Power of Analytics. *Supply Chain Quarterly*, *4*, 28-31.

Davenport, T. (2014). *Big data at work: dispelling the myths, uncovering the opportunities*. Harvard Business Review Press. doi:10.15358/9783800648153

Davenport, T. H. (2006). *Competing on analytics, Harvard Business Review*. Harvard Business Press.

Davenport, T. H. (2018). *The AI advantage: How to put the artificial intelligence revolution to work*. MIT Press. doi:10.7551/mitpress/11781.001.0001

Davenport, T. H., Barth, P., & Bean, R. (2012). How Big Data is different. *MIT Sloan Management Review*, (Fall), 22–24.

Davenport, T. H., & Dyche, J. (2013). *Big Data in Big Companies. Thomas H.* Davenport and SAS Institute Inc.

Davenport, T. H., & Harris, J. G. (2007). *Competing on analytics – the new science of winning*. Harvard Business School Publishing Corporation.

Davenport, T. H., Harris, J. G., & Morison, R. (2010). *Analytics at work – smart decisions, better results*. Harvard Business Press.

Davenport, T. H., & Prusak, L. (2000). *Working knowledge: how organizations manage what they know*. Harvard Business Press.

Davenport, T. H., & Ronanki, R. (2018). Artificial intelligence for the real world. *Harvard Business Review*, *96*(1), 108–116.

Davis-Sramek, B., Germain, R., & Iyer, K. (2010). Supply Chain Technology: The Role of Environment in Predicting Performance. *Journal of the Academy of Marketing Science*, *38*(1), 42–55. doi:10.100711747-009-0137-1

de Carvalho, M. I., Relvas, S., & Barbosa-Póvoa, A. P. (2022). A roadmap for sustainability performance assessment in the context of Agri-Food Supply Chain. *Sustainable Production and Consumption*, *34*, 565–585. doi:10.1016/j.spc.2022.10.001

De Virgilio, R., Di Sciascio, E., Ruta, M., Scioscia, F., & Torlone, R. (2011). Semantic-based rfid data management. In *Unique Radio Innovation for the 21st Century* (pp. 111–141). Springer.

Debauche, O., Mahmoudi, S., & Guttadauria, A. (2022). A new edge computing architecture for IoT and multimedia data management. *Information (Basel), 13*(2), 89. doi:10.3390/info13020089

Decker, C., Berchtold, M. L., Chaves, W. F., Beigl, M., Roehr, D., & Riedel, T. (2008). Cost benefit model for smart items in the supply chain. In: The Internet of Things, 155–172. Springer. doi:10.1007/978-3-540-78731-0_10

DEFRA. (2019, March 21). *Department for Environment, Food & Rural Affairs*. GOV.UK. https://www.gov.uk/government/organisations/department-for-environment-food-rural-affairs

Dekker, R., Fleischmann, M., Inderfurth, K., & van Wassenhove, L. N. (2019). *Reverse logistics: Quantitative models for closed-loop supply chains* (2nd ed.). Springer.

Deloitte & MHI. (2014). *The 2014 MHI Annual Industry Report – Innovation the driven supply chain*. MHI.

Deloitte & MHI. (2016). *The 2016 MHI Annual Industry Report – Accelerating change: How innovation is driving digital, always-on Supply Chains*. MHI.

Demchenko, Y., De Laat, C., & Membrey, P. (2014), Defining architecture components of the Big Data Ecosystem, in: *International Conference on Collaboration Technologies and Systems (CTS)*. IEEE. 10.1109/CTS.2014.6867550

Demestichas, K., Peppes, N., & Alexakis, T. (2020). Survey on security threats in agricultural IoT and smart farming. *Sensors (Basel), 20*(22), 6458. doi:10.339020226458 PMID:33198160

Demirkan, H., & Delen, D. (2012). Levering the Capabilities of Service-oriented Decision Support Systems: Putting Analytics and Big Data in Cloud. *Decision Support Systems, 55*(1), 412–421. doi:10.1016/j.dss.2012.05.048

Denga, E. M., & Rakshit, S. (2022). Supply Chain Logistics Risk Mitigation: Impact of the COVID-19 Pandemic. In Global Risk and Contingency Management Research in Times of Crisis (pp. 99-121). IGI Global.

Dev, N. K., Shankar, R., Gupta, R., & Dong, J. (2018). Multi-criteria evaluation of real-time key performance indicators of supply chain with consideration of big data architecture. *Computers & Industrial Engineering, 128*, 1076–1087. doi:10.1016/j.cie.2018.04.012

Dey, P. K., Malesios, C., De, D., Chowdhury, S., & Abdelaziz, F. B. (2019). Could lean practices and process innovation enhance supply chain sustainability of small and medium-sized enterprises? *Business Strategy and the Environment, 28*(4), 582–598. doi:10.1002/bse.2266

Dhoopar, A., Sihag, P., Kumar, A., & Suhag, A. K. (2022). Organizational resilience and employee performance in COVID-19 pandemic: The mediating effect of emotional intelligence. *The International Journal of Organizational Analysis, 30*(1), 130–155. doi:10.1108/IJOA-06-2020-2261

Di Vaio, A., & Varriale, L. (2020). Blockchain technology in supply chain management for sustainable performance: Evidence from the airport industry. *International Journal of Information Management, 52*, 102014. doi:10.1016/j.ijinfomgt.2019.09.010

Dietrich, B., Plachy, E. C., & Norton, M. F. (2014). *Analytics across the enterprise: How IBM realize business value from big data and analytics*. IBM Press Books.

Dietrich, B., Plachy, E. C., & Norton, M. F. (2014). *Analytics across the enterprise: How IBM realizes business value from big data and analytics*. IBM Press Books.

Difrancesco, R. M., Meena, P., & Kumar, G. (2022). How blockchain technology improves sustainable supply chain processes: a practical guide. *Operations Management Research*. doi:10.1007/s12063-022-00343-y

Dong, Z., Liang, W., Liang, Y., Gao, W., & Lu, Y. (2022). Blockchained supply chain management based on IoT tracking and machine learning. *EURASIP Journal on Wireless Communications and Networking*, *2022*(1), 1–19. doi:10.118613638-022-02209-0 PMID:36597502

Dora, M., Kumar, M., & Gellynck, X. (2016). Determinants and barriers to lean implementation in food-processing SMEs–a multiple case analysis. *Production Planning and Control*, *27*(1), 1–23. doi:10.1080/09537287.2015.1050477

Duan, Y., Edwards, J. S., & Dwivedi, Y. K. (2019). Artificial intelligence for decision making in the era of Big Data–evolution, challenges and research agenda. *International Journal of Information Management*, *48*, 63–71. doi:10.1016/j.ijinfomgt.2019.01.021

Dubey, R., Gunasekaran, A., & Childe, S. J. (2018a). Big data analytics capability in supply chain agility: The moderating effect of organizational flexibility. *Management Decision*.

Dubey, R., Gunasekaran, A., Childe, S. J., Blome, C., Papadopoulos, T., & Luo, Z. (2019). Sustainable supply chain management: Framework and further research directions. *Journal of Business Ethics*, *156*(2), 299–326.

Dubey, R., Gunasekaran, A., Childe, S. J., Fosso Wamba, S., Roubaud, D., & Foropon, C. (2019a). Empirical investigation of data analytics capability and organizational flexibility as complements to supply chain resilience. *International Journal of Production Research*, 1–19.

Dubey, R., Gunasekaran, A., Childe, S. J., Luo, Z., Wamba, S. F., Roubaud, D., & Foropon, C. (2018b). Examining the role of big data and predictive analytics on collaborative performance in context to sustainable consumption and production behaviour. *Journal of Cleaner Production*, *196*, 1508–1521. doi:10.1016/j.jclepro.2018.06.097

Dubey, R., Gunasekaran, A., Childe, S. J., Roubaud, D., Wamba, S. F., Giannakis, M., & Foropon, C. (2019b). Big data analytics and organizational culture as complements to swift trust and collaborative performance in the humanitarian supply chain. *International Journal of Production Economics*, *210*, 120–136. doi:10.1016/j.ijpe.2019.01.023

Dubey, R., Gunasekaran, A., Childe, S. J., Wamba, S. F., & Papadopoulos, T. (2016). The impact of big data on world-class sustainable manufacturing. *International Journal of Advanced Manufacturing Technology*, *84*(1–4), 631–645. doi:10.100700170-015-7674-1

Durand, A., Harms, L., Hoogendoorn-lanser, S., & Zijlstra, T. (2018). Mobility-as-a-Service and changes in travel preferences and travel behaviour : a literature review. *KiM| Netherlands Inst. Transp. Policy Anal.*

Dwivedi, Y. K., Hughes, L., Ismagilova, E., Aarts, G., Coombs, C., Crick, T., Duan, Y., Dwivedi, R., Edwards, J., Eirug, A., Galanos, V., Ilavarasan, P. V., Janssen, M., Jones, P., Kar, A. K., Kizgin, H., Kronemann, B., Lal, B., Lucini, B., & Williams, M. (2021). Artificial Intelligence (Ai): Multidisciplinary Perspectives On Emerging Challenges, Opportunities, and Agenda For Research, Practice And Policy. *International Journal of Information Management*, *101994*(57), 101994. doi:10.1016/j.ijinfomgt.2019.08.002

Edreira, J. I. R., Guilpart, N., Sadras, V., Cassman, K. G., van Ittersum, M. K., Schils, R. L., & Grassini, P. (2018). Water productivity of rainfed maize and wheat: A local to global perspective. *Agricultural and Forest Meteorology*, *259*, 364–373. doi:10.1016/j.agrformet.2018.05.019 PMID:30224833

Ekinci, E., Mangla, S. K., Kazancoglu, Y., Sarma, P. R. S., Sezer, M. D., & Ozbiltekin-Pala, M. (2022). Resilience and complexity measurement for energy efficient global supply chains in disruptive events. *Technological Forecasting and Social Change*, *179*, 121634. doi:10.1016/j.techfore.2022.121634 PMID:35400766

El Baz, J., Cherrafi, A., Benabdellah, A. C., Zekhnini, K., Beka Be Nguema, J. N., & Derrouiche, R. (2023). Environmental Supply Chain Risk Management for Industry 4.0: A Data Mining Framework and Research Agenda. *Systems*, *11*(1), 46. doi:10.3390ystems11010046

El Ouarrak, Y., & Hmioui, A. (2023). Communication Between Supply Chain Actors: A Risk Reduction Factor in Supply Chains. *Lecture Notes in Networks and Systems*, 695–703. doi:10.1007/978-981-99-3043-2_56

Esmaeilian, B., Sarkis, J., Lewis, K., & Behdad, S. (2020). Blockchain for the future of sustainable supply chain management in Industry 4.0. *Resources, Conservation and Recycling*, *163*, 105064. doi:10.1016/j.resconrec.2020.105064

Esper, T. L. (2022). In Artificial Intelligence (Ai) We Trust: A Qualitative Investigation Of Ai Technology Acceptance. *Journal of Business Logistics*, *3*(43), 388–412. doi:10.1111/jbl.12301

Fang, C., Liu, X., Pardalos, P. M., & Pei, J. (2016). Optimization for a three-stage production system in the Internet of Things: Procurement, production and product recovery, and acquisition. *International Journal of Advanced Manufacturing Technology*, *83*(5-8), 689–710. doi:10.100700170-015-7593-1

Fang, J., & Ma, A. (2020). IoT application modules placement and dynamic task processing in edge-cloud computing. *IEEE Internet of Things Journal*, *8*(6), 12771–12781.

Fang, J., Qu, T., Li, Z. G., Xu, G., & Huang, G. Q. (2013). Agent-based gateway operating system for RFID-enabled ubiquitous manufacturing enterprise. *Robotics and Computer-integrated Manufacturing*, *29*(4), 222–231. doi:10.1016/j.rcim.2013.01.001

Farooq, M. S., Riaz, S., Abid, A., Umer, T., & Zikria, Y. B. (2020). Role of IoT technology in agriculture: A systematic literature review. *Electronics (Basel)*, *9*(2), 319. doi:10.3390/electronics9020319

Farooque, M., Zhang, A., Liu, Y., & Hartley, J. L. (2022). Circular supply chain management: Performance outcomes and the role of eco-industrial parks in China. *Transportation Research Part E, Logistics and Transportation Review*, *157*, 102596. doi:10.1016/j.tre.2021.102596

Fawcett, S. E., Magnan, G. M., & McCarter, M. W. (2008). Benefits, barriers, and bridges to effective supply chain management. *Supply Chain Management*, *13*(1), 35–48. doi:10.1108/13598540810850300

Fawcett, S. E., & Waller, M. A. (2014). Supply chain game changers—mega, nano, and virtual trends—and forces that impede supply chain design (ie, building a winning team). *Journal of Business Logistics*, *35*(3), 157–164. doi:10.1111/jbl.12058

Feng, Y., Lai, K. H., & Zhu, Q. (2022). Green supply chain innovation: Emergence, adoption, and challenges. *International Journal of Production Economics*, *248*, 108497. doi:10.1016/j.ijpe.2022.108497

Ferdows, K., & de Meyer, A. (2018). Lasting improvements in manufacturing performance: In search of a new theory. *Journal of Operations Management*, *59*, 1–6.

Field, C. B. (2014). Impacts, adaptation and vulnerability: Working Group II contribution to the fifth assessment report of the Intergovernmental Panel on Climate Change. *Climatic Change*.

Foley, J. A., Ramankutty, N., Brauman, K. A., Cassidy, E. S., Gerber, J. S., Johnston, M., Mueller, N. D., O'Connell, C., Ray, D. K., West, P. C., Balzer, C., Bennett, E. M., Carpenter, S. R., Hill, J., Monfreda, C., Polasky, S., Rockström, J., Sheehan, J., Siebert, S., & Zaks, D. P. (2011). Solutions for a cultivated planet. *Nature*, *478*(7369), 337–342. doi:10.1038/nature10452 PMID:21993620

Food and Agriculture Organization of the United Nations (FAO). (2018). *The future of food and agriculture: Alternative pathways to 2050*. FAO. https://www.fao.org/3/a-i6583e.pdf

Foote, B. (2021). *Ford Blockchain Initiative Aims to Identify Unethically Sourced Materials*. Ford Authority. https://fordauthority.com/2021/12/ford-blockchain-initiative-aims-to-identify-unethically-sourced-materials/

Forslund, H., & Jonsson, P. (2007). The Impact of Forecast Information Quality on Supply Chain Performance. *International Journal of Operations & Production Management*, *27*(1), 90–107. doi:10.1108/01443570710714556

Forward, S. (2004). The Prediction of Travel Behaviour Using the Theory of Planned Behaviour. *Traffic Transp. Psychol*, (January), 481–492. doi:10.1016/B978-008043925-9/50045-1

Fosso Wamba, S., Gunasekaran, A., Papadopoulos, T., & Ngai, E. (2018). Big data analytics in logistics and supply chain management. *International Journal of Logistics Management*, *29*(2), 478–484. doi:10.1108/IJLM-02-2018-0026

Fraga-Lamas, P., Lopes, S. I., & Fernández-Caramés, T. M. (2021). Green IoT and edge AI as key technological enablers for a sustainable digital transition towards a smart circular economy: An industry 5.0 use case. *Sensors (Basel)*, *21*(17), 5745. doi:10.339021175745 PMID:34502637

Francis, O. (1997). *G.P.R.T.U National Secretariat-Accra.* Kwame Nkrumah University.

Free, C., & Hecimovic, A. (2021). Global supply chains after COVID-19: The end of the road for neoliberal globalisation? *Accounting, Auditing & Accountability Journal*, *34*(1), 58–84. doi:10.1108/AAAJ-06-2020-4634

Frempong, M. A., & Hiran, K. K. (2014). Awareness and Understanding of Computer Forensics in the Ghana Legal System. *International Journal of Computer Applications*, *975*, 8887.

Frieden, R. (2019). Two-Sided Internet Markets and the Need to Assess Both Upstream and Downstream Impacts. American University Law Review, 68(3).

Fróna, D., Szenderák, J., & Harangi-Rákos, M. (2019). The challenge of feeding the world. *Sustainability (Basel)*, *11*(20), 5816. doi:10.3390u11205816

Frynas, J. G., Mol, M. J., & Mellahi, K. (2018). Management innovation made in China: Haier's Rendanheyi. *California Management Review*, *61*(1), 71–93. doi:10.1177/0008125618790244

Gadi, T., Benslimane, R. (2000), de Segmentation hiérarchique floue Fuzzy hierarchical segmentation. *Traitement du Signal 2000, 17*, 59-67.

Gande, A. (2020). Emerging ai & ml-based technologies & applications in supply chain management (scm): Future prospects. *International Journal of Marketing and Technology*, *10*(12), 1–6.

García Márquez, F. P., Papaelias, M., & Marini, S. (2022). Artificial Intelligence in Marine Science and Engineering. *Journal of Marine Science and Engineering*, *10*(6), 711. doi:10.3390/jmse10060711

Garg, R., Kiwelekar, A. W., & Netak, L. D. (2021). Logistics and Freight Transportation Management: An NLP based Approach for Shipment Tracking. *Pertanika Journal of Science & Technology*, *29*(4). doi:10.47836/pjst.29.4.28

Gaustad, G., Krystofik, M., Bustamante, M., & Badami, K. (2018). Circular economy strategies for mitigating critical material supply issues. *Resources, Conservation and Recycling*, *135*, 24–33. doi:10.1016/j.resconrec.2017.08.002

Gazis, A. (2021). What is iot? the internet of things explained. *Academia Letters, 2.*

Ge, H., Gray, R., & Nolan, J. (2015). Agricultural supply chain optimization and complexity: A comparison of analytic vs simulated solutions and policies. *International Journal of Production Economics*, *159*, 208–220. doi:10.1016/j.ijpe.2014.09.023

George, R. V., Harsh, H. O., Ray, P., & Babu, A. K. (2019). Food quality traceability prototype for restaurants using blockchain and food quality data index. *Journal of Cleaner Production*, *240*, 118021. doi:10.1016/j.jclepro.2019.118021

Gereffi, G. (1999). International trade and industrial upgrading in the apparel commodity chain. *Journal of International Economics, 48*(1), 37–70. doi:10.1016/S0022-1996(98)00075-0

Ghabak, V., & Seetharaman, A. (2023, March). Integration of Machine Learning in Agile Supply Chain Management. In *2023 15th International Conference on Computer and Automation Engineering (ICCAE)* (pp. 6-12). IEEE. 10.1109/ICCAE56788.2023.10111340

Ghadimi, P., Wang, C., & Lim, M. K. (2019). Sustainable supply chain modeling and analysis: Past debate, present problems and future challenges. *Resources, Conservation and Recycling, 140*, 72–84. doi:10.1016/j.resconrec.2018.09.005

Gia, T. N., Qingqing, L., Queralta, J. P., Zou, Z., Tenhunen, H., &Westerlund, T. (2019, September). Edge AI in smart farming IoT: CNNs at the edge and fog computing with LoRa. In *2019 IEEE AFRICON* (pp. 1-6). IEEE.

Giannakis, M., & Louis, M. (2016). A multi-agent based system with big data processing for enhanced supply chain agility. *Journal of Enterprise Information Management, 29*(5), 706–727. doi:10.1108/JEIM-06-2015-0050

Giannakis, M., & Papadopoulos, T. (2016). Supply chain sustainability : A risk management approach. *International Journal of Production Economics, 171*, 455–470. doi:10.1016/j.ijpe.2015.06.032

Gilbert, D. U., & Huber, K. (2023 Forthcoming). *Labour rights in global supply chains. Corporate Responsibility, Second Edi-tion*. Cambridge University Press.

Giunchiglia, F., Shvaiko, P., & Yatskevich, M. (2004). S-Match: an algorithm and an implementation of semantic matching. *The 1st European Semantic Web Symposium (ESWS), 3053*, 61-75.

Godde, C. M., Boone, R. B., Ash, A. J., Waha, K., Sloat, L. L., Thornton, P. K., & Herrero, M. (2020). Global rangeland production systems and livelihoods at threat under climate change and variability. *Environmental Research Letters, 15*(4), 044021. doi:10.1088/1748-9326/ab7395

Golub, A., Balassiano, R., Araújo, A., & Ferreira, E. (2009). Regulation of the informal transport sector in Rio de Janeiro, Brazil: Welfare impacts and policy analysis. *Transportation, 36*(5), 601–616. doi:10.100711116-009-9215-y

Gouda, S. K., & Saranga, H. (2018). Sustainable supply chains for supply chain sustainability: Impact of sustainability efforts on supply chain risk. *International Journal of Production Research, 56*(17), 5820–5835. doi:10.1080/00207543.2018.1456695

Govindan, K. (2018). Sustainable consumption and production in the food supply chain: A conceptual framework. *International Journal of Production Economics, 195*, 419–431. doi:10.1016/j.ijpe.2017.03.003

Govindan, K., Cheng, T. C. E., Mishra, N., & Shukla, N. (2018). Big data analytics and application for logistics and supply chain management. *Transportation Research Part E, Logistics and Transportation Review, 114*, 343–349. doi:10.1016/j.tre.2018.03.011

Govindan, K., Fattahi, M., Keyvanshokooh, E., & Diabat, A. (2017). Supply chain network design under uncertainty: A comprehensive review and future research directions. *European Journal of Operational Research, 263*(1), 108–141. doi:10.1016/j.ejor.2017.04.009

Grant, D. B., Wong, C. Y., & Trautrims, A. (2017). *Sustainable logistics and supply chain management: principles and practices for sustainable operations and management*. Kogan Page Publishers.

Gružauskas, V., & Pačėsaitė, K. (2021). Expert system for the freight coordination based on artificial intelligence. In *14th international scientific-methodical-practical conference on sustainable regional development: Economics, management, law and technology opportunities 2021 Klaipeda, Lithuania*. Hungarian University of Agriculture and Life Science.

Gubbi, J., Buyya, R., Marusic, S., & Palaniswami, M. (2013). Internet of Things (IoT): A vision, architectural elements, and future directions. *Future Generation Computer Systems*, *29*(7), 1645–1660.

Guest, G., Namey, E. E., & Mitchell, M. L. (2013). Collecting qualitative data: A field manual for applied research. *Sage (Atlanta, Ga.)*. doi:10.4135/9781506374680

Guha, S., Harrigan, P., & Soutar, G. (2018). Linking social media to customer relationship management (CRM): A qualitative study on SMEs. *Journal of Small Business and Entrepreneurship*, *30*(3), 193–214. doi:10.1080/08276331.2017.1399628

Gu, M., Yang, L., & Huo, B. (2021). The impact of information technology usage on supply chain resilience and performance: An ambidexterous view. *International Journal of Production Economics*, *232*, 107956. doi:10.1016/j.ijpe.2020.107956 PMID:33071462

Gunasekaran, A., Papadopoulos, T., Dubey, R., Wamba, S. F., Childe, S. J., Hazen, B., & Akter, S. (2017). Big data and predictive analytics for supply chain and organizational performance. *Journal of Business Research*, *70*, 308–317. doi:10.1016/j.jbusres.2016.08.004

Gupta. (2022). Management of Agriculture Supply Chain. *Food Logistics*. www.foodlogistics.com. https://www.foodlogistics.com/sustainability/agriculture/article/22159660/allied-market-research-management-of-agriculture-supply-chain

Gupta, D., Gujre, N., Singha, S., & Mitra, S. (2022). Role of existing and emerging technologies in advancing climate-smart agriculture through modeling: A review. *Ecological Informatics*, *71*, 101805. doi:10.1016/j.ecoinf.2022.101805

Gupta, M., Abdelsalam, M., Khorsandroo, S., & Mittal, S. (2020). Security and privacy in smart farming: Challenges and opportunities. *IEEE Access : Practical Innovations, Open Solutions*, *8*, 34564–34584. doi:10.1109/ACCESS.2020.2975142

Gurtu, A., & Johny, J. (2019). Potential of blockchain technology in supply chain management: A literature review. *International Journal of Physical Distribution & Logistics Management*, *49*(9), 881–900. doi:10.1108/IJPDLM-11-2018-0371

Haipeter, T., Helfen, M., Kirsch, A., Rosenbohm, S., & Üyük, C. (2021). Industrial relations at centre stage: Efficiency, equity and voice in the governance of global labour standards. *Industrielle Beziehungen. Zeitschrift für Arbeit. Organisation und Management*, *28*(2), 148–171.

Hald, K. S., & Kinra, A. (2019). How the blockchain enables and constrains supply chain performance. *International Journal of Physical Distribution & Logistics Management*, *49*(4), 376–397. doi:10.1108/IJPDLM-02-2019-0063

Handfield, R. (2006). *Supply Market Intelligence: A Managerial Handbook for Building Sourcing Strategies*. Taylor & Francis. doi:10.4324/9780203339527

Handfield, R., & Nichols, E. Jr. (2004). Key Issues in Global Supply Base Management. *Industrial Marketing Management*, *33*(1), 29–35. doi:10.1016/j.indmarman.2003.08.007

Hashim, M., Nazam, M., Zia-Ur-Rehman, M., Abrar, M., Baig, S. A., Nazim, M., & Hussain, Z. (2021). Modeling Supply Chain Sustainability-Related Risks and Vulnerability : Insights from the Textile Sector of Pakistan. *AUTEX Research Journal*, *22*(1), 123–134. doi:10.2478/aut-2021-0008

Hazen, B. T., Boone, C. A., Ezell, J. D., & Jones-Farmer, L. A. (2014). Data quality for data science, predictive analytics, and big data in supply chain management: An introduction to the problem and suggestions for research and applications. *International Journal of Production Economics*, *154*, 72–80. doi:10.1016/j.ijpe.2014.04.018

Hazen, B. T., Skipper, J. B., Ezell, J. D., & Boone, C. A. (2016). Big Data and predictive analytics for supply chain sustainability: A theory-driven research agenda. *Computers & Industrial Engineering*, *101*, 592–598. doi:10.1016/j.cie.2016.06.030

Hazra, A., Adhikari, M., Amgoth, T., & Srirama, S. N. (2021). A Comprehensive Survey on Interoperability for IIoT: Taxonomy, Standards, and Future Directions. *ACM Computing Survey, 55*(1).

Heal, G., & Millner, A. (2014). Reflections: Uncertainty and decision making in climate change economics. *Review of Environmental Economics and Policy*, *8*(1), 120–137. doi:10.1093/reep/ret023

Herrero, M., Addison, J., Bedelian, C., Carabine, E., Havlík, P., Henderson, B., Van De Steeg, S. J., & Thornton, P. K. (2016). Climate change and pastoralism: Impacts, consequences and adaptation. *Revue Scientifique et Technique (International Office of Epizootics)*, *35*(2), 417–433. doi:10.20506/rst.35.2.2533 PMID:27917982

Hessel, V. (2015). *Smart Mobility – A tool to achieve sustainable cities.* IOP Science.

Hessel, V. (2015). *Smart Mobility-A tool to achieve sustainable cities.*

Hickel, J. (2019). The contradiction of the sustainable development goals: Growth versus ecology on a finite planet. *Sustainable Development (Bradford)*, *27*(5), 873–884. doi:10.1002d.1947

Hiran, K. K., & Doshi, R. (2014). *The Proliferation of Smart Devices on Mobile Cloud Computing*. Lambert Academic Publishing.

Hmioui, A., Bentalha, B., & Alla, L. (2020). Service supply chain: A prospective analysis of sustainable management for global performance. In *2020 IEEE 13th International Colloquium of Logistics and Supply Chain Management (LOGISTIQUA)* (pp. 1-7). IEEE. 10.1109/LOGISTIQUA49782.2020.9353940

Hofmann, E., Sternberg, H., Chen, H., Pflaum, A., & Prockl, G. (2019). Supply chain management and Industry 4.0: Conducting research in the digital age. *International Journal of Physical Distribution & Logistics Management*, *49*(10), 945–955. doi:10.1108/IJPDLM-11-2019-399

Hofmann, H., Busse, C., Bode, C., & Henke, M. (2013). Sustainability-Related Supply Chain Risks : Conceptualization and Management. *Business Strategy and the Environment*, *23*(3), 160–172. doi:10.1002/bse.1778

Holmberg, J., & Sandbrook, R. (2019). Sustainable development: what is to be done? In *Policies for a small planet* (pp. 19–38). Routledge. doi:10.4324/9780429200465-1

Hsieh, T. Y., Lu, S. T., & Tzeng, G. H. (2004). Fuzzy MCDM approach for planning and design tenders selection in public office buildings. *International Journal of Project Management*, *22*(7), 573–584. doi:10.1016/j.ijproman.2004.01.002

Hsu, C.-H., Yu, R.-Y., Chang, A.-Y., Chung, W.-H., & Liu, W.-L. (2021). Resilience-Enhancing Solution to Mitigate Risk for Sustainable Supply Chain—An Empirical Study of Elevator Manufacturing. *Processes (Basel, Switzerland)*, *9*(4), 596. doi:10.3390/pr9040596

Hsu, C.-H., Yu, R.-Y., Chang, A.-Y., Liu, W.-L., & Sun, A.-C. (2022). Applying Integrated QFD-MCDM Approach to Strengthen Supply Chain Agility for Mitigating Sustainable Risks. *Mathematics*, *10*(4), 552. doi:10.3390/math10040552

Huang, L., Zheng, W. (2022). Hotel Demand Forecasting: a Comprehensive Literature Review. *TR, 1*(78), 218-244. doi:10.1108/TR-07-2022-0367

Huang, M. H., & Rust, R. T. (2021). Engaged to a robot? The role of AI in service. *Journal of Service Research*, *24*(1), 30–41. doi:10.1177/1094670520902266

Hugos, M. H. (2018). *Essentials of supply chain management.* John Wiley & Sons.

Hu, W., Dong, J., Hwang, B. G., Ren, R., & Chen, Z. (2020). Hybrid optimization procedures applying for two-echelon urban underground logistics network planning: A case study of Beijing. *Computers & Industrial Engineering*, *144*, 106452. doi:10.1016/j.cie.2020.106452

IBM. (2023). *Benefits of Blockchain.* IBM. https://www.ibm.com/topics/benefits-of-blockchain

IKEA. (2021). *Climate action.* IKEA. https://www.ikea.com/gb/en/this-is-ikea/climate-environment/climate-action

Inamdar, Z.Z., Raut, R.D., Narwane, V.S., Gardas, B.B., Narkhede, B.E., & Sagnak, M., (2020). A systematic literature review with bibliometric analysis of big data analytics adoption from period 2014 to 2018. *J. Enterprise Informat. Manage.*

ISACA. (2013). *Big Data: impacts and benefits.* ISACA White Paper.

Ishikawa, A., Amagasa, M., Shiga, T., Tomizawa, G., Tatsuta, R., & Mieno, H. (1993). The max-min Delphi method and fuzzy Delphi method via fuzzy integration. *Fuzzy Sets and Systems, 55*(3), 241–253. doi:10.1016/0165-0114(93)90251-C

Issaoui, Y., Khiat, A., Haricha, K., Bahnasse, A., & Ouajji, H. (2022). An Advanced System To Enhance and Optimize Delivery Operations In A Smart Logistics Environment. *IEEE Access : Practical Innovations, Open Solutions, 10*(10), 6175–6193. doi:10.1109/ACCESS.2022.3141311

Ivanov, D., & Dolgui, A. (2020). Viability of intertwined supply networks: Extending the supply chain resilience angles towards survivability. A position paper motivated by COVID-19 outbreak. *International Journal of Production Research, 58*(10), 2904–2915. doi:10.1080/00207543.2020.1750727

Ivanov, D., & Tsipoulanidis, A. (2019). Sustainability and resilience in supply chain management. *International Journal of Production Research, 57*(3), 829–846. doi:10.1080/00207543.2018.1488086

Jabbar, M. A., Prasad, K. M., & Aluvalu, R. (2021). *Future challenges for cyber-security in a smart city environment in Indian context.*

Jabbarzadeh, A., Fahimnia, B., & Sabouhi, F. (2018). Resilient and sustainable supply chain design: Sustainability analysis under disruption risks. *International Journal of Production Research, 56*(17), 5945–5968. doi:10.1080/00207543.2018.1461950

Jakl, A., Schoffer, L., Husinsky, M., & Wagner, M. (2018). Augmented Reality for Industry 4.0: Architecture and User Experience. *Proceeding of the 11th Forum Media Technology, CER-WS*, 38-42.

Jandl, C., Nurgazina, J., Schoffer, L., Reichl, C., Wagner, M., & Moser, T. (2019). SensiTrack – A Privacy by Design Concept for Industrial IoT Applications. *Proceeding of the 24th IEEE International Conference on Emerging Technologies and Factory Automation*, 1782-1789.

Javaid, M., Haleem, A., Singh, R. P., & Suman, R. (2022). Enhancing smart farming through the applications of Agriculture 4.0 technologies. *International Journal of Intelligent Networks, 3*, 150–164. doi:10.1016/j.ijin.2022.09.004

Javed, A. R., Shahzad, F., Rehman, S., Zikria, Y. B., Razzak, I., Jalil, Z., & Xu, G. (2022). Future smart cities requirements, emerging technologies, applications, challenges, and future aspects. *Cities (London, England), 129*, 103794. doi:10.1016/j.cities.2022.103794

Jayarathna, C. P., Agdas, D., & Dawes, L. (2023). Exploring sustainable logistics practices toward a circular economy: A value creation perspective. *Business Strategy and the Environment, 32*(1), 704–720. doi:10.1002/bse.3170

Jeschke, S., Brecher, C., Meisen, T., Ozdemir, D., & Eschert, T. (2017). Industrial Internet of Things and Cyber Manufacturing Systems. In Industrial Internet of Things. Springer.

Jha, K., Sahid, K., Hassan, M., Mukhtar, S., Ghimire, A., & Thapa, S. (2021). A Review of AI for Urban Planning: Towards Building Sustainable Smart Cities. *6th International Conference on Inventive Computation Technologies (ICICT)*, (pp. 937–944). Research Gate.

Jiang, J., Li, Z., Tian, Y., & Al-Nabhan, N. (2020). A review of techniques and methods for IoT applications in collaborative cloud-fog environment. *Security and Communication Networks, 2020*, 1–15. doi:10.1155/2020/8849181

Jinru, L., Changbiao, Z., Ahmad, B., Irfan, M., & Nazir, R. (2022). How do green financing and green logistics affect the circular economy in the pandemic situation: Key mediating role of sustainable production. *Ekonomska Istrazivanja, 35*(1), 3836–3856. doi:10.1080/1331677X.2021.2004437

Jüttner, U., & Maklan, S. (2019). Supply chain resilience in the global financial crisis: An empirical study. *Supply Chain Management, 24*(2), 184–199.

Kaewkluengklom, R., Satiennam, W., Jaensirisak, S., & Satiennam, T. (2017). Influence of psychological factors on mode choice behaviours: Case study of BRT in Khon Kaen City, Thailand. *Transportation Research Procedia, 25*, 5072–5082. doi:10.1016/j.trpro.2017.05.213

Kakkar, S. (2017). How to Use Big Data And Predictive Analytics For Your Next Digital Marketing Campaign, [Online]. *The Next Scoop.* https://thenextscoop.com/big-data-predictive-analytics-digital-marketing-campaign/

Kalyani, Y., & Collier, R. (2021). A systematic survey on the role of cloud, fog, and edge computing combination in smart agriculture. *Sensors (Basel), 21*(17), 5922. doi:10.339021175922 PMID:34502813

Kamalahmadi, M., & Mellat-Parast, M. (2016). Developing a resilient supply chain through supplier flexibility and reliability assessment. *International Journal of Production Research, 54*(1), 302–321. doi:10.1080/00207543.2015.1088971

Kamble, S. S., Gunasekaran, A., & Gawankar, S. A. (2018). Sustainable Industry 4.0 framework: A systematic literature review identifying the current trends and future perspectives. *Process Safety and Environmental Protection, 117*, 408–425. doi:10.1016/j.psep.2018.05.009

Kamble, S. S., Gunasekaran, A., Kumar, V., Belhadi, A., & Foropon, C. (2021). A machine learning based approach for predicting blockchain adoption in supply Chain. *Technological Forecasting and Social Change, 163*, 120465. doi:10.1016/j.techfore.2020.120465

Kamble, S. S., Gunasekaran, A., Subramanian, N., Ghadge, A., Belhadi, A., & Venkatesh, M. (2021). Blockchain technology's impact on supply chain integration and sustainable supply chain performance: Evidence from the automotive industry. *Annals of Operations Research*, 1–26. doi:10.100710479-021-04129-6

Kamilaris, A., Kartakoullis, A., & Prenafeta-Boldú, F. X. (2017). A review on the practice of big data analysis in agriculture. *Computers and Electronics in Agriculture, 143*, 23–37. doi:10.1016/j.compag.2017.09.037

Karakostas, B. (2013). A DNS architecture for the Internet of things: A case study in transport logistics. *Procedia Computer Science*, 594–601.

Karmaker, C. L., Bari, A. M., Anam, M. Z., Ahmed, T., Ali, S. M., de Jesus Pacheco, D. A., & Moktadir, M. A. (2023). Industry 5.0 challenges for post-pandemic supply chain sustainability in an emerging economy. *International Journal of Production Economics, 258*, 108806. doi:10.1016/j.ijpe.2023.108806

Karumanchi, M. D., Sheeba, J. I., & Devaneyan, S. P. (2022). Blockchain Enabled Supply Chain using Machine Learning for Secure Cargo Tracking. *International Journal of Intelligent Systems and Applications in Engineering, 10*(4), 434–442.

Kashem, M. A., Shamsuddoha, M., Nasir, T., & Chowdhury, A. A. (2023). Supply Chain Disruption versus Optimization: A Review on Artificial Intelligence and Blockchain. *Knowledge (Beverly Hills, Calif.), 3*(1), 80–96.

Kashi B. & Carello, S. (2020). *Urban Transport Solutions For Accra.* ISSU.

Katasonov, A., Kaykova, O., Khriyenko, O., Nikitin, S., & Terziyan, V. (2008). Smart Semantic Middleware for the Internet of Things. *Proceedings of the 5th International Conference of Informatics in Control, Automation and Robotics*, 11-15.

Kearney, V., Chan, J. W., Valdes, G., Solberg, T. D., & Yom, S. S. (2018). The application of artificial intelligence in the IMRT planning process for head and neck cancer. *Oral Oncology*, *87*, 111–116. doi:10.1016/j.oraloncology.2018.10.026 PMID:30527225

Kechagias, E. P., Gayialis, S. P., Konstantakopoulos, G. D., & Papadopoulos, G. A. (2020). An application of an urban freight transportation system for reduced environmental emissions. *Systems*, *8*(4), 49. doi:10.3390ystems8040049

Keskinock, P., & Tayur, S. (2001). Quantitive analysis of Internet-enabled supply chain. *Interface*, *31*(2), 70–89.

Khan, S. A. R., Yu, Z., Rehman Khan, S. A., & Yu, Z. (2019). Introduction to supply chain management. *Strategic Supply Chain Management*, 1-22.

Khan, R. U., Salamzadeh, Y., Iqbal, Q., & Yang, S. (2022). The impact of customer relationship management and company reputation on customer loyalty: The mediating role of customer satisfaction. *Journal of Relationship Marketing*, *21*(1), 1–26. doi:10.1080/15332667.2020.1840904

Khan, R., Khan, S. U., Zaheer, R., & Khan, S. (2012). Future internet: the internet of things architecture, possible applications and key challenges. *Proceedings of the 10th International Conference on Frontiers of Information Technology (FIT '12)*, 257–260.

Kharas, H., & Zhang, C. (2014). New agenda, new narrative: What happens after 2015? *SAIS Review (Paul H. Nitze School of Advanced International Studies)*, *34*(2), 25–35. doi:10.1353ais.2014.0019

Kharlamov, A., Del Vecchio, M., & Porgrenba, G. (2021). Innovation In Entertainment Industries. *Journal of the Operational Research Society*, *5*(72), 1110-1137. doi:10.1080/01605682.2019.1705194

Kim, S., & Chae, S. (2022). Shareholder value effects of ethical sourcing: Comparing reactive and proactive initiatives. *Journal of Business Ethics*, *179*(3), 887–906. doi:10.100710551-021-04841-0

Knight, A. T., Cowling, R. M., Rouget, M., Balmford, A., Lombard, A. T., & Campbell, B. M. (2008). Knowing but not doing: Selecting priority conservation areas and the research–implementation gap. *Conservation Biology*, *22*(3), 610–617. doi:10.1111/j.1523-1739.2008.00914.x PMID:18477033

Koh, L., Orzes, G., & Jia, F. J. (2019). The fourth industrial revolution (Industry 4.0): technologies disruption on operations and supply chain management. *International Journal of Operations & Production Management*, *39*(6/7/8), 817-828.

Kohli, R., & Grover, V. (2008). Business Value of IT: An Essay on Expanding Research Directions to Keep up with the times. *Journal of the Association for Information Systems*, *9*(1), 23–39. doi:10.17705/1jais.00147

Kolberg, D., Knobloch, J., & Zühlke, D. (2017). Towards a lean automation interface for workstations. *International Journal of Production Research*, *55*(10), 2845–2856. doi:10.1080/00207543.2016.1223384

Kota, L. (2018). Artificial Intelligence In Logistics. *ALS*, *1*(12), 47–60. doi:10.32971/als.2019.004

Kotler, P., & Keller, K. (2012). Marketing Management (14 ed.). Pearson Education.

Kouhizadeh, M., Saberi, S., & Sarkis, J. (2021). Blockchain technology and the sustainable supply chain: Theoretically exploring adoption barriers. *International Journal of Production Economics*, *231*, 107831. doi:10.1016/j.ijpe.2020.107831

Kouhizadeh, M., & Sarkis, J. (2018). Blockchain practices, potentials, and perspectives in greening supply chains. *Sustainability (Basel)*, *10*(10), 3652. doi:10.3390u10103652

Kozma, D., Varga, P., & Hegedüs, C. (2019, March 1). *Supply Chain Management and Logistics 4.0 - A Study on Arrowhead Framework Integration*. IEEE. doi:10.1109/ICITM.2019.8710670

Kudtarkar, A. & Shaikh, D. (2021). Applications of Machine Learning Techniques in Supply Chain Management. *International journal of creative research thoughts – IJCRT.*

Kumar, A., & Kumar, T. V. (2021). A Multi-Objective Approach to Big Data View Materialization. [IJKSS]. *International Journal of Knowledge and Systems Science*, *12*(2), 17–37. doi:10.4018/IJKSS.2021040102

Kumar, A., Liu, R., & Shan, Z. (2020). Is Blockchain a Silver Bullet for Supply Chain Management? Technical Challenges and Research Opportunities. *Decision Sciences*, *51*(1), 8–37. doi:10.1111/deci.12396

Kumar, K., Sen, N., Azid, S., & Mehta, U. (2017). A fuzzy decision in smart fire and home security system. *Procedia Computer Science*, *105*, 93–98. doi:10.1016/j.procs.2017.01.207

Kumar, V., Ramachandran, D., & Kumar, B. (2021). Influence of new-age technologies on marketing: A research agenda. *Journal of Business Research*, *125*, 864–877. doi:10.1016/j.jbusres.2020.01.007

Kyriakopoulos, G. L. (2021). Environmental legislation in european and international contexts: Legal practices and social planning toward the circular economy. *Laws*, *10*(1), 3. doi:10.3390/laws10010003

Lacity, M., & Van Hoek, R. (2021). *Requiem for reconciliations: DL Freight, a blockchain-enabled solution by Walmart Canada and DLT Labs.* University of Arkansas Blockchain Center for Excellence Research.

Lahkani, M. J., Wang, S., Urbański, M., & Egorova, M. (2020). Sustainable B2B E-commerce and blockchain-based supply chain finance. *Sustainability (Basel)*, *12*(10), 3968. doi:10.3390u12103968

Lahoti, N. (2019). Uber Business Model Explained: From Start to Finish. *Mobisoft.* https://mobisoftinfotech.com/resources/blog/uber-business-model-explained/.

Lai, J. Y., Wang, J. T., & Chiu, Y. H. (2021). Evaluating blockchain technology for reducing supply chain risks. *Information Systems and e-Business Management*, *19*(4), 1089–1111. doi:10.100710257-021-00533-4

Lakhwani, K., Gianey, H., Wireko, J., & Hiran, K. (2020). Internet of Things (IOT)-Principles, Paradigms and Applications of IoT. BPB Publications, India.

Lakhwani, K., Gianey, H. K., Wireko, J. K., & Hiran, K. K. (2020). *Internet of Things (IoT): Principles, paradigms and applications of IoT.* Bpb Publications.

Lan, S., Tseng, M. L., Yang, C., & Huisingh, D. (2020). Trends in sustainable logistics in major cities in China. *The Science of the Total Environment*, *712*, 136381. doi:10.1016/j.scitotenv.2019.136381 PMID:31940512

Lasi, H., Fettke, P., Kemper, H.-G., Feld, T., & Hoffmann, M. (2014). Industry 4.0. *BISE*, *6*(4), 239–242.

Lastanto, W. K. R., Dilini, K. A., & Kulawansa, T. (2018). A Review of Big Data Analytics for Customer Relationship Management. In *2018 3rd International Conference on Information Technology Research (ICITR)* (pp. 1-6). IEEE

Lastra, J. L. M., & Delamer, I. M. (2006). Semantic Web Services in Factory Automation: Fundamental Insights and Research Roadmap. *IEEE Transactions on Industrial Informatics*, *2*(1), 1–11.

Lavalle, S., Lesser, E., Shockey, R. H., & Crosthwait, N. M. (2011). Big Data, Analytics and the Path from Insight to Value. *MIT Sloan Management Review*, *52*(2), 21–32.

Lee, D., & Yoon, S. N. (2021). Application of artificial intelligence-based technologies in the healthcare industry: Opportunities and challenges. *International Journal of Environmental Research and Public Health, 18*(1), 271. doi:10.3390/ijerph18010271 PMID:33401373

Lee, H. L., & Billington, C. (1992). Managing supply chain inventories: Pitfalls and opportunities. *Sloan Management Review, 33*(3), 65–77.

Lee, H. L., & Zhang, H. (2019). Introduction to the Special Issue on Innovations and Sustainability. *Production and Operations Management, 28*(12), 2929–2929. doi:10.1111/poms.13113

Lee, J., Kao, H.-A., & Yang, S. (2014). Service Innovation and Smart Analytics for Industry 4.0 and Big Data Environment. *Procedia CIRP, 16*, 3–8.

Lefort, L., Henson, C., Taylor, K., Barnaghi, P., Compton, M., Corcho, O., Garcia-Castro, R., Graybeal, J., Herzog, A., & Janowicz, K. (2005). *Semantic Sensor Network XG Final Report.* W3C Incubator Group Report. http://www.w3.org/2005/Incubator/ssn/XGR-ssn/

Lemoine, P. (2014). La nouvelle grammaire du succès. La transformation numérique de l'économie française. *Rapport au gouvernement.*

Leng, J., Sha, W., Wang, B., Zheng, P., Zhuang, C., Liu, Q., Wuest, T., Mourtzis, D., & Wang, L. (2022). Industry 5.0: Prospect and retrospect. *Journal of Manufacturing Systems, 65*, 279–295. doi:10.1016/j.jmsy.2022.09.017

Lennon, M. (2019). 10 Countries Where Uber Isn't Available *The Travel.* https://www.thetravel.com/countries-uber-rides-unavailable/.

Leveling, J., Edelbrock, M., & Otto, B. (2014). Big data analytics for supply chain management. In *2014 IEEE international conference on industrial engineering and engineering management* (pp. 918-922). IEEE.

Li, B., Yang, C., & Huang, S. (2014). Study on supply chain disruption management under service level dependent demand. *Journal of Networking, 9*(6), 1432–1439. doi:10.4304/jnw.9.6.1432-1439

Liberatore, M., & Luo, W. (2010). The Analytics Movement. *Interfaces, 40*(4), 313–324. doi:10.1287/inte.1100.0502

Li, D. (2016). Perspective for smart factory in petrochemical industry. *Computers & Chemical Engineering, 91*, 136–148. doi:10.1016/j.compchemeng.2016.03.006

Liébana-Cabanillas, F., Molinillo, S., & Ruiz-Montañez, M. (2019). To use or not to use, that is the question: Analysis of the determining factors for using NFC mobile payment systems in public transportation. Technol. Forecast. Soc. Change, 139, 266–276.

Li, J., & Kassem, M. (2021). Applications of distributed ledger technology (DLT) and Blockchain-enabled smart contracts in construction. *Automation in Construction, 132*, 103955. doi:10.1016/j.autcon.2021.103955

Li, L., & Horrocks, I. (2004). A software framework for matchmaking based on semantic web technology. *International Journal of Electronic Commerce, 8*(4), 39–60.

Liu, C. H., Lin, Q., & Wen, S. (2018). Blockchain-enabled data collection and sharing for industrial IoT with deep reinforcement learning. *IEEE Transactions on Industrial Informatics, 15*(6), 3516–3526. doi:10.1109/TII.2018.2890203

Liu, C., & Ma, T. (2022). Green logistics management and supply chain system construction based on internet of things technology. *Sustainable Computing: Informatics and Systems, 35*, 100773. doi:10.1016/j.suscom.2022.100773

Liukkonen, M., & Tsai, T. N. (2016). Toward decentralized intelligence in manufacturing: Recent trends in automatic identification of things. *International Journal of Advanced Manufacturing Technology, 87*(9-12), 2509–2531. doi:10.100700170-016-8628-y

Liu, W., Liang, Y., Bao, X., Qin, J., & Lim, M. K. (2020). China's Logistics Development Trends In the Post Covid-19 Era. *International Journal of Logistics, 6*(25), 965–976. doi:10.1080/13675567.2020.1837760

Liu, W., Wei, W., Yan, X., Dong, D., & Chen, Z. (2020). Sustainability risk management in a smart logistics ecological chain : An evaluation framework based on social network analysis. *Journal of Cleaner Production, 276*, 124189. doi:10.1016/j.jclepro.2020.124189

Liu, Y., Zhang, Y., Batista, L., & Rong, K. (2019). Green operations: What's the role of supply chain flexibility? *International Journal of Production Economics, 214*, 30–43. doi:10.1016/j.ijpe.2019.03.026

Li, X., Lu, W., Xue, F., Wu, L., Zhao, R., Lou, J., & Xu, J. (2022). Blockchain-enabled IoT-BIM platform for supply chain management in modular construction. *Journal of Construction Engineering and Management, 148*(2), 04021195. doi:10.1061/(ASCE)CO.1943-7862.0002229

Lobell, D. B., Bänziger, M., Magorokosho, C., & Vivek, B. (2011). Nonlinear heat effects on African maize as evidenced by historical yield trials. *Nature Climate Change, 1*(1), 42–45. doi:10.1038/nclimate1043

Lobov, A., Lopez, F. U., Herrera, V. V., Puttonen, J., & Lastra, J. L. M. (2008). Semantic Web Services framework for manufacturing industries. In *Int. Conf. on Rob. and Biomim.* (pp. 2104–2108). IEEE.

Loladze, I. (2014). Hidden shift of the ionome of plants exposed to elevated CO2 depletes minerals at the base of human nutrition. *elife, 3*, e02245.

Lopez, J., Roman, R., & Alcaraz, C. (2009). Analysis of security threats, requirements, technologies and standards in wireless sensor networks. In A. Aldini, G. Barthe, & R. Gorrieri (Eds.), *Foundations of Security Analysis and Design V: FOSAD 2007/2008/2009 Tutorial Lectures* (pp. 289–338). Springer. doi:10.1007/978-3-642-03829-7_10

Lotfi, R., Mehrjerdi, Y. Z., Pishvaee, M. S., Sadeghieh, A., & Weber, G. W. (2021). A Robust Optimization Model For Sustainable And Resilient Closed-Loop Supply Chain Network Design Considering Conditional Value At Risk. *Numerical algebra, control & optimization, 11*(2).

Lusch, R. F., Vargo, S. L., & Tanniru, M. (2010). Service, value networks and learning. *Journal of the Academy of Marketing Science, 38*(1), 19–31. doi:10.100711747-008-0131-z

Maass, W., Filler, A. (2006). Towards an infrastructure for semantically annotated physical products. In *INFORMATIK 2006–Informatik für Menschen–Band 2, Beiträge der 36.* Jahrestagung der Gesellschaft für Informatik eV (GI).

Madakam, S., Holmukhe, R. M., & Jaiswal, D. K. (2019). The Future Digital Work Force: Robotic Process Automation (Rpa). *Journal of Information Systems and Technology Management, 16*, 1–17. doi:10.4301/S1807-1775201916001

Magazine, I. N. (2023). Connected farming – How can it be beneficial for agriculture manufacturers, customers, and the environment. *IoT Now News*. https://www.iot-now.com/2023/03/09/128547-connected-farming-how-can-it-be-beneficial-for-agriculture-manufacturers-customers-and-the-environment/

Mahon, B. (2004). *The Man Who Changed Everything: The Life of James Clerk Maxwell*. John Wiley & Sons Ltd.

Mangla, S. K., Sharma, Y. K., Patil, P. P., Yadav, G., & Xu, J. (2019). Logistics and distribution challenges to managing operations for corporate sustainability: Study on leading Indian diary organizations. *Journal of Cleaner Production, 238*, 117620. doi:10.1016/j.jclepro.2019.117620

Manisha, N., & Jagadeeshwar, M. (2023). BC driven IoT-based food quality traceability system for dairy product using deep learning model. *High-Confidence Computing*, *3*(3), 100121. doi:10.1016/j.hcc.2023.100121

Manners-Bell, J., & Lyon, K. (2019). *The logistics and supply chain innovation handbook: disruptive technologies and new business models*. Kogan Page Publishers.

Markus, S., & Buijs, P. (2022). Beyond the hype: How blockchain affects supply chain performance. *Supply Chain Management*, *27*(7), 177–193. doi:10.1108/SCM-03-2022-0109

Maroua, B., Rachida, A. A., & Abdelaziz, M. (2022). Smart farming architectures based on IoT review: Comparative study. *Procedia Computer Science*, *203*, 783–788. doi:10.1016/j.procs.2022.07.117

Marrella, A. (2018). *Automated Planning for Business Process Management*. Academic Press.

Mashal, I., Alsaryrah, O., Chung, T. Y., Yang, C. Z., Kuo, W. H., & Agrawal, D. P. (2015). Choices for interaction with things on Internet and underlying issues. *Ad Hoc Networks*, *28*, 68–90.

Matthias Weber, K., Heller-Schuh, B., Godoe, H., & Roeste, R. (2014). ICT-enabled system innovations in public services: Experiences from intelligent transport systems. *Telecommunications Policy*, *38*(5–6), 539–557. doi:10.1016/j.telpol.2013.12.004

Mayika, J. M., Chui, B., Brown, J. Bughin, R., Dobbs, Roxburgh, C., & Byers, A. (2011). Big Data: The Next Frontier for Innovation, Competition, and Productivity. *McKinsey Report*. McKinsey.

Mc Carthy, U., Uysal, I., Badia-Melis, R., Mercier, S., O'Donnell, C., & Ktenioudaki, A. (2018). Global food security–Issues, challenges and technological solutions. *Trends in Food Science & Technology*, *77*, 11–20. doi:10.1016/j.tifs.2018.05.002

McAfee, A., & Brynjolfsson, E. (2012). Big data: The management revolution. *Harvard Business Review*, *90*(10), 61–68. PMID:23074865

McCartney, L., & Lefsrud, M. (2018). Protected agriculture in extreme environments: A review of controlled environment agriculture in tropical, arid, polar, and urban locations. *Applied Engineering in Agriculture*, *34*(2), 455–473. doi:10.13031/aea.12590

Meera, A. J., Kantipudi, M. V. V., & Aluvalu, R. (2019, December). Intrusion detection system for the IoT: A comprehensive review. In *International Conference on Soft Computing and Pattern Recognition* (pp. 235-243). Springer.

Meerburg, B. G., Verhagen, A., Jongschaap, R. E. E., Franke, A. C., Schaap, B. F., Dueck, T. A., & Van Der Werf, A. (2009). Do nonlinear temperature effects indicate severe damages to US crop yields under climate change? *Proceedings of the National Academy of Sciences of the United States of America*, *106*(43), E120–E120. doi:10.1073/pnas.0910618106 PMID:19850868

Meghla, T. I., Rahman, M. M., Biswas, A. A., Hossain, J. T., & Khatun, T. (2021, July). Supply Chain Management with Demand Forecasting of Covid-19 Vaccine using Blockchain and Machine Learning. In *2021 12th International Conference on Computing Communication and Networking Technologies (ICCCNT)* (pp. 01-07). IEEE. 10.1109/ICCCNT51525.2021.9580006

Mehdizadeh, M. (2020). Integrating ABC analysis and rough set theory to control the inventories of distributor in the supply chain of auto spare parts. *Computers & Industrial Engineering*, *139*, 105673. doi:10.1016/j.cie.2019.01.047

Melnyk, S. A., Schoenherr, T., Speier-Pero, C., Peters, C., Chang, J. F., & Friday, D. (2022). New challenges in supply chain management: Cybersecurity across the supply chain. *International Journal of Production Research*, *60*(1), 162–183. doi:10.1080/00207543.2021.1984606

Mhaisen, N., Fetais, N., Erbad, A., Mohamed, A., & Guizani, M. (2020). To chain or not to chain: A reinforcement learning approach for blockchain-enabled IoT monitoring applications. *Future Generation Computer Systems*, *111*, 39–51. doi:10.1016/j.future.2020.04.035

Mihálovits, Z., & Tapaszti, A. (2018). Green bond, the financial instrument that supports sustainable development. *Public Finance Quarterly*, *63*(3), 303.

Minor, M., Montani, S., & Recio-García, J. A. (2014). Process-oriented Case-based Reasoning. *Information Systems*, *40*, 103–105.

Mirón, I. J., Linares, C., & Díaz, J. (2023). The influence of climate change on food production and food safety. *Environmental Research*, *216*, 114674. doi:10.1016/j.envres.2022.114674 PMID:36341795

Mishra, D., Gunasekaran, A., Papadopoulos, T., & Childe, S. J. (2018). Big Data and supply chain management: A review and bibliometric analysis. *Annals of Operations Research*, *270*(1-2), 313–336. doi:10.100710479-016-2236-y

Mishra, S., & Sharma, S. K. (2023). Advanced contribution of IoT in agricultural production for the development of smart livestock environments. *Internet of Things*, *22*, 100724. doi:10.1016/j.iot.2023.100724

Misic, V. V., & Perakis, G. (2020). Data analytics in operations management: A review. *Manufacturing & Service Operations Management*, *22*(1), 158–169. doi:10.1287/msom.2019.0805

Misra, N. N., Dixit, Y., Al-Mallahi, A., Bhullar, M. S., Upadhyay, R., & Martynenko, A. (2020). IoT, big data, and artificial intelligence in agriculture and food industry. *IEEE Internet of Things Journal*, *9*(9), 6305–6324. doi:10.1109/JIOT.2020.2998584

Mitchell, J., & Guile, D. (2021). Fusion skills and industry 5.0: conceptions and challenges. In *Insights Into Global Engineering Education After the Birth of Industry 5.0*. IntechOpen.

Mithas, S., Ramasubbu, N., & Sambamurthy, V. (2011). How Information Management Capability Influences Firm Performance. *Management Information Systems Quarterly*, *35*(1), 237–256. doi:10.2307/23043496

Modgil, S., Singh, R., & Hannibal, C. (2021). Artificial Intelligence For Supply Chain Resilience: Learning From Covid-19. *International Journal of Logistics Management*, *4*(33), 1246–1268. doi:10.1108/IJLM-02-2021-0094

Moher, D., Liberati, A., Tetzlaff, J., & Altman, D. G.The PRISMA Group. (2009). Preferred reporting items for systematic reviews and meta-analyses : The PRISMA statement. *PLoS Medicine*, *6*(7), e1000097. doi:10.1371/journal.pmed.1000097 PMID:19621072

Moktadir, M. A., Ali, S. M., Paul, S. K., & Shukla, N. (2019). Barriers to big data analytics in manufacturing supply chains: A case study from Bangladesh. *Computers & Industrial Engineering*, *128*, 1063–1075. doi:10.1016/j.cie.2018.04.013

Monostori, L. (2014). Cyber-physical Production Systems: Roots, Expectations and R&D Challenges. *Procedia CIRP*, *17*, 9–13.

Montenegro, G., Kushalnagar, N., Hui, J., & Culler, D. (2007). Transmission of IPv6 packets over IEEE 802.15.4 networks. Internet Proposed Standard RFC, vol. 4944.

Moosavi, J., Fathollahi-Fard, A. M., & Dulebenets, M. A. (2022). Supply chain disruption during the COVID-19 pandemic: Recognizing potential disruption management strategies. *International Journal of Disaster Risk Reduction*, *75*, 102983. doi:10.1016/j.ijdrr.2022.102983 PMID:35475018

Muangprathub, J., Boonnam, N., Kajornkasirat, S., Lekbangpong, N., Wanichsombat, A., & Nillaor, P. (2019). IoT and agriculture data analysis for smart farm. *Computers and Electronics in Agriculture*, *156*, 467–474. doi:10.1016/j.compag.2018.12.011

Müller, G. (2018). *Workflow Modeling Assistance by Casebased Reasoning*. Springer Fachmedien.

Munir, M. S., Bajwa, I. S., Ashraf, A., Anwar, W., & Rashid, R. (2021). Intelligent and smart irrigation system using edge computing and IoT. *Complexity*, *2021*, 1–16. doi:10.1155/2021/6691571

Muzellec, L., Ronteau, S., & Lambkin, M. (2015, February). Two-sided Internet platforms: A business model lifecycle perspective. *Industrial Marketing Management*, *45*(1), 139–150. doi:10.1016/j.indmarman.2015.02.012

Nagarajan, S. M., Muthukumaran, V., Vinoth Kumar, V., Beschi, I. S., & Magesh, S. (2021). *Fine Tuning Smart Manufacturing Enterprise Systems: A Perspective of Internet of Things-Based Service-Oriented Architecture*. IGI Global.

Naidoo, M., & Gasparatos, A. (2018). Corporate environmental sustainability in the retail sector: Drivers, strategies and performance measurement. *Journal of Cleaner Production*, *203*, 125–142. doi:10.1016/j.jclepro.2018.08.253

Naim, A. (2021). New Trends in Business Process Management: Applications of Green Information Technologies. *British Journal of Environmental Studies*, *1*(1), 12–23.

Nalluri, V., & Chen, L.-S. (2022). Risk assessment for sustainability on telecom supply chain : A hybrid fuzzy approach. *Uncertain Supply Chain Management*, *10*(2), 559–576. doi:10.5267/j.uscm.2021.11.007

Nara, E. O. B., da Costa, M. B., Baierle, I. C., Schaefer, J. L., Benitez, G. B., do Santos, L. M. A. L., & Benitez, L. B. (2021). Expected impact of industry 4.0 technologies on sustainable development: A study in the context of Brazil's plastic industry. *Sustainable Production and Consumption*, *25*, 102–122. doi:10.1016/j.spc.2020.07.018

Narwane, V. S., Gunasekaran, A., & Gardas, B. B. (2022). Unlocking adoption challenges of IoT in Indian agricultural and food supply chain. *Smart Agricultural Technology*, *2*, 100035. doi:10.1016/j.atech.2022.100035

Natanelov, V., Cao, S., Foth, M., & Dulleck, U. (2022). Blockchain smart contracts for supply chain finance: Mapping the innovation potential in Australia-China beef supply chains. *Journal of Industrial Information Integration*, *30*, 100389. doi:10.1016/j.jii.2022.100389

Naumann, A., Dörr, L., Salscheider, N. O., & Furmans, K. (2020). Refined Plane Segmentation For Cuboid-shaped Objects By Leveraging Edge Detection. *2020 19th IEEE International Conference on Machine Learning and Applications (ICMLA)*. IEEE. 10.1109/ICMLA51294.2020.00096

NCAS. (2020) *Air pollution falling across UK cities, latest data shows*. NCAS. https://ncas.ac.uk/air-pollution-falling-across-uk-cities-latest-data-shows/

Newsroom of IBM. (2019). *Ford Motor Company, Huayou Cobalt, IBM, LG Chem and RCS Global launch blockchain pilot to address concerns in strategic mineral supply chains*. IBM. https://newsroom.ibm.com/2019-01-16-Ford-Motor-Company-Huayou-Cobalt-IBM-LG-Chem-and-RCS-Global-Launch-Blockchain-Pilot-to-Address-Concerns-in-Strategic-Mineral-Supply-Chains

Ng, I. C., & Wakenshaw, S. Y. (2017). The Internet-of-Things: Review and research directions. *International Journal of Research in Marketing*, *34*(1), 3–21. doi:10.1016/j.ijresmar.2016.11.003

Ng, K. K., Chen, C. H., Lee, C. K., Jiao, J. R., & Yang, Z. X. (2021). A systematic literature review on intelligent automation: Aligning concepts from theory, practice, and future perspectives. *Advanced Engineering Informatics*, *47*, 101246. doi:10.1016/j.aei.2021.101246

Nguyen, T., Li, Z. H. O. U., Spiegler, V., Ieromonachou, P., & Lin, Y. (2018). Big data analytics in supply chain management: A state-of-the-art literature review. *Computers & Operations Research*, *98*, 254–264. doi:10.1016/j.cor.2017.07.004

Nicastro, R., & Carillo, P. (2021). Food Loss and Waste Prevention Strategies from Farm to Fork. *Sustainability (Basel)*, *13*(10), 5443. doi:10.3390u13105443

Ning, H., & Wang, Z. (2011). Future internet of things architecture: Like mankind neural system or social organization framework? *IEEE Communications Letters*, *15*(4), 461–463.

Novo, R., & Neves, J. M. S. (2013). Inovação na inteligência analítica por meio do Big Data: Características de diferenciação da abordagem tradicional. *Workshop de Pós-Graduação e Pesquisa do Centro Paula Souza, São Paulo*, *8*, 32–44.

O'dwyer, J., & Renner, R. (2011). The Promise of Advanced Supply Chain Analytics, Supply Chain. *Management Review*, *15*, 32–37.

Ocker, F., Kovalenko, I., Barton, K., & Tilbury, D., & VogelHeuser, B. (2019). A Framework for Automatic Initialization of Multi-Agent Production Systems Using Semantic Web Technologies. *IEEE Robotics and Automation Letters*, *4*(4), 4330–4337.

Odlyzko, A., & Tilly, B. (2005). A refutation of Metcalfe ' s Law and a better estimate for the value of networks and network interconnections. *Technology (Elmsford, N.Y.)*, 1–11.

Ogli, G. B. B., & Buribayevich, E. O. (2022). Development of Logistics Processes in Transport Enterprises. Vital Annex. *International Journal of Novel Research in Advanced Sciences*, *1*(3), 138–142.

Ojha, T., Misra, S., & Raghuwanshi, N. S. (2015). Wireless sensor networks for agriculture: The state-of-the-art in practice and future challenges. *Computers and Electronics in Agriculture*, *118*, 66–84. doi:10.1016/j.compag.2015.08.011

Oliva, R., & Watson, N. (2011). Cross-Functional Alignment in Supply Chain Planning: A Case Study of Sales & Operations Planning. *Journal of Operations Management*, *29*(5), 434–448. doi:10.1016/j.jom.2010.11.012

Orenga-Rogla, S., & Chalmeta, R. (2016). Social customer relationship management: Taking advantage of Web 2.0 and Big Data technologies. *SpringerPlus*, *5*(1), 1462. doi:10.118640064-016-3128-y PMID:27652037

Orji, I. J., Kusi-Sarpong, S., & Gupta, H. (2020). The critical success factors of using social media for supply chain social sustainability in the freight logistics industry. *International Journal of Production Research*, *58*(5), 1522–1539. doi:10.1080/00207543.2019.1660829

Othmeni, I., Abdallah, R. B., Aribi, H. B., Amara, E. B., & Fattouch, S. (2023). Artificial Intelligence Applications in Agricultural Sustainability: Enhancing Efficiency and Resilience. In Convergence of Cloud Computing, AI, and Agricultural Science (pp. 187-209). IGI Global.

Pagell, M., & Wu, Z. (2017). Building a more complete theory of sustainable supply chain management using case studies of 10 exemplars. *The Journal of Supply Chain Management*, *53*(4), 3–23.

Paksoy, T., Karaoğlan, I., Gökçen, H., Pardalos, P. M., & Torğul, B. (2016). Experimental research on closed loop supply chain management with internet of things, Journal of Economy. *Bibliograph.*, *3*, 1–20.

Pal, K. (2016). Supply Chain Coordination Based on Web Services. In Chan H K, Subramanian, N. and Abdulrahman, M D (eds.), Supply Chain Management in the Big Data Era, 137-171. IGI Global.

Pal, K. (2018). A Big Data Framework for Decision Making in Supply Chain. IGI Global.

Pal, K. (2018). A Big Data Framework for Decision Making in Supply Chain. P K Gupta, Tuner Oren, Mayank Singh (eds) Predictive Intelligence Using Big Data and the Internet of Things, 51-76. IGI Global Publication.

Pal, K. (2019). Quality Assurance Issues for Big Data Applications in Supply Chain Management. In P K Gupta, Tuner Oren, Mayank Singh (eds.) Predictive Intelligence Using Big Data and the Internet of Things, 51-76. IGI Global Publication.

Pal, K. (2020). *Information Sharing for Manufacturing Supply Chain Management Based on Blockchain Technology*. IGI Global.

Pal, K. (2020). Information sharing for manufacturing supply chain management based on blockchain technology. In I. Williams (ed.) Cross-Industry Use of Blockchain Technology and Opportunities for the Future. IGI Global Publication.

Pal, K. (2021a). Applications of Secured Blockchain Technology in Manufacturing Industry. In Subhendu Kumar Pani, Biju Patnaik, Sian Lun, & Xingcheng Liu (eds.), Blockchain and AI Technology in the Industrial Internet of Things. IGI Global Publication.

Pal, K. (2022). A Decentralized Privacy-Preserving Healthcare Blockchain for IoT, Challenges, and Solutions. In Malaya Dutta Borah, Pen Zhang, Ganesh Chandra Deka (eds.), Prospects of Blockchain Technology for Accelerating Scientific Advancement in Healthcare. IGI Global Publication.

Pal, K. (2023a). Security Issues and Solutions for Resource-Constrained IoT Applications Using Lightweight Cryptography. In Suhasini Verma, Vidhisha Vyas, and Keshav Kaushik (eds.), Cybersecurity Issues, Challenges, and Solutions in the Business World. IGI Global Publication.

Pal, K. (2023b). Drivers of Sustainable Supply Chain Management Using Internet of Things-Based Blockchain Technology. In Atour Taghipour (eds.), Government Impact on Sustainable and Responsible Supply Chan. IGI Global Publication.

Pal, K., & Ul-Haque, A. (2000). Internet of Things and Blockchain Technology in Apparel Manufacturing Supply Chain Data Management. *Procedia Computer Science*, 450-457.

Pal, K. (2017). Supply Chain Coordination Based on Web Services. In H. K. Chan, N. Subramanian, & M. D. Abdulrahman (Eds.), *Supply Chain Management in the Big Data Era* (pp. 137–171). IGI Global Publication.

Pal, K. (2021b). Privacy, Security and Policies: A Review of Problems and Solutions with Blockchain-Based Internet of Things Applications in Manufacturing Industry. *Procedia Computer Science*, *191*, 176–183. doi:10.1016/j.procs.2021.07.022

Pal, K., & Karakostas, B. (2014). A Multi Agent-Based Service Framework for Supply Chain Management, In the proceeding of International Conference on Ambient Systems, Networks and Technology. *Procedia Computer Science*, *32*, 53–60.

Pal, K., & Yasar, A. (2020). Internet of Things and blockchain technology in apparel manufacturing supply chain data management. *Procedia Computer Science*, *170*, 450–457. doi:10.1016/j.procs.2020.03.088

Pal, K., & Yasar, A.-U.-H. (2023). Internet of Things Impact on Supply Chain Management. *Procedia Computer Science*, *220*, 478–485. doi:10.1016/j.procs.2023.03.061

Pandian, A. P. (2019). Artificial Intelligence Application In Smart Warehousing Environment For Automated Logistics. *JAICN*, *2*(2), 63–72. doi:10.36548/jaicn.2019.2.002

Pan, Y., & Zhang, L. (2021). Roles of artificial intelligence in construction engineering and management: A critical review and future trends. *Automation in Construction*, *122*, 103517. doi:10.1016/j.autcon.2020.103517

Papadopoulos, T., Gunasekaran, A., Dubey, R., Altay, N., Childe, S. J., & Fosso-Wamba, S. (2017). The role of Big Data in explaining disaster resilience in supply chains for sustainability. *Journal of Cleaner Production*, *142*, 1108–1118. doi:10.1016/j.jclepro.2016.03.059

Parise, S., Iyer, B., & Vesset, D. (2012), Four strategies to capture and create value from big data. *Ivey Business Journal*. https://iveybusinessjournal.com/publication/four-strategies-to-capture-and-create-value-from-big-data/

Patel, A. S., Brahmbhatt, M. N., Bariya, A. R., Nayak, J. B., & Singh, V. K. (2023). Blockchain technology in food safety and traceability concern to livestock products. *Heliyon*, *9*(6), e16526. doi:10.1016/j.heliyon.2023.e16526 PMID:37265625

Pena-opez, I. (2005). *Internet Report 2005: The Internet of Things, 2005.* Academic Press.

Persdotter Isaksson, M., Hulthén, H., & Forslund, H. (2019). Environmentally sustainable logistics performance management process integration between Buyers and 3PLs. *Sustainability (Basel)*, *11*(11), 3061. doi:10.3390u11113061

Pilkington, M. (2019). *Retail Therapy: Why The Retail Industry Is Broken–And What Can Be Done To Fix It.* Bloomsbury Publishing.

Piramuthu, S. (2022). IoT, Environmental Sustainability, Agricultural Supply Chains. *Procedia Computer Science*, *204*, 811–816. doi:10.1016/j.procs.2022.08.098

Pirsa, S., Sani, I. K., & Mirtalebi, S. S. (2022). Nano-biocomposite based color sensors: Investigation of structure, function, and applications in intelligent food packaging. *Food Packaging and Shelf Life*, *31*, 100789. doi:10.1016/j.fpsl.2021.100789

Pizoń, J., & Gola, A. (2023). Human–Machine Relationship—Perspective and Future Roadmap for Industry 5.0 Solutions. *Machines*, *11*(2), 203. doi:10.3390/machines11020203

Poku-Boansi, M., & Adarkwa, K. (2014). The determinants of demand for public transport services in Kumasi, Ghana. *Journal of Science and Technology*, *33*(3), 60.

Poluha, R. G. (2007). *Application of the SCOR Model in Supply Chain Management.* Youngstown.

Porter, J. R., Xie, L., Challinor, A. J., Cochrane, K., Howden, S. M., Iqbal, M. M., & Travasso, M. I. (2014). *Food security and food production systems.*

Porter, M. E. (1985). *Competitive Advantage: Creating and Sustaining Superior Performance.* Free Press.

Power, D. J. (2007). *A Brief History of Decision Support Systems.* DSS. http://DSSResource.COM/history/dsshistory.html

Prahalad, C. K., & Mashelkar, R. A. (2010). Innovation's Holy Grail. *Harvard Business Review*, (July-August), 2010.

Prakash, A., Pathak, N., Muralidharan, C., & Maas, G. (2017). Sustainable supply chain management: A review and research agenda. *International Journal of Management Reviews*, *19*(1), 18–38.

Pretty, J. (2018). Intensification for redesigned and sustainable agricultural systems. *Science*, *362*(6417), eaav0294. doi:10.1126cience.aav0294 PMID:30467142

Priyadarshi, N., Padmanaban, S., Hiran, K. K., Holm-Nielson, J. B., & Bansal, R. C. (Eds.). (2021). *Artificial Intelligence and Internet of Things for Renewable Energy Systems* (Vol. 12). Walter de Gruyter GmbH & Co KG. doi:10.1515/9783110714043

Proctor & Gamble. (2023). *Environmental Sustainability.* Proctor and Gamble. https://us.pg.com/environmental-sustainability/

Puttonen, J., Lobov, A., & Lastra, J. L. M. (2013). Semantics-Based Composition of Factory Automation Processes Encapsulated by Web Services. *IEEE TII*, *9*(4), 2349–2359.

Puttonen, J., Lobov, A., Soto, M. A. C., & Lastra, J. L. M. (2010). A Semantic Web Services-based approach for production systems control. *Advanced Engineering Informatics*, *24*(3), 285–299.

Queiroz, M. M., Ivanov, D., Dolgui, A., & Fosso Wamba, S. (2022). Impacts of epidemic outbreaks on supply chains: Mapping a research agenda amid the COVID-19 pandemic through a structured literature review. *Annals of Operations Research*, *319*(1), 1159–1196. doi:10.100710479-020-03685-7 PMID:32836615

Queiroz, M. M., Telles, R., & Bonilla, S. H. (2020). Blockchain and supply chain management integration: A systematic review of the literature. *Supply Chain Management*, *25*(2), 241–254. doi:10.1108/SCM-03-2018-0143

Qureshi, R., Mehboob, S. H., & Aamir, M. (2021). Sustainable green fog computing for smart agriculture. *Wireless Personal Communications*, *121*(2), 1379–1390. doi:10.100711277-021-09059-x

Rad, F. F., Oghazi, P., Palmié, M., Chirumalla, K., Pashkevich, N., Patel, P. C., & Sattari, S. (2022). Industry 4.0 and supply chain performance: A systematic literature review of the benefits, challenges, and critical success factors of 11 core technologies. *Industrial Marketing Management*, *105*, 268–293. doi:10.1016/j.indmarman.2022.06.009

Raian, S., Ali, S. M., Sarker, M., Sankaranarayanan, B., Kabir, G., Paul, S. K., & Chakrabortty, R. K. (2022). Assessing sustainability risks in the supply chain of the textile industry under uncertainty. *Resources, Conservation and Recycling*, *177*, 105975. doi:10.1016/j.resconrec.2021.105975

Rajakumar, A. G., Anthony, A., & Kumar, V. (2021). Application Of Deep Learning Methods For Urban Water Demand Forecast Modelling. https://doi.org/ doi:10.5194/egusphere-egu21-9572

Rajanarthagi, D. (2021), Role of Big data in digital marketing. *The Future*. https://gecdesigns.com/blog/role-of-big-data-in-digital-marketing

Rajasekaran, A. S., Azees, M., & Al-Turjman, F. (2022). A comprehensive survey on blockchain technology. *Sustainable Energy Technologies and Assessments*, *52*, 102039. doi:10.1016/j.seta.2022.102039

Raj, E. F. I., Appadurai, M., & Athiappan, K. (2022). Precision farming in modern agriculture. In *Smart Agriculture Automation Using Advanced Technologies: Data Analytics and Machine Learning, Cloud Architecture, Automation and IoT* (pp. 61–87). Springer Singapore.

Rajkumar, M. N., Abinaya, S., & Kumar, V. V. (2017, March). Intelligent irrigation system—An IOT based approach. In *2017 International Conference on Innovations in Green Energy and Healthcare Technologies (IGEHT)* (pp. 1-5). IEEE.

Ramankutty, N., Mehrabi, Z., Waha, K., Jarvis, L., Kremen, C., Herrero, M., & Rieseberg, L. H. (2018). Trends in global agricultural land use: Implications for environmental health and food security. *Annual Review of Plant Biology*, *69*(1), 789–815. doi:10.1146/annurev-arplant-042817-040256 PMID:29489395

Raman, R., Shamim, R., Akram, S. V., Thakur, L., Pillai, B. G., & Ponnusamy, R. (2023, January). Classification and Contrast of Supervised Machine Learning Algorithms. In *2023 International Conference on Artificial Intelligence and Smart Communication (AISC)* (pp. 629-633). IEEE. 10.1109/AISC56616.2023.10085338

Rana, A. (2023). An Analysis Of Warehouse Management Systems. *International Journal for Research in Applied Science and Engineering Technology*, *6*(11), 1154–1157. doi:10.22214/ijraset.2023.53808

Rana, S. (2022). Consumer Awareness and Perception Towards Green Marketing: An Empirical Study In Bangalore City. *Journal of Positive School Psychology*, *6*(5), 4240–4245. http://journalppw.com

Raut, R. D., Mangla, S. K., Narwane, V. S., Gardas, B. B., Priyadarshinee, P., & Narkhede, B. E. (2019). Linking big data analytics and operational sustainability practices for sustainable business management. *Journal of Cleaner Production*, *224*, 10–24. doi:10.1016/j.jclepro.2019.03.181

Reinartz, W., Krafft, M., & Hoyer, W.D. (2004). The Customer Relationship Management Process: Its Measurement and Impact on Performance. *Journal Of Marketing Research, 41*(3), 293-305.

Ren, R., Hu, W., Dong, J., Sun, B., Chen, Y., & Chen, Z. (2020). A systematic literature review of green and sustainable logistics: Bibliometric analysis, research trend and knowledge taxonomy. *International Journal of Environmental Research and Public Health*, *17*(1), 261. doi:10.3390/ijerph17010261 PMID:31905934

Rharoubi, I., & Talmenssour, K. (2022). Understanding the role of supply chain digitalization in the quality of buyer-supplier relationship: Case studies of Moroccan companies. *Revue Française d'Economie et de Gestion, 3*(7).

Riahi, Y., Saikouk, T., Gunasekaran, A., & Badraoui, I. (2021). Artificial intelligence applications in supply chain: A descriptive bibliometric analysis and future research directions. *Expert Systems with Applications, 173*, 114702. doi:10.1016/j.eswa.2021.114702

Richey, R. G. Jr, Chen, H., & Kahle, L. R. (2016). The changing landscape of the US logistics industry: A content analysis of Fortune 100 firms. *Transportation Journal, 55*(3), 275–295.

Rickardo, N. G., & Gladson, N. V. (2023). Disruptive Technologies In Supply Chain Management Such As Artificial Intelligence and Blockchain. *World J. Adv. Res. Rev., 1*(18), 604–608. doi:10.30574/wjarr.2023.18.1.0656

Ritchie, H., Roser, M., & Rosado, P. (2020). CO_2 and greenhouse gas emissions. *Our world in data.*

Romano, A. L., Ferreira, L. M. D. F., & Caeiro, S. S. F. S. (2021). Modelling Sustainability Risk in the Brazilian Cosmetics Industry. *Sustainability (Basel), 13*(24), 13771. doi:10.3390u132413771

Rosendorff, A., Hodes, A., & Fabian, B. (2021). Artificial Intelligence For Last-mile Logistics - Procedures and Architecture. *OJAKM, 1*(9), 46–61. doi:10.36965/OJAKM.2021.9(1)46-61

Rossitto, C., Comber, R., Tholander, J., & Jacobsson, M. (2022, April). Towards Digital Environmental Stewardship: The Work of Caring for the Environment in Waste Management. In *Proceedings of the 2022 CHI Conference on Human Factors in Computing Systems* (pp. 1-16). ACM. 10.1145/3491102.3517679

Russomanno, D. J., Kothari, C. R., & Thomas, O. A. (2005). Building a Sensor Ontology: A Practical Approach Leveraging ISO and OGC Models. *2005 International Conference on Artificial Intelligence*, 637-643.

Ruta, M., Colucci, S., Scioscia, F., Di Sciascio, E., & Donini, F. M. (2011). Finding commonalities in RFID semantic streams. *Procedia Computer Science, 5*, 857–864.

S. A. O. (2014). Towards quasi - formal management of paratransit in informal transport dependent cities of Nigeria. *IOSR J. Humanit. Soc. Sci., 19*(12), 75–80. doi:10.9790/0837-191247580

Saberi, S., Kouhizadeh, M., Sarkis, J., & Shen, L. (2019). Blockchain technology and its relationships to sustainable supply chain management. *International Journal of Production Research, 57*(7), 2117–2135. doi:10.1080/00207543.2018.1533261

Saddier, S., Patterson, Z., Johnson, A., & Wiseman, N. (2017). Fickle or flexible?: Assessing paratransit reliability with smartphones in Accra, Ghana. *Transportation Research Record: Journal of the Transportation Research Board, 2650*(1), 9–17. doi:10.3141/2650-02

Said, O., & Masud, M. (2013). Towards internet of things: Survey and future vision. *International Journal of Computer Networks, 5*(1), 1–17.

Saini, H. K., Jain, K. L., Hiran, K. K., & Bhati, A. (2021). Paradigms to make smart city using blockchain. *Blockchain 3.0 for Sustainable Development, 10*, 21.

Sajjad, A., Eweje, G., & Tappin, D. (2020). Managerial perspectives on drivers for and barriers to sustainable supply chain management implementation: Evidence from New Zealand. *Business Strategy and the Environment, 29*(2), 592–604. doi:10.1002/bse.2389

Salam, A., & Salam, A. (2020). Internet of things in agricultural innovation and security. *Internet of Things for Sustainable Community Development: Wireless Communications. Sensory Systems*, 71–112.

Saniuk, S., Grabowska, S., & Straka, M. (2022). Identification of Social and Economic Expectations: Contextual Reasons for the Transformation Process of Industry 4.0 into the Industry 5.0 Concept. *Sustainability (Basel), 14*(3), 1391. doi:10.3390u14031391

Sargani, G. R., Zhou, D., Raza, M. H., & Wei, Y. (2020). Sustainable entrepreneurship in the agriculture sector: The nexus of the triple bottom line measurement approach. *Sustainability (Basel), 12*(8), 3275. doi:10.3390u12083275

Sarkar, I., Adhikari, M., Kumar, N., & Kumar, S. (2021). Dynamic task placement for deadline-aware IoT applications in federated for networks. *IEEE Internet Things Journal, 1*, 2021.

Sarkar, T. K., Mailloux, R. J., Oliner, A. A., Salazar-Palma, M., & Sengupta, D. L. (2006). *History of Wireless*. John Wiley & Sons Inc.

Sarmah, S. S. (2018). Understanding blockchain technology. *Computing in Science & Engineering, 8*(2), 23–29. doi:10.5923/j.computer.20180802.02

SAS. (2012). *Supply Chain Analytics: Beyond ERP and SCM*. SAS.

Sathi, A. (2012). Big data analytics: Disruptive technologies for changing the game. MC Press Online.

Saunders, M. N., Lewis, P., Thornhill, A., & Bristow, A. (2015). *Understanding research philosophy and approaches to theory development.* The Open University.

Saurabh, S., & Dey, K. (2021). Blockchain technology adoption, architecture, and sustainable agri-food supply chains. *Journal of Cleaner Production, 284*, 124731. doi:10.1016/j.jclepro.2020.124731

Schneider, M., Hippchen, B., Abeck, S., Jacoby, M., & Herzog, R. (2018). Enabling IoT platform interoperability using a systematic development approach by example. *Proceedings of the Global Internet of Things Summit (GIoTS'18),* 1-6.

Schutzer, D. (1990). Business expert systems: The competitive edge. *Expert Systems with Applications, 1*(1), 17–21. doi:10.1016/0957-4174(90)90065-3

Scur, G., & Barbosa, M. E. (2017). Green supply chain management practices: Multiple case studies in the Brazilian home appliance industry. *Journal of Cleaner Production, 141*, 1293–1302. doi:10.1016/j.jclepro.2016.09.158

Seiger, R., Huber, S., & Schlegel, T. (2018). Toward an execution system for self-healing workflows in cyber-physical systems. *Software & Systems Modeling, 17*(2), 551–572.

Sekaran, U., & Bougie, R. (2016). *Research methods for business: A skill building approach.* John Wiley & Sons.

Seuring, S., Aman, S., Hettiarachchi, B. D., de Lima, F. A., Schilling, L., & Sudusinghe, J. I. (2022). Reflecting on theory development in sustainable supply chain management. *Cleaner Logistics and Supply Chain, 3*, 100016. doi:10.1016/j.clscn.2021.100016

Seuring, S., & Gold, S. (2019). Sustainability management beyond corporate boundaries: From stakeholders to performance. *Journal of Cleaner Production, 207*, 1084–1094.

Seydanlou, P., Jolai, F., Tavakkoli-Moghaddam, R., & Fathollahi-Fard, A. M. (2022). A multi-objective optimization framework for a sustainable closed-loop supply chain network in the olive industry: Hybrid meta-heuristic algorithms. *Expert Systems with Applications, 203*, 117566. doi:10.1016/j.eswa.2022.117566

Sgarbossa, F., Grosse, E. H., Neumann, W. P., Battini, D., & Glock, C. H. (2020). Human factors in production and logistics systems of the future. *Annual Reviews in Control, 49*, 295–305. doi:10.1016/j.arcontrol.2020.04.007

Shaban, A., Zaki, F. E., Afefy, I. H., Di Gravio, G., Falegnami, A., & Patriarca, R. (2022). An Optimization Model for the Design of a Sustainable Municipal Solid Waste Management System. *Sustainability (Basel)*, *14*(10), 6345. doi:10.3390u14106345

Shaikh, T. A., Rasool, T., & Lone, F. R. (2022). Towards leveraging the role of machine learning and artificial intelligence in precision agriculture and smart farming. *Computers and Electronics in Agriculture*, *198*, 107119. doi:10.1016/j.compag.2022.107119

Shamim, R. (2022). Machine learning's algorithm profoundly impacts predicting the share market stock's price. *IJFMR-International Journal For Multidisciplinary Research, 4*(5).

Shankar, R., Choudhary, D., & Jharkharia, S. (2018). An integrated risk assessment model : A case of sustainable freight transportation systems. *Transportation Research Part D, Transport and Environment*, *63*, 662–676. doi:10.1016/j.trd.2018.07.003

Shapiro, J. (2010). Advanced Analytics for Sales & Operations Planning. *Analytics Magazine*, (May-June), 20–26.

Sharifnasab, H., Mahrokh, A., Dehghanisanij, H., Łazuka, E., Łagód, G., & Karami, H. (2023). Evaluating the use of intelligent irrigation systems based on the IoT in grain corn irrigation. *Water (Basel)*, *15*(7), 1394. doi:10.3390/w15071394

Sharma, A., Kaur, J., & Singh, I. (2020). Internet of things (IoT) in pharmaceutical manufacturing, warehousing, and supply chain management. *SN Computer Science*, *1*(4), 1–10. doi:10.100742979-020-00248-2

Sharma, R., Kamble, S. S., Gunasekaran, A., Kumar, V., & Kumar, A. (2020). A Systematic Literature Review On Machine Learning Applications For Sustainable Agriculture Supply Chain Performance. Computers &amp. *Computers & Operations Research*, *104926*(119), 104926. doi:10.1016/j.cor.2020.104926

Sharma, S., Gahlawat, V. K., Rahul, K., Mor, R. S., & Malik, M. (2021). Sustainable Innovations In the Food Industry Through Artificial Intelligence And Big Data Analytics. *Logistics*, *4*(5), 66. doi:10.3390/logistics5040066

Shekarian, E., Ijadi, B., Zare, A., & Majava, J. (2022). Sustainable supply chain management: A comprehensive systematic review of industrial practices. *Sustainability (Basel)*, *14*(13), 7892. doi:10.3390u14137892

Sheng, J., Amankwah-Amoah, J., Khan, Z., & Wang, X. (2021). COVID-19 pandemic in the new era of big data analytics: Methodological innovations and future research directions. *British Journal of Management*, *32*(4), 1164–1183. doi:10.1111/1467-8551.12441

Shen, Z. M., & Sun, Y. (2023). Strengthening supply chain resilience during COVID-19: A case study of JD. com. *Journal of Operations Management*, *69*(3), 359–383. doi:10.1002/joom.1161

Shin, T. H., Chin, S., Yoon, S. W., & Kwon, S. W. (2011). A service-oriented integrated information framework for RFID/WSN-based intelligent construction supply chain management. *Automation in Construction*, *20*(6), 706–715. doi:10.1016/j.autcon.2010.12.002

Shi, P., Li, P., Li, Z., Sun, J., Wang, D., & Min, Z. (2022). Effects of grass vegetation coverage and position on runoff and sediment yields on the slope of Loess Plateau, China. *Agricultural Water Management*, *259*, 107231. doi:10.1016/j.agwat.2021.107231

Shoman, W., Yeh, S., Sprei, F., Koehler, J., Plötz, P., Todorov, Y., . . . Speth, D. (2022). A Review Of Big Data In Road Freight Transport Modeling–gaps and Potentials. SSRN Journal. https://doi.org/ doi:10.2139/ssrn.4156400

Shrivastav, M. (2022). Barriers Related To Ai Implementation In Supply Chain Management. *Journal of Global Information Management*, *8*(30), 1–19. doi:10.4018/JGIM.296725

Sibanyoni, J. J., & Tabit, F. T. (2019). An assessment of the hygiene status and incidence of foodborne pathogens on food contact surfaces in the food preparation facilities of schools. *Food Control*, *98*, 94–99. doi:10.1016/j.foodcont.2018.11.009

Siegel, E. (2013). *Predictive analytics: The power to predict who will click, buy, lie or die*. John Wiley & Sons Inc.

Silvestre, B. S. (2015). Sustainable supply chain management in emerging economies: Environmental turbulence, institutional voids and sustainability trajectories. *International Journal of Production Economics*, *167*, 156–169. doi:10.1016/j.ijpe.2015.05.025

Simonetto, M., Sgarbossa, F., Battini, D., & Govindan, K. (2022). Closed loop supply chains 4.0: From risks to benefits through advanced technologies. A literature review and research agenda. *International Journal of Production Economics*, *253*, 108582. doi:10.1016/j.ijpe.2022.108582

Singh, A. K., Zhu, X., Chen, C., Wu, J., Yang, B., Zakari, S., Jiang, X. J., Singh, N., & Liu, W. (2022). The role of glomalin in mitigation of multiple soil degradation problems. *Critical Reviews in Environmental Science and Technology*, *52*(9), 1604–1638. doi:10.1080/10643389.2020.1862561

Singhania, M., & Saini, N. (2022). Systems approach to environment, social and governance (ESG): Case of Reliance industries. *Sustainable Operations and Computers*, *3*, 103–117. doi:10.1016/j.susoc.2021.11.003

Singh, S. K., Azzaoui, A. E., Kim, T. W., Pan, Y., & Park, J. H. (2021). DeepBlockScheme: A deep learning-based blockchain driven scheme for secure smart city. *Human-centric Computing and Information Sciences*, *11*(12), 1–13.

Sodhi, M. S., & Tang, C. S. (2016). *Supply chain risk management* (2nd ed.). Springer.

Song, M. L., Fisher, R., Wang, J. L., & Cui, L. B. (2018). Environmental performance evaluation with big data: Theories and methods. *Annals of Operations Research*, *270*(1–2), 459–472. doi:10.100710479-016-2158-8

spglobal *(2023) UK carbon prices swing back to premium as EUA rally halts*. SP Global. https://www.spglobal.com/commodityinsights/en/market-insights/latest-news/electric-power/020923-uk-carbon-prices-swing-back-to-premium-as-eua-rally-halts#

Srivastava, P. R., Zhang, J. Z., & Eachempati, P. (2023). Blockchain technology and its applications in agriculture and supply chain management: A retrospective overview and analysis. *Enterprise Information Systems*, *17*(5), 1995783. doi:10.1080/17517575.2021.1995783

Srivastava, S. K. (2017). Green supply-chain management: A state-of-the-art literature review. *International Journal of Management Reviews*, *19*(1), 63–84.

SSATP. (2017). *Case Study : Accra, Ghana Overview Objectives of the Road Passenger Transport Stakeholders Strategies for improvement of Urban Road Passenger Transport National Transport Policy*. SSATP.

SSATP. (2018). *Policies for Sustainable Accessibility and Mobility in Cities of Rwanda*. SSATP.

Starbucks. (2023). *C.A.F.E. Practices: Starbucks Approach to Ethically Sourcing Coffee*. Starbucks. https://stories.starbucks.com/press/2020/cafe-practices-starbucks-approach-to-ethically-sourcing-coffee/ [Accessed Date: 28 June, 2023]

statista. (2022). *UK: carbon price growth for industry & services 2040*. Statista. https://www.statista.com/statistics/496288/carbon-price-growth-industry-service-uk/

Sternberg, H. S., Hofmann, E., & Roeck, D. (2021). The Struggle is Real: Insights from a Supply Chain Blockchain Case. *Journal of Business Logistics*, *42*(1), 71–87. doi:10.1111/jbl.12240

Stern, N. (2007). *The Economics of Climate Change: The Stern Review*. Cambridge University Press. doi:10.1017/CBO9780511817434

Stiglitz, J. (2017). *Globalization and its Discontents Revisited: Anti-Globalization in the Era of Trump.* Penguin.

Stock, J. R. (2013). Supply chain management: A look back, a look ahead. *Supply Chain Quarterly, 2*, 22–26.

Stock, T., & Seliger, G. (2016). Opportunities of sustainable manufacturing in industry 4.0. *Procedia CIRP, 40*, 536–541. doi:10.1016/j.procir.2016.01.129

Stojmenovic, I., & Wen, S. (2014). The fog computing paradigm: scenarios and security issues. *Proceedings of the Federated Conference on Computer Science and Information Systems (FedCSIS' 14),* 1–8.

Strauss, J. & Frost, R.D. (2016). *E-marketing: Instructor's Review Copy.* Springer.

Stuart, I., McCutcheon, D., Handfield, R., McLachlin, R., & Samson, D. (2002). Effective case research in operations management: A process perspective. *Journal of Operations Management, 20*(5), 419–433. doi:10.1016/S0272-6963(02)00022-0

Sudusinghe, J. I., & Seuring, S. (2022). Supply chain collaboration and sustainability performance in circular economy: A systematic literature review. *International Journal of Production Economics, 245*, 108402. doi:10.1016/j.ijpe.2021.108402

Suifan, T., Alazab, M., & Alhyari, S. (2019). Trade-off among lean, agile, resilient and green paradigms: An empirical study on pharmaceutical industry in jordan using a TOPSIS-entropy method. *Int. J. Adv. Oper. Manage., 11*(1–2), 69–101. doi:10.1504/IJAOM.2019.098493

Sulaiman, M. A. (2020). Evaluating data mining classification methods performance in Internet of things applications. *Journal of Soft Computing and Data Mining, 1*(2), 11–25.

Sulkowski, A. (2018). Blockchain, business supply chains, sustainability, and law: The future of governance, legal frameworks, and lawyers. *SSRN, 43*, 303. doi:10.2139srn.3262291

Sun, Z. Strang, K. Firmin, S. (2017). *Business analytics-based enterprise information systems.*

Sundarakani, B., Ajaykumar, A., & Gunasekaran, A. (2021). Big data driven supply chain design and applications for blockchain: An action research using case study approach. *Omega, 102*, 102452. doi:10.1016/j.omega.2021.102452

Sunitha, G., Pushpalatha, M. N., Parkavi, A., Boyapati, P., Walia, R., Kohar, R., & Qureshi, K. (2022). Modeling of chaotic political optimizer for crop yield prediction. *Intelligent Automation and Soft Computing, 34*(1), 423–437. doi:10.32604/iasc.2022.024757

Supply Chain Council (2010). http://supply-chain.org/f/down-load/726710733/SCOR10.pdf.

Sutrisno, A., & Kumar, V. (2022). Supply chain sustainability risk assessment model using integration of the preference selection index (PSI) and the Shannon entropy. *International Journal of Quality & Reliability Management, 40*(3), 674–708. doi:10.1108/IJQRM-06-2021-0191

Sutrisno, A., & Kumar, V. (2022). Supply chain sustainability risk decision support model using integrated Preference Selection Index (PSI) method and prospect theory. *Journal of Advances in Management Research, 19*(2), 316–346. doi:10.1108/JAMR-06-2021-0193

Suweis, S., Carr, J. A., Maritan, A., Rinaldo, A., & D'Odorico, P. (2015). Resilience and reactivity of global food security. *Proceedings of the National Academy of Sciences of the United States of America, 112*(22), 6902–6907. doi:10.1073/pnas.1507366112 PMID:25964361

Svilvar, M., Charkraborty, A. & Kanioura, A. (2013). Big data analytics in marketing. *OR/MS Today.*

Swaminathan, J. M. (2000). *Supply chain management.* In International Encyclopedia of the Social and Behavioural Sciences. Elsevier Sciences.

Tajul Baharuddin, M. F., Taib, S., Hashim, R., Abidin, M. H. Z., & Rahman, N. I. (2013). Assessment of seawater intrusion to the agricultural sustainability at the coastal area of Carey Island, Selangor, Malaysia. *Arabian Journal of Geosciences*, *6*(10), 3909–3928. doi:10.100712517-012-0651-1

Talavera, J. M., Tobón, L. E., Gómez, J. A., Culman, M. A., Aranda, J. M., Parra, D. T., Quiroz, L. A., Hoyos, A., & Garreta, L. E. (2017). Review of IoT applications in agro-industrial and environmental fields. *Computers and Electronics in Agriculture*, *142*, 283–297. doi:10.1016/j.compag.2017.09.015

Talón-Ballestero, P., González-Serrano, L., Soguero-Ruiz, C., Muñoz-Romero, S., & Rojo-Álvarez, J. L. (2018). Using big data from customer relationship management information systems to determine the client profile in the hotel sector. *Tourism Management*, *68*, 187–197. doi:10.1016/j.tourman.2018.03.017

Tan, J., & Koo, S. (2014). A survey of technologies in internet of things, in IEEE Computer Society, 269-274. *The Economist* (10). https://www.economist.com/node/15557443

Tan, K. H., Zhan, Y., Ji, G., Ye, F., & Chang, C. (2015). Harvesting big data to enhance supply chain innovation capabilities: An analytic infrastructure based on deduction graph. *International Journal of Production Economics*, *165*, 223–233. doi:10.1016/j.ijpe.2014.12.034

Tan, R., Zhang, T., Liu, D., & Xu, H. (2021). How will innovation-driven development policy affect sustainable urban land use: Evidence from 230 Chinese cities. *Sustainable Cities and Society*, *72*, 103021. doi:10.1016/j.scs.2021.103021

Taylor, D., & Pettit, S. (2009). A consideration of the relevance of lean supply chain concepts for humanitarian aid provision. *International Journal of Services Technology and Management*, *12*(4), 430–444. doi:10.1504/IJSTM.2009.025817

Thakur, T., Mehra, A., Hassija, V., Chamola, V., Srinivas, R., Gupta, K. K., & Singh, A. P. (2021). Smart water conservation through a machine learning and blockchain-enabled decentralized edge computing network. *Applied Soft Computing*, *106*, 107274. doi:10.1016/j.asoc.2021.107274

The Economist (2010). *Data, Data Everywhere*, http://www.economist.com/node/15557443

Tokkozhina, U., Martins, A. L., & Ferreira, J. C. (2023). Uncovering dimensions of the impact of blockchain technology in supply chain management. *Operations Management Research : Advancing Practice Through Research*, *16*(1), 99–125. doi:10.100712063-022-00273-9

Toolsense. (). *Which type of equipment tracker should you use.* Tool Sense. https://toolsense.io/equipment-management/which-type-of-equipment-tracker-should-you-use/,

Toorajipour, R., Sohrabpour, V., Nazarpour, A., Oghazi, P., & Fischl, M. (2021). Artificial intelligence in supply chain management: A systematic literature review. *Journal of Business Research*, *122*, 502–517. doi:10.1016/j.jbusres.2020.09.009

Torre-Bastida, A. I., Laña, I., Ilardia, M., Bilbao, M. N., & Campos-Cordobés, S. (2018). Big Data For Transportation and Mobility: Recent Advances, Trends And Challenges. *IET Intelligent Transport Systems*, *8*(12), 742–755. doi:10.1049/iet-its.2018.5188

Torres-Ruiz, A., & Ravindran, A. R. (2018). Multiple criteria framework for the sustainability risk assessment of a supplier portfolio. *Journal of Cleaner Production*, *172*, 4478–4493. doi:10.1016/j.jclepro.2017.10.304

Townsend, D. M., & Hunt, R. A. (2019). Entrepreneurial action, creativity, & judgment in the age of artificial intelligence. *Journal of Business Venturing Insights*, *11*, e00126. doi:10.1016/j.jbvi.2019.e00126

Travis Fried, I. A. (2019). *Putting Paratransit on the Map*. ZBW.

Treiblmaier, H. (2018). The impact of the blockchain on the supply chain: A theory-based research framework and a call for action. *Supply Chain Management, 23*(6), 545–559. doi:10.1108/SCM-01-2018-0029

Tripathi, A. D., Mishra, R., Maurya, K. K., Singh, R. B., & Wilson, D. W. (2019). Estimates for world population and global food availability for global health. In *The role of functional food security in global health* (pp. 3-24). Academic Press.

Trkman, P., McCormack, K., de Oliveira, M. P. V., & Ladeira, M. B. (2010). The Impact of Business Analytics on Supply Chain Performance. *Decision Support Systems, 49*(3), 318–327. doi:10.1016/j.dss.2010.03.007

Tsai, C. Y., & Huang, S. H. (2015). A data mining approach to optimise shelf space allocation in consideration of customer purchase and moving behaviours. *International Journal of Production Research, 53*(3), 850–866. doi:10.1080/00207543.2014.937011

Tsang, Y. P., Yang, T., Chen, Z. S., Wu, C. H., & Tan, K. H. (2022). How is extended reality bridging human and cyber-physical systems in the IoT-empowered logistics and supply chain management? *Internet of Things, 20*, 100623. doi:10.1016/j.iot.2022.100623

Tseng, M. L., Bui, T. D., Lim, M. K., Fujii, M., & Mishra, U. (2022). Assessing data-driven sustainable supply chain management indicators for the textile industry under industrial disruption and ambidexterity. *International Journal of Production Economics, 245*, 108401. doi:10.1016/j.ijpe.2021.108401

Tsouros, D. C., Bibi, S., & Sarigiannidis, P. G. (2019). A review on UAV-based applications for precision agriculture. *Information (Basel), 10*(11), 349. doi:10.3390/info10110349

Turban, E., & Sepehri, M. (1986). Applications of Decision Support and Expert Systems in Flexible Manufacturing Systems. *Journal of Operations Management, 6*(34), 433–448. doi:10.1016/0272-6963(86)90015-X

Turban, E., Sharda, R., Delen, D., & King, D. (2011). *Business Intelligence: A Managerial Approach* (2nd ed.). Prentice-Hall.

Tzounis, A., Katsoulas, N., Bartzanas, T., & Kittas, C. (2017). Internet of Things in agriculture, recent advances and future challenges. *Biosystems Engineering, 164*, 31–48. doi:10.1016/j.biosystemseng.2017.09.007

Udeagha, M. C., & Muchapondwa, E. (2023). Green finance, fintech, and environmental sustainability: Fresh policy insights from the BRICS nations. *International Journal of Sustainable Development and World Ecology, 30*(6), 1–17. doi:10.1080/13504509.2023.2183526

UN. (2015). *Transforming our world: The 2030 agenda for sustainable development.* United Nations.

United Nations. (2021). *Transforming our world: The 2030 Agenda for Sustainable Development.* UN. https://sdgs.un.org/2030agenda

Valinejad, F., & Rahmani, D. (2018). Sustainability risk management in the supply chain of telecommunication companies : A case study. *Journal of Cleaner Production, 203*, 53–67. doi:10.1016/j.jclepro.2018.08.174

Valinejad, F., Safaie, N., Rahmani, D., & Saadatmand, M. R. (2022). A Hybrid Model for Supply Chain Risk Management Based on Five-dimensional Sustainability Approach in Telecommunication Industry. *International Journal of Engineering, 35*(6), 1096–1110. doi:10.5829/IJE.2022.35.06C.01

Van Engeland, J., Beliën, J., De Boeck, L., & De Jaeger, S. (2020). Literature review: Strategic network optimization models in waste reverse supply chains. *Omega, 91*, 102012. doi:10.1016/j.omega.2018.12.001

Vanalle, R. M., Barbieri, J. C., & Arantes, A. F. (2021). Sustainability assessment model for logistics service providers. *Journal of Cleaner Production, 318*, 128611.

Varelas, G., Voutsakist, E., Raftopoulout, P., Petrakis, E. G. M., & Milios, E. (2005). Semantic Similarity methods in WordNet and their application to information retrieval on the Web. In *Proceedings of the 7th annual ACM international workshop on web information and data management*. ACM.

Vargas-Florez, J., Medina-Rodríguez, R., & Alva-Cabrera, R. (2015, September). A clustering optimization approach for disaster relief delivery: A case study in lima-Peru. In *Annual International Symposium on Information Management and Big Data* (pp. 69-80). Cham: Springer International Publishing.

Varsei, M., Azadegan, A., & Ivanov, D. (2019). A systematic literature review on sustainable supply chain finance: Current trends and future directions. *Annals of Operations Research*, *283*(1-2), 375–416.

Vecchio, M. D., Kharlamov, A. A., Parry, G., Pogrebna, G. (2020). *Improving Productivity In Hollywood With Data Science: Using Emotional Arcs Of Movies To Drive Product and Service.*

Verdouw, C. N., Wolfert, J., Beulens, A. J. M., & Rialland, A. (2016). Virtualization of food supply chains with the internet of things. *Journal of Food Engineering*, *176*, 128–136. doi:10.1016/j.jfoodeng.2015.11.009

Verma V., & Chandra, B. (2017). *An Application of Theory of Planned Behavior to Predict Young Indian Consumers' Green Hotel Visit Intention*. Research Gate.

Verma, M. (2023). Integration of AI-Based Chatbot (ChatGPT) And Supply Chain Management Solution To Enhance Tracking And Queries Response. *International Journal for Science and Advance Research in Technology.*

Vermesan, O., Friess, P., & Guillemin, P. (2011). Internet of things strategic research roadmap. *Internet of Things. Global Technological and Societal Trends, 1*, 9–52.

Veza, I., Mladineo, M., & Gjeldum, N. (2015). Managing innovative production network of smart factories. *IFAC-PapersOnLine*, *48*(3), 555–560. doi:10.1016/j.ifacol.2015.06.139

Vilariño, M. V., Franco, C., & Quarrington, C. (2017). Food loss and waste reduction as an integral part of a circular economy. *Frontiers in Environmental Science*, *5*, 21. doi:10.3389/fenvs.2017.00021

Villars, R. L., Olofson, C. W., & Eastwood, M. (2011). *Big data: what it is and why you should care.* (White Paper). IDC.

Vinodh, S., Ben Ruben, R., & Asokan, P. (2016). Life cycle assessment integrated value stream mapping framework to ensure sustainable manufacturing: A case study. *Clean Technologies and Environmental Policy*, *18*(1), 279–295. doi:10.100710098-015-1016-8

Vinodh, S., Devadasan, S. R., Vimal, K. E. K., & Kumar, D. (2013). Design of agile supply chain assessment model and its case study in an Indian automotive components manufacturing organization. *Journal of Manufacturing Systems*, *32*(4), 620–631. doi:10.1016/j.jmsy.2013.04.001

Viswanathan, N., & Sadlovska, V. (2010). *Supply Chain Intelligence: Adopt Role-based Operational Business Intelligence and Improve Visibility.* Aberdeen Group.

Vosburg, J., & Kumar, A. (2011). Managing Dirty Data in Organizations Using ERP: Lessons from a Case Study. *Industrial Management & Data Systems*, *101*(1), 21–31. doi:10.1108/02635570110365970

Wadmann, S., & Hoeyer, K. (2018). Dangers of the digital fit: Rethinking seamlessness and social sustainability in data-intensive healthcare. *Big Data & Society*, *5*(1). doi:10.1177/2053951717752964

Waller, M. A., & Fawcett, C. (2013). Click Here for a Data Scientist: Big Data, Predictive Analytics, and Theory Development in the Era of a Maker Movement Supply Chain. *Journal of Business Logistics*, *34*(4), 249–252. doi:10.1111/jbl.12024

Wang, J., & Feng, T. (2022). Supply chain ethical leadership and green supply chain integration: A moderated mediation analysis. *International Journal of Logistics Research and Applications*, 1-27.

Wang, T., Zhang, Y., & Zang, D. (2016) Real-time visibility and traceability framework for discrete manufacturing shop-floor. *Proceedings of the 22nd International Conference on Industrial Engineering and Engineering Management*,(pp. 763–772). Springer. 10.2991/978-94-6239-180-2_72

Wang, B., Luo, W., Zhang, A., Tian, Z., & Li, Z. (2020). Blockchain-enabled circular supply chain management: A system architecture for fast fashion. *Computers in Industry*, *123*, 103324. doi:10.1016/j.compind.2020.103324

Wang, H., Zhang, M., Ying, H., & Zhao, X. (2021). The impact of blockchain technology on consumer behavior: A multimethod study. *Journal of Management Analytics*, *8*(3), 371–390. doi:10.1080/23270012.2021.1958264

Wang, L., Laszewski, G. V., Young, K. M., & Tao, J. (2010). Cloud Computing: A Perspective Study. *New Generation Computing*, *28*(2), 137–146. doi:10.100700354-008-0081-5

Wang, L., & Rani, P. (2021). Sustainable supply chains under risk in the manufacturing firms : An extended double normalization-based multiple aggregation approach under an intuitionistic fuzzy environment. *Journal of Enterprise Information Management*, *35*(4/5), 1067–1099. doi:10.1108/JEIM-05-2021-0222

Wang, X., Sethi, S. P., & Chang, S. (2022). Pollution abatement using cap-and-trade in a dynamic supply chain and its coordination. *Transportation Research Part E, Logistics and Transportation Review*, *158*, 102592. doi:10.1016/j.tre.2021.102592

Watson, M., Lewis, S., Cacioppi, P., & Jayaraman, J. (2013). *Supply chain network design – applying optimization and analytics to the global supply chain*. FT Press.

Watson, H. J. (2009). Tutorial: Business Intelligence – Past, Present, and Future. *Communications of the Association for Information Systems*, *39*(25). doi:10.17705/1CAIS.02539

Weaver, C. P., Lempert, R. J., Brown, C., Hall, J. A., Revell, D., & Sarewitz, D. (2013). Improving the contribution of climate model information to decision making: The value and demands of robust decision frameworks. *Wiley Interdisciplinary Reviews: Climate Change*, *4*(1), 39–60. doi:10.1002/wcc.202

Wee, H., & Wu, S. (2009). Lean supply chain and its effect on product cost and quality: A case study on Ford Motor Company. *Supply Chain Management*, *14*(5), 335–341. doi:10.1108/13598540910980242

Wei, Z., Alam, T., Al Sulaie, S., Bouye, M., Deebani, W., & Song, M. (2023). An efficient IoT-based perspective view of food traceability supply chain using optimized classifier algorithm. *Information Processing & Management*, *60*(3), 103275. doi:10.1016/j.ipm.2023.103275

Wells, P., Abouarghoub, W., Pettit, S., & Beresford, A. (2020). A socio-technical transitions perspective for assessing future sustainability following the COVID-19 pandemic. Sustainability: Science. *Sustainability*, *16*(1), 29–36. doi:10.1080/15487733.2020.1763002

Weyrich, M., & Ebert, C. (2016). Reference architectures for the internet of things. *IEEE Software*, *33*(1), 112–116.

WHIG, P. (2023). Leveraging AI for Sustainable Agriculture: Opportunities and Challenges. *Transactions on Latest Trends in Artificial Intelligence*, *4*(4).

Whittington, R., Regnér, P., Angwin, D., Johnson, G., & Scholes, K. (2022). *Exploring Strategy* (12th ed.). Pearson.

Wichaisri, S., & Sopadang, A. (2017). Integrating sustainable development, lean, and logistics concepts into a lean sustainable logistics model. *International Journal of Logistics Systems and Management*, *26*(1), 85. doi:10.1504/IJLSM.2017.080631

Widder, D. G., Nafus, D., Dabbish, L., & Herbsleb, J. (2022, June). Limits and Possibilities for "Ethical AI" in Open Source: A Study of Deepfakes. In *2022 ACM Conference on Fairness, Accountability, and Transparency* (pp. 2035-2046). ACM. 10.1145/3531146.3533779

Wilson, M. W., Paschen, J., & Pitt, L. (2021). The Circular Economy Meets Artificial Intelligence (Ai): Understanding the Opportunities Of Ai For Reverse Logistics. *Management of Environmental Quality*, *1*(33), 9–25. doi:10.1108/MEQ-10-2020-0222

Wireko, J. K., Hiran, K. K., & Doshi, R. (2018). Culturally Based User Resistance to New Technologies in the Age of IoT In Developing Countries: Perspectives From Ethiopia. *International Journal of Emerging Technology and Advanced Engineering*, *8*(4), 96–105.

Wong, C. W., Wong, C. Y., & Boon-itt, S. (2018). How does sustainable development of supply chains make firms lean, green and profitable? A resource orchestration perspective. *Business Strategy and the Environment*, *27*(3), 375–388. doi:10.1002/bse.2004

World Bank Group. (2016). *World development report 2016: Digital dividends*. World Bank Publications.

World Commission on Environment and Development. (1987). *Our Common Future*. Oxford University Press.

World Economic Forum. (2021). Net Zero Challenge: The supply chain opportunity. I*nsight Report.* https://www3.weforum.org/docs/WEF_Net_Zero_Challenge_The_Supply_Chain_Opportunity_2021.pdf

World Health Organization. (2022). *UN Report: Global hunger numbers rose to as many as 828 million in 2021*. WHO.

Woschank, M., Rauch, E., & Zsifkovits, H. (2020). A Review Of Further Directions For Artificial Intelligence, Machine Learning, and Deep Learning In Smart Logistics. *Sustainability (Basel)*, *9*(12), 3760. doi:10.3390u12093760

Wu, M., Lu, T. J., Ling, F. Y., Sun, J., & Du, H. Y. (2010). Research on the architecture of internet of things. *Proceedings of the 3rd International Conference on Advanced Computer Theory and Engineering (ICACTE' 10), 5*, 484-487.

Wu, K. J., Liao, C. J., Tseng, M. L., Lim, M. K., Hu, J., & Tan, K. (2017). Toward sustainability: Using big data to explore the decisive attributes of supply chain risks and uncertainties. *Journal of Cleaner Production*, *142*, 663–676. doi:10.1016/j.jclepro.2016.04.040

Xian, F. (2022). Quantifying the Impact Of Artificial Intelligence Technology On China's Manufacturing Employment. *International Conference on Computer, Artificial Intelligence, and Control Engineering (CAICE 2022).* Spie. 10.1117/12.2640987

Xing, B., Gao, W. J., Battle, K., Nelwamondo, F. V., & Marwala, T. (2012). e-RL: the Internet of things supported reverse logistics for remanufacture-to-order. *International Conference in Swarm Intelligence: Advances in Swarm Intelligence,* (pp. 519–526). IEEE.

Xu, M., David, J. M., & Kim, S. H. (2018). The fourth industrial revolution: Opportunities and challenges. *International journal of financial research, 9*(2), 90-95.

Xu, G., Dong, T., Cobbinah, P. B., Jiao, L., Sumari, N. S., Chai, B., & Liu, Y. (2019). Urban expansion and form changes across African cities with a global outlook: Spatiotemporal analysis of urban land densities. *Journal of Cleaner Production*, *224*, 802–810. doi:10.1016/j.jclepro.2019.03.276

Xu, M., Cui, Y., Hu, M., Xu, X., Zhang, Z., Liang, S., & Qu, S. (2019). Supply chain sustainability risk and assessment. *Journal of Cleaner Production, 225*, 857–867. doi:10.1016/j.jclepro.2019.03.307

Xu, X., Tatge, L., Xu, X., & Liu, Y. (2022). Blockchain applications in the supply chain management in German automotive industry. *Production Planning and Control*, 1–15. doi:10.1080/09537287.2022.2044073

Yadav, S., Choi, T. M., Kumar, A., Luthra, S., & Naz, F. (2023). A meta-analysis of sustainable supply chain practices and performance: The moderating roles of type of economy and innovation. *International Journal of Operations & Production Management, 43*(5), 802–845. doi:10.1108/IJOPM-05-2022-0328

Yadav, V. S., Singh, A. R., Gunasekaran, A., Raut, R. D., & Narkhede, B. E. (2022). A systematic literature review of the agro-food supply chain: Challenges, network design, and performance measurement perspectives. *Sustainable Production and Consumption, 29*, 685–704. doi:10.1016/j.spc.2021.11.019

Yan, B., & Huang, G. (2009). *Supply chain information transmission based on RFID and internet of things in Computing*. Communication, Control, and Management, ISECS International Colloquium on, (pp. 166–169). ISECS.

Yansui, L., Xiaoyu, Z., Yongsheng, W., Zhi, C., Yuheng, L., Wenhao, W., ... & Rui, L. (2018). Land consolidation engineering and modern agriculture: A case study from soil particles to agricultural systems.

Yan, Z., Ismail, H., Chen, L., Zhao, X., & Wang, L. (2019). The Application Of Big Data Analytics In Optimizing Logistics: A Developmental Perspective Review. J. of Data. *Information & Management, 1-2*(1), 33–43. doi:10.100742488-019-00003-0

Yingfei, Y., Mengze, Z., Zeyu, L., Ki-Hyung, B., Avotra, A. A. R. N., & Nawaz, A. (2022). Green logistics performance and infrastructure on service trade and environment-measuring firm's performance and service quality. *Journal of King Saud University. Science, 34*(1), 101683. doi:10.1016/j.jksus.2021.101683

Yin, R. K. (2009). Case Study Research: Design and Methods. *Sage (Atlanta, Ga.)*.

Yoshioka, N., Honiden, S., & Fnkelstein, A. (2004). Security Patterns: A Method for Constructing Secure and Efficient Inter-Company Coordination Systems. *Proceedings of Enterprise Distributed Object Computing Conference 2004 (EDOC'04)*, 84–97.

Younis, H., Sundarakani, B., & Alsharairi, M. (2022). Applications of artificial intelligence and machine learning within supply chains: Systematic review and future research directions. *Journal of Modelling in Management, 17*(3), 916–940. doi:10.1108/JM2-12-2020-0322

Yusufkhonov, Z., Ravshanov, M., Kamolov, A., & Kamalova, E. (2021). Improving the position of the logistics performance index of Uzbekistan. In *E3S Web of Conferences* (Vol. 264, p. 05028). EDP Sciences. doi:10.1051/e3sconf/202126405028

Yuvaraj, S., & Sangeetha, M. (2016). Smart supply chain management using internet of things (IoT) and low power wireless communication systems. In Wireless Communication, Signal Processing and Networking, International Conference, 555-558.

Yu, X., Xu, S., & Ashton, M. (2023). Antecedents and outcomes of artificial intelligence adoption and application in the workplace: The socio-technical system theory perspective. *Information Technology & People, 36*(1), 454–474. doi:10.1108/ITP-04-2021-0254

Zach F. & Fesenmaier, D. R. (2016). *ScholarWorks@UMass Amherst The Changing Impact of the Internet on Travel Planning Behavior*. University of Massachusetts.

Zawadzki, P., & Zywicki, K. (2016). Smart product design and production control for effective mass customization in the industry 4.0 concept. *Management of Production Engineering Review, 7*(3), 105–112. doi:10.1515/mper-2016-0030

Zeppel, M. J. B., Wilks, J. V., & Lewis, J. D. (2014). Impacts of extreme precipitation and seasonal changes in precipitation on plants. *Biogeosciences, 11*(11), 3083–3093. doi:10.5194/bg-11-3083-2014

Zerbino, P., Aloini, D., Dulmin, R., & Mininno, V. (2018). Big Data-enabled Customer Relationship Management : A holistic approach. *Information Processing & Management, 54*(5), 818–846. doi:10.1016/j.ipm.2017.10.005

Zhang, D., Pee, L. G., & Cui, L. (2021). Artificial intelligence in E-commerce fulfillment: A case study of resource orchestration at Alibaba's Smart Warehouse. *International Journal of Information Management, 57*, 102304. doi:10.1016/j.ijinfomgt.2020.102304

Zhang, F., & Song, W. (2022). Sustainability risk assessment of blockchain adoption in sustainable supply chain : An integrated method. *Computers & Industrial Engineering, 171*, 108378. doi:10.1016/j.cie.2022.108378

Zhang, S., & Chen, W. (2022). China's energy transition pathway in a carbon neutral vision. *Engineering (Beijing), 14*, 64–76. doi:10.1016/j.eng.2021.09.004

Zhang, Z., Yu, X., Wu, P., & Han, W. (2015). Survey on water-saving agricultural internet of things based on wireless sensor network. *International Journal of Control and Automation, 8*(4), 229–240. doi:10.14257/ijca.2015.8.4.23

Zhao, J., & Kumar, V. V. (2021). *Handbook of Research on Innovations and Applications of AI, IoT, and Cognitive Technologies*. IGI Global Publication.

Zhao, R., Liu, Y., Zhang, N., & Huang, T. (2017). An optimization model for green supply chain management by using a big data analytic approach. *Journal of Cleaner Production, 142*, 1085–1097. doi:10.1016/j.jclepro.2016.03.006

Zhong, R. Y., Huang, G. Q., Lan, S., Dai, Q. Y., Chen, X., & Zhang, T. (2015). A big data approach for logistics trajectory discovery from RFID-enabled production data. *International Journal of Production Economics, 165*, 260–272. doi:10.1016/j.ijpe.2015.02.014

Zhong, R. Y., Lan, S., Xu, C., Dai, Q., & Huang, G. Q. (2016). Visualization of RFID-enabled shopfloor logistics Big Data in Cloud Manufacturing. *International Journal of Advanced Manufacturing Technology, 84*(1–4), 5–16. doi:10.100700170-015-7702-1

Zhou, Y., Gao, X., & Nie, J. J. (2023, April 10). Value of blockchain-enabled supply chain traceability under competition. *International Transactions in Operational Research*, itor.13295. doi:10.1111/itor.13295

Zhu, X., Shi, Y., & Liu, N. (2022). Artificial Intelligence Technology In Modern Logistics System. *IJTPM, 1/2*(22), 66. doi:10.1504/IJTPM.2022.122537

Zkik, K., Sebbar, A., Nejjari, N., Lahlou, S., Fadi, O., & Oudani, M. (2023). Secure Model for Records Traceability in Airline Supply Chain Based on Blockchain and Machine Learning. In *Digital Transformation and Industry 4.0 for Sustainable Supply Chain Performance* (pp. 141–159). Springer International Publishing. doi:10.1007/978-3-031-19711-6_6

Zreik, M. (2022). The Regional Comprehensive Economic Partnership (RCEP) for the Asia–Pacific region and world. *Journal of Economic and Administrative Sciences*.

Zreik, M. (2020). The Dimensions of the US-China trade war. *Open Political Science, 3*(1), 47–55. doi:10.1515/openps-2020-0004

Zreik, M. (2023). Analytical study on Foreign Direct Investment Divestment Inflows and Outflows in Developing Economies: Evidence of China. *Chinese Economy*, 1–16. doi:10.1080/10971475.2023.2193118

Zreik, M., Syed Marzuki, S. Z., & Iqbal, B. A. (2023). Deepening Financial Inclusion through Digitization: A Case Study of Microfinance in China. [AEJ]. *ASEAN Entrepreneurship Journal, 9*(2), 9–21.

About the Contributors

Badr Bentalha is a Professor of Economics and Management at the National School of Business and Management, University Sidi Mohamed Ben Abdellah in Fez, Morocco. He received his Ph.D. in Service Logistics and Performance at Sidi Mohammed Ben Abdellah University, Fez, Morocco. Dr. Bentalha has a wealth of experience in auditing and optimizing business operations, which he brings to his teaching and writing. In addition to his academic work, Dr. Bentalha has authored several articles and participated in various international conferences. He is a member of numerous scientific committees for international journals and conferences. Dr. Bentalha has also worked extensively with companies to implement audit systems, resolve issues, and improve performance. Since 2009, he has helped many organizations, including banks, manufacturers, and logistics providers, optimize their operations and improve their bottom line. His expertise in internal auditing has helped these companies identify areas for improvement and implement effective solutions. Dr. Bentalha's most recent books, "Internal Audit of Treasury and Cash Management" and "Netnography: Principles, Method, and Ethics," are a testament to his expertise in auditing and optimizing business operations. Disciplines Managerial Economics Business Administration Supply chain management Qualitative Social Research Skills and expertise Management Marketing Management Management studies AuditSupply Chain Supply Chain Management Green Supply Chain Account Management Operations Research Organization and Administration Service Service Operations Management Service Supply Chain Languages English French

Aziz Hmioui received his PhD in Industrial Economics and is a Professor at Sidi Mohammed Ben Abdellah University, Fez. His research focuses on tourism, logistics and territorial attractiveness. He is the author of numerous scientific articles. He has participated in numerous international scientific events (Algeria, Brazil, Canada, Egypt, Spain, France, Tunisia and Vietnam). He is a member of several scientific committees of international journals and conferences.

Lhoussaine Alla is a Teacher-researcher at the National School of Applied Sciences of Fez, Sidi Mohamed de Ben Abdellah University His research focuses on tourism, logistics and territorial attractiveness. He is the author of numerous scientific articles. He has participated in numerous international scientific events

***

Belem Barbosa received her PhD in Business and Management Studies – Specialisation in Marketing and Strategy from the University of Porto, Portugal. She is Assistant Professor at the School of Economics and Management of the University of Porto. She is full researcher at GOVCOPP, the Research Unit of Governance, Competitiveness, and Public Policies, and Invited Researcher at cef.up Center for Economics and Finance at the University of Porto. Her research interests lie primarily in the areas of digital marketing and consumer behavior.

Sophia Barroso is a young researcher studying economics of business and strategy at the master's level.

Rim Ben Abdallah is a postdoctoral researcher in biological sciences with a particular interest in the application of food biochemistry, molecular biology in the areas of nutrition, food processes and technologies. Possesses strong analytical skills and resolutions developed through professional, academic and voluntary practice. Experienced in the execution and design of quantitative and qualitative analyzes acquired as part of scientific research projects.

Eya Ben Amara is a biology researcher.

Gonçalo Castro is a young researcher studying economics of business and strategy at the master's level.

Marcelo Corrêa is a young researcher studying economics of business and strategy at the Master's level.

Ruchi Doshi has more than 16 years of academic, research and software development experience in Asia and Africa. Currently she is working as research supervisor at the Azteca University, Mexico and Adjunct Professor at the Jyoti Vidyapeeth Women's University, Jaipur, Rajasthan, India. She worked in the BlueCrest University College, Liberia,West Africa as Registrar and Head, Examination; BlueCrest University College, Ghana, Africa; Amity University, Rajasthan, India; Trimax IT Infrastructure & Services, Udaipur, India. She worked as a Founder Chair, Women in Engineering (WIE) and Secretary Position in the IEEE Liberia Subsection. She worked with Ministry of Higher Education (MoHE) in Liberia and Ghana for the Degree approvals and accreditations processes. She is interested in the field of Machine Learning and Cloud computing framework development. She has published numerous research papers in peer-reviewed international journals and conferences. She is a Reviewer, Advisor, Ambassador and Editorial board member of various reputable International Journals and Conferences.

Yasser El Ouarrak is a PhD student at the National School of Business and Management, Sidi Mohamed Ben Abdellah University. He is working on various topics related to Supply Chain Risk Management, Supply Chain Sustainability, and Smart Supply Chains.

Sami Fattouch is a Professor of Biological Engineering at the University of Carthage.

Mohamed Hedi Ghidaoui is a scientific researcher who starts his career with a licence of anesthesia obtained from the higher school of health sciences and Techniques of Tunis in 2018 after three years of studying, also he studied in the Higher Institute of Medical Technologies of Tunis for almost one year (2019) in the field of biomedical engineering, then in 2021 he starts the master's degree course of "research and promotion of pain management" for two years.Mohamed Hedi has the keen interest for discovering new things, collaborate in the scientific works and researches in which he hopes to succeed. Now he's a member of a scientific group working in the National Institute of Applied Sciences and Technology, University of Carthage, Tunis- department of Biological and Chemical Engineering. For his interests, he cannot get enough of practicing sport among other things.

Rafael Godinho is a young researcher studying economics of business and strategy at the Master's level.

Kamal Kant Hiran has over 18 years of experience in academia, research, and administration in Asia, Africa, Europe, and North America. Currently he is working as Associate Professor in the School of Computer Science and IT, Symbiosis University of Applied Sciences, Indore, India and Adjunct Research Fellow at the Aalborg University, Copenhagen, Denmark. He has published 15 International books with repute publishers like BPB Publications, IGI Global, De Gruyter from India, Germany, USA, UK. He has made significant contributions to our society's technological transformation. He has several awards to his credit such as International travel grant for attending the IEEE Region 8 Committee Meeting at Warsaw, Poland; International travel grant for Germany from ITS Europe, Passau, Germany; Best Research Paper Award at the University of Gondar, Ethiopia; IEEE Liberia Subsection Founder Award; Gold Medal Award in MTech (Hons.); IEEE Ghana Section Award-Technical and Professional Activity Chair; IEEE Senior Member Recognition, Best IEEE Student Branch Award, Elsevier Reviewer Recognition Award. He has published 75 scientific research papers in SCI/Scopus/Web of Science and IEEE Transactions Journal, conferences, 2 Indian Patents, 1 Australian Patent Grants. He has made several international visits to Denmark, Sweden, Germany, Norway, Ghana, Liberia, Ethiopia, Russia, Dubai, Mexico, and Jordan for research exposures. His research interests focus on Artificial Intelligence, Cloud-edge computing, Machine-deep learning and Intelligent IoT.

Tahir Iqbal is an Associate Professor of Operations & Supply Chain Management. He earned his Ph.D. from Bradford University School Of Management United Kingdom. He has been working at Imam Abdulrahman Bin Faisal University Dammam KSA. I Possesses Over 18 years of teaching, administrative, and training experience: Experience in teaching, specialized training for junior faculty, curriculum development, programs' articulations, and accreditations, supervision of undergraduate and graduate students, leadership roles, and academic-related administrative experience. I am a multidisciplinary academic whose research interests include diverse topics such as Occupational Health & Safety practices, Blockchain, Humanitarian Logistics, Public Health, Networking & E-commerce are among those. I have published many publications, including Book, Book chapters and refereed journal articles.

Maad M. Mijwil is an Iraqi Academician; he is born in Baghdad, Iraq, in 1987. He received his B.Sc. degree in software engineering from Baghdad college of economic sciences university, Iraq, in 2009. He received a M.Sc. degree in 2015 from the computer science department, university of Baghdad in the field of wireless sensor networks, Iraq. Currently, he is working as a Lecturer and an academic member of staff in the computer techniques engineering department at Baghdad college of economic sciences university, Iraq. He has over ten years of experience in teaching and guiding projects for undergraduates. He has authored more than 100 publications, including papers/ chapters(published 70 peer reviewed papers in national/international conferences and journals), preprints, presentations, and posters. He is also an editor in more than 10 international/national journals and a reviewer in more than 100 international/national journals (English and Turkish manuscripts). He has served on technical program committees for many prestigious conferences. Also, he graduated from Publons academy as a peer reviewer. His Google citations are over 900 mark.

Shakerod Munuhwa is a seasoned logistics and supply chain practitioner. He is an academic, a researcher and industrialist.

Leon Niemann is a young researcher studying economics of business and strategy at the Master's level.

Kamalendu Pal is with the Department of Computer Science, School of Science and Technology, City, University of London. Kamalendu received his BSc (Hons) degree in Physics from Calcutta University, India, Postgraduate Diploma in Computer Science from Pune, India, MSc degree in Software Systems Technology from the University of Sheffield, Postgraduate Diploma in Artificial Intelligence from Kingston University, MPhil degree in Computer Science from the University College London, and MBA degree from the University of Hull, United Kingdom. He has published over hundred international research articles (including book chapters) widely in the scientific community with research papers in the ACM SIGMIS Database, Expert Systems with Applications, Decision Support Systems, and conferences. His research interests include knowledge-based systems, decision support systems, teaching and learning practice, blockchain technology, software engineering, service-oriented computing, sensor network simulation, and supply chain management. He is on the editorial board of an international computer science journal and is a member of the British Computer Society, the Institution of Engineering and Technology, and the IEEE Computer Society.

Renan Rocha is a young researcher studying economics of business and strategy at the Master's level.

Mohamad Zreik, is a recognized scholar in International Relations. His extensive knowledge spans Middle Eastern Studies, China-Arab relations, East Asian and Asian Affairs, Eurasian geopolitics, and Political Economy, providing him a unique viewpoint in his field. Dr. Zreik is a proud recipient of a PhD from Central China Normal University (Wuhan). He's written numerous acclaimed papers, many focusing on China's Belt and Road Initiative and its Arab-region impact. His groundbreaking research has established him as a leading expert in his field. His significant contributions make him a crucial figure in understanding contemporary international relations.

Index

F

G

I

L

M

N

O

P

R

www.ingramcontent.com/pod-product-compliance
Lightning Source LLC
LaVergne TN
LVHW062135300926
849161LV00010B/2541

* 9 7 9 8 3 6 9 3 0 2 2 5 5 *